Didier Pollefeyt & Jan F

CW01024077

Identity in Dialog

Christian Religious Education and School Identity

edited by

Prof. Dr. Didier Pollefeyt
(KU Leuven)

and

Jan Bouwens
(KU Leuven)

Volume 1

LIT

Didier Pollefeyt & Jan Bouwens

IDENTITY IN DIALOGUE

Assessing and enhancing Catholic school identity

Research methodology and research results
in Catholic schools in Victoria, Australia

LIT

Gedruckt auf alterungsbeständigem Werkdruckpapier entsprechend
ANSI Z3948   DIN ISO 9706

Bibliographic information published by the Deutsche Nationalbibliothek
The Deutsche Nationalbibliothek lists this publication in the Deutsche
Nationalbibliografie; detailed bibliographic data are available in the Internet at
http://dnb.d-nb.de.

ISBN 978-3-643-90550-5

A catalogue record for this book is available from the British Library

©LIT VERLAG GmbH & Co. KG Wien,   LIT VERLAG Dr. W. Hopf
Zweigniederlassung Zürich 2014   Berlin 2014
Klosbachstr. 107   Fresnostr. 2
CH-8032 Zürich   D-48159 Münster
Tel. +41 (0) 44-251 75 05   Tel. +49 (0) 2 51-62 03 20
Fax +41 (0) 44-251 75 06   Fax +49 (0) 2 51-23 19 72
E-Mail: zuerich@lit-verlag.ch   E-Mail: lit@lit-verlag.de
http://www.lit-verlag.ch   http://www.lit-verlag.de

Distribution:
In the UK: Global Book Marketing, e-mail: mo@centralbooks.com
In North America: International Specialized Book Services, e-mail: orders@isbs.com
In Germany: LIT Verlag Fresnostr. 2, D-48159 Münster
Tel. +49 (0) 2 51-620 32 22, Fax +49 (0) 2 51-922 60 99, E-mail: vertrieb@lit-verlag.de

In Austria: Medienlogistik Pichler-ÖBZ, e-mail: mlo@medien-logistik.at
e-books are available at www.litwebshop.de

The ECSIP team at KU Leuven wishes to dedicate this book to Mgr Thomas M. Doyle, former *Director of Catholic Education* in the Archdiocese of Melbourne and one of the initiators of the Project, to thank him for his vision, dedication, inspiration and utter excellence.

'A shoot will come up from the stump of Jesse;
from his roots a branch will bear fruit.'

Isaiah 11.1 (New International Version, © 2011)

'Do not put your faith in what statistics say
until you have carefully considered what they do not say.'

after William W. Watt

Table of contents

The *Enhancing Catholic School Identity Project*

§1. ECSIP: a general introduction

The Enhancing Catholic School Identity Project (ECSIP) is a research and implementation project carried out by the *Centre for Academic Teacher Training* of the *Faculty of Theology and Religious Studies* of the *Catholic University of Leuven* in Belgium.

ECSIP was initiated in 2006 in a modest way and has been growing in size and relevance ever since. Since its inception until this day, ECSIP has been conducted under the auspices of the *Catholic Education Commission of Victoria Ltd* (CECV) located in Melbourne, Australia. Over the years, a multitude of related projects and research activities arose out of the prime collaboration between Leuven and Victoria.

The ECSIP Project is promoted by Prof. Dr. Didier Pollefeyt (°1965), full professor at the *Faculty of Theology and Religious Studies* and current Vice President for Education KU Leuven. The chief scientific researcher assigned to ECSIP is Drs. Jan Bouwens (°1978).

In the context of ECSIP, the *Faculty of Theology and Religious Studies* in Leuven has been developing a new empirical and practical theological methodology to assess and enhance the identity structure of Catholic educational organisations. The project focuses on the religious identity of Catholic schools and other institutions involved in Catholic education facing the challenge today of *Recontextualising* their Catholic identity in a detraditionalising, secularising and pluralising culture.

Three theoretical models were developed into *multivariate attitude scales* and complemented by three additional surveys that collect relevant background variables, all integrated into the automated web platform www.schoolidentity.net. The suite of ECSIP survey instruments can be used to quantitatively assess a Catholic organisation's identity structure in a statistically accurate and reliable way. After consecutively analysing, describing and interpreting the results, the acquired data allows for informed recommendations concerning the policy steps aimed at the further development and enhancement of Catholic institutional identity.

The ECSIP process always consists of two stages. First, Catholic identity is *assessed* by means of quantitative and qualitative research methodologies. Next, Catholic identity is *enhanced* by means of various kinds of *practical-theological instruments* (PTI's).

The ECSIP Project offers support to ongoing processes of *self-assessment* that form the basis for ongoing dynamics of *self-improvement* of Catholic institutional identity. The identity research enables Catholic schools and other institutions to understand themselves more completely and thoroughly, so that they are in a better position to improve their Catholic identity in ways that are both theologically legitimate and culturally plausible in the short and long term.

§2. A brief chronology of the *Enhancing Catholic School Identity Project* (2006-2014)

- ECSIP was initiated in August 2006 at the initiative of the *Catholic Education Office Melbourne*. Initially the project was planned to run for three years. During this time, the empirical research instruments were created and trialled in Belgium and in Australia.

- Soon, the other three dioceses in the state of Victoria, Australia (Ballarat, Sandhurst and Sale) began to show interest in joining ECSIP.

- In 2008, a first large-scale trial run was held in 67 primary and 10 secondary schools in Victoria, as well as 2 *Catholic Education Offices*, for a total of 5365 respondents.

- In February 2009, people responsible for Religious Education at all four *Catholic Education Offices* attended a two-week intensive *CEO Staff Training* in Leuven.

- In 2009, the research project was extended for two more years, under the auspices of the *Catholic Education Commission of Victoria Ltd* (CECV) chaired by Bishop Tim Costelloe SDB. Through continuous testing and refining, the survey instruments gained statistical validity and practical applicability.

- In 2010, a final large-scale trial run was held in 48 primary and 24 secondary schools throughout Victoria (2645 respondents). The promising results of this trial were presented to the assembled Victorian bishops, chaired by Archbishop Denis Hart.

- From 2011-2015: first large-scale implementation phase. The ECSIP research became a core component of the official *School Improvement Framework* in Catholic schools throughout Victoria. Over the course of four years, all primary and secondary schools in Victoria implemented the empirical research. Each school received an individual report that contained an analysis, description and interpretation of its identity profile, leading to constructive suggestions for enhancing it further during the following school improvement cycle. ECSIP 2011, 2012 and 2013 comprised of 244 primary schools, 57 secondary colleges and 6 assessments in *Catholic Education Offices* for a total of 56603 respondents. At the time of publication, ECSIP 2014 was underway.

- In September 2011, Prof. Dr. Didier Pollefeyt presented a well-attended keynote lecture on ECSIP at the *National Catholic Education Convention* in Adelaide, Australia.

- Gradually, other Australian dioceses began to express a growing interest in taking part in the ECSIP research as well. At the initiative of *Catholic Education South Australia* (CESA) in Adelaide, a pilot round was conducted in 2012 and the survey research was applied in 49 schools and *Catholic Education Offices* throughout Australia – for a total of 18716 respondents.

- A follow-up round of this *National Enhancing Catholic School Identity Project* (NECSIP) was organised in 2013-2014 when 11 schools throughout Australia applied not only the survey research, but also various qualitative research components that complemented the surveys, such as document analysis, interviews, school founding and history, as well as a photo documentary on Catholic identity. 2994 respondents completed the surveys as part of the *NECSIP 2013 Project*.

- Based on the momentum generated by the ECSIP research, three dioceses in the state of Queensland (Townsville, Brisbane and Cairns) have been showing considerable interest in applying the identity research to their Catholic schools as well.

- Next to Australia, the ECSIP methodology has been applied extensively in Flanders, Belgium. At the time of publication, the research has been carried out in 78 Catholic institutions: primary and secondary schools, diocesan Catholic education offices, special education facilities, the *Association KU Leuven*, psychiatric hospitals and one Catholic youth movement — for a total of 23656 survey respondents.

- Also in other parts of the world the ECSIP research methodology is being trialled in preparation for wide-scale implementation: The Netherlands, England, Ireland, Germany, Lithuania, The Philippines and the United States of America.

- In March 2014, the ECSIP Project was presented by Prof. Dr. Didier Pollefeyt to the Vatican *Congregation of Catholic Education (for Educational Institutions)* in Rome, in the presence of the prefect of the congregation, Mgr Zenon Grochlewski. Also present were the governing body of the KU Leuven led by Rector Rik Torfs, as well as Archbishop André-Joseph Léonard of Mechelen-Brussels and Bishop Johan Bonny from Antwerp. The research and monitoring trajectory received ample support.

§3. Ensor's *Christ's Entry Into Brussels in 1889*. An analysis of the cover painting in the light of ECSIP theology

A Flemish painter of the late 19th and early 20th Century James Ensor was a product of his context and having mastered the mainstream impressionist painting style of his time he achieved much early success with his works. Yet not content with the impressionism of his time Ensor sought to be emotionally expressive and engaged with his canvas personally, dramatically making physical his feelings.

Christ's Entry Into Brussels in 1889 is a fusion of the triumphant entry of Christ into Jerusalem on Palm Sunday with the modern bawdy rites of Mardi Gras, which modernity has hijacked with its hedonism. Ensor portrays his future Brussels of 1889, set one year after he completed his work, as a maelstrom of disorder, alienation and hypocrisy. The viewer feels almost trampled by Ensor's portrayal of modern society as an ugly, chaotic and dehumanised sea of masks, frauds, clowns and caricatures that swell toward the viewer like a wave.

In *Christ's Entry*, Ensor captures the carnival of humanity, made up of frauds, buffoons and misfits, full of ugliness, yet exhilarating in its turbulence and tumbling chaos. We are presented with an uncompromising modernity; in all its vulgarity and hedonism, yet Christ is to be found there. In a 'future Brussels' where religion, politics and traditional powers are satirised, mocked and jeered we find Christ quietly present at the centre.

Although the title of the painting reveals Christ is the central figure, he is almost an afterthought, forced to the back of the marching crowd, small (albeit haloed), but insignificant. He has been relegated to the back seat – propped up as a puppet as opposed to a Saviour. Are we also guilty of this practice? Of having Christ or the Saints in the names of our schools, while letting Christ exist there only in the name, but not at the core of what we do in Catholic schools?

Do you see Christ's entry into Brussels amidst the chaos of the painting? Have you flicked back to the front cover in disbelief that he is indeed at the centre of this piece? Finding Christ in Ensor's paintings is akin to finding Christ in the 'chaos' of our lives, or more specifically in the busyness of our modern Catholic schools, we need someone to point out Christ to us, to equip us with the necessary tools to find him and search him out. Christ is present, but we do not see him. It takes someone to guide us, to point out what is later obvious, to show us his golden halo. Even if he is at the very heart of the panting, we can miss him. So too Christ can be at the heart of our school, work, endeavours, life, reality, yet we let him stand in the middle unnoticed, without recognising him. We are distracted by the chaos, by the bright gaudy colours of life's fast pace and by a myriad of other distractions.

As Ensor's artwork still catches its viewers off guard and causes them to pause, reflect and search for Christ, so too, we at ECSIP, hope that our work will offer the same lens to see and experience Christ in a new light, a fresh perspective and help us keep him at the centre of our modern and *Recontextualising* Catholic schools. Ensor calls us to search for and recognise Christ in a new context, so too we hope our work at ECSIP will direct our search to find Christ anew and bring him to the fore of who we are and what we do at Catholic schools.

Ensor offers us a *Recontextualised* portrayal of *Christ's Entry*. Although reminiscent of Christ's triumphant entry into Jerusalem on Palm Sunday, Ensor portrays Christ entering the city of Brussels at the end of the 19th century during carnival celebrations. Ensor's painting begs the question: Would we recognise Christ amidst the hedonism of a modern carnival celebration, which is in itself almost completely stripped of its original Christian meaning? At ECSIP we seek to ask this same question in relation to our Catholic schools. Where, how and when do we find Christ in our schools in a post-Christian context? It is the task of religious educators and our project to show people where Christ is and to help discern his presence amidst the daily reality of school life. Ensor chooses an unexpected occasion for his depiction of *Christ's Entry*, which again challenges our conception of when, where and on whose terms Christ should enter in. Perhaps it is not when, where, how or what we expect. The Spirit is at work but we may not recognise its activity; Christ enters into our school but we may overlook his presence.

What we wish to learn from Ensor and ECSIP is the hermeneutic to find Christ in unexpected ways, to have the flexibility of mind, spirit, creativity and inventiveness so that things appear in a new way. Christ is clearly present in Ensor's painting, yet he is hard to see, but once he is pointed out to us we will never look at the painting in the same light again. So too we at ECSIP hope that our research findings and recommendations will *interrupt* your expectations and encourage contemporary Catholic schools to do as Ensor did: to paint the picture of *Christ's Entry into Our Catholic Schools in 2014 and Beyond* in as vibrant, stimulating and refreshing manner as Ensor himself.

§4. Structure of this book

This book consists of two main parts, a number of attachments and a selected bibliography. *Part One* describes in detail the empirical instruments and the research methodology that are being employed by ECSIP. Quantitative ways of *assessing* Catholic school identity receive most attention. *Chapter One* opens with discussing ECSIP's central research aims and questions. *Chapter Two* talks extensively about the empirical and statistical research methodology. Having a good grasp of these 'statistical building blocks' is required to understand and interpret the research results. In *Chapter Three*, the survey instruments are being introduced and explained, as well as much of the typical ECSIP vocabulary that has been developed to reflect on Catholic school identity in a detailed and nuanced way. *Chapter Four* deals briefly with a number of complementary qualitative research methodologies. The indispensable first step of assessing school identity is followed by structured attempts at enhancing it. *Chapter Five* introduces the way this is being undertaken by the ECSIP Project. The *Sixth Chapter* does deeper into the *ECSIP Research Website*, an online platform for administering and analysing the identity surveys.

In *Part Two*, the research methodology explored in the first part of the book is being applied in a large-scale research in 96 Catholic schools in Victoria, Australia in the year 2012. *Chapter Seven* provides an introduction to the ECSIP 2012 Research. *Chapter Eight* describes the research sample and determines its representivity and validity. *Chapter Nine* explores the identity of Catholic schools in Victoria by means of the results of the *Profile* and the *Doyle Questionnaires*. *Chapter Ten* is central to Part Two: it deals extensively with the results of the three multivariate attitude scales that form the core of the ECSIP research. After dealing with the *Post-Critical Belief Scale*, the *Melbourne Scale* and the *Victoria Scale* separately, the intercorrelations between the scales are being examined at close range. Next, we summarise the findings by means of four *Subpopulations*. The final chapter of the book, *Chapter Eleven*, contains conclusions and recommendations based on the ECSIP 2012 Research data. It begins with the distinction between a *Kerygmatic* and a *Recontextualising* style of *Dialogue*. It continues with a summary of qualities and strengths as well as challenges and critical questions and it ends with an extensive array of recommendations that could help Catholic schools in Victoria to enhance their identity in the ways of *Post-Critical Belief*, *Recontextualisation* and the *Dialogue School* model. The text closes with a brief biblical reflection on the well-known but ever captivating parable of the *Good Samaritan* (Luke 10:25-37).

Next come three clusters of *Attachments* that cover about a third of the book. First, all quantitative empirical research instruments that were used in the ECSIP 2012 Research are published in full. Second, an extensive summary of tables that contain statistical research results on the ECSIP 2012 Research are included for the purpose of scientific review. Third, we illustrate the ECSIP Project with a brief photo report. The book concludes with a *Bibliography* that contains a selection of relevant references to additional literature.

PART 1. Assessing and enhancing Catholic school identity. Empirical instruments and research methodology

Chapter 1. Research aims and questions

The ECSIP research has both a descriptive and an evaluative component. In a first step, we assess the identity of Catholic organisations in an objective, neutral and scientifically validated way. In a second step, we evaluate these findings in the light of the normative-theological views developed and defended by the *Faculty of Theology and Religious Studies* of the KU Leuven, Belgium. This evaluation will give rise to non-committal recommendations for enhancing the Catholic identity of the school or Catholic organisation in question.

§1. It is always best to know. Assessing the identity of Catholic organisations

> Descriptive research question: How does a Catholic organisation shape the religious and specifically Catholic components of its institutional identity in a cultural context characterised by increasing *secularisation, detraditionalisation* and *pluralisation*?

The research question is deliberately broad and comprehensive, enabling us to delve into Catholic institutional identity with great nuance and detail, taking into account its manifold relevant aspects. Also, the scope of the research remains open for the exploration of new avenues leading to discoveries that could not have been foreseen. The drawback of this approach is the extensiveness of the research that could lead to difficulties in managing the research data. This drawback is countered by methodological design and practical application in any way possible.

This first research question departs from an analysis of the 'late-modern' cultural context of Western countries today in terms of processes not only of *secularisation* but also *pluralisation, detraditionalisation* and *individualisation*.[1] This point of view directs the focus of the research in particular towards the relationship and the interaction between the specificity and the irreducible character of the Catholic faith on the one hand, and a cultural context characterised by religious and philosophical diversity on the other.

Note that, in this publication, we focus on Catholic *educational* institutions, mostly primary and secondary schools. *Mutatis mutandis*, the methodology presented here, can also be applied to other Catholic organisations, inside and outside the educational sector, for example: universities and high schools, diocesan education offices, Catholic health and social services, Catholic youth movements, Catholic political parties and unions, various Catholic societies, groups, clubs, et cetera.

---

[1] For a further elaboration of this cultural analysis and its consequences for Catholic theology, see: L. Boeve, *God Interrupts History. Theology in a Time of Upheaval*, London - New York, Continuum, 2007, 15-45.

§2. Theology is a normative science. Evaluating and enhancing the identity of Catholic organisations

> *Evaluative research question: Based on the assessment of the perceived current practice in the Catholic organisation and the ideal perspectives of its members, what does KU Leuven recommend to the leadership of this organisation, in case it wishes to maintain and enhance the religious and specifically Catholic components of its institutional identity, in order to Recontextualise it in a hermeneutical-communicative theological perspective in a pluralising cultural context?*

The suite of empirical and practical-theological instruments enables those responsible for the Catholic identity of schools and other institutions to plan future growth and development in a rational and informed way. Policies and procedures regarding staff professional development, parent education and enrolment will be informed by accurate data on the organisation, contributing to a multi-year strategic and integrated development program.

Obviously, the leadership of an organisation remains free to determine its policy decisions. Through their Catholic identity project, the CECV and KU Leuven can assess, inform, explain and make recommendations intended to help people see and understand the current practice and the possible future of their organisation. However, as indicated by the second research question, the project can and will never impose anything. Catholic identity is something people must want for themselves and do for themselves freely. If that is their decision, then they will find support and guidance in the empirical and practical-theological instruments we develop in the course of this project.

Chapter 2. Research methodology. Operationalisation of the first research question

§1. Empirical survey instruments: an introduction

What follows is an overview of the suite of empirical instruments designed for ECSIP. Further in this publication, each of these instruments is described in detail.

- **Identification Diagram**
Short, preceding, interactive diagram designed to assess the respondents' place and function within the organisation.

- **Profile Questionnaire**
A questionnaire designed to collect background variables that determine the personal religious profile of the respondents. *Profile Questionnaire* graphs have a white background.

- **Doyle Questionnaire** (dual level measurement: current practice + ideal school)
A questionnaire designed to collect background variables that determine the religious profile of the school or Catholic organisation the respondents belong to. It consists of individual items that focus on relevant aspects of Catholic identity in relation to increasing religious diversity. *Doyle Questionnaire* graphs have a pink background.

- ***Post-Critical Belief* Scale (*PCB Scale*)**
Multivariate attitude scale that determines the cognitive belief styles present among the respondents. These personal religious faith attitudes are the building blocks for Catholic institutional identity. *PCB Scale* graphs have a blue background.

- **Melbourne Scale** (dual level measurement: current practice + ideal school)
Multivariate attitude scale based on a typology of *theological* school identity options in a detraditionalising and pluralising cultural context. *Melbourne Scale* graphs have a brown background.

- **Victoria Scale** (dual level measurement: current practice + ideal school)
Multivariate attitude scale based on a typology of *pedagogical* school identity options in a detraditionalising and pluralising cultural context. *Victoria Scale* graphs have a green background.

The *Melbourne Scale* typology, based on the theological analysis of the contemporary relation between faith and culture designed by Prof. Dr. Lieven Boeve[2] and operationalised by the ECSIP research team, forms the core of the ECSIP Research. It is highly recommended to supplement the *Melbourne Scale* with the two other attitude scales, namely the *Post-Critical Belief Scale* and the *Victoria Scale*. That way, valuable information is collected on the belief styles of the school population and the way a school deals with the tension between Catholic identity and diversity. Next, the background variables collected by the *Profile Questionnaire* and the *Doyle Questionnaire* provide additional information that is less central but nonetheless valuable and very revealing, especially when this data is cross-referenced with the scale results. It is the case, here too, that the whole is more than the sum of its parts.

Despite the extensiveness of the entire suite of ECSIP surveys and the practical difficulties some schools experience when administering them to a large number of respondents, experience teaches that their combined application yields the best results. In those few cases when one or more surveys have been omitted, afterward the schools have expressed regret to have collected only part of the information. Organising survey research may be an administrative burden at the time, but afterward the rewards are plenty. And if there is one thing schools usually excel at, it is organisation.

---

[2] BOEVE, L., *The Identity of a Catholic University in Post-Christian European Societies: Four Models*, in Louvain Studies 31 (2006), 238-258.

§2. Twenty-one respondent groups: 10 single + 11 combined groups

The respondent groups form a key component of the ECSIP research methodology. In total, there are ten distinct respondent groups. These correspond to the existing social structure of the school or Catholic organisation. Each respondent belongs to exactly one of the ten single respondent groups. The *Identification Diagram* determines for each respondent to which respondent group he/she belongs. Each respondent group has its own colour that consistently identifies that group in the graph results. Knowing the respondent groups inside out is essential to be able to read and understands the results.

	Single respondent groups in school contexts	General description
RG1	Primary school students, year 5-6	Children 9-12 years old.
RG2	Secondary college students, year 7-8	Teenagers 12-13 years old.
RG3	Secondary college students, year 9-10	Teenagers 14-15 years old.
RG4	Secondary college students, year 11-12	Teenagers 16-18 years old.
RG5	Tertiary education students	Young adults 19-25 years old.
RG6	School teachers and other staff	Adults who implement policy, but do not make it themselves.
RG7	School leadership	Adults who make policy on a local level.
RG8	Educational policy makers	Adults who make policy on a supra-local level.
RG9	Parents or guardians of students	The social context of an organisation.
RG10	Individual respondents	Individual respondents who do not belong to any other group, or whose RG is unknown.

Figure I-1. Overview of 10 single respondent groups.

In addition to these ten single respondent groups, there are eleven combined respondent groups that add together the research data of two or more single groups. Combined respondent groups are used frequently to aggregate multiple single respondent groups so that the profile of a larger group of people can be ascertained. Also, the combined respondent groups provide a practical sample size if the single groups are too small to stand on their own.

Combined respondent groups in school contexts		General description
RG11	Students year 7-10	Combination of secondary college students grades 7-8 and 9-10
RG12	Students year 9-12	Combination of secondary college students grades 9-10 and 11-12
RG13	Secondary college students	Combination of all secondary college students, grades 7 to 12
RG14	All students	Combination of all students, primary as well as secondary
RG15	School staff (teachers + leadership)	Combination of school teachers and school leadership
RG16	School staff and parents	Combination of school teachers, school leadership and parents
RG17	Students year 5-12 + tertiary education	All students combined: PRIM + SEC + TER
RG18	Educational policy makers	Combination of local leadership and supra-local leadership.
RG19	Adults excl. individual respondents	Combination of all adults, except individual respondents
RG20	All adults	Combination of all adults, including individual respondents
RG21	All respondents (students + adults)	Combination of all respondents, students as well as adults

Figure I-2. Overview of 11 combined respondent groups.

Frequently used combined respondent groups are:
- RG13: secondary college students taken together.
- RG14: a combination of all school students, primary and secondary school
- RG20: a combination of all adult groups.
- RG21: the aggregation of ALL respondent groups.

Differentiated mean scores
The ability to differentiate research results according to these pre-established respondent groups is a powerful feature of the ECSIP methodology. It allows us to track variations in responses in constituent groups (e.g. younger students, older students, staff, parents and other members of the school community). This enables age-based and constituency-based comparisons and trends to be compared and identified.

Adjustment factors

In order to combine single respondent groups, they are *adjusted* in relation to each other. If the research sample is sufficiently large, then single respondent groups stand to each other in a 1:1 relationship. This implies that the score of the combined group is simply the mathematical mean of mean scores of the single groups that are combined, no matter their individual size. This adjustment occurs in order to prevent accidental differences in sample size between single respondent groups skewing the combined score. If the sample size is reduced in size, as is the case in many individual schools, then the 'relative weight' of the constituent respondent groups in the overall result may vary according to the following principles: (a) the older a student, the more he/she will impact on the combined score; and (b) school leaders and Catholic Education Office staff will impact a little more than teachers, who in turn impact a little more than parents. These adjustments are applied in order to provide the best possible prediction of the actual impact on the identity of a school by the various respondent groups. Nevertheless, in most cases the effect of the adjustments remains marginal.

The n ≥ 30 rule

In order to create differentiated results per respondent group, a sufficient number of respondents is needed in each group. The mathematical mean of a small group of individuals tends to become devoid of meaning and therefore needs to be avoided (unless a small group of respondents all have similar scores). As a general rule, we need at least thirty people per respondent group. When a group contains fewer than thirty respondents, it is automatically combined with one or more other groups until the total sum exceeds thirty. For example, in most schools 'School leadership' (RG7) and 'school teachers' (RG6) are combined to form a new group called 'school staff' (RG15). The reason for this is that there are usually insufficient school board members to form a group on their own. Subsequently, in many schools 'school staff' (RG15) and 'parents' (RG9) are combined to form a group called 'adults' (RG19) because of insufficient participation numbers in one or more single respondent groups.

A flexible model that can be adapted to other research contexts

Although the 21 respondent groups as such remain constant, they can be applied to new groups, strata or structures in Catholic organisations. Applying the respondent groups is an essential part of the implementation of the research methodology in a new context. For example, if the ECSIP research is carried out in a psychiatric care institution, then RG1-4 are designated to patients younger than 18 years of age, RG5 is meant for adult patients, RG6 for doctors, nurses and other staff, RG7 for the leaders of the organisation, RG8 for higher-level policy makers in the psychiatric sector and RG9 for friends and family of the patients or for externally involved medical professionals.

§3. Different survey versions for different respondent groups

After the online *Identification Diagram* has identified the appropriate respondent group for each respondent, he/she is automatically directed towards the corresponding survey version, adapted to the respondent group in question. The diagram below shows the corresponding survey version for each of the ten single respondent groups for each of the empirical instruments.

	students year 5-6	students year 7-10	students year 9-10	students year 11-12	students tertiary education	teachers & staff	school leader- ship	policy makers	parents
Identification Diagram	same diagram for all								
Profile Questionnaire	same questionnaire for all								
Doyle Questionnaire	student version (shorter version)			adult version (variable length)					parent formulation
PCB Scale	student version (24-item scale)			adult version (33-item scale)					
Melbourne Scale	student version (the mind maps)			adult version (45-item scale)					parent formulation
Victoria Scale	student version (the blackboards)			adult version (40-item scale)					parent formulation

Figure I-3. Survey instruments in relation to the 10 single respondent groups.

Note that the students and adults fill in different survey versions. This was decided in order to make the survey process easier and shorter for children and teenagers. The parents and guardians of the students complete the adult survey versions with slightly adapted formulations that fit the perspective of the parents. For example, on the factual measurement level, 'my school' is changed into: 'my son's/daughter's school'.

§4. Sample design: a *randomised disproportional stratified sample*, sample size, sample quality, validity and representivity

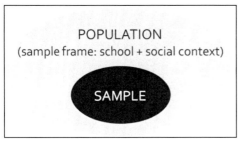

POPULATION
(sample frame: school + social context)

SAMPLE

Figure I-4. Basic sampling theory.

A good sample is a 'representative miniature' of the population in such a way that it proportionately mirrors all characteristics that are relevant to the research.

A sample must be drawn as randomly as possible
Within each respondent group, the sample must be randomised. This means that, ideally, each element (respondent) must have the same opportunity to be included in the sample, when compared with any other element in the respondent group. In order to guarantee the quality and representivity of the sample, *non-response errors of observation* must be avoided.

A sample must have an adequate size in relation to the population
General guidelines: in school settings, samples should have a minimum size of 15-20% of the population, although more is always better. In absolute figures, the minimal sample size in a single school is 30 respondents.[3] The smaller the school, the bigger the relative sample size needs to be. When generalising the sample to an entire school population, certain margins of error need to be taken into account.

All respondent groups should be accounted for
The total sample in a school should consist of adequate samples from all respondent groups that are present in that school's sample frame. The picture will be incomplete and thus not representative, if one or more respondent groups are missing.

For the research results to be statistically *representative*, an adequate sample from all respondent groups is required. If these requirements are not met, the sample may still be *indicative* of the characteristics of the population as a whole, although margins of error need to be taken into account.

---

[3] See the n ≥ 30 rule, see Chapter 2 §2.

§5. A dual measurement level: factual and normative

The application of the *dual measurement level* is a crucial component of the ECSIP methodology. Most empirical instruments measure an organisation's identity on two levels in which case the survey items appear twice in a slightly different formulation according to the following distinction:

FACTUAL MEASUREMENT LEVEL: "the current practice in my school"
The way in which school members perceive and interpret the reality of their school as it unfolds today. It concerns the subjective perception by the respondents of the current practice in their school.

NORMATIVE MEASUREMENT LEVEL: "my ideal school"
The personal ideal of the school members regarding the 'perfect' identity of Catholic schools. It concerns the normative standpoint from which they perceive and evaluate the reality in their school. It reveals how the respondents would prefer their school to be in the future.

Factual measurement level	Normative measurement level
"My school is a Catholic school."	"My ideal school is a Catholic school."
"All people in my school believe in God."	"I'd like to go to a school where all people believe in God."
"In my school, religious beliefs are a private matter."	"In my opinion, religious beliefs are a private matter."
"My school used to be Catholic, but Christianity has slowly disappeared from school life."	"I find it no problem that Christianity is slowly disappearing from school life."

Figure I-5. Examples of survey items on both measurement levels: factual and normative.

The dual measurement level applies only when institutional identity is being assessed and a distinction can be made between 'the factual' and 'the ideal'. For this reason, the *Profile Questionnaire* and the *Post-Critical Belief Scale* do not employ a dual measurement level: these empirical instruments assess facts, personal opinions and attitudes that apply to the respondents themselves instead of their school.

The *comparison* between both measurements levels yields valuable insights:

1. **It reveals the support basis for a school's current identity.** Are people satisfied and happy with the situation at school, as it is being shaped today? To what degree is the school's current identity supported by the people involved? The more the factual and the normative scores coincide, the more people agree with their school's identity and feel comfortable and content to be there. However, the more the factual and the normative scores deviate, the more people would like things to be different compared with the current practice. Which aspects of school life are met with resistance, by whom, and why?

2. **It reveals the potential for change and points at the school's most likely future development.** It can be assumed that a school will evolve in the direction desired by the majority of its community members. In this way, the dual measurement level is able to 'predict the future' of a school's development or at least the potential for change in a certain direction, namely from its current profile today towards the normative ideal profile projected by its members. What is the preferred direction of the school's future development according to its members? How big is this desire for change and renewal? To what degree are people prepared to support and assist change in a certain direction? What are the normative tensions between the people involved regarding their school's future development?

3. **It provides indications to school leaders for making policy decisions that realise their normative vision.** Given the respondents' perception of their school's current practice, as well as their ideal perspectives regarding the school's future development and given the normative view on a specific kind of desired school identity envisioned by its leadership, what are the policy options available to school leaders and high-level policy makers to guide the school's development in their normatively preferred direction? How to proceed in order to assist – and, if necessary, correct – a school's development towards the desired type of (Catholic) identity? What are the school's strengths, weaknesses, opportunities, challenges and pitfalls when it comes to leading it towards the ideal vision? When answering this question in a satisfactory way, it is essential to take into account the support basis and the potential for change that is present among the school population.

§6. A twofold normativity: empirical and theological

Dual empirical measurement level: CURRENT PRACTICE (factual level) **the current identity of a school,** **perceived by the respondents** IDEAL SCHOOL (normative level) **perspectives on ideal school identity** *empirical normativity*	NORMATIVE PREFERENCE **Our preference on theological grounds** 'hermeneutical theology' a post-critical belief style, symbolically mediated a recontextualisation of Catholic school identity a dialogue school model: identity in diversity the hermeneutical-communicative didactical model *theological normativity*
Step 1 A neutral and objective description of the research results without reference to our normative preference; 'the graph put into words'	Step 2 Our evaluation and critique of the research results in the light of our normative preference Recommendations for future policy

Figure I-6. Diagram twofold normativity.

The *Empirical normativity* denotes the ideal perspective of the people involved in the school or Catholic organisation that is being investigated (cf. first research question). It is clearly distinguished from the *theological normativity* used by the ECSIP Project to evaluate the Catholic identity of the school in question (cf. second research question).

The *Enhancing Catholic School Identity Project* has a practical-theological focus. To obtain its goal, it employs empirical and statistical techniques that were initially developed by the social sciences and it applies these techniques to the issue of Catholic school identity. ECSIP is not just a sociological endeavour that merely attempts to describe unfolding realities in an objective and neutral way. Such description is important and must be handled according to the scientific rigour that is appropriate for any empirical research – but this is only the first step in the ECSIP methodology. The second step is theological and therefore *normative* in nature. It concerns the evaluation of empirical findings according to a theological ideal option: ECSIP promotes a genuine *Recontextualisation* of Catholic school identity through a *Dialogue School* pedagogy in view of a *Post-Critical Believing* attitude towards the Catholic faith tradition[4]. Empirical and theological normativity can coincide but they can also differ: it is not because a majority of the respondents in a school desire a certain approach

---

[4] The precise content, meaning, scope and justification of ECSIP's normative theological view is treated extensively in chapters 3, 10 and 11.

towards Catholic identity (cf. the *normative measurement level*), that ECSIP is to yield to this perspective. ECSIP's theological normative might *confront* the empirical normativity expressed by school members. This could happen, for example, if the respondents indicated a desire for an exclusive *Monological* Catholic identity or if they opted for an *Institutional Secularisation* of their school's Catholicity.

Three possible responses to ECSIP's theological normativity
When confronted with the ECSIP's theological normativity and the conclusion would be that the Catholic identity of the school finds itself under pressure, then its leadership could respond in three different ways:

1. **"That is not true" – disagreement.** "We reject the empirical instrumentation and/or the theological views proposed by the ECSIP Project and we therefore disagree with the analysis."

2. **"So what?" – acknowledge and ignore.** "It is okay that our school is gradually *Secularising*. Also without a specifically Catholic identity we can offer excellent education and formation to our students."

3. **"O dear, help us!" – acknowledge and act.** "We accept the analysis and realise the severity of the situation. What can we do to enhance and – if necessary – re-establish our school's Catholic identity?"

In the case of response two or two, ECSIP will respect the school's decision but will try to initiate an open dialogue about its views on Catholic identity and the theological justification and educational consequences of its decision not to go with ECSIP's proposal. If the school's decision stands, then the cooperation will end. In the case of response three, the school might pose its candidacy to take part in a process of enhancement of its Catholic identity by means of the *Practical-Theological Instruments* (PTI's) developed by the ECSIP Project[5].

---

[5] Chapter 5 of this book goes deeper into the process of *enhancing* Catholic school identity by means of PTIs.

§7. The seven-point Likert scale used in the ECSIP surveys

7-point Likert Scale
1. I strongly disagree
2. I disagree
3. I somewhat disagree
4. I neither agree, nor disagree
5. I somewhat agree
6. I agree
7. I strongly agree

Figure I-7. The seven-point Likert scale used in the ECSIP surveys.

A so-called *Likert scale* is a psychometric response scale often used in survey research. When responding to a Likert questionnaire item, respondents specify their level of agreement or disagreement to a statement. The scale is named after Rensis Likert, an American psychologist (1903-1981) who developed the scale and used it for the first time in his PhD thesis in 1932.[6]

Most ECSIP survey instruments employ a seven-point Likert scale to gather responses. This extensive scale offers significant opportunity for the respondents to react in a nuanced way with great exactness to the survey items and to provide a wealth of statistical information. The same seven-point Likert scale is used in the surveys for all respondent groups alike so that a fair comparison between them is possible. The graphs' Y-axes are scaled according to the same seven-point Likert scale used in the surveys.

The seven-point scale has an odd number of response options, which means there is a neutral 'middle point' (4) that denotes "I neither agree, nor disagree". The respondents are not forced to make a choice between 'agreement' and 'disagreement'. Not only is this practice appropriate regarding the complex subject matter, but the resulting scores are also more reliable compared to a 'forced choice method'. Since people have the opportunity to opt for a neutral middle position, the occasion of their 'agreeing' or 'disagreeing' can be considered to denote just that.

---

[6] L.R. FREY, C.H. BOTAN e.a., *Investigating Communication. An Introduction to Research Methods*, Prentice Hall, NJ, Englewood Cliffs, 1991.

Eight items in the *Doyle Questionnaire* form an exception and use a five-point Likert scale (more-less) instead of the usual seven-point scale (agreement-disagreement). These items assess 'features of Catholic school identity' on the normative measurement level only:

1 = a lot more
2 = more
3 = neither more, nor less
4 = less
5 = a lot less

There are three typical biases connected to Likert response scales. The ECSIP survey process actively attempts to avoid these biases:

- **central tendency bias**: respondents may avoid using extreme response categories.
- **acquiescence bias**: respondents may agree too easily with the statements.
- **social desirability bias**: respondents may try to portray themselves or their school in a more favourable light.

When citing research results in the form of mathematical means, then the numbers are indicated as a fraction with denominator 7, for example: "2/7" or "5.5/7". This means that the mean score has to be interpreted as a result on the seven-point Likert scale that ranges from 1 to 7. If a five-point response scale has been used, then the denominator changes likewise.

§8. Criteria for valid participation

Not in every occasion when a respondent completes a survey he/she does this in a valid way. An ECSIP survey is considered *valid* on the following conditions:

1. The respondent must have completed the *Identification Diagram* without inconsistencies so that it is known to which research project, research group and respondent group he/she belongs.

2. The respondent has completed at least one questionnaire in a valid way (either the *Doyle Questionnaire*, the *PCB Scale*, the *Melbourne Scale* or the *Victoria Scale*).

3. In the case of the three multivariate attitude scales (*PCB Scale*, *Melbourne Scale*, *Victoria Scale*): at least one third of the questions must be answered, so that it is possible to calculate the scale mean results.

4. In the case of the three attitude scales (*PCB Scale*, *Melbourne Scale*, *Victoria Scale*): no more than half of the given answers may be a 4 on the Likert scale ('I don't know, I have no opinion'). If an inordinate number of fours has been ticked, then it is assumed that the respondent either actually did not know or did not have an opinion about the survey items (he/she might never have thought about Catholic identity or he/she did not understand the questions), or the respondent did not feel like taking the research seriously. In either case the data contains little or no information about the respondent's actual views. In order to improve the validity of the remaining research data, the *de facto* 'non-participations' are removed from the sample.

5. The given scores should not contain artificial or illogical patterns, indicating that the answers were ticked randomly regardless of the questions (for example 7-7-7-7-7-7-7-7; 1-1-1-1-1-1-1-1; 1-2-3-4-5-6-7; 7-6-5-4-3-2-1; 1-1-2-2-3-3-4-4-5-5-6-6-7-7; 2-2-6-6-2-2-6-6; et cetera).

An invalid survey is disregarded as if it were never completed. The data it contains is automatically omitted when computing research results. This is the reason why the official respondent numbers per survey might be a bit lower than the actual total number of participants: some of them might have completed one or more surveys in an invalid way.

Respondents who fill in one or more surveys but ALL in an invalid way, are de facto non-respondents who are therefore disregarded as if they never participated in the research at all. This elimination usually occurs for only a few respondents, since most of them do manage to complete at least one or more surveys in a valid way.

§9. Evaluation questions

The following two evaluation questions, scored on a seven-point Likert scale, are always added to both the student and the adult versions of the *Doyle Questionnaire*, the *PCB Scale*, the *Melbourne Scale* and the *Victoria Scale*:

1. The questions in this survey made sense to me.	2. I liked completing this survey.
1 I strongly disagree 2 I disagree 3 I somewhat disagree 4 I neither agree, nor disagree 5 I somewhat agree 6 I agree 7 I strongly agree	1 I strongly disagree 2 I disagree 3 I somewhat disagree 4 I neither agree, nor disagree 5 I somewhat agree 6 I agree 7 I strongly agree

Figure I-8. Two evaluation questions on a 7-point Likert scale.

With these questions valuable feedback is collected both about the reliability of the collected data and about the data collection process itself. The same questions apply to all respondent groups, which makes it possible to compare their feedback.

The most important evaluation question is the first one, namely whether or not the questions in the survey made sense to the respondents. If a large number of respondents indicated that they cannot make sense of the questions, then we must treat the results with care. Fortunately, that rarely happens.

The results of the evaluation questions are presented as graphs that differentiate the mean score of various respondent groups (see the example graph on the left hand side). Additionally, the relative number of respondents who agree or disagree with the two evaluation questions can also be presented as percentages in stacked bar graphs (see the example graph on the right hand side).

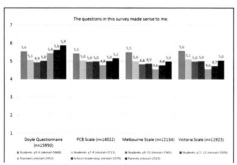
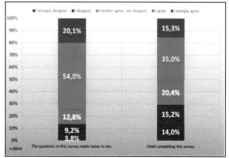

Figures I-9 & I-10. Examples of graphs that present the evaluation questions.

§10. Reading and interpreting the scale mean results

The results of the empirical instruments are graphically presented in a variety of different but complementary ways. Below, we explain how the most important type of graph should be read and interpreted: the graph that presents the scale means. Chapter 3 contains examples of written interpretations for fictitious results for each of the three attitude scales. In Chapter 10, the actual results of the *ECSIP 2012 Research* are being described and analysed.

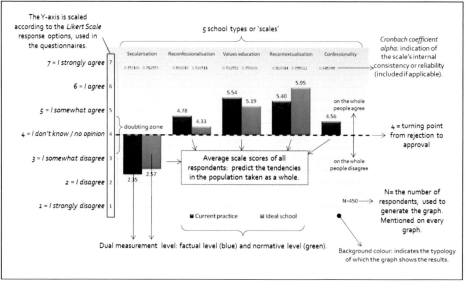

Figure I-11. Composition of the Melbourne Scale graph showing mean scores on the factual and normative level.

The scale means graphs of the *PCB Scale*, the *Melbourne Scale* and the *Victoria Scale* contain similar elements:

- The background colour reveals which scale is being shown.

- The Y-axis is scaled according to the same seven-point Likert scale used in the surveys.

- This means that the dotted line at 4 marks the turning point between 'agreement' (the bars point upwards) and 'disagreement' (the bars point downwards).

- Mean scores on the factual level are displayed by blue bars. Mean scores on the normative level are displayed by green bars.

- Each graph contains an 'n-number' indicating the number of respondents that contribute to that graph (this number may differ from one graph to another depending on the sample size and the number of invalidly completed surveys).

§11. Pearson Linear correlation coefficients

The *Pearson product-moment correlation coefficient* (typically denoted by r) is a measure of the *linear dependence* between two variables, giving a value between +1 (perfect positive correlation) and −1 (perfect negative correlation):

- **Positive correlation** (r>0): all data points lie on a straight line for which Y increases as X increases.
- **Negative correlation** (r<0): all data points lie on a straight line for which Y decreases as X increases.
- **No correlation** (r=0): there is no linear correlation between the variables.

Linear correlation coefficients are commonly used in the statistical analysis of empirical research data. A number of ECSIP graphs make use of linear correlation coefficients to visualise the associations between various types of the multivariate attitude scales, for example the *internal correlations* graphs that show the interrelations between the types that belong to the same scale, or the *intercorrelation bubble graphs* that show the interrelations between types that belong to two different scales.

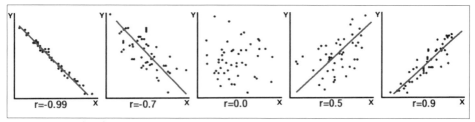

Figure I-12. Examples of scatter plots visualising positive and negative linear correlations.

Chapter 3. Empirical instruments

§1. *The Identification Diagram*

For each respondent, the research opens with the *Identification Diagram*, a short interactive questionnaire that serves to assess the place and function of each respondent within the school or Catholic organisation he/she belongs to, and to place him/her exclusively in one of the ten basic respondent groups.

The *Identification Diagram* also collects some additional information about the respondents, such as:

- Whether a secondary college student did or did not attend a Catholic primary school.

- The staff group, function or title of a Catholic Education Office member.

- For adult respondents: are you a Roman-Catholic priest? Are you a religious brother or sister?

- Where the respondent is a tertiary education student: the education program he/she is enrolled in, as well as the study year he/she is in.

- Where the respondent fulfils a specific role in an educational institution: the year he/she teaches in, whether he/she teaches religious education, humanities and/or sciences, whether he/she has an executive or leadership function, whether he/she is a member of the administrative and support staff, and whether he/she works in an academic institution as a scientific researcher or assistant.

- Where the respondent is a parent or guardian of school aged children or tertiary students: whether his/her children are in kindergarten, primary school, secondary college or a tertiary education institution.

Note that the interactive *Identification Diagram* becomes significantly shorter for primary and secondary school students and consequently quicker to complete because the options that only apply to adults are automatically left out.

It is very important that the privacy of the respondents is guaranteed at all times. Respondent are never asked to provide their names, nor do we attempt to identify an individual respondent indirectly by means of the available background variables or scale results. All research data is treated confidentially.

§2. Assessing the respondents' personal religious profile: *The Profile Questionnaire*

The interactive *Profile Questionnaire*, to be completed by all respondents at the start of the research, collects a carefully selected range of background variables that determine the personal religious profile of the respondents, such as:

General background variables:
- What is your gender?
- What is your age?
- Are you a baptised Catholic?
- Are you a Catholic priest?
- What is the highest level of education you received and completed? (Only in case of Catholic Education Office members)
- What is your main ethnic background?

Personal religion or philosophy of life:
- Are you a Catholic or do you come from a Catholic background?
- How strong is your personal Christian faith?
- If you are a Catholic, are you a Roman or an Eastern rite Catholic?
- If you are Christian but not Catholic, what is the church or Christian denomination you belong to?
- If you are not a Christian believer, what is your religion?
- If you are a non-religious person, what is your personal philosophy of life?
- If none of the above options apply to you, manually enter the preferred description of your personal religion or philosophy of life.

Attitude towards the Catholic faith, church praxis and prayer life:
- To what degree do you support the Catholic faith?
- When did you last attend a celebration of the Eucharist in your own time?
- How often do you pray to God individually?

§3. Assessing the school's religious profile: *The Doyle Questionnaire*

The next survey is the *Doyle Questionnaire*, named after Monsignor Tom Doyle, one of the inspiring pioneers of the ECSIP Project to whom this book is dedicated. The *Doyle Questionnaire* consists of a number of individual questions, both on the factual and on the normative measurement level. It is conceived as a flexible questionnaire that can be adapted to particular research contexts.

It consists of a number of standard relevant themes additional to the results of the three scales. This set of questions about relevant aspects of Catholic school identity cannot be omitted from a thorough investigation of school identity but may not be represented, or may be under-represented, in the multivariate attitude scales. It deals with topics such as:

- the recognition of the school's Catholic identity
- religious education practices
- the school's relation to the Church and its leadership
- moral education, ethics and values
- social commitment
- community formation
- the school buildings, facilities and grounds
- using the Scriptures at school
- Prayer and faith celebrations
- diversity within in relation to faith affiliation and practice
- ... and other themes.

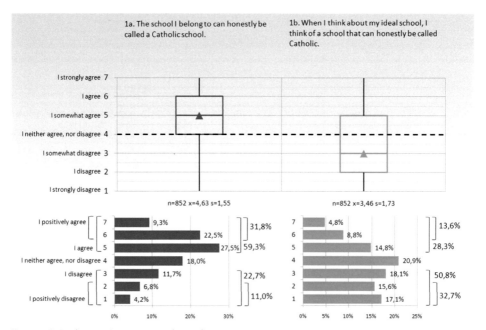

Figure I-13. *Doyle Questionnaire* example graph.

Figure I-13 is an example graph of the *Doyle Questionnaire*'s first question on the factual level (left) and the normative level (right). 852 respondents answered both questions and contributed to this graph.

The 'box-and-whisker plot' at the top conveniently displays the dispersal of responses. The box contains the 'middle 50%' of the scores ranked from high to low and points at the main tendency, while the 'whiskers' indicate the range of responses that are still relevant relative to the main tendency. The little triangle at the centre of the box denotes the median or 50th percentile, while an 'x' points at an 'outlier' i.e. an extreme response that is exceptionally far removed from the main tendency.

Additionally, the 'histogram' at the bottom displays the same research data in a different yet complementary way. It counts the number of times each of the seven possible *Likert scale* responses is given and expresses this figure relative to the total number of responses in the form of a percentage. The sum of the percentages (plus a possible number of missing values) is always 100%. For the reader's convenience, the graph also contains cumulative percentages of agreement and disagreement. The results of the adults are displayed on the left hand side (factual and normative level), while the results of the students are displayed on the right hand side (factual and normative level).

§4. Cognitive belief styles: *The Post-Critical Belief Scale*

In the three following paragraphs, the three multivariate attitude scales are being introduced: the *Post-Critical Belief Scale*, the *Melbourne Scale* and the *Victoria Scale*. Each time, the internal structure of the underlying typologies is presented schematically and briefly described. We will then describe in some detail the various ideal-typical school identity options used in our research. We continue with a written interpretation of a basic example result taken from our Flemish educational context[7].

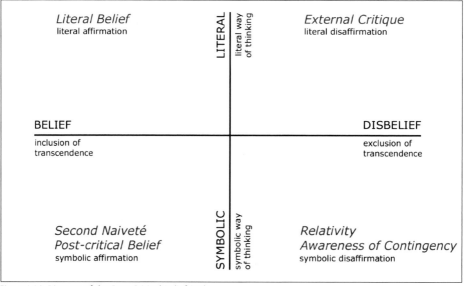

Figure I-14. Diagram of the *Post-Critical Belief Scale*.

The *Post-Critical Belief Scale* is an empirical instrument that was developed in the 1990s by the Leuven psychologist of religion Dirk Hutsebaut.[8] The questionnaire operationalises the typology by David M. Wulff on the four different ways that people deal with belief content.[9] These four cognitive belief styles or religious attitudes result from the combination of two dimensions. In the diagram, the horizontal line refers to whether or not someone has personal belief in God: inclusion/exclusion of belief in transcendence. The vertical line concerns the way in which religious faith is

---

[7] The content of paragraph 4 (*PCB Scale*), paragraph 5 (*Melbourne Scale*) and paragraph 6 (*Victoria Scale*) are re-edited texts that have been published in 2009 the following peer-reviewed article: POLLEFEYT, D., & BOUWENS, J., *Framing the identity of Catholic schools. Empirical methodology for quantitative research of the Catholic identity of an education institute*, in *International Studies in Catholic Education* 2-2 (2010).

[8] D. HUTSEBAUT, *Post-Critical Belief. A New Approach to the Religious Attitude Problem*, in *Journal of Empirical Theology* 9/2 (1996), 48-66.

[9] D.M. WULFF, *Psychology and religion. Classic and contemporary views*, New York, Wiley, 1991 & 1997.

experienced and processed: literal/symbolic interpretation of religious content. The combination of these two dimensions results in four different ways of dealing with religiosity. The *PCB Scale* is not so much concerned with the content of belief but rather with the ways in which people hold beliefs. Notice that these faith styles are ideal-typical, meaning that they are theoretical, extreme positions in a continuum with many in-between positions and mixed forms.

A. *Literal Belief* (*First Naiveté*)

Literal Belief stands for a literal affirmation of doctrinal belief content. Theologically speaking, this religious attitude assumes a direct, immediate access to the transcendent reality. The literally believing human being stresses the possibility and the desirability to present God unmediated, to meet him directly in words and rituals. He believes in a personal, immutable God and in fixed religious truth claims. Religious metaphors and truths of faith are objectified and interpreted literally. Biblical texts are mostly read literally and just accepted: often, Bible stories are read literally as 'reportage', describing actual historical events. Great value is attached to the Catholic tradition's objective shape. In particular cases, literal faith goes together with a need for stability, certainty, security, and familiarity. The literally believing person is often uncertain and afraid of new, complicating problems and therefore desires absolute certainty on matters of faith. On each question of faith, one single, exact, certain and unchangeable answer should be given. Authority, ecclesiastical hierarchy and obedience are of great importance. A subjective, critical faith interpretation is risky since interpretation results in uncertainty and doubt. Critical reflection about faith is seen as risky and a possible threat to religious certainty. One meritorious aspect of *Literal Belief* is the care for the ontological referent of the Christian faith: faith may not 'become symbolised' in such a way that belief in the objective existence of God would no longer be significant. However, in a pure form *Literal Belief* runs the risk of becoming a rigid, forced faith experience, often characterised by intolerance for alternative religious positions. At its worst, we can even speak of religious fanaticism and fundamentalism.

B. *External Critique* (*literal disbelief*)

External Critique or *Literal Disbelief* stands for a literal rejection of the belief content, in other words a direct critique on religion from an external point of view. Just like *Literal Belief*, this type starts from the immediate presence of the transcendent and from a literal interpretation of religious language, doctrines, and rites. But *External Critique* draws the harsh conclusion that all this 'religiousness' must be nonsense, because the literal interpretation – reasonably speaking – is untenable. Bible texts are also read literally and subsequently rejected: many facts in the Bible are considered untenable and, moreover, they are mutually contradictory. *External Critique* is an attitude of explicit disbelief that denies the existence of a transcendent reality. An external critic cannot imagine how it is possible to experience and envisage reality religiously. *Literal disbelief* is often framed in a modernistic, positivistic-scientific epistemology. External faith critics desire clarity and objective certainty, just as can be found in the positive sciences. They are afraid of the uncertainty in matters of faith and associate religion mostly with negative feelings. They emphasise freedom and personal autonomy, in opposition to the dependence associated with religious faith. They are stressed by the tension between human autonomy and the submission to God. Even though the use of critical reason certainly has its merits, *External Critique* runs the risk of exaggerating unilaterally and of losing any symbolic awareness. The holder of this belief position may see belief as a form of dependence or weakness. To live this kind of lifestyle might be demanding and burdensome. In the end, they maintain what can be in some cases an empty and gloomy worldview and this requires a fanaticism that frightens many people. At its worst, we can even speak of an intolerant anti-religious fundamentalism.

C. *Relativism* (*Contingency Awareness*)

Relativism or *Contingency Awareness* stands for a symbolic approach to religiosity, but without belief in a transcendent reality. Relativists are thoroughly aware of the symbolic and hermeneutical nature of religious faith. However, they hold no personal belief in God: relativists do not believe in the existence of a transcendent reality outside or beyond the human being, a reality to which we relate and in which religious faith grounds itself. The different religions are merely mutually interchangeable, human constructions. The one, true religion does not exist. Anyone's way of believing is just *one* possibility among many others. Relativists emphasise the contingency and the relativity of the contents of religion. These are all different paths to the top(s) of the mountain without one path or one top being privileged. The relativist's motto reads: "it is all equal to me what someone believes; it all comes down to the same anyway". All religions are 'equally true' and thus, actually, 'equally untrue'; there exists no God and so finally religion comes down to nothing. *Relativism* is permeated by the historical contingency of all religiosity. What is said about God, doctrines, faith confessions and morals is historically determined. Their content and form are only a reflection of the accidental historical context in which they came into being. The same is true for a believing person: what somebody believes depends on the accidental familial and cultural situation in which he or she grew up. For these people, religious content cannot be objectified and has no significance that reaches beyond the individual; they are merely subjective. Religion is not rejected resolutely by relativists (as external critics would do) but it is put into perspective. There remains a positive interest in religion, sometimes even a sympathy or fascination for religion. Relativists cultivate a great openness and receptivity towards various philosophical and religious traditions, as long as no coercion is used. *Relativism* is often a (temporary) position of *non-commitment*: they prefer not to commit themselves and they refrain from a positive choice for or against any religious stance. They postpone the choice, keeping their options open. At its worst, *Relativism* can lead to apathy, indifference and a lack of solidarity.

To illustrate this point, this is what former Pope Benedict XVI said about *Relativism* at the occasion of the *World Youth Days* in 2011[10]:

"Many people have no stable points of reference on which to build their lives, and so they end up deeply insecure. There is a growing mentality of *Relativism*, which holds that everything is equally valid, that truth and absolute points of reference do not exist. But this way of thinking does not lead to true freedom, but rather to instability, confusion and blind conformity to the fads of the moment. As young people, you are entitled to receive from previous generations solid points of reference to help you to make choices and on which to build your lives: like a young plant which needs solid support until it can sink deep roots and become a sturdy tree capable of bearing fruit."

D. *Post-Critical Belief (Second Naiveté)*

Post-Critical Belief stands for a symbolic affirmation of faith content. It is characterised by faith in a transcendent God and in a religious interpretation of reality in which the transcendent is not considered literally present but is represented symbolically. God is the radical Other to whom we relate through a symbolic representation, through the interpretation of a sign that refers to the transcendent. People relate to the transcendent reality only through mediations: through stories, rituals, traditions, institutions, churches, ministries, communities, social organisations and so forth. Faith is acquired through the active, creative and interpretative handling of these mediations. According to *Post-Critical Belief*, to believe is a continuous process of symbol-interpretation; the revelation of new layers of significance in the symbolic relationship with God. To believe is only possible and meaningful after interpretation. Here, critical reason plays an important role, so that we do not believe in nonsense

---

[10] JOSEPH RATZINGER, *Message Of His Holiness Pope Benedict Xvi For The Twenty-Sixth World Youth Day* (2011), Libreria Editrice Vaticana (2010), §1. (http://www.vatican.va/; access 18-08-2011).

against our better judgment. Biblical texts and other religious writings can only be understood and believed in after interpretation. The Bible is written in a specific historical context and employs (sometimes obsolete) mythological, symbolic and religious language in which the story of God with human beings is told. To read the Bible then requires interpretation, deciphering and translation: the post-critical believer tries to distinguish the mythological images from the religious message for us, alive in the here and now. The term *Post-Critical Belief* refers to a well-considered faith in God despite critical reasons not to believe. After a renewed interpretation, religious content becomes meaningful again. Destructive criticism on the literal understanding of faith is surmounted by a renewed faith understanding that lasts despite the ongoing possibility of rational critique. *Post-Critical Belief* is a continuous 'searching for' religious significance and meaning without ever finding a final, absolute, established and certain answer. Symbolic believers live with the existential tension between uncertainty and trust. They feel called to constantly question the religious content and personal convictions from which they live. They are prepared for reinterpretation, are open to change and are receptive to complex faith questions that feed the hermeneutical process. Since they are searching themselves, *Post-Critical Believers* are sympathetic to the spiritual search of others even though these people live within different worldviews than they do. They have an essential openness and receptivity vis-à-vis other religious perspectives and practices. Because of the hermeneutical nuances and the continuous 'searching', *Post-Critical Belief* is a complex and vulnerable faith position. We sometimes have difficulty with an existential confidence in faith in the first person, without a clear, established and immediately comprehensible meaning structure. Moreover, *Post-Critical Belief* is under pressure both from *Literal Belief* (which denounces it as relativism and a watering down of literal faith understanding) as well as from *External Critique* and *Relativism* (which both suspect it of being disguised *Literal Belief*). At its worst, this belief style can slide into a 'religious' attitude that has a very general and unspecified content without a clear point of reference, in which any interpretation remains possible.

We openly acknowledge that the *Post-Critical Belief* type is the faith style promoted at the *Centre for Academic Teacher Training* of our Faculty of Theology. Based on theological arguments and on empirical research results, we defend that a symbolic style of faith is the most fruitful for the development of the identity of Catholic schools in a pluralising society, today and tomorrow.[11] To promote a *Post-Critical Belief* attitude among youth is the intention of the current course curriculum of religious education in Flemish schools, as well.

---

[11] D. POLLEFEYT, *Hoe aan onze (klein)kinderen uitleggen dat Sinterklaas (niet) bestaat. Over levensbeschouwelijke en religieuze maturiteit*, in *H-ogelijn* 17-1 (2009) 31-35.

E. Empirical operationalisation: approaches to measuring cognitive belief styles

This typology was developed by Hutsebaut into an empirical instrument called the *Post-Critical Belief* Scale.[12] It involves a multivariate questionnaire with 33 items on a seven-point scale which can be filled out by individuals or groups. For respondents under 18 years of age, we created a simpler 'teenage version'. After statistical analysis, we get a view of how the four belief styles are supported or rejected, as well as insight into their mutual relations. Obviously, it is not the intention to label people. The four belief styles are not mutually exclusive; they do not need to exclude each other in practice. One and the same person can show features of several faith attitudes, depending on the subject, the point in time or the situation. Equally, tendencies of several belief styles can be present at the same time in one population. When we want to research an institutions' Catholic identity, an insight into the faith attitudes of its members is very illuminating. Such insights explain not only the current religious identity of the organisation, but throw light on the potential to evolve in a certain direction in the future as well.

Below is an example graph of the scale averages of the PCB Scale, obtained from a sample of 852 respondents. The vertical line is scaled according to the seven-point Likert scale used in the questionnaire. The white horizontal line at No. four indicates the turning point from rejection (<4) to approval (>4). It is immediately clear that *Post-Critical Belief* is the most prominent faith attitude here (5.45). This main tendency is followed by an equally clear positive score for *Relativism* (4.92). A majority of the respondents deals with belief content in a symbolic-hermeneutical way, but there is no unanimity about the transcendent-believing interpretation. A debate seems to be taking place about the desirability of a personal faith in God amidst a plurality of philosophical positions, whereby, in general, the symbolic-believing attitude is most appreciated. Furthermore, among these respondents, there is a clear united tendency to reject a literal dealing with religious faith (2.42). A literal-disbelieving attitude is also rejected among all respondents (3.44). However, this rejection is not very strong. In this sample, there is a minority tendency which positions itself externally-critically vis-à-vis faith, whereas a small majority takes a doubting or rather rejecting position.

---

[12] B. DURIEZ, D. HUTSEBAUT et al, *An Introduction To The Post-Critical Belief Scale. Internal Structure And External Relationships*, in *Psyke & Logos* 28 (2007), 767-793. See also: B. DURIEZ, R.J. FONTAINE & D. HUTSEBAUT, *A further elaboration of the post-critical belief scale: evidence for the existence of four different approaches to religion in Flanders-Belgium*, in *Psychologica Belgica* 40-3 (2000).

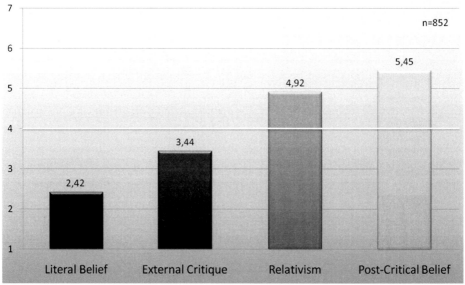

Figure I-15. *Post-Critical Belief Scale* example graph.

Suppose this sample comes from a Catholic school context. How can these PCB-results be interpreted and what recommendations would we make to this school, starting from a normative preference for a symbolic-believing attitude? To make the Catholic identity work, the widespread appreciation of *Post-Critical Belief* definitely sounds promising. It is also positive that a symbolic-hermeneutical attitude towards religion is generally accepted, and that a multiplicity of philosophies of life is appreciated. However, the high score for *Relativism* or Contingency Awareness may threaten the Catholic school identity because it strongly tones down its particularity. It should be recommended that *Post-Critical Believers* exemplify in word and deed that a Catholic faith attitude by no means contradicts the recognition of religious and philosophical multiplicity or an authentic appreciation of other-minded people. From the idea that a dogmatic, *Literal-Believing* interaction with the Catholic tradition would be unfruitful for the identity of Catholic schools in our contemporary pluralising culture, we can rejoice in the rejection of *Literal Belief*. However, an all too strong rejection of traditional faith content is unfortunate as well, because symbolic-believing people also entrust themselves to the reality and truth of the triune God who reveals himself in the Christian tradition. Without an ontological referent, the symbol remains empty and meaningless. It is the closed, totalising attitude of *Literal Belief* that causes danger, not the traditional faith contents to which one relates in a symbolic-hermeneutical way. The greatest threat for a school's Catholic identity lies in the minority tendency to *External Critique*. We recommend further research on this tendency (e.g. through stratification in respondent groups) and invite adherers of *External Critique* to at least take a symbolic-hermeneutical attitude vis-à-vis religion. To this end, imagination and hermeneutical skills should be promoted, for instance through contact with literature or art, or by stimulating the dialogue between different religions and philosophies of life.

§5. Catholic identity options from a theological perspective: *The Melbourne Scale*

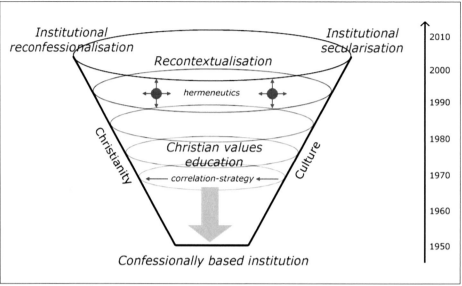

Figure I-16. Diagram of the *Melbourne Scale*.

Up until the 1950s, the confessional identity of schools from the Catholic network in Flanders was guaranteed. Since then, we have seen that our cultural context, including the educational field, has increasingly secularised, detraditionalised and more recently also pluralised. The Catholic identity of schools is under pressure.[13] The gap between culture and Catholic faith becomes larger and larger. The challenge for Catholic schools consists therefore in bridging the gap time and again and to communicate the Catholic faith to children and youth who grow up in contemporary culture.[14] Against the background of this analysis, the systematic theologian Lieven Boeve, the present Dean of the Faculty of Theology, has developed a typology of identity options which Catholic schools can adopt to give shape to their identity in a changing cultural context.[15]

---

[13] L. BOEVE, *Interrupting Tradition. An Essay on Christian Faith in a Postmodern Context* (Louvain Theological and Pastoral Monographs 30), Leuven, Peeters, 2002; L. BOEVE, *God onderbreekt de geschiedenis. Theologie in tijden van ommekeer*, Kapellen, Pelckmans, 2006.

[14] D. POLLEFEYT, *Het leven doorgeven. Religieuze traditie in de katholieke godsdienstpedagogiek. Ontwikkelingen en toekomstperspectieven*, in H. van Crombrugge & W. Meijer (ed.), *Pedagogiek en traditie. Opvoeding en religie*, Tielt, Lannoo Campus, 2004.

[15] L. BOEVE, *The Identity of a Catholic University in Post-Christian European Societies: Four Models*, in *Louvain Studies* 31 (2006), 238-258.

A. *Confessional School Identity*

The traditional *Confessional* identity of the Catholic education system has not yet completely eroded. The *Confessional School* type indicates to what extent a traditional-Catholic school identity is continued today, despite the tension between culture and Catholicism. It indicates how far a Catholic school adheres to the traditional elements of its confessional nature, as a leftover of cultural Christianity. An 'old style' *Confessional* school identity is simply continued out of habit, out of the desire to remain recognisably 'Catholic', as an expression of a passive, awaiting attitude, or also just to not to engage with the issue.

B. *Values Education in a Christian perspective*

As the gap between the Catholic faith and culture became wider from the 1960s onwards, Catholic schools started to use a new method to bridge the gap, called *Values Education* in a Christian Perspective. This school type aims at *a compromise between culture and Catholic tradition* in an attempt to maintain a Catholic school identity that 'keeps up with the time' and with which anybody can reconcile. More specifically, this involves an attempt to link a generally shared awareness of 'a good life' to the Catholic faith as the fulfilment of this intuition. For instance, this approach might start with the experience of love between two human beings, give a Catholic explanation to it, and arrive at the love of God for all people. Ethics especially functions as mediator between culture and Catholic faith; Catholic inspiration is translated into an education in Christian values and norms that are thought to be universally recognisable. In this way, the hope is that a pluralising student population can continue to be addressed on the subject of faith. It is expected that students can recognise themselves (again) in the Catholic faith by this *Christian Values Education* that grounds, deepens and brings to completion these values and norms. *Values Education* uses a secularisation paradigm: the school population consists of Catholic believers and 'not-any-more' Catholics, and the aim is to bring back into the Church as many 'astray' and 'anonymous' Catholics as possible. Despite the inductive didactical approach, this remains in fact a strategy with confessionalising intentions. This type of school stimulates civic responsibility and supports social welfare projects, solidarity with the poor and the vulnerable, volunteer work and so forth. The school community consists of Catholics and people who positively value the Catholic faith. Since the Christian inspiration is presented as 'doing good', this school can also appeal to post-Christians, other-believers and other-minded people. This type of school is thus assured of a broad support basis.

Even though the belief in the universal communicability of the salvific message is typically Catholic and this strategy did function well for many years, it implies some risks. After all, it starts with the presupposition that all school members, even though they are not Catholic believers, can always be addressed with the Catholic message in a way that is open and evident. For a long time this was indeed the case. But the more culture detraditionalises and pluralises, and the more culture and Catholicism drift apart, the harder it becomes to reconnect the two. When the gap becomes too wide, this strategy will malfunction. If present-day experiences are difficult to explain and categorise from a Catholic perspective, then the correlation movement is in danger of running aground half way. If in the long term this ineffectiveness is linked to predictability (students see the attempt at correlation coming a long way off), then this strategy can end up being counterproductive. Furthermore, *Values Education* runs the risk of a 'horizontalisation' of the Catholic teachings: those elements that are easy to link to present-day experience are selected spontaneously. Catholic faith is then reduced to just an ethical code, which, moreover, is broadly shared. Since all those involved should be able to recognise themselves in the compromise, it could be feared that personal particularity is erased and that an active dialogue among different life visions is curtailed. If the movement runs aground half way without bringing up the Catholic faith explicitly, would that be specific enough for Catholic schools? Can one still rightly speak of a 'Catholic school' when God and Jesus Christ are not being talked about? In practice, this approach usually results in a post-Christian school environment in which it is good to sojourn, but where little explicitly Catholic faith remains present. De facto, *Values Education in a Christian Perspective* is an intermediate phase towards a secularisation of school identity. Often, it is more an unconscious sliding of Catholic identity than an intentional strategy. Often *Values Education* itself is an exponent of detraditionalising and pluralising tendencies.

C. Institutional *Reconfessionalisation*

An obvious reaction to the secularisation of educational institutes is to actively promote the confessional Catholic identity again. Boeve calls this *Institutional Reconfessionalisation*. This school type wishes to make its Catholic identity stronger and more general again by means of an active strategy of *Reconfessionalisation*. In an attempt to bring the school culture closer to Catholicism again, the Catholic nature of the school is explicitly and publicly profiled. It is taken for granted that a substantial part of the school population is practising Catholic or should be, and the aim is faith formation for all students in a Catholic environment. The ties with the Church and the local parish are tightened. An active participation with the ecclesiastical community life is encouraged. Priests are actively present at school. Classes in religious education, pastoral care, celebrations of the Eucharist, sacraments, school prayer, first communion, confirmation preparations, et cetera are considered essential components of school life.

What is the difference between a *Confessional* and a *Reconfessionalising* Catholic school? Both school models possess all the markers of traditional Catholicity, but *the intention* behind their identity profiles differs:

➤ A *Confessional School* is said to be one that has not wavered from its long-standing Catholic identity in the face of a changing society, and thus still bears strong resemblance to the Catholic identity it possessed a half century ago.

➤ A *Reconfessionalising School* is said to be one which intentionally re-injects traditional Catholicity into its identity as a way of combating the forces of secularisation and pluralisation – with the specific intention of reforming young people as traditional Catholics.

In itself, a *Confessional* Catholic school identity is of course a legitimate option in the midst of plurality: one aims to be one's authentic self amid the multiplicity. It is certainly not the case that a *Reconfessionalising* identity strategy automatically and necessarily would be promoted out of a closed, narrow-minded mentality (as would be the case in a *Monologue School*, see below). Moreover, it is a service to those parents who wish an undivided Catholic education for their children. Yet, it is not unlikely that this school type would adopt a critical-rejective stance against the secularised and pluralist culture. In this way, the Catholic faith and the Catholic lifestyle are defended and promoted as a counter-story. The fact that students are possibly alienated from the outside, non-Catholic world, is considered an unavoidable consequence rather than an objection. Despite the possible justifications, one can wonder if in present-day society there is sufficient support for this identity option.

D. *Institutional Secularisation*

The opposite reaction to the growing gap between culture and Christianity is to let go of the Catholic school identity. Boeve calls this *Institutional Secularisation*. This school type parallels the cultural context: just as the Catholic faith gradually disappears in culture, this happens at school as well. The Catholic nature and the preferential option for Catholicism erode away slowly until nothing is left of them in daily school life. Catholic signs and symbols disappear, rituals no longer take place and references to religion vanish from everyday discourse. Over the course of time, the school's original Catholic background and inspiration hardly play any role anymore. This gradual erosion is often more an implicit process than a conscious and guided option. The presence of *Christian Values Education*, which for a long time has often been employed as a compromise model, can disguise this hidden secularisation process for quite some time. However, when the tension between Christianity and culture becomes insurmountable in the end, the decision is made to adopt the *Secularisation* process on an organisational and institutional level. At a certain moment, voices are raised to call the school no longer 'a Catholic school' officially and to strike off the 'C' from the school's name. Also, people desire to replace mandatory, Catholic religious education with a broad, comparative, philosophical formation, with Catholic religion as an optional course. The school population of such a secularised school is characterised by philosophical and religious diversity without a preferential option for the Catholic faith. Everyone has the right to be him or herself and is called to respect and show tolerance towards others (see also the *Colourful School* and the *Colourless School* below).

E. *Recontextualisation* of Catholic identity (Identity formation in a plural context)

The fifth and last identity type is called *Recontextualisation of Catholic School Identity*, also known as *Identity Construction in a Pluralist Perspective*. This school type is deliberately in search of a renewed Catholic profile in and through conversation with plurality. It tries to understand the Catholic faith re-interpreted in a contemporary cultural context. On the one hand plurality is recognised and valued as such; on the other hand the focus on the Catholic identity is maintained. After all, the evangelical message remains relevant for people of today and tomorrow. But the changing cultural context should be integrated into 'being Catholic' (recontextualisation) so that it remains recognisable, credible and meaningful for contemporary people (tradition development). The question then is how to live a Catholic life and how to build a Catholic school in the middle of contemporary culture. It is important to understand that recontextualisation of Catholic school identity starts from a pluralisation paradigm. In fact, Catholicism is *one* option among a multiplicity of philosophical and religious positions. Catholics believe that God, in his own way, is near to all people in their search for value and meaning. This plurality is not only formally recognised, but also appreciated as a positive challenge and a chance to enrich one's own Catholic identity. Openness to and dialogue with otherness (including non-Catholic) is encouraged without aiming at the greatest common denominator. Multiplicity is played out; multi-vocality needs to resound. *Recontextualisation* is not substantiated by an attitude of consensus (as in *Values Education*) but is propelled by dissimilarity. Young people are taught to relate to other religions and philosophies of life from a personal profile (whether Catholic or not). In dialogue with otherness they learn to know themselves, and how to take responsibility for personal choices. Show your individuality in tension with dissimilarities — precisely out of respect for the other. This way, the Catholic faith is treated as the preferential perspective. The conversation between religious and philosophical visions is reflected upon from a preferential option for Catholicism. From its own power and depth, the voice of Catholicism resonates amid the multiplicity of voices. So it is not the intention that all students become

Catholic believers per se, but that they let themselves be challenged and enriched by the offer of the Catholic narrative. A *Recontextualising* school environment challenges people to give shape to their personal identity in conversation with others, against the background of a dialogue and sometimes a confrontation with the Catholic tradition (see the *Dialogue School* elsewhere in this book). The basis for this is shaped by at least a significant minority of Catholics who are recognisable as such and who want to enter into dialogue explicitly. Next to them there is a diverse school population that opens up to what Catholicism has to offer.

F. Empirical operationalisation: approaches to measuring theological identity options

This typology has been developed into an empirical instrument called the *Melbourne Scale*. We developed a multivariate questionnaire with a factual and a normative measurement level (except for the Confessional School, which is only measured at a factual level). For respondents under 18, we created a shorter and simpler 'teenage version'. The theoretical identity options of the Melbourne Scale were empirically tested both in Flanders and in Australia, and retrieved in practice as latent thinking patterns. The result is an empirical instrument that provides us with a nuanced in-depth image of the various tendencies and their mutual relations both now and in the future regarding the complex dynamics of the Catholic institutional identity.

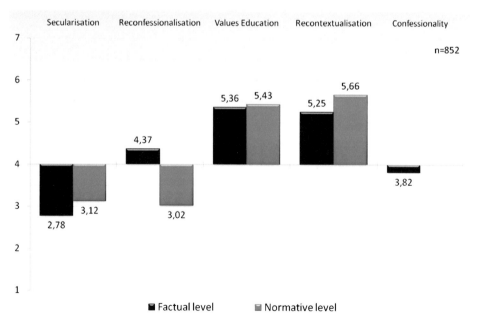

Figure I-17. *Melbourne Scale* example graph.

Figure I-18 is an example graph of the scale means of the *Melbourne Scale* on the factual (F) and the normative (N) level. We notice that the traditional *Confessionality* of this school is still recognised, but that it is obviously under pressure (F 3.82). In general, the respondents recognise that the Catholic confessionality is disappearing. We see this trend in the *Secularisation* scores as well. Even though the school is experienced as not being secularised at this time (F 2.78), the resistance to *Secularisation* is crumbling (N 3.12). The scores on the factual level for the three Catholic school types are all positive. Here we see a school that practices *Christian Values Education* (F 5.36) and in parallel is trying to *Recontextualise* its Catholic identity (F 5.25). In addition, the current practice shows a small tendency to *Reconfessionalisation* (F 4.37). On the normative level, the implosion of *Reconfessionalisation* is striking (N 3.02); the intention to make the school more traditionally Catholic again, cannot count on any sympathy. On the other hand, the respondents do agree with *Values Education* but its growth has nearly halted and as such it seems to have reached its high point (N 5.43). The most plausible perspective for the future appears to be a further *Recontextualisation* of the school (N 5.66); the score rises significantly compared with the factual level and takes the lead over from *Values Education*.

Starting from a preference for *Identity Formation in a Pluralist Perspective*, how should these results be interpreted and which recommendations should be made to an organisation with these empirical results? The high score for the *Recontextualising* school type, which moreover is the main tendency at the normative level, is encouraging in this perspective. Together with the high score for *Values Education*, this indicates a desire for a Catholic school identity that is open to contemporary experiences. Furthermore, a certain appreciation for the pluralist culture is acceptable, even its apparently non-Catholic aspects. But this school has to take care that resistance to *Secularisation* does not crumble too much among certain groups (particularly among students, as differentiations show). Moreover, it is worthwhile warning against the continuation of *Values Education* when the confessional structures are in the process of disappearing. Latent *Confessionality* is the 'petrol tank', as it were, of *Values Education*. When the tank runs empty, the correlation strategy might sputter and *Values Education* can just undermine the Catholic identity. Attempts to makes this school more traditionally Catholic do not have a future perspective either. In view of the manifest rejection of *Reconfessionalisation* on the normative level, pushing through this identity option could even harm the school's Catholic identity. Not only is it useless to impose top-down an identity for which there exists no support among school members, it would also increase the fear for a curtailing Catholic preferential perspective. Tendencies towards *External Critique* and *Relativism* would turn against *all* sorts of Catholic identity, even against the more open types like *Values Education* and *Recontextualisation*. We summarise that the people of this school are generally attached to their institution's Catholic identity, but on the condition that the latter takes an open and communicative stand towards contemporary cultural developments. They wish to distance themselves from the 'old style' Catholic identity but still demonstrate a preference for the Catholic narrative. It should be hoped that this school leaves behind the hidden *Reconfessionalising* agenda of *Values Education*, recognises and values plurality even more, and, being a Catholic school, openly enters into dialogue with plurality in search of a recognisable Catholic identity amidst a religious and philosophical multiplicity as a service to the personal development of all.

§6. Catholic identity options from a pedagogical perspective: *The Victoria Scale*

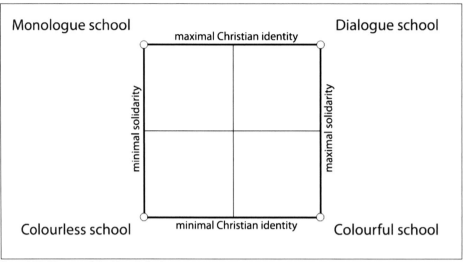

Figure I-18. Diagram of the *Victoria Scale*.

The *Victoria Scale* is an empirical instrument inspired by a typology of the Dutch researchers Wim ter Horst[16] and Chris Hermans[17] on the pedagogical basic options of Catholic schools in a pluralising cultural context. Just like the *PCB Scale*, the *Victoria Scale* is constructed of two dimensions. The vertical line refers to an organisation's Christian identity: the measure in which its members live out of a generally shared, Catholic inspiration. The horizontal line concerns the solidarity with people from subcultures other than the Catholic one: the measure of openness to and receptivity of other life visions and life attitudes. Every confessional organisation faces the task of making pedagogical and organisational choices concerning its Catholic identity, in combination to its solidarity with otherness. Putting together these two dimensions results in what is called the *identity square*. On the angles we find four ideal-typical strategies that schools can adopt to give shape to their pedagogical responsibility vis-à-vis their faith education in a multicultural society. The *Victoria Scale* explores the ways in which a Catholic school, in a multicultural and multi-religious society, manages the two-fold challenge of defining its identity on the one hand and exercising solidarity with the wider community on the other.

---

[16] W. TER HORST, *Wijs me de weg. Mogelijkheden voor een christelijke opvoeding in een post-christelijke samenleving*, Kampen, Kok, 1995, p.63-75.

[17] C.A.M. HERMANS & J. VAN VUYGT (ed.), *Identiteit door de tijd. Reflectie op het confessionele basisonderwijs in een geseculariseerde en multiculturele samenleving*, Den Haag, ABKO, 1997, 5-27.

A. The *Monologue School*

The *Monologue School* is typified by a combination of maximal Christian identity with minimal solidarity. It concerns a traditional Catholic school of, aimed at, and run by Catholics. This school puts a strong emphasis on its *Catholic* Identity. It promotes a traditionalist, non-emancipatory form of Catholicism in which the Catholic faith is interpreted as a 'closed story' with a resolute truth claim. The Catholic confession and praxis of the majority of the school members is taken for granted and, if necessary, is realised through an active recruitment policy. This school stresses safety within its own Catholic circle. In fact, its education is a service to its own sub-cultural group. However, this school deliberately does not choose receptivity of other religions and philosophies of life. There is little solidarity with the non-Catholic external world, which is considered a threat to the Catholic specificity. It is considered *unsafe* to discuss issues that dare to challenge Catholic doctrines. This school offers its members a sense of certainty, security and safety. It likes to promote itself as an 'air raid shelter', emphasising its role in protecting its members from the possible ravages of the secularising culture. However, this risks fostering a tendency toward isolation and unworldliness. This school type can therefore be described as a 'shelter' or a walled 'Catholic ghetto'.

In many empirical research results, we detect a pairing of perceived *Monologue* tendencies (current practice) and a desire for more *Colourless School* characteristics (ideal school). People who feel intimidated by a strong, 'top-down' Catholic identity that is being imposed upon them, often show the self-protective reaction to retreat into the private realm. They defend the right for a personal opinion and believe that the school should show more tolerance and respect for people's individual freedom. An imposed Catholic identity risks eliciting a counter reaction that leads to individualism, formal tolerance and relativism.

B. The *Colourless School*

The *Colourless School* is typified by a combination of a minimal Christian identity with minimal solidarity. It concerns a secularised and pluralist school environment where contact between individuals is non-committal. The attention to a specific Catholic ethos has been gradually watered down in this type of school to such an extent that it has taken up a *secularistic* standpoint: philosophy of life and religion have no place in the public sphere. The school takes a 'neutral' standpoint, in the sense that philosophies of life cannot be imposed or steered from above. The school limits its task to the provision of sound education but considers religious formation not as its responsibility. The school shows great openness and tolerance for all kinds of philosophies of life and religions, but this openness is not framed in a common religious project. It is not up to the collective to care for the individual's mental welfare. Life-reflection and giving meaning is a personal matter, for which every individual is personally responsible in freedom. Connected to individualistic and liberalistic tendencies in society, the focus lies on the individual rather than on the school community. The school is composed of individuals and small groups of people with little mutual solidarity or community spirit. The *Colourless School* limits itself to a minimalistic ethics based on the no-damage principle: the focus lies on personal freedom on the condition that nobody hinders anyone else's freedom. Even though many encounters and exchanges take place, the contacts with the others remain superficial and free from obligation or mutual commitment. People live quasi non-committally next to each other; the prevalent mentality is one of *laisser faire, laisser passer*. Although this school is very accessible, pluralistic and open, there is little authentic engagement or care for others and little pedagogical security. The risk is that formal tolerance and respect for personal freedom slide down into a culture of non-commitment and indifference.

C. The *Colourful School*

The *Colourful School* is typified by a combination of minimal Christian identity with maximal solidarity. It concerns a secularised and pluralist school environment where one takes a very social, committed, united and solidary position. This school type is characterised by a rich and visible diversity and this internal plurality is taken into account seriously. The school spends a lot of effort on its pedagogical responsibility and the care for the spiritual well-being of others. Authentic attention and interest is shown for each other's differences. Encounters and exchanges testify to depth and mutual solidarity. There is sincere involvement and care for one another's well-being. 'One for all, all for one' is the motto. This is a community of doers and caregivers who put themselves to service for people in need. The school actively engages in social projects and volunteer work. However, few school members are still concerned about the school's Catholic character. Little or no room is available for the proclamation of the Gospel and for pastoral education at school. Catholicism as a preferential option above other views is rejected. The *Colourful School* thinks that every (in)doctrinal direction should be avoided as much as possible. It puts itself in a neutral-pluralist position: the dialogue among different views should be encouraged but without any preference for one particular perspective. The school board devotes itself to giving the many religious and philosophical views of its members every chance to flourish, but it will not take any preferential option itself. It is feared that a preferential option for the Catholic faith (or any other view) would undermine solidarity with other-minded people and that it would form a hindrance for living together in plurality. A preferential option can lead to alienation, exclusion, and even aversion. To value the other *as other* implies the respect of each other's personal freedom. To impose one or other 'truth' collectively would lead to the suppression of the individual's 'personal truth'. Of course, Catholic believers can be present at this school. They enjoy the same openness, freedom of speech, chances to growth, and appreciation that is offered to other-minded people too. But despite the edifying ethos of involvement and solidarity, in which Catholics can also find themselves, the *Colourful School* cannot be called a Catholic school.

D. The *Dialogue School*

The *Dialogue School*, finally, is typified by a combination of maximal Catholic identity with maximal solidarity. It concerns a Catholic school in the middle of cultural and religious plurality in which both Catholics and other-believers can develop themselves maximally. A *Dialogue School* explicitly chooses to emphasise its Catholic inspiration and individuality through and thanks to a hermeneutical-communicative dialogue with the multicultural society. The multiplicity of voices, views and perspectives, is recognised as a positive contribution to an open Catholic school environment. Receptivity and openness to what is different is a chance to re-profile the Catholic faith amidst contemporary plurality (*Recontextualisation*). A preferential option for the Catholic message sets the tone for this dialogue. The conversation among philosophical views is conducted with a preferential option for Catholicism in mind. In the midst of plurality, one is looking to be a Catholic; from being a Catholic, one lives in plurality. It is this open relation to the other/Other that typifies a typical Catholic life attitude. Just like for Catholic believers, the intense conversation enriches the other-minded people at school too. Not only by what the Catholic faith has to offer to them, even though they do not believe themselves. But also because, through dialogue, they get to know themselves better, become more distinctly aware of their own philosophical choices, learning to take responsibility for them, and so deepen their identity (Identity Formation in a Pluralist Perspective). The pluralisation process challenges the Catholic school to be at the service of the personal formation of all youngsters, regardless their cultural or religious background. The *Dialogue School* takes its responsibility for all, also on the level of personal development. Starting from its Catholic individuality and through a dialogue with different life views, it wants to be a guide for the philosophical and religious growth of all students. As such, Catholic school identity and solidarity with otherness are not only perfectly combinable but they both come to full flourishing when combined.

E. Empirical operationalisation: approaches to measuring pedagogical identity options

This typology was developed into an empirical instrument called the *Victoria Scale*. We developed a multivariate questionnaire with a factual and a normative measurement level. As with the *Melbourne Scale*, we created a shorter and more simple 'teenage version' for respondents under 18 years of age. After empirical research, the theoretical identity options were retrieved in practice as latent thinking patterns. Because of its focus on the pedagogical dealing with multi-culturality and multi-religiosity, the *Victoria Scale* is a meaningful addition to the *Melbourne Scale*. Moreover, the *Victoria Scale* splits the *Institutional Secularisation* type into two distinct types that handle philosophical and religious multiplicity differently: the Colourless and the Colourful School.

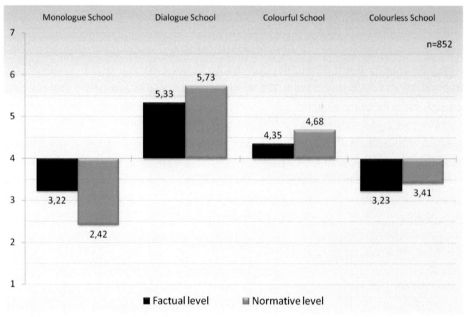

Figure I-19. *Victoria Scale* example graph.

Figure I-19 is an example graph of the scale averages of the *Victoria Scale* on the factual (F) and on the normative (N) level. It is immediately clear that the respondents consider this school a *Dialogue School* (F 5.33) and that the desire can be felt to strengthen this pedagogy in the future (N 5.73). Next to this main trend, there is a second, smaller tendency that is also backed by a majority of the respondents: the *Colourful School*. The graph shows that the respondents recognise this solidary but non-Catholic approach in the current practice (F 4.35) and its adherents still increase when they think of their ideal school environment (N 4.68). What this school is definitely not and never will be is a *Monologue School*. It is striking how great the distance is between the measure of absence perceived on average (F 3.22) and the resistance felt for this type (N 2.42). Also the *Colourless School* type is not applicable to this school environment (F 3.23), even though the resistance to this individualistic school environment slightly decreases among all respondents (N 3.41).

§7. Assessing the validity of the multivariate attitude scales

When creating results for the *PCB Scale*, the *Melbourne Scale* and the *Victoria Scale*, we have to ensure as much as possible that the measurements in the graphs actually indicate what they are supposed to measure, namely the conceptual constructs of the underlying typologies. So that, if we conclude based on the measurements that, for example, a school's traditional Catholic *Confessionality* is fading away (*Melbourne Scale*), the measurement in question actually measures *Confessionality* instead of something else. Moreover, we must ensure that the corresponding measurements on the factual and the normative level actually refer to the same underlying construct. How is this achieved?

Mostly the scale's *standardised reading keys* produce valid and correct results without the need for manual adjustment. Still we always keep a close eye on the validity of the research results we produce. After each new research project with a sufficient number of respondents, we spend time carrying out a thorough statistical analysis. When evaluating the validity of the subscale measurements, we always combine a variety of checks:

1. The meaning of the constituting items should adequately refer to the conceptual constructs they are supposed to measure. The items should formulate the constructs in a correct, concise and understandable way. The formulations should be varied and yet form a coherent group.
2. We examine the *Pearson correlation matrixes* of all the items. These matrixes should contain clear 'blocks' of highly correlating items that belong to the same type.
3. We examine the *internal consistencies and reliabilities* of all subscales by means of the *Cronbach Alpha coefficient*.
4. We conduct a *factor analysis* (principal component). After orthogonal rotation the factor structure should reveal latent variables that coincide with the conceptual constructs behind the items, whose factor loads should cluster accordingly. We also examine the factors' Eigen values and the amount of variance that is explained by them.
5. Finally, we also examine the meaning of the result: the resulting graph should be clearly interpretable, believable and free of inconsistencies or paradoxes.

Based on this combined information, we decide how to summarise the many items into the subscale measurements that appear in the graphs. Mostly we cannot improve upon the standardised reading keys. However, in some cases a manual adjustment can be required in order to *guarantee the best possible measurement*. We can make various adjustments, in combination if needed:

a) We could simply delete an item that does not function as it is supposed to, while making sure that sufficient items remain.
b) We could move an item from one subscale to another, if it appears to function better there.
c) We could, exceptionally, even invert an item (agreement becomes disagreement).
d) Based on the analysis, we could suggest an alternative formulation that might function better and update the scale itself.

The empirical instruments were designed and tested to work even in cases where people become 'tired' or complete them in a careless manner. Where the multivariate attitude scales are concerned: as long as there is *any* relation between the content of the questions and the answers on the Likert scale, we are able to determine general attitudinal tendencies that exist within all the answers taken together. This becomes all the more true when we combine data from larger numbers of respondents.

During the course of the *Enhancing Catholic School Identity Project* we carried out numerous trials in Belgium, in Victoria and elsewhere in the world. Based on these trial data sets, we gradually improved the validity and stability of the attitude scales. At present, we can confidently say that our empirical research instruments produce reliable estimates of all the subscale measurements, *at least* approximating the 'actual' score of the school population. However, whenever possible we continue to conduct small-scale experiments in order to improve the scales where possible. Some item formulations will also need to be cross-culturally adapted to the educational context of a new country.

Chapter 4. Complementary qualitative research methodologies – Introduction

The ECSIP survey research methodology is a form of *quantitative* research because it quantifies representative trends in a population using numbers and statistical calculations. In addition, ECSIP offers a range of *qualitative* research methodologies that complement the survey research process. They collect non-numerical information of a more qualitative nature, often in the form of texts, images, sound or video that needs to be analysed in an interpretative manner. The practice of complementing the ECSIP survey research with qualitative research methods has been trialled extensively in Belgium as well as Australia in the past years. For the purpose of researching Catholic school identity, qualitative research entails a combination and integration of the following four research activities:

- *Document analysis*
- *Analysis of the founding and the history of the school*
- *An annotated photo report*
- *Interview research*

In the ECSIP approach, qualitative research does not stand on its own but always follows the survey research as a second step in the process. Based on the representative findings of the standardised online surveys, a limited number of *qualitative research questions* are formulated, aimed at a further exploration of the Catholic identity of a particular school. These are the purposes and advantages of using additional qualitative research techniques:

- To gain a deeper understanding of underlying reasons and motivations;
- To uncover prevalent trends in thought and opinion;
- To apply the graph results better to the concrete context of a particular school;
- To sharpen our understanding of the quantitative research findings;
- To clear up ambivalent or unclear survey results.

First step: preparation
Preferably, the ECSIP qualitative research is to be executed by a qualified researcher external to the school. The first step of the process consists of thorough preparation. First, the findings of the survey research, which need to be available, are analysed in detail and a number of *qualitative research questions* are detected and written down. Next, with the help of the school, the researcher puts together a *School Identity Portfolio* that consists of relevant written documents and other materials that are directly or indirectly informative about the school's Catholic identity. Likewise,

information is collected about the school's founding and history, with a special focus on the development of its religious features over the years, including the most recent period. Next, a number of digital pictures are assembled in an annotated *Photo Report*. Finally, the interview research is prepared by selecting people to talk to, making the appointments and developing a good number of *interview questions* appropriate for the target audiences that operationalise the more general *qualitative research questions*.

Second step: school visit
The second step of the process consists of a visit to the school. Typically, such a visit begins with a guided tour of the school campus. During the visit, there is the opportunity to take additional photographs and have brief informal conversations with students and teachers. It continues with an extensive interview with the principal, possibly accompanied by members of the school leadership team. If time allows, then a number of additional interviews can be organised with members of the teaching staff, the parents of the students and of course also with the students themselves. Other people that could be interviewed are the parish priest or the college chaplain, the religious education teacher(s), people responsible for pastoral care at school, a student leader, administrative and maintenance staff and basically everyone who might have something relevant to contribute regarding the school's Catholic identity. The school visit typically concludes with a second meeting with the principal and the leadership team. At this meeting, the researcher shares his/her findings in an informal, open and constructive way. The remaining and/or additional research questions can be discussed and people can dialogue about the application and interpretation of the collected research data. Throughout the entire school visit, the researcher attempts to acquire additional documents and printed materials for the *School Identity Portfolio*. It is advisable to schedule short breaks in between each of the activities. This private reflection time can be used to recollect and structure newly obtained information, to re-think the research questions or come up with new questions and to prepare for the subsequent activity.

Alternatively although less ideal, the qualitative research could be executed from a distance without an actual school visit. The document portfolio, the picture report and written information about the school's founding and history can be collected by the school and sent to the researcher by postal or electronic mail. The interview(s) can be executed by video-conference of telephone. The ECSIP team at KU Leuven in Belgium have applied this long-distance research successfully in the eleven schools that took part in the *NECSIP 2013 Research*.

Third step: creating the research report

The third and final step of the research process is the creation of a research report. First, the survey research results are inserted into the report and carefully interpreted in written form. Next, the researcher analyses the entire *School Identity Portfolio* and the annotated *Photo Report* and creates a structured summary of the available information. He/she also writes up the *School History*, starting from its founding until the present. The recorded interviews are transcribed and subsequently analysed as well. When working with qualitative data, it is good to keep in mind that its findings can never be used to make generalisations about the population simply because the investigated sample is too small. Finally, the all the quantitative and qualitative information is integrated into the *School Identity Profile*. This concluding section of the report contains conclusions and recommendations based on all available information taken together. The *qualitative research questions* that emerge from the examination of the quantitative data are met with appropriate responses. It follows a fixed, three-fold structure: (a) qualities and strengths; (b) challenges and critical questions; and (c) recommendations from the ECSIP point of view. Figure I-20 summarises the basic structure of the ECSIP research report.

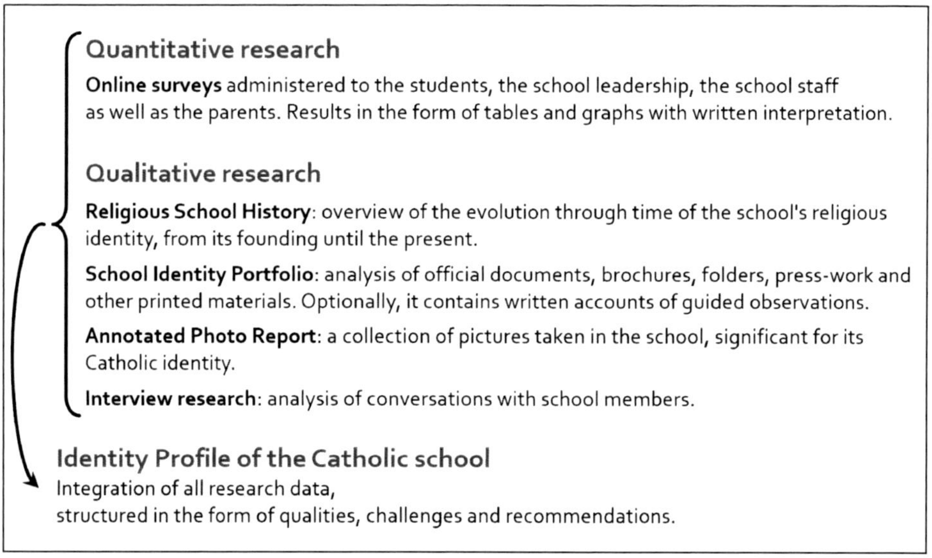

Quantitative research
Online surveys administered to the students, the school leadership, the school staff as well as the parents. Results in the form of tables and graphs with written interpretation.

Qualitative research
Religious School History: overview of the evolution through time of the school's religious identity, from its founding until the present.

School Identity Portfolio: analysis of official documents, brochures, folders, press-work and other printed materials. Optionally, it contains written accounts of guided observations.

Annotated Photo Report: a collection of pictures taken in the school, significant for its Catholic identity.

Interview research: analysis of conversations with school members.

Identity Profile of the Catholic school
Integration of all research data, structured in the form of qualities, challenges and recommendations.

Figure I-20. Basic structure of the ECSIP school reports. Integration of quantitative and qualitative data.

Chapter 5. Enhancing Catholic school identity

§1. Training and formation by means of *practical-theological instruments*

The proper *assessment* of a school's Catholic identity is the first step in the process of its successful *enhancement* towards the future. The ECSIP team at KU Leuven is investing heavily in the development of tools and materials that can assist Catholic schools and other organisations in the process of enhancing their identity. The following types of materials are being developed:

- Practical-theological instruments (PTI's);
- Impulses and ingredients;
- Good (and bad) practices of *Recontextualisation*;
- Didactic techniques and approaches;
- Expressions of (*Recontextualised*) Catholic identity.

These materials are designed to be used by a variety of target audiences:

- School leadership and staff;
- Catholic Education Office staff;
- Staff at offices of congregationally owned school networks;
- Members of the clergy involved with Catholic education;
- Staff employed at Catholic universities and other tertiary education institutions;
- Tertiary students in teacher training programs;
- Theology students;
- Parents of students in Catholic schools.

Typically, the materials under development are being used during *identity coaching sessions* administered to an assembled group of people and led by a classified teacher. It is also possible, though, that they are used for the individual study and formation.

There exist four kinds of *Practical-Theological Instruments* (PTI's), depending on their specific function and purpose:

1. *Explorative PTI's*: instruments that make the user familiar with the ECSIP research methodology, instruments and results. For example, the online *MIND THE GAP!* game (presented in the second paragraph of this chapter) is designed as an exploration, instruction and practice of the *Melbourne Scale* typology.

2. *Recontextualisation PTI's*: instruments that make the user reflect on the meaning, purpose and justification of a *Recontextualisation* of Catholic (school) identity. These instruments are designed to effect a transition from *Literal Belief* to *Post-Critical Belief*, from the *Monologue School* model to the *Dialogue School* model and from *Reconfessionalisation* to *Recontextualisation* — see the red arrows in the diagrams below.

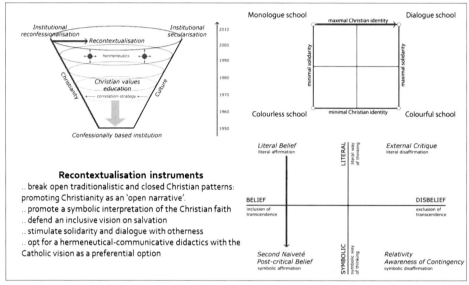

Figure I-21. Recontextualisation instruments.

3. *Confrontation PTI's*: instruments that make the user reflect critically on *External Religious Critique*, the *Colourless School* model and an *Institutional Secularisation* of a Catholic school's identity, in the hope of breaking open and transforming existing *Secularising* patterns, creating new opportunities for a Catholic school identity — see the blue arrows in the diagrams below.

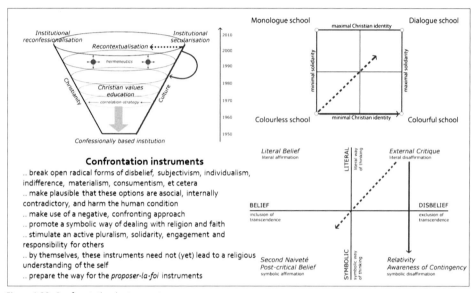

Figure I-22. Confrontation instruments.

4. 'Proposer-la-foi' PTI's: instruments that 'propose the faith' to people who have become unfamiliar with Catholicism but who are nonetheless (still or again) receptive to it. This type of PTI seeks to promote a transcendent belief and Catholic school identity, to effect the transition from *Relativity / Awareness of Contingency* to *Post-Critical Belief,* from the *Colourful School* model to the *Dialogue School* model and from *Institutional Secularisation* to *Recontextualisation* — see the green arrows in the diagrams below.

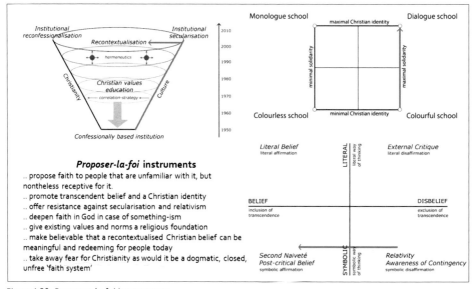

Figure I-23. Proposer-la-foi instruments.

§2. Sampling some *practical-theological instruments*

MIND THE GAP! (*Melbourne Scale*)

MIND THE GAP! is an online game, to be published on the *ECSIP Website*, designed to familiarise the players with the typology of theological school identity models that form the background of the *Melbourne Scale*. This explorative PTI can be played by individuals or by groups.

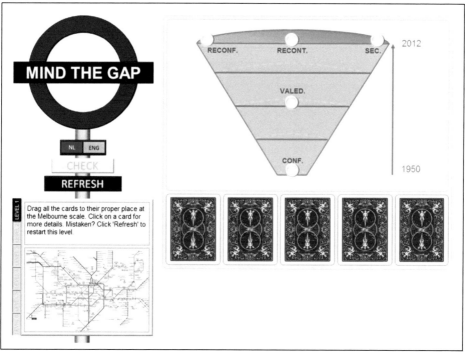

Figure I-24. Screenshot of the online MIND THE GAP! game.

The objective of the game is to drag-and-drop various pictures, most of them taken in Catholic schools in Victoria, to their correct location on the *Melbourne Scale* diagram. Online tips and hints guide the player to the correct solution – and more importantly to an understanding of the reason *why*. There are six consecutive game levels that increase in complexity and difficulty.

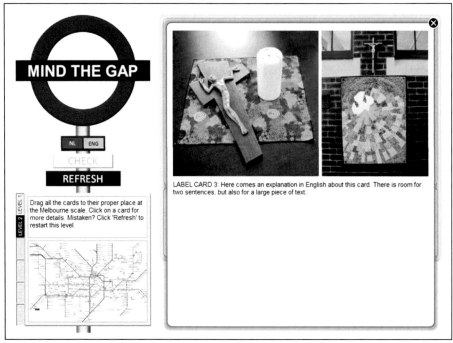

Figure I-25. Screenshot of the online MIND THE GAP! game.

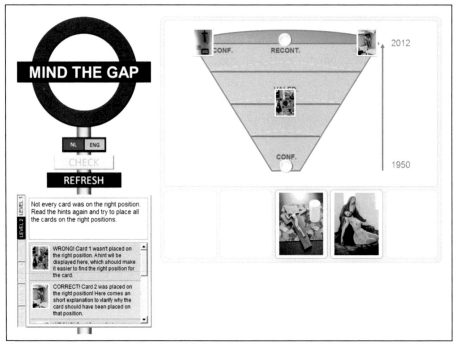

Figure I-26. Screenshot of the online MIND THE GAP! game.

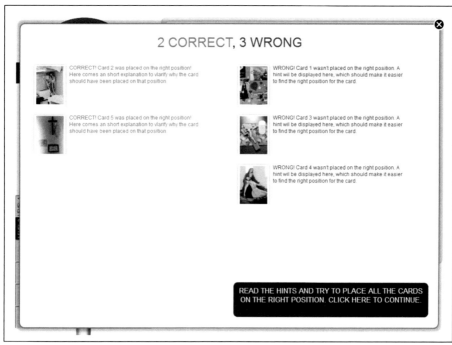

Figure I-27. Screenshot of the online MIND THE GAP! game.

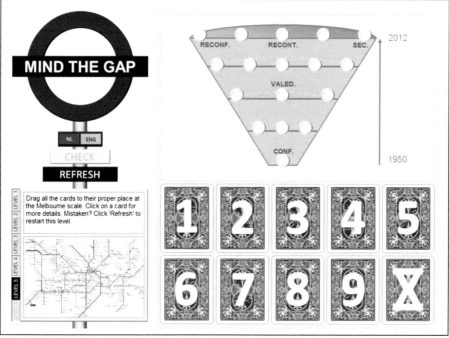

Figure I-28. Screenshot of the online MIND THE GAP! game.

Grandmother's ring (*Post-Critical Belief Scale*)

The explorative PTI titled *Grandmother's ring* tells a provocative story of a ring that is stolen an replaced by a replica. It is designed to help people reflect on the typology of four types of cognitive belief that lies behind the *Post-Critical Belief Scale*.

A gift from grandma

"A little girl called Anna is blessed with a close relationship with her grandma. They are always together and the girl loves her grandma deeply. One day grandma is stricken with severe pneumonia. It is not sure whether she will survive this illness. Grandma feels that she hasn't got long to live, so she decides to let Anna come to her bed. With tear-filled eyes, she hands over a golden ring to the girl and tells her to keep it with her, in memory of her beloved grandma. In that way, they will always be close together. Knowing that her grandma might die soon, Anna accepts the precious gift in tears. She promises her grandma that she will keep the ring forever. A couple of days later, the beloved grandmother dies."

"A few years later, on a certain night, when Anna is away on a summer camp, burglars break into the girl's parental house. When her mother awakens the morning after, she discovers that, amongst other valuable jewellery and possessions, the ring has been stolen. She knows that Anna will be inconsolable when she discovers that the precious ring is gone. So she decides to go to a jeweller with a picture of grandma wearing the ring while she was still alive, in order to have him create an exact replica of the ring. When Anna returns a few days later and when she finds out that there had been a burglary while she was away, the first thing she does, is to check in her room whether the ring is still there. When she discovers that the ring is still intact, she is very relieved. For it would have been terrible if the ring that meant so much to her was gone."

"For more than thirty years, Anna, who is now a grown woman, goes on with her life, thinking that the ring that she keeps with her, is the same ring that her grandmother gave her. One day, her mother, who suffers from a severe and fatal form of cancer, calls her with her and says that she needs to tell her something that she has kept secret for her for many years. She informs Anna about the fact that the ring that she treasured for so many years in fact is not the ring her grandma gave her, but a replica that she ordered to be made when burglars broke in to the house, many years ago."

How does Anna react to this fact? When Anna's mother has told her what has happened, multiple reactions are possible. Put yourself in Anna's position. How would you react to the news that your ring was in fact replaced with a replica? What would you say to your mother after she had given you this news? What would you do with the 'counterfeit' ring?

Now reread the text, with one difference: imagine that the ring represents the Catholic faith. When you were young, you received from your beloved grandmother a ring that you identified with the gift of faith in God. Years later, you learn that the ring is actually just another piece of metal. How would you react? How would a discovery like this affect your faith in God, and your relation to the Catholic tradition?

Assignment: study the PCB Scale typology by means of the interpretation manual. Now apply this typology to the story. Try to think of four alternative reactions, each representing one of the four belief attitudes of the PCB Scale. Read the four possible reactions to the news of the replicated ring on the following pages. Make the connection between each of these reactions and the four dimensions on the PCB Scale. What do you consider to be the most realistic reaction? What's the most desirable reaction? Which reaction corresponds with your own attitude towards faith?

Four possible reactions:

1) "Anna suddenly bursts into tears. How could her mother do this to her? How could she lie for so many years about something so important? Anna is furious and at the same time so disappointed. She feels deceived, not only by her mother, but also by the ring. That ring was the connection to her deceased grandmother and now that it is proven that the ring is not real, this connection was based on a lie. The ring is meaningless. The only ring that establishes a real connection with her grandmother is the ring that the burglars took with them, so many years ago. The first thing Anna does when she comes home is throw away the ring. Then a few minutes later, Anna picks the ring out of the bin and decides to take it to a jeweller. He needs to determine how old the ring is and whether it is the original ring or merely a replica, because she cannot take her mother's words for granted. If the ring turns out to be a replica, she will throw it away immediately. How could she keep it, knowing that it is fake?" (***External Critique***)

2) "Anna bursts into tears. She really didn't expect this kind of confession. At first she is disappointed, but soon she realises that her mum didn't want to spoil the memory of her grandmother. Although she understands her mother's loving intentions, Anna also knows that the theft of the ring would have hurt her a lot, but that it would not have ruined the memory of and connection with her deceased grandmother. After all, it is not the ring per se that means the most (although it does mean a lot) but the

act of giving the ring. The ring in itself is mostly a reminder of that gift and of her beloved grandmother, and a substitute ring is also capable of evoking the memory of the gift and of her grandmother. Besides, the ring will from now on stand for two things, namely the love of her grandmother and the love of her mother. Although the original referent is lost, an intermediate referent that refers to the original referent remains. Anna does blame her mother a bit for not telling the truth to her, and she tells her mother that it might have been better if she had told her right away that the ring had been stolen. But she knows her mother so well and she also knows that everything she has ever done has been in her daughter's best interest, so she reassures her that she is not mad at her and that she understands her motives since she did it out of love for her daughter, although she regrets the loss of the original ring deeply." (*Post-Critical Belief*)

3) "Anna is perplexed and shocked. The ring means nothing to her anymore, for it is not real. She cannot accept this situation. Most of all, she is disappointed in her mother for not going to the police to make a declaration about the theft of the ring. Anna decides to go to the police office to make a declaration, although many years have passed since. The police officer does not understand why this is so important for Anna. At home, she decides to purchase a safe to protect her other jewels. Since the confession of her mother, Anna has become much more anxious and even a bit more negative towards the world. Anna's mother understands her daughter's feelings and decides to give Anna another piece of her grandmother's legacy, namely a vase. Anna places the vase in the living room of her house. Although she knows that the vase is not an expression of the relation between her and her grandmother, at least it is an authentic piece that was once in the possession of her grandmother. She is proud of the vase, but is hesitant to tell the real story behind it to guests visiting the house. She just tells visitors that this was once the vase of her grandmother whom she loved very much. To make this even more obvious for visitors, she places a framed photograph of her grandmother in front of the vase. Despite her calmness on the outside, deep inside she continues to struggle with the fact that she does not succeed in building up a relation with her grandmother through the vase in her house." (*Literal Belief*)

4) "Anna, contrary to what her mother might have expected, reacts very calmly. She tells her mother that she does not care at all whether the ring is real or not. When she was a child, she might have cared, but now she knows that it does not really matter. In fact it is just the same to her: real ring, replica – who cares. It is the memory that counts, not the ring. Anna's mother is somewhat disappointed in Anna's reaction. She has struggled to keep the information a secret for so many years, and now, Anna does not even seem to mind." (*Relativism*)

This PTI serves as an exercise in the typology of the *Post-Critical Belief Scale*. It could also serve as a starting point to create a common vision about Catholic school identity. How would you like the people in your school to deal with the discovery of the replicated ring? What does this reveal about what you find important? Can you find consensus about the desired reaction?

Further suggestions for assimilation:
- This instrument is an excellent starting point for role playing, in which the participants place themselves in the role of one of the characters and bring the story to life and enrich it with new meanings. Possible characters are: Anna, grandmother, mother, father, the true ring, the counterfeit ring or the thief. It is possible to focus the role playing on one specific moment or one can also depict the events in a chronological manner.
- A task for the participants could be to write a letter in which they take up the position of one of the characters of the story. This character writes a letter to one of the other characters. For instance Anna can write a letter to her mother or to her deceased grandmother; Anna's mother can write a letter to Anna. Participants would try to render the feelings, motivations, thoughts and inner barriers of the character as well as possible.

Out of the Box (*Post-Critical Belief* Scale)

Out of the Box is an explorative PTI in the form of a board game that focuses on the *PCB Scale* typology. By playing the game, people assimilate and practice the four different ways to cognitively deal with religious belief. The game is played by four pairs of players. The players are asked to respond to a number of 'issue explorations', i.e. fictitious scenarios that view a particular subject or problem from four different 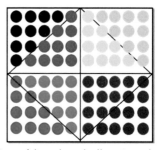 perspectives (thereby challenging the players to think 'out of the box'). Each player is then asked to choose and justify one of these normative-theological positions (he or she has to come 'out of the box'). As the game progresses, the PCB profile of the group gradually becomes apparent on the coloured game board.

Figures I-29; I-30 & I-31.

The Melbourne Jigsaw Puzzle (*Melbourne Scale*)

Figure I-32.

The Melbourne Jigsaw Puzzle is an explorative PTI in the form of a giant wooden puzzle, designed to familiarise people with the *Melbourne Scale* typology. In several rounds, the players need to solve the puzzle by arranging the pieces into their correct positions, justifying each move. Each puzzle piece has different things printed on it: photographs, cartoons, artwork, still lifes, newspaper headlines, quotes, statements, stories, issue explorations, et cetera.

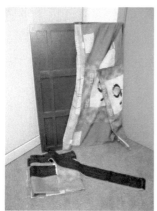

Figures I-33 & I-34.

Victorian Pursuit (*Victoria Scale*)

Victorian Pursuit is a board game designed to familiarise people with the *Victoria Scale* typology. Four players attempt to complete the board as quickly as possible. Along the way, they need to evaluate a series of 'issue explorations' concerning the appropriate pedagogical response to the tension between Catholic identity and increasing plurality in schools. Also, they need to discuss 'narrative scenarios' and evaluate 'non-verbal impulses', designed to explore the *Victoria Scale* typology. Gradually, the normative preference of each player becomes apparent, both to himself/herself and to the other players.

Figure I-35. *Victoria Pursuit* game board.

Issue explorations

Issue explorations are impulses in the form of a single page or *PowerPoint* slide. In the middle of the page, the diagram of one of the three scales is being displayed. Overlaying the diagram, a particular 'issue' (i.e. a question, dilemma, problem, point of contention) is being explored from the perspectives of the belief styles or school identity types of the *PCB Scale*, the *Melbourne Scale* or the *Victoria Scale*. *Issue explorations* help people to make the typology behind the scales more concrete and clear and to apply them creatively in their own school context. Below are two *issue explorations* based on the *PCB Scale* by way of example.

A burglar stole my wedding ring! How do I respond?

Literal Belief

I am so sad and angry that my wedding ring is stolen! What fiendish person would do such a thing? This was the ring that my wife gave to me at our wedding. It has great value and is irreplaceable. Being separated from my ring, our bond of marriage itself seems to be damaged. I'm going to go to the police at once to report the theft. I count on them to catch the thief and retrieve the ring!

External Critique

I didn't wear that ring anymore, anyway. It may just as well be gone. To be honest: I don't really understand my wife and daughters' hysteria about the significance of a piece of metal. Let's be clear: I hate thieves, but I am more upset that they took our stereo as well.

BELIEF

My wedding ring means a lot to me. I am very sad that it is stolen, because for my husband and I, it is an irreplaceable symbol of our love in marriage. However, we realise that what matters is not the ring itself, but what it refers to: our eternal love for each other. Therefore, we should search creatively for new ways to symbolically express our love, in line with our history as a couple. Perhaps we could once more present each other our engagement rings, along with a love letter and our favorite flower? We could have the new old rings consecrated and renew our marriage vows at the occasion of the Baptism of our youngest daughter. Perhaps something good can come from this loss.

DISBELIEF

What a pity, I was rather fond of that ring. But hey, it is not the end of the world. In fact, I saw a gorgeous golden ring at the jewellery store the other day. I will ask my partner to present it to me during our cruise in the Caribbean next Summer, to celebrate good times. I am not too upset about the lost wedding ring. After all, unmarried couples in a common law relationship don't wear rings either, although they do love each other too. There are many ways to show affection.

Post-Critical Belief

Relativity

What is it like to believe in a *post-critical* way, in distinction from the alternatives?

Figure I-36. *Issue Exploration PCB Scale*: stolen wedding ring.

88

A group of students from sixth grade who are to receive the sacrament of Confirmation during a Mass in our Catholic school, were encouraged to think of ways to make the ceremony more relevant to their daily lives. Their most striking proposal was to replace the sacramental wine with *Coca Cola*. "We are not allowed to drink wine because we are too young", they argued, "while Coca Cola is our daily drink".

Literal Belief

I find this proposal ludicrous and even blasphemous. How dare these children even ask! Without wine the Eucharist would simply not be valid. If they have no respect for the Church's tradition they should not be admitted to Confirmation at all.

External Critique

To me, it's all equally meaningless, regardless whether you use Coca Cola, wine or water. I don't think most of these students believe in it anyway. In my experience, they only go to Confirmation to please their grandmas and receive presents.

BELIEF

DISBELIEF

I am pleased that the students find sacraments important enough to engage with them critically. However, the Eucharist needs to be rooted in historical tradition as well as in the daily lives of believers. From the beginning, bread and wine have been crucial elements of this sacrament. Letting go of the wine runs the risk of rendering the symbol unintelligible and no longer related to the person of Christ. Still, the children are right that the Mass should also be linked to their experiences. Perhaps they can make that connection in some other creative way, for example offering something form their daily lifes together with the bread and the wine?

What a fun and creative idea! It is an expression of the children's individual conviction and that is what really matters. If they are willing to believe that Christ can be present in a cup of Cola, it is just the same as them thinking that He is present in wine, wouldn't it be?

Post-Critical Belief

Relativity

What is it like to believe in a *post-critical* way, in distinction from the alternatives?

Figure I-37. *Issue Exploration PCB Scale*: Coca cola instead of wine.

Chapter 6. The *ECSIP Research Website*

The ECSIP surveys and empirical methodology are integrated in a comprehensive automated online research platform with which individuals, groups and schools can carry out empirical research into their Catholic identity. The *ECSIP Website* can be used to organise quantitative survey research as well as to assist with qualitative research methodologies. The password protected *ECSIP Website* can be visited by surfing to the following URL: http://www.schoolidentity.net/.

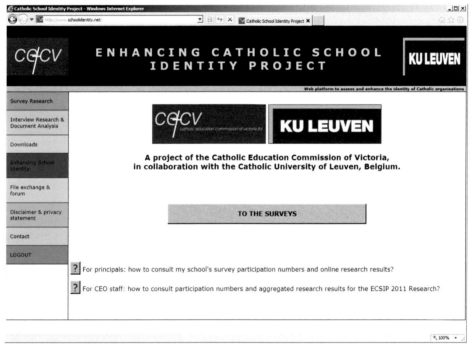

Figure I-38. Screenshot of the *ECSIP Website* – Main portal (08-05-2013).

The *ECSIP Website* has been developed and is being maintained by the ECSIP team at KU Leuven. The general access password is updated regularly. The system is designed and tested to run on all commonly used desktop and laptop computer systems. It should also work fine on most mobile devices with access to the internet, such as tablet computers and smartphones. The website is hosted from the powerful KU Leuven university web server in order to minimise issues with limited access, bandwidth and time delays. A disclaimer and a privacy statement are available to all visitors. http://www.schoolidentity.net/ is available in the English language only. There exists a Dutch counterpart of the *ECSIP Website* that can be accessed at the following location: http://www.identiteitsonderzoek.be/.

Overview of the main online features available on http://www.schoolidentity.net/

User Access Level (wooden keyhole)
- Password protection: individual Login-ID and password.
- Respondents can complete all ECSIP surveys online.
- Personal Login-ID and password: log out and continue later.
- View and download personal results (protected by a personal password).
- Print a certificate of successful completion of the surveys.

Principal Access Level (silver keyhole)
- Password protection: school code and password.
- A group manager can register his/her school online.
- Automatically filled-in forms for school registration.
- A group manager can choose which survey instruments to use for the research.
- A group manager can manage his/her school's registration online.
- *Sample size calculator*: the *ECSIP Website* calculates required survey participation.
- Provide confirmation that the group registration information is accurate.
- Customisable school password.
- Feedback functionality to provide info about the ECSIP survey process.
- Render inactive test users or false user registrations.
- Track participation numbers during the data collection period.
- Automatically generated tables and graphs show a school's results in real-time.
- Write and save personal comments on the online graph results.
- Create an automated PDF research report with graphs and written texts.

CEO Access Level (golden keyhole)
- Password protection: CEO Access Level password.
- View and download aggregated research results from multiple schools.
- Manually aggregate multiple research groups and view their results.
- Data filter functionality: select respondents based on a number of criteria.
- Create new research projects and manage them.
- Track the survey progress of multiple schools at once (research projects, dioceses).
- Render inactive test users or false user registrations.
- Activate or de-activate research groups.
- Update the built-in school registration data to help schools register quickly.
- Export research data for backup and further statistical analysis.
- Download extensive ECSIP documentation.

Qualitative research methodologies
- Password protection: school code and password.
- Formulate *qualitative research questions.*
- Select appropriate interview questions and prepare the interview.
- Transcribe interview recordings directly into the *ECSIP Website*.
- Analyse and summarise interview transcriptions.
- Input written reports of guided observations during school visits.
- Build an online *School Identity Portfolio* by uploading documents.
- Build an online *Picture Report* by uploading and annotating photographs.
- Analyse and summarise the *School Identity Portfolio* and the *Photo Report*.
- Integrate all research data and create a *School Identity Profile*.
- Create an automated PDF research report that contains all research data.

General functionalities
- Automated database clean-up and statistical analysis.
- Detailed instructions, online help files and interactive interpretation manuals.
- *myECSIP*-ID: users can complete the surveys multiple times and examine trends.
- Tracking date and time of user registrations and survey completion.
- Detailed user statistics.
- View and download information about the ECSIP Research.
- Learn about the Catholic school identity typologies.

Concerning the enhancement of Catholic school identity, the ECSIP team is preparing the online publication of a new section on the *ECSIP Website*: a portal that offers different types of content in a structured overview: practical-theological instruments, impulses and ingredients, good and bad practices, didactic techniques and expressions of Catholic identity that will help schools and other Catholic organisations to develop and enhance their Catholic identity. ECSIP's long-term goal is to create an online platform that guides the entire process step by step: from conducting the survey research, complementing the results with qualitative research methods, creating a comprehensive research report to the practical-theological enhancement of Catholic school identity.

Selected screenshots of http://www.schoolidentity.net/

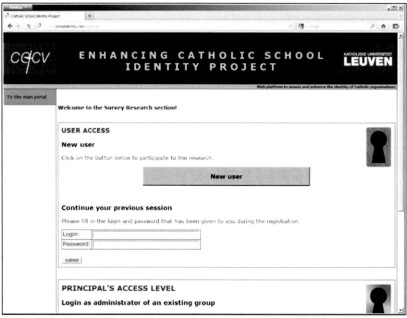

Figure I-39. Screenshot of the *ECSIP Website*: create a new user or login as existing user.

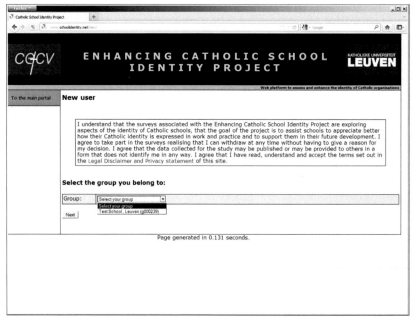

Figure I-40. Screenshot of the *ECSIP Website*: select the school you belong to.

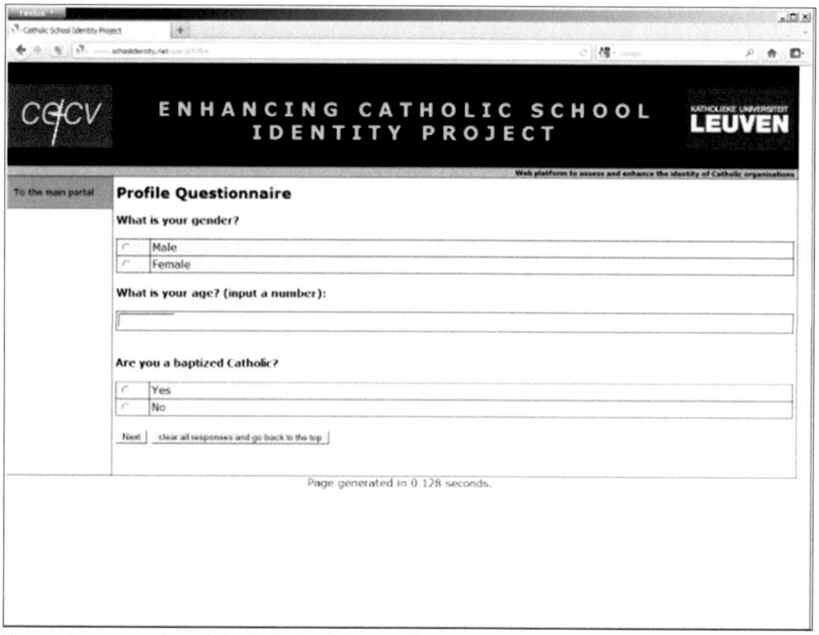

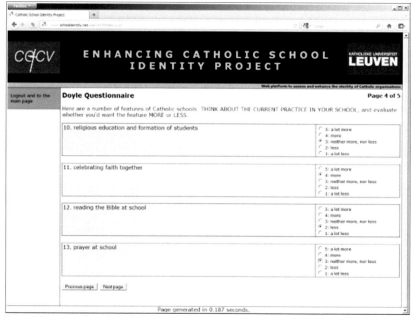

Figure I-41. Screenshot of the *ECSIP Website*: *Profile Questionnaire*.

Figure I-42. Screenshot of the *ECSIP Website*: *Doyle Questionnaire*.

94

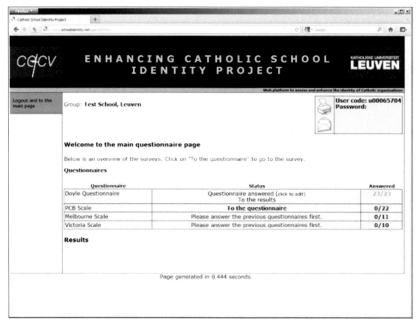

Figure I-43. Screenshot of the *ECSIP Website*: main questionnaire page.

Figure I-44. Screenshot of the *ECSIP Website*: *Melbourne Scale*, student version.

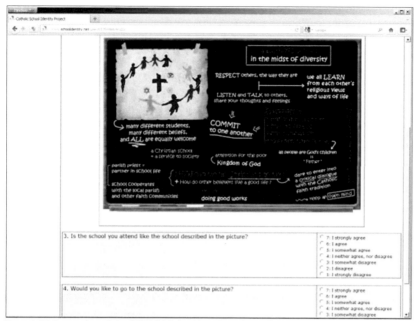

Figure I-45. Screenshot of the *ECSIP Website*: *Victoria Scale*, student version.

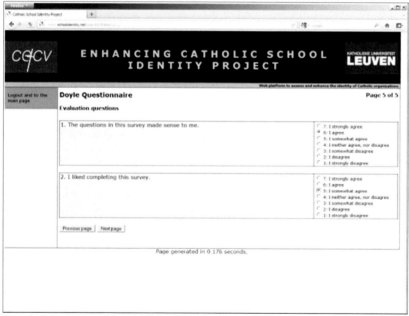

Figure I-46. Screenshot of the *ECSIP Website*: evaluation questions.

PART 2. The *ECSIP 2012 Research* in Victoria, Australia

Chapter 7. Introduction to the *ECSIP 2012 Research*

§1. What is the *ECSIP 2012 Research*?

From 2006 to 2011, the ECSIP research methodology was gradually created, tested and refined. The empirical instruments were subjected to multiple trials in Belgian, Australian and other international research settings – educational and otherwise. In Belgium, the research methodology was tested in dozens of small trials in schools, Catholic education offices and tertiary education institutes. In Australia, the large 2008 trial (5365 respondents) and the 2010 trial (2645 respondents), as well as multiple small runs in Catholic education offices and schools, are worth mentioning. By early 2011, the empirical instruments had reached their final form – although some small adjustments and improvements might still be made in the coming years. During this period, the *ECSIP Research Website* http://www.schoolidentity.net/ was also gradually created, tested and put into use[18].

The period from 2011 to 2015 marks the implementation phase of the *Enhancing Catholic School Identity Project* in the Archdiocese of Melbourne and in the Dioceses of Ballarat, Sale and Sandhurst. During this period, the quantitative and qualitative assessment of Catholic school identity is being implemented throughout Victoria in alignment with the *School Improvement Framework* (SIF). The SIF is a systematic process, overseen by the *Catholic Education Commission of Victoria* Ltd (CECV), to address the dual purpose of satisfying legitimate expectations of government and sector authorities about accountability for the outcomes of schooling whilst seeking to continuously improve student learning outcomes. Each of the four Victorian Dioceses meets these requirements through their own processes and procedures. The ECSIP surveys are completed as part of the cyclical review process and assess the status of education in each Catholic school – including the state of its religious education and Catholic school identity.

The *ECSIP 2012 Research* round constitutes the second year of the 4-year implementation phase of the ECSIP in Victoria. In the first implementation round, the *ECSIP 2011 Research*, 17923 respondents from 84 primary and 19 secondary schools in four dioceses (Melbourne, Ballarat, Sandhurst and Sale) took part in the research. During the *ECSIP 2012 Research*, 16899 respondents from 82 primary and 14 secondary schools from three dioceses (Melbourne, Ballarat and Sale) participated. In this publication, the research data from the 2012 round is presented and analysed. Two

---

[18] See paragraph 2 of the introduction, titled: *A brief chronology of the Enhancing Catholic School Identity Project (2006-2014)*, for a more detailed overview of ECSIP's development over the years.

more implementation rounds are scheduled in the years 2013 and 2014. At that time, upon completion of the first four-year rotation, all Catholic schools in Victoria will have participated to the ECSIP research at least one time. In the years to come, follow-up research can be scheduled.

§3. Purposes of the ECSIP 2012 Research

The purposes of the *ECSIP 2012 Research* are fourfold:

I. **To gather representative research samples from 96 primary and secondary Catholic schools** that are scheduled to participate in the second ECSIP implementation round. Each school receives its own research report based on these individual school samples in the course of 2012 and 2013, containing data tables, graph results and interpretative texts including written conclusions and recommendations, tailoured to that particular school.

II. **To acquire a large, varied and balanced research sample to be used in the second part of this publication**, namely, as the application of the research methodology described in the first part. So, the aggregated research data used to create the 96 individual school reports for the 2012 implementation phase also constitutes the large sample that is analysed in this publication.

III. **To continue testing and refinement of the ECSIP empirical survey instruments.** The ECSIP surveys have reached their final structure and content, but still we continue to look for ways to enhance them. We especially continue to simplify and shorten the surveys as much as possible while maintaining their scope, effectiveness and validity.

IV. **To continue development and field testing of the *ECSIP Research Website*.** More precisely, the opportunity of the *ECSIP 2012 Research* round was used to redesign the school registration procedure, to refine the automated clean-up of inputted data, to upgrade the data export routines, to expand and debug the on-the-fly graphs that report individual and aggregated schools results, to create a convenient interface to manage online *Research Projects*, to program a new interface that allows research managers to monitor in real-time the progress of the data entry process for an entire *Research Project* as well as for each individual school separately, and to track down and fix multiple little software *bugs*.

§4. Timetable of the ECSIP 2012 Research

- 9 February 2012: the *Catholic Education Office Melbourne* sent the most recent population numbers for all Catholic schools in Victoria to KU Leuven. Based on this information, a representative sample was calculated for each participating school.
- School registrations by the principals: the week from Monday 26 March until Friday 30 March 2012. Upon registration, the *ECSIP Website* communicated the *requested participant numbers* to the school principals.
- In the three weeks between the school registrations and the start of the research period, the *ECSIP Website* was prepared to receive almost 17000 new respondents.
- 16 April 2012: paper questionnaire bundles for students, school staff and parents are delivered to the *ECSIP Steering Committee*. These bundles contained the exact same surveys that appear online. Some schools had parents complete the surveys on paper and input the data in the *ECSIP Website* at a later date. The paper questionnaire bundles were also used by schools to assist the respondents with completing the surveys online.
- The data collection process started on Monday 23 April 2012 and ran until Friday 22 June 2012. So, the total running time was nine weeks.
- The *ECSIP Website* remained available a little longer, namely until Tuesday 3 July 2012. On that day, the last data export was done. From that day on, it was no longer possible to participate in the *ECSIP 2012 Research*.
- July and August 2012: data clean-up, followed by a thorough statistical analysis of the research data.
- September 2012 until February 2013: production of individual school reports.

§5. Sample design: about the *requested participant numbers*

The goal of the *ECSIP research* in schools is to draw a representative sample from each participating school. To achieve this goal, the principal receives the *requested participant numbers* upon registering his/her school in the *ECSIP Website*. The *requested participant numbers* are based upon the minimum required sample size relative to the total population in each respondent group, augmented with a group-specific expected margin of dropouts. The *requested participant numbers* are calculated by the built-in *sample size calculator* in the *ECSIP Website*, which is based on a model of average expected respondent group sizes relative to the total population size of primary and secondary schools in Victoria. The task for participating schools is to achieve the *requested participant numbers* in all respondent groups. When this number of participants is attained, then the resulting research sample is sufficient to be considered as representative.

Chapter 8. Description of the research sample

When interpreting empirical research results, it is important to know exactly *whose results* they are. After all, the interpretation depends on the composition, the size, the quality and the representivity of the research sample.

§1. Determination of the sample frame

A *sample frame* is the precise description of the total number of people in the population that is being investigated. From the sample frame, we draw the research sample. Each element in the sample frame has a certain probability to end up in the research sample. (An element that is excluded from the sample frame cannot be part of the sample, while an element that should not be part of the sample is excluded from the sample frame.)

The sample frame for the ECSIP 2012 Research is defined as follows:
- RG1: primary school students, year 5-6.
- RG2: secondary college students, year 7-8.
- RG3: secondary college students, year 9-10.
- RG4: secondary college students, year 11-12.
- RG6+7: teachers and leadership from primary and secondary schools.
- RG9: parents from children in primary and secondary schools.

It is to be noted that the primary school students in year 1 to 4 are not selected to participate in the research because they are too young. Presumably, the views of the students in years 5 and 6 are representative for the younger children as well.

From each *family unit*, which may consist of one or more parents or guardians, a single respondent is invited to participate in the research. To determine the total number of respondents in the 'parent' group, we count the number of *family units*.

In 2012, a number of *Catholic Education Office* personnel from the three participating dioceses also completed the online surveys, for various purposes. These respondents were not included in the research data.

In total, the sample frame of the ECSIP 2012 Research consists of 54246 potential respondents (see Figure II-1 on the next page). From this population, a research sample is drawn.

§2. Research sample composition and size

The following tables present the participation numbers obtained in primary schools (P-6 and P-8) and secondary colleges (7-12) that took part in the ECSIP 2012 Research.

The total achieved sample size in Catholic schools in Victoria during the ECSIP 2012 Research is **16899 respondents**. Each of these people completed at least one valid survey. The following table breaks down the participation numbers according to the respondent groups:

Respondent groups	Achieved sample	Population (sample frame)	Sample ratio
Students year 5-6	5668	6652	85.2%
Students year 7-8	2111	5201	40.6%
Students year 9-10	1565	4968	31.5%
Students year 11-12	1509	4436	34.0%
School staff (teachers + leadership)	3531	4316	81.8%
Parents	2515	28673	8.8%
TOTAL incl. parents	16899	54246	31.2%
TOTAL excl. parents	14384	25573	56.2%

Figure II-1. Table of overall participation numbers of the ECSIP 2012 Research.

The column on the right hand side of the table expresses the achieved sample size in relation to the total population size at the time of the research. The sample ratio varies according to the respondent groups.

Note that the parents' sample ratio is lowest (8.8%). Considerable efforts were undertaken to reach as many parents as possible, resulting in an impressive number of 2515 participating mothers, fathers and guardians of students. Nevertheless, for practical reasons the very extensive parent respondent group remains the hardest to reach.

In total, 96 different schools took part in the ECSIP 2012 Research.[19] The 96 research schools have different organisational structures:

School types	n	Participating respondent groups
P-6 primary schools (preparatory to year 6)	81	students y5-6 teachers, school leadership, parents
P-8 primary schools (preparatory to year 8)	1	students y5-6, *y7-8* teachers, school leadership, parents
7-12 secondary colleges (students from year 7 to 12)	14	students y7-8, y9-10, y11-12 teachers, school leadership, parents
TOTAL	96	**students y5-6, y7-8, y9-10, y11-12 teachers, school leadership, parents**

Figure II-2. Table of participating school types and respondent groups.

The participating schools were located in the following three dioceses in Victoria:

Participating dioceses	Achieved sample	Population (sample frame)	Sample ratio
MELBOURNE Archdiocese	12921 (76.5%)	42693	30.3%
BALLARAT Diocese	2382 (14.1%)	7709	30.9%
SALE Diocese	1596 (9.4%)	3844	41.5%
TOTAL	**16899 (100%)**	**54246**	**31.2%**

Figure II-3. Table of participating dioceses and the participation numbers in each diocese.

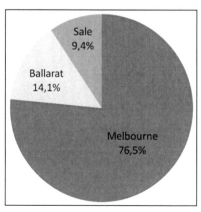

Figure II-4. Dioceses in the research sample.

Note that 76.5% of the ECSIP 2012 Research data comes from schools in the Melbourne Archdiocese, which is by far the largest diocese in Victoria. The Ballarat Diocese delivers 14.1% of the research data. The Sale Diocese delivers 9.4% of the data.

Note: the Sandhurst Diocese had most of its Catholic schools take part in the previous ECSIP research in 2011 and hence is not represented here.

---

[19] The attached table on pages 302-303 contains an overview of all 96 participating schools.

Participation numbers in primary schools (P-6 & P-8)

Most research results are broken down into primary schools (P6 and P8) and secondary colleges (7-12). We present here a detailed overview of the participation numbers in both cohorts.

	Profile Quest.	Doyle Quest.	PCB Scale	Melbourne Scale	Victoria Scale	TOTAL	Relative share
Students y5-6	5632	5347	4832	4067	3958	5668	57,0%
Students y7-8	34	31	14	4	10	34	0,3%
Teachers	1511	1487	1355	1350	1232	1520	15,3%
School leadership	731	702	658	644	601	732	7,4%
Parents	1988	1957	1714	1717	1560	1993	20,0%
TOTAL	9896	9524	8573	7782	7361	9947	

	Achieved sample	Population (sample frame)	Relative participation
Students y5-6	5668	6652	85,2%
Students y7-8	34	36	94,4%
School staff	2252	2411	93,4%
Parents	1993	16806	11,9%
TOTAL incl. parents	9947	25905	38,4%
TOTAL excl. parents	7954	9099	87,4%

Figure II-5. Participation numbers in primary schools (P-6 and P-8).

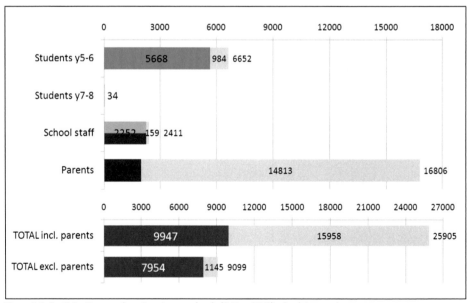

Figure II-6. Participation numbers in primary schools (P-6 and P-8), absolute numbers.

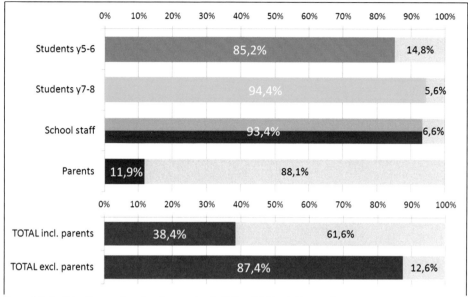

Figure II-7. Participation numbers in primary schools (P-6 and P-8), relative numbers.

Participation numbers in secondary colleges (7-12)

	Profile Quest.	Doyle Quest.	PCB Scale	Melbourne Scale	Victoria Scale	TOTAL	Relative share
Students y7-8	2077	2000	1662	1324	1287	2077	29,9%
Students y9-10	1536	1519	1278	1012	1055	1565	22,5%
Students y11-12	1477	1445	1188	920	963	1509	21,7%
Teachers	931	922	803	804	733	932	13,4%
School leadership	344	337	306	307	290	347	5,0%
Parents	522	505	394	378	338	522	7,5%
TOTAL	6887	6728	5631	4745	4666	6952	

	Achieved sample	Population (sample frame)	Relative participation
Students y7-8	2077	5165	40,2%
Students y9-10	1565	4968	31,5%
Students y11-12	1509	4436	34,0%
School staff	1279	1905	67,1%
Parents	522	11867	4,4%
TOTAL incl. parents	6952	28341	24,5%
TOTAL excl. parents	6430	16474	39,0%

Figure II-8. Participation numbers in secondary colleges (7-12).

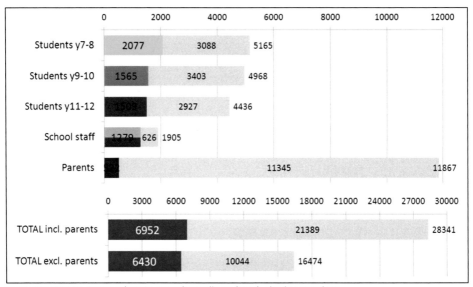

Figure II-9. Participation numbers in secondary colleges (7-12), absolute numbers.

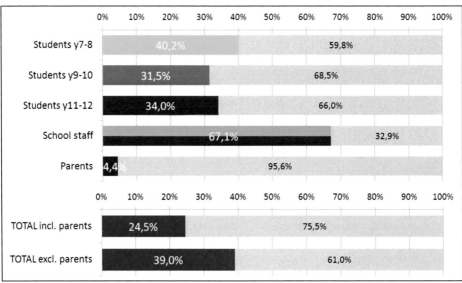

Figure II-10. Participation numbers in secondary colleges (7-12), relative numbers.

§3. Description and evaluation of the research sample

From a total sample frame of 54246 potential respondents, we were able to draw a sample of 16899 respondents. Each of these individuals completed at least ONE of the surveys in a valid way. This coverage results in an overall sample ratio of 31.2%. If we disregard the parents in this calculation, then 14384 of 25573 school members took part in the research, which results in a ratio of 56.2%.

Are the results based on this sample representative for the entire population in the participating schools? In other words, do they predict the scores of the sum of all the school communities with sufficient accuracy? In order to evaluate this data, we need to separately study the representivity of each different respondent group. First, we examine the student sample; after that, we look at the adult respondents.

Primary school students, year 5-6
In total, 5668 year 5-6 students took part in the research. Relative to a total number of 6652 students, this results in a sample ratio of 85.2%. This ratio means that about 17 in 20 children in year 5-6 have taken part in the survey research. Obviously, this is a notable achievement. Based on the presumption that the 14.8% of the children who did NOT participate do not have significantly different views compared with the children who DID take part, the results of this sample may be generalised and called representative. (Note: the 17949 children in year one to four did not participate in the research because they are still too young. Therefore, these children fall outside the sample frame.[20])

Secondary college students, year 7-8
A total of 2111 year 7-8 students (in 14 secondary colleges and one P-8 primary school) took part in the ECSIP 2012 Research. Relative to a total population of 5201 students, this results in a sample fraction of 40.6%. This turnout shows that only a significant minority of year 7-8 students completed one or more surveys in a valid way. Provided the respondents were selected in a random way, these results could provide a reliable indication of the population scores in the cohort of students in year 7-8.

Secondary college students, year 9-10
In total, 1565 year 9-10 students participated in the research. The total number of students in the group at the time of the research was 4968. So, 31.5% of them completed one or more surveys. In other words, about one third of the year 9-10 students (more precisely: 4 in 13) completed at least one survey in a valid way. Strictly

---

[20] See the determination of the ECSIP sample frame, Chapter 8 §1.

speaking, we should presume that this sample ratio is not representative for the whole group. However, given the large absolute number of respondents and assuming the randomness of the research sample, we may conclude that the obtained sample at least gives a reliable indication of the population scores among the students in year 9-10.

Secondary college students, year 11-12
A total number of 1509 students in year 11-12 participated in the survey research. Relative to a total number of 4436 potential students, 34.0% took part. As with the year 9-10 students, we should presume that a sample ratio of one third is not representative for the whole group. However, the large number of respondents in absolute figures allows for very small margins of error when generalising the results. Moreover, we can assume that the students were selected at random so that each student has the same probability to be included in the research sample. Therefore, we may conclude that the obtained sample at least provides a reliable indication of the population scores among the students in year 11-12.

School staff
No less than 3531 staff members from 96 primary and secondary schools, among whom teachers, members of the school leadership, administrative personnel as well as support staff, took part in the ECSIP 2012 Research. Relative to a total number of 4316 staff members, this turnout results in a sample ratio of 81.8%. In other words, about 9 in 11 school staff members took part in the empirical research, which is an excellent achievement on the part of the schools and the Catholic Education Offices. Assuming that the views of the not-participating minority (18.2%) are similar to the views of the people who did participate, then the research results based on this sample may be generalised to the sum of all the school staff teams. In other words, provided the sample selection was randomised, we may call the school staff results representative.

Parents
Of all the target groups that are part of the sample frame, the students' parents are the most difficult group to include in the research. Even still, they were also invited to take part. In total, 2515 parents or guardians filled in at least one survey in a valid way. At the time of the research, there were 28673 family units that sent one or more children to the research schools. From each family unit, one adult (mother, father or guardian) was invited to participate. This means that 8.8% of those invited took part in the survey research, which comes down to about 1 in 11. *Strictly speaking, this sample ratio is insufficient to be representative.* Moreover, it is not unlikely that a selection of respondents occurred which might endanger the randomness of the parent sample. It

has been reported that the increasingly engaged, committed and religiously inspired parents are more likely to complete surveys on Catholic identity, compared with the other parents. Despite the low sample fraction and the possible non-response bias, we can attempt to draw conclusions about the views of the parents based on the available information. In absolute numbers we are dealing with a sample of considerable size, which minimises the probability of mistakes when generalising the results. But when doing so, it is advisable always to keep in mind the composition of the parent sample and include this knowledge in the process of interpretation.

Conclusion: is the sample taken from the combined adult groups representative?
Taken together, 6046 of the 32989 adult respondents (school staff + parents) took part in the ECSIP 2012 survey research. This results in a total ratio of 18.3%. It must be noted, however, that there is a considerable difference in participation rate between the school staff and the parents: while 81.8% of the teachers and school leadership took part in the research, the sample frame among the parents does not exceed 8.8%. Therefore, each sample differs significantly in terms of our ability to claim they are representative of the respective respondent group. This should be taken into account when interpreting any aggregated research results for the adult groups.

§4. Result of the evaluation questions

At the end of each of the four Catholic identity surveys, the *ECSIP Research Website* invites the respondents to evaluate the survey by means of two simple evaluation questions. In this way we obtain valuable feedback about the surveys' level of difficulty and the respondents' satisfaction with the data gathering process.

1. *The questions in this survey made sense to me.*
2. *I liked completing this survey.*

Did the questions in the surveys make sense to the respondents? It is important to assess the surveys' level of difficulty in order to ensure the relation between the research results and the content of the survey questions. The results are scaled according to the seven-point Likert scale, ranging from 'I strongly disagree' to 'I strongly agree'.

The first graph (Figure II-11) summarises the mean scores on the second evaluation question of the students and the adults (in primary and secondary schools combined) for each of the four Catholic identity surveys.

The second graph (Figure II-12) breaks down the mean scores on the second evaluation question of all the respondent groups that took part in the ECSIP 2012 Research (in primary and secondary schools combined) for each of the four Catholic identity surveys.

The third composite graph (Figure II-13) presents the mean scores on both evaluation questions of the students and the adults (in primary and secondary schools combined) for each of the four Catholic identity surveys.

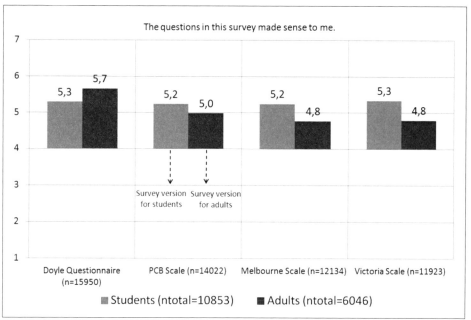

Figure II-11. Second evaluation question on four surveys, students compared with adults.

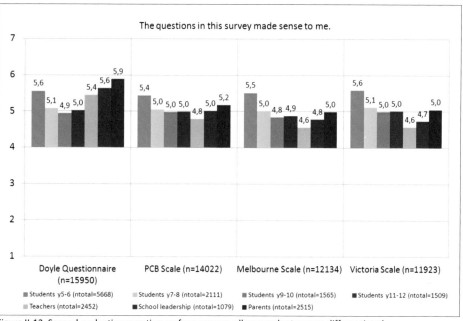

Figure II-12. Second evaluation question on four surveys, all respondent groups differentiated.

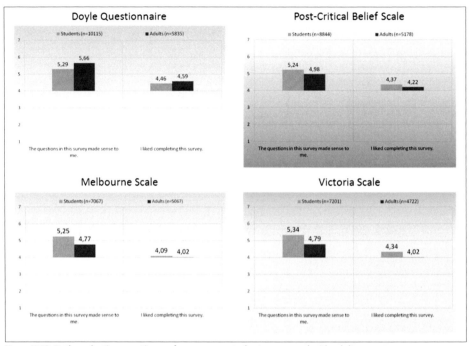

Figure II-13. Both evaluation question on four surveys, students compared with adults.

In short, the evaluation questions reveal that, though some of the surveys are not light or particularly easy, both the student and the adult groups are nonetheless capable of completing them successfully. A clear majority of both students and adults agree to a greater or lesser extent that the surveys' difficulty level is acceptable. This is the case for each of the four Catholic identity surveys and for all respondent groups. This is also true for the primary school children and the younger students in secondary colleges. Therefore, we can conclude that the ECSIP 2012 Research data is of good quality.

However, completing the ECSIP surveys is, admittedly, not a job that comes easily. Having all the surveys completed by large groups of people is an organisational challenge that was added on top of many other tasks and responsibilities. What is more, most people are not particularly fond of filling in questionnaires, which is something they are asked to do often. Consequently, in general, people expressed a moderate dissatisfaction about the arduous process of the ECSIP data collection. Especially the students indicated that, on the whole, they were not very keen on completing questionnaires. If we look more closely then, the students appear to be divided. Some students are highly motivated and pleased to participate, while others find it a burden they would rather avoid. The adults are generally more motivated and appreciative of the ECSIP surveys.

§5. Internal consistency and validity of the multivariate attitude scales

After having collected, downloaded, sorted and cleaned up the empirical research data, a thorough statistical analysis is performed with special attention to the multivariate attitude scales in the attempt to produce research results that are *as correct and reliable as possible*.

In total, the ECSIP 2012 Research employed four multivariate attitude scales:
1. *Post-Critical Belief Scale*, 24(20)-item student version[21] (Pollefeyt & Bouwens).
2. *Post-Critical Belief Scale*, 33-item adult version (Hutsebaut).
3. *Melbourne Scale*, 45-item adult version (Pollefeyt & Bouwens).
4. *Victoria Scale*, 40-item adult version (Pollefeyt & Bouwens).

The following sets of statistical analysis of all four multivariate attitude scales are included in this publication as attachments:
- **Basic summary statistics**, such as: number of observations, mean, standard deviation, variance, minimum score, maximum score, median, first and third quartile, lower and upper 99% confidence limits for the mean, t-value and probability under t.
- **Pearson linear correlation matrices** for all individual survey items as well as the scale means (which are basically adjusted linear combinations of individual survey items), including the probability estimates of the correlation coefficients.
- **Cronbach's Coefficient Alpha**: measures for internal consistency of all the types described by the 4 attitude scales, both on the factual and the normative measurement levels.
- **Principal Component factor analysis** without and with varimax rotation in three or four latent factors, including scree plots, eigenvectors, ratios of explained variance and the orthogonal transformation matrix.

The statistical analysis is executed using the following computer software:
- *SAS Institute Inc., SAS 9.3 TS Level 1M0*
- *SAS Institute Inc., SAS enterprise guide 4.3 (4.3.0.11123) C44010*
- *Microsoft Excel 2010*

---

[21] In the case of the ECSIP 2012 Research, at the request of the ECSIP Steering Committee, the 24-item student version of the *PCB Scale* was reduced to 20 items by deleting a set of questions about the adequate interpretation of miracle stories in the Bible. Statistical analysis showed that the negative effect of the deletion of these 4 items on the stability of the scale remains minimal.

Cronbach's Alpha coefficients: internal consistencies of the scale types

The (standardised) *Cronbach's Alpha coefficients* of the various subscales in the ECSIP research in Victoria in 2012 are as follows:

PCB Scale, 24(20)-item student version (n≈9812):
- *Literal Belief*: 0.818683
- *External Critique*: 0.882739
- *Relativism*: 0.657559
- *Post-Critical Belief*: 0.906989

PCB Scale, 33-item adults version (n≈5604):
- *Literal Belief*: 0.815922
- *External Critique*: 0.852742
- *Relativism*: 0.548271
- *Post-Critical Belief*: 0.642263

Melbourne Scale, 45-item adult version (n≈5396):
- Secularisation, factual level: 0.691715
- Secularisation, normative level: 0.788714
- Reconfessionalisation, factual level: 0.332871
- Reconfessionalisation, normative level: 0.624504
- Values Education, factual level: 0.406967
- Values Education, normative level: 0.506622
- Recontextualisation, factual level: 0.686939
- Recontextualisation, normative level: 0.586747
- Confessionality (only factual level): 0.755562

Victoria Scale, 40-item adult version (n≈5147):
- Monologue School, factual level: 0.594042
- Monologue School, normative level: 0.769371
- Dialogue School, factual level: 0.622038
- Dialogue School, normative level: 0.663192
- Colourful School, factual level: 0.671429
- Colourful School, normative level: 0.785695
- Colourless School, factual level: 0.598369
- Colourless School, normative level: 0.721999

We determined that most of the clusters of items that constitute the various scale types showed sufficient mutual correlations and internal consistencies. These findings point at the conclusion that they indeed refer to a single latent construct, which makes it possible to combine them to form a new subscale measurement.

As expected, the consistencies on the factual measurement level are sometimes lower compared with the normative measurement level. When thinking about the current practice of a complex school reality, there are many complicated latent variables that influence and steer people's Likert scale responses. However, reflection on the normative, 'ideal school' level is naturally more abstract, less complicated and more simple. For this reason, the internal consistencies are usually higher on the normative level.

After carrying out and examining the statistical analysis of the ECSIP 2012 Research data, we can conclude that all research results are sufficiently representative, consistent and valid to be used to assess and enhance the Catholic identity of schools, taking into consideration the modalities, conditions and limitations that are inherent to the empirical research method in use.

Chapter 9. Exploring Catholic school identity. Results of the Profile Questionnaire and the Doyle Questionnaire

§1. The religious identity profile of Catholic school members (Profile Questionnaire)

Prior to the analysis of the *Doyle Questionnaire* and the three multivariate attitude scales, that form the core of the ECSIP research, we analyse a selection of background variables about the personal religious identity of the respondents themselves.

After having registered as a new user in the *ECSIP Website*, each respondent is categorised into a respondent group by the *Identification Diagram*. The first survey that follows – the first actual survey – is the *Profile Questionnaire*. It consists of individual questions regarding the following subjects (standard version)[22]:
- *gender*
- *age*
- *highest level of education*
- *main ethnic background*
- *Catholic baptism*
- *personal religion or philosophy of life*
- *personal Christian faith*
- *support for the Catholic faith*
- *familiarity with the Bible*
- *church praxis: attendance at the Eucharist*
- *personal prayer life*

In this publication, we present a selection of some of the most relevant results (the underlined items), although the other items in the questionnaire are also worth exploring.

---

[22] The results of the underlined survey items are displayed and interpreted in the remainder of this paragraph.

Personal religion or philosophy of life

All respondents are required to choose one single option from a predefined list of religious and philosophical profiles. Optionally, they can include additional information in an open text input field. The following table contains the answers from the ECSIP 2012 Research, differentiated between the students and the adults in primary and secondary schools.

Personal religion or philosophy of life	Students 5-6	Students 7-12	Adults PRIM	Adults SEC
Roman rite Catholic	68.2%	40.7%	74.7%	57.6%
Eastern rite Catholic	1.0%	0.5%	0.8%	0.6%
Episcopal / Anglican Church	0.9%	1.1%	2.8%	4.1%
Orthodox	4.0%	5.5%	2.1%	4.2%
Reformed church	0.0%	0.0%	0.0%	0.1%
Calvinist	0.0%	0.0%	0.1%	0.1%
Evangelical	0.0%	0.1%	0.0%	0.3%
Mormon / Church of Latter-Day Saints	0.1%	0.2%	0.1%	0.2%
Assemblies of God / Pentecostal	0.1%	0.2%	0.2%	0.2%
Methodist	0.0%	0.1%	0.1%	0.6%
Lutheran	0.2%	0.7%	0.2%	0.5%
Presbyterian	0.1%	0.1%	0.7%	1.2%
Baptist	1.5%	1.5%	0.6%	0.9%
Churches of Christ	1.6%	2.7%	0.5%	0.4%
Uniting Church / United Church of Christ	0.5%	1.1%	2.0%	3.6%
Just Christian (no denomination)	2.3%	4.7%	1.3%	1.5%
Muslim	1.0%	2.5%	0.4%	1.1%
Jewish	0.1%	0.2%	0.0%	0.2%
Hindu	2.0%	1.9%	0.3%	0.9%
Sikh	0.4%	0.4%	0.0%	0.2%
Buddhist	2.6%	3.1%	0.5%	1.0%
Just religious (I believe in God but I don't belong to an established religion.)	1.8%	3.2%	2.0%	1.4%
Agnostic (I don't know, I'm still searching)	0.6%	3.4%	0.8%	1.4%
Indifferent or nihilistic	0.3%	2.6%	0.3%	1.3%
New age	0.6%	1.5%	0.8%	1.5%
Something-ism	0.2%	2.4%	1.5%	2.1%
I believe in science.	1.0%	2.7%	0.4%	0.7%
Humanistic	0.3%	2.2%	2.0%	3.5%
Atheist	0.2%	3.3%	1.0%	3.5%
Other	2.2%	4.7%	1.0%	3.2%
Unknown	6.1%	6.8%	2.7%	2.0%
	n=5668	n=5151	n=4245	n=1801

Figure II-14. Detailed table of personal religions and philosophies of life, differentiated between students and adults in primary and secondary schools.

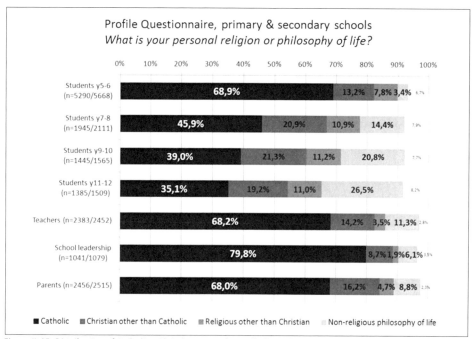

Figure II-15. Distribution of Catholics, Christians, members of other religions and non-religious people in Catholic schools across all respondent groups.

This graph summarises the respondents' personal religion or philosophy of life into four categories, expressed as a percentage of the total number of respondents in each group:

Roman Catholic	black colour
Christian, other than Catholic, e.g. Orthodox, Protestant	dark grey colour
Religious, other than Christian, e.g. Hindu	middle grey colour
Non-religious philosophy of life, e.g. atheist, humanist, agnostic	light grey colour
Respondents who gave an alternative response or who did not answer the question	white gap on the right

Figure II-15 tells many stories. We summarise the most relevant story lines:

- A clear majority of primary school children in year 5-6 identify themselves as Roman-Catholic (68.9%). There are also minorities of Christians 'other than Catholic' (13.2%) and religious people 'other than Christian' (7.8%). Encountering a non-religious primary school student is rather an exception (3.4%).

- There is a drop in the percentages of students who identify themselves as Catholics between primary and secondary schools: from 68.9% in primary schools to 45.9% in year 7-8 in secondary colleges.

- In secondary colleges, the percentage of Catholics among the students in year 7-8 (45.9%) is higher compared with students in year 9-10 (39.0%), which in turn is higher compared with students in year 11-12 (35.1%). This drop is accompanied by an increase of students with a non-religious philosophy of life (from 14.4% to 20.8% to 26.5%). The ratio of Christians 'other than Catholic' and religious people 'other than Christian' remain stable across secondary education. There are two possible ways to explain the drop in Catholics among the students:
  - ➢ In recent years, secondary colleges have been enrolling an increasing number of Catholic students in year 7, while reducing the number of non-religious students.
  - ➢ The older the students become, the less they identify themselves as Catholic. Some students lose their Catholic identity along the way.

- A clear majority of the adult groups (primary and secondary levels combined) identify themselves as Roman-Catholic: 68.0% of the parents and guardians, 68.2% of the teachers, and 79.8% of the school leadership.

- The percentage of Catholics is highest among the school leadership (79.8%). This either means that Catholic believers are more likely to take up leadership positions or being a school leader reinforces an affiliation with the Catholic faith.

- In all adult groups, there exist minority groups of Christians 'other than Catholic' (16.2% and 14.2% among parents and teachers respectively; 8.7% among the school leadership).

- Non-religious people constitute another minority group among the adults. 8.8% of the parents (about 1 in 11) indicate a philosophy of life that is clearly not religious in nature. This indication also applies to 11.3% of the school teachers (about 1 in 9) and to 6.1% of the school leadership (about 1 in 16).

- Further, there are non-Christian religious people involved in Catholic schools, although their numbers are small (4.7% and 3.5% among parents and teachers respectively; 1.9% among the school leadership).

Personal Christian faith

By means of an initial exploration, we assess the personal faith in Jesus Christ present among the people in Catholic schools. All respondents simply choose from the following three options: do you consider yourself to have STRONG faith in Christ, AVERAGE faith in Christ, or NO faith in Christ? Though this approach is not very nuanced, it provides a reliable first exploration of the Christian profile in Catholic schools.

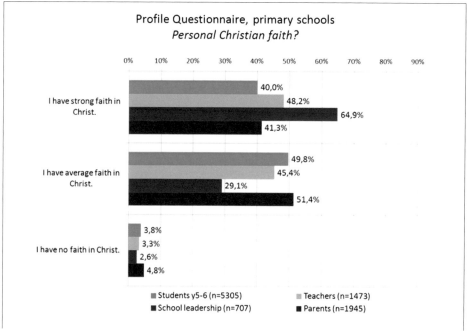

Figure II-16. Personal Christian faith in primary schools, all respondent groups differentiated.

The results in primary schools show that a clear majority of the adults believe in Christ (Figure II-16). Many say that they have 'deep' faith in Christ, while a considerable additional number express having 'average' faith in Christ. Two thirds of the school leadership confess to have *strong* faith in Christ, which is significantly more than the teachers (48.2%) and the parents (41.3%). Those who say they do not have faith in Christ are only a tiny fraction: 1 in 38 school leaders (2.6%), 1 in 30 teachers (3.3%), and 1 in 21 parents (4.8%). Compared with these results among the adult respondents, what is the children's faith profile? The graph shows that most of the year 5-6 students in primary schools can be considered believers, with 40% saying they have deep faith in Christ and about 50% (49.8%) who say they are average believers in Christ. Only a very small number say they are unbelievers (3.8%). Therefore, we presume that

Catholic school identity is very well supported by the majority of both the adults and the students in primary schools.

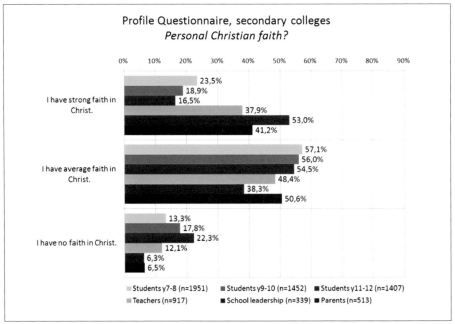

Figure II-17. Personal Christian faith in secondary colleges, all respondent groups differentiated.

In Figure II-17, the results in secondary colleges show that the adults who profess faith in Christ (either 'deep' or 'average') form a clear majority, despite a small group which is characterised as having no faith in Christ. Again, more school leadership members claim to have 'deep' faith (53%) compared with teachers (37.9%) and parents (41.2%). Yet, all percentages are somewhat lower compared with the very strong Catholic profile of adults in primary schools (see Figure II-16 above). Notice the minority of adults who do not profess faith in Christ: 1 in 16 school leaders (6.3%), 1 in 15 parents (6.5%), and 1 in 8 secondary school teachers (12.1%). How about the students' faith profile? The graph shows that those who describe themselves as having 'average' faith in Christ constitute the majority of the students (about 56% on the average). Those who have 'deep' faith in Christ include 20.1% of the students. Those who deny believing in Christ are almost the same: 17.3% on the average (nearly 1 in 6). Notice the little 'staircase shape' in the students' results: it is striking that the older students in secondary schools tend to profess less faith in Christ compared with the younger students. While 23.5% of the year 7-8 students say they have 'deep' faith, the same is true for 16.5% of the year 11-12 students. While 13.3% of the year 7-8 students consider themselves as having 'no faith', the same is true for 22.3% of the oldest students (which is 1 in 4.5 students).

Despite some non-Christian and non-religious diversity, we can conclude that the indicators of personal faith profile of the people in secondary colleges reach high levels. These encouraging results assure the Catholic religious profile of these colleges for many years to come.

Support for the Catholic faith

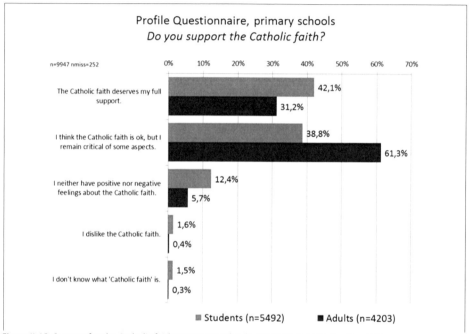

Figure II-18. Support for the Catholic faith in primary schools, students compared with adults.

Of the adults in primary schools, a majority of 92.6% claims to support the Catholic faith. This breaks down to 31.2% who say they 'strongly' support it, plus 61.3% who show support despite a critical attitude towards some aspects of the Catholic faith. 5.7% of the adult respondents (about 1 in 18) say they neither have positive nor negative feelings about it – which could be interpreted as acceptance and tolerance towards the Catholic faith, without actively supporting it though. Very few adults are formal in their rejection: 0.4% (about 1 in 236) claim they dislike Catholicism, while 0.3% of the adult respondents say they do not know what the term 'Catholic faith' means.

Concerning the children in year 5-6, no less than 80.8% claims to support the Catholic faith. This breaks down to 42.1% who strongly support it and 38.7% who show support despite a critical attitude towards some aspects. Not all students show active support for the Catholic faith: 12.4% (about 1 in 8) say they neither have positive nor negative feelings about it. Few say that they dislike Catholicism, namely 1.6% of the students (about 1 in 62). 1.5% of the students say they do not know what the 'Catholic faith' is. We conclude that the support for the Catholic faith is very strong in primary education in Victoria, with a vast majority of adults and students expressing strong to moderate support. Nevertheless, a minority express indifference or criticism for the Catholic faith.

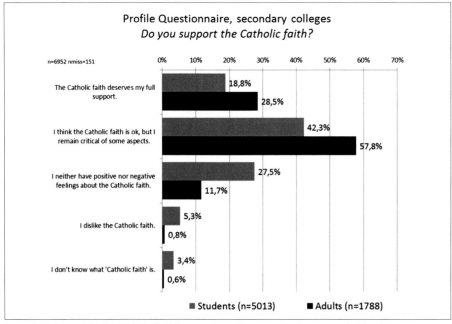

Figure II-19. Support for the Catholic faith in secondary colleges, students compared with adults.

Secondary colleges have a somewhat different profile, especially on the part of the students. First, on the part of the adult respondents, a total of 86.3% support the Catholic faith: 28.5% favour it strongly while an additional 57.8% are more critical about some aspects of their Catholic faith. 11.7% of the adult respondents say they neither have positive nor negative feelings about it (about 1 in 9). Those who dislike Catholicism remain a tiny minority comprising only 0.8% (about 1 in 129). Notably, 0.6% do not know what 'Catholic faith' is.

Next, concerning the student groups, those who align themselves with the Catholic faith reaches a total of 61.1%: 18.8% support it strongly while 42.3% show support despite some criticism. One in 3.6 students (a relatively large proportion of 27.5%) say they neither have positive nor negative feelings about the Catholic faith, which most likely means that they accept and tolerate the Catholic faith but they do not actively support it. In secondary colleges, 5.3% of students (which is about 1 in 19) say that they dislike Catholicism. About 3.4% of the students indicate not knowing what 'Catholic faith' means.

We summarise that most adults at the secondary education level express strong or at least moderate support for the Catholic faith. Many students also lend their support, but it should be noted that a significant minority takes a 'neutral' and rather 'indifferent' position vis-à-vis the Catholic faith, or even unambiguously dislikes it. These students may be open to strengthening their support for the Catholic faith, provided the adults lead the way in this respect.

The endorsement of the Catholic faith given by school members determines the way a school's Catholic identity can take shape. Investigating the way in which people at school relate to the religious faith reveals the 'building blocks' for the school's religious identity, so to speak. Background variables from the *Profile questionnaire* (such as this one) as well as a number of *Doyle Questionnaire* items pave the way for a more systematic and thorough exploration of religious attitudes by the *Post-Critical Belief Scale* (see chapter 10 paragraph 1).

Personal prayer life

Personal prayer life is an important background variable. Not surprisingly, we detect direct correlations between personal prayer life and the cognitive belief styles examined by the *Post-Critical Belief Scale*[23], as well as the inclination to endorse or reject various Catholic school identity models described by the *Melbourne Scale* and the *Victoria Scale*.

In general, the ECSIP research shows that the relation between prayer life and Catholic identity is *positive*. Catholic identity – personal identity as well as school identity – is eminently expressed in prayer, while prayer in turn constitutes Catholic identity. Therefore, if the intention is to communicate the Catholic faith to a new generation, and to foster a living and authentic Catholic school community, then the recommendation is apparent: *teach them how to pray*. The better way to do that is to be a living example of someone who prays.

---

[23] Cf. the elaboration of the relation between the *Post-Critical Belief Scale* and *Personal Prayer Life*.

128

We asked both students and adults how often they pray to God *on their own*, that is, without taking communal prayer in church or at school into consideration. To respond, there are six options to choose from:

- *'I pray on a daily basis'*
- *'I pray regularly'*
- *'I sometimes pray, but not regularly'*
- *'I only pray in times of great happiness or trouble'*
- *'Once I did pray, but not anymore'*
- *'I have never prayed before'*.

We analyse the result by counting the frequency of each option and expressing it as a percentage of the total number of respondents. Next, we summarise the results into three categories: 'I have an active prayer life' (option 1+2), 'I sometimes pray, but not regularly' (option 3+4) and 'I never pray' (option 5+6). Consequently, this summary is differentiated according to different respondent groups.

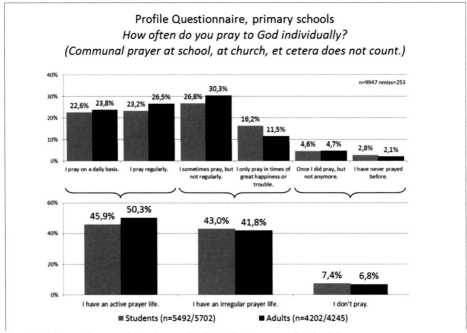

Figure II-20. Personal prayer life in primary schools, students compared with adults.

Where the adult respondents in primary schools are concerned, it is noteworthy that the options on the left are favoured most. Adults who pray with great regularity clearly form a majority: 23.8% make time for personal prayers on a daily basis; 26.5% pray at least regularly; and another 30.3% say that they pray at least sometimes, though not regularly. This is confirmed by our examination of the summary of the adult profile in the bottom graph: in total, 50.3% of the adult respondents have an active prayer life. A further 41.8% say that they pray sometimes though not regularly, while 6.8% indicate not to have a personal prayer life at all. We conclude that most of the adults are familiar with personal prayer to a greater or lesser extent: the largest proportion has an active prayer life, followed by a smaller but significant subgroup of people who pray to God at least occasionally. Adults who indicate that they never pray to God at all in their own time constitute a small minority (6.8%; about 1 in 15). We conclude that the adults in primary schools have a well-developed personal prayer life that most likely coincides with wide-spread support for Catholic school identity.

Like the adults, the primary school students also prefer the options on the left. A majority indicate that they pray in their own time with great regularity: 22.6% pray on a daily basis, while an additional 23.3% pray at least regularly. Another 26.8% of the children pray at least sometimes, but not regularly. This is confirmed by the summary in the bottom graph: overall, 45.9% of the students indicate having an active personal prayer life. 42.9% have an irregular prayer life, while 7.4% indicate not to have a personal prayer life at all. In other words, most of the students are familiar with personal prayer to a greater or lesser extent. However, there exists some diversity where the intensity of their prayer life is concerned. Only relatively few children have no personal prayer life of any kind. Based on the common practice of personal prayer, we may assume that the children support the Catholic identity of their school.

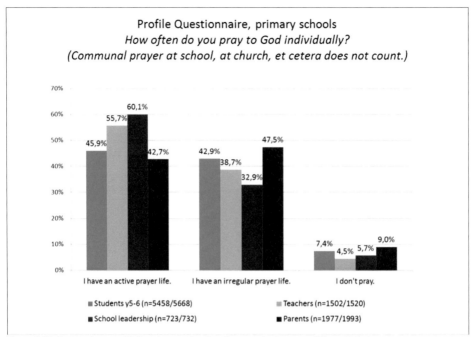

Figure II-21. Personal prayer life in primary schools, all respondent groups differentiated.

When examining the differentiation of the respondent groups in primary schools, we notice some differences between them. In general, people in school leadership positions claim to have a more regular prayer life (active prayer life: 60.1%) compared with the teachers (active prayer life: 55.7%) and the parents (active prayer life: 42.7%). Further, we notice that the personal prayer life of the parents is relatively weaker than that of the school staff: 47.5% only pray from time to time, while 9% claim they never pray on their own. The practice of personal prayer of the children is related to that of their parents, i.e. strong but not as regular compared with the staff in primary schools. Next, we will examine the personal prayer life in secondary colleges.

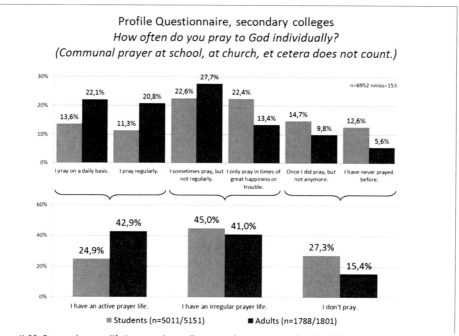

Figure II-22. Personal prayer life in secondary colleges, students compared with adults.

As we have come to expect after examining several background variables so far, the adults in secondary education show a strong Catholic faith profile, even if by comparison it is a little less strong than in primary education. A majority of the adults in secondary schools pray in their own time with great regularity: 22.1% of them make time for personal prayer daily, and 20.8% pray at least regularly. This results in 42.9% active prayer life. Another 41.0% of the adult respondents pray at least sometimes or only in times of great happiness or trouble, but not regularly. A minority of 15.4% (about three in twenty) indicate not having a personal prayer life at all. So, taking into account some diversity regarding the frequency of prayer, most of the staff and parents in secondary colleges are familiar with personal prayer to a greater or lesser extent.

Once more, the students in secondary education show a different profile from those in primary education. When examining the aggregated student groups, we notice that the percentages are spread over all six options. So, there are students with an active prayer life, with an irregular prayer life, as well as those without any personal prayer life. The bottom graph summarises this finding. Overall, a quarter of the students (24.9%) indicate having an active personal prayer life. A little under half of the students (45.0%) have an irregular prayer life, while another quarter (27.3%) never make time for personal prayer. We conclude that most of the students in secondary education have a prayer life that is rather erratic: in general, the students are not so likely to have an active prayer life.

At this stage, it is important to note that there exist different and sometimes opposite religious profiles among the students in secondary colleges. In this instance, we see a subgroup that has a very active prayer life, another group that has no prayer life at all, and a large group in-between that shows a moderate prayer life that could go either way. Apparently, the student population is pluralised regarding its affinity for prayer, and by extension most likely also regarding its views on Catholic identity in general – but more on that later.

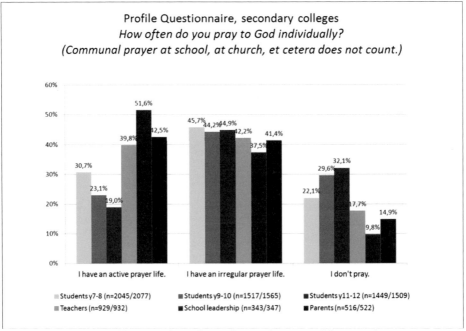

Figure II-23. Personal prayer life in secondary colleges, all respondent groups differentiated.

When examining the differentiation of the respondent groups in secondary colleges, we detect interesting variations between them. On the part of the adults, it is striking that the school leadership prays relatively more often (active prayer life: 51.6%) than the teachers (active prayer life: 39.8%) and the parents (active prayer life: 42.5%). In comparison with the primary schools, the parents are likely to pray a little less frequently (41.4% irregular prayer life and 14.9% absent prayer life), compared with the school staff. On the part of the students, we encounter the 'staircase shape' again. As the students grow older, the subgroup that favours an active prayer life becomes smaller in size, while the subgroup without prayer life grows. At the end of secondary education, approximately 19% of the students (about 1 in 5) pray daily or at least regularly, while 44.9% pray on an irregular basis, and 32.1% (about 1 in 3) admit to not praying on their own.

§2. The religious identity profile of Catholic schools (Doyle Questionnaire)

The *Doyle Questionnaire* is named after Mgr Tom Doyle, one of the initiators of the *Enhancing Catholic School Identity Project*. It consists of a number of varied, individual questions that assess the philosophical and religious profile of schools as an educational institutions.

Most questions are posed on both the factual measurement level and the normative measurement level. So, in the *Doyle Questionnaire*, the respondents are asked to assess the current practice of their school where its religious identity is concerned, and compare it with what they consider to be the ideal.

The graphs that show the results of the *Doyle Questionnaire* all have a pink background. They may consist of various combined objects, such as differentiated mean scores and percentages, cumulative mean scores and percentages, histograms, box-and-whisker plots and explanatory texts. Together, the composite graphs provide a clear presentation of the data that assists the interpretation of the results.

In this publication we present a selection of results from the *Doyle Questionnaire*. All research data originates from the ECSIP 2012 Research.

Support for Catholic school identity

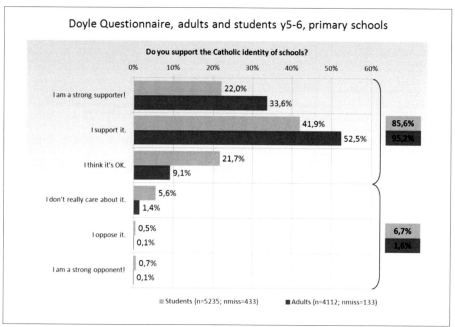

Figure II-24. Doyle Questionnaire, support for Catholic school identity in primary schools.

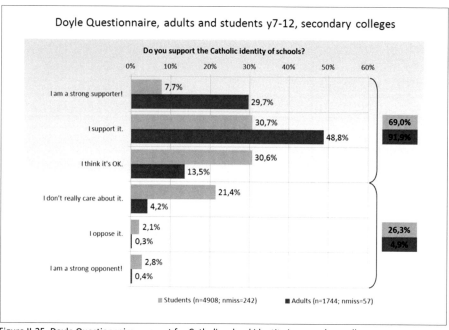

Figure II-25. Doyle Questionnaire, support for Catholic school identity in secondary colleges.

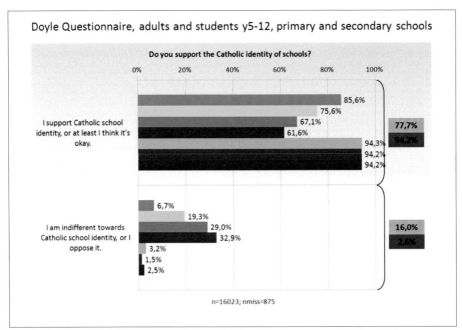

Figure II-26. Doyle Questionnaire, support for Catholic school identity, summary & differentiation.

To what extent is a Catholic educational project supported by the various respondent groups in Catholic schools in Victoria? What are the differences in support levels between the various respondent groups in primary schools and secondary colleges?

To respond to this question, people choose one of the following six responses:
- I am a strong supporter!
- I support it.
- I think it is OK.
- I don't really care about it.
- I oppose it.
- I am a strong opponent!

In total, no less than 16023 respondents answered this *Doyle Questionnaire* item; about 63% of them were students and 37% of them were adults.

Figures II-24 and II-25 show the results of primary and secondary school respectively, the students differentiated from the adults. Figure II-26 combines the three responses that express support on the one hand, and the three responses that express indifference or opposition on the other hand, and differentiates the combined results according to the various respondent groups. Note that, in the latter graph, the adult data from primary and secondary schools has been aggregated. The graphs show that a majority of both students and adults in primary and secondary schools in Victoria support a Catholic education project, although there are differences in levels of support.

In primary schools, no less than 95.2% of the adult respondents pledge their support to the Catholicity of schools: 33.6% are strong supporters, 52.5% just support it, while 9.1% think it is 'okay' without explicitly supporting it. No more than 1.6% of the adults refrain from expressing interest in Catholic education.

In comparison with the adults in secondary colleges, the support for the Catholic identity of schools is also overwhelming: 91.9% pledge their support. This breaks down as follows: 29.7% are strong supporters, 48.8% just support it, while 13.5% think it is merely 'okay'. However, though very supportive of Catholic identity, there is a tiny decrease in percentage compared with the primary schools. The number of adults who remain indifferent or oppose Catholic identity rises to 4.9% – about one in twenty.

The above observation is also somewhat true of the number of students who are very supportive of Catholic identity, although they tell a different story. No less than 85.6% of the primary school children in years 5 and 6 say they support the Catholic identity of schools: 22.0% are strong supporters, 41.9% just support it, while 21.7% think it is merely okay. Further, 5.6% do not really care about it, while 1.2% oppose it. In primary schools, the children follow the adults' lead where Catholic school identity is concerned. Nevertheless, their levels of support are somewhat lower, compared with the teachers and the parents. In particular, there are significantly more students (1 in 4.6) who do not explicitly express support but say that Catholic identity is merely 'okay', compared with the adult groups (1 in 11).

In secondary colleges, a total of 69.0% of the students in years seven to twelve indicate support for the Catholic identity of schools: 7.7% are strong supporters, 30.7% just support it, while 30.6% think it is merely 'okay'. Further, 26.3% refrain from expressing any form of support: 21.4% do not really care about it, 2.1% opposes it and 2.8% strongly opposes it. Although a large majority of the secondary college students pledge their support and very few explicitly refrain from doing so, the support levels for Catholic school identity are reduced compared with the children in primary schools.
Also noteworthy are the differences between the support levels of the students and the adults in primary and secondary schools respectively. Most children in primary schools (85.6%) join the adults in their support for Catholic identity (95.2%). However, the gap between the support of the students (69.0%) and the adults (91.9%) in secondary colleges is significantly larger.

Relevant additional information is provided in Figure II-26 that shows the differentiated percentages for all respondent groups. There is a clear connection between the support for a Catholic education project on the one hand, and the age of the students on the other. As the students get older, their cumulative support for Catholic school identity decreases, while the percentages that show indifference and resistance increase. The 85.6% of primary school children who support Catholic identity are reduced to 75.6% in grades 7-8, to 67.1% in grades 9-10, to 61.6% in grades 11-12. Although Catholic identity always enjoys the support of a clear majority of the student population, it is striking that the general levels of support diminish the further the students' progress in the school curriculum.

Most likely, one of the reasons for the reduction of the support for Catholic identity among secondary college students can be found in the composition of the school population, which is more pluralised in secondary colleges. Also, in general, secondary college students demonstrate a reduced interest and passion vis-à-vis Catholic education, a finding that is confirmed by many other research results. In particular, the analysis of the students' results on the *Post Critical Belief Scale* will shed more light on this finding.[24]

---

[24] See the student results on the *Post Critical Belief Scale*, chapter 10 paragraph 1.

Catholic school characteristics

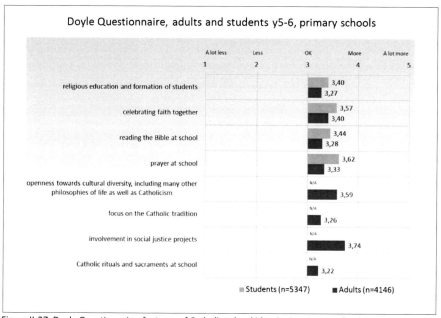

Figure II-27. Doyle Questionnaire, features of Catholic school identity in primary schools.

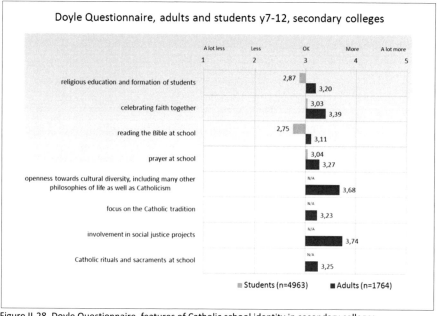

Figure II-28. Doyle Questionnaire, features of Catholic school identity in secondary colleges.

In this set of Doyle Questionnaire items, the respondents are requested to consider the following typical features of Catholic school identity. Keeping in mind the current practice in their school, would they like these features *more or less* (normative measurement level)?

These four features are presented to both students and adults:
- *religious education and formation of students*
- *celebrating faith together*
- *reading the Bible at school*
- *prayer at school*

The following four features are presented only to the adult respondents (in order to shorten and simplify the survey for children and teenagers):
- *openness towards cultural diversity, including many other philosophies of life as well as Catholicism*
- *focus on the Catholic tradition*
- *involvement in social justice projects*
- *Catholic rituals and sacraments at school*

The following five-point Likert scale, generally assessing quantity, extent or frequency, is used in this question:
1 = a lot less
2 = less
3 = neither more, nor less
4 = more
5 = a lot more

We need to note here that mean scores that approach the middle line (3 = 'neither more, nor less') indicate that people are satisfied about the current practice in their school concerning the feature in question. The more a mean score deviates from the middle line, the more critical the respondents are – either wishing for more or less of the feature in question.

In the P-6 and P-8 primary schools in Victoria, ALL respondents desire MORE of all eight Catholic school characteristics. Not only is the Catholic character of most schools already strong today, but people desire to make it even more apparent in the future. On the average, children in years 5 and 6 seem enthusiastic about religious education (3.40/5), celebrating faith (3.57/5), Bible reading (3.44/5) and school prayer (3.62/5).

They want more of these religious activities, even more than the staff and the parents desire (who score 3.27/5, 3.40/5, 3.28/5 and 3.33/5 respectively).

The adult respondents in primary schools indicate that there is room for a little more focus on the Catholic tradition (3.26/5) as well as Catholic rituals and sacraments at school (3.22/5), compared with the usual practice today. It should be noted that the adults clearly indicate that there is room for improvement regarding involvement in social justice projects (3.75/5), which they desire significantly more than is already the case today. Moreover, many adults also tend to be critical of their primary school's openness towards cultural diversity, including many other philosophies of life as well as Catholicism (3.59/5). Is this typical feature of Catholic identity, present in the faith tradition as well as theologically desirable, sometimes lacking in schools in Victoria?

In the secondary colleges, the adult respondents indicate that they also want more of all Catholic school characteristics. Staff and parents desire a little more religious education and formation of the students (3.20/5), prayer at school (3.27/5), focus on the Catholic tradition (3.23/5) and Catholic rituals and sacraments (3.25/5). Their desire for a more communal celebration of faith is a little stronger (3.39/5). Just like in primary schools, many adult respondents tend to be critical about a perceived lack of involvement in social justice projects (3.75/5). Because of their Catholic identity, they also would like more openness towards cultural diversity, which is present outside but also inside the secondary colleges (3.68/5).

In contrast to the primary school children, who appear to be very eager where Catholic identity is concerned, the teenagers and adolescents in secondary colleges seem to be generally satisfied about their schools' level of Catholicity. On the average, they either think that things are 'okay' the way they are now, or they desire a little less the Catholic characteristics featured in the survey. However, when we examine the data more closely (see Figure II-29 below), we find that there are differences of opinion that tend to cancel each other out. On the average, the largest subgroup of students is satisfied with the current status quo and like their college the way it is. Next, there is a subgroup of about 21% of the secondary college students who want more Catholic identity. Another equally sized subgroup of about 22% of the students want less Catholic identity. These findings confirm what we find in many other parts of the ECSIP research: secondary college students fracture into opposing subgroups where the Catholic identity of their college is concerned.

COLLEGE STUDENTS	a lot less	less	OK	more	a lot more	nmiss
religious education and formation of students	7 .8%	14 .2%	56 .3%	13 .4%	3 .1%	5 .1%
celebrating faith together	6 .5%	12 .3%	50 .8%	20 .0%	5 .3%	5 .1%
reading the Bible at school	14 .0%	15 .8%	47 .0%	14 .0%	4 .1%	5 .1%
prayer at school	7 .8%	10 .6%	51 .4%	18 .1%	7 .0%	5 .1%
MEAN %	9 .0%	13 .2%	51 .4%	16 .4%	4 .9%	5 .1%

Figure II-29. Frequency of Likert scale responses of secondary college students.

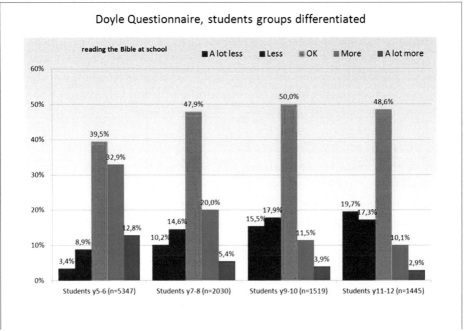

Figure II-30. Frequency of Likert scale responses on Bible reading at school, primary and secondary school students differentiated.

Special attention goes to the difficult issue of reading and working with Bible stories at school. In general, secondary college students show some fatigue where Bible reading is concerned: on the average they wish a little less of it compared with the current practice (2.75/5). However, we notice that the resistance to Bible use at school increases significantly as students grow older. While no more than 12.3% of the primary school children want less Bible reading at school, this percentage increases to 24.8% in years 7-8, 33.4% in years 9-10 and 37.0% in years 11-12. So, while most students remain satisfied with the amount of Bible reading at school, an increasing subgroup tends to resist it. The adults in secondary colleges admit that the current practice suffices, with perhaps a little room for increase but not much (3.11/5).

Although a thorough acquaintance with the Holy Scriptures ought to be part of any Christian religious formation, it is apparently difficult to bridge the many gaps that make it hard to work with the Bible in schools. Despite the difficulties, presenting the Bible to young people at school in a justified way deserves attention, creativity, courage and patience. It would be good to gain more insight in the exact nature and the causes of the 'Bible fatigue' that affects young people today, by searching for a new theological understanding of the dynamics of revelation in the Scriptures and how this could be made relevant for religious pedagogy.[25]

---

[25] D. POLLEFEYT & R. BIERINGER, *The Role of the Bible in Religious Education Reconsidered. Risks and Challenges in Teaching the Bible*, in *International Journal of Practical Theology* 9(1) (2005) 117-139.

Do people at school believe in God?

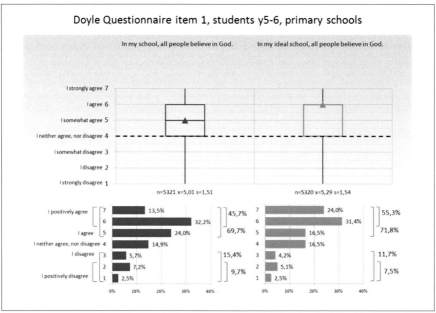

Figure II-31. Doyle Questionnaire item 1, students y5-6 in primary schools.

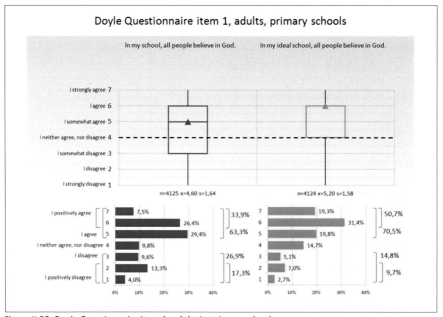

Figure II-32. Doyle Questionnaire item 1, adults in primary schools.

145

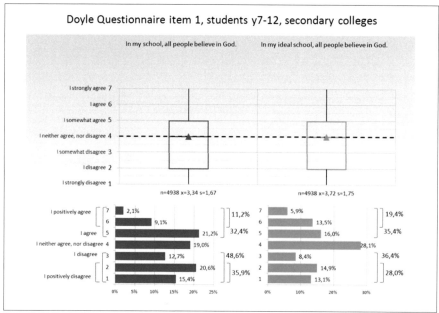

Figure II-33. Doyle Questionnaire item 1, students y7-12 in secondary colleges.

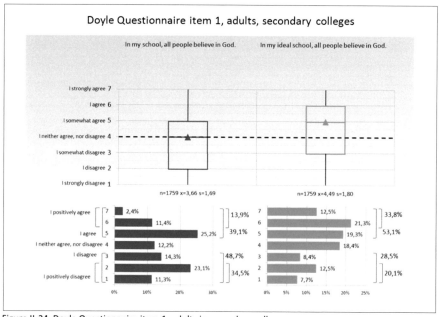

Figure II-34. Doyle Questionnaire item 1, adults in secondary colleges.

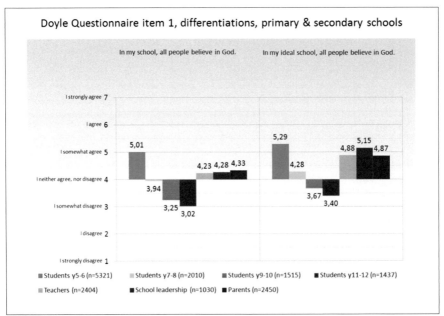

Figure II-35. Doyle Questionnaire item 1, all groups differentiated.

To what extent do the people in Catholic schools in Victoria believe in God? Since a Catholic education project is always carried by the personal faith of its members, this is a relevant background variable when assessing the religious identity of schools. How do the various respondent groups perceive the current practice of belief in God among their fellow school members (factual level)? And to what extent is belief in God important to them when they think about the ideal school context (normative level)? Are there differences between adults and students or between primary and secondary schools regarding people's perceptions and their desires when faith in God in concerned?

To respond to this question, people choose one of these seven Likert scale options:
1. I strongly disagree
2. I disagree
3. I somewhat disagree
4. I neither agree, nor disagree
5. I somewhat agree
6. I agree
7. I strongly agree

In total, no less than 6697 respondents answered this *Doyle Questionnaire* item; about 74% of them were students and 26% of them were adults.

Figures II-31, II-32, II-33 and II-34 show the detailed results in primary and secondary schools respectively, the students separated from the adults. Each of these four composite graphs contains *box-and-whisker plots* and corresponding *histograms*, both on the factual level (on the left hand side in blue colour) and on the normative level (on the right hand side in green colour).

A *box-and-whisker plot*[26] conveniently displays the dispersal of the respondents' scores. The box contains the 'middle 50%' of the scores ranked from high to low and points at the main tendency, while the 'whiskers' indicate the range of responses that are still relevant relative to the main tendency. The little triangle at the centre of the box denotes the median or 50th percentile, while an 'x' points at an 'outlier' i.e. an extreme response that is exceptionally far removed from the main tendency.

A *histogram*[27] displays the same research data in a different yet complementary way. It simply counts the number of times each of the seven possible responses is given and expresses this figure relative to the total number of responses in the form of a percentage. The sum of the seven percentages (plus a possible number of missing values) is always 100%. For the reader's convenience, the graph also contains the cumulative percentages of agreement and disagreement:
- "I positively agree"% = sum of responses 6 and 7.
- "I agree"% = sum of responses 5, 6 and 7.
- "I positively disagree"% = sum of responses 1 and 2.
- "I disagree"% = sum of responses 1, 2 and 3.

Figure II-35 shows the differentiated mean scores on the seven-point scale of all respondent groups, so it is convenient to compare them one to the other and examine the differences. (Note that, in this graph, the adult data from primary and secondary schools has been aggregated.)

Most children in years 5 and 6 agree that many people in their primary school believe in God (mean score: 5.01/7; 69.7% agreement). Yet, few children indicate that *all* people believe in God (13.5%), while there is also a minority that claims that only *some* school members actually believe in God (15.4% disagreement, including 9.7% positive disagreement). The adult school members are a little more critical about the current practice. Although it is very common for people in primary schools to believe in God, the adults indicate that not all of them do (mean score: 4.60/7; 63.3% agreement;

---

[26] For more information on *box-and-whisker plots*, see: D.S. MOORE & G.P. MCCABE, *Statistiek in de Praktijk. Theorieboek*, 5de herziene druk, Den Haag, Sdu Uitgevers bv, 2006 (repr. 2007), p.31-35.
[27] For more information on *histograms*, see: *Ibid.*, p.13-16.

148

26.9% disagreement, including 17.3% positive disagreement). Ideally speaking, both the children and the adults in primary schools would like a little more belief in God at school (mean scores: 5.29/7 and 5.20/7 respectively; in both cases over 70% agreement). Only a minority group prefers a school where people have no faith in God (7.5% of the students and 9.7% of the adults.

In secondary colleges, people have a lower estimation of belief in God, compared with primary schools. At the secondary level, both the students and the adults indicate that quite a few school members believe in God, but certainly not all (about 1/3 tends to agree; almost 1/2 disagrees; mean scores: 3.34/7 and 3.66/7, respectively). Despite the consensus on the factual measurement level, on the normative level we notice a divergence between students and adults. A majority of 53.1% of the adults opt for a school where belief in God is very common (mean score: 4.49/7). The same holds for 35.4% of the students (mean score: 3.72/7). And while 28.5% of the adults prefer a school with little or no belief in God, the same holds for 36.4% of the students – well over 1 in 3.

Once more, the graph that shows differentiated mean scores (Figure II-35) provides relevant additional information. It indicates that primary school students have an idealised perception about people at school believing in God, even more so than the adult groups. Contrary to this, in secondary colleges fewer and fewer students testify for belief in God in the current practice. Also ideally speaking, year after year the students tend to attach less importance to people at school believing in God. The mean scores on the normative level drop as the students grow older and start to indicate an overall rejection by the students in years 9-10 and 11-12 (5.29/7 > 4.28/7 > 3.67/7> 3.40/7).

Again we conclude that the children in primary schools bear witness to strong levels of Catholic identity, both in their perception of the current practice and in their ideal views – even stronger than the staff and the parents. Also we conclude that the staff and the parents in secondary colleges have a generally strong Catholic identity profile, but that the students are divided into subgroups with opposing views concerning Catholic school identity: some are in favour of it while others tend to be sceptical, especially when belief in God is expected of *all* those involved.

School as a good place to grow closer to God?

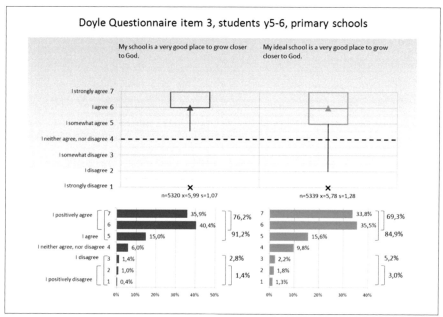

Figure II-36. Doyle Questionnaire item 3, students y5-6 in primary schools.

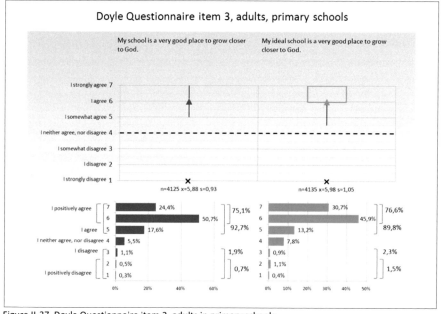

Figure II-37. Doyle Questionnaire item 3, adults in primary schools.

150

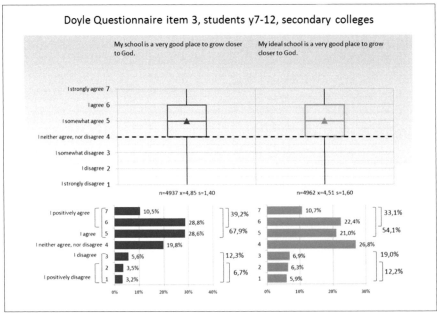

Figure II-38. Doyle Questionnaire item 3, students y7-12 in secondary colleges.

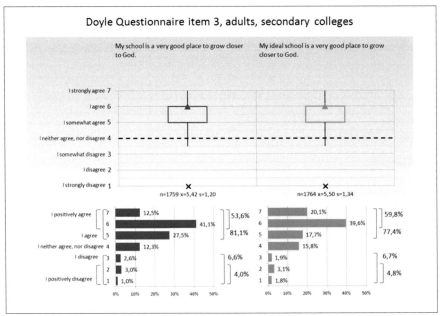

Figure II-39. Doyle Questionnaire item 3, adults in secondary colleges.

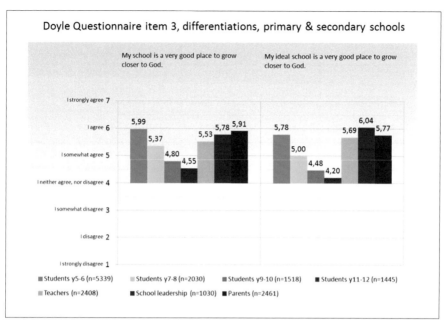

Figure II-40. Doyle Questionnaire item 3, all groups differentiated.

Even though not all people in a Catholic school believe in God or can be expected to have religious faith, one might expect that a Catholic school – by definition – is a good place to *grow closer to God*. Catholic identity is not just a formal characteristic or a 'quality label', but it contains an existential dynamic that is continuously evolving and growing – like revelation itself. This *Doyle Questionnaire* item examines to what degree people in Catholic schools in Victoria actually consider their school to be a good place to grow closer to God (factual measurement level). It also examines to what degree they would like this to be the case, ideally speaking (normative measurement level). Again we separate the primary schools from the secondary colleges and the student groups from the adult staff and parents.

It is striking how both the adults and the children in primary schools have a very high estimate of their school being a good place to grow closer to God (adults' mean score: 5.88/7; 92.7% agreement; hardly any disagreement / students' mean score: 5.99/7; 91.2% agreement; hardly any disagreement). This trend is confirmed on the normative level: vast majorities of both students (mean score: 5.78/7; 84.9% agreement) and adults (mean score: 5.98/7; 89.8% agreement) are eager to agree that a school should be suitable for religious growth. Although we notice a small decline from the factual to the normative level (2.3% of the adults and 5.2% of the children disagree), the levels of support for religious education and formation remain overwhelmingly positive in primary schools.

Similarly to the primary schools, the staff and the parents in the secondary colleges in Victoria also have a high estimate of their college being a good place to grow closer to God (adults' mean score: 5.42/7; 81.1% agreement), although we notice a subgroup of adults who regard the college with more scepticism (6.6% disagreement). This sceptical minority is larger among the students (12.3% disagreement), which results in the lower overall mean score (5.85/7). Moreover, the students' estimate about their college being a good place to grow closer to God declines significantly as they grow older (the overall mean score drops from 5.99/7 in primary schools to 4.55/7 in year 11-12). Opposite to this sceptical group stands a majority of students who agree, to varying degrees, that their college is indeed suitable to grow closer to God (69.9% agreement, including 39.2% positive agreement).

Normatively speaking, the adult groups in secondary colleges have no hesitation that their college ought to remain a good place to grow closer to God (mean score: 5.5/7; 77.4% agreement). A small majority of the students agree with this point of view (mean score: 4.51/7; 54.1% agreement). The 'not so good news' is that the students' desire for a college that fosters Christian faith declines when compared with their estimate of the current practice (the mean score declines from 4.85/7 to 4.51/7), and that this decline is mainly due to a growing scepticism among the older students (the overall mean score drops from 5.78/7 in primary schools to 4.20/7 in year 11-12). However, the 'good news' is that *all* respondent groups, including the year 11-12 students in secondary colleges, show a general willingness to remain part of a school that is suitable to grow closer to God.

We can confirm here what we concluded earlier about the high levels of Catholic identity in Victorian Catholic schools and we summarise as follows:
- All adult groups in primary and secondary schools support Catholic identity, which guarantees a sustained Catholic education system in the long run.
- The identity profile of adult groups in primary schools is a little stronger, than that of the adults groups in secondary colleges.
- Members of the school leadership teams have the strongest normative profile of all adult groups, closely followed by the teachers and the parents.
- Primary school children show remarkably strong levels of Catholic identity. They are almost unanimous in their high scores, both regarding their perception of the current practice and their views of the ideal school context. Often, the children's Catholic views are even more idealised than that of the adults.
- On the whole, secondary college students show mild support for Catholic school identity. However, a deeper analysis reveals a division into subgroups with opposing views.

- It should be noted that the minority of students who are sceptical vis-à-vis Catholic identity grows as the students proceed through the education curriculum.

Chapter 10. Catholic school identity *in dialogue*? Results of the three multivariate attitude scales

§1. Cognitive belief styles as building blocks for Catholic school identity. Results of the *Post-Critical Belief* Scale

In this section we consider the ways in which students, staff and parents cognitively handle religious content: what are the cognitive belief styles of the people that make up the school community? The prevailing tendencies among students and adults of *Literal Belief, Post-Critical Belief, Relativism/Contingency Awareness* and *External Critique* reveal the potential (or lack thereof) to develop the school's Catholic identity. We examine this by means of the *Post-Critical Belief Scale* developed in the 1990s by the Leuven psychologist of religion Dirk Hutsebaut.[28]

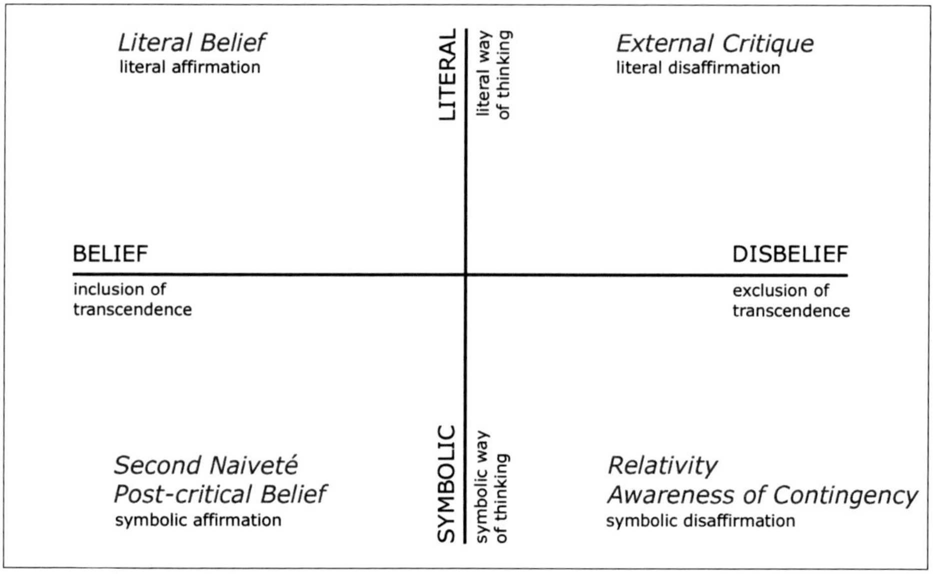

Figure II-41. The *PCB Scale* diagram.

The *Post-Critical Belief Scale* is an empirical instrument that operationalises the typology conceived of by David M. Wulff on the four different ways that people deal with belief content. These four *cognitive belief styles* or *religious attitudes* result from the combination of two dimensions. In the above diagram, the horizontal line refers to whether or not someone has personal belief in God: *inclusion/exclusion of belief in transcendence*. The vertical line concerns the way in which religious faith is

---

[28] See the presentation of the *Post-Critical Belief Scale* in the first part of this publication, chapter 3 §4.

experienced and processed: *literal/symbolic interpretation of religious contents*. The combination of these two dimensions results in four different ways of dealing with religiosity: *Literal Belief, Post-Critical Belief, Relativism/Contingency Awareness* and *External Critique*. Notice that these faith styles are ideal-typical, meaning that they are theoretical, extreme positions in a continuum with many in-between positions and mixed forms. It is never the intention to put people into 'boxes'; instead we try to describe tendencies within groups of people.

Brief recapitulation of the four cognitive belief styles of the PCB Scale:

Literal Belief
Literal affirmation of belief content. Belief in the possibility of direct access to a transcendent God. Literal acceptance of doctrinal belief content. If dominant, then the Catholic faith tradition tends to become a 'closed narrative'. However, when combined with high levels of *Post-Critical Belief*, the believer becomes a positive and constructive guardian of the faith.

Literal Disbelief / External Critique
Literal disaffirmation of belief content. Destructive criticism of religion and faith from an external position. Faith is contrary to reason, and must therefore be dismissed. Generally destructive for Catholic school identity!

Relativism/Awareness of Contingency
Ultimately, belief content is contingent and merely relative. A symbolic approach to religion, however belief in a transcendent God is excluded. Positive aspect: points at a fundamental openness towards otherness and receptivity for the potentially valuable impact of the encounter with people who differ.

Post-Critical Belief / Second Naiveté
Symbolical affirmation of belief content. Only through a symbolic mediation and an on-going interpretation can people enter into a relationship with the transcendent Reality. High correlation with a *Recontextualisation* of Catholic school identity in a pluralistic context (see the *Melbourne Scale*).

Below are the empirical research results for the four religious attitudes, for the adult groups on the one hand and the students on the other. The same result is being displayed in two different but complementing ways: as *scale mean results* and as *percentages*.

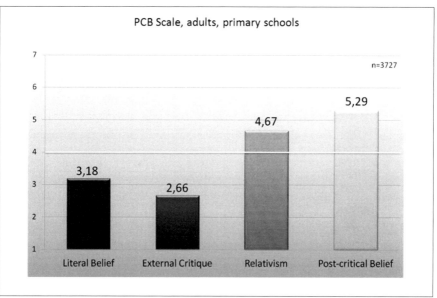

Figure II-42. PCB Scale, scale means for all the adults in primary schools.

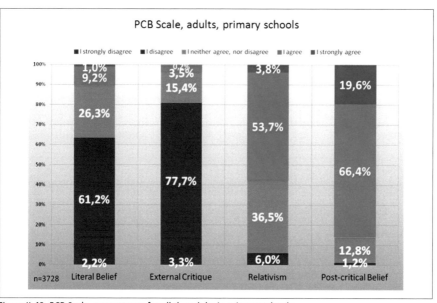

Figure II-43. PCB Scale, percentages for all the adults in primary schools.

158

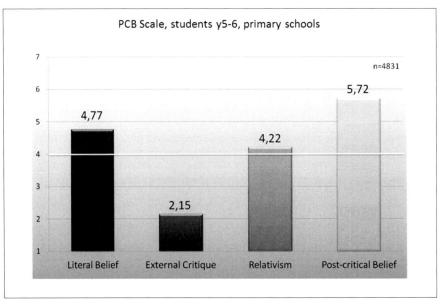

Figure II-44. PCB Scale, scale means for all the students year 5-6 in primary schools.

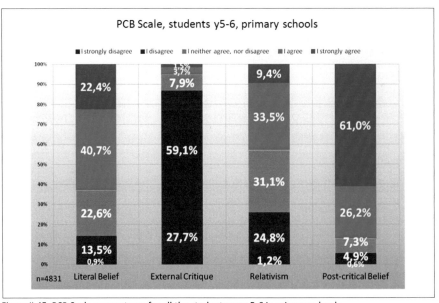

Figure II-45. PCB Scale, percentages for all the students year 5-6 in primary schools.

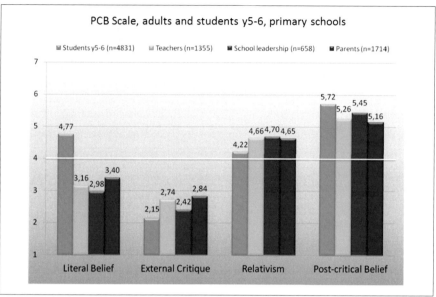

Figure II-46. PCB Scale, differentiated scale means in primary schools.

Figures II-42, II-43, II-44, II-45 and II-46 present the *PCB Scale* results in all primary schools together (P-6 and P-8, excluding the small group of students year 7-8 in the P-8 school):

- the scale means and the percentages of the combined adult groups.
- the scale means and the percentages of the combined student groups.
- the differentiated scale means for students, school staff and parents.

The scale mean results are adjusted, average scores expressed on a seven-point Likert scale ranging from 1 ('I strongly disagree') to 7 ('I strongly agree'). The horizontal white line at the number 4 ('I neither agree, nor disagree') indicates the turning point from disagreement to agreement or vice versa: when the bar remains under the white line, then the respondents disapprove of the type in question; when the bar reaches above the white line, then the respondents approve of it. The *n-number* in the top corner indicates the total number of people who contribute to the graph. The scale mean graph shows *general tendencies* that emerge when an entire group of people is observed *as a whole*.

The percentage graph is based on the same data and shows the same results, but in a distinctive way. Here we count the number of respondents who strongly disagree (dark red), who disagree (red), who are doubting or unsure (orange), who agree (green) and who strongly agree (dark green), and express these as ratios of the total number of contributors. The percentages graph often offers valuable additional information that complements the scale mean results: it reveals different subgroups and underlying tendencies that exist within a group of people.

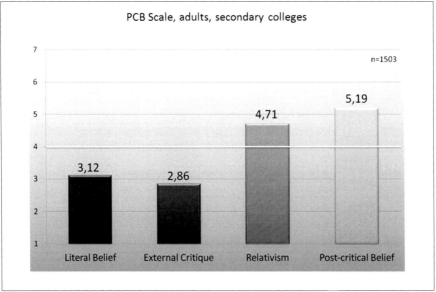

Figure II-47. PCB Scale, scale means for all the adults in secondary colleges.

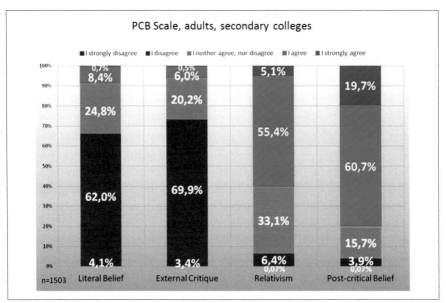

Figure II-48. PCB Scale, percentages for all the adults in secondary colleges.

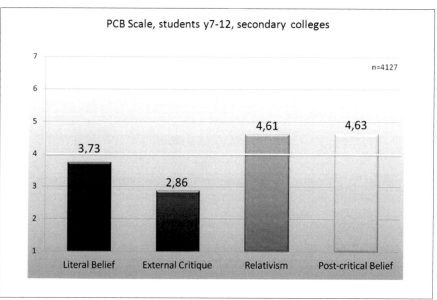

Figure II-49. PCB Scale, scale means for all the students year 7-12 in secondary colleges.

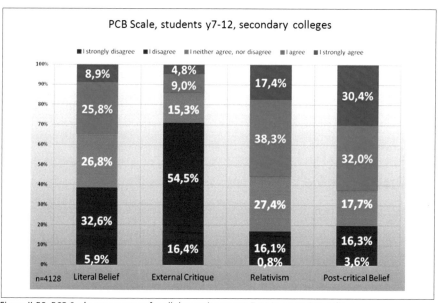

Figure II-50. PCB Scale, percentages for all the students year 7-12 in secondary colleges.

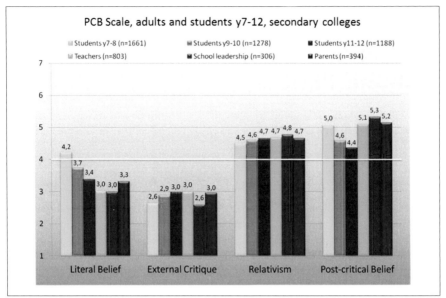

Figure II-51. PCB Scale, differentiated scale means in secondary colleges.

Figures II-47, II-48, II-49, II-50 and II-51 present the *PCB Scale* results in all secondary colleges together (7-12):

- the scale means and the percentages of the combined adult groups.
- the scale means and the percentages of the combined student groups.
- the differentiated scale means for three student groups, teachers, school leadership and parents.

This graph presents data collected from a total of 5630 respondents.

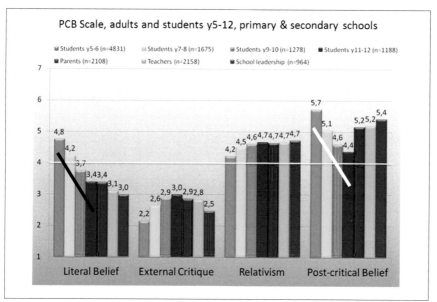

Figure II-52. PCB Scale, differentiated scale means in primary and secondary schools.

Figure II-52 on this page summarises all *PCB Scale* results. It differentiates the mean Likert scale scores of all seven respondent groups, combining the data from P-6, P-8 and 7-12 schools. For example, the yellow bars contain all students in year 7-8 in the 14 secondary colleges *including* those in the single P-8 primary school. The blue, green and brown bars combine the *PCB Scale* results for parents, teachers and school leadership respectively, in primary and secondary schools *together*.

This graph presents data collected from a total of 14204 respondents.

The black trend line indicates a sharply decreasing mean score on *Literal Belief* as the students grow older, while the white trend line indicates a simultaneous drop in the mean scores for *Post-Critical Belief*.

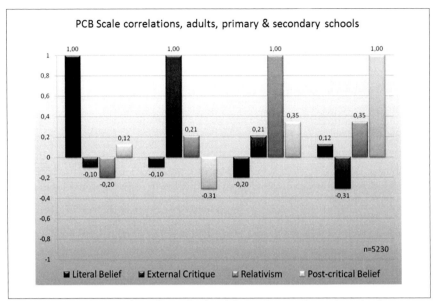

Figure II-53. PCB Scale, internal correlations for the adults in primary and secondary schools.

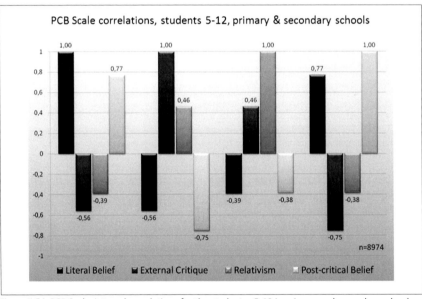

Figure II-54. PCB Scale, internal correlations for the students y5-12 in primary and secondary schools.

The two graphs on this page (Figures II-43 and II-54) are visual representations of the 4x4 matrices that contain the Pearson linear correlation coefficients between the religious attitudes described by the *Post-Critical Belief Scale* for both the combined adult groups and the combined student groups in all ECSIP 2012 schools.

A general tendency towards *Post-Critical Belief*

Among students, staff and parents in Catholic schools in Victoria, the predominant attitude towards religion – the main tendency shared by most people – is *Post-Critical Belief* (adults PRIM: 5.29/7; adults SEC: 5.19/7; students PRIM: 5.72/7; students SEC: 4.63/7). 86% of the adults in primary schools and 80.4% of the adults in secondary colleges agree or even strongly agree with PCB. Further, 87.2% of the primary school children and 62.4% of the secondary college students also support or strongly support a PCB attitude. Generally speaking, the people in schools in Victoria clearly confess that they personally believe in a transcendent reality while dealing with belief content in a symbolic, interpretative way. No doubt this is a point of strength for Catholic schools since *as an historical religion, the Christian faith and practice are inherently hermeneutical, interpretative and symbolically mediated.*

However, it must be noted that the students' interest in *Post-Critical Belief*, especially where the older students are concerned, is diminishing. On the whole, it remains the preferential option in all student grades, but *Post-Critical Belief* is slowly being caught up by tendencies of *Relativism* and even *External Religious Critique* as the students mature. It is striking how PCB loses support as the students grow up: the mean score drops from 5.7/7 in primary schools, to 5.1/7 in year 7-8, to 4.6/7 in year 9-10, and finally to 4.4/7 in year 11-12. This trend shows that among the oldest students in secondary colleges, a majority does not adopt a *Post-Critical Believing* attitude.

Post-Critical Belief is backed up by a strong *Awareness of Contingency*

Apart from this dominant tendency, there is another approach that finds wide-spread support, namely, 'Relativism', which is also labelled as 'Awareness of contingency' in the specific context of the PCB Scale typology. A majority of staff and parents (PRIM: 57.5%; SEC: 60.5%) agrees that a multiplicity of religious commitments should be accepted, welcomed and valued, without – in principle – any one of these interchangeable options being more true or valuable than the others. *Awareness of Contingency* is also backed up by about 42.9% of the students in primary schools and 55.7% of the students in secondary colleges. Another third of the students lean towards it. Moreover, the differentiated scale means reveal that the students are growing in *Contingency Awareness* as they get older, approaching adult levels by the age of 18.

A love-hate relationship between *Post-Critical Belief* and *Relativism/Awareness of Contingency*

On the one hand, from a theological point of view, a wide-spread *Awareness of Contingency* can be a hopeful sign, provided it is accompanied by an even stronger appreciation for *Post-Critical Belief*. This would indicate that people value an attitude of openness, receptiveness and hospitality towards a diversity of cultural and religious commitments, appreciating the contribution each of them could make. When outflanked by a high score for *Post-Critical Belief*, there is no need to worry that a high score for 'Relativism' would mean that the school members actually think 'relativistically'. Instead, in line with the Catholic tradition, it is to be understood that they merely accept, tolerate and value the identity and the input of other-believers in their school – an attitude that contributes to a truly Catholic ethos. This holds for the adult groups and also for the biggest part of the student population.

On the other hand, a strong tendency towards *Relativism* could potentially undermine a school's Catholic identity structure, especially when it is not balanced by a significant *Post-Critical Belief* tendency. The positive correlation (adults: r=0.21; students: r=0.46) between *Relativism* and *External Critique* (while *External Critique* and *Post-Critical Belief* are strongly opposed to each other) might point towards this danger: as an unbelieving stance, an increasing *Relativistic* trend might lead to increasing *External Critique* levels – a perspective that looms on the horizon where the students are concerned.

In the current context, the tension between the desirability of *Contingency Awareness* and the corresponding openness towards other beliefs and lifestyles on the one hand, and the fear that such openness and receptivity could potentially be harmful to a school's specific Catholic identity on the other, seem to be a key discussion in Victorian Catholic schools. Although a majority have religious faith and agrees that religious contents should be dealt with in a symbolical-hermeneutical way (*Post-Critical Belief*), there is disagreement about the extent in which openness towards other than Catholic views and practices should be embraced. There exist many different opinions about how the schools, in being Catholic, should relate to a plural outside culture and deal with 'otherness'.

This discussion is taking place within the various adults groups, and even more outspoken within the student population. The students are divided regarding *Contingency Awareness/Relativism*. In primary schools, 42.9% clearly support it, 31.1% lean towards it and 26% openly oppose it. In secondary colleges, there is a little more support: 60.5% strongly support it, 33.1% lean towards it and another 6.4% clearly oppose it. This division is correlated to the students' age: the younger students are less *Aware of Contingency* or do not see much need for it in contrast with the older students. On the whole, the primary school students tend to dismiss *Contingency Awareness* in favour of a generally shared faith affiliation that can hinge upon a direct and literal understanding. However, the more years the students spend in the Catholic school system, the more their personal religious identities come under pressure in favour of an *Awareness of Contingency* and in some groups a straightforward *Relativistic* or even *Externally Critical* attitude. The oldest students are most aware of the multiplicity and relativity of philosophical and religious claims. For many of them, this development has an impact on their own religious identity.

From a theological point of view, it is important to stress that *Post-Critical* Catholic believers should keep showing in words and deeds that a believing attitude is, in its very essence, not in conflict with their acknowledgement of plurality, nor with their authentic appreciation of other people's identity, their values, beliefs and ways of life. On the contrary, it is the ongoing search for a Recontextualisation of Catholic identity that requires and needs the encounter, the dialogue, the empathy and the understanding among different peoples, promoting the personal growth and identity construction of all involved – Catholics, Christians, as well as other-believers.

Literal Belief: a minority tendency though a central debate

As stated, the results clearly reveal that a symbolic, hermeneutical approach towards religious content is the preferred approach in schools in Victoria: the survey shows that both *Post-Critical Belief* and *Contingency Awareness* are well supported. On the whole, the school members are keen to reject a literal interpretation of religious belief content: both *Literal Belief* and *External Critique* are met with resistance. The difference between a literal versus a symbolic understanding of religious beliefs is clearly relevant to describe the religious attitudes of the people in Victorian Catholic schools.

Despite a strong tendency towards *Post-Critical Belief*, it is striking that *Literal Belief* is not rejected strongly, not by the adults and certainly not by the students. The attitude of *Literal Belief* is rejected by many adult respondents, but there is also hesitation and some approval (mean score PRIM: 3.18/7; mean score SEC: 3.12/7; which is relatively close to the white line). A majority of almost 63.4% of the adults in primary schools and 66.1% of the adults in secondary colleges reject a literal understanding of religious faith. However, about a quarter of them hesitate and are in doubt, neither clearly accepting nor rejecting it (adults PRIM: 26.3%; adults SEC: 24.8%). It is a relevant finding that a minority of about 10.2% of the adults in primary schools and 9.1% of the adults in secondary colleges straightforwardly favour *Literal Belief*.

The students, on the other hand, show a different profile: a notable 63.1% of the primary school children in year 5-6 straightforwardly favour a literal, direct, unmediated and non-interpretative faith understanding. It is revealing, however, that this religious attitude shifts when the students grow older. In secondary colleges, year after year, more and more teenagers let go of a *Literal Believing* approach in favour of more *Contingency Awareness*, *Relativism* and even *External Critique* (year 5-6: 4.8; year 7-8: 4.2; year 9-10: 3.7; year 11-12: 3.4, which is an overall rejection). In Figure II-52 on page 58, which shows the differentiated scale means for all respondent groups, this shift is indicated by the black trend line.

It is generally hoped that teenagers transform the *Literal Believing* attitude they may have been taught during childhood in primary education into a more mature and complex *Post-Critical Believing* attitude – similar to the religious faith that is lived and shared by the adults. However, in many cases, this is not what actually happens. The decline of a *Literal Believing* attitude – which is not unusual and even desirable when children enter puberty and make the transition towards adulthood – is not compensated by an increase in a more mature, hermeneutical, post-critical and symbolically mediated faith. On the contrary, parallel to the general loss of *Literal Belief*, we notice a sharp decrease of *Post-Critical Belief* as well: from 5.7/7 in primary schools to a barely positive mean score of 4.4/7 among the oldest students at the secondary level (indicated by the white trend line in Figure II-52). Not only *Literal Belief*, but also *Post-Critical Belief* becomes less attractive and is adopted by subgroups of students that grow smaller and smaller. Despite the good intentions of many educators, the literal and unmediated faith understanding that is acquired during childhood does not transform into strong levels of *Post-Critical Belief* as the students grow older. The data shows that both religious attitudes (*Literal* and *Post-Critical Belief*) decrease hand in hand, in favour of both unbelieving attitudes (*Contingency Awareness* and *External Critique*).

The most plausible hypothesis is that overly strong levels of *Literal Belief* among primary school children in this day and age have the effect of reducing support for *any* kind of religious life style, including a *Post-Critical Believing* attitude, during their time in secondary college. Once the children leave the safe haven of primary education to enter the larger world of secondary college, a *Literal Believing* attitude tends to lose its enchantment, is unmasked, increasingly rejected and consequently replaced by *Relativism* and even religious scepticism (*External Critique*). This PCB data suggests that in the current time frame a strong (and initially seemingly successful) focus on *Literal*

Belief when dealing with primary school children actually risks undermining the development of a more mature faith in many young people as they grow older. Do these developments suggest the need for a (continued) paradigm shift in religious pedagogy? We propose fostering a *Post-Critical Believing* attitude as early as possible, as early as in the first years of primary education. The secondary Catholic colleges also need to take on the challenge to withstand *Literal Believing* tendencies among teenagers and guide them in the direction of a more hermeneutical and symbolically mediated religious identity instead.

A debate between a literal and a symbolic understanding of faith

The research data shows that there exist firm minority tendencies towards *Literal Belief* in Catholic education in Victoria. About 36.5% of the adults in primary schools, 33.9% of the adults in secondary colleges, 85.7% of the primary school children and 61.5% of the secondary college students support or at least tolerate a direct, unmediated, literal understanding of Catholic faith doctrines. A considerable number of people, on the other hand, clearly dismiss *Literal Belief*. This is the case for about 63.4% of the adults in primary schools, 66.1% of the adults in secondary colleges, 14.4% of the primary school children and 38.5% of the secondary college students. These opposing views among the adults and even more among the student population suggest a debate – either implicit or explicit – concerning a literal versus a symbolic understanding of religious faith. The issue is: at this point in time, should we hold on to a direct and literal approach when dealing with religious content, in order to preserve a tradition-minded Catholic school identity? Or should we allow for more interpretative openness, for a more symbolic understanding of religion and for more hermeneutical challenges, in order to 're-profile' the school's religious identity in today's pluralising cultural context?

Both sides of the debate make strong points. On the one hand, there are indeed good reasons for safeguarding important elements of the Catholic tradition as well as the *ontological referent*, i.e. the objective existence of God as the basis for all religious claims. On the other hand, one must be careful not to appropriate God directly in words and practice, not to objectify religious truth thereby turning it into an ideology, and to keep in mind that all relation with the transcendent reality happens through mediation and the interpretation of symbols that point at 'the other Reality'. From a theological point of view, the ideal would be a balanced combination of some levels of *Literal Belief* included in a predominant *Post-Critical Believing* attitude, sailing between the cliffs of a rigid, fundamentalist faith on the one hand, and a relativistic dilution of faith on the other. Therefore, it is positive that the high scores for *Post-Critical Belief* in Victoria (combined with *Awareness of Contingency*) show that this position prevails over *Literal Belief*. Still, the minority tendency towards a rather dogmatic, literal understanding of religious faith – albeit under pressure – continues to have heavy influence on the religious identity of Catholic schools in Victoria.

External Critique is rejected by adults, not so strongly by the older students

Regarding *External Critique*, there is less disagreement. *External Critique* is clearly rejected by the adult groups (a strong overall rejection of 2.66/7 in primary schools and 2.86/7 in secondary colleges). Most adults agree that a direct, critical rejection of religious practice is undesirable. In primary schools, 81% dismiss this attitude, 15.4% is in doubt, while only 3.7% approve of it. In secondary colleges, 73.7% dismiss *External Critique*, 20.2% are in doubt, while 6.5% support it. It is neither unusual nor alarming to detect small minority tendencies towards *External Critique* in Catholic schools. On the contrary, the presence of some voices that are critical of religion could be beneficial for a *Post-Critical* Catholic education project, provided all school members contribute to it in a supportive and constructive way.

On the whole, students also dismiss *External Critique*. The overall student score in primary schools is 2.15/7 and the percentage of disagreement amounts to 86.8%, which means that students in year 5-6 dismiss *External Critique* even more strongly than the staff and the parents do. Secondary college students, on the contrary, reveal a different tendency: the overall score is 2.86/7 and the percentage of agreement plus hesitation grows to 29.1% (13.1% in primary schools). This means that, among the secondary college students, there is dissension about *External Critique*: the student population fractures in faithful believers (still the majority) versus *Externally Critical* disbelievers (a growing minority). Moreover, it is striking that the levels of *External Critique* tend to spread – while the resistance to it fades – as the students grow older. This growing tendency of *External Critique* among the students should be monitored, lest they become threatening for a religious educational project. The internal correlations show significant, inverse relationships between *External Critique* on the one hand, and *Post-Critical Belief* and *Literal Belief* on the other (-0.75 and -0.56 respectively).

The significance of prayer

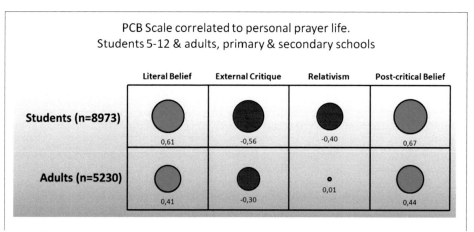

Figure II-55. PCB Scale means correlated to the background variable 'personal prayer life', for students year 5-12 and adults in primary and secondary schools.[29]

On comparing the results of the *Post-Critical Belief* scale among students and adults with their score on *Personal Prayer Life*, an important background variable in the *Profile Questionnaire*, we detect notable links between them. As Figure II-55 shows, there seem to be direct and significant associations between the cognitive belief styles and personal prayer life, regardless of age or gender. Figures II-56 and II-57 on the next page clearly show that the more people pray on their own, the higher they score on both *Literal Belief* and *Post-Critical Belief* (the two believing types) and the lower they score on *Relativism* and *External Critique* (the two unbelieving types). Conversely, the more people believe in either a *Literal* or a *Post-Critical* way, the more active their personal prayer life is likely to be. And the more people tend towards *Relativism* and *External Critique*, the less they tend to pray. This holds true for the adults and it is even stronger among the student groups. The data suggest that prayer is a vital component of personal and institutional Catholic identity. What one might expect is true: while Catholic school identity is expressed through prayer, promoting prayer enhances the Catholic identity of schools. Both processes reinforce each other and go hand in hand.

---

[29] Interesting is the zero-correlation between *Relativism/Awareness of Contingency* and *Post-Critical Belief* among the adult groups. As explained above, this result reveals that most adults are faithful people who understand *Contingency Awareness* as supporting their predominant *Post-Critical Believing* stance. Others, however, reveal traces of pure *Relativism* that tend to undermine Catholic identity.

172

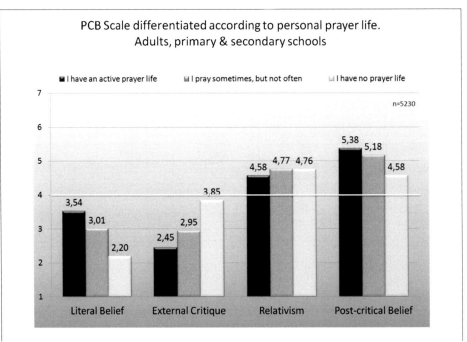

Figure II-56. PCB Scale mean scores differentiated according to the background variable 'personal prayer life', for all adult groups in primary and secondary schools.

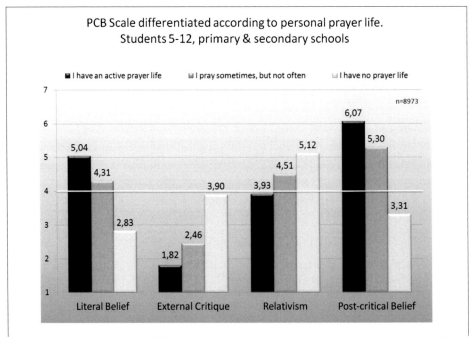

Figure II-57. PCB Scale mean scores differentiated according to the background variable 'personal prayer life', for students year 5-12 in primary and secondary schools.

§2. Catholic school identity options from a theological perspective. Results of the *Melbourne Scale*

In this section we examine the school's Catholic identity itself. The *Melbourne Scale* is based on a theological typology of five different ways of establishing Catholic identity in a secularising and pluralising cultural context: *Confessionality*, *Secularisation*, *Reconfessionalisation*, *Values Education in a Christian Perspective* and *Recontextualisation*. This scale reveals not only the perceived current practice in the school today, but also the students' and adults' ideal perspectives on future identity development. As such it is construed as a prediction of what's most likely going to happen in the future. The *Melbourne Scale* was invented by the systematic theologian Lieven Boeve and operationalised by the Leuven ECSIP research team.

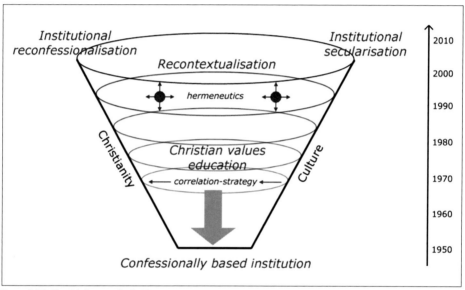

Figure II-58. The *Melbourne Scale* Diagram.

Brief recapitulation of the five school identity models of the *Melbourne Scale*:

The Confessionally based school
A traditional Catholic institution, still largely unaffected by tendencies of detraditionalisation and secularisation. Typical confessional elements and identity structures endure in a passive and unreflective way. A classic Catholic school identity is being continued unproblematically and unchallenged.

Values Education in a Christian perspective
An identity model often adopted when the school population is gradually diversifying while most people are still rooted in Christian culture. Trying to link a generally shared awareness of 'a good life' to the Catholic faith, perceived as the ultimate fulfilment of this intuition (*mono-correlation*). Catholic school identity is mediated by Christian values and norms that can appeal to everyone. By teaching values, it is hoped that the students can continue to recognise themselves in the Catholic life style and faith. However, in reality it risks to become a compromise model, reducing the Catholic faith to its ethical aspects and thereby 'hollowing it out'. As the gap between culture and faith widens, *Values Education* tends to become predictable and reductive, hence ineffective and even counterproductive – producing further secularisation.

Institutional Secularisation
In daily school life, Catholic particularity fades away. Catholic signs and symbols disappear, rituals no longer take place, and references to religion vanish from everyday discourse. A preferential option for the Catholic faith is replaced by a preference for neutrality, equality and relativism. Gradually this trend is taken over also on the institutional level. Often it is more an implicit process than a conscious and guided option.

Institutional Reconfessionalisation
Actively promoting a classic, confessional Catholic school identity withstanding tendencies of detraditionalisation and secularisation. Deliberately attempting to bring the school culture closer to Catholicism again. The Catholic nature of the school is explicitly and publicly profiled. Faithful and practicing Catholics are given preference to enter the school. Moral and religious education programs for all students. There is little desire to engage with diversity or to develop the Catholic Tradition in interaction with changing times.

> ***Identity formation in a plural context (Recontextualisation of Catholic school identity)***
>
> A Catholic school with a diverse school population, among whom is at least a significant and recognisable group of Catholic believers. Deliberately engaged in a common search of a renewed Catholic profile for the school, in and through a conversation with plurality, aiming at a reinterpreted understanding of the Catholic faith in the contemporary diversifying world (tradition development). Withstanding a consensus paradigm, it is propelled by difference and 'otherness'. The encounter and conversation between different views is being moderated by a clear preferential option for the Catholic faith. Out of its own inherent strength and depth, Christianity's voice is allowed to resonate amid a multiplicity of voices (*multi-correlation*). Promoted by the *hermeneutical-communicative didactic model*.

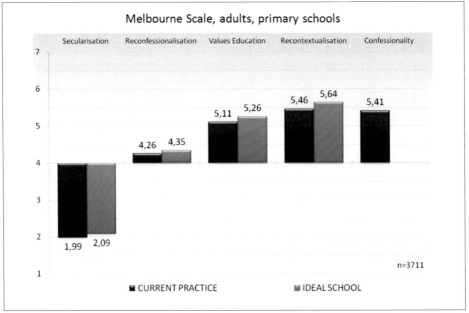

Figure II-59. Melbourne Scale, scale means for all the adults in primary schools.

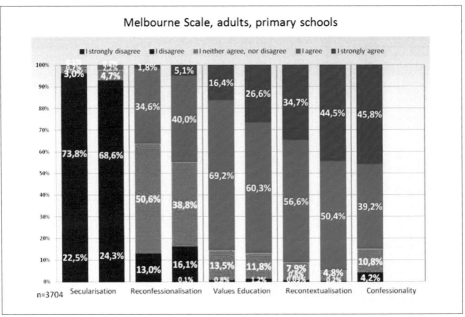

Figure II-60. Melbourne Scale, percentages for all the adults in primary schools.

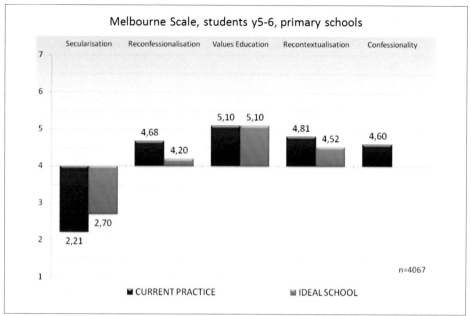

Figure II-61. Melbourne Scale, scale means for all the students year 5-6 in primary schools.

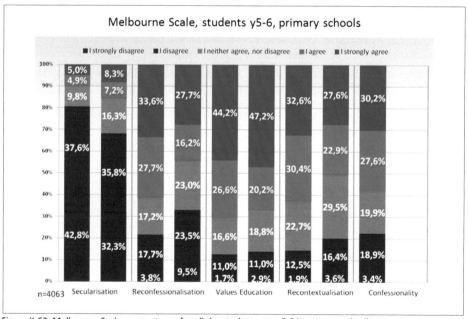

Figure II-62. Melbourne Scale, percentages for all the students year 5-6 in primary schools.

178

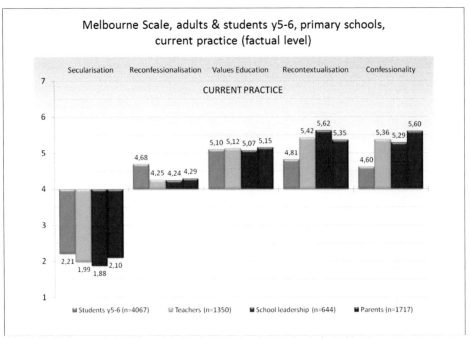

Figure II-63. Melbourne Scale, differentiated scale means in primary schools, factual level.

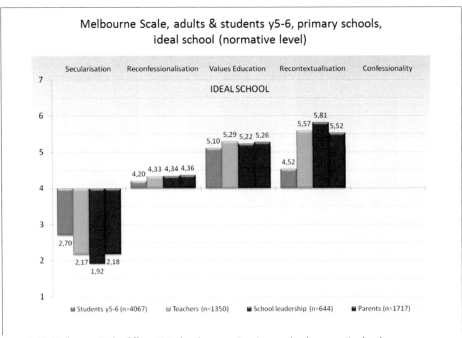

Figure II-64. Melbourne Scale, differentiated scale means in primary schools, normative level.

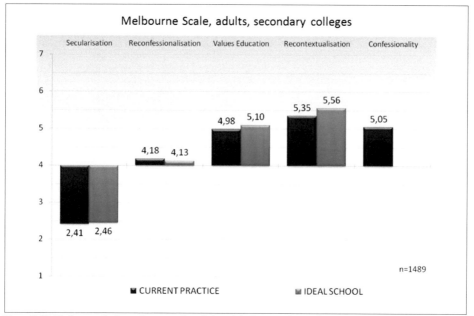

Figure II-65. Melbourne Scale, scale means for all the adults in secondary colleges.

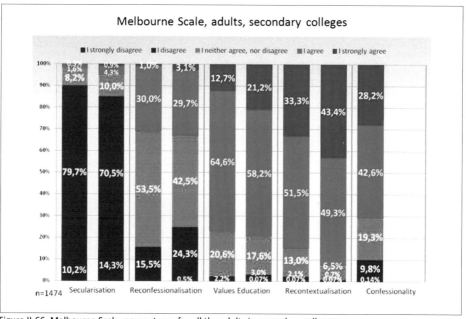

Figure II-66. Melbourne Scale, percentages for all the adults in secondary colleges.

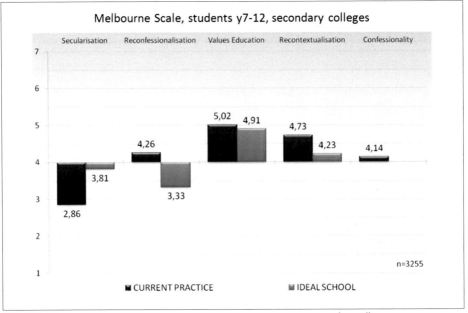

Figure II-67. Melbourne Scale, scale means for all the students year 7-12 in secondary colleges.

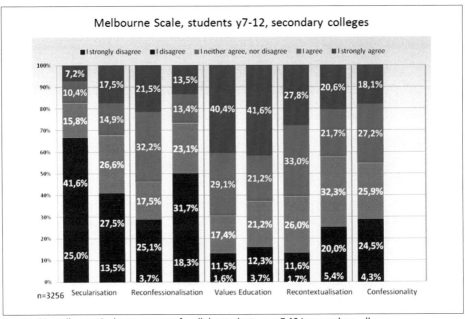

Figure II-68. Melbourne Scale, percentages for all the students year 7-12 in secondary colleges.

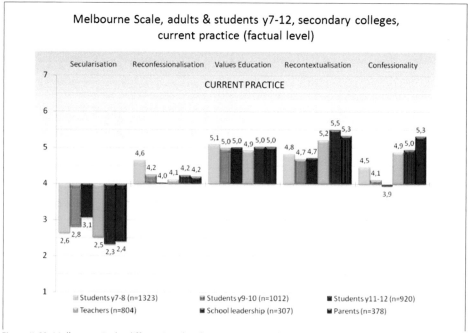

Figure II-69. Melbourne Scale, differentiated scale means in secondary colleges, factual level.

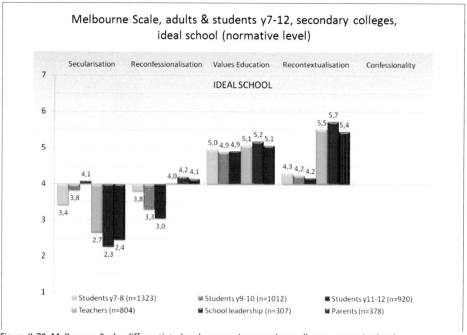

Figure II-70. Melbourne Scale, differentiated scale means in secondary colleges, normative level.

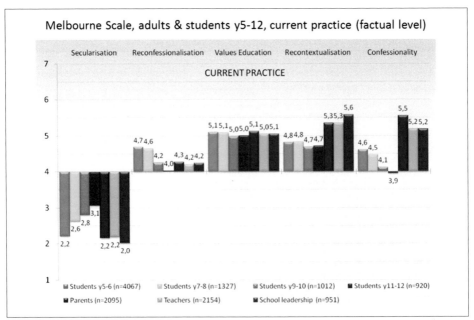

Figure II-71. Melbourne Scale, differentiated scale means in primary and secondary schools, factual level.

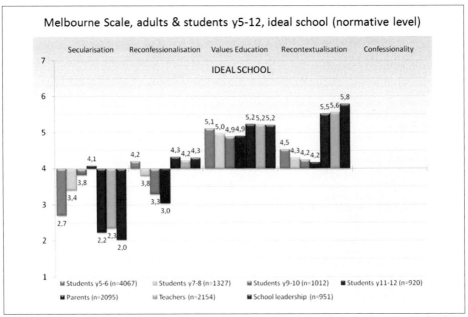

Figure II-72. Melbourne Scale, differentiated scale means in primary and secondary schools, normative level.

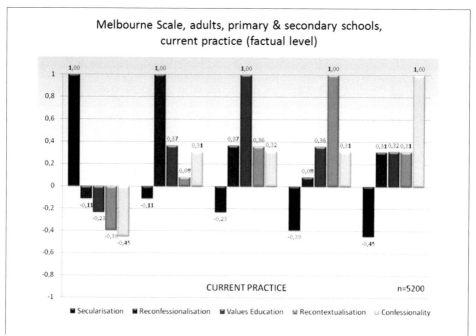

Figure II-73. Melbourne Scale, internal correlations for the adults in primary and secondary schools, the factual level related to the factual level.

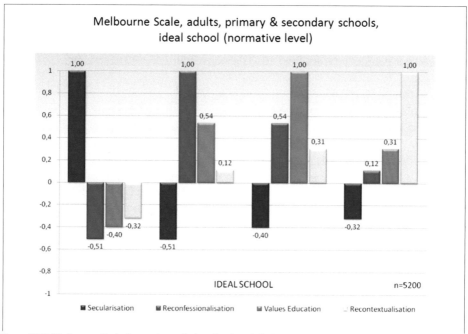

Figure II-74. Melbourne Scale, internal correlations for the adults in primary and secondary schools, the normative level related to the normative level.

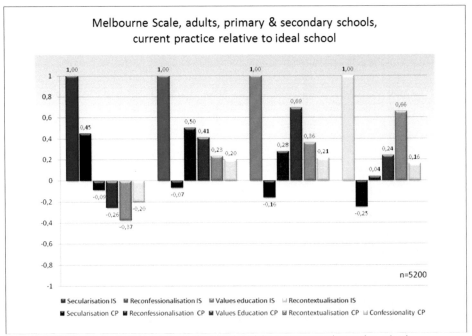

Figure II-75. Melbourne Scale, internal correlations for the adults in primary and secondary schools, the factual level related to the normative level.

Figures II-73, II-74 and II-75 visually represent the 5x4 (factual level), 4x4 (normative level) and 4x5 (factual related to normative level) matrices that contain the Pearson linear correlation coefficients between the school identity models described by the *Melbourne Scale* for the combined adults groups in all ECSIP 2012 schools.

Earlier in this publication we learned from the *Doyle Questionnaire* results that, on the 'current practice' level, the people in Catholic schools in Victoria perceive their school as a good place to grow closer to God. On the 'ideal school' level, a recognisable Catholic school identity remains the ideal in the future, but the resistance to a strong Catholic identity is increasing, especially among the student population. Let us now examine these findings more closely and in more detail by means of the *Melbourne Scale*.

Current practice (the factual measurement level).

A first glance at the 'current practice' level of the *Melbourne Scale* results of the adult groups confirms the apparent Catholic identity of the schools: all Catholic identity models receive positive means scores, while *Institutional Secularisation* is strongly rejected. For staff and parents, the question of whether the education system is *Secularising* on an institutional level, whether it is 'doing away' with its religious features, is answered negatively by all adult groups. Despite this unanimity, on the whole the secondary colleges are perceived to be a little more *Secular*, compared to the primary schools (PRIM: 1.99/7; SEC: 2.41/7).

On the average, the students also somewhat agree that Catholic schools in Victoria are not *Secularising*, although they currently perceive less resistance to it (PRIM: 2.21/7; SEC: 2.86/7). Even more, there are a significant number of students, especially the older ones, who see *Secularisation* happen many times and in many places in daily school life. So it seems that the school members are somewhat divided in their experience of the schools' Catholic identity: more than the adults, the students acknowledge the presence of some secular culture inside the school.

All adults agree that many of the traditional Catholic 'identity markers' are still in place today (PRIM: 5.41/7; SEC: 5.05/7): there are still crucifixes, religious education classes, communal prayer, Scripture texts, Eucharistic celebrations, sacraments, an active parish priest or college chaplain, etc. Also a majority of primary school children agree that their schools are still *Confessionally based* (4.60/7). However, a number of mainly secondary college students perceive school reality in a different way; for them, the above mentioned Catholic 'identity markers' are not quite as visible and notable as the adults believe. On the whole, the secondary college students indicate that these traditional elements are fading away (4.14/7). This perception tends to be more common as the students get older. On the average, the year 11-12 students tend to overlook the existence of these traditional *Confessional* elements (3.9/7). It is also worth noting that the 2095 participating parents somewhat overestimate the traditional Catholic identity of the Catholic school or college they send their children to: they suspect more *Confessionality* (PRIM: 5.60/7; SEC: 5.3/7) than is actually perceived by the people inside the school.

Although the Catholicity of the school is still recognised today, with many of the elements that characterise a traditional Catholic school still in place, it is clearly under pressure. How do Victorian Catholic schools respond to this situation?

One possibility would be to *Re-confessionalise* the college: to actively promote and enhance its specific Catholic features, for example by attempting to re-introduce the Catholic identity markers that have faded over time. As a reaction against the perceived pressure on the schools' Catholicity, people want to safeguard and protect its traditional Catholic features; they feel the need to maintain and, if needed, to re-establish them. Pure *Reconfessionalising* schools have a clear preference for the Catholic faith and prefer to avoid situations where this preference is put into question. They try hard to be and to remain clearly Catholic and want to guarantee the Catholic faith formation of all their students. Such schools stress the importance of religious education classes because learning about faith promotes a Catholic way of life. Unless the encounter with diversity provides an opportunity to 'present the faith' to others, they are worried that an overly strong presence and appreciation for 'other-than-Catholic' views and practices might threaten the specific Catholic identity of schools.

Though most Catholic schools in Victoria cannot be identified as such, we do detect *Reconfessionalising* tendencies: both students and adults recognise traces of *Reconfessionalisation* of Catholic school identity (adults PRIM: 36.4% agreement on the factual level; adults SEC: 31% agreement; students PRIM: 61.3% agreement; students SEC: 53.7% agreement). Again it is noteworthy that, as the students grow older, their perception of *Reconfessionalising* tendencies becomes less outspoken (year 5-6: 4.7/7; year 7-8: 4.6/7; year 9-10: 4.2/7; year 11-12: 4.0/7). Attempts at *Reconfessionalisation* are, therefore, more likely to be noticed by the younger students and less likely by the older students.

But this is not the only response; there are also other ways to deal with the growing gap between Christianity and pluralising culture. Many Victorian Catholic schools are also strongly characterised by a *Christian Values Education* strategy. This popular approach is clearly recognised by all respondent groups, students (PRIM: 5.10/7; SEC: 5.02/7) as well as adults (PRIM: 5.11/7; SEC: 4.98/7). Few people doubt or deny that this strategy is being employed. To maintain the schools' Catholic character, people tend to employ a didactic method, called *mono-correlation*. The model of *Christian Values Education* aims at a compromise between culture and Catholic tradition in an attempt to maintain a Catholic school identity that 'keeps up with the times' and with which anybody can reconcile. More specifically, there is a prevailing discourse that attempts to directly link or correlate the students' personal life-experiences and moral awareness to the Catholic religion and way of life. The school tries to link a generally shared awareness of 'a good life' to the Catholic faith as the fulfilment of this intuition. *Ethics* is especially suited to function as mediator between culture and Catholic faith (hence the label 'values education'): Catholic inspiration is translated into an education in Christian values and norms that are believed to be universally recognisable. In this way, the school hopes to continue to address a pluralising student population on faith. This approach might seem evident to some, but from a theological and empirical point of view it should nevertheless be criticised.[30]

Next to this *mono-correlation* approach, the school members also perceive a tendency towards *Identity Formation in a Plural Context*. This is a hermeneutical attitude that attempts to *Recontextualise Catholic school identity*, deliberately searching for a renewed Catholic profile in and through an encounter and a conversation with plurality. Instead of a *mono-correlation* approach (reducing diversity in an attempt to forcibly correlate it to the Catholic faith), it employs a *multi-correlation* approach: as a Catholic I stand in the middle of diversity, relating myself to a range of diverse people whose neighbour I try to be; therefore, I need to search for new and original ways to

---

[30] For a critical evaluation of the *Christian Values Education* approach, see: POLLEFEYT, D., & BOUWENS, J., *Framing the identity of Catholic schools. Empirical methodology for quantitative research of the Catholic identity of an education institute*, in *International Studies in Catholic Education* 2-2 (2010), pages 11-12.

express my specific religious identity in ever changing situations. To achieve this goal, encounter and dialogue with diversity are obviously crucial. This identity strategy tries to understand the Catholic faith re-interpreted in a pluralised, contemporary cultural context. On the one hand plurality is recognised and valued as such; on the other hand the focus on Catholic identity is maintained. After all, the Gospel message remains relevant for people today and tomorrow. But the changing cultural context must first be integrated into my 'being Catholic' so that it remains recognisable, credible, authentic and meaningful for contemporary people (ongoing tradition development). The question then is how to live a Catholic life and how to build a Catholic school in the middle of contemporary culture. That this approach is being realised in Catholic schools in Victoria is confirmed by no less than 91.3% of the adults in primary schools and 84.8% of the adults in secondary colleges. The students agree, although they are less convinced. About 63% of the primary school children and 60.8% of the secondary school student respondents positively confirm that *Recontextualisation* happens in their school. However, in primary schools, about 22.7% of the students remain unsure about this; while 14.4% deny its existence on the factual level. In secondary colleges, about 26% of the students remain unsure, while 13.3% deny it happens in daily school life.

The perceived inclinations toward *Values Education* and *Recontextualisation* do not stand on their own. In daily school life they are combined and intertwined, resulting in mixed forms. Both school types correlate with each other, which indicates that when people promote or reject the one type, they are likely to promote or reject the other. Often (but not always) there is an interaction and a cooperation between *Values Education* and *Recontextualisation*; often they occur simultaneously. Furthermore, both strategies also correlate with the tendency towards *Reconfessionalisation* we noted above. This indicates that, to some extent, both strategies are motivated by the desire to be open and receptive towards 'the outside world' while still firmly keeping in mind the school's specific religious identity (a *Kerygmatic Dialogue* model). Nevertheless, the 'marriage' between *Values Education* and *Recontextualisation* is not devoid of matrimonial tension – but more of that later.

To conclude: at present, where the 'current practice' is concerned, many changes are taking place in Victorian Catholic schools. The many people involved in Catholic education not only experience things differently, but also respond to them in different ways. Simultaneously, multiple strategies are at work that play into each other in complex interaction. Next, the 'ideal school' level will tell us which directions people would like to take in the future.

Ideal school (the normative measurement level).

On the 'ideal school' level we notice significant shifts, compared with the current practice. We see new patterns, new combinations of school identity strategies that are shaping the future Catholic identity of Catholic schools.

Where the adults are concerned, they are united in their desire to hold on to the Catholic identity of the schools. The current resistance to *Secularisation* will be carried on into the future (PRIM: from 1.99/7 to 2.09/7; SEC: from 2.41/7 to SEC: 2.46/7). It is virtually certain that the current school leadership and staff do not intend to let their Catholic schools *Secularise* on the institutional level. Instead, all Catholic identity types gain in strength: the adults want more *Christian Values Education* (PRIM; from 5.11/7 to 5.26/7; SEC: from 4.98/7 to 5.10/7) and more *Recontextualisation* (PRIM: 5.46/7 to 5.64/7; SEC: from 5.35/7 to 5.56/7) than they currently already perceive. Both strategies are related to the concern not to lose the college's *Confessional* structures and, if necessary, the preparedness to *Reconfessionalise* what has being lost (PRIM: 4.32/7; SEC: 4.13/7). The adults take a clear stand here, and apart from diverging opinions about the extent and the methods of *Reconfessionalisation*, they appear to show notable agreement.

This determination on the part of the adult groups is shared by a number of students, but it is important to realise that the general resistance to *Secularisation* is fading, especially among the students in secondary colleges. Certainly, there exists a subgroup of students in primary and secondary schools who share the adults' enthusiasm and concern about Catholic identity (PRIM: about 68.1% resistance to *Secularisation*; SEC: about 41% resistance). Nevertheless, the research data show that significant and growing number of students express different views.

On the whole, primary school children lose some resistance to *Secularisation*, compared with the current practice (from 2.21/7 to 2.70/7). The reason is that a subgroup of about 15.5% desire a secular school over a Catholic one, while an additional 16.3% are inclined towards it. Where the secondary college students are concerned, for many of them, the already fading resistance to *Secularisation* (2.86/7) may just as well continue and even grow weaker in the near future (3.81/7, very close to the middle line). On the 'ideal school' level, a significant number of secondary college students would not really mind if their school let go of its Catholic identity (32.4% agreement + 26.6% hesitation). Moreover, there is a clear trend of declining support for Catholic school identity as the students grow older. On the normative level, the general resistance to *Secularising* tendencies in primary schools turns into a hesitant overall approval among the oldest students in secondary colleges (year 5-6: 2.7/7; year 7-8: 3.4/7; year 9-10: 3.8/7; year 11-12: 4.1/7 which is a positive score). The generally fading resistance to *Secularisation* on the part of many students in Catholic schools is one of the important findings of the ECSIP research.

In line with this outcome, we notice a generally fading enthusiasm among students for *any* type of Catholic school identity. Be it *Recontextualisation, Reconfessionalisation* or *Christian Values Education*, all three religious school models lose support on the normative level, both in primary and in secondary schools. (An exception is the mean score for *Values Education* that remains *status quo* in primary schools.)

The existing division regarding a *Recontextualisation* of Catholic school identity becomes stronger on the 'ideal school' level, while the general mean scores drop. In primary schools, the students who oppose *Recontextualisation* (PRIM: 20%) and those who hesitate (PRIM: 29.5%) grow in numbers, at the cost of those in favour (PRIM: 50.5%). This tendency is the same in secondary colleges, where both the resistance (SEC: 25.4%) and the hesitation (32.3%) about *Recontextualisation* grow, while support is lost (SEC: from 60.8% to 42.3% which is less than half).

Moreover, it is revealing that the students show a significant drop in their appreciation for a continued *Reconfessionalisation* approach (PRIM: from 4.68/7 to 4.20/7; SEC: from 4.26/7 to 3.33/7). While the students in primary school and in year 7-8 still show a general doubt about *Reconfessionalisation* (4.2/7 and 3.8/7 on the 'ideal school' level), the older student groups increasingly distance themselves from this approach (year 9-10: 3.3/7; year 11-12: 3.0/7). Comparing the current practice to the normative ideal, the student population expresses a clear desire for a less stringent Catholic identity approach that does not impose itself too strongly. On the part of the students, this growing resistance to *Reconfessionalisation* coincides with a growing desire to *Secularise* the schools. Is it conceivable that the latter is a reaction against the former?

The school model that loses least support on the normative level is *Christian Values Education* (PRIM: from 5.10/7 to 5.10/7); SEC: from 5.02/7 to 4.91/7). Concerning the students' 'ideal school', *Values Education* is their favourite approach. However, we do not believe this to be a particularly good sign. We ought to be critical of the way the students make use of *Values Education*, because at the same time the general resistance to *Secularisation* drops significantly, and the support for the other Catholic school types declines. We explore this critique more deeply below.

At this juncture, we arrive at an important question: where is this 'separation of minds' between adults and students coming from? Why do the adults have such difficulty in communicating their Catholic convictions to many of the students, especially while teenagers make progress through college? Why is the Victorian Catholic education system losing such student support for Catholic identity?

Dissension about *Institutional Reconfessionalisation*

The identity option that stirs most disagreement among students as well as adults is *Institutional Reconfessionalisation*. Among young and old, it has advocates as well as opponents, and at times the discord is serious.

A significant minority of the adults (PRIM: 45.1%; SEC: 32.8%) feel attracted to a continuing *Reconfessionalisation* of Catholic schools. However, a growing minority (PRIM: 16.2%; SEC: 24.8% – nearly one in four) clearly resists this and expresses their objections out loud. A significant group of adults (PRIM: 38.8%; SEC: 42.5%) finds itself in between, undecided and unsure what to think.

A similar dissension exists among the student groups, only here the group of outspoken adversaries is significantly bigger: in primary schools, 33% of the children disagree or strongly disagree with *Reconfessionalisation*; in secondary colleges, 50% of the students disagree or strongly disagree. At the other end of the spectrum, 43.9% of the primary school children agree or strongly agree that their school should *Reconfessionalise* further, while 26.9% of the secondary college students agree or strongly agree. In between these opposing subgroups, about 23% of the students hesitate and are unsure which side to choose.

These findings suggest that there is a debate going on about the theological merits and continuing effectiveness of a *Reconfessionalising* approach. Obviously, this debate parallels the issue we encountered when analysing the PCB Scale results: behind it lies a theological discussion about a *Literal* versus a *Post-Critical* faith understanding. Some people, young and old, remain convinced that stressing the traditionally recognisable features of a typically Catholic education, thereby avoiding change and 'adaptation', is necessary in order to safeguard a 'truly' Catholic school identity. Many other people, adults and certainly students, have serious objections to a school identity that *Reconfessionalises*. The older the students become, the more they let go of Catholic identity and become distrustful of every attempt to *impose* a Catholic view. The data show that continuing to push for a *Reconfessionalisation* actually results in unexpected, undesirable and even opposite effects on a significant part of the students. Given this dissension, it seems more and more unlikely that the future of Victorian Catholic schools will follow the path of a clear and univocal *Reconfessionalisation*. Nevertheless, the tendency towards *Reconfessionalisation* – albeit under pressure – will continue to have heavy influence on the religious identity of Catholic schools in Victoria.

The risks of *Christian Values Education*

Another reason, according to our theological analysis, that schools are losing student support for Catholic identity, can be found in the continued *mono-correlation* didactics of the *Values Education in Christian Perspective*. It should be noted that the school staff and the parents continue to believe in a *Values Education* approach: it is strongly perceived in the current practice (PRIM: 5.11/7; SEC: 4.98/7) and these adult respondents wished for it to be even stronger (PRIM: 5.26/7; SEC: 5.10/7). Many students also agree that *Values Education* is an important trait of Catholic school today (PRIM: 5.10/7; SEC: 5.02/7), and say they will keep supporting it in the future (PRIM: 5.10/7; SEC: 4.91/7).

Values Education in Christian Perspective can only be effective and justified when it is backed up by reasonably high levels of *Confessionality*. As long as a school retains its distinct Catholic *Confessional* structures, which are recognised, expected and accepted by all involved, then *Values Education* remains an effective strategy that deserves our support. In a *Confessional* Catholic school setting without much diversity where *mono-correlation* is still evident, and where people expect and desire that a direct link is made between their experiences and the Catholic faith – in such schools where *Christian Values Education* actually still works, there can be no objections against it.

However, the *Melbourne Scale* results show that the adults in Victorian schools exaggerate the remaining *Confessionality* and are misled by this perception into believing that *Christian Values Education* is still working and could keep working in the future, and even that they are *Reconfessionalising* the school's Catholic identity while doing so. However, most of the students perceive the same reality quite differently. In their view, the school's *Confessional* structures are fading. The gap between youth culture and the Catholic preference of schools is becoming increasingly difficult to bridge, especially as students become older. The time has passed when all students were able and willing to go along with *Values Education* and its *mono-correlation* attempt to link and possibly reduce their everyday experience to a pre-defined, self-evident, confessional belief structure. Although a minority of the students still rejoice when this is attempted, most of them have had enough.

The *Melbourne Scale* results suggest that a prolonged use of *Christian Values Education* in a pluralising and detraditionalising cultural context is a dangerous endeavour. Confessional identity structures are, so to speak, the 'petrol tank' of *Values Education*. As long as the students are still well inculturated in a Catholic life style, it remains evident for them to interpret their experiences in a Catholic frame of reference. However, the more teenagers outgrow traditional Catholic structures, the wider the gap between culture and Christianity, and the more pressure there is on the *Confessionality* of schools – the more difficult it will be to *correlate* experience and faith. When the petrol tank runs empty, the engine of *Values Education* begins to sputter. It will become less effective, more predictable, and increasingly undesirable. In the end, it even risks becoming *counterproductive*.

The Belgian experience

The above effect is what, according to our analysis, occurred in Belgian Catholic schools over the past decades. Driven by necessity, when it was almost too late, we had to adopt a new approach, one that does take diversity as well as Catholic identity seriously. We had to look for a *Recontextualisation* of Catholic school identity, and promoted *Identity Construction in a Plural Context* as the new paradigm for Catholic schools in the 21st Century. To that end we developed a new didactical approach, called the *Hermeneutical Communicative Model for religious education* (HCM). Nowadays we encourage our schools to become *Dialogue Schools*: as Catholic schools, they are called to engage in encounter and communication between people, assisting in the personal growth, education, identity formation and integration of all involved. We shall go

192

deeper into this approach when analysing the results of the last multivariate attitude scale, the *Victoria Scale*.

§3. Catholic school identity options from a pedagogical perspective. Results of the *Victoria Scale*

The third multivariate attitude scale is called the *Victoria Scale*. It is based on another pedagogical typology that identifies four different ways of combining Catholic school identity with religious and philosophical diversity: the *Monologue School*, the *Dialogue School*, the *Colourful School* and the *Colourless School*. Again, we examine both the current practice in the school and the ideal perspectives of students as well as adults. The Victoria Scale was invented by the Dutch pedagogues Wim Ter Horst and Chris Hermans, and operationalised by the Leuven ECSIP research team.

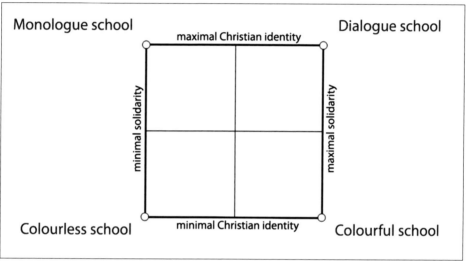

Figure II-76. The *Victoria Scale* Diagram.

The *Victoria Scale* is an empirical instrument inspired by a typology of the Dutch researchers Wim ter Horst and Chris Hermans on the pedagogical basic options of Catholic schools in a pluralising cultural context. Just like the *PCB Scale*, the *Victoria Scale* is constructed of two dimensions:

1. The vertical axis refers to an organisation's **CHRISTIAN IDENTITY**: the measure in which its members live out of a generally shared, Catholic inspiration.
2. The horizontal axis concerns the **SOLIDARITY** with people from subcultures other than the Catholic one: the measure of openness and receptivity towards other life views and attitudes.

194

Today, every confessional organisation faces the task of making pedagogical and organisational choices concerning its Catholic identity, in combination with its solidarity with otherness.

Putting together these two dimensions results in the so called **IDENTITY SQUARE**. On the four angles we find ideal-typical strategies that schools can adopt to shape their pedagogical responsibility towards faith education in a multicultural society: the *Monologue School* type, the *Dialogue School* type, The *Colourful School* type and the *Colourless School* type.

Just like the *Melbourne Scale*, the *Victoria Scale* assesses school identity both on the 'current practice' measurement level and the 'ideal school' measurement level. The comparison between both measurements can be very revealing.

Brief recapitulation of the four school identity models of the Victoria Scale:

The Monologue school (maximal Christian identity, minimal solidarity and openness to diversity)
A traditional Catholic school by Catholics and for Catholics, putting strong focus on its religious identity. Emphasis on unity, security, solidarity and pedagogical responsibility inside their own Catholic circle. However, this school deliberately rejects openness and receptivity towards other religions and life philosophies, which are considered to be untrue, undesirable and even threatening. There is little solidarity with the non-Catholic outside world.

The Dialogue School (maximal Christian identity, maximal solidarity and openness to diversity)
A Catholic school in the midst of cultural and religious plurality. This school deliberately puts emphasis on its Catholic inspiration, while simultaneously it takes our multicultural world seriously. A multiplicity of voices, views and perspectives are recognised and engaged as contributions to the dialogue. A preferential option for the Christian story and message sets the tone for this dialogue. Receptivity and openness to what is different is a prerequisite to re-profile the Catholic faith in the middle of plural culture (*Recontextualisation*). In the midst of plurality we search for what it means to be Christian today; as Christians we search for a way to live in the middle of plurality.

The Colourful School (minimal Christian identity, maximal solidarity and openness to diversity)

A secularised and plural school environment where people relate to each other in a social, engaged and solidary way. This school expends significant effort towards genuine pedagogical responsibility. The internal plurality is taken to heart seriously; there is authentic desire and interest in recognising the 'otherness' of the fellow school members. However, few students or staff members are still concerned about the school's original Catholic heritage. A preferential option for Christianity over and above other religions and life philosophies is rejected, because it is considered to hinder personal freedom and free interaction. Akin to *active pluralism*.

The Colourless School (minimal Christian identity, minimal solidarity and openness to diversity)

A secularised and plural school environment where the relation between individuals remains free of engagement or obligations. The school adopts a radically 'neutral' stand: philosophies of life or religions must never be imposed top-down; never suggest what another person should or should not think or do. There is strong openness and tolerance for all kinds of religions and life philosophies. However, this openness is not framed in a common pedagogical project. Religion is a private matter: each individual makes up his/her own mind. Formation is a personal responsibility, not the school's. There is little unity or security; people live next to each other in a non-committed way. Formal tolerance risks ending up in indifference. This is akin to *neutral pluralism*.

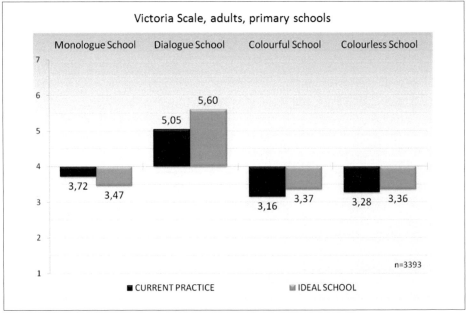

Figure II-77. Victoria Scale, scale means for all the adults in primary schools.

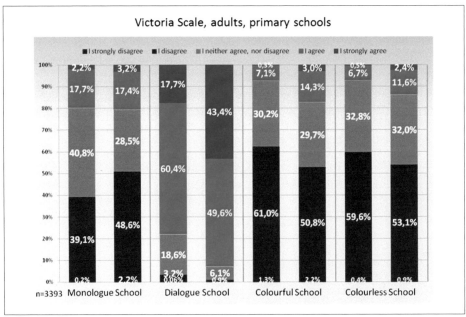

Figure II-78. Victoria Scale, percentages for all the adults in primary schools.

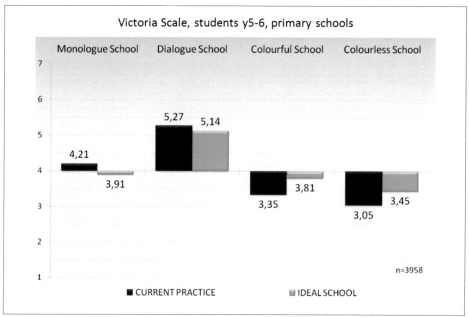

Figure II-79. Victoria Scale, scale means for all the students year 5-6 in primary schools.

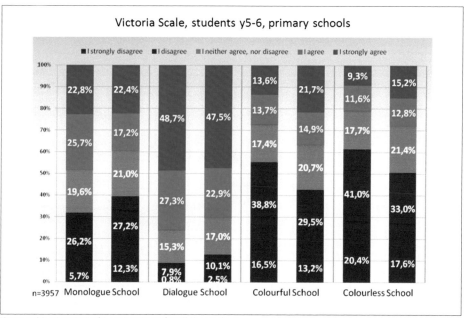

Figure II-80. Victoria Scale, percentages for all the students year 5-6 in primary schools.

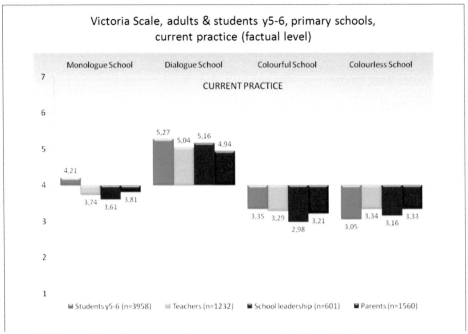

Figure II-81. Victoria Scale, differentiated scale means in primary schools, factual level.

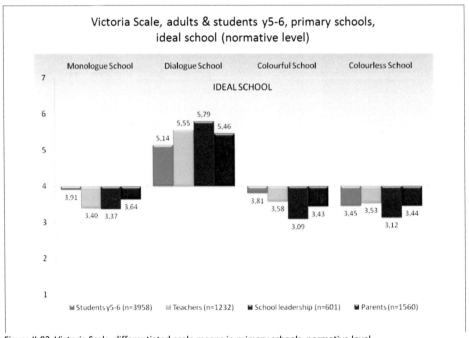

Figure II-82. Victoria Scale, differentiated scale means in primary schools, normative level.

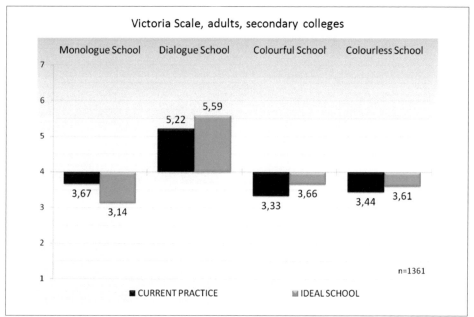

Figure II-83. Victoria Scale, scale means for all the adults in secondary colleges.

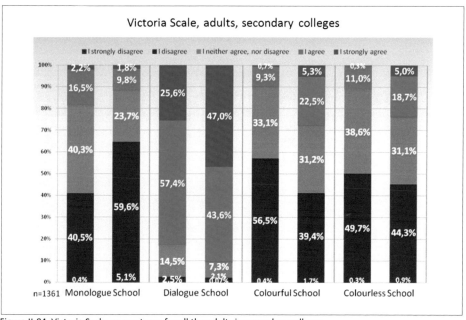

Figure II-84. Victoria Scale, percentages for all the adults in secondary colleges.

200

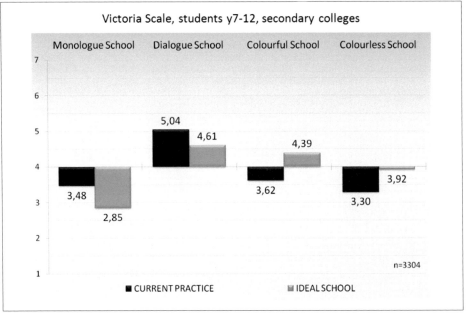

Figure II-85. Victoria Scale, scale means for all the students year 7-12 in secondary colleges.

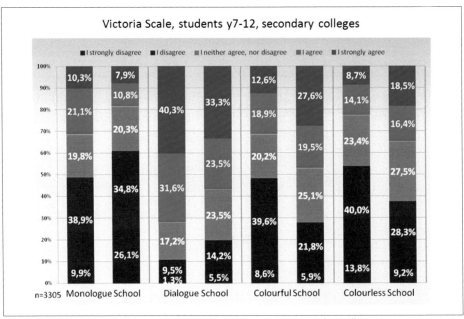

Figure II-86. Victoria Scale, percentages for all the students year 7-12 in secondary colleges.

201

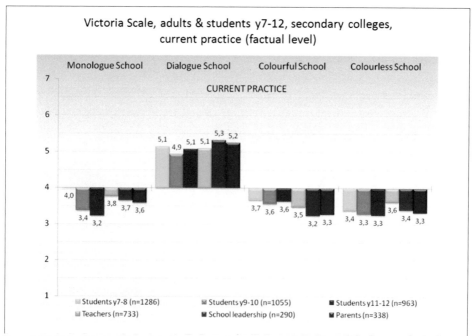

Figure II-87. Victoria Scale, differentiated scale means in secondary colleges, factual level.

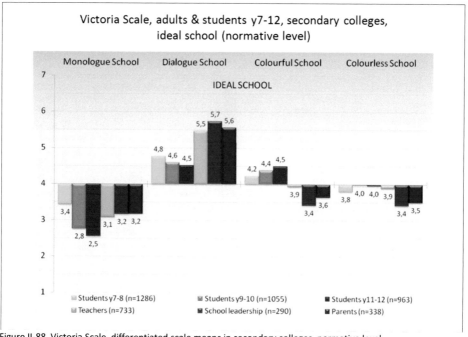

Figure II-88. Victoria Scale, differentiated scale means in secondary colleges, normative level.

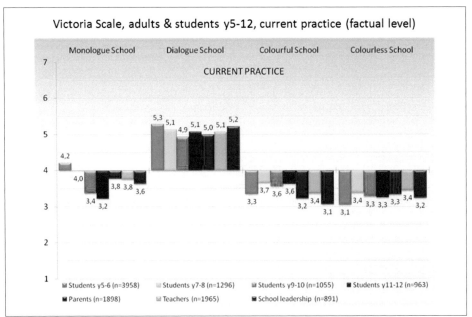

Figure II-89. Victoria Scale, differentiated scale means in primary and secondary schools, factual level.

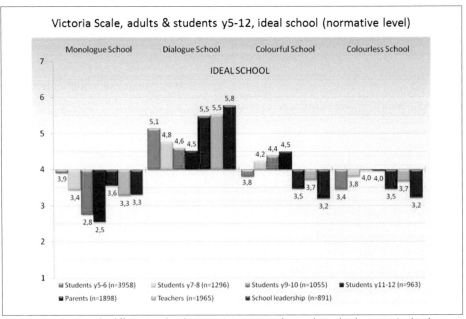

Figure II-90. Victoria Scale, differentiated scale means in primary and secondary schools, normative level.

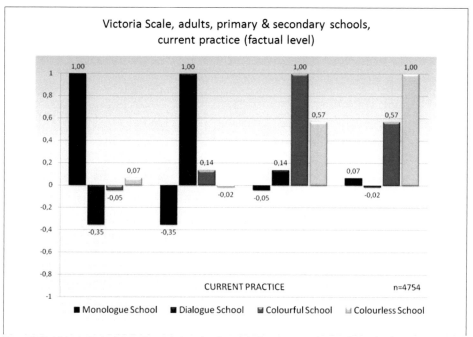

Figure II-91. Victoria Scale, internal correlations for the adults in primary and secondary schools, the factual level related to the factual level.

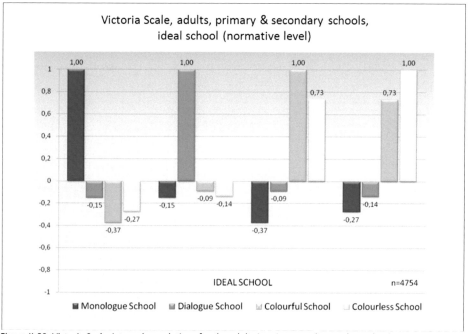

Figure II-92. Victoria Scale, internal correlations for the adults in primary and secondary schools, the normative level related to the normative level.

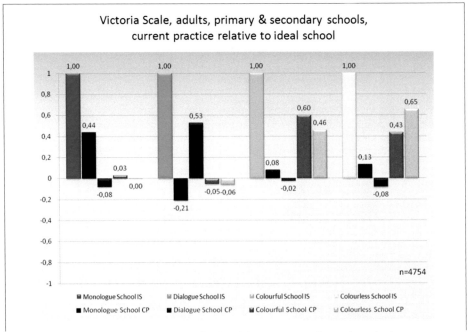

Figure II-93. Victoria Scale, internal correlations for the adults in primary and secondary schools, the factual level related to the normative level.

Figure II-91, II-92 and II-93 are visual representations of the 4x4 (factual as well as normative levels) and 4x5 (factual level related to normative level) matrices that contain the Pearson linear correlation coefficients between the school identity models described by the Victoria Scale for the combined adults groups in all ECSIP 2012 schools.

A *Dialogue School* model: the preferential model for all people involved

As we saw earlier in this publication, the Catholic faith and practice is the preferred perspective for Victorian Catholic schools. At the same time, background variables show that there is a religious and non-religious diversity in the schools. Most likely, this diversity, which remains mainly in the background so far, will increase in the future. As for Catholic schools all over the world, the population gradually becomes more and more pluralised, not only because of the influx of non-Christian school members, but also from within the Catholic community. Although there are significant differences by country and region, we notice a general trend of religious and philosophical *pluralisation*, accompanied by tendencies of *individualisation* (individuals decide each for themselves what to believe) and *detraditionalisation* (the process of passing on traditions across generations falters). To some extent, these changes put the traditional Catholic identity of schools under pressure.

Rather than 'contaminating' Catholic specificity, it must be emphasised that a growing diversity constitutes an opportunity, especially for schools, to actively *Recontextualise* Catholic identity (personal and institutional) in a changing world. The new key question becomes: what does it mean for me as a Catholic believer and for my school as a Catholic school to live out the original Christian inspiration in an increasingly plural world? What can we do as a Catholic school in a present-day context to support and nurture every person's potential in a way that reveals the radical love that Jesus Christ taught us, so many years ago and in a different context? Bringing this love and care into reality within a specifically educational context that services a pluralising student population, and while doing so giving testimony to what inspires and drives us, is the new way in which Catholic schools today fulfil their time-honoured mission, namely to spread God's Word across the world. The pedagogy that makes this possible is being promoted by the *Dialogue School* model: maximal Catholic identity in combination with maximal openness and solidarity with 'otherness'. A *Dialogue School* fosters a hermeneutical Catholic theology, explicitly aiming at encounter and dialogue about philosophical, religious and moral issues, regarding the Catholic story as a privileged conversational partner. Being open for diversity, the *Dialogue School* aims for a deep encounter between tradition and context, in which the Catholic tradition is renewed and revitalised for people today.

Currently, people in Catholic schools in Victoria clearly experience their school first and foremost as a *Dialogue School* (adults PRIM: 5.05/7; adults SEC: 5.22/7; students PRIM: 5.27/7; students SEC: 5.04/7). What is more, according to school staff and parents, there is a substantial margin for growth of the *Dialogue School* pedagogy on the normative level (adults PRIM: from 5.05/7 to 5.60/7; adults SEC: from 5.22/7 to 5.59/7;

almost all contributors agree or strongly agree with the *Dialogue School* on the normative level). For the adults, despite different views on other topics, there is no doubt that the *Dialogue School* is *the* way of the future for Catholic schools.

Student groups also like this kind of school which combines Catholic identity with openness and solidarity. The *Dialogue School* continues to be the preferred option for most students, which is important. However, according to the students, there is no need to increase the *Dialogue School* model in the future. Alongside the rejection of a *Monologue School* model (see below), we note that the support for a *Dialogue* model is also diminishing, while the resistance grows. In primary schools, this results in a small drop in overall appreciation for the *Dialogue School* (students PRIM: from 5.27/7 to 5.14/7; resistance grows to 12.6%; 17% hesitation; 70.4% remain supportive). In secondary colleges, the drop in appreciation is more notable (students SEC: from 5.04/7 to 4.61/7; resistance grows to 19.7%; 23.5% hesitation; 56.8% support). The *Dialogue School*, which exerts a clear preference for a Catholic school identity, is becoming a point of contention among secondary college students: while a shrinking majority continues to support it, a growing minority express critique on the *Dialogue School*. Once more, we find that the oldest students are relatively more critical: the mean score on the *Dialogue School* drops as the students grow older (year 5-6: 5.1/7; year 7-8: 4.8/7; year 9-10: 4.6/7; year 11-12:4.5/7).

The *Monologue School* model: a minority tendency giving rise to contrasts

Enthusiasm for the *Dialogue School* model stands in contrast to a general rejection of a *Monologue School* environment, a school type that stresses Catholic specificity *in opposition* to other worldviews and lifestyles. A *Monologue School* focuses only on Catholic identity and tends to exclude other-than-Catholic voices (in contrast to the *Reconfessionalisation* strategy described in the *Melbourne Scale* that might very well be open and receptive for diversity). On the whole, most adults disagree that Catholic schools could be identified as *Monological*, while on the normative level the rejection grows stronger (PRIM: from 3.72/7 to 3.47/7; SEC: from 3.67/7 to 3.14/7). Hence, a majority of the staff and the parents dismisses a *Monologue School* approach.

Among primary school children, we detect notable differences in views where the *Monologue School* model is concerned. Almost half of the children in year 5-6 experience their school as *Monological* (48.5%), while the other half hesitates (19.6%) or denies this (31.9%). On the normative level, the differences between the students' preference is growing: 39.6% agreement (including no less that 22.4% strong agreement), 21% hesitation and 39.5% disagreement. The net result of these shifts is a slightly diminishing mean score for the *Monologue School* (from 4.21/7 to 3.91/7).

We, thus, conclude that many children in primary schools (more than the adults) recognise traces of a *Monologue* Catholic pedagogy, while growing opposition offers resistance.

Likewise, some secondary college students experience *Monologue* tendencies at school (3.48/7; 31.4% agreement on the factual level) and would continue to support them in the future (18.7% agreement on the normative level). Despite this minority support, most secondary college students surpass the adults in their rejection of the *Monologue School*: the mean score drops from 3.48/7 to 2.85/7, 48.8% deny that Catholic colleges would be *Monologue*, while 60.9% clearly resists such an identity on the normative level (including 26.1% strong disagreement). It is to be noted that, the older the students become, the less tolerance they show for a *Monologue School* model: year by year, the mean score drops (from 3.9/7 in primary schools, to 3.4/7, 2.8/7 and 2.5/7 in secondary colleges). The oldest students are strong in their rejection of a closed Catholic school environment, where they clearly would not feel at home. It is therefore conceivable that the increasing doubt and protest on the part of some students against certain manifestations of Catholic school identity is related to their increasing objection to and fear of being caught up in *Monologue* tendencies.

To summarise: among both students and staff, there exists a sharp contrast between a minority that dream of a closed, protected, 'truly Catholic' *Monologue School* model that safeguards Catholic tradition and avoids contamination on the one hand, and a majority that favour solidarity in an open, *Recontextualising Dialogue School* model on the other hand. Today and also in the future, the latter choice will take the lead – though the former option remains influential.

The conclusions we drew while analysing the *PCB Scale* and the *Melbourne Scale*, namely that the diverging opinions about *Literal Belief* and *Reconfessionalisation* give rise to a debate that is as yet unresolved, also seem to apply to the *Victoria Scale*. We find similar tensions between the *Dialogue* and the *Monologue School* models, referring to two different pedagogical identity options entailed in a debate. The negative correlations on the factual and the normative level between the *Dialogue* and the *Monologue School* (-0.35 and -0.15) also point at this opposition: in daily school life, people experience a general contrast between a closed, self-protective, 'turned-inward' pedagogical stance on the one hand, and an open, accepting, communicative stance on the other.

Simultaneously we detect emerging *Colourful* and even *Colourless* traits

It seems important that this theological discussion amongst the adults in Catholic schools and the subsequent policy making regarding the schools' religious identity is carried through thoroughly and with due haste. This is because the schools are currently being subjected to *Secularising* tendencies, which erode their religious identity from the inside out.[31]

Let us look at the results to substantiate this claim: the mean score on the factual level for the *Colourful School*, which stresses solidarity above Catholic identity, comes close to the turning point (PRIM: 3.35/7 with 27.3% agreement; SEC: 3.62/7 with 31.5% agreement). On the normative level, many students are beginning to appreciate a *Colourful* outlook, which means that their preference for a Catholic school identity is vanishing (PRIM: from 3.35/7 to 3.81/7, with 36.6% agreement; SEC: from 3.62/7 to 4.39/7 with 47.1% agreement). In secondary colleges, the desire for a *Colourful School* is becoming a majority point of view. Its mean score on the normative level (4.39/7) is nearing the mean score for the *Dialogue School* (4.61/7). As we noted above, it is true that most students continue to prefer a *Dialogue School* environment, but their second best choice – and rising in appreciation – is the *Colourful School*. It could be seen that as the students grow older, the *Colourful School* receives more support (3.8/7 in primary schools, to 4.2/7, 4.4/7 and 4.5/7 in secondary colleges). On the whole, no less than 27.6% of the students in secondary colleges strongly agree and an additional 19.5% just agree with the *Colourful School* blackboard picture[32], which clearly states: *"Christianity should no longer be important at school, (...) because a preference for Christianity would hinder living together in harmony."*

A *Colourless School* is a secularistic school environment that does not involve itself in its members' philosophical, religious or moral affairs, because these are considered personal issues belonging to the private realm. We detect growing *Colourless School* tendencies among the student population. In primary schools, the resistance to a *Colourless* approach is diminishing (from 3.05/7 to 3.45/7). Likewise in secondary schools (from 3.30/7 to 3.92/7), where a significant minority of 34.9% approves of a *Colourless School* on the normative level. Increasing levels of *Colourless* approaches indicate a desire to be 'left alone' where religion or philosophy of life is concerned. According to the *Colourless School* pedagogy, a school should limit its responsibility to teaching alone and refrain from moral or religious education of any kind.

---

[31] This was one of the conclusions of the *Melbourne Scale*, confirmed here by the *Victoria Scale* results.
[32] Cf. the student version of the *Victoria Scale*, see the attachments, survey Instruments, paragraph 10.

Given their strong Catholic profile, it is no surprise that among the adults the resistance to both the *Colourful* and the *Colourless School* types receives majority support. Unlike the students, the adults hardly perceive *Colourful School* tendencies at the present time (PRIM: 3.16/7; SEC: 3.33/7). Also, many deny the existence of *Colourless School* tendencies (PRIM: 3.28/7; SEC: 3.44/7). On the normative level, a majority dismisses the outlook of becoming a *Colourful School* (PRIM: 3.37/7; SEC: 3.66/7) or a *Colourless School* (PRIM: 3.36/7; SEC: 3.61/7). Despite this clear trend, however, we do detect a minority support for both secular school types, especially among the adults in secondary colleges (PRIM: 17.3% support the *Colourful School* and 14% support the *Colourless School*; SEC: 27.8% support the *Colourful School* and 23.7% support the *Colourless School*). We therefore perceive here that the adults also show some *Colourful* and even *Colourless* traits: solidarity without Catholic preference (*Colourful*) and formal neutrality without interference (*Colourless*) also have their appeal. Nevertheless, given the adults' overwhelming preference for a *Dialogue School* approach, these findings are interesting but not alarming.

If the school leadership wishes to maintain a Catholic school identity, it would be advisable to keep a close eye on the emerging *Colourful* and *Colourless School* tendencies among the students – just as it would be advisable to guard against *Christian Values Education*[33] that tends to result in *Colourful* and even *Colourless* practices. Despite its apparent attractiveness, its warmth and positive values, its solidarity, openness and readiness for dialogue, a *Colourful School* in principle does not support a preference for the Catholic faith. Instead, it will opt for a 'neutral' and 'relativistic' stance, thereby 'hollowing out' Catholic school identity from the inside out. A Catholic school on the other hand is not only concerned with solidarity, with doing good things, but also with the motivation, inspiration, sources, et cetera, behind the solidarity practices that make them explicitly identifiable as Catholic. Therefore, it is important to distinguish the commitment to solidarity that comes from a Catholic conviction (*Dialogue School*) from solidarity that is a value on its own without being grounded in a believing option (*Colourful School*). The *Colourful* and *Colourless* tendencies that erode a school's Catholic identity might need to be responded to imaginatively and critically, even at their germinating stage.

---

[33] See the warnings against *Christian Values Education* in Chapter 11, §3.

§4. Intercorrelations between the three multivariate attitude scales

Intercorrelation graphs, also referred to as 'bubble graphs', are visual representations of the 4x4 matrices that contain the *Pearson linear correlation coefficients*[34] between the types of three multivariate attitude scales on the normative measurement levels.

Three intercorrelation graphs are described in this publication:
1. The *Post-Critical Belief Scale* related to the *Melbourne Scale* (normative level).
2. The *Post-Critical Belief Scale* related to the *Victoria Scale* (normative level).
3. The *Melbourne Scale* related to the *Victoria Scale* (in each case normative level).

Intercorrelation graphs are created using only the data from the adult groups. We examine the normative measurement levels, because that is where people reveal their personal point of view.

Pearson linear correlation coefficients can have a value that ranges from -1 to +1. Positive correlations are represented by a blue bubble, while negative correlations are represented by a red bubble. The bigger the bubble, the higher the correlation coefficient. The smaller the bubble, the smaller the correlation coefficient.

It is best to read these graphs by first examining the horizontal rows, and then by evaluating the vertical columns. In other words, we first analyse the 16 correlations from the perspective of the first scale; and, after that, we consider them again from the perspective of the second scale. Although this method creates some overlap as each correlation is examined twice, the advantage is that they are viewed in a new light and, therefore, reveal new meanings depending on the perspective of the scale under examination.

Most correlations or lack thereof are logical and to be expected because they merely represent the interrelated internal structures of the combined scales. For example, it is to be expected, and therefore not very revealing, that *Literal Belief* correlates with *Reconfessionalisation* and the *Monologue School*. However, special interest is aroused by those correlations that are unexpectedly high, low, positive, negative or missing.

In this instance, a correlation that exceeds +/- 0.35 is considered to be significant in principle, because it indicates that a particular linear association between two types is detected. In itself, a small or absent correlation does not reveal anything other than

---

[34] For thorough insight into the nature of linear correlation coefficients, see: D.S. MOORE & G.P. MCCABE, *Statistiek in de Praktijk. Theorieboek*, 5de herziene druk, Den Haag, Sdu Uitgevers bv, 2006 (repr. 2007), p.77-82.

that there is no linear association. Such a figure is only then meaningful provided there is an external reason why the absence of a significant correlation would be meaningful, which could very well be the case, as we shall see.

Intercorrelations between the *Melbourne Scale* and the *PCB Scale*

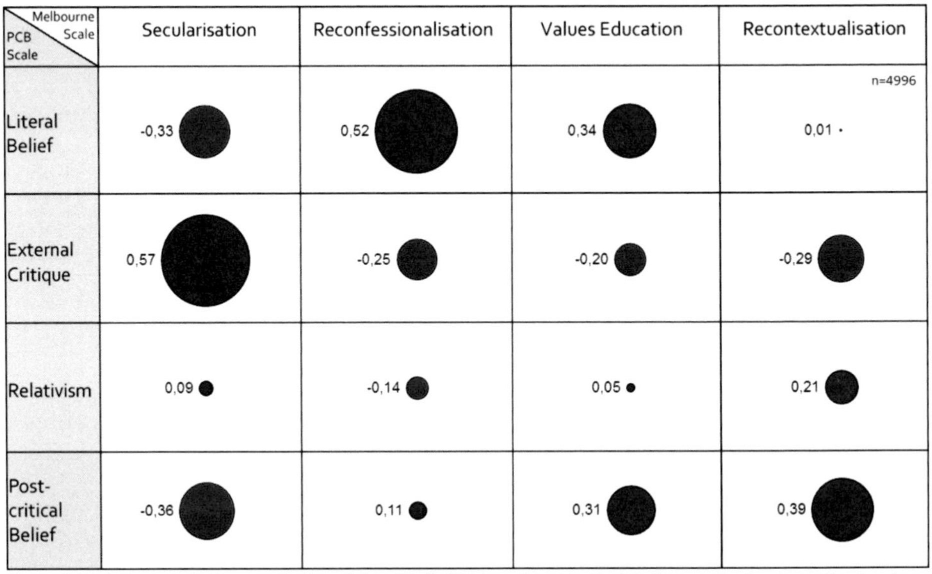

Melbourne Scale / PCB Scale	Secularisation	Reconfessionalisation	Values Education	Recontextualisation
Literal Belief	-0,33	0,52	0,34	0,01 ·
External Critique	0,57	-0,25	-0,20	-0,29
Relativism	0,09	-0,14	0,05	0,21
Post-critical Belief	-0,36	0,11	0,31	0,39

n=4996

Figure II-94. Intercorrelation graph: *Post-Critical Belief* Scale related to the *Melbourne Scale*, normative level.

	Secularisation	Reconfessionalisation	Christian Values Education	Recontextualisation
Literal Belief	-0,32585	0,52242	0,33888	0,01339
External Critique	0,57285	-0,25233	-0,19856	-0,29263
Relativism	0,08835	-0,13612	0,04791	0,20514
Post-Critical Belief	-0,35551	0,11068	0,30742	0,39416

Figure II-95. Correlation coefficients: *Post-Critical Belief* Scale related to the *Melbourne Scale*, normative level.

The first intercorrelation bubble graph represents the relation between the *Post-Critical Belief Scale* and the normative measurement level of the *Melbourne Scale*. No less than 4996 adult respondents of the ECSIP 2012 Research completed both surveys and, therefore, contributed to the correlation matrix.

First row: Literal Belief

On the top left corner, we detect a small inverted linear association between a *Literal Believing* attitude and the *Institutional Secularisation* of schools (r=-0.32585). Most respondents mildly reject *Literal Belief* and strongly reject the process of

Secularisation.[35] Yet, speaking in general, when people score higher on *Literal Belief*, they tend to be more opposed to *Secularisation*. As we would expect, *Literal Believing* tendencies (to the extent that they exist within the adult population) offer resistance to the *Secularisation* of a school's Catholic identity. Conversely, the more strongly people dismiss *Literal Belief*, the smaller their resistance to *Secularisation*. In other words, people show more openness and receptivity towards other-than-Catholic views and values to the extent that they more strongly resist *Literal Believing* cognitive patterns, which is the case among many adult respondents in Catholic schools in Victoria.

In line with this result, we notice a significant positive correlation between *Literal Belief* and *Reconfessionalisation* (r=0.52242), as well as a positive correlation with *Christian Values Education* (r=0.33888). As *Literal Belief* stands in opposition to *Secularisation*, it clearly supports those identity models which actively improve and strengthen a school's specifically Catholic character, either by means of a direct *Reconfessionalisation* or by means of a *mono-correlational Christian Values Education* didactic. So, approving *Literal Belief* goes hand in hand with approving the practice of *Reconfessionalisation*. Conversely, we can say that people who dismiss a literal, direct and dogmatic way of dealing with the Christian faith wish to avoid for the same reasons an overly strong stress on confessional Catholic school identity. The rejection of *Literal Belief* and the rejection of *Reconfessionalisation* go hand in hand.

We also learn that *Literal Belief* expects *Christian Values Education* to be a strategy with a *Reconfessionalising* aim, intending to mediate the Catholic faith through moral education, hoping to encourage stronger religious faith in the students. By teaching Catholic values and mores to the students, *Literal Believers* intend and hope to induce and improve the Catholic faith of young people today. Conversely, people with the opposite profile also contribute to this positive correlation: because they reject a direct and literal understanding of faith, they fear *Christian Values Education's Reconfessionalising* agenda that, according to them, should be avoided. If this distrust of *Values Education* were to spread, then its continuation might have the subversive effect to actually undermine the Catholic identity of the school.

Further, it is significant to note that *Literal Believing* people are not overly enthusiastic about a *Recontextualising* Catholic educational project (r=0,01339), although they do not seem to oppose it either. Here is an example of a zero-correlation that is meaningful because we might expect *Literal Believers* to take a clear stand on *Recontextualisation*, either in favour of it or rejecting it. What in fact happens is that

---

[35] Cf. *PCB Scale* means, Figure II-42 and Figure II-47.

both tendencies occur simultaneously and cancel each other out. There is a tendency of *Literal Belief* that favours *Recontextualisation* because of its genuine concern for Catholic identity, while there is also a propensity for *Literal Belief* to distrust *Recontextualisation* because it supposedly risks to 'adapt' or 'sell out' Catholic identity to plural culture and thereby damaging it from the inside out. The net result of both tendencies playing at the same time amounts to the zero-correlation we see in the bubble graph. It reveals a debate among the adults in Victoria about the nature and relationship of both *Literal Belief* and the ongoing *Recontextualisation* process. The prevailing *Literal Belief* discourse among adults is in doubt about a renewed contextual interpretation of the Catholic faith. It accepts and tolerates *Recontextualising* efforts to a certain extent, but without much enthusiasm or active support.

Second row: *External Critique*

The clear positive correlation between *External Critique* and *Secularisation* (r=0.57285) is not surprising yet very relevant. It shows that the tendencies of *External Critique* present among school members are a direct threat to the religious identity of schools. Because it rejects all religious faith, *External Critique* wants just one thing, namely to *Secularise* the school. Although this does apply to a minority of the respondents, most adults take the opposite position: they clearly reject both *External Critique* and *Institutional Secularisation*. The more they reject the one, the more they also reject the other – hence, a clear positive correlation displayed by the big blue bubble.

Further, *External Critique* shows negative correlations with all other three Catholic school identity models. As it aims for *Secularisation*, *External Critique* is a threat to any kind of Catholic school identity, be it *Reconfessionalising* (r=-0.25233), *Values Education* based (r=-0.19856) or *Recontextualising* (r=-0.29263). We therefore advise detecting and resisting in an unambiguous way any form of hard external religious critique in Catholic schools, especially the sort that is unwilling to contribute in a constructive way to a religious school project. Although such religious critique is rare among the adult groups, it should not be underestimated among the student groups, as the PCB scale mean graphs reveal.[36]

Third row: *Relativism / Awareness of Contingency*

It is striking that all correlation coefficients between *Relativism / Awareness of Contingency* on the one hand, and the school models of the *Melbourne Scale* on the other, are near zero. Again, this is not unexpected. To the extent that we are dealing with a *Relativistic* attitude, it is often a non-committed and non-engaged stance that is

---

[36] Cf. *PCB Scale* means, Figure II-42 and Figure II-47.

ultimately indifferent about the philosophical and religious positions adopted by people and institutions. From the perspective of *Relativism*, it does not really matter what kind of school one goes to. For a relativist, a school may have any pedagogical project provided it respects my personal freedom to believe whatever I want – just as anyone else's freedom of belief and freedom of expression ought to be respected. Because there are no discernible associations but only a scatter plot that shows a 'dispersed cloud of dots' between people's scores on *Relativism* and their scores on the four school identity models, there are no significant correlations between them.

Nevertheless, to the extent that we are dealing with *Awareness of Contingency*, perhaps the weak positive correlation with *Recontextualisation* (r=0.20514) could be reflected on a little further. When we examine the combined scores of nearly 5000 adults on these two variables, we detect a weak general tendency of linear association: the higher people score on *Recontextualisation*, the higher they also tend to score on *Awareness of Contingency*, and vice versa. Conversely, the lower they score on *Awareness of Contingency*, the lower they also tend to score on *Recontextualisation*, and vice versa. This could point to two underlying mechanisms playing simultaneously. On the one hand, it could be that an increasing *Awareness of Contingency* among faithful people, like the ones we are dealing with here, supports the move towards more *Recontextualisation* of Catholic school identity. Attempts at *Recontextualisation* can thus build in a positive way on patterns of *Contingency Awareness*. This is to be expected since an awareness of the diversity of philosophical and religious stances and the willingness to engage in dialogue with them are requirements for a successful *Recontextualisation* process. On the other hand, neither is it surprising that the process of *Recontextualising* Catholic identity arouses an increasing awareness of the multiplicity of identities that constitute today's school communities, including a growing understanding of the significance of a specifically *Catholic* identity for those communities. Searching for a renewed Catholic profile in a plural context implies an increased awareness of this diversity and the special relation of Catholicity towards it.

Moreover, if this interpretation holds for the weak positive association between *Contingency Awareness* and *Recontextualisation* (r=0.20514), then the inverse explanation could be true for the weak negative association with *Reconfessionalisation* (r=-0.13612): people who are *Aware of Contingency* tend to dismiss a school model that uniquely stresses a Catholic perspective, while a *Reconfessionalising* school model prefers to avoid too much non-Catholic diversity within school communities.

Fourth row: *Post-Critical Belief*

The positive linear correlation between *Post-Critical Belief* and *Recontextualisation* (r=0.39416) is very significant. There is an obvious correspondence between a cognitive belief style that deals with religious content in a symbolically mediated and hermeneutical way on the one hand, and a school identity model that deliberately searches for a renewed *Recontextualisation* of Catholic identity in today's context on the other. A *Post-Critical Believing* attitude is obviously allied to a *Recontextualisation* of Catholic identity. Conversely, to the extent that people experience their religiousness in a direct and non-mediated way, the less trust they put in a *Recontextualising* identity process.

According to the adult respondents in Victoria, the process of *Recontextualisation* driven by a *Post-Critical Believing* attitude ought to take place through a *Christian Values Education* pedagogy (r=0.30742) and against the background of a *Reconfessionalising* intention (r=0.11068). As such, it clearly opposes a *Secularisation* of Catholic school identity (r=-0.35551).

It is important to note the small positive correlation between *Post-Critical Belief* and *Reconfessionalisation* (r=0.11068). Although *Reconfessionalisation* is mainly supported by *Literal Belief* (r=0.52242; see above), it is not rejected by a *Post-Critical* religious attitude, as some might suspect. On the contrary, *Post-Critical Believers* also find it important to maintain and strengthen the specifically Catholic features of a school community, although their approach to it differs from *Literal Believers*. While the latter unilaterally stress the value and importance of a traditionally Catholic school culture, *Post-Critical Believers* stand in the dialectic between tradition and context. They attempt to reintegrate the Catholic faith in contemporary pluralising culture, so that it can enjoy a renewed credibility and authenticity for people today, in line with the Faith Tradition (*Recontextualisation*). ECSIP promotes a *Post-Critical Believing* religious attitude because it is the most promising approach for a *Recontextualisation* of Catholic school identity that is both culturally plausible and theologically valid, while keeping *Secularisation* at bay.

Given the possible critiques on a continued pedagogy of *Christian Values Education*[37], the relatively high correlation between *Post-Critical Belief* and *Values Education* (r=0.30742) may constitute a warning. Apparently, the many respondents who consider themselves *Post-Critically Believing* adults remain convinced that *Christian Values Education* is an effective and appropriate way to *Recontextualise* the Catholic

---

[37] See the critical assessment of *Christian Values Education*, Chapter 11 §3.

faith among young people today. However, given the profile of many students[38], a prolonged *Values Education* approach may put into danger the Catholic identity of schools in Victoria. Despite the adults' admirable intentions, *Values Education* might not only become ineffective, predictable and even counterproductive, but it might also flatten and reduce the religious aspects of Catholic education at school.

First column: *Secularisation*

Now that we have analysed the intercorrelation bubble graph by reading it horizontally from the perspective of the religious coping styles of the *Post-Critical Belief Scale*, we now proceed to read it vertically from the perspective of the *Melbourne Scale* school identity models. The first vertical column shows the correlations between *Institutional Secularisation* on the one hand, and the four religious attitudes on the other.

The first column reveals that, if we wished to *Secularise* our Catholic schools, we should give clear priority to people who profess *External Critique*, as is shown by the big positive correlation between the two (r=0.57285). The more this unbelieving pattern is present at schools, the more swiftly the *Secularisation* process proceeds. Conversely, the more *External Critique* is opposed (as is the case in the adult sample under consideration), the more the *Secularisation* process is delayed and transformed.

Both *Literal Believers* (r=-0.32585) and *Post-Critical Believers* (-0.35551) wish to avoid the *Secularisation* of Catholic schools. Both belief styles attempt to safeguard and strengthen the Catholic identity of schools in Victoria. *Post-Critical Belief* pushes this option a bit stronger compared with *Literal Belief*. According to the adult respondents in Victoria, people with a balanced combination of literal and symbolic belief are needed in Catholic schools in order to slow down and transform current processes of *Secularisation*.

From the perspective of *Relativism/Awareness of Contingency*, it is not particularly relevant whether the school *Secularises* or remains Catholic (r=0.08835). On the one hand, pure *Relativists* might favour *Secularisation* to the extent that they believe it is better suited to guarantee every person's personal freedom in a formal way. On the other hand, those faithful people who cherish an *Awareness of Contingency* might want to avoid *Secularisation* because it risks relativising all philosophical, ethical and religious positions, dismisses a Catholic preferential option and destroys its religious truth claims. The net result is a 'dispersed cloud of dots' with a correlation that is close to zero.

---

[38] See for example the analysis of the students' results on the *Melbourne Scale*.

Second column: Reconfessionalisation

Which cognitive belief styles are suited best in order to *Reconfessionalise* schools? The bubbles in the second column reveal that especially *Literal Believing* faith patterns lead on to *Reconfessionalisation* (r=0.52242), which is as we would expect. *Post-Critical Believing* faith patterns also support to some extent *Reconfessionalising* identity strategies (r=0.11068). A certain amount of *Reconfessionalisation* might be needed in order to maintain or reintroduce elements of Catholic identity where they are in danger of being neglected or even vanishing. On the other hand, it is not surprising that the unbelieving cognitive belief styles, namely *External Critique* (r=-0.25233) and *Relativism / Awareness of Contingency* (r=-0.13612), both resist a straightforward *Reconfessionalisation* of schools.

Third column: Christian Values Education

Despite possible critiques, *Christian Values Education* is a prominent didactical approach in Catholic schools in Victoria, clearly supported both by *Literal Believing* (r=0.33888) and *Post-Critical Believing* (r=0.30742) tendencies. Since most adults in Catholic schools profess to a combination of these two belief styles, it is clear that the majority believe *Christian Values Education* to be and remain an essential strategy in religious education in primary and secondary schools.

However, as the bubble graph shows, people with *Literal Believing* and *Post-Critical Believing* tendencies clearly perceive *Values Education* in a different way. *Literal Believers* wish to employ *Christian Values Education* in its full *mono-correlation* capacity in order to benefit the *Reconfessionalisation* which is their ultimate goal (r=0.52242). In other words, *Literal Believers* wish to give the students a Christian moral education in order to stir up religious awareness and turn them towards a Catholic religious life style. In this way, moral education directly mediates religious formation.

Post-Critical Believers, on the other hand, wish to employ *Christian Values Education* in order to benefit a *Recontextualisation* of Catholic school identity, which is their ultimate goal (r=0.39416). In other words, *Post-Critical Believers* are likely to focus more on how Christian values can be universally recognised and approved of, and how this unanimity can serve the communication of the Catholic faith in a pluralising context.

It might be feared, however, that neither use of *Christian Values Education* suffices, when continued unreflectively in the future, to address the increasing detraditionalisation and pluralisation in contemporary culture. For that, we need a *multi-correlation* dynamic that connects the Catholic faith to a manifold of interpretational tracks, transforming both the interpreters and faith itself, thereby *Recontextualising* it once more. In other words, the time has come for a conscious (*multi-correlational*) *Recontextualisation* to take the lead from a (*mono-correlational*) *Christian Values Education* didactic.

Fourth column: Recontextualisation of Catholic identity

As the negative correlation shows, *Recontextualisation* is clearly rejected by *External Critique* (r=-0.29263). It is no surprise that people, to the extent that they externally criticise religious claims, get in conflict with a school identity model that focuses on a continued Catholic identity. It may be surprising, however, that the negative correlation of *External Critique* with *Recontextualisation* (r=-0.29263) is slightly more pronounced when compared with its negative correlation with *Reconfessionalisation* (r=-0.25233). Could it be that a *Recontextualising* didactic is somewhat more challenging and demanding to non-believing people, compared with a *Reconfessionalising* approach? Perhaps, the reason why *Recontextualisation* stirs more resistance from *External Critique* is that it continuously questions people's views, critically challenges them to justify their positions, to enter into an open dialogue about various points of view, to search openly for value and truth in various places – in short: to take part in the dynamics of a *Recontextualisation* process? On the other hand, despite that fact that they are diametrically opposed about religious truth claims, *External Critique* and *Reconfessionalisation* share similarities on the epistemological level that might explain why the negative correlation between them is not that pronounced. Both types are akin to a *Literal Believing* cognitive style that objectifies truth claims and departs from a direct and unmediated relation to religious contents.

Apart from *External Critique*, none of the other cognitive belief styles offer rejection to *Recontextualisation*. Obviously, the greatest level of support comes from *Post-Critical Belief* (r=0.39416). Also *Relativism / Awareness of Contingency* offers a support basis for a *Recontextualising* Catholic identity project (r=0.20514). *Literal Believing* tendencies, to the extent that they are present in the sample, do not oppose a *Recontextualising* project, although they do not promote it either (r=0.01339). As explained above, *Literal Belief* is in doubt about a renewed contextual interpretation of the Catholic faith: while it is willing to accept and tolerate *Recontextualising* efforts to a certain level, it also tends to distrust it.

Taken into consideration the composition of the adult respondent groups in terms of their cognitive belief patterns (a clear majority of *Post-Critical Belief*, backed up by firm levels of *Contingency Awareness*, a general dismissal of *Literal Belief* and a strong rejection of *External Critique*)[39], it is clear that the school identity model of *Recontextualisation* is the option that enjoys most empirical support as well as normative plausibility.

---

[39] Cf. *PCB Scale* means, Figure II-42 and Figure II-47.

Intercorrelations between the *Victoria Scale* and the *PCB Scale*

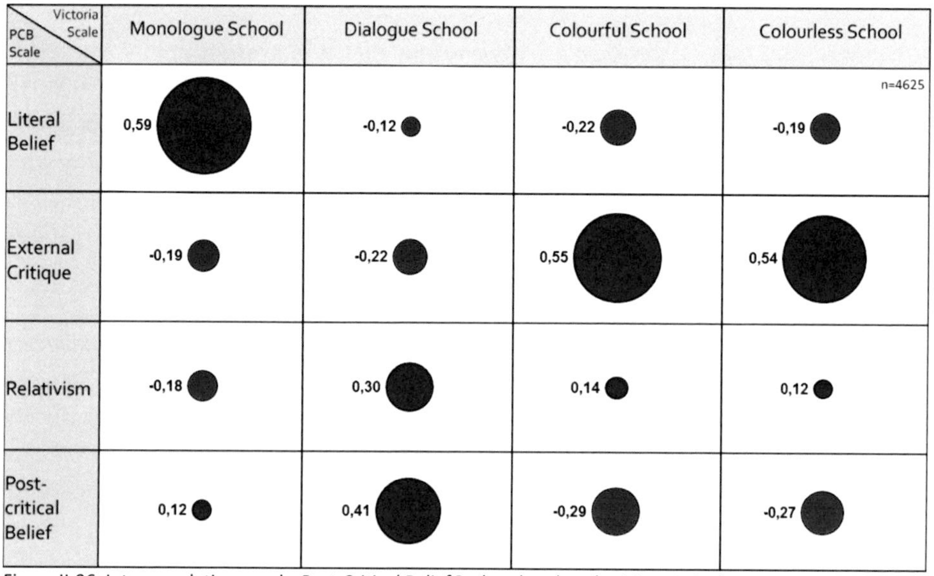

Victoria Scale / PCB Scale	Monologue School	Dialogue School	Colourful School	Colourless School
Literal Belief	0,59	-0,12	-0,22	-0,19
External Critique	-0,19	-0,22	0,55	0,54
Relativism	-0,18	0,30	0,14	0,12
Post-critical Belief	0,12	0,41	-0,29	-0,27

n=4625

Figure II-96. Intercorrelation graph: *Post-Critical Belief* Scale related to the *Victoria Scale*, normative level.

	Monologue School	Dialogue School	Colourless School	Colourful School
Literal Belief	0,59301	-0,11705	-0,21712	-0,18544
External Critique	-0,19248	-0,21615	0,54735	0,53508
Relativism	-0,18457	0,29741	0,13547	0,11539
Post-Critical Belief	0,12120	0,40556	-0,29368	-0,26652

Figure II-97. Correlation coefficients: *Post-Critical Belief* Scale related to the *Victoria Scale*, normative level.

The second intercorrelation bubble graph represents the relation between the *Post-Critical Belief Scale* and the normative measurement level of the *Victoria Scale*. 4625 adult respondents of the ECSIP 2012 Research completed both surveys and contribute to this graph.

Basic interpretations when reading the graph horizontally

From the perspective of the cognitive belief styles of the *PCB Scale*, this bubble graph shows many results that are logical and expected. For example, it is no surprise that the religious faith attitude of *Literal Belief* correlates positively with a *Monologue School* model (r=0.59301), while the three other *Victoria Scale* types are being rejected

(*Dialogue School*: r=-0.11705; *Colourful School*: r=-0.21712; *Colourless School*: r=-0.18544).

It is interesting that *Literal Belief*, to the extent that it is present among the adult respondents, shows a significant correlation with the *Monologue School* (r=0.59301). The minority of *Literal Believing* adults imagine a *Monological Catholic School* as the ideal[40]: a school by and for Catholics only, with little or no openness or solidarity with other-than-Catholic perspectives. In this sample, however, the big blue bubble mainly indicates a general mutual rejection of both *Literal Belief* and the *Monologue School*. When one is rejected, so is the other; hence a positive correlation.

Just as they distrust a *Recontextualisation* of Catholic school identity[41], *Literal Believers* are also wary of the *Dialogue School* model, even though the overall rejection remains small (r=-0.11705). In this sample, however, the small negative correlation is mainly caused by the inverse tendency of a vast majority of adults who support a *Dialogue School* model while somewhat rejecting *Literal Belief*. Further, also both secular school models of the *Victoria Scale* typology, namely the *Colourful* and the *Colourless School*, are inversely related to *Literal Belief* (r=-0.21712 and r=-0.18544 respectively).

This intercorrelation bubble graph makes it overwhelmingly clear why significant levels of *External Critique* ought to be avoided in Catholic schools. On the one hand, it shows high positive correlations with both secular school types, namely the *Colourful School* (r=0.54735) and the *Colourless School* (r=0.53508). Conversely, the rejection of *Colourful* and *Colourless Schools* goes hand in hand with the rejection of *External Critique* among most adult respondents in this sample, which explains the correlation in this case. On the other hand, *External Critique* is inversely related to both Catholic school types, namely the *Monologue School* (r=-0.19248) and the *Dialogue School* (r=-0.21615).

As was the case with *Recontextualisation*[42], *Relativism/Awareness of Contingency* shows a moderately positive association with the *Dialogue School* model (r=0.29741). This means that the *Dialogue School* can count on the support of existing tendencies of *Contingency Awareness*, while simultaneously it gives rise to the awareness of the existence of a multiplicity of philosophical and religious views and practices, and the need to enter into conversation and dialogue with them. Despite this correspondence, *Relativism / Contingency Awareness* remains a non-believing way to deal with religious content, as is evidenced by the mild approval of both the *Colourful* (r=0.13547) and the

---

[40] See the *Victoria Scale* mean results for the adult groups.
[41] See the explanation of the correlation between *Literal Belief* and *Recontextualisation*.
[42] See the explanation of the correlation between *Relativism* and *Recontextualisation*.

Colourless Schools (r=0.11539). It is no surprise that *Relativism* and the *Monologue School* are inversely correlated (r=-0.18457).

The bottom row reveals a clear, positive correlation between *Post-Critical Belief* and the *Dialogue School* (r=0.40556). Similar to the correlation with *Recontextualisation*[43], *Post-Critical Belief* is ideally suited to support a *Dialogical School* identity. The *Monologue School* model also shows a small general correlation with *Post-Critical Belief* (r=0.12120). On the one hand, this is to be expected since both school types share a preference for the Catholic faith. On the other hand, it is good to know that among the *Post-Critically Believing* adults in Victoria there exists some sympathy for a *Monological Catholic School* approach. Finally, we detect the expected rejection, from the perspective of *Post-Critical Belief*, of both the *Colourful School* model (r=-0,29368) and the *Colourless School* model (r=-0.26652).

Basic interpretations when reading the graph vertically

The column on the left of the bubble graph shows the correlations between the *Monologue School* model of the *Victoria Scale* and the four cognitive belief styles of the *Post-Critical Belief Scale*. According to the adults in our sample, in order to create a *Monologue School* environment, one can count on the support of the *Literal Believers* (r=0.59301) and perhaps also on the support of *Post-Critical Believing* people (r=0.12120), although their support is much more hesitant and uncertain. It is evident that both *External Critique* (r=-0.19248) and *Relativism/Awareness of Contingency* (r=-0.18457) are expected to resist *Monologue School* tendencies.

The two cognitive belief patterns that are most present in the adult sample are the ones that provide a clear support for a *Dialogue School* model: *Post-Critical Belief* (r=0.40556) and *Awareness of Contingency* (r=0.29741). Therefore we can conclude that continuing to nourish *Dialogue Schools* in Victoria is both empirically supported and theologically plausible among the adult groups. On the other hand, a *Dialogical School* model is hindered by *External Critique* (r=-0.21615) but also a little by *Literal Belief* (r=-0.11705) that probably suspects it of being too 'open' and 'compromising' where its Catholic identity is concerned.

On the whole, the adult respondents reject both the *Colourful* and the *Colourless School* types[44]. The rejection of these secularised school models strongly correlates with the rejection of *External Critique* (a positive correlation of r=0.54735 and

---

[43] See the explanation of the correlation between *Post-Critical Belief* and *Recontextualisation*.
[44] See the analysis of the *Victoria Scale* mean results.

r=0.53508 respectively). Also logical is the rejection of *Colourful* and *Colourless Schools* from the perspective of *Literal Believing* tendencies (r=-0.21712 and r=-0,18544 respectively) and even more so from the perspective of *Post-Critical Belief* (r=-0.29368 and r=-0.26652 respectively). Finally, *Relativism/Contingency Awareness* reveals its ties to a secular way of thinking by supporting, though only slightly, both *Colourful* and *Colourless Schools* (r=0.13547 and r=0.11539 respectively). From the perspective of the four cognitive belief styles of the *PCB Scale*, the intercorrelation bubble graph reveals little difference in assessment between the *Colourful School* and the *Colourless School*: both secular school types relate in a very similar way to the four religious coping styles.

Intercorrelations between the *Melbourne Scale* and the *Victoria Scale*

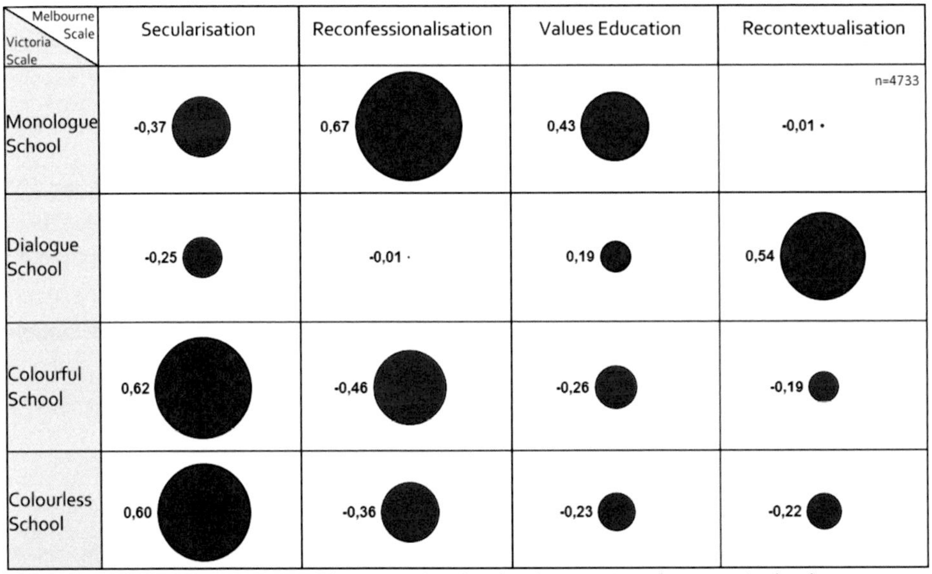

Victoria Scale \ Melbourne Scale	Secularisation	Reconfessionalisation	Values Education	Recontextualisation
Monologue School	-0,37	0,67	0,43	-0,01 · (n=4733)
Dialogue School	-0,25	-0,01 ·	0,19	0,54
Colourful School	0,62	-0,46	-0,26	-0,19
Colourless School	0,60	-0,36	-0,23	-0,22

Figure II-98. Intercorrelation graph: *Melbourne Scale* related to the *Victoria Scale*, normative level.

	Secularisation	Reconfessionalisation	Christian Values Education	Recontextualisation
Monologue School	-0,37070	0,66964	0,42512	-0,01418
Dialogue School	-0,24669	-0,00697	0,18993	0,54100
Colourless School	0,62205	-0,45695	-0,26438	-0,18706
Colourful School	0,59691	-0,36207	-0,23095	-0,21606

Figure II-99. Correlation matrix: *Melbourne Scale* related to the *Victoria Scale*, normative level.

The third intercorrelation bubble graph visualises the relation between the normative measurement levels of the *Victoria Scale* and the *Melbourne Scale*. 4733 adult respondents completed both scales and therefore contribute to this graph.

Basic interpretations when reading the graph horizontally

This bubble graph consists of correlations that reveal the internal structures of the two combined typologies and that are, therefore, mostly logical and expected. Nevertheless, there are also some striking and rather unexpected correlations that deserve extra attention.

Not surprisingly, on the normative measurement level, the *Monologue School* model is at odds with the *Institutional Secularisation* strategy described by the *Melbourne Scale* (-0.37070). More precisely: the more strongly people dismiss *Secularisation*, the less negative (though in most cases still negative) they tend to score on a *Monologue School* pedagogy. Conversely, the more strongly people repudiate *Monologue School* tendencies, the more openness is revealed towards secular culture.

Further, the *Monologue School* model is clearly supported by both *Reconfessionalisation* (r=0.66964) and *Christian Values Education* (r=0.42512). The former correlation is no surprise. The latter correlation reveals how, for a majority of the respondents, *Values Education* employs a *mono-correlation* pedagogy in order to 'bridge the gap' between plural culture and the Catholic faith, attempting to bring all students closer to Catholicism out of an evangelising intention. This way, *Values Education* serves a *Reconfessionalising* and even *Monological* approach to the Catholic faith.

Also interesting is the zero-correlation between the *Monologue School* and *Recontextualisation of Catholic Identity* (r=-0.01418). Similar to the zero-correlation between *Literal Belief* and *Recontextualisation*[45], this indicates that there is a debate about the nature and relationship of the *Monologue* and the *Recontextualising* school models. Among the advocates of *Monological* education, some tend to support *Recontextualisation* while others distrust its hermeneutical openness and prefer to avoid it. Among the opponents of *Monological* Catholic identity, some tend to support *Recontextualisation* more and others less. The result is a scatter plot with a 'dispersed cloud of dots' resulting in a near zero correlation.

---

[45] See the explanation of the correlation between *Literal Belief* and *Recontextualisation*.

It is clear that a *Dialogue School* is related in many ways to a *Recontextualisation* of Catholic school identity as is evidenced by the significant positive correlation in the second horizontal row (r=0.54100). A *Dialogical* religious pedagogy is a prerequisite for a successful *Recontextualisation* of the Catholic faith, while such a *Recontextualisation* evidently assists and sustains the *Dialogue* between different viewpoints at school. *Christian Values Education* (r=0.18993) as well as *Reconfessionalisation* (r=-0.00697) tend to support *Dialogue School* efforts, although to a decreasing extent: while *Values Education* can still favour a *Dialogue School* environment, *Reconfessionalisation* hesitates and is divided between proponents and opponents – hence the zero-correlation. Finally, it is not surprising that the *Dialogue School* correlates negatively with *Institutional Secularisation* (r=-0.24669). After all, a *Dialogue school* is characterised by maximum Christian identity combined with maximum solidarity.

The *Colourful* and *Colourless School* types are secularised environments that aim at an *Institutional Secularisation* of Catholic school identity (cf. the positive correlations of r=0.62205 and r=0.59691 respectively). In the minds of the adult respondents, these three school models are clearly linked. Consequently, all correlations between the *Colourful* and *Colourless School* on the one hand and the three Catholic school identity models of the *Melbourne Scale* on the other hand, are negative. More precisely, *Colourful* and *Colourless* tendencies clearly strive against *Reconfessionalisation* (r=-0.45695 and r=-0.36207 respectively), but also resist *Christian Values Education* (r=-0.26438 and r=-0.23095 respectively) as well as Recontextualisation (r=-0.18706 and r=-0.21606 respectively). In other words, more appropriately applied to this sample, to the extent that people favour a Catholic school identity of whatever sort, then for the same reason they reject both the *Colourful* and *Colourless School* models described by the *Victoria Scale*.

Basic interpretations when reading the graph vertically

If we desired to do away with Catholic identity and *Secularise* Catholic schools, then we would find allies in both the *Colourful* and the *Colourless* pedagogical approaches (r=0.62205 and r=0.59691 respectively), while both the *Monologue* and the *Dialogue School* tendencies would object (r=-0.37070 and r=-0.24669 respectively).

However, if we desired to *Reconfessionalise* Catholic schools in order to actively strengthen their traditional Catholic character, then we would find a strong ally in the *Monologue School* tendencies (r=0.66964) that exist in a minority capacity among the adults in Victoria[46]. On the other hand, the majority of adults who dismiss the

---

[46] See the *Victoria Scale* means and percentages for the adult groups.

Monologue School are expected to resist *Reconfessionalisation* as well. Additional resistance is to be expected from those enthusiastic about the *Colourful School* (r=-0.45695) and the *Colourless School* (r=-0.36207).

Similar to the discussion regarding *Recontextualisation*[47], there exists a debate among the proponents of the *Dialogue School* model about the desirability of *Reconfessionalisation* (cf. the zero-correlation of r=-0.00697). While some believe that a certain extent of *Reconfessionalisation* is inevitable in order to safeguard a truly Catholic preferential perspective in a *Dialogue School*, others dispute the amount of *Reconfessionalisation* that is needed and desired, as well as the way in which it can fruitfully contribute to the solidary encounter and dialogue of different viewpoints at school.

The *mono-correlational* strategy of *Christian Values Education* is promoted especially by those who imagine *Monologue Schools*, as expected (r=0.42512). Conversely, those who reject the one, also tend to reject the other. *Values Education* also enjoys some support from the side of the *Dialogue School*, although significantly less compared with the *Monologue School* (r=0.18993). This too is expected, because in a pluralising context a *Dialogue School* pedagogy is preferably affiliated with a *multi-correlational* (*Recontextualising*) approach. Because of its confessionalising intentions that strive to avoid the perceived *Secularisation* of Catholic schools, both the *Colourful School* model and the *Colourless School* model take position against *Christian Values Education* (r=-0.26438 and r=-0.23095 respectively).

The column on the right hand side of the bubble graph reveals a significant positive correlation between *Recontextualisation* of Catholic school identity and a *Dialogue School* pedagogy (r=0.54100). As stated above, an open-minded, solidary and dialogical approach is a prerequisite for an ongoing *Recontextualisation* of the Catholic faith. From the perspective of a *Monological* Catholic identity, however, the support for *Recontextualisation* is divided: while some are willing to pledge their support, others are more hesitant (r=-0.01418). Finally, *Recontextualisation* is objected to by the *Colourful School* as well as the *Colourless School* (r=-0.18706 and r=-0.21606 respectively), although the focus on a culture of openness, debate and solidarity somewhat mitigates their rejection.

We conclude that the analysis of the intercorrelation between the three multivariate attitude scales offers in-depth insights and understandings of the viewpoints and the

---

[47] See the explanation of the correlation between *Post-Critical Belief* and *Reconfessionalisation*.

intricate relations between them that exist among the adult respondents connected to Catholic schools in Victoria.

§5. *Subpopulations*: clusters of respondents who share similar views on Catholic school identity

Introduction

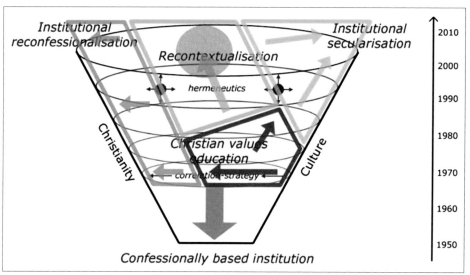

Figure II-100. Overview of the four *Subpopulations*, situated on the *Melbourne Scale* diagram.

Subpopulations are a special technique to identify the main trends regarding Catholic school identity that exist within any researched population and to summarise these trends in a clear, visual way. They are a convenient tool for integrating and summarising the main findings of the ECSIP research in one overview, making it easier to grasp the tendencies and conclusions that are being detected.

All respondents are being classified in one of four pre-established '*Subpopulations*', namely the one to which someone *most likely* belongs. This classification is based on a large number of indicators, selected from all available empirical data (scale results as well as background variables). Based on this classification, we can estimate percentage-wise the relative existence of the four *Subpopulations* within the entire population of primary and secondary schools in Victoria, adults and students differentiated.

The four *Subpopulations* group people together based on similar views on Catholic school identity (on the normative measurement level), not unlike the way in which a *political party* consists of a community of people who share similar ideals and practices. People who belong to the same *Subpopulation* share convictions, ways of thinking and practices that are at least related. Although they do not necessarily agree with each other on all relevant points, at least they tend to think in a similar way and desire to move in a similar direction.

The four pre-established *Subpopulations* are characterised and visually presented by means of the typology that frames the *Melbourne Scale*, i.e. the theological distinction of different school identity models against the background of a secularising and pluralising cultural context. This typology determines the central theological analysis of Catholic school identity and forms the heart of the ECSIP project.

Each *Subpopulation* can be recognised by its own fluorescent colour:

YELLOW: *Subpopulation* of people who want to *Secularise* Catholic identity.

BLUE: *Subpopulation* of people who want to *Reconfessionalise* Catholic identity.

RED: *Subpopulation* of people who want to employ *Christian Values Education*.

GREEN: *Subpopulation* of people who want to *Recontextualise* Catholic identity.

Subpopulation 1. Trends of *Secularisation*

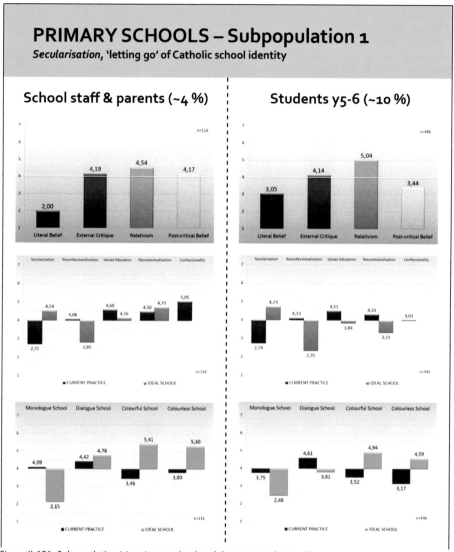

Figure II-101. *Subpopulation* 1 in primary schools, adults compared to students.

About 3.9% of the adults in primary schools are part of this *Subpopulation*:
- Teachers: about 3.8% (1 in 26)
- School leadership: about 2.0% (1 in 50)
- Parents: about 4.7% (1 in 21)

About 10.2% of the students in year 5-6 are part of this *Subpopulation*:
- Primary school children year 5-6: about 10.2% (1 in 10)

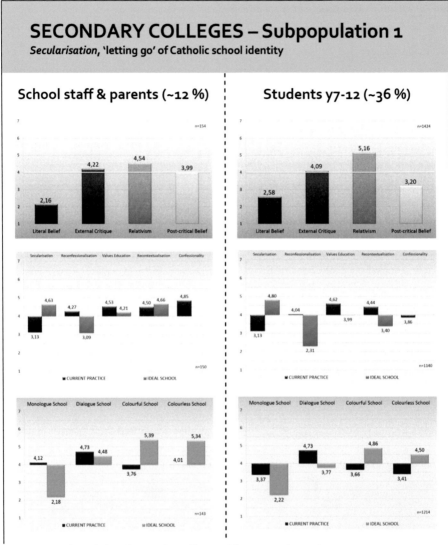

Figure II-102. *Subpopulation* 1 in secondary colleges, adults compared to students.

About 12.2% of the adults in secondary colleges are part of this *Subpopulation*:

- Teachers: about 15.7% (2 in 13)
- School leadership: about 6.1% (2 in 33)
- Parents: about 10.0% (1 in 10)

About 35.6% of the students in year 7-12 are part of this *Subpopulation*:

- Secondary college students year 7-8: about 28.2% (2 in 7)
- Secondary college students year 9-10: about 38.2% (3 in 8)
- Secondary college students year 11-12: about 43.0% (3 in 7)

The first *Subpopulation* denotes trends of *Secularisation* or a 'letting go' of Catholic school identity. This group will express a desire for the school to be a religiously neutral environment and will shun notions of a religiously underpinned ethos, faith formation and expressions of belief at school. This group thinks that religion and faith should be privatised and has no role in the public sphere, including in school. They will typically present with non-believing stances on the *Post-Critical Belief* Scale, be pro-*Institutional Secularisation* and against *Reconfessionalisation* on the *Melbourne Scale* and against a *Monologue School* but pro-*Colourful* and pro-*Colourless Schools* on the *Victoria Scale*.

Adults

About 3.9% of the adult respondents from the primary schools group (that is to say 1 in every 26) are part of this *Subpopulation*; specifically this represents 3.8% of teachers (1 in 26), 2% of those in school leadership (1 in 50) and 4.7% of parents or 1 in every 21 parents. Interestingly the number of adults falling into this category increases by over three-fold once we examine the figures for adults in secondary colleges. Some 12.2% of the adults, or 1 in 8, surveyed as part of the secondary college research fit into this *Subpopulation*. A particularly large jump can be noted from the teacher's results, which spring from 3.8% at primary school level (1 in 26) to 15.7% (2 in 13), this represents a four-fold increase. It will later become apparent that the didactic technique of teachers changes to match that of the students who flock into this *Subpopulation* during their secondary college years. It could also be proposed that these teachers are more *Secular* and non-believing themselves due to personal choice and hence fall into this category. The number of members of school leadership at secondary college level falling into this category is 2 in 33, or 6.1%, which is again a three-fold increase from their equivalents in primary school. Finally 10%, or 1 in 10, parents of secondary college students identify themselves in this *Subpopulation*; which represents a two-fold increase from parents of primary school children. The fact that these parents of secondary college students are in general drawn from a larger and more diverse cultural, ethical, geographical and religious background, results in a diversity of opinion than one would not encounter in a smaller, localised and more homogenous primary school.

Examining the adult's graphs for the *Post-Critical Belief, Melbourne* and *Victoria* Scales in Figures II-101/102 lets one see the main characteristics in diagram form and to track the trends from the adult population in both primary and secondary schools. Firstly, a clear preference is noted in the *Melbourne Scale* for *Institutional Secularisation* on the normative level, scoring 4.54/7 in primary schools and increasing to 4.63/7 in secondary colleges. For both groups they note that their current school is resistant towards *Secularisation* (2.71/7 for primary, 3.13/7 secondary), but they clearly desire this to change. A very positive appreciation for both *Colourful* and *Colourless Schools* is also noted, with support for each increasing on the secondary college level, from 5.41/7 to 5.39/7 and 5.30/7 to 5.34/7, respectively. On the factual level the adults do not view their school as either *Colourful* (3.46/7 primary, 3.76/7 secondary) or *Colourless* (3.80/7 primary, 4.01/7 secondary; which represents an overall neutral score). In terms of the *PCB Scale* a similar high score for the non-believing stance of *External Critique* is observed for primary school adults (4.19/7) and among the secondary college adult group (4.22/7). So too for *Relativism*, which holds that a multiplicity of religious commitments should be accepted, welcomed, valued and considered as interchangeable options, with no one being more true or valuable than another, achieving an equally high 5.54/7 among both groups. *Post-Critical Belief* is noted to be lower than both *External Critique* and *Relativism*, at 4.17/7 in the primary group and 3.99/7 among the secondary college adult group.

Literal Belief is opposed, as it represents a literal believing stance, with scores of 2.00/7 at primary level and 2.15/7 at secondary level. *Reconfessionalisation* is strongly opposed at primary level (2.81/7) where it is factually somewhat recognised (4.08/7). Among the secondary college group *Reconfessionalisation* is perceived to be more present factually (4.27/7) and is less resisted than on the primary level (3.09/7). The *Monologue School* is factually somewhat recognised by both groups (4.09/7, 4.12/7 respectively) and almost equally strongly resisted on the normative level (2.15/7, 2.18/7 respectively).

As has been noted *Post-Critical Belief* decreases among the secondary college group from 4.17/7 at primary level to 3.99/7. There is recognition of *Recontextualisation* to a similar degree in their current schools (both at 4.50/7) with a slight increase in desire on the ideal level for both groups (4.73/7 and 4.66/7 respectively). Among the adults in the primary school group they recognise some *Dialogue School* tendencies currently (4.42/7) and desire more on the ideal level (4.78/7). A dissimilar trend is noted in our latter grouping, with a higher level of recognition of *Dialogue* factually (4.73/7) but a decrease in desire on the normative level (4.48/7). It is interesting to note that this group is not against the idea of the *Dialogue/Recontextualising School* but it is found that they do not support this model in a fully committed manner but rather will go along with these identity options in a manner, which will 'hollow out' their significance in the long term. That is to say that while they exhibit an exterior following of these trends their support is not derived from being rooted in faith or care about maintaining the schools Catholic identity. This point is evidenced already in the three-fold increase in those supporting this *Secularisation Subpopulation* among the adults in the secondary college group (12.2%) compared to the primary school group (3.9%).

While there are similarities among those in this *Subpopulation* from both the primary and secondary college groups, certain patterns can also be discerned. To that end one notes a decreasing *Post-Critical Belief*, increasing desire for *Secularisation* and decreasing desire for a *Dialogue School*. It can be noted that while there is a three-fold increase in the raw numbers falling into this *Subpopulation* one also notes more pronounced tendencies within this group at secondary level.

Students

About 10.2% of the students in year 5-6 from the primary schools group (that is to say 1 in every 10) are part of this *Subpopulation*. Worryingly the number of students falling into this category increases by three and a half-fold once we examine the figures for students in secondary college. Some 35.6% of secondary college students, or 5 in 14, surveyed as part of the secondary college research fit into this *Subpopulation*. A rather notable progressive trend can be discerned within this overall data. Beginning from the level of 10.2% (1 in 10) among year 5-6 in primary school, the numbers in this *Secularisation Subpopulation* jump upon their move to secondary college, with 28.2% (2 in 7) among the year 7-8 students falling into this *Subpopulation*. This grows steadily to 39.2% (3 in 8) among the year 9-10's and again increases to 43% (3 in 7) among the year 11-12's. Hence one observes a significant and steady migration into this *Subpopulation* as students age, with a particularly large leap made during the liminal moment of moving from primary to secondary college (a threefold difference from 10.2% to 28.2%). A similar general comment can be made to that of the adults in relation to the composition of secondary colleges, which, in general, draw students from a larger and more diverse cultural, ethical, geographical and religious background, results in a diversity of opinion than one would not encounter in a smaller, localised and more homogenous primary school.

When we examine the characteristics of the students in this *Secularising Subpopulation*, it is not surprising that we note a clear preference in the *Melbourne Scale* for *Institutional Secularisation* on the normative level, with a mean score of 4.73/7 in primary school and increasing to 4.80/7 in secondary colleges. For both groups they note that their current school is resistant towards *Secularisation* (2.74/7 for primary, 3.13/7 secondary) but they clearly desire this to change. Most striking from the *PCB Scale* is the very low score for *Post-Critical Belief,* which among the year 5-6 at primary school is 3.44/7, which further decreases among the secondary college students to 3.20/7. Although characteristics of a *Colourful School* are not currently present in their school according to the year 5-6's (3.17/7), they express a clear desire for a *Colourful school* (4.94/7) on the ideal level. The same pattern is present among the secondary college students with the factual level of the *Colourful School* at 3.66/7 and the normative reading 4.86/7. A similar trend is also noted for the *Colourless*

School with primary school students expressing a desire for this model (4.59/7) where currently their school Is resistant to it (3.17/7). Likewise for the secondary college students although it is currently less resisted in their school (3.41/7) their desire is similar to that of their younger counterparts (4.50/7). The year 5-6's have a high level of *Relativism* (5.04/7) which continues to increase among the year 7-12's (5.16/7). A high level of *External Critique* is also present among both primary school (4.14/7) and secondary college (4.09/7) students.

Literal Belief is opposed with scores of 3.05/7 at primary level and 2.58/7 at secondary level. *Reconfessionalisation* is strongly opposed at primary level (2.35/7) where it is factually somewhat recognised (4.13/7). Among the secondary college group *Reconfessionalisation* is perceived to be less present factually (4.04/7) but similarly resisted as on the primary level (2.31/7). The *Monologue School* is not factually recognised in either primary or secondary college (3.75/7, 3.37/7 respectively) and is strongly resisted on the normative level (2.48/7 in primary school), particularly among the secondary college students (2.22/7).

As has been noted *Post-Critical Belief* decreases among the secondary college group from 3.44/7 at primary level to 3.20/7. Although there is recognition of *Recontextualisation* in their current schools (4.33/7 in year 5-6 and 4.44/7 in year 7-12), it is opposed normatively among both groups (4.33/7 and 4.40/7 respectively), with the secondary college students recognising more *Recontextualisation* in their school than their primary school counterparts while also expressing greater resistance normatively. The students in the primary school group recognise their school currently as a *Dialogue School* (4.61/7) but resist this model on the ideal level (3.81/7). The secondary college students have a higher recognition of a *Dialogue School* factually (4.73/7) but similarly resist it on the normative level (3.77/7).

While there are similarities among those in this *Subpopulation* from both the primary and secondary college groups, for example their strong resistance against a *Monologue School*, certain trends can also be discerned. To that end one notes a decreasing *Post-Critical Belief*, decreasing *Literal Belief,* growing desire for *Secularisation*, increasing *Relativism* and a growing resistance against a *Monologue School*. Yet in general the students are more or less consistent from year 5-6 to years 7-12, in terms of scale results. The most notable dynamic is the rapidly increasing numbers falling into this *Subpopulation*, which increases exponentially as the students age; 10.2% in year 5-6, 28.2% in year 7-8, 38.2% in year 9-10 and 43% in year 11-12.

Hence it is observed that in relation to the adult group the student group express more pronounced characteristics of this *Secularisation Subpopulation*.

Primary school – secondary school comparison

To speak in broad terms, Catholic primary schools in Victoria often tend to be small and localised, attracting Catholic families to send their Catholic children there. Hence one does not expect to find a large-scale tendency which goes against the notion of a faith based education. Compare this situation to that of secondary colleges, which have a tendency to be much larger and are hence more centrally located and attract a more diverse student population from a wider geographical area. Students commonly travel longer distances to their secondary college, due to both necessity (from rural areas) and by choice (for reasons of quality, etc.). Students more commonly come into contact with students from different areas, religions, cultures, diverse backgrounds and so forth. One thus expects a different population demographic that might effect a larger tendency towards *Secularisation*.

When one juxtaposes the primary and secondary school groups as a whole, it is fair to say that there is a clear trend towards this *Subpopulation* in terms of number of adherents, and within this group its characteristics become somewhat more pronounced at the secondary college level. Concretely this means a decreasing *Post-Critical Belief*, increased resistance to *Reconfessionalisation* and a decreasing desire for a *Dialogue School*. While other key traits remain constant with high scores for non-believing stances, pro-*Institutional Secularisation* against a *Monologue School* and pro-*Colourful* and *Colourless Schools*.

In conjunction with this, as earlier observed, the students are also more pronounced in their views, for instance the adults show a desire for *Recontextualisation* while students actively resist. This feeds into the general conclusion that the students are more extreme in their expression of this *Secularisation Subpopulation*. Students, especially secondary college students, are more questioning and asking: "Why? Why the need for this Catholic identity? Why is it important? Why should it affect my life? Why should I care?"

Generally this group prefers a non-Catholic school but being in a Catholic school, they are nonetheless unwilling to contribute to its Catholic identity. Instead, they prefer to *Secularise* their school, turning it into a *Colourful* or even a *Colourless* environment. This observation is supported by a strong rejection of *Reconfessionalising* and *Monologue school* tendencies. While the schools are perceived to be *Dialogue School* environments that attempt to *Recontextualise* the Catholic faith while still employing a large amount of *Christian Values Education*, these people express doubt and suspicion of these school identity models.

It is important to see that even these non-religious school members are willing and able to contribute to the dialogue between Catholic identity and plural culture – though in this dialogue they choose the side of secular culture. Having this minority *Subpopulation* present in Catholic schools need not be counterproductive per se. As long as there is an openness to acknowledging the value of religion and a willingness to enter into conversation with it, these people could play a valuable role as critical representatives of secular culture. However, when *Reconfessionalising* tendencies attempt to 'recuperate' the non-religious people in this *Subpopulation*, their resistance will become more outspoken and could turn against Catholic school identity. This leads to the need to *Recontextualise* more authentically and more clearly. Students would be open to *Recontextualisation* if schools truly *Recontextualise* in a proper and plausible manner.

Subpopulation 2. An active strategy of *Re-confessionalisation*

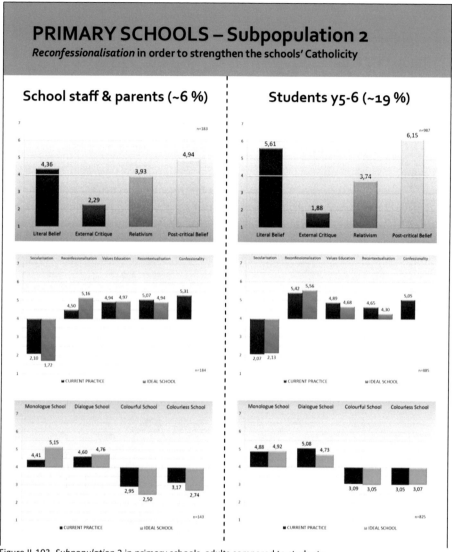

Figure II-103. *Subpopulation* 2 in primary schools, adults compared to students.

About 6.0% of the adults in primary schools are part of this *Subpopulation*:
- Teachers: about 5.2% (1 in 20)
- School leadership: about 4.9% (1 in 20)
- Parents: about 7.0% (1 in 14)

About 19.3% of the students in year 5-6 are part of this *Subpopulation*:
- Primary school children year 5-6: about 19.3% (1 in 5)

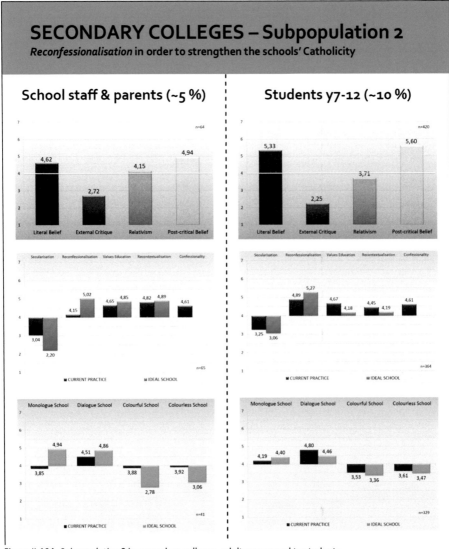

Figure II-104. *Subpopulation* 2 in secondary colleges, adults compared to students.

About 5.3% of the adults in secondary colleges are part of this *Subpopulation*:
- Teachers: about 5.4% (1 in 19)
- School leadership: about 4.9% (1 in 20)
- Parents: about 5.6% (1 in 18)

About 10.2% of the students in year 7-12 are part of this *Subpopulation*:
- Secondary college students year 7-8: about 14.2% (1 in 7)
- Secondary college students year 9-10: about 8.0% (2 in 25)
- Secondary college students year 11-12: about 7.0% (1 in 14)

People who show a consistent attraction to the second *Subpopulation* prefer *Reconfessionalisation* and mono-correlative *Christian Values Education* in order to strengthen their school's Catholicity. They have little appreciation for dialogue with plurality, rather they are rooted in a strong personal Catholic identity and wish to maintain and if necessary re-establish a clearly recognisable, tradition minded Catholic school identity.

Adults

About 6.0% of the adult respondents from the primary schools group (that is to say 1 in every 17) are part of this *Subpopulation*; specifically this represents 5.2% of teachers (1 in 20), 4.9% of those in school leadership (1 in 20) and 7.0% of parents or 1 in every 14 parents. There is a very slight decline in numbers of adults falling into this category among the secondary college group. Some 5.3% of the adults, or 1 in 19, surveyed as part of the secondary college research fit into this *Subpopulation*. Specifically this represents 5.4% of teachers (1 in 19), 4.9% of school leadership (1 in 20) and 5.6% of parents (1 in 18). Hence the slight overall decline in this group at the secondary college level is attributed to the 1.4% decrease in the parent group, which fell from 7.0% to 5.6%.

A high level of *Literal Belief* is very prominent among the primary school adult group (4.36/7) and increases even further among the secondary college group (4.62/7). A strong desire for their school to become a *Reconfessionalising School* is expressed (5.16/7 in the primary school where it is also factually acknowledged with a score of 4.50/7 and 5.02/7 in the secondary college where it is also slightly factually present with a score of 4.15/7). Characteristics of a *Monologue School* are recognised on the factual level in the primary school (4.41/7) but are not in the secondary college (3.85/7), however both groups express a clear desire for this school type on the ideal level (5.15/7 and 4.94/7 respectively). The primary school group recognise a very high level of *Confessionality* in their school (5.31/7) and although on a much lower level, so too do their secondary college counterparts (4.61/7).

A very strong resistance against *Secularisation* is currently expressed among the primary school group (2.10/7) while an even greater resistance is desired on the ideal level (1.72/7). A corresponding trend is noticeable among their secondary college counterparts although to a much lesser degree, with the factual resistance at 3.04/7 and the ideal at 2.20/7. The primary school group exhibit a very clear rejection of the *Colourful School* on the factual (2.95/7) and the ideal level (2.50). This is echoed somewhat less definitively among their secondary college counterparts, with a factual resistance of 3.53/7 and an ideal resistance of 3.36/7. A similar pattern is present with regard to the *Colourless School* with 3.17/7 factual and 2.74/7 ideal resistance among the primary school group and 3.61/7 factual and 3.47/7 ideal resistance among their secondary college counterparts. Correspondingly both groups are against the non-believing stance of *External Critique* (2.29/7 for the primary and 2.72/7 for the secondary college adult group). The other non-believing stance of *Relativism* is scored at an essentially neutral 3.93/7 and 4.15/7 respectively. Given that this is the culturally dominant pattern the results, which flirt with the neutral line, are significantly lower than an expected norm. Hence one might suggest that those in this *Subpopulation* are somewhat doubtful of diversity, not overly aware of contingency and are not particularly open towards change. They tend to have a fixed view of one particular outlook or lifestyle that is preferential and are not really interested in other views.

A positive and consistent result for *Post-Critical Belief* is noted, with both groups scoring 4.94/7. This will serve a positive interpretation of both *Recontextualisation* and *Reconfessionalisation*. A *Dialogue School* model is recognised in both groups (4.60/7 and 4.80/7 respectively), with a greater desire for a *Dialogue School* expressed by the primary school group (4.76/7) while the secondary college adult group are less enthusiastic on the ideal level (4.86/7). This shift towards a decreasing desire for a *Dialogue School* is interesting in that it expresses a decreasing willingness to engage with the 'other'. While this *Subpopulation* agrees with some aspects of a *Dialogue School* their support is not so genuine, as it does not serve their *Reconfessionalising* goal, hence a decrease on the secondary college level is noted, while at the primary school level it is dwarfed by tendencies towards a *Monologue School*.

Once these two groups of primary school staff and parents are juxtaposed alongside the secondary college adult group certain trends begin to emerge. In particular a decreasing resistance to *Secularisation* is noted although it still remains a strong resistance. This gives primary schools a stronger position in which to *Reconfessionalise* and according to the data they do this with more successful vigour than their secondary college counterparts (factual level of *Reconfessionalisation* is 4.50/7 in primary school compared to 4.15/7 in secondary college). Their desire for continued *Reconfessionalisation* is also higher on the ideal level. There is increasing openness to a *Dialogue School* among the secondary college group; which interpreted in tandem with the high factual and ideal level of *Monologue School* at primary level shows that they are less open to diversity than their secondary college counterparts. The primary school group seem somewhat content to enjoy their singularity amidst the bubble of the *Monologue School*. Resistance against both *Colourful* and *Colourless School* types decreases among the secondary college group. It is hence evident that primary schools are more radical in their *Reconfessionalisation* tendencies overall.

Students

To begin it is evident that there is a large core of support among the year 5-6 students for this *Reconfessionalising Subpopulation* with 19.3%, or 1 in 5, of year 5-6 students falling into this bracket. But as the students age they move away from this grouping at a rapid rate, with 10.2%, or 1 in 10, falling into this category at secondary college. The continuous decline is more evident once the students are broken into their year groups with 14.2%, or 1 in 7, year 7-8's falling into this category, 8.0%, or 2 in 25, of year 9-10's and finally the lowest level of 7.0%, or 1 in 14, among the year 11-12's. These figures are representative of a cohort of students who live in the safety of the Church-school world. They tend to be very proud of their own and their school's Catholic identity (which in itself is a positive characteristic). It is often true that some adults project their preference to these students, who have a desire to please their parents or superiors, and hence fall into this trend as a result. It is hence interesting to note that as the students grow older the number falling into this category comes very much into line with that of their parents (7.0% of year 11-12's compared to 5.6% of parents).

The students in the primary school group exhibit a very high level of *Literal Belief* (5.61/7) and *Post-Critical Belief* (6.15/7). The high level on both demonstrates that at their young age the students do not differentiate between symbolic and non-symbolic belief and hence give assent to any creedal or belief statement. A similar pattern is true for the secondary college group albeit on a somewhat reduced level of extremity (5.33/7 for *Literal Belief* and 5.60/7 for *Post-Critical Belief*). This suggests that among his group there is still significant room for the growth of *Literal Belief* into a mature understanding of *Post-Critical Belief*. The students at primary school strongly recognise on-going *Reconfessionalisation* in their school (5.42/7) and desire even more of it on the ideal level (5.56/7). So too with the secondary college group if in a less enthusiastic manner, *Reconfessionalisation* is clearly their first preference on the factual level (4.99/7) and on the ideal level (5.27/7). Going hand in hand with this option is the recognition of (4.88/7) and desire for (4.92/7) a *Monologue School*. Again the same pattern in a less enthusiastic manner is evident among secondary college students (4.19/7 and 4.40/7 respectively).

There is definitive rejection of *External Critique* among the primary students (1.88/7) and the secondary college students (2.25/7). The primary students very strongly resist *Secularisation* on the factual (2.07/7) and the ideal (2.13/7) level. For the secondary college students they recognise the factual need to resist *Secularisation* (3.25/7) and desire a stronger resistance in the future (3.06/7). As a consequence both *Colourful* (3.09/7 factual, 3.05/7 ideal) and *Colourless* (3.05/7 factual, 3.07/7 ideal) *Schools* are resisted among the primary school students. Again a similar milder pattern is noted among the secondary students (*Colourful School* 3.53/7 and *Colourless School* 3.61/7

244

on the factual level), although the resistance to both school types increases on the ideal level (3.36/7 and 3.47/7 respectively).

The student's recognise *Recontextualisation* efforts present in their schools (primary students 4.65/7, secondary students 4.45/7) and although this decreases on the ideal level there is still an openness expressed towards *Recontextualisation* (primary students 4.30/7, secondary students 4.19/7). It is proposed that this level of openness expressed as *Recontextualisation* can be used as a tool to ultimately *Reconfessionalise* further. A similar reason can be attributed to the recognition of the *Dialogue School* factually (primary students 5.08/7, secondary students 4.80/7) and the continued openness towards it although support decreases on the normative level (primary students 4.73/7, secondary students 4.46/7).

Comparing these two groups of primary school students and secondary college students one can observe that the characteristics of this *Subpopulation* are much more pronounced among primary school students where things appear to be viewed more in black and white. Concretely they are more opposed to *Secularisation,* have a higher level of *Confessionality*, a greater desire for a *Monologue School,* a higher level of *Literal Belief* and a higher level of *Reconfessionalisation*. Secondary colleges have all these desires but have the sharp corners filed off so to speak as they come into contact with an even increasing diversity. It is natural that their desires are still clear but they must be applied in a softer manner due to the nature of their environment. Yet to this end there is still a decreasing openness towards *Recontextualisation* and a decreasing desire for a *Dialogue School* expressed among the secondary college students.

In relation to the adults the students have remarkably similar expressions of desire in regards to the way forward in *Reconfessionalising* Catholic school identity. Worthy of note is the students much lower recognition and desire for *Recontextualisation* hence hinting that *Recontextualisation* is not well communicated to the students. Although also in this vein as has been suggested earlier they use it as a vehicle to *Reconfessionalise.* Particularly strong *Literal Believing* tendencies are shared and although the adults' scores are lower than that of the students, this is to be expected in older adults, and still represents a high value.

Primary – secondary school comparison
The primary difference to be noted between the primary school group as a whole taken against their secondary college counterparts is the number falling into this category with the numbers of students identified in this *Subpopulation* having halved and a decrease is also evident among the adult group. This represents a general shift away from this perspective on Catholic identity in schools. As has been noted above the

primary school as a whole expresses more intensively and radically this position and it softens on the level of the secondary college. The secondary college adults and students have all the desires of their primary school counterparts but have the sharp corners filed off so to speak as they come into contact with an even increasing diversity. It is natural that their desires are still clear but they must be applied in a softer manner due to the nature of their environment.

It is clear that the adults and students in this *Subpopulation* have a strong passion for Catholic identity and reject any notion of *Secularisation*, whether it be *Colourful* or *Colourless*. On the whole, they take a defensive and restorative stand, desiring to combat the rising *Secularisation* that is targeting the schools. They believe that the downfall should be stopped and the movement turned around: Catholic schools should be 'truly Catholic' again. Among these people, there is little taste for hermeneutics (there is no need for interpretation), little search for truth (since they believe they have found it already), and little tradition development (tradition should be kept unaffected by change). The answers to the questions of life are already known; there is no need for a conversation with alterity or a search for the truth.

This group believes that Catholic schools are part of the Church and share its mission: to spread the Gospel in the world today. To do so, schools should open their doors and invite all those who are willing to accept the Word of God. "Come and see for yourself what it means to be Catholic today. The Catholic faith has lots to offer, and you will discover that it is for you as well." However, they are wavering between openness and hospitality on the one hand, which is expressed as a high score for the *Dialogue School*, and a protective and restorative stand on the other, which is expressed as a positive and rising score for the *Monologue School*. When today's plural culture is concerned, they are caught in a tension between hospitality and suspicion. Should 'non-Catholics' be considered a potential opportunity or a potential threat?

They believe in a mono-correlative *Christian Values Education* didactics with a clear *Reconfessionalising* agenda. They wish to appeal to the hearts and minds of present-day students in order to bring them closer to the Catholic faith, away from other views or life styles. Plurality is either denied, avoided, enclosed or tolerated only to a certain level. The 'dialogue' tends to be *Kerygmatic* in nature; it is unidirectional communication rather than a mutual encounter. It tends to exclude those that do not fit into the pre-established framework. Ultimately, views and practices that are not compatible with Catholicism do not belong in a Catholic school – in extremis, it could even threaten a genuine Catholic school project.

Among the adult respondents, this is a minority group that has a strong influence, nonetheless. Primary school children, especially those who have adopted a strong *Literal Believing* attitude, support an unambiguous *Reconfessionalisation* of their school. The student respondent groups are at least as strong in this identity option, compared with the adults. In opposition to the adults, they do not really see the need to enter into an active dialogue with plurality in order to present the Catholic faith hence a fading support for *Recontextualisation*.

Subpopulation 3. *Recontextualisation* of Catholic school identity

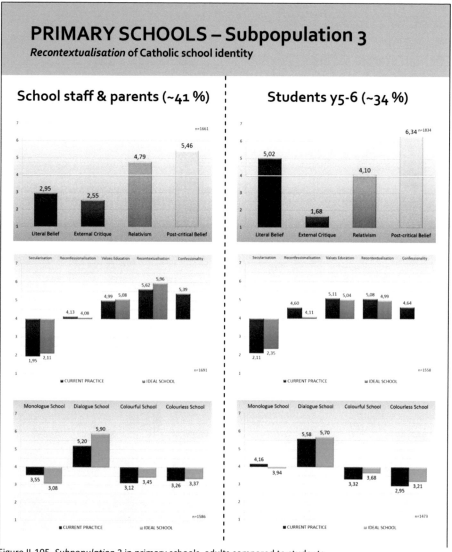

Figure II-105. *Subpopulation* 3 in primary schools, adults compared to students.

About 41.3% of the adults in primary schools are part of this *Subpopulation*:
- Teachers: about 41.6% (5 in 12)
- School leadership: about 53.3% (8 in 15)
- Parents: about 36.8% (3 in 8)

About 34.3% of the students in year 5-6 are part of this *Subpopulation*:
- Primary school children year 5-6: about 34.3% (1 in 3)

248

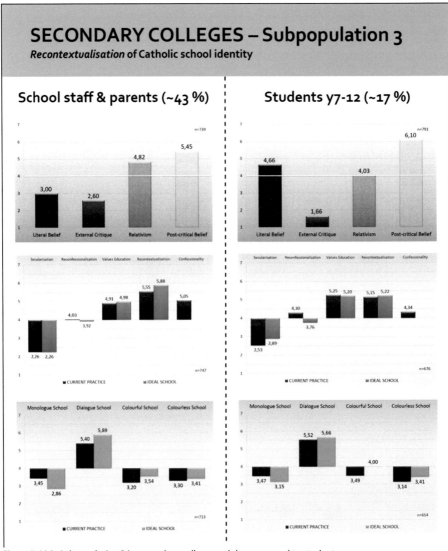

Figure II-106. *Subpopulation* 3 in secondary colleges, adults compared to students.

About 43.5% of the adults in secondary colleges are part of this *Subpopulation*:
- Teachers: about 44.0% (4 in 9)
- School leadership: about 53.3% (8 in 15)
- Parents: about 36.0% (4 in 11)

About 17.5% of the students in year 7-12 are part of this *Subpopulation*:
- Secondary college students year 7-8: about 21.1% (3 in 14)
- Secondary college students year 9-10: about 16.2% (1 in 6)
- Secondary college students year 11-12: about 13.7% (3 in 22)

This *Subpopulation* contains those who have a consistent attraction to a *Recontextualisation* of Catholic school identity, though many are still strongly rooted in *Christian Values Education* didactics.

Adults

About 41.3% of the adult respondents from the primary schools group (that is to say 5 in every 12) are part of this *Subpopulation*; this is a significant proportion and hence is an important *Subpopulation* to analyse. Specifically this group represents 41.6% of teachers (5 in 12), 53.3% of those in school leadership (8 in 15) and 36.8% of parents or 3 in every 8 parents. A similar number of adults (43.5%, or 4 in 9) fall into this category among the adults in the secondary college group, with an again similar breakdown among the constituent groups: 44.0%, or 4 in 9, of teachers, 53.3%, or 8 in 15, of school leadership and 36.0%, or 4 in 11, of parents. With over half of the members of school leadership falling into this category one can see the direction which schools are most likely to be guided in. While a much smaller, although still significant, number of parents are part of this *Subpopulation*.

It seems obvious that the primary characteristic of this *Subpopulation* is a very high level of *Recontextualisation*. For the adults in the primary school group this score is 5.62/7 with an increasing desire expressed on the normative level of 5.96/7. Adults in the secondary college grouping have a similar factual score of 5.55/7 with a shared increasing desire expressed as 5.88/7. The next main characteristic is strong support for a *Dialogue School,* which is evidenced in both groups factually (5.20/7 and 5.40/7 respectively) and normatively (5.90/7 and 5.89/7 respectively). This expresses a huge leap in terms of increased desire on the ideal level. Hand in hand with these developments goes a high level of *Post-Critical Belief* which is 5.46/7 among the primary school group of adults and 5.45/7 among the adults linked to the secondary colleges. This is combined with a positive level of *Relativism* (4.79/7 and 4.82/7 respectively), which can be interpreted as a healthier *Awareness of Contingency,* or awareness of other life options while still priding one's own approach. In this case the *Literal Belief* of these adults (2.95/7 and 3.00/7 respectively) does not work towards *Relativism* but towards offering a firm grounding in an *Awareness of Contingency.*

There is a recognition of *Confessionality* in the schools of these adults with the primary school noting a higher level (5.39/7) than that of the secondary colleges (5.05/7). *Secularisation* is very strongly and consistently resisted factually (1.96/7 in the primary school group and 2.26/7 in the secondary colleges group) and normatively (2.11/7 and 2.26/7 respectively). There is currently resistance to both a *Colourful* (3.12/7 and 3.20/7 respectively) and *Colourless* (3.26/7 and 3.30/7 respectively) *School* model in both primary schools and secondary colleges with only a slight increase in resistance on the ideal level (3.45/7 and 3.53/7 respectively for a *Colourful School* and 3.37/7 and 3.41/7 respectively for a *Colourless School*). In itself a slight decreasing score for a *Colourful School* is not particularly harmful as long as it is represented by only a minority subgroup and in the context of all the strong positive characteristics expressed above. A greater caveat is attached to the *Colourless School, which* is opposed to and hinders true dialogue that is so essential for this *Recontextualising* model. It is very important to avoid *Colourless* tendencies and it is important that that this group are made aware of the dangers of this perspective.

An almost neutral overall score on *Reconfessionalising* at both primary and secondary level factually (4.13/7 and 4.03/7 respectively) and normatively (4.08/8 and 3.92/7 respectively) demonstrates a neutral stance towards *Reconfessionalisation.* Yet it is often the case that in a modern and fairly secular secondary college environment there is a need to insert some *Confessional* elements, but this should be done in a *Recontextualising* manner. To this end it is important to remember that occasionally one needs to introduce *Reconfessionalising* moments so that there is something of substance and import to *Recontextualise.* The *Monologue School* is resisted in both primary schools (3.55/7) and secondary colleges (3.45) with resistance significantly increasing among the adult groups on the normative level (3.08/7 and 2.86/7 respectively). This increasing resistance to a *Monologue School* is a positive trend and leaves the door open for increasing support for a *Dialogue School,* a trend which was noted earlier.

A high level of *Christian Values Education* is recognised on the factual level in both the primary schools (4.99/7) and in the secondary colleges (4.91/7) with a desire expressed to see further *Christian Values Education* in the future (5.08/7 and 4.98/7 respectively). It is very important that a warning be offered in this regard. Even though *Christian Values Education* is the second preference to *Recontextualisation* its score is high enough to warrant a caution. The key problem with embracing *Christian Values Education* is that it reduces the Christian message to universal human values that can easily be disconnected from the Christian story. So while it supports a Catholic ethos in the short term it 'hollows out' the foundation and core of Catholic education in the long term, replacing it instead with a secular value system. This is discussed at more length under the next *Subpopulation.* The approach of *Christian Values Education* is in sharp contrast to an authentic *Recontextualisation*, which creates a deeper, more complex interaction between life and faith.

In general the adult groups associated with the primary schools and secondary colleges exhibit the same characteristics as have been discussed above; a high level of *Recontextualisation* and strong support for a *Dialogue School,* supported by a strong level of *Post-Critical Belief,* a resistance to Secularisation and a similar resistance for a *Monologue, Colourful and Colourless School.* Variations from this pattern are a slightly higher level of appreciation for *Reconfessionalisation*, a stronger resistance to *Secularisation* and slightly more resistance for a *Monologue School.*

Students

About 34.3% of the students in year 5-6 from the primary schools group (that is to say 1 in every 3) are part of this *Subpopulation*. Worryingly the number of students falling into this category decreases by a half once we examine the figures for students in secondary college. Some 17.5% of secondary college students, or 3 in 17, surveyed as part of the secondary college research fit into this *Subpopulation*. A rather notable trend can be discerned which shows a constant decrease in the numbers of students falling into this *Subpopulation* as they age. Beginning from the level of 34.3% (1 in 3) among the year 5-6's in primary school, the numbers in this *Recontextualisation Subpopulation* fall significantly upon their move to secondary college, with 21.1% (3 in 14) among the year 7-8 students falling into this *Subpopulation*. This decreases steadily to 16.2% (1 in 6) among the year 9-10's and again decreases to 13.7%, or 3 in 22, among the year 11-12's. Hence one observes a significant and steady migration out of this *Subpopulation* as student's age; with a particularly large leap made during the liminal moment of moving from primary to secondary college.

Students in primary school demonstrate a very high level of *Post-Critical Belief* (6.34/7), which only decreases slightly among the secondary college students (6.10/7). This is linked to a neutral level of *Relativism/Awareness of Contingency* among the primary children (4.10/7) and is similar to that of the secondary college students (4.03/7). In primary school the students recognise a high level of *Recontextualisation* (5.08/7), as do their secondary college cotemporaries (5.15/7). Interestingly, among the primary students their support drops somewhat on the ideal level to 4.99/7 whereas on the secondary level it increases to 5.22/7. There is a strong preference for a *Dialogue School* expressed among the primary students (5.58/7) and their secondary college counterparts (5.52/7) with both groups expressing an increased desire on the normative level (5.70/7 and 5.66/7 respectively).

A particularly strong resistance to *External Critique* is noted (1.68/7 for primary children and 1.66/7 for secondary students). Naturally a corresponding strong resistance to *Secularisation* is expressed among the primary students currently (2.11/7) with a slight increase in resistance expressed on the ideal level (2.35/7). A similar slight decreasing resistance is observable among the secondary college students whose results fall from 2.53/7 to 2.89/7. Resistance is expressed for the *Colourful School* (3.32/7 in primary school and 3.49/7 in secondary colleges), with a slight decrease for the primary children on the ideal level (3.68/7) but a total decrease in resistance for the students in secondary colleges (4.00/7). The *Colourless School* is resisted by both student groups (2.95/7 and 3.14/7 respectively) with resistance decreasing for both on the ideal level (3.21/7 and 3.41/7 respectively).

A high level of *Literal Belief* (5.02/7 for primary children and 4.66/7 for secondary students) goes hand in hand with the high level of *Post-Critical Belief* in that it is often the case that young students cannot differentiate between literal and symbolic belief, but it is positive that *Post-Critical Belief* remains the highest. A positive level of *Reconfessionalisation* is factually present among both primary (4.60/7) and secondary (4.30/7) students, but decreases in both cases; to 4.11/7 for the former and to a negative and resistant 3.76/7 for the latter. A certain amount of *Reconfessionalisation* is needed to achieve the goal of *Recontextualisation* in that there needs to be something of substance present before it can be re-imagined in a new context, that being said it is not a goal in itself. In the primary school the perception of and desire for a *Monologue School* skirts around the neutral level (4.16/7 factually and 3.94/7 normatively). This is in contrast to the secondary school students who resist a *Monologue School* factually (3.47/7) and express increasing resistance on the ideal level (3.15/7).

Christian Values Education is still very prominent among both groups. The primary children acknowledge their school is a *Christian Values* school (5.11/7) and show only a slight drop in support on the ideal level (5.04/7). So too for the secondary students who recognise *Christian Values Education* as their schools main choice (5.25/7) with only a slight decrease in support on the normative level (5.20/7). Again, as mentioned above, this is a dangerous trend as it will ultimately draw good intentioned student's into purely *Christian Values Education* thinking.

In terms of differentiating between the adults and students one observes a significantly lower level of support for *Recontextualisation* among the students than the adults. This is a situation requiring an adequate response in terms of educating the students to the advantages of *Recontextualisation*. This decreased level of support for *Recontextualisation* among the students also has the effect of making *Christian Values Education* the first preference option for the students. The student's higher level of *Literal Belief* is the final major difference. Otherwise a similar pattern of expression can be discerned.

Primary-secondary comparison

In comparing the primary and secondary school overall results a key difference is that among the student groups the secondary school has a more pronounced expression of the main characteristics than the primary school, while among the adult groups very little deviation can be noted.

Similarly high levels of support for a *Dialogue School* are present across all groups and schools, so too is the strong resistance against *Secularisation*, a strong *Post-Critical Belief*, a resistance against (even if somewhat decreasing) both *Colourful* and *Colourless Schools*. A deviation from this trend is noticeable among the students in the secondary colleges who have no resistance against the *Colourful School* and a lower and decreasing level of *Secularisation*. A certain cohort within this *Subpopulation* group are migrating towards *Subpopulation 1 (Secularisation)* and this is evidenced from the ever increasing number considered part of this *Subpopulation* plus the presence of certain distinct trends. These movements between *Subpopulations* will be discussed later at a greater length.

In this *Subpopulation*, two qualities are combined: a strong religious awareness and the desire to maintain a recognisable Catholic school identity on the one hand, and a genuine openness for the religious and philosophical diversity people bring to the school and a corresponding desire for tolerance, solidarity and respect of the other. These people wish to *Recontextualise* Catholic school identity in the middle of pluralising Australian culture today. If the Catholic faith is to remain authentic and meaningful for people today and tomorrow, we need to revitalise its original religious, ethical and social inspiration in a new context and look for new, original, contemporary ways to do this.

These people are standing, so to speak, with one foot in the Christian tradition and with the other foot in a yet unwritten future. They are writing a new paragraph in the book of the Christian story, while continuously re-reading the previous chapters. Rooted in the past they shape the present in the light of the future – the light of God's eschatological dream with humankind that is yet to come but in which we already participate today.

Although the profile shown in the above scale results comes very close to the normative-theological preference defended by the research, it is to be noted that the people who belong to this *Subpopulation* are still strongly rooted in *Christian Values Education*: the *Values Education* scores are rather high. Driven by the circumstances that surround them, many have to take part in the *Kerygmatic* type of Dialogue. Nevertheless, their intention is to evolve further in the direction of a *Recontextualisation* of Catholic school identity. It is important to support this *Subpopulations* cultural analysis and theological position, and enable them to continue to foster the creative tension between faith and culture, between continuity and discontinuity, between past manifestations of Catholicism and eschatological promises.

Subpopulation 4. Trends of *Christian Values Education*

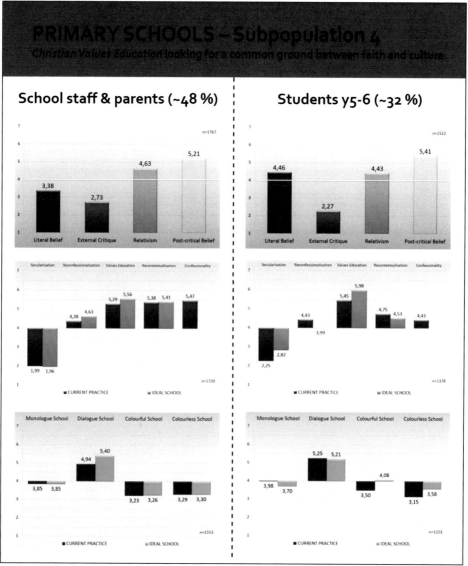

Figure II-107. *Subpopulation* 4 in primary schools, adults compared to students.

About 47.6% of the adults in primary schools are part of this *Subpopulation*:
- Teachers: about 48.4% (1 in 2)
- School leadership: about 37.6% (3 in 8)
- Parents: about 50.7% (1 in 2)

About 32.3% of the students in year 5-6 are part of this *Subpopulation*:
- Primary school children year 5-6: about 32.3% (1 in 3)

256

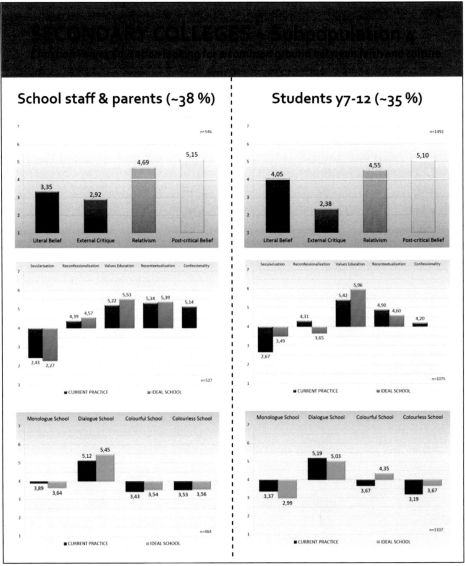

Figure II-108. *Subpopulation* 4 in secondary colleges, adults compared to students.

About 37.5% of the adults in secondary colleges are part of this *Subpopulation*:
- Teachers: about 33.7% (1 in 3)
- School leadership: about 34.9% (1 in 3)
- Parents: about 46.2% (6 in 13)

About 34.5% of the students in year 7-12 are part of this *Subpopulation*:
- Secondary college students year 7-8: about 33.8% (1 in 3)
- Secondary college students year 9-10: about 36.0% (3 in 8)
- Secondary college students year 11-12: about 34.0% (1 in 3)

People in this *Subpopulation* show a consistent attraction to *Christian Values Education*. They are looking for a common ground between faith and culture, often at the cost of Catholic particularity. There is a need to be aware of the potentially *Secularising* effects of this *Christian Values Education* approach.

Adults

Finally one arrives at the most densely populated *Subpopulation*. Some 47.6% of the adult respondents from the primary schools group (that is to say 9 in every 19 or very close to half) are part of this *Subpopulation*; specifically this represents 48.4% of teachers (1 in 2), 37.6% of those in school leadership (3 in 8) and 50.4% of parents or 1 in every 2 parents. Noteworthy is that the school leadership are present in this *Subpopulation* to a lesser extent than parents and teachers; with the majority of members of school leadership falling into the *Recontextualisation Subpopulation*. There is a rather significant decline in numbers of adults falling into this category among the secondary college group; some ten percentage points overall. 37.5% of the adults, or 3 in 8, surveyed as part of the secondary college research fit into this *Subpopulation*. Specifically this represents 33.7% of teachers (1 in 3), 34.9% of school leadership (1 in 3) and 46.2% of parents (6 in 13). Hence the overall decline of ten percentage points in this group at the secondary college level is mostly attributed to a drop if fifteen percentage points in the teacher group. It is proposed that as secondary school teachers recognise that *Christian Values Education* is working less effectively they also try less in this vein and a sizeable portion shift their didactic approach. In the next section this pattern of change will be discussed.

Naturally this *Subpopulation* presents with a high level of *Christian Values Education* with the primary school group of adults scoring a factual 5.29/7 with increased desire expressed on the normative level (5.56/7). These figures are mirrored among the secondary colleges adult group with the current level at 5.22/7 and the ideal at 5.53/7. This high level of *Christian Values Education* searches for the middle ground between faith and culture, seeking to attach values to the Christian faith, and demonstrate this particular expression of Christianity to the world and within the school context.

A high level of *Recontextualisation* is also noted with a factually high level of 5.38/7 and 5.34/7 respectively, with a slight increase in desire on the normative level (5.42/7 and 5.39/7 respectively). This expresses that this *Subpopulation* also has a clear *Recontextualising* desire. This is supported by a high *Post-Critical Belief* of 5.21/7 among the adult group at the primary school and 5.19/7 for the adults among the secondary colleges group. Correspondingly a positive appreciation for a *Dialogue School* is noted (4.94/7 and 5.12/7 respectively), with an even greater desire expressed on the normative level (5.40/7 and 5.45/7 respectively).

A positive value for *Reconfessionalisation* is expressed in the primary school (4.38/7) and the secondary college (4.39/7) group, with an increased desire on the normative level expressed by both (4.63/7 and 4.57/7 respectively). This *Reconfessionalising* tendency is supported by a higher than normal level of *Literal Belief* (3.38/7 among the primary school group and 3.35/7 in the secondary colleges group). Their attitude to a *Monologue School* is mixed with scores just sitting below the neutral position (3.85/7 factually and normatively in the primary school group with a factual 3.89/7 and a normative 3.64/7 in the secondary colleges group). As such a relatively strong *Reconfessionalising* undercurrent is also discerned in this *Subpopulation*. Later a pattern of intention of movement away from this *Subpopulation* to that of the second *Reconfessionalising Subpopulation* will be noted, although this only effects a small cohort of this overall *Subpopulation*. It will be demonstrated that although the intention upholds that *Christian Values Education* is the best way to *Reconfessionalise* Catholic school identity and make it plausible, in reality this is an illusion as, in reality, a *Secularising* trend results.

A high level of *Confessionality* is noted, especially among the primary school group (5.47/7), although the secondary colleges also score a high 5.14/7, it also represents a decrease worthy of note. A high level of *Confessionality* is required to support *Christian Values Education* in order that there is enough creedal faith expressed which can have values attached and joined in a neutral manner to the surrounding culture and context. If the level of *Confessionality* declines so too does the success of *Christian Values Education*.

Secularisation is strongly opposed among the primary school group (1.99/7 factually and 1.96/7 normatively). This sentiment is echoed, albeit to a lesser extent, in the secondary colleges (2.43/7 factually and 2.27/7 normatively). This decreasing resistance to *Secularisation* is a negative step and is further supported by an increasing appreciation for the non-believing stances, particularly *External Critique* (2.73/7 in primary school increasing to 2.92/7 in the secondary colleges). Likewise *Relativism* shows a slight increase from the primary school (4.63/7) to the secondary colleges (4.69/7) group. *Colourful* and *Colourless Schools* are resisted across the board among the primary school group (*Colourful*: 3.23/7 factually and 3.26/7 normatively, *Colourless* 3.29/7 factually and 3.30/7 normatively), while the same pattern is reproduced with a decreased resistance among in the secondary colleges (*Colourful*: 3.43/7 factually and 3.54/7 normatively, *Colourless* 3.53/7 factually and 3.56/7 normatively).

Overall the trends of increasing support for *Christian Values Education,* decreasing *Confessionality,* decreasing resistance to *Secularisation* and decreased resistance to both *Colourful* and *Colourless Schools* can be observed when comparing the these two groups of adults across the primary and secondary school groups.

Students
Although this *Subpopulation* is less popular than among the adults a very sizeable portion of students are part of this *Subpopulation* with 32.3%, or 1 in 3, of year 5-6 students falling into this bracket. As the students age and move to secondary school

the size of this group remains sees a slight increase, with 34.5%, or 1 in 3, falling into this category at secondary college. Once the students are divided into their year groups one notes a gradual small increase until the year 9-10's with a slight drop among the year 11-12's, with 33.8%, or 1 in 3, year 7-8's falling into this category, 36.0%, or 3 in 8, of year 9-10's and finally 34.0%, or 1 in 3, among the year 11-12's. At secondary school a similar number of students fall into this *Subpopulation* as teachers and school leadership, it is only the parents who are present in this group in larger lumbers.

While a high appreciation of *Christian Values Education* is currently expressed among both primary and secondary school students (5.45/7 and 5.42/7 respectively) a significant jump in enthusiasm in noted on the normative level (5.98/7 in primary school and 5.96/7 in secondary colleges). This makes *Christian Values Education* a clear first preference among the students, who wish their Catholic school identity to be expressed as a search for the middle ground between faith and culture, seeking to attach values to the Christian faith, and demonstrate this particular expression of Christianity to the world and within the school context. *Christian Values Education* is often applied with a greater emphasis on the Values Education without any real religious faith underpinning it. Hence one can give assent to this system of belief without holding to the faith that is supposedly its foundation.

A positive level of *Recontextualisation* is currently acknowledged by both primary (4.75/7) and secondary school (4.90/7). A not insignificant decrease is noted among both groups (4.53/7 and 4.60/7 respectively). This openness is supported by a high *Post-Critical Belief* of 5.41/7 among primary school children and a lower but still positive 5.10/7 for the secondary college students. Correspondingly a positive appreciation for a *Dialogue School* is present (5.25/7 and 5.19/7 respectively), with a decreased desire expressed on the normative level (5.21/7 and 5.03/7 respectively). While it is encouraging to see an openness for a *Recontextualising Dialogue School* among the student groups this *Subpopulation* uses these tools as means to an end and are not wholeheartedly behind this agenda.

Reconfessionalisation is recognised factually by the primary school children (4.43/7) and the secondary college students (4.31/7). But they have not desire for this trend to continue in the future with the primary school children expressing a neutral 3.99/7 normative value and the secondary college students resisting *Reconfessionalisation* on the ideal level (3.65/7). To this end one is surprised by the higher than normal level of *Literal Belief* (4.46/7 among the primary school children and 4.05/7 for the secondary college students), but it can be reasoned that combined with the high level of *Post-Critical Belief* that many of the student simply are not yet able to distinguish between symbolic and non-symbolic belief and hence give accent to all creedal statements. They reject the notion of a *Monologue School* both factually (3.98/7 and 3.37/7 respectively) and resist it even more so normatively (3.70/7 and 2.99/7 respectively). As such, unlike the adults, no strong *Reconfessionalising* undercurrent present among the students in this *Subpopulation*.

A low level of *Confessionality* is noted among the primary school group (4.43/7), with a further decrease on the secondary colleges level (4.20/7). As has been mentioned before a high level of *Confessionality* is required to support *Christian Values Education* in order that there is enough creedal faith expressed which can have values attached and joined in a neutral manner to the surrounding culture and context. If the level of *Confessionality* declines so too does the success of *Christian Values Education*. From the students' results, there is not much *Confessionality* that can serve as 'petrol' for a one to one correspondence between the Catholic faith and the increasingly plural context. In the long run, *Christian Values Education* cannot uphold the specificity of the Christian tradition and settles with the least common denominator in comparison with the other life options. Consequently, the values are kept but the Christian identity is lost, leading to inadvertent but gradual lack of need and desire to maintain the school's Catholic identity.

Secularisation is strongly opposed factually in both primary and secondary school (2.25/7 and 2.67/7 respectively). Yet a significant decrease in resistance it noted in both instances (2.82/7 and 3.49/7 respectively), resulting in secondary college students being only mildly resistant to *Secularisation.* This decreasing resistance to *Secularisation* is a negative step and is supported by an increasing appreciation for the non-believing stances, particularly *External Critique* as the students age (2.27/7 in primary school increasing to 2.38/7 in the secondary colleges). Likewise *Relativism* shows a slight increase from the primary school children (4.43/7) to the secondary college students (4.55/7). The *Colourful School* is resisted by both primary and secondary school students currently (3.50/7 and 3.67/7 respectively), but this resistance turns to a desire for a *Colourful School* on the normative level (4.08/7 and 4.35/7 respectively). A decreasing resistance for a *Colourless School* is noted in both groups, with a factual 3.15/7 reducing to a normative 3.58/7 among the primary students and a factual 3.19/7 decreasing to a mild resistance of 3.67/7 among the secondary college students.

Similarly to the adult group the trends of increasing support for *Christian Values Education,* decreasing *Confessionality,* decreasing resistance to *Secularisation,* decreased resistance for a *Colourless School* and a switch from resistance to appreciation for a *Colourful School* can be observed when comparing the primary school children to the secondary college students. In addition a decreasing support for *Recontextualisation,* an increased resistance for a *Monologue School* and a decreased appreciation for a *Dialogue School* are observed. Overall once can say that this *Subpopulation* represents a diversity of opinions within its overall outlook with a movement from this *Subpopulation* to others present, which will be discussed in the next section. For instance while many in this group use *Christian Values Education* to avoid *Secularisation* others use it to the opposite effect.

Primary – secondary school comparison

A *Christian Values Education* approach is very much ingrained among a vast number of Catholic primary and secondary schools in this research. This does not seem surprising because it appears to be successful — at first. Due to the considerable level of Catholic *Confessionality* that is still present in many primary schools, it is evident that Catholic values are being linked directly to a religious foundation: people expect and desire this *mono-correlation* to occur. Little children, who easily comply with the role models presented to them, are a grateful target group for *Christian Values Education*, with their higher level of *Literal Belief*, lower resistance against a *Monologue School* and greater appreciation for *Reconfessionalisation*. However, as they grow up and become more aware of the complex and diverse world they live in, as they begin to think individually and critically, as they meet new people and gain life experiences outside the rather protected environment of Catholic primary schools, the adverse effects of *Christian Values Education* due to its inadequacy to adapt the Catholic faith to the more complex life situations become apparent. Although most of the problems and challenges surface in the secondary colleges, it seems that the seeds of the problem are sown at the primary school level.

To this end adults and students in the primary school choose the 'half-way house' of *Christian Values Education* believing they are going towards a strong *Values Education* model, but in reality the adherents scatter, with a diminishing support for a *Dialogue School*, a growth towards a *Colourful* and *Colourless School* and a general abandoning of *Christian Values Education* in favour of the *Secularising Subpopulation*. While it is true that some adherents will develop positively in this didactic approach the majority trend is not to be ignored.

Contrary to the adults' intention, the students opt for *Christian Values Education* as the 'path of least resistance' in the direction of a gradual *Secularisation* and pluralisation, both on the personal and the institutional level. They recognise the compromising nature of the *Christian Values Education* approach and the desire of the teachers to make it work, and are eager to make it serve their own purpose. They see it is an opportunity to 'get away' with a growing scepticism, disinterest and disengagement, while keeping the teachers satisfied nonetheless. Complying in one way or another to a desired moral attitude is one thing; developing a Christian spirituality is another. So long as the teachers are satisfied with proof of the former in the expectation that *Christian Values Education* will eventually be effective, there is no need for the students to engage in the latter and develop a genuine personal religious identity.

Based on the large decrease in the numbers of teachers falling into this category on the secondary college level one assumes that they have realised that this vision of *Christian Values Education* is not working as it has become ineffective, predictable, counterproductive by producing further *Secularisation* and reduces the Catholic faith to its moral aspects and thereby 'hollowing it out'.

It is easy and attractive for many students to 'ride along' with *Christian Values Education*, pleasing their parents and teachers. But while the education in moral and social values is appreciated and successful, many students neglect and ultimately abandon the religious formation that comes with it. Many students incorporate the values they learn at school but leave behind the Catholic religious foundation that deepens and grounds those values. In a rapidly changing and pluralising cultural context where there often exists a gap between generations, faith communication by means of *Christian Values Education* becomes increasingly problematic and progressively inadequate.

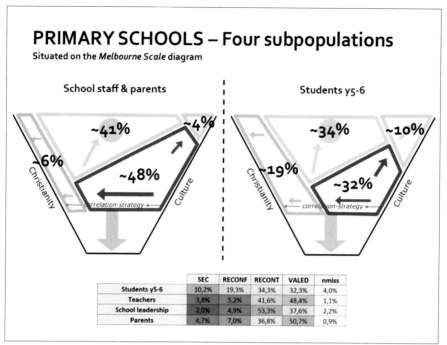

Figure II-109. Summary of *Subpopulations* in primary schools.

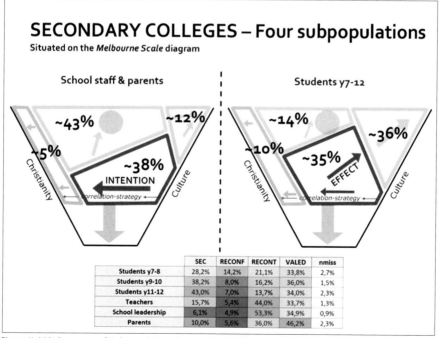

Figure II-110. Summary of *Subpopulations* in secondary colleges.

In these diagrams, the four *Subpopulations* among both the adults and the students in primary and secondary schools are presented in a schematic way on top of the *Melbourne Scale* diagram, including their estimated proportions and the directions in which each *Subpopulation* is inclined to move. This presentation effectively summarises the ECSIP research findings into one comprehensive scheme.

School staff & parents

It is visually very obvious from Figure II-109 that the vast majority of school staff and parents fall into either the green section, i.e. the *Recontextualising Subpopulation*, or the pink section which represents the *Christian Values Education Subpopulation.* These are the dominant categories representing ±41% and ±48% of the adults respectively. The *Recontextualising Subpopulation* aims towards the model position as represented by the grey circle in the middle of the diagram, which offers the ideal balance of a firm faith-based educational experience which is authentic to its own tradition, while remaining firmly situated amidst the modern world and in constant dialogue with the surrounding culture, yielding a situation in which the culture, faith, institution and the individual agent are mutually enriched. While the *Christian Values Education Subpopulation* attempts to offer a correlation strategy linking the surrounding culture to Christianity through a particular interpretation of shared common ground. ±6% form the blue section on the far left of the diagram, representing the *Reconfessionalising Subpopulation*. This group will guard and preserve the remaining tradition present in the school context, while not being numerous enough to have a negative effect on the school in terms of moving back towards an entire traditional understanding and expression of the Catholic faith and school identity. An essentially negligible ±4% of the adults are part of the yellow section representing the *Secularising Subpopulation*.

From the secondary college staff and parents *Subpopulation* results, diagrammatically represented in Figure II-110, it is evident that an evolution has occurred compared to their primary school counterparts. Firstly a clear shift into the left yellow section representing the *Secularising Subpopulation* is evidenced, with the ±12% falling into this category representing a three-fold increase from the primary school group. With the *Reconfessionalising Subpopulation* remaining essentially constant at ±5% in addition to the *recontextualising Subpopulation* at ±43%, it is evident that the shift into the *Secularising Subpopulation* comes from the *Christian Values Education Subpopulation,* which has dropped ten percentage points to ±38%. Once the students at secondary colleges observe their parents and teachers not taking their schools Catholic identity seriously (by desiring an increasingly secular school) then it's easier for the students to go along also, a trend which is to be observed on the secondary college students diagram.

The migration patterns of each subgroup can be traced from the breakdown offered under the relevant diagram. Specifically the number of teachers in the *Secularising Subpopulation* increases from 3.8% among the primary school group to 15.7%, or in other words a four-fold increase. This is a significant movement and will have detrimental effects on the schools Catholic identity and the attitude of the students in secondary colleges. The number of teachers in the *Reconfessionalising Subpopulation* remains relatively constant at 5.2% and 5.4% as do those in the *Recontextualising Subpopulation* at 41.6% and 44%. There is a marked reduction in the *Christian Values Education Subpopulation,* with numbers dropping from 48.4% to 33.7%.

The number of members of school leadership in the *Secularising Subpopulation* increases from 2.0% among the primary school group to 6.1%, or in other words a three-fold increase. While these numbers are small they are still significant as people in school leadership have a very central role in guiding the schools direction with regard to Catholic identity and this could have a significant effect on the future development of secondary colleges in particular. The number of in the *Reconfessionalising Subpopulation* remains constant at 4.9%, as do those in the *Recontextualising Subpopulation* at 53.3%. The large percentage, over half, of people in school leadership supporting the ideal type of *Recontextualisation*, is a very positive finding and offers good hope moving forward. Finally there is a slight reduction in the *Christian Values Education Subpopulation,* with numbers dropping from 37.6% to 34.9%.

Over half of the parents of primary schoolchildren are in the *Christian Values Education Subpopulation,* specifically 50.7%, but this number drop slightly to 46.2% among parents of secondary college students. The number in the *Secularising Subpopulation* doubles from 4.7% among the primary school group to 10% among parents of secondary school students. As with the other adults this will have a significant effect on the attitudes of the students. The number in the *Reconfessionalising Subpopulation* falls only slightly from 7.0% to 5.6%. Finally the numbers in the *Recontextualisation Subpopulation* remain essentially constant at 36.8% and 36.0% respectively.

Students

Figure II-110 demonstrates that ±34% of primary school students in year 5-6 fall into the *Recontextualising Subpopulation,* while ±32% are in the *Christian Values Education Subpopulation.* A sizeable ±19% occupy the blue section on the far left of the diagram, representing the *Reconfessionalising Subpopulation.* Finally ±10% of the children are part of the yellow section representing the *Secularising Subpopulation* on the far right of the diagram. Concretely this represents ±19% who wish to keep the faith in a traditional Catholic school, ±34% who wish to be faithful in a *Recontextualised* way in a *Dialogue School,* ±32% who wish to make a correlation between faith and culture and finally ±10% who wish to abandon the faith entirely in have a secular school environment.

From the secondary college student *Subpopulation* results, diagrammatically represented in Figure II-110, it is evident that an evolution has occurred compared to their primary school counterparts. Firstly a clear shift from the blue and green of *Reconfessionalisation* and *Recontextualisation* towards the pink and yellow of *Christian Values Education* and *Secularisation* is evident. The number in the *Reconfessionalising Subpopulation* has halved to some ±10% and is left fighting the corner of traditional faith and the traditional *confessional* Catholic school. While a mere ±14% of students are trying to be Catholic in an open manner and promote a *Dialogical* and *Recontextualised* school. ±35% fall into the *Christian Values Education Subpopulation* and wish to become good citizens with values learned from Christianity but who will eventually leave faith elements at school. Finally the *Secularising Subpopulation* becomes the largest at ±36%, having increased almost four-fold from the primacy school group.

The migration patterns of the students into the different *Subpopulations* as they age can be traced from the breakdown offered under the relevant diagram. Most noticeably there is a clearly increasing *Secularising* trend evidenced beginning with 10.2% of year 5-6's falling into this *Subpopulation* then increasing significantly to 28.2% among the year 7-8's as they begin secondary college, progressing to 38.2% in year 9-10 and finally to 43% among the year 11-12's. Next a decreasing *Reconfessionalising* trend is noted falling from 19.3% among the year 5-6's to 14.2% among the year 7-8's, 8.0% among the year 9-10's and finally 7.0% among the year 11-12's. The number of adherents to the *Recontextualising Subpopulation* also falls dramatically from 34.2% among the year 5-6's, to 21.1% among the year 7-8's, 16.2% among the year 9-10's and finally 13.7% among the year 11-12's. Finally it is noted that the *Christian Values Education Subpopulation,* remains essentially constant with a slight growth noted, from 32.3% among the year 5-6's, to 33.8% among the year 7-8's, 36.0% among the year 9-10's and finally 34.0% among the year 11-12's.

It is hence evidenced that the *Secularisation* tendency increases at the expense of *Reconfessionalisation* and *Recontextualisation*, while *Christian Values Education* is used as a 'half-way house'. That is to say that students originally in the *Reconfessionalising Subpopulation* move into the *Christian Values Education Subpopulation* while others move out of *Christian Values Education* into the *Secularising Subpopulation*; as time passes those who joined the *Christian values Education Subpopulation* from the *Reconfessionalising Subpopulation* will end up in the

Secularising Subpopulation also, even though this was not their intention. Although the exact internal shifts are not clear from this data, this is found to be the case.

It is the expressed intention of *Christian Values Education* to draw the culture closer to the faith through its *mono-correlational* strategy, this is visually represented in Figure II-110 by an arrow marked 'intention' which points towards the left (Christianity) side of the diagram. Yet looking to the students diagram also in Figure II-110 we see the arrow marked 'effect', which is pointing towards the culture side; specifically towards the *Secularising Subpopulation*. The *Christian Values Education Subpopulation* is unique in that its movement is in two directions, although in reality the intention arrow is not fulfilled by actual movement in that direction.

The responsibility for these movements away from a Catholic school identity to a secular one can be attributed to secondary colleges, as this is where the problem presents itself, but really the problem has its seeds sown at primary school. Hence the key to solving this trend lies in the primary schools. In primary school ±34% of the students and ±41% of the school staff and parents are willing to *Recontextualise,* and it is the findings of this research that if they are supported in their position then in the long term they would never abandon this stance. In reality the required support is not given, instead schools focus on *Christian Values Education* with a *Reconfessionalising* pull being promoted to the expense of *Recontextualisation.*

Conclusion. Everybody likes dialogue

ECSIP promotes *Catholic school identity – in a context of diversity*. In order for present-day schools to establish a true, authentic and living Catholic identity in present-day times, it is necessary to engage in a 'dialogue between faith and culture'.

But what exactly is meant by such a 'dialogue between faith and culture'? In Australia, dialogue between faith and culture is the predominant discourse shared by all parties involved. It is striking that nearly all *Subpopulations* show a positive mean score on the *Dialogue School* model on the factual and normative measurement levels, in primary and secondary schools and for adults and students alike. The description of the *Dialogue School* sounds recognisable and attractive for nearly all Australian respondents despite the differences that are being revealed by their adjacent belief styles and school types in the graphs on the previous pages.

We can induce that people understand 'dialogue' in different ways and use it for different purposes. The overview below provides a summary of four key types of dialogue between faith and culture uncovered by the *Subpopulations*.

From the perspective of *Secularisation*: dialogue between faith and culture = opening up to the postmodern world, accepting the erosion of Catholic school identity. Dialogue is an opportunity to create openness and room for secular human values, sensitivities and lifestyles in a Catholic institution. Dialogue provides an opportunity to relinquish religion gradually and defend more and more the merits and values of modernity and postmodernity, thereby accepting a gradual erosion of Catholic school identity.

From the perspective of *Reconfessionalisation*: dialogue between faith and culture = an opportunity to proclaim the Catholic faith in the contemporary world, undiluted and clear. By increasing the access to a larger audience of potential believers, dialogue is a way to counteract a lack of faith, postmodern philosophical views and secular morality.

From the perspective of *Christian Values Education*: dialogue between faith and youth culture = an opportunity to *equalise* the human and the Catholic. Still presuming an overlap between Christian faith and youth culture (cf. the *Confessional* Catholic school model), the students' religious identity, believed to be implicitly present, is made explicit. Dialogue is an opportunity to directly 'couple' faith and culture (*mono-correlation*) in order to (Re-)Confessionalise the student population. Generally shared 'Christian values' serve as convenient mediators between culture and faith.

From the perspective of *Recontextualisation*: dialogue between faith and culture = a chance to renew Catholic identity by *reconfiguring* it in a new context, creating a dynamic interplay between both, at the service of the identity formation of all involved. Dialogue is a way of searching for a renewed Catholic profile in changing times. Out of its own inherent strength and depth, Christianity's voice is allowed to resonate amid a multiplicity of voices, at the service of all.

Everybody likes dialogue, which comes as no surprise. And as such this is beneficial, certainly. However, 'Dialogue' risks to turn into a *buzzword* that becomes so common, popular and 'correct' that it can mean many things depending on who does the talking. Exactly what kind of 'dialogue between faith and culture' does the ECSIP Project promote, and why? What are the theological underpinnings of 'Catholic identity in dialogue'? How does this dialogue relate to its different interpretations and uses discovered by the *Subpopulations*? These crucial questions are stepping stones to the next and final chapter that describes the *identity profile* of Catholic schools in Victoria.

Chapter 11. The identity profile of Catholic schools in Victoria. Conclusions and recommendations.

Chapter 11 describes the *identity profile* of Catholic schools in Victoria based on the survey results of the *ECSIP 2012 Research*. The first paragraph talks about the important difference between a *Kerygmatic* and a *Recontextualising Dialogue School* type: while the former is the prevalent approach in Victoria, ECSIP actually advises the latter as the most promising way forward and legitimises this claim. Paragraph two presents a summary of selected research results, namely those findings that show the ample qualities and strengths of the participating schools with regard to their Catholic identity. Paragraph three continues this summary of the state of Catholic education in Victoria by focussing on the potential challenges and critical questions that are revealed by the research as well. Paragraph four rounds up the book with an extensive number of recommendations that may help Catholic schools in Victoria to enhance their identity in light of the ECSIP empirical findings and its underpinning theological view.

§1. Everybody is in favour of dialogue between faith and culture. But is the dialogue *Kerygmatic* or is it *Recontextualising*?

The *Recontextualising Dialogue School* model

Regarding the identity of Catholic schools in Australia and elsewhere in the world, the *Enhancing Catholic School Identity Project* recognises the urgent need for a conscious, fundamental and authentic application of the *Dialogue School* model that *Recontextualises* the Catholic faith in a pluralising culture based on a strong *Post-Critical Belief*. This normative theological view applies the insights and directions provided by the *Second Vatican Council* (1962-1965) and has been developed throughout the years in a dialogue between all theological sub-disciplines at the *Faculty of Theology and Religious Studies* of KU Leuven, Belgium. ECSIP builds on this legacy and applies it consistently to the issue of Catholic school identity. The following remarks summarise the theological view that underpins the ECSIP Project.

- *Recontextualisation* **of Catholic school identity and the dynamics of revelation.** In every new historical context throughout history, the Catholic faith necessarily 're-profiles' itself according to the new situation it finds itself in, that is to say it is *Recontextualised*. This process of manifold *Recontextualisations*, which is the dynamic of the Christian tradition itself, has been going on since the dawn of Christianity. Without it, Christianity would have ceased to exist long ago! Now it is up to us to become part of this dynamic and to continue the tradition of *Recontextualisation* into the 21st century. Now it is our time to look for new ways to express the Gospel as authentic, alive and fresh, and to look for new practices to make it come true in our world today. We are standing with one foot in the Christian tradition, so to say, and with the other in a yet unwritten future. As God walks with us on our path, new revelation occurs and the faith tradition keeps expanding itself. While re-reading previous entries, we write a new chapter in the book of the Catholic story.

- **A future-oriented hermeneutics.** From a theological point of view, ECSIP opts for an eschatological, future-oriented hermeneutics: today we are called to reach out and contribute to God's salvific 'dream for humankind' that is being developed throughout history. The normative point that inspires and shapes our living faith lies in the eschatological future, not in the preservation of the past.

- **A *Post-Critical*, hermeneutical theology.** Catholic theology is to adopt an open hermeneutical approach, especially when 'faith is seeking understanding' in a multi-religious cultural context. The truth of Christianity is not fixed, but is to be rediscovered and made real through a continuous search for it. We should look creatively and with an open mind for renewed insights into what it could mean to be Catholic in the 21st century. Catholic school identity re-profiles itself in the hermeneutic activity of giving meaning and purpose to those things that really matter in life.

- **Searching for a renewed Catholic identity profile in a context of diversity.** It has become a prime mission of Catholic schools to render a service of education, personal up building, grace, freedom, righteousness and 'humanisation' to the diverse student population that is entrusted to their care – whoever these students may be. Catholic schools tend to this responsibility wholeheartedly not just because of their *Catholic* identity, but also because of their being inspired by the person and life of Jesus Christ and by the Gospel stories — because of the God of Jesus Christ, who is *Love*. Through this quest for service and unconditional love, Catholic believers in the school *Recontextualise* and live their faith.

- **Genuine encounter and dialogue between Catholic faith and plural culture** is the prerequisite to *Recontextualise* Catholic school identity today. In and through the dialogue with pluralising culture, *Recontextualisation* of personal and institutional Catholic identity occurs. Being 'open-minded' and welcoming a plurality of other-believers into the school is a first step. It is even more important to acknowledge and accept the new and different generation for who they really are, without prejudice or judgment. Grow closer to them and allow them to grow closer to you, while simultaneously being the best possible Catholic you could ever be. Serve your students in order to gain their respect and love. Take their hand and guide them in their education as well as personal formation and growth, each in his/her specific way. Such a genuine, bi-lateral dialogical process quasi-automatically results in *Recontextualisation* – how else could you live your Catholicity fully while being recognised as such by a new generation in a new world? (Schools do not only *Secularise* because the students have 'lost the faith', somehow became disengaged and nihilistic – but because Catholic schools have gradually become unable to relate to them in a genuine and meaningful way.)

- **Identity formation in a plural context.** Catholics, Christians, other-believers as well as non-religious people benefit from the particular educational approach in *Catholic* schools. They can all be accepted, taken seriously and challenged to realise their potential and to become more fully human. For the Catholics among them, this growth implies a personal, religious and spiritual formation.

- **The important place of the *Kerygma* in *Recontextualising* dialogue.** It is important to note that *Recontextualising* dialogue is not devoid of the *Kerygma*. The process of *Recontextualisation* has at its centre a privileged place for Christianity. Within the school Catholicism will stand as the favoured interpretive key around which dialogue takes place. By introducing the perspectives of the Catholic faith, proclamation does indeed take place. At the same time the sensitivity of *Recontextualising Dialogue* ensures that the *Kerygma* does not obliterate the others' point of view before it is even heard or put forward. The *Kerygma* can also actively engage with difference. In this way *Recontextualisation* can occur when the tradition and its proclamation is challenged, purified, and taken more deeply into the truth of its claim.

- **A realistic outlook.** An added advantage is that, unlike the alternatives that present themselves, ECSIP promotes a *realistic* option that holds a promise for the future in the short and the long run. It is not ignoring, denying or fighting cultural shifts that cannot be stopped nor is it waiting for a miraculous 'counter-revolution' that will never take place.

The *Kerygmatic Dialogue School* model

Everybody is in favour of dialogue between faith and culture. However, as the *Subpopulations* make clear[48], there are various ways to conduct such dialogue giving rise to various outcomes. The *Recontextualising Dialogue School* model is a particular paradigm of dealing with the complicated relation between faith and culture. Through statistical analysis of empirical research data we identified a second paradigm that exerts significant influence in Catholic schools in Victoria: the *Kerygmatic Dialogue School* model. Although both approaches can be situated within the *Dialogue School* quadrant of the *Victoria Scale* typology, there are significant theological and educational differences between them. ECSIP identifies with the *Recontextualising* approach much more than the *Kerygmatic* approach. The following remarks summarise the main characteristics of a *Kerygmatic Dialogue School* model:

- **Catholic proclamation.** The *Kerygmatic Dialogue School* is very eager to create opportunities to communicate and promote a Catholic point of view and it is very active and creative in finding ways to achieve this. Its motto sounds a little like: "Come to our school all of you and see just how great Catholicism is!" The view that underscores much of what happens at school comes down to proclaiming the plausibility, greater value and universal truth of the gospel of Jesus Christ. This proclamation happens within an 'open dialogue' with all who are prepared to enter into the discussion and receive the message. However, far less or little attention is paid to differing points of view, religious beliefs or cultural practices that are nonetheless increasingly present within the school community.

- **Exclusive/inclusive truth-claim.** Like the *Monologue School* type, *Kerygmatic Dialogue* presumes that the Catholic faith tradition presents a message that is ultimately meaningful and valuable as such for *all* people. It is thought that the truth offered by the Catholic faith is literally more fundamental and fulfilling than the ideas offered by other religions and philosophies of life. Catholicism is to be

---

[48] See the analysis of the *Subpopulations* in Chapter 10 §5.

preferred above other views and therefore should be heard by everyone. It should be 'proposed' to all, regardless of their varied backgrounds. A Catholic school must therefore, in principle, give priority to the Catholic faith and Catholic practices, placing them over and above other beliefs and life views (*apologetics*). Conversely, it is best to avoid clearly non-Catholic and certainly all anti-Catholic attitudes and practices, because these could undermine the mission of the Catholic school itself.

A more moderate variant of *Kerygmatic Dialogue* is not exclusive but inclusive regarding its religious truth-claim: other religions or world views are not condemned, rejected or avoided but seen as implicit manifestations in which the logic of Christ is at work even if its members and adherents are not aware of it. In other words, people of other religions and worldviews are considered to be *anonymous Christians*: they are accepted and even appreciated *as far as* they are confirming the Catholic truth.

Despite the apparent variety of views present in the school community, the typical discourse in a *Kerygmatic Dialogue School* is converging towards one single point of view: *Catholicism*. The parents of the students have consciously chosen to enrol their children in a *Catholic* institution; it is therefore not unreasonable to expect that all participate in the school's religious project, even though levels of participation may vary.

- **A pre-determined message.** The 'Catholic package' of faith convictions and truth claims, specific rites and rituals, concrete moral and socio-political attitudes, distinctive prayers and music – in other words the 'traditional Catholic *way of life*' as it was developed by past generations – is considered more or less fixed and immutable. Generally speaking, it is not desirable to change the content and form of Catholic beliefs and practices too much in order to make it 'conform' or 'resonate' better with the constantly changing present-day cultural maelstrom. The essence of Catholicism is to a large extent defined by the tradition and must be preserved and, if necessary, protected from other ideas and influences.

- **All people are presumably receptive.** *Kerygmatic Dialogue* presumes that all staff and students are actually sensitive and receptive to the same Catholic message and in fact are longing for it, either explicitly or implicitly. Based on their being *human* and the universal applicability of the Catholic faith, it is justified to invite all to come to know the Catholic faith presented as the deeper meaning and fulfilment of their lives.

- **Dialogue as opportunity to witness.** Unlike the *Monologue School*, a *Kerygmatic* type of the *Dialogue* does not go so far as to expect that all of the students are, should be or will become Catholic. It remains a *Dialogical* instead of a *Monological* approach. It is true that the school doors are open and a great variety of students are welcomed and accepted. The school places itself deliberately in the midst of a pluralistic society with an attitude of hospitality, inclusion, tolerance, solidarity and friendship for all people. The atmosphere is welcoming, peaceful, caring and open-minded so that people from diverse backgrounds feel comfortable and safe. This impression does not negate the fact, however, that the *Kerygmatic Dialogue School* holds on firmly to its Catholic convictions that are positively and optimistically communicated to all school members. In fact, the encounter and the dialogue with others are an *opportunity* to witness to those convictions in both word and deed. Being enthusiastic about Jesus Christ and Catholic faith and inviting others to embrace the Catholic vision can be *captivating* indeed – and engaging oneself this way is certainly not incompatible with a Catholic educational project.

- **'Schools in a bubble'.** Problems may arise, however, when *alterity* becomes real and even radical, when the post-Catholic, non-Catholic and other-than-Catholic diversity at school grows less receptive and more resistant to the school's invariable Catholic climate – an evolution which has been ruled out as a pre-supposition of *Kerygmatic Dialogue*. Problems may arise when Catholic school identity becomes something artificially created by the (no doubt well-intended) ambition to uphold a certain tradition. This may lead to a 'school in a bubble' phenomenon where school members 'play their expected parts' but leave their role behind as soon as they put off the school uniform and put on their 'real clothes' (cf. *Colourless School* tendencies). Could a continuation of *Kerygmatic Dialogue* in those circumstances, at least for some of the students, come down to a form of *indoctrination*?

- **A new 'public relations policy'.** *Kerygmatic Dialogue* is looking for a fresh way of expressing unaltered Catholic points of view and for new didactic techniques to carry it forth to people today. It is looking for a new 'wrapping' to present the faith in an attractive way, for a new 'public relations policy' to positively portray a school's religious profile in today's Australia. However, there is little concern for new, fundamental religious or theological developments or genuine spiritual renewal that could make Catholic faith alive again in the hearts of people today.

- **'Implanting Catholic identity'.** Another proposed metaphor to describe a *Kerygmatic* style of dialogue would be a 'transplantation' or 'implantation' of a predetermined Catholic *Confessionality* in the middle of a pluralising school culture. Similar to the transfer of an organ from a host body to a sick patient, an external 'Catholic package' is implanted in a diversifying school context hoping that it will somehow 'fit in' and be accepted in its new environment. While avoiding genuine and intrinsic dialogue with the new context, it is just a matter of finding a way to avoid or counteract any symptoms of rejection of the implant by the receiving body.

Below we summarise the description of the *Kerygmatic Dialogue School* model by formulating three fundamental critiques.

1. An ethical critique. From an ethical point of view, in a pluralising context *Kerygmatic Dialogue* ultimately risks not completely accepting and taking seriously the people entrusted to its care. It risks replacing them with a projection of its own desires instead of taking them for whom they really are. *Kerygmatic Dialogue* risks not taking seriously the 'difference of alterity'. In the *Kerygmatic Dialogue School* model, the 'open doors policy' can result in no more than a rather superficial interest in what 'other-believers' and 'non-believers' have to offer that might be new and truly relevant for a Catholic school project — whereas for sure the opposite is the case. *Kerygmatic Dialogue* moves out to meet the other, *but only up to a certain level*. When diversity becomes 'radical', ultimately unable to conform to Catholic beliefs and practices', then continuing to pursue a Kerygmatic Dialogue runs the risk of being *recuperative* or even *manipulative*.

On the other hand, the starting point for any Christian relationship of love and compassion is to acknowledge the personhood of the other for who he/she really is, even though this may be difficult or even painful. Receptivity towards the (radical) other is fundamental. The Christian faith has a fundamentally relational and dialogical character. The Christian point of view is one of respect and appreciation for all people including their philosophical and religious beliefs and practices. Christians have no choice but to respect people's freedom of choice always. Faith neither can nor may ever be imposed on others, whether by explicit or implicit coercion — trying this would be contradictory to the message itself. Instead, Christians welcome other voices in their midst with humility and respect, looking for new ways to serve them, inspired by the Word of the Gospel. In order to meet people and be their neighbours, they must first be allowed to come near us. Only when we actually do this, we become a Catholic school. Only when we look the other in the eye, can we see the face of Jesus. When we offer shelter to 'the stranger', God reveals Himself in new, unexpected ways.

2. A theological critique. *Kerygmatic Dialogue* inhibits, avoids or counteracts fundamental tradition development that is needed to *Recontextualise* Catholic identity in the light of changing times. *Kerygmatic Dialogue* tends to 'close the narrative' and inhibits the spontaneous development and organic growth that is necessary to revitalise the Catholic faith in the new millennium. Instead, it wishes to 'conserve' and restate the religious content and form adopted by Catholics of former generations, which were in turn the result of a genuine process of *Recontextualisation* of the faith tradition in a past historical context. Today, in a new context that is changing more radically and quickly than ever before in human history, a new *Recontextualisation* of the faith tradition is required – as it will be again in the future.

3. A pragmatic critique. In a pluralising culture that unavoidably pervades school communities as well, a *Kerygmatic Dialogue* model risks becoming increasingly ineffective and even counterproductive. A culturally implausible, maladjusted and top-down imposed proclamation of Catholic faith will falter – or worse, if the 'gap' between faith and culture becomes too wide and the students detraditionalise, pluralise and secularise further. Paradoxically, a continued practice of *Kerygmatic Dialogue* risks producing further *Secularisation* instead of slowing it down. Furthermore, imposing *Kerygmatic Dialogue* risks alienating present-day students to the extent even that the Christian message ceases to be the 'good news' of love and compassion it is supposed to be. It might confirm existing doubt and cultural prejudice regarding religion in general and Catholicism in particular. Consequently, a growing subgroup of students are tempted to distance themselves from religion all together.

Empirical ground for the distinction between a *Recontextualising* and a *Kerygmatic Dialogue School* model

In the ECSIP 2010 Research we were able to statistically discern two types of dialogue within the raw data of the *Victoria Scale*. After performing and analysing an *orthogonal rotated factor analysis* on the adult data, we empirically discovered that two subtypes exist within the *Dialogue School* type of the *Victoria Scale* on the factual and the normative measurement level alike. Upon close examination of their structure and meaning, we christened these subtypes *Recontextualising* and *Kerygmatic Dialogue*.

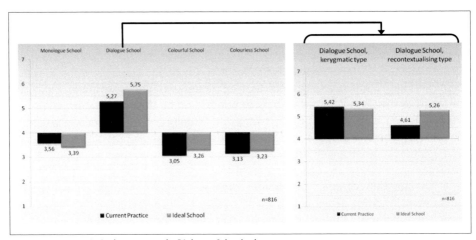

Figure II-111. *Victoria Scale* mean graph, *Dialogue School* subtypes.

Figure II-111 shows the *Victoria Scale* results of the school staff and the parents that took part to the ECSIP 2010 Research. The graph on the left hand side makes clear that the vast majority of the adults perceive their school as a *Dialogue School* (5.27/7) and wish to continue building a *Dialogue School* model towards the future (5.75/7). The graph on the left hand side shows their mean scores for both the *Kerygmatic* and the *Recontextualising* variant of the *Dialogue School* model. By distinguishing these two subtypes, the graph on the right goes deeper into the meaning of the broad support for dialogue revealed by the graph on the left.

On the factual level, the school staff and the parents identify the schools more with the *Kerygmatic Dialogue* type (5.42/7) than the *Recontextualising Dialogue* type (4.61/7). At the time of the research, *Kerygmatic Dialogue* was more commonly practised compared to *Recontextualising Dialogue*. However, on the normative level we detect a gradual shift in the future. The *Kerygmatic Dialogue* type remains popular but is slowly losing some of its potency (from 5.42/7 to 5.34/7) while the *Recontextualising Dialogue* type is gaining in strength significantly (from 4.61/7 to 5.26/7). *Kerygmatic Dialogue* receives the highest normative score but is being caught up by *Recontextualising Dialogue*.

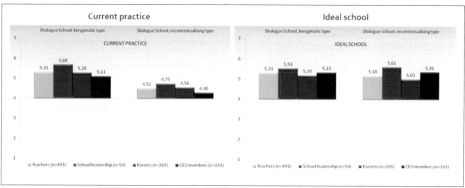

Figure II-112. *Victoria Scale* differentiation adult groups, *Dialogue School* subtypes.

Figure II-112 breaks down the mean scores for the two subtypes according to the four respondent groups that make up the sample: teaching staff (n= 493), school leadership (n=54), parents (n=269) and members of diocesan Catholic education offices (n=143). The gradual shift from *Kerygmatic* to *Recontextualising Dialogue* can be perceived in all four respondent groups.

A comparison between the factual and the normative levels reveals that *Kerygmatic Dialogue* loses some of its plausibility for school leadership (from 5.68/7 to 5.53/7) and parents (from 5.28/7 to 5.19/7). The teaching staff hold on to the current level of *Kerygmatic Dialogue* (5.31/7 on both levels). CEO members indicate a desire for a small increase of *Kerygmatic Dialogue* in the future (from 5.11/7 to 5.33/7).

Regarding the *Recontextualising Dialogue* subtype, all adult respondent groups clearly acknowledge the need to make it stronger and invest in it more. The desire to turn to a *Recontextualising* direction is strongest with the CEO members (from 4.30/7 to 5.36/7 which is an increase of more than 1 point). They are followed by the school leadership teams (increase of 0.86), the teachers (increase of 0.67) and finally the parents as well (increase of 0.45).

In Australian Catholic schools, a *Kerygmatic* style of dialogue between faith and culture remains widespread and strong. However, we detect that the desire to evolve towards a more *Recontextualising* style of dialogue is growing stronger across the board.

For many years, the paradigm of *Kerygmatic Dialogue* has been very successful in Australian Catholic schools. Today, the reality of a pluralising culture outside and inside the school is resulting in a growing crisis of the *Kerygmatic Dialogue School* model. This crisis of faith communication is especially noticeable in secondary colleges, but increasingly present in primary schools as well. In order to face this challenge constructively without giving up on the Catholic education project, the ECSIP Project promotes the alternative of a *Recontextualising Dialogue School*. Empirical research results point in the same direction.

§2. The state of Catholic education in Victoria, Australia. Qualities and strengths

Introduction
The comprehensive outcomes of the *ECSIP 2012 Research* clearly indicate that Catholic primary and secondary schools in Victoria have in place the foundations needed to achieve their mission as Catholic schools and their commitment to religious education. They possess many qualities and strengths where Catholic identity is concerned, both in the current practice and regarding future prospects.

A diverse population with a majority of Catholics
It is observed that Catholic schools in Victoria are generally populated by a good balance of Roman-Catholics, other Christians, people with other religious affiliations and non-religious philosophies of life. Yet these diverse school communities are still characterised by a majority of Catholic believers (see Figures II-14/15). This observation is a fundamental strength in upholding and fostering the school's Catholic identity.

Faith in Christ
This is supported by the numbers expressing faith in Christ (as per Figures II-16/17). A clear majority of school staff and parents in primary and in secondary schools indicate having faith in Christ, including no less than 46.0% of adults who claim to have 'strong faith' in Christ. Parents indicate high levels of faith in Christ (strong faith: 41.3%; average faith: 51.3%), which vouches for their continued support for the Catholic identity of their children's schools. Among the primary school students, a vast majority indicate having faith in Christ (strong faith: 40.0%; average faith: 49.8%). Also among the students in secondary colleges, faith in Christ is widespread (strong faith: 20.1%; average faith: 56.1%).

Belief in God
In primary schools, a majority of the children (69.7%) and the adults (63.3%) agree that most people in their school believe in God, unmistakably a feature of Catholic school identity. They would even like to raise this high level of belief in God (students: from 69.7% to 71.8%; adults: from 63.3% to 70.5%). Only a small minority would feel at home in a school where people did not believe in God (students: 11.7%; adults: 14.8%) (see Figures II-31/32). In secondary colleges, 32.4% of the students and 39.1% of the adults claim that most people at school believe in God. An increasing proportion would prefer more belief in God at school (students: from 32.4% to 35.4%; adults: from 39.1% to 53.1%). Although these figures are not as high as for the primary schools, believing in God is very common in secondary colleges (see Figures II 33/34).

Personal prayer life

Positive is also the respondents' self-description about their personal prayer life where almost half of the students and over a half of the adults confess that they have an active personal prayer life (students: 45.9%; adults: 50.3%). Further, many school members pray sometimes but not regularly (students: 43.0%; adults: 41.8%). While just a few people never pray (see Figures II-11-20). In secondary colleges, having a personal prayer life is common among staff members and parents (active prayer life: 42.9%; irregular prayer life: 41.0%). Also many students confess praying on their own regularly (active prayer life: 24.9%; irregular prayer life: 45.0%). Those in school leadership express this combination of strong belief in Christ and an active prayer life particularly, with 64.9% of those in primary and 53.0% of those in secondary college leadership expressing a strong faith in Christ (see Figures II-16/17), while 57.4% pray daily or at least regularly, and 34.4% pray sometimes or only in times of great happiness or trouble (see Figures II-21/23).

Supporting the Catholic faith

Almost all adults connected to Catholic education support the Catholic faith, either giving it their full support (30.4%) or supporting it despite criticism of some aspects (60.3%). Adult respondents who dislike the Catholic faith are very much an exception to the rule (0.53%) (see Figure II-18/19). Likewise among the student population, a majority render support to the Catholic faith with 42.1% of primary school children demonstrating their full support, while 38.8% support it despite criticism. Among secondary colleges there is a smaller cohort of 18.8% demonstrating their full support, while 41.3% support the Catholic faith despite criticism.

Supporting Catholic school identity

Based on the strong religious profile of people in Victorian schools, we expect a wide support basis for the Catholic identity of these same schools. Indeed, 95.2% of the adults in primary schools and 91.9% of the adults in secondary colleges support, to varying degrees, the Catholic identity of schools. Adults, who do not care about it or even oppose it, constitute a low percentage. This is true for teachers, school leadership members and parents alike. In primary schools, 85.6% of the children claim to support Catholic school identity. 22.0% of them even pledge their 'strong support'. Also in secondary colleges, a majority of the students support the Catholic identity of their institutions: 69.0% claim to support it to a varying degree. 7.7% pledge their 'strong support' (see Figures II-24/25/26).

Features of Catholic school identity

Both at the primary and the secondary level, the adult school members are eager to invest more in all the typical features that define the Catholic character of schools, such as: religious education and formation of the students (3.25/5), celebrating faith together (3.40/5), reading the Bible at school (3.23/5), prayer at school (3.31/5), focus on the Catholic tradition (3.26/5) and Catholic rituals and sacraments at school (3.23/5) (see Figures II-27/28). Primary school students are eager to have more religious education and formation (3.40/5), communal celebration of faith (3.57/5), Bible activities (3.44/5) and prayer at school (3.62/5) (see Figures II-27/28).

Social justice

Many adults in primary and secondary schools desire more involvement in social justice projects, compared with the current practice in their schools (3.74/5). The desire for social action and justice is certainly an important trait of Catholic school identity (see Figures II-27/28). Through social justice activities, Catholic schools inspire students to actively help those who are in need, explicitly framed in a Catholic perspective. Through specific prayers and a long-term Catholic ecological education schools can foster a sense of stewardship amongst the students.

Growing closer to God

In connection with this, the majority of the respondents concur and desire that their school continue to be a very good place to grow closer to God. According to both the students (91.2% with a mean score of 5.99/7) and the adults (92.7% with a mean score of 5.88/7), primary schools are excellently suited to grow closer to God. Further, a clear majority would also like to maintain this quality in the future (students: 84.9% with a mean score of 5.78/7 and adults: 89.8% with a mean score of 5.98/7) (see Figure 11-36/37). It is positive that a majority of the students (67.9% with a mean score of 4.85/7) and the adults (81.1% with a mean score of 5.42/7) in secondary colleges believe their college to be a good place to grow closer to God. Also, on the normative level there remains majority support to continue on this track (students: 54.1% with a mean score of 4.51/7; adults: 77.4% with a mean score of 5.50/7). Few staff members or parents (6.7%) disagree with this item. Though not as high as in primary schools, also at the secondary education level the desire to grow closer to God is generally shared (see Figures II-38/39). Again reiterating the strong believing profile of members of school leadership, it is observed that of the adult groups the people who belong to the school leadership are most enthusiastic about creating school environments that are good places to grow closer to God (6.04/7) and where belief in God is common (5.15/7) (see Figure II-38/40).

Post-Critical Belief

The *Post-Critical Belief Scale* results demonstrate that the majority of the respondents prefer *Post-Critical Belief*. A 86% majority of adults in primary school and 80.4% in secondary college with 87.2% of students in primary school and 62.4% in secondary college showing a *Post-Critical Believing* attitude (see Figures II-43/45/48/50). Standing in the tradition of the *Second Vatican Council*, they are interpreters who are searching for religious truth in all things, wishing to make it 'come alive' in and be relevant to a present-day context. In doing so, they resist the inclination to fix religious truth claims, attitudes and practices in past formulations and forms.

Awareness of Contingency

This predominant *Post-Critical Believing* attitude is supported by reasonable degrees of *Awareness of Contingency* among the adults, with 57.5% agreeing in the primary school group and 60.5% among the secondary college adults. This is also true to a lesser extent among the students with 42.9% agreement among the primary school children and 55.7% among the secondary college students (see Figures II-43/45/48/50). This constitutes a genuine openness and receptivity to diversity needed to *Recontextualise* Catholic identity in a *Post-Critically Believing* way.

Hence, *Post-Critical Believers* are aware of the, sometimes justified, religious criticism and of the growing multitude of religious and philosophical fundamental life options within present society. Nevertheless, they choose to relate themselves intrinsically to the symbols of a particular religion, namely the Catholic tradition, in order to establish a personal relationship with a transcendent reality. *Post-Critical Belief* attempts a new, fresh, outside-of-the-box and creative way of looking and interpreting the present context in order to shape Christ's dream for mankind in a new time. This option of *Symbolic Belief* is a very significant building block for the school's Catholic identity. It offers the best support for the processes that most likely encourage the Catholic identity of schools such as *Recontextualisation* efforts and *Dialogical* endeavours.

Traditional *Confessional* elements are present and recognised

Many adults indicate that there are many *Confessional* Catholic elements present in primary schools (85% agreement and 10.8% hesitation) as well as secondary colleges (70.8% agreement and 19.3% hesitation). The same is true for many students in primary schools (57.8% agreement and 19.9% hesitation) as well as secondary colleges (45.3% agreement and 25.9% hesitation). This means that many traditional 'identity markers' that are typical of Catholic schools, are still in place, especially in primary schools (see Figures II-60/62/68). In other words, there is still a fair amount of 'petrol in the tank' that allows the engine of Catholic school identity to run. This implies that the approach of *Christian Values Education* might still be effective, although only in some schools and in specific circumstances.

Recontextualising Catholic school identity

The outcome of the *Melbourne Scale*, which considers the theological perspective concerning the growing gap between a pluralising context and Christianity, exhibits that the School Leadership in both primary (5.62/7) and secondary (5.5/7) schools is the largest supporter for *Recontextualisation*, where the Catholic faith is reinterpreted and understood in the midst of a quickly changing and pluralising world. While there is commonality around the support for *Values Education* among students, teachers and leaders, it is in *Recontextualisation* that the leadership differentiates itself. The school leadership are followed by the teachers and parents (teachers ahead of parents in primary school and teachers and parents together in secondary colleges) (see Figure II-63/71). These results are both a strength and a challenge for school leadership teams as they pave the way forward for *Recontextualising* the school.

Partnership with parents to *Recontextualise* the school

Results show that the Parents of students at both primary and secondary schools strongly recognise the *Confessional* basis of the Catholic school. Along with the leadership and the staff they are also supportive of *Recontextualising* the school and of resisting the *Secularisation* tendencies (see Figure II-71/72). These results indicate that there is an opportunity for a renewed focus on a partnership between school leadership and parents to *Recontextualise* Catholic schools.

The popularity of the *Dialogue School*

The results of the *Victoria Scale* show that nearly all adults and a majority of students want to create a *Dialogue School* environment. This option is taken by 93% of the adults in primary schools and 90.6% of the adults in secondary schools. The students also show a willingness to establish a *Catholic identity in dialogue*: 70.4% support among primary school children and 56.8% support among secondary students (see Figures II-78/80/84/86).

This means that people in Victorian Catholic schools set up an active and creative conversation with plural culture inspired by a preference for the Catholic faith. This is a very promising result because this school type combines a maximal openness for social and religious diversity with an explicit choice for the Catholic tradition as a preferred partner in the conversation. Important to point out is that dialogue not only implies the conversation with religious diversity in society, but also with the religious tradition in which the school is situated. Furthermore, within the context of the *Dialogue School* attention is focused on the specific manner in which the dialogue inspires and shapes the school community in words and actions.

Openness towards cultural diversity
In particular, relative to the current practice, many adults desire more 'openness towards cultural diversity, including many other philosophies of life as well as Catholicism' (3.62/5). This high normative score vouches for their solidarity and their willingness to establish Catholic identity through the dialogue with a diverse range of religious and philosophical views and practices (see Figures II-27/28). From the perspective of the ECSIP research, this attention and openness for diversity is considered a major strength for Catholic schools.

The *Dialogue School*, which is the theologically preferable point of view, is after all the obvious combination of Christian identity *within* a religiously diverse society. Jesus himself went from place to place to encounter a vast diversity of people. He strived to build a respectful and pedagogical relationship with all those he encountered, always referring to his ceaseless testimony of the love of God. Therefore, Catholic *Dialogue Schools* are a service to society in their effort to offer quality education and personal formation to a very diverse student population. Being a Catholic school implies helping diverse students to achieve the best of their abilities, taking each student's specific background and talents into account. Religious and cultural diversity can serve as a positive opportunity for developing a *Dialogue School* pedagogy that fosters a *Recontextualisation* of Catholic identity, both personal and institutional.

The importance of a Catholic school identity
To summarise, almost all adult respondents wish to hold on to a Catholic school model of *Recontextualisation*, *Reconfessionalisation* or *Values Education* or a combination of these strategies. Clearly, the staff are instilled with a sense of the importance of working on Catholic school identity. Also, almost all adults (92.9% in primary school and 84.8% in secondary school) reject the prospect of a *Secularisation* of the school. So, the *Melbourne Scale* reveals that the adult support basis for Catholic identity is very strong (see Figure II-60/66).

External Critique is rejected
External Religious Critique is strongly rejected by a clear majority of the respondents. In primary schools, no more than 3.7% of the adults (plus 15.4% hesitation) and 5.2% (plus 7.9% hesitation) of the children consistently dismiss religious belief. In secondary colleges, minorities of 6.5% of the adults (plus 20.2% hesitation) and 13.8% of the students (plus 15.3% hesitation) opt for *Literal Disbelief*. The others disagree with nearly all items that express *External Critique* (see Figures II-43/45/48/50), meaning that they avoid criticising and undermining religion from a closed, rigid and literal atheist stance.

Secularisation is resisted

No doubt, this attitude takes the wind out of the sails of those who desire to *Secularise* the schools. There are very few adults present in the Catholic education system who would want to dismiss Catholic identity: no more than 2.4% agreement and 4.7% hesitation among adults in primary schools; 5.2% agreement and 10.0% hesitation among adults in secondary colleges. A vast majority of the adults cherish the opposite opinion. A clear majority of the students actively resist *Secularising* tendencies as well: 68.1% disagreement and 16.3% hesitation among children in primary schools; 41% disagreement and 26.6% hesitation among students in secondary colleges (see Figures II-60/62/66/68).

Colourful or *Colourless Schools* under pressure

Though there exist *Colourful* and *Colourless School* traits among the adults, these remain a minority. Well over half the adults clearly dismiss both *Secularising* pedagogical models. Also a part of the students dismiss both the *Colourful* and the *Colourless School* model (see Figures II-78/80/84/86). Survey items that clearly express hesitation or dismissal of Catholic identity are singled out and rejected by many adults and students. This is a clear sign of strong support for Catholic school identity.

Epilogue

The survey outcome signifies that most of the ECSIP respondents presently recognise and continue to support their schools' Catholic identity, not only as a formal label but also experienced and lived. Many respondents show that they have the aptitude to confirm, uphold and contribute to a *Post-Critical* understanding of the Christian faith in their context and exert efforts that allow the *Dialogical* manner of *Recontextualising* their school's Catholic identity to prosper.

§3. The state of Catholic education in Victoria, Australia. Potential challenges and critical questions

Introduction
With their qualities and strengths as Catholic schools demonstrated, it is also important to delve into the challenges that they face today and in the future. A close look at the results points out that the Catholic identity of Victorian schools also finds itself under pressure today, especially among the student groups. This claim can be substantiated by the empirical evidence summarised below.

Literal Belief
According to the ECSIP 2012 Research results, almost two-thirds (63.1%) of the primary school children favour a *Literal Believing* way to deal with religious content while they seem to have difficulty making the distinction with a more hermeneutic cognitive belief style (see Figures II-44/45). A significant amount of *Literal Belief* is transmitted to children in primary schools, actually more than is present among the school staff and the parents themselves (10.2% are *Literal Believers*; see Figures II-42/43). In secondary colleges, about one third of the students agree with all *Literal Belief* items (34.7%) (see Figures II-49/50). Also this figure is higher than the 8.6% of the adults at the secondary level who are *Literal Believers* (see Figures II-47-48).

Hence there is a need to guide the *Literal Belief* among children and adolescents to a more interpretative and symbolically mediated faith attitude: *Post-Critical Belief*. The *Literal Belief* tendency among a great deal of students raises critical questions about the possibility of this stance becoming dominant and thereby threatening the *hermeneutical space* required for new religious discovery and growth and for the continuous revitalisation of faith. It is important that young believers are made aware of the mediated character of all religious references and discourses and of the historic, collective and human context of religious symbolism.

It can be considered fortunate that many of those among the primary and secondary school children who show a tendency to *Literal Belief* simultaneously show a strong *Post-Critical Believing* attitude as well (see Figures II-44/45/49/50). Unfortunately, however, the results show that while the primary school students set out with a high *Literal Believing* attitude, the faith of many students weakens as they proceed through the curriculum of secondary college, without their initial *Literal Believing* attitude being *transformed* into a more mature *Post-Critical Believing* attitude. Instead, both non-believing coping styles take over (see Figure II-52). There is a tendency among the students to take refuge in *Relativistic* and even *External Critical* attitudes in an attempt to cope with rising tensions regarding their school's religious profile. This trend seems to increase as the students grow older (see Figures II-45/50).

Different perceptions of *Confessionality* by adults and students

Due to their varied backgrounds (see Figures II-14/15) and given the inevitably changing cultural context and the *generational gap* between students and adults, the results of the *Melbourne Scale* (see Figures II-59 to 75) show a growing difference in how the adults (5.41/7 in primary schools; 5.05/7 in secondary colleges) and the students (4.60/7 in primary schools; 4.14/7 in secondary colleges) perceive their school's Catholic *Confessionality*. Adults and students tend to have a different experience of the typical, traditional identity markers that define a school context as Catholic, as if they wear 'different sets of glasses' as they move about the school. They observe the same reality differently and interpret the explicit and implicit references to the school's Catholic identity in quite different ways.

Christian Values Education leads to *Secularisation* instead of Catholic identity

Consequently, there is a growing distinction in what the adults believe could uphold a Catholic school identity in the short and the long run on the one hand, and the students' experience of this religious project and their capacity to turn in into reality on the other. The general trend among the adults is to employ *Christian Values Education* to a large extent with the intention to create a *Reconfessionalising* dynamic and they believe that this is what it means to effectively *Recontextualise* Catholic identity in a pluralising school population. However, the increasing difference between the adults' and the students' perception of *Confessionality* will tend to negatively influence the effectiveness of *Christian Values Education*. Many students do recognise the strategy of *Christian Values Education* but they use it as a way to gradually *Secularise*. It does not reinforce a strategy of active *Reconfessionalisation* which is, on the contrary, increasingly resisted. Moreover, the outcome in terms of recognisable *Recontextualisation* remains ambiguous at best: many students perceive far less *Recontextualisation* than the adults intend to create; moreover, an increasing number of students critically question the plausibility of their schools' attempts to have Catholicism resonate with their actual life experiences. To their educators they ask the question: "show us how the Catholic faith can be truly relevant and recognisably meaningful for my actual life because often this is unclear".

The remaining level of perceived *Confessionality* is like the 'petrol in the tank' of *Christian Values Education*: the more it runs out, the more its engine begins to sputter and ultimately stops running. The adults overestimate the amount of remaining petrol in the tank and continue to use *Christian Values Education* while the students disconnect the values from their religious foundation and leave the latter behind.

However, when *Christian Values Education* is disconnected from the obvious Catholic background that was present in former times (*Confessionality*), it ceases to be effective and can even become counterproductive (see Figures II-62/68). Many adults rely too strongly on a direct, one-to-one *mono-correlation* of the Catholic faith to present-day values and sensitivities. While the *Christian Values Education* approach functioned well in the past, the continuous use of a *Christian Values Education* strategy against the background of disappearing *Confessionality* and a growing pluralisation is leading to an ever-increasing *Secularisation* among the student groups.

Despite this analysis that is based on representative empirical observation, all adult groups continue to support *Christian Values Education* on the normative level. There is even an increase compared with the perception of the current practice with support among adults in primary schools increasing from 5.11/7 to 5.26/7 and from 4.98/7 to 5.10/7 among secondary college adults (see Figures II-59/65).

This means we are confronted with a miscommunication between generations: while the adults *intend* to use *Christian Values Education* in order to strengthen Catholic school identity, the actual *effect* it has on many students goes the opposite way. The only way out of this conundrum is to intend and effect true *Recontextualisation* of Catholic identity in a way that corresponds to the experience and the needs of a new generation of believers.

Secularising trends: Catholic identity under pressure

Indicative of this trend is the rising level of *Institutional Secularisation* on the normative level among the student groups. In primary schools, *Secularisation* remains a minority option among the students that is slowly increasing nonetheless (from 2.21/7 to 2.70/7 with 15.5% agreement and 16.3% hesitation on the normative level). In secondary colleges, *Secularisation* becomes increasingly popular among the students to the extent that the overall mean score almost turns to agreement (from 2.86/7 to 3.81/7 with 32.4% agreement and 26.6% hesitation) (see Figures II-62/68). It is striking that this trend corresponds to the students' age: the older they become, the more they opt for *Secularisation* on the normative level (year 7-8: 3.4/7; year 9-10: 3.8/7; year 11-12: 4.1/7) (see Figure II-70). In secondary colleges, a significant part of the students agree with the *Melbourne Scale* mind map about *Secularisation* which clearly states, for example: "having faith in God sounds a bit strange"; or "Tim's schools used to be a Catholic school but, overtime, its religious identity has vanished"; or "the school makes no fuss about the beliefs and lifestyles of its students"; or "Cheers to NEUTRALITY!"

External Religious Critique in Catholic schools

The observed trend towards *Secularisation* is supported by a minority tendency of *External Critique* in secondary colleges, among the adult groups (6.5% agreement and 20.2% hesitation) and most of all among the students (13.8% agreement and 15.3% hesitation). This is a worrisome trend; if these anti-religious tendencies are allowed to thrive in the discourse about religion, then they are likely to further undermine the schools' Catholic identity, as the intercorrelation 'bubble graphs' reveal (see Figures II-48/50/49/96).

Growing closer to God?

Secularising tendencies are detectable in many research results. For example, even though a good number of students find it important that their Catholic school helps them to grow closer to God, their overall results show that they appreciate it less and less. Particularly as the students grow older, more and more confess that their ideal school need not be a suitable place to grow closer to God (year 7-8: 5.00/7; year 9-10: 4.48/7; year 11-12: 4.20/7) (see Figure II-40). In secondary colleges, 1 in 5 students (19.0%) do not find it important that their 'ideal school' would be a good place to grow closer to God. Another 26.8% neither agree, nor disagree with this statement (see Figure II-38).

Declining self-identification with Catholicism

68.9% of the children in year 5-6 in primary schools confess to be Catholic. The remaining 31.1% self-identify either with various other Christian denominations, with other religious profiles or with non-religious philosophies of life (only 3.4%). However, the number of secondary college students who self-identify as Catholic lies under 50% and drops steadily as the students grow older (45.9% in year 7-8 to 39.0% in year 9-10 to 35.1% in year 11-12). This drop is accompanied by an increase of various non-religious philosophies of life, while the ratios of Christians and students with other religious profiles remain unchanged. In year 11-12, a little over one-third of the students profess to be Catholic while 26.5% claim not to be religious at all. Regarding the adults, throughout primary and secondary schools 11.3% of the teachers (1 in 9) and 6.1% of the school leadership (1 in 16) identify with a philosophy of life that is not religious in nature (see Figures II-14/15).

Declining support for Catholic school identity

In the same way, on the part of the students, a minority of 1.2% in primary schools and 4.9% in secondary colleges, which is almost 1 in 20, declare active opposition or even strong opposition against Catholic school identity (see Figures II-24/25). As the students grow older, their support for Catholic school identity diminishes year after year (year 7-8: 75.6%; year 9-10: 67.1%; year 11-12: 61.6%). Conversely, the minority group who are indifferent or opposed to Catholic identity increases steadily (year 5-6: 6.7%; year 7-8: 19.3%; year 9-10: 29.0%; year 11-12: 32.9%) (see Figure II-26).

A steadily declining religious profile

Other background variables indicate a similar trend. As the students grow older, we detect an increasing minority who claim not to have faith in Christ (year 5-6: 3.8%; year 7-8: 13.3%; year 9-10: 17.8%; year 11-12: 22.3% which is 1 in 4.5 students) (see Figure II-16/17). Noteworthy also is that 12.1% (about 3 in 25) of the teaching staff have no personal faith in Christ. In secondary colleges, 5.3% of the students, or 1 in 19, admit they dislike the Catholic faith while 3.4% claim not to know what the 'Catholic faith' is (see Figure II-19). They also indicate that they desire a little less religious education and formation of students at school (2.87/5). Although this represents only a small average rejection, it means that there is no general support basis for *more* religious education in the future (see Figure II-28). In secondary colleges, 36.4% of the students indicate that it is not important to them whether people at school believe in God (see Figure II-33). Both the perception of people at school believing in God and the desire for it, plummet year after year (current practice: 5.01/7 > 3.94/7 > 3.25/7 > 3.02/7; ideal school: 5.29/7 > 4.28/7 > 3.67/7 > 3.40/7) (see Figure II-35). Believing in God becomes 'less popular' among teenagers as they mature. The adults seem to recognise this trend and desire to counteract it, as is shown by their increasing mean score on the normative level (from 3.66/7 in the current practice to 4.49/7 normatively). Moreover, secondary college students generally dislike working with Bible texts at school (2.75/5). Moreover, the subgroup that desires less reading of the Bible at school increases over a number of years (from 12.3% in year 5-6, to 24.8% in year 7-8, to 33.4% in year 9-10, to 37.0% in year 11-12). It is necessary to gain more insight in the exact nature and the causes of the 'Bible fatigue' that affects young people today (see Figures II-28/30).

The challenge of fostering a personal prayer life

7.4% of primary school students and 6.8% of the adults never pray in their own time. In secondary colleges, these percentages increase to 27.3% for the students and 15.4% for the adults (see Figures II-20/22). The ratio of students who never pray increases as they grow older (year 5-6: 7.4%; year 7-8: 22.1%; year 9-10: 29.6%; year 11-12: 32.1% which is almost 1/3) (see Figures II-21/23). Active prayer lives tend to become more irregular and irregular prayer lives tend to disappear steadily throughout the students' academic career. Given the importance of personal prayer life for any Catholic identity both personal and institutional, these observations indicate an upcoming religious crisis in Catholic schools.

Colourful and Colourless Schools

Considering the pedagogical typology of school identity types, the results of the *Victoria Scale* demonstrate an increasing number of students leaning towards minimal Christian identity by supporting both the *Colourful* and *Colourless School* types. A declining resistance and a growing support for a school type with maximal solidarity but minimal Christian identity is identified: the *Colourful School*. The rising mean score for the *Colourful School* model must be noted (from 3.35/7 to 3.81/7 in primary schools and from 3.62/7 to 4.39/7 in secondary colleges). This means that secondary college students generally approve of the *Colourful School*, which mean score approaches the declining score for the *Dialogue School* model (see Figures II-79/85). Moreover, there is an increasing difference of opinion about a school with minimal Christian identity and minimal solidarity: the *Colourless School*. The rising appreciation of the *Colourless School* model is a challenge to be addressed, especially among the student respondents. In primary schools, 28% agree with and 21.4% express hesitation for this school type. In secondary colleges, 34.9% approve of and 27.5% show hesitation towards a *Colourless School* on the normative level (see Figures II-80/86).

Regarding these evolutions, the crucial and decisive shift is the one from the *Dialogue School* to the *Colourful School*. In the latter school model, Christianity ceases to be the privileged conversational partner and *Secularisation* will emerge. When the way of a *Colourful School* is chosen, the shift to a *Colourless School* is seductive and almost inevitable. There is, therefore, a need to be cautious about activities that gradually water down the inherent solidarity with others in the Christian tradition and eventually albeit inadvertently lead to the gradual embracing of the *Colourful* and *Colourless School* types.

A subgroup of students doubt the *Dialogue School* model

Noteworthy is also the decreasing support for a *Dialogue School* model among students in primary schools (from 5.27/7 to 5.14/7; 12.6% resistance and 17.0% hesitation) and among students in secondary colleges (from 5.04/7 to 4.61/7; 19.7% resistance and 23.5% hesitation). It is positive, however, that a majority of the students keep supporting the *Dialogue School* while it remains the adults' preferred identity option by far.

Diversity among the students

It would be good not to underestimate the diversity that exists among the student population regarding Catholic identity, both personal and institutional, especially in secondary colleges but also in primary schools. Some might be tempted to represent the student population as a uniform group of children or teenagers who share similar views and practices. The ECSIP research indicates that this is not the case. On the contrary, we discover that one of the actual effects of the current Catholic identity management in Victorian Catholic schools is a *fragmentation* of the student population into subgroups with very different experiences and opinions. Among them, there exists different 'parties' or 'fractions' that have a hard time communicating with each other about the sensitive issue of Catholic identity. Becoming aware of this effect is an important first step.

The influence of cultural surroundings

When reflecting on *Secularisation* tendencies among student groups, it is important to note that this drop in openness for religious belief is not automatically the consequence of what happens in the school alone. It is also both the expression of puberty and adolescence and of the cultural surroundings that are often characterised by pluralism and *Secularisation*. A central challenge for Catholic schools is to be aware of these influences and patterns and to respond to them in a creative way, given that they are part of school life.

Relativism in relation to *Post-Critical Belief*

When viewing the ECSIP research results, the relationship between *Post-Critical Belief* and *Relativism* needs to be closely considered. Regarding the adult groups, their overall score for *Post-Critical Belief* clearly dominates their inclination to *Relativise* religious claims, which is positive (adults in primary schools: 5.29/7 for *Post-Critical Belief* and 4.67/7 for *Relativism*; adults in secondary colleges: 5.19/7 for *Post-Critical Belief* and 4.71/7 for *Relativism*) (see Figures II-42/47). The same is true for the children in year 5-6 (5.72/7 for *Post-Critical Belief* and 4.22/7 for *Relativism*) albeit their *Post-Critical Belief* is somewhat 'tainted' by an overly high mean score for *Literal Belief* (4.77/7) (see Figure II-44). The results among secondary college students tell a different story, though. Their mean scores for *Post-Critical Belief* and *Relativism* have become nearly identical (4.63/7 for *Post-Critical Belief* and 4.61/7 for *Relativism*) (see Figure II-49). A closer examination of these results shows disagreement among various subgroups of students regarding both *Post-Critical Belief* and *Relativism* (see Figure II-50). What is at stake in the current debate among secondary college students with regard to Catholic school identity is the relation between a believing and a non-believing symbolically mediated approach to religious contents. In other words, the students have become undecided about the surplus value of a religious outlook and a Christian preferential point of view. *Relativism* is ready to take over.

It is important that students do not exchange *Post-Critical Belief* with *Relativism*, which is a hermeneutic but religiously unbelieving cognitive stance. This point is important since *Post-Critical Belief* functions as the basis that enables the reinterpretation of the Catholic faith tradition today (*Recontextualisation*) in a way that is mindful of the pluralising cultural context (*Dialogue School*). *Post-Critical Belief* differs from *Relativism* because people are existentially engaged with a particular perspective – the Christian faith! – and a personal relationship with the God of Jesus Christ. For *Post-Critical Believers*, religious symbols refer to a transcendent reality and are not simply interchangeable with other symbols and frames of reference that are supposedly merely culturally and historically determined and therefore contingent.

The risk of *Reconfessionalisation*

The decreasing student support for *Reconfessionalisation*, particularly as they move through secondary school, is a challenge for the adults who appear unsure as to which way to go with the *Reconfessionalising* approach. At present, the prime debate among adults concerns the level of *Reconfessionalisation* required to face *Secularising* challenges, whereas a majority of the students indicate how unlikely it is that this is the way of the future. In primary schools, 32.5% of the children in year 5-6 decline *Reconfessionalisation* with an additional 23.0% hesitation. In secondary colleges, 50.0% of the students decline *Reconfessionalisation* with an additional 23.1% hesitation (see Figures II-62/68). As the students advance in their school career, their resistance becomes stronger: from a mean score of 4.2/7 in year 5-6, to 3.8/7 in year 7-8, to 3.3/7 in year 9-10 and finally to 3.0/7 in year 11-12 (see Figures II-64/70).

The debate about *Reconfessionalisation* is a continuing one in Victorian Catholic education. However, it is a potentially polarising discussion that could stall and even harm the identity development of Catholic schools. The question of the plausibility of the Catholic tradition in relation to the living environment of people today and to the presence of other religious and philosophical options risk to be left unspoken or approached in merely apologetic terms whereby the plurality of views and practices is not a theme nor a source of richness.

Great care should be taken to keep the conversations at school from becoming *Reconfessionalising* in a *Monological* way. Though some level of *Reconfessionalisation* is necessary to cherish and rediscover treasures from the faith tradition and for *Recontextualisation* to occur, these efforts must be carried out in *Dialogue* which the growing diversity that exists at school. *Reconfessionalisation* and *Recontextualisation* can be framed as processes that work together, always moving forward, relating faith symbolically to its surroundings and yet affirming its uniqueness. A clear and effective communication of *Recontextualisation* of the Catholic faith may reassure students that adults are not simply trying to reinstate some 'old-fashioned', uncompromising Catholic *Confessionality*, but rather bringing the tradition to life and applying it to their actual existence. ECSIP advises against a one-sided *Reconfessionalising* approach to Catholic identity formation lest the gap between students and teachers becomes so wide that *Reconfessionalisation* becomes ineffective and even straightforwardly counterproductive. Going against a mainstream dynamic in a new generation of students is unlikely to succeed and might effect increasing doubt and resistance.

§4. *ECSIP 2012 Research* – Recommendations

Introduction
In this concluding paragraph a number of recommendations are being considered that could assist Catholic schools in Victoria to further develop and enhance their Catholic identity in the normative direction proposed by ECSIP. The various remarks in this paragraph, although rooted in a theoretical framework, attempt to be as concrete and practical as possible. They serve a double purpose: not only do they apply the theoretical framework to the everyday reality inside the school, but in addition they illustrate the theological view behind ECSIP with concrete examples and thus make it more conceivable and accessible. Finally, it needs to be stressed that recommendations are indeed just that – recommendations – and it will be up to each school to engage with and take ownership of the ECSIP research in a practical, inclusive and engaging manner.

Cherish and nurture the (remaining) *Confessional* elements.
A Catholic school is true to its name only when it maintains and nurtures a clearly recognisable *Catholic* identity. Central to Catholic identity is that, in all aspects of life, schools relate in a preferential way to the person, the message and the future offered by Jesus Christ, Son of God, through the particular mediations that are offered by the Catholic Church. *Confessional* Catholic identity markers (such a crucifixes, Bibles and Scripture quotations, statues and artwork, the school chapel, prayer tables, celebrations, posters, icons, candles, and so on) play a constitutive role in *any* type of Catholic institutional identity because they are not only markers but also symbols that enable us to relate in an unique and vivid way to Jesus Christ.

Therefore we recommend that schools cherish and nurture the *Confessional* elements that constitute their identity. It would be good to put them in the picture, to refurbish them, to restore them if necessary, to reintroduce them and to manifest their meaning. The students should be invited to contribute actively and creatively to this process whenever possible. While doing so, it is important to *Recontextualise Confessional* references, so that they continue to be carriers of authentic religious meaning for people today and tomorrow.

This first and central recommendation is all the more important because of the *Secularising* trends that have been described earlier in this volume. Gradual *Secularisation* becomes apparent especially in the results of the students in secondary colleges. However, it threatens the entire Catholic education network and primary schools certainly do not escape it either. The *ECSIP 2012 Research* results show that for many students the Catholic identity markers have become somehow invisible: the students accept their presence as something evident, but an increasing number do not really notice, understand and incorporate their meaning anymore. In many instances, one of the reasons why a *Christian Values Education strategy* fails, is because the students are becoming less and less familiar with and accepting of *Confessional* Catholic views and practices.

Focus on prayer life, spirituality, rituals and liturgy
Empirical research shows that there is a positive relationship between spirituality manifested through prayer and Catholic (school) identity. There is hardly a more fitting way to communicate the Christian faith to a new generation and to foster a true and living religious school community than to *teach its members how to pray*. The best way to achieve this is to teach by example: adults must be authentic and show a new generation how valuable prayer is for living a true religious life. That way, at school a *culture of prayer* can grow. The same holds true for the ritualistic expression and the liturgical celebration of the Catholic faith, on the personal as well as the communal level. As always, there is a dynamic between *continuation* and *discontinuation*. Inevitably, the way young people shape their faith through prayers and rituals is informed and inspired by the Catholic tradition. Yet it is not limited to past contents and forms. We recommend encouraging the students to creatively search for new ways to pray and to celebrate their faith.

Theological differences among the adult groups (*Subpopulations*)
At first sight, there might seem to be a relative unanimity among the adult groups. When we look closer, however, we discover different theological positions that exist in various degrees among all Catholic school staff and parents across Victoria, in primary as well as in secondary schools. ECSIP summarises these theological differences among the adult groups in terms of four *Subpopulations* (that in turn summarise the three *multivariate attitude scales*), modelled on the typology of theological school identity types that underpins the *Melbourne Scale*[49].

First subpopulation: *Secularisation*. About 4% of the adults in primary schools and about 12% of the adults in secondary colleges adhere to this point of view (see Figures II-109/110). These people appear to go along with their school's Catholic identity, but in fact they desire to let go of it and to *Secularise* the school even at the institutional level. Although only a minority with little real impact, it is important to recognise that this tendency is present in the Catholic education system and might even increase towards the future.

---

[49] The *Subpopulations* are elaborated in Chapter 10, paragraph 5.

Second subpopulation: *Reconfessionalisation*. The desire to react against perceived trends of *Secularisation* by going the opposite way and opting for an active and uncompromising strategy of *Reconfessionalisation* is shared by about 6% of the adults in primary schools and about 5% in secondary colleges. These minority subgroups tend towards a *Literal Believing* faith orientation and a *Monological* Catholic identity. They want to continue to preserve a specific traditional manifestation of Catholic identity, thereby resisting too much 'change' or 'adaptation' in the light of present-day cultural developments. They feel the need to 'pass on' the Catholic faith to new generations preferably without significant change. They also tend to mistrust the increasing plurality that is considered a (potential) threat to Catholic identity.

Third subpopulation: *Recontextualisation of Catholic identity*. About 41% of the staff members and the parents in primary schools and about 43% in secondary colleges sincerely believe in a *Catholic identity in dialogue* approach. They see the need to *Recontextualise* Catholic school identity in present-day times, thereby combining Catholic identity with a genuine openness towards plural culture. These people have a predominant *Post-Critical Belief* attitude and prefer a *Dialogue School* environment. They are searching for new, creative and original ways of realising the Catholic faith in a changed context, thereby redefining the school's religious identity and mission. Instead of avoiding plurality, they acknowledge it, respect it and engage with it in an open and constructive way.

Fourth subpopulation: *Christian Values Education*. This approach to Catholic identity attracts significant proportions of the adults as well: about 48% at the primary education level and about 38% at the secondary level. These people still perceive a significant amount of traditional Catholic *Confessionality* in their school. Based on this (often exaggerated) perception, they remain convinced of a significant overlap between the Catholic faith and present-day student culture. Consequently, they continue to try to directly *link* the students' experiences to the Catholic faith (*mono-correlation*) without seeing a real need to engage with plurality at a deeper level. They prefer to deny, ignore or reduce the growing existence of (radical) differences, thereby creating a risk that true encounter and genuine dialogue does not take place. Often, diverse perspectives are joined under the same denominator, thereby declaring plurality merely a kind of *anonymous Christianity*. Either non-believing people are simply wrong, or they have not (yet) reached the insight that what they believe in and what they desire is actually *Catholic deep down*. Adopting this approach in a pluralising context risks becoming ineffective and even counterproductive, 'hollowing out' the Catholic message from the inside out and paradoxically contributing to a *Secularisation* of Catholic schools.

Despite these fundamental differences, *everybody likes dialogue*: the *Dialogue School* identity option is the prevailing discourse among the adult population in Victorian Catholic schools. It is the current paradigm everyone seems to adhere to. However, beneath the surface there exist multiple theological positions. Depending on their preference and perspective, people interpret the proposed 'dialogue' differently, as the four *Subpopulations* show.

First of all, it is recommendable to acknowledge the different points of view that exist among the adults engaged in the Catholic education system. After all, it is crucial for any successful management process to start from a correct analysis and understanding of the unfolding reality. Although we might not appreciate certain positions or practices, it is nonetheless necessary to receive the people involved with an open mind, to take their experiences seriously and to listen to their concerns with empathy and care, without judgement or rejection.

The various understandings of dialogue provide a rich basis on which teachers in schools could explore and reflect on the very meaning and attitudes towards dialogue that exist in the school. The existence of and tension between *Kerygmatic Dialogue* and *Recontextualising Dialogue* within Catholic schools in Victoria requires further discussion and understanding. The opportunity to delve more deeply into the insights of the Second Vatican Council, in particular the relationship between the Church and the world could assist in this clarification of what type of dialogue is called for today.

Educational leaders and policy makers are challenged to look for effective ways to manage and lead the reality in Catholic schools in a desired direction based on an adequate, consistent and generally shared long-term vision. Providing proper training as well as on-going personal formation of all staff, teachers, school leaders and Catholic education personnel is paramount. No doubt, Catholic tertiary education institutions have an important role to play in this regard.

Literal Believing trends

As the results of the *PCB Scale* show, adults and students in both primary and secondary schools reveal a significant minority tendency towards *Literal Belief*. On the one hand, from a theological point of view, it is positive for Catholic identity that a minority of *Literal Believers* keep reminding people of the importance of respecting the ontological references of religious beliefs (first of all the reality of God) and of transmitting the many elements in the Catholic tradition that make this faith tangibly and recognisably Catholic. A balanced combination of *Post-Critical Belief* backed up by some levels of *Literal Belief* is the theological ideal.

On the other hand, tendencies of *Literal Belief* grow remarkably strong in many primary schools and, to a lesser degree, but still significantly, in many secondary colleges. On the whole, over 60% of the children in primary schools and about one third of the students at the secondary level agree with most items that assess *Literal Belief* (see Figures II-45/50). In both cases, the mean score for *Post-Critical Belief* is still higher. Nevertheless, the preferred balance between both approaches seems to be out of kilter. We can wonder whether most young people understand or even notice the difference between a literal and a symbolic religious approach? This raises the question why Catholic schools accept that some students develop a religious attitude they themselves do not accept? The adults' mean score on *Literal Belief* is significantly lower, compared with that of the students'. Theologically, it is preferable not to allow *Literal Belief* to develop to such proportions among young people in schools. It is preferable to situate this in relation to a predominant *Post-Critical Believing* approach of the Christian and Catholic story and tradition.

Finding the right balance when employing
Reconfessionalisation and *Monologue School* policies

As stated, the continuous preservation, integration and *Recontextualisation* of Catholic identity markers, prayer, rituals and liturgy, is very relevant for any type of Catholic school identity. However, the research results warn against a unilateral *Reconfessionalising* approach. As the research results show, in the current circumstances the danger is real that this approach would possibly provoke scepticism, resistance and even a counter reaction among many students. The generally fading enthusiasm among students for *any* type of Catholic school identity (especially among the older students) is partly due to their resistance to a Catholicity that imposes itself.

From a theological point of view, we believe that retreating into an established Catholic identity, unilaterally focussing on continuity instead of tradition development and development of doctrine, avoiding contact and exchange between Catholic believers and the plural culture we live in, and reducing the Christian heritage to a 'closed narrative' only available for insiders, is generally undesirable.

Based on the ECSIP 2012 *Research* results, a strong *Reconfessionalising* and *Monologue School* approach is very unlikely to achieve its intended objectives. On the contrary, despite its good intentions and best efforts, in reality tensions would rise and resistances would grow. Hypothetically, there is only one way a *Reconfessionalising* Catholic school identity policy could work: *downsize* the Catholic education system significantly so that only those staff, leaders, families and students remain who are 'truly' faithful and practicing Catholics in the intended way. Given the view and mission of Catholic schools, this option is theologically undesirable – not to speak of the social, educational, political and economic consequences of such a drastic decision.

Interpreting student results: a *psycho-dynamic perspective*
Children and teenagers go through a process of growth and change, developing their minds and personalities as they gain knowledge and life experience. It could be argued that a *psycho-dynamic perspective* should be taken into account when interpreting student research results. It is conceivable that children and teenagers, from a certain age on, adopt a critical stance towards all proposed frames of reference and expectations – religious and otherwise. Usually this is considered a temporary stage in their normal personal development, surpassed when they reach an adult age. It is recommended that the empirical findings be interpreted in the light of such a *psycho-dynamic perspective*.

The impact of adults on Catholic school identity
The question could be raised as to what extent the attitudes and opinions of the students are actually relevant to assess the Catholic identity of a school. Some people argue that the relevance of student results should be minimised:
- After all, it is mainly the adults – the teachers, the school leadership and the parents – who determine and shape a school's Catholic identity. Since they are in charge of the school and make and implement the relevant decisions, the adults weigh much more on the school's current practice and future course, compared with the student population. The students participate in the school's Catholic identity, but their contribution in shaping it remains minimal.
- It can be argued moreover, that the adult population is usually more united and less divided, compared with the students. Because of their training, selection and pedagogical responsibility as a group, the school staff members are motivated to conform to the role they play in the school community and to speak in a similar voice. The students, on the other hand, are usually more divided and less able to exercise influence on their school's educational and religious course.
- It can be also argued that the view of the adult school members not only carries more weight, but it is also more stable over time, enduring on the long run, thereby ensuring the continuity of the school's religious mission over time. Every so often the student population is entirely replaced, while most school staff members remain present in the school for many years. Because of their prolonged presence and conserving influence, it is the adult school population that actually determines the school's identity and development, much more so than the students.

Because many staff members build their teaching career remaining in the same school over the course of many years, educational institutions tend to change slowly and only gradually. When it comes to adapting to new circumstances, schools are structurally rather 'inert' institutions. Although they continuously evolve and incorporate new things, there is always a gap between the prevailing culture in a school and the fast changes that occur in the surrounding world. Every once in a while, if the gap becomes too wide, the institution feels the need to abruptly 'catch up' with the changes in the surrounding context – normally this happens when new leadership is installed. Organisations that have their leadership replaced by a new and younger generation in a much shorter time span, as is the case for example in youth movements, tend to evolve more quickly, compared with schools.

Students at the centre
Notwithstanding the much stronger impact of the adults in the identity of Catholic schools, we must never overlook that it is the outcome in terms of the human development and spiritual growth of *the student population* that is the prime measure and core objective of a successful Catholic educational project. Obviously, a school does not find its purpose in itself but in the educational service it renders to the students. The reason Catholic schools exist is to give young people the opportunity to be educated in a Catholic spirit. Ultimately, the criterion to ascertain the outcome of a Catholic school's educational and religious mission is the effect it actually has on the students. This is the reason that the students are involved in the ECSIP research in the first place and why their empirical results need to be taken seriously.

Although it is recommended to interpret the students' empirical results in the light of a psycho-dynamic perspective, when relating to them personally it is very important to take them seriously and listen to what they have to say. Using processes of proper dialogue, school leaders should invite students to share their opinions on significant matters, for example the organisation of school events and activities, in ways that genuinely take the students' ideas into account. This will show students that their views and voices are important to figures of authority. By providing a model of 'Catholics as listeners' as well as speakers, leaders can help lend legitimacy to the process of *Dialogue*. This will, in turn, aid efforts at *Recontextualisation* as well as *Reconfessionalisation*. In all this, dialogue among the staff should serve as a model of dialogue among and with the students.

The possible dangers of *Christian Values Education*,
especially when little traditional *Confessionality* remains
The research results show that the continued and unambiguous use of a mono-correlation *Christian Values Education* strategy within a cultural context that is detraditionalising and *Secularising*, holds great risks. The more that traditional

Confessional Catholic identity fades away, the more a *Christian Values Education* approach could and does become:

1. **Ineffective**: the correlation movement is stalling.
2. **Predictable**, boring and even manipulative.
3. **Counterproductive**, actually producing further *Secularisation*!
4. **Reducing the Christian faith** to its moral aspects and thereby 'hollowing it out'.

Presumably, every good school teaches good values and norms. Every decent education is also 'values education'. Like any school, a self-respecting Catholic school induces in its students a sense of self-esteem and personal decency, interpersonal skills and civil responsibility. However, it is not in this sense that the *Melbourne Scale* typology uses the concept 'values education'. With the pedagogical and theological category of '*Christian Values Education*' we mean something different. By warning against '*Christian Values Education*', by no means are we implying that schools should drop their moral education programs!

Christian Values Education, understood in the context of the *Melbourne Scale* typology, only works with those students who are *already* initiated in the Christian story and who therefore expect and desire their experiences and sense of value to be connected to and illuminated by the Catholic faith. It only works when there is still sufficient overlap, when the gap between Catholicism and student culture has not become too wide. If it has, then a *Values Education* approach becomes not only ineffective, but even counterproductive.

It is striking how many adults still support *Christian Values Education*, still believing that it is actually working and will keep on working in the future. Most of the staff intend to use a *Christian Values Education* didactic to bridge the gap between faith and student culture. However, their efforts are increasingly unsuccessful. The research data suggests that there is a dichotomy between the *intention* of the school staff and the parents compared to the actual *effect* it has on many students.

It is possible that, in some cases, the adults are being 'misled' by the students, who know the game all too well and merely 'play along'. After years of being immersed in *Christian Values Education*, the students suspect the prepossession that typifies it, and they know the answers that will satisfy the teachers in advance. The teachers can feel easily reassured when the students seem to follow where 'Christian values' are concerned. But while the adults still tend to believe that this moral education has the potential to carry the students closer to a Christian *religious* life, many students actually adapt the moral sensibility taught at school and integrate it into their own, increasingly diverse, life philosophies. Though they may not feel that they are taken entirely seriously, the students do grasp the nature of this compromise model that allows them to 'get away' easily with their reluctance and disengagement regarding the Catholic faith, while the teachers keep believing they are doing a 'good job'. It is likely that the students find it is easier to 'go with the flow' of the conventional *Christian Values Education* pedagogy instead of opting for *Recontextualisation*. Many students hide behind the minimum acceptable 'proper' behaviour, and a valuable opportunity to engage them on a religious level is lost.

That may be why, contrary to its purpose, *Christian Values Education* allows *Secularising* tendencies to continue and to spread – a process of which it itself becomes an exponent, as the communication of faith is replaced more and more by values. The result is a spiral of ever more de-confessionalisation, rather than a genuine religious education.

A Gospel attitude reaching out to the world: diversity and *Recontextualisation*
Catholic schools have a mission in the world: as Christians, we go out into the world to encounter other people and to spread the Gospel of love, in the footsteps of Jesus. If we are to live up to this calling, Catholic schools should exist in the middle of the world, sharing its life.

Our unique position in history is marked by detraditionalisation and pluralisation on the individual level: people find themselves disconnected from traditions, having to construct a personal life-view. In reality, this is no less true for Christians, than it is for other-believers. In this context, Catholic schools receive a new mission – or more precisely a *Recontextualised* form of the same mission they have always had: to assist the *'identity formation in a plural context'* of all students, in the light of the Gospel.

We are on a quest for original ways to relate the Christian message to a multitude of new discoveries about what it means to be human. We need a *multi-correlation didactics* instead of a *mono-correlation* approach. The latter presumes it already knows the answers and is not really interested in 'new discoveries'. *Multi-correlation*, on the other hand, is more humble and tries to *listen* to what others have to say, to the good and the bad. The Spirit whispers in our hearts in new and unexpected ways and is at work through each human being. New revelation happens all over, waiting to be recognised. Simultaneously, this process also enriches the Catholic tradition itself.

In order to live up to this mission, we believe it is crucial to acknowledge, accept, welcome and engage cultural, philosophical and religious diversity in Catholic schools – in accord with the demography of particular areas.

For how can we, as a Catholic school, be of service to our neighbours if they are not present in the school? How can we encounter other people, if we do not allow them to be visible in daily school life? How can we respect and value the personal identity of each individual, if they can only become part of our community by conforming to a pre-established point of view? How can we stand beside a student and share his/her life, if we prefer not to acknowledge the unique identity and contribution everyone brings to the school, whoever he/she is? How can we live out an authentic and appealing Christian life, if we do not listen to others' (religious) discoveries, values and meanings – to what others try to *teach us* about being Christian, either directly or indirectly? The question is not who does or does not belong to the circle of the faithful; instead my calling is to *become the neighbour* of all I find on my path.

Prof. Dr. Lieven Boeve, the current Dean of the *Faculty of Theology and Religious Studies* at KU Leuven and soon[50] to be promoted to the post of Director-General of the *Flemish Secretariat for Catholic Education* (VSKO), puts it as follows: "Thinking in terms of pluralisation does not mean less but *more* Catholic identity, though at the same time *different* Catholic identity. It is about an identity that knows where it comes from and what it stands for, while it allows itself to be challenged and renewed through the dialogue with others. After all, a dialogical Catholic perspective does make a difference."[51]

Being truly open and receptive towards 'otherness' is an integral part of what it means to be Catholic. This has always been true, but in the pluralising context we live in, it becomes more apparent than ever. Only through the mutual relationships with others can we realise the Catholic mission of our school. Herein lies the key for a culturally plausible and theologically justified *Recontextualisation* of Catholic school identity in a world that is characterised by detraditionalisation and pluralisation: as Christians, we need to welcome other voices in our midst with humility and respect, looking for new ways to serve them, inspired by the Word of the Gospel. In order to meet people, we must first allow them to come near us. Only when we actually do that, we become a Catholic school.

Open the narrative and invite people to input their own narrative. That's when you really engage the students. This process cannot be directed; it happens. But you can *facilitate* it by creating the right circumstances for it to happen.

---

[50] Lieven Boeve will take up his function as Director-General of the *Flemish Secretariat for Catholic Education* (VSKO) from 1 August 2014 onwards.

[51] This quote is an excellent summary of Lieven Boeve's position on Catholic school identity, published in many of his articles and books. The quote itself is an English translation of a text fragment that can be found in: L. BOEVE, *Vakantiebrief 2012* (unpublished letter to the members of the *Faculty of Theology and Religious Studies*, KU Leuven), Leuven, July 2012.

Using the Scriptures and reading the Bible at school

From a Catholic point of view, the Scriptures and the Tradition are being referred to as fundamental sources of faith. When establishing a Catholic school identity, a prime question is: are the Scriptures in fact being used at school? If the answer is negative, then the Catholic identity of a school must be put into question. If the answer is positive, then it is worth considering the questions which Bible or Bibles are being used at school and in what way they are being used?

Figure II-30 on page 142 compares the responses of four age groups of students in Catholic schools in Victoria regarding the issue of reading the Bible at school. These research results show that the resistance against the use of the Bible grows steadily. An increasing subgroup of students suffers from 'Bible fatigue', are unfamiliar with it, feel alienated and resist its use at school. This trend corresponds not only to the increasing *Relativism*, *External Critique* and *Secularisation* among the students as they grow older, but also to the continued practice of *Christian Values Education* that uses and commonly misuses biblical texts in the attempt to *mono-correlate* the Catholic faith to the students' moral sensitivities. Moreover, it is a fundamental problem that using the Bible is becoming increasingly difficult as human cultures evolve and change over time so that the Bible becomes more and more a book of the past and increasingly difficult to read and interpret. There are several serious gaps that inhibit the use of biblical texts by people today and in the future.[52]

Attempting to respond to the necessary challenge that is the Bible at school, here are some suggestions on how to relate to biblical texts or to other texts from the Christian tradition in ways that express and promote *Post-Critical Belief*, *Recontextualisation* and a *Dialogue School* approach.

- The very nature of biblical texts necessitates the application of the *historical-critical method* of interpretation so that we come to know and understand the specific historical and contextual origins of all biblical texts and integrate this historical consciousness into our interpretation. The Bible does not intend to be a direct revelation of timeless truths. Instead, it contains the written testimony of events and experiences where God reveals himself within human history.

- Next, it is up to us to apply this historical consciousness to our present-day existence. For we can only be faithful to the proper intention of biblical texts if we

---

[52] A more comprehensive treatment of the difficulties and opportunities of using the Scriptures in the Catholic school, see: D. POLLEFEYT & R. BIERINGER, *The Role of the Bible in Religious Education Reconsidered. Risks and Challenges in Teaching the Bible*, in *International Journal of Practical Theology* 9(1) (2005) 117-139.

keep trying to discover the religious faith dimension that is being expressed in the heart of their formulation and if we try to link this faith dimension to our own religious experience. Only in this way may we recognise that the word of God is living and addressed to each of us in the here and now of our lives.[53]

- Three pitfalls with regard to the use of biblical texts should be knowingly avoided:
  1. Objectification of the Bible. If we unilaterally focus on the historical and cultural background of biblical texts, their historical origins and evolution through time, then the Bible risks becoming merely an object of scientific study and curiosity that is detached from the religious faith dimension that is nonetheless the essence of its existence. We must not overlook the religious experience that forms the foundation of Biblical stories, or else the critical question comes up as to why these ancient texts are worth studying at all?

  2. Functionalisation of the Bible. It is wrong to introduce and use the Bible in an authoritative way in discourses and debates that as such are disconnected from the world of the Bible itself. A typical example is the use of biblical quotes as authoritative arguments that presumably support a pre-determined position (*proof reading*) while the Bible itself plays no further role in the development of the view that is being defended. Unfortunately, this mistake often occurs with regard to ethical issues whereby the Bible is reduced to a 'recipe book' that contains a proper response to each moral dilemma.

  3. Uniformisation of the Bible. Sometimes, the Bible is presented as a consistent story that gradually unfolds itself and that contains a clear, constant and reliable message: a salvation history starting with Abraham until the first Christian generations whereby all characters and events appear to have an unambiguously positive nature. However, the only way to obtain this kind of consistency is to create a 'canon within the canon' that contains only those texts and passages that fit within a pre-determined framework while ignoring the existence of other texts. The presupposition of this pitfall is that the Bible is expected to express a perfect and ideal message, whereas in reality this is not the case. The Bible is not a book but rather a library that contains a great diversity of texts written by a host of authors in different times and cultural contexts, writing in different languages, expressing different points of view for different purposes. The Bible contains also many sensitive or difficult stories, events, characters and statements that can be harmful or offensive, such as e.g. the creation account, parables, miracle stories,

---

[53] POPE BENEDICT XVI, *Post-Synodal Apostolic Exhortation Verbum Domini. On the Word of God in the Life and Mission of the Church*, 2010, §37.

androcentric accounts, the anti-Jewish character of the Gospel of John, eschatological descriptions, acts of violence and murder, etc. In this regard, the bible is a *mirror* of our human reality, including the good and the bad. Intellectual honesty compels us nonetheless not to avoid these 'problematic' passages.

Each of these approaches of the Bible leaves insufficient room for the interpretation and the response of the reader. If we intend letting the Bible be a 'living word', then we must accept that its meaning is not fixed and determined in advance. Instead, giving meaning to biblical texts is a complex interaction between (a) the text itself including all the difficulties it contains, (b) the text's history of interpretation (c) and its interpretation by the current reader.

- By strengthening the school members' attitude of *Post-Critical Belief*, they can become more aware of the essentially interpretative nature of Biblical texts and therefore sensitive to the hermeneutical quality of any act of reading them. There is a need to change the perspective from merely 'Bible reading' to the more apt 'interpreting the Bible' at school. It is important to realise that even the task of reading the Bible itself is already an act of interpretation. A participatory approach might be helpful where students learn to interpret the text instead of only being given one interpretation. *Post-Critical Believers* will want to listen and communicate one's interpretation of biblical texts and respect others' varying interpretations. They can articulate questions coming from the Bible itself and also ask the Bible questions that can sometimes be critical. They would also be receptive, for example, to the important distinction between the 'world behind the text', the 'world of the text' and the 'world before the text' when they engage the Bible and other texts of the Christian tradition.

- As is the case for all elements of the faith tradition, the use and the interpretation of biblical texts are subject to a continuous process of *Recontextualisation*. Revitalise the *Recontextualisation* of biblical interpretative methods and incorporate these insights on biblical texts, taking the students' abilities and spiritual needs into account. We encourage the discovery of new ways of approaching the Bible that promote critical hermeneutical processes and integrating them in the Catholic identity of schools. It is important to underscore the *multi-correlational nature* of the interaction between the biblical text and the person-in-community's plural and changing contexts

- In relation to the these remarks, it is clear how the pedagogical approach of a genuine *Dialogue School* is indispensable for taking on the challenge of using the Bible in a Catholic school in a correct, meaningful and fruitful way. Dealing with the

Bible is an act of *Dialogue* in various ways. We advocate training teachers and students to acquire *Dialogical* skills: they are invited to enter into an active *Dialogue* with (1) the biblical text itself, (2) with the history of its interpretation that continues today, (3) with other people within the Catholic tradition, (4) with other Christian communities, and (5) with other religions, especially Judaism with whom Christians share the Torah or Old Testament.

- It is important that the school members, especially the teachers, get acquainted with the most recent methodologies and approaches in biblical interpretation. We encourage teachers to take part in on-going formation that includes updated exegetical scientific research findings about the interpretation of biblical texts that are used at school.

- Finally, it is important to acknowledge that biblical interpretation does not only happen in the classroom during course times but that it permeates various expressions of a school's Catholic identity at any given moment. Working with the Bible and applying newfound meaning to daily school life should be made part of many activities at school. For example, the students and the adults should be able to recognise and integrate biblical interpretation at school in personal and communal prayers as well as in liturgy and sacramental celebrations. Biblical texts ought to be recognised as a foundation of ethical commitments such as the schools' involvement in social justice projects. The Bible can also be vital in grounding people's critical openness to plurality not only in terms of biblical interpretations but also in terms of the diversity of people, cultures, traditions and philosophies of life. Make sure that in doing so, one's own Catholic identity is nourished by interpreting the Bible with an accompanying respect for those who do not share one's conviction without watering down one's own identity in the process. In a Catholic school, the Holy Bible is a living text that inspires people and leaves traces everywhere.

The implications for Religious Education

With many adults continuing to support *Christian Values Education*, there is a danger that Religious Education programs could be reduced to *mono-correlation* activities reducing Christianity to its ethical dimension alone. On the other hand there is a significant number of adults who support a *Reconfessionalising* strategy and who are more likely to support a deductive approach to religious education. We have seen that among the large group of adults who favour a *Recontextualising* strategy to Catholic identity formation they also favour both *Christian Values Education* and to a lesser degree *Reconfessionalisation.* We have also noted a tendency among the adults to use *Christian Values* and *Recontextualisation* in order to *Reconfessionalise* the school and we have noted the limitations of this approach. It is time for Victorian Catholic schools to evaluate the approach to Religious Education in light of these findings. In this regard, the *hermeneutical-communicative* approach to Religious Education developed by KU Leuven has some insights to offer Catholic Schools in Victoria into the future[54].

The implications for religious education leaders

Religious education leaders in Victorian Catholic Schools have great challenges in conjunction with their leaders to create opportunities for growth and development for both staff and students in Catholic schools. It would seem advisable that religious education leaders in particular are provided with the opportunities to read, analyse and understand the school data on Catholic Identity. Catholic religious education leaders should be equipped with the tools to explore the theological and pedagogical approaches behind the ECSIP Project and lead staff into deeper reflection on their practices and identity formation outcomes.

Pre-service training and on-going teacher formation

It will become increasingly important for new teachers entering Catholic schools to be aware of the cultural environment in which Catholic schools exist today. They will need to be appraised of the changed nature of the Catholic school and the varying levels of support for Catholic schools today (both on the factual and the normative level). It is recommended that those students involved in teacher training in Catholic institutions are exposed to the findings of the *Enhancing Catholic School Identity Project* and introduced to the various scales and questionnaires that are now part of the landscape of Catholic Identity in school improvement across Victoria. The CECV should ensure that enhancing the identity of Catholic Schools is a key part of the induction process into the Catholic education system.

Understanding *Recontextualisation*

In the *Melbourne Scale* we see that *Recontextualisation* is favoured on the normative level by the majority of adults. For many adults within Victorian schools this approach is coupled with support for *Christian Values Education* and with small amounts of *Reconfessionalisation*. This has exhibited itself in the research as the *Kerygmatic Dialogue* approach. The ECSIP normative position is for a *Recontextualising Dialogue School* model. It is recommended that the following elements of this approach be further explored by Catholic schools in Victoria: (a) the *Recontextualisation* of revelation from the Second Vatican Council onwards; (b) an exploration of hermeneutical theology and religious education; (c) a pedagogy of dialogue; (d) further

---

[54] H. LOMBAERTS & D. POLLEFEYT, *Hermeneutics and Religious Education* (BETL, 180), Leuven, Peeters, 2004.

deepening an understanding of *Post-Critical Belief* and in particular the interpretation of Scripture in the Church today.

It is certainly true that Catholics tell and teach the great stories about the relationship between God and men in a past age, written in old language. *Recontextualising* Catholic identity also implies that we ourselves continue the tradition of story-telling, creating and telling new stories about God humankind and the world today, written in our current language.

Personalised learning and Catholic Identity
Catholic Schools in Victoria strive for educational excellency with a growing emphasis on personalised learning, characterised by a dynamic interaction of teacher led delivery, group work, individual research by students, the sharing and presentation of findings by students to each other, grouping of students together to work on chosen projects, the attention to open environments in schools and the targeted organisation of curriculum. However, at the same time an unsophisticated *Kerygmatic Dialogue* approach to Catholic identity can tend to keep the reigns very tight on religious questions. The shift to a *Recontextualising Dialogue* is akin to the letting go of the total teacher directed learning to an approach that allows individual responsibility for goal setting, discovery and insight into learning. Is it timely for Victorian Catholic Schools to explore further implications for religious learning with the framework of personalised learning and contemporary learning spaces?

Visible practices of *Catholic identity in Dialogue*
There exists a challenge for Victorian Catholic schools to make the confessional Catholic elements visible and meaningful within the schools. Visible practices of Catholic Identity go beyond the *Recontextualising* of traditional iconography, art and statues (as important as they can be) to the practices of *Dialogue*, decision-making, disciplinary practices, financial policies, communication protocols and practices of inclusion. It is recommended that Catholic Schools in Victoria reflect on a range of current practices and policies to identify where *Catholic identity in Dialogue* is visible and recognisable in the school.

Governance and identity of Catholic schools
More and more the issue of governance of Catholic schools is coming to the fore with Catholic schools in Victoria experiencing a decline in the number of priests and members of religious orders involved as school personnel. Schools are increasingly led by delegated lay boards or incorporated boards (in the case of secondary colleges) and lay principals under the authority of a canonical administrator (parish priest in the case of primary schools) who may be responsible for one or more schools. Those

responsible for the governance of the once *Confessional* system of Catholic schools are charged with the responsibility of ensuring that a clearly articulated and relevant vision for their Catholic school is stated. They are also responsible for appointing and supporting the leadership they have in place for these schools. It is recommended that governance boards and canonical administrators reflect and act on the ECSIP data. The overwhelming majority of leaders in the ECSIP data support a *Post-Critical, Recontextualising Dialogue School*. However, there are small pockets even within the leadership of schools who prefer to let go of the Catholic school identity and would be happy to move to a *Colourful* or even *Colourless School*. It is recommended that the governance personnel of the school involve themselves in questions of the future identity of the school.

School Improvement Framework

Victorian Catholic Schools have already now embedded the diagnostic tools of ECSIP into their *School Improvement Framework* protocols. To ensure quality analysis and targeted strategies are occurring in Catholic schools it will be important for ECSIP professional learning to be part of the support provided for those involved in *School Improvement* support and validation. A clear understanding of the theological normative position of ECSIP and a year by year tracking of the ECSIP data to monitor longer term trends is essential for those involved in assisting schools in setting goals for enhancing and strengthening Catholic Identity.

Implications for the wider Church community

The ECSIP Project data has uncovered patterns of belief and pedagogical practices among adults and children that are likely to be at work in the wider Catholic community and its institutions and at local, parochial and diocesan level. Catholic schools never exist as isolated institutions of the Church. They are part of the broader ecclesial environment in which they exist. The findings of the ECSIP Project could be shared with the wider diocesan communities within each of the diocese of Victoria. The process of *Recontextualising* the Catholic school would benefit from wider support from parishes, theologates, Catholic universities and other agencies of the various dioceses. The challenges facing Catholic schools today are not isolated to the school itself but are shared with the wider Catholic community which is also experiencing the effects of a pluralising and detraditionalising cultural context. Schools working together within and across dioceses and in dialogue with other Catholic community organisations may be better equipped to tackle the task of creating a school which truly reflects *Catholic identity in Dialogue*.

Implications for enrolment policies

Diverse demographic, social economic and religious situations should be taken into account as schools are implementing enrolment policies. The theologically normative position of the ECSIP Project – *Post-Critical Belief, Recontextualised* school identity in *Dialogue* – envisages a school were a diversity of voices and views sit side by side. This does not mean that enrolment policies should not give priority to Catholic students or teachers. It is clear that a critical number of committed Catholic teachers and students is essential to the process of identity formation in a Catholic school. But the process of identity formation in *Dialogue* also means that other voices are present, heard and respected. These voices may also be challenged and challenge the views of the Catholic school and its adherents. Managed carefully this internal pluralist environment can lead to a stronger sense of identity for all.

Recruitment of staff

The school leadership and staff play a key role in shaping the identity of the Catholic school. Correlations between the *Melbourne Scale* and the *Post-Critical Belief Scale* indicate that the overwhelming majority of Catholic school staff in Victoria are supportive of the Catholic school. At the same time there are differing combinations of believing styles and hopes of the ideal school among staff. There is a need for all staff to have openness to their own continuing education and formation in theology, pedagogy and human development.

Epilogue

In all successful leadership, the first step is an adequate analysis of the current state of affairs. A correct understanding of the problem has the solution already embedded within it. Only when we properly *understand* what is happening, can we properly *act*.

As is the case in other parts of the world, Catholic schools in Victoria are confronted with *Secularising* tendencies. The Catholic education leadership in Victoria cooperate with KU Leuven in order to come to grips with a difficult and at times escalating situation. ECSIP endeavours to analyse and understand the unfolding reality in Victorian Catholic schools, looking at the situation from a fresh point of view. To this end, we have developed a new vocabulary and new conceptualisations needed to reflect upon the original, complex but exciting historical situation we live in today.

The ECSIP Project sets out to serve the Catholic educational system in Victoria by describing both the strengths and the challenges it faces and by formulating open-ended recommendations to enhance its identity. We are invited to be part of the living and on-going Catholic story. Catholic schools remain privileged venues to continue telling and living this great story. It is hoped that the ECSIP approach to Catholic education sparks new ways of looking, new ideas and visions, new encounter and dialogue, a new potential to 'break open' narratives that tend to be closed, and new hope and faith in the bright future of Catholic education in Australia and the rest of the world.

Coda. A biblical reflection (Luke 10:25-37)

One day an expert in the law, critical of Jesus' teachings, stands up to test Him: "Tell me, *teacher*, what shall I do to inherit eternal life?" Jesus refers to the famous commandment in the book of Leviticus: "You shall love the Lord your God with all your heart, with all your soul, with all your strength, and with all your mind; <u>and you shall love your neighbour as yourself</u>." (Lev 19.18)

Desiring to justify himself, the lawyer asks Jesus, "*Who is my neighbour?*" Who am I to love as myself? Surely it would be undoable to show unconditional love to all people in an equal way. Who belongs to the circle of those deserving my love, and who does not? Where do I draw the line, reasonably speaking? Surely it does not include those who do not belong to the people of Israel? Surely it does not imply harming my own (religious) interests? Jesus avoids answering this trick question; instead, He tells a rather provocative story, which has become known as the famous parable of the *Good Samaritan*.

Figure II-113. Rembrandt van Rijn: *The Good Samaritan* (1632-1633).

A man fell victim to robbers on the dangerous road from Jerusalem to Jericho. It is not stated who the victim was. His identity is unimportant to the story; it could have been anyone. Two devout Jews, a priest and a Levite, passed by, saw the wounded man, but did nothing. However, a Samaritan traveller stopped and helped him. Even more so: he does everything that is humanly possible – more than can be reasonably expected – to help the victim. Since Samaritans were unwanted outsiders who were generally despised by Jesus' target audience, this plot must have come as a shock to them.

Then Jesus turns the initial question upside down and asks: "*Which of these three has been the neighbour to him who fell among the robbers?*" The challenger has no other choice than to answer: "He who showed mercy on him." After which Jesus sends him out into the world: "Go and do likewise."

318

Martin Luther King once explained this reversal as follows[55]. The priest and the Levite wondered by themselves: "If I stop to help this man, what will happen TO ME?" (think of purification rites, avoiding uncleanness at the eve of the Passover Festival, et cetera). But the Good Samaritan reversed the question: "If I do not stop to help this man, what will happen TO HIM?"

The right question is not: "Who is MY neighbour?" In other words: to what degree is it justified to potentially harm myself and my circle of peers when making sacrifices for another person? Where to draw the line, reasonably speaking, keeping in mind my own (religious) interests? Instead, the calling is for me to BECOME the neighbour of all the people I encounter on my path, just because I have no other choice than to love them as myself. And not just the happy and collaborative ones, but especially also those who are in need. Only then I testify that I love the Lord my God – *who is love* – and inherit eternal life.

As always, Jesus breaks open closed narratives that – though they were originally intended to set people free and advance the good – tend to imprison people resulting in evil side-effects. Jesus frees us of self-serving impulses and then sends us into the world to 'show mercy' on our neighbours.[56]

Our present-day challenge is not how to safeguard a 'circle of the faithful' and to advance its interests, so that the Catholic identity of our schools can be saved. Instead, our continuous calling as *Catholic* schools is to become the servants of young people who are entrusted to our care, in a way that testifies of an authentic Christian inspiration.

Thus, the challenge is not so much theological as *practical*. HOW to do this as Catholic schools, in an era when time-honoured traditions fragment, people individualise and school populations pluralise? The question is HOW to *Recontextualise* Catholic school identity so that we are enabled to serve a pluralising school population?

The key is to be open to dialogue with plurality and to encounter each of these young people as they really are – even if it hurts. We need to enter into a pedagogical relationship with them and become their neighbours through acts and words of love and compassion – also if that means sacrificing our (religious) interests. The challenge is to walk alongside them, listening to their despair and aspirations, sharing their joy and their pain, making all of them good people. How do we create a stillness and an openness in their hearts – so that God is able to touch them? How do we let them meet

[55] MARTIN LUTHER KING, JR, *I've Been to the Mountaintop*, speech delivered on 3 April 1968, Memphis, Tennessee at Stanford University. See online: http://mlk-kpp01.stanford.edu/index.php/encyclopedia/documentsentry/ive_been_to_the_mountaintop/ (access 4-09-2011).
[56] BOEVE, L., *Onderbroken traditie. Heeft het christelijk verhaal nog toekomst?*, Kapellen, Pelckmans, 1999, p.101-102.

Jesus and allow ourselves to meet Jesus through them? Let us proclaim the Gospel in word and practice and have it proclaimed to us. Let us find ways to pray and to share the *Bread of Life* together.

Catholic identity is *a verb*. It has to be done and made real through acts of love and compassion. Only when this happens – which is always a moment of grace – do we *become* Catholics. When we 'act out' our Catholic identity, freely and courageously, and make God's unconditional love come alive in all the aspects of school life, then we *become* Catholic schools – and the appeal will be irresistible.

Attachments

The empirical instruments used in the ECSIP Research

§1. Research Group Registration Diagram

An organisation that takes part in the ECSIP research is called a 'research group'. It can be a primary or a secondary school, a tertiary education institution (or part thereof), a Catholic education office, a Catholic youth movement, a health care or social institution, or any group of people who complete the surveys as a group.

Before its members can take part in the ECSIP research, the research group must first be registered on the *ECSIP Website*. This group registration process is accomplished by completing the online *Research Group Registration Diagram*. When researching a Catholic school, the following information is collected:

VARIABLE	CONTENT (in school contexts)
Registration date	Date and time of the group registration.
Group manager	The email address of the person who registers the research group and receives the group's login information.
Group name	Full name of the school.
Location	Name of town or city.
Province / state	Name of broader geographical region the school belongs to.
E-number	In Victoria, each Catholic school is identified by a unique E-number, e.g. E1050.
Logo	JPG-file that contains the school's logo, crest or shield.
Organisation type	Primary, secondary, tertiary, CEO.
Education type	Code indicating the grades of the students' being taught, e.g. P-6, 1-6, P-8, 1-12, P-12, 7-12, 9-12, 10-12, etc.
Affiliation / congregation	Sometimes schools are part of a larger affiliation, network or congregation.
Diocese	Name of the diocese the school belongs to.

Region	Sometimes dioceses are being split up in different regions, e.g. Northern, Southern, Eastern, Western.
Zone	Sometimes dioceses are split up further in specific zones, e.g. North Eastern, Central, Peninsula, Bendigo, etc.
Parish	Name of the parish or group of parishes the school belongs to or is affiliated with.
Geographical location / regional indicator	Rural, provincial, outer-urban, metropolitan, inner-urban.
Student gender	CO-ED, boys only, girls only.
Surveys	Overview of the surveys that are to be used for researching this group.
Extra info	Any additional information about the research group that is pertinent to the ECSIP research.
Population numbers	A list of figures indicating the total number of people who are part of the research group at the time of the research. Added together, these people constitute the sample frame. Population numbers are collected for all the respondent groups present in the organisation: students of different grades, teaching staff, leadership, parents and CEO staff.
Cultural diversity	A list of characteristics that assess the cultural diversity within the school population, e.g. ethnic background or country of origin, different religious or philosophical affiliations, etc.

After being registered on the system, a research group receives a unique *Group ID* and 6-digit password. Using these codes, the group manager can login into the *Principal's Access Level* at any time to view the group's aggregated research results.

When registered, the research group (Name, location and E-number) appears in the dropdown list presented to new respondents upon accessing the *ECSIP Website*. It can then be used immediately to take part in the research. Each respondent is required to select a single research group from the list.

§2. Respondent Identification Diagram

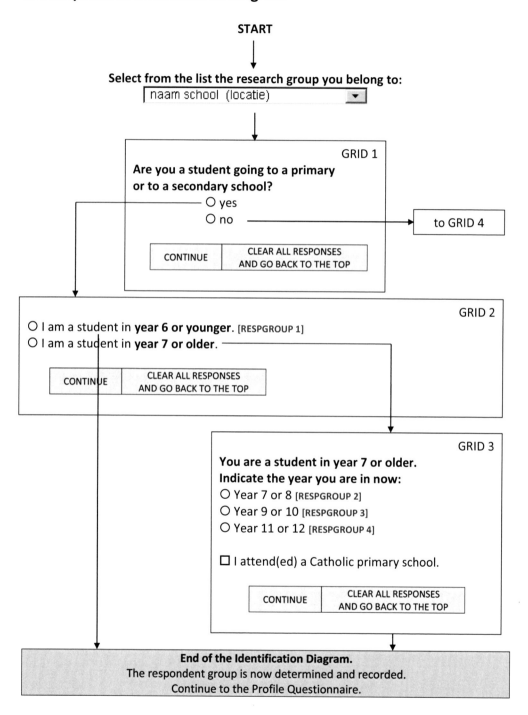

START

Select from the list the research group you belong to:

naam school (locatie) ▼

GRID 1

Are you a student going to a primary or to a secondary school?

○ yes
○ no — to GRID 4

CONTINUE | CLEAR ALL RESPONSES AND GO BACK TO THE TOP

GRID 2

○ I am a student in **year 6 or younger**. [RESPGROUP 1]
○ I am a student in **year 7 or older**.

CONTINUE | CLEAR ALL RESPONSES AND GO BACK TO THE TOP

GRID 3

You are a student in year 7 or older.
Indicate the year you are in now:
○ Year 7 or 8 [RESPGROUP 2]
○ Year 9 or 10 [RESPGROUP 3]
○ Year 11 or 12 [RESPGROUP 4]

☐ I attend(ed) a Catholic primary school.

CONTINUE | CLEAR ALL RESPONSES AND GO BACK TO THE TOP

End of the Identification Diagram.
The respondent group is now determined and recorded.
Continue to the Profile Questionnaire.

```
GRID 1
```

GRID 4

In what capacity are you participating in this survey?
Choose the ONE option that most applies to you.

I participate in this survey as ..
O as a tertiary education student
[RESPGROUP 5]
O as a teacher, a lecturer, or a member of the administrative or support staff in a school or tertiary institution
[RESPGROUP 6]
O as a parent or guardian of school aged children or tertiary students
[RESPGROUP 9]
O as a 'local decision maker' (*)
[RESPGROUP 7]
O as a member of a Catholic Education Office
[RESPGROUP 8]
O as an individual respondent, NOT belonging to any of the groups above
[RESPGROUP 10]

(*) All people who make policy decisions, contribute to school planning initiatives and help lead the school, for example: the principal, the deputy principal, the parish priest, the school board, the governance team, the school leadership team, the staff representative, the college chaplain, the religious education coordinator, the canonical administrator, the business manager, the department head, the college organiser, et cetera. Teachers, parents or guardians to whom this description applies, should also tick this option.

If you are a member of a Catholic Education Office, then please list your staff group:

(text input field)

☐ **I am a Catholic priest.**
☐ **I am a Religious Brother or Sister.**

CONTINUE	CLEAR ALL RESPONSES AND GO BACK TO THE TOP

Fill in this page only if you are a tertiary student. If not, click on 'continue'.

Indicate in which program you are enrolled at this moment.
You can select multiple options.
☐ diploma of education
☐ bachelor of education
☐ other bachelor program
☐ master program
☐ doctoral program
☐ theological or religious education unit
☐ other diploma

Indicate in which year you are now:
(dropdownlist 1-10)

CONTINUE	CLEAR ALL RESPONSES AND GO BACK TO THE TOP

Fill in this page only if you have a specific role in a school or tertiary institution. If not, click on 'continue'.

I am a teacher or lecturer..
☐ .. in a kindergarten.
☐ .. in a primary school.
☐ .. in a secondary school, year 7 or 8.
☐ .. in a secondary school, year 9 or 10.
☐ .. in a secondary school, year 11 or 12.
☐ .. in a tertiary education institution

I am a teacher or lecturer..
☐ .. and I teach 'science and technology" [1]
☐ .. and I teach 'humanities'. [2]
☐ .. and I teach religious education.

1 Science and technology: physics, earth sciences and geography, chemistry, astronomy, mathematics, economics and business management, engineering, architecture, biological sciences, medicine and biomedical sciences, pharmaceutical sciences, kinesiology and rehabilitation sciences, dentistry, technology, electrical engineering, mechanics, computer sciences and ICT, et cetera.
2 Humanities: languages and literature, philosophy, theology, religious studies and religious education, pedagogical sciences, social sciences, society and culture, law, history, aesthetics, arts, music, physical education, health, personal care and nursing, et cetera.

Were you educated in a Catholic or in a non-Catholic institution?
○ I received my education / teacher training mainly in (a) CATHOLIC institution(s).
○ I received my education / teacher training mainly in (a) NON-CATHOLIC institution(s).

Tick the options that apply to you:
☐ I have an executive / leadership function, e.g. I'm a member of the board, the school leadership or management team.
☐ I'm a member of the administrative or support staff.
☐ I work in an academic institution as a scientific researcher or assistant.

CONTINUE	CLEAR ALL RESPONSES AND GO BACK TO THE TOP

GRID 7

Fill in this page only if you're the parent or guardian of school aged children or tertiary students. If not, click on 'continue'.

I'm the parent or guardian of..
☐ .. a child in a kindergarten.
☐ .. a child in a primary school, year 1-4.
☐ .. a child in a primary school, year 5-6.
☐ .. a student in a secondary school.
☐ .. a student enrolled in a tertiary education institution.

CONTINUE	CLEAR ALL RESPONSES AND GO BACK TO THE TOP

End of the Identification Diagram.
The respondent group is now determined and recorded.
Continue to the Profile Questionnaire.

§3. Profile Questionnaire (standard version)

GRID 1

What is your gender?
- O   Male.
- O   Female.

What is your age?
At this moment I am y[   ]

Are you a baptised Catholic?
- O   Yes
- O   No

What's the highest level of education you received and completed?
(Additional question in *Catholic Education Offices*)
- O   Primary education
- O   Secondary education
- O   TAFE / Trade / apprenticeship
- O   University degree
- O   Post-graduate degree
- O   Post-graduate diploma
- O   Other (fill in): [   ]

| SUBMIT | CLEAR ALL RESPONSES AND GO BACK TO THE TOP |

What is your MAIN ethnic background? In other words: what is your country of origin, or the country of origin of your parents or grandparents? Choose the ONE option that applies most.

O	Argentina	O	Italy
O	Australia	O	Japan
O	Austria	O	Lebanon
O	Canada	O	Malaysia
O	Chile	O	Malta
O	China	O	The Netherlands
O	Colombia	O	New Zealand
O	Croatia	O	Poland
O	Egypt	O	Scotland
O	England	O	Serbia
O	Ethiopia	O	South Africa
O	The Philippines	O	Spain
O	France	O	Sri Lanka
O	Germany	O	Sudan
O	Greece	O	the United States of America
O	Hungary	O	Vietnam
O	India	O	Wales
O	Ireland	O	other (tick the button and fill in):
O	Israel		

SUBMIT	CLEAR ALL RESPONSES AND GO BACK TO THE TOP

330

What's your personal affiliation to the Christian faith?
Choose the option that applies to you most.
- ○ I have strong faith in Christ.
- ○ I have average faith in Christ.
- ○ I have no faith in Christ.

What's your personal religion or philosophy of life?
Choose ONE option from the list that applies to you most.
Optionally, you can type additional information in the text field below.
- ○ Roman Rite Catholic
- ○ Eastern Rite Catholic
- ○ Orthodox (Greek, Russian, Lebanese, Antiochian, Ethiopian, Coptic and others)
- ○ Lutheran
- ○ Calvinist
- ○ Episcopal / Anglican Church
- ○ Evangelical
- ○ Uniting Church / United Church of Christ
- ○ Baptist
- ○ Churches of Christ
- ○ Presbyterian
- ○ Methodist
- ○ Assemblies of God / Pentecostal
- ○ Mormon / Church of Latter-Day Saints
- ○ Just Christian (I don't belong to a particular church or denomination.)
- ○ Muslim (either Sunni or Shiite)
- ○ Jewish
- ○ Buddhist
- ○ Hindu
- ○ Sikh
- ○ Just religious (I believe in God but I don't belong to an established religion.)
- ○ New age
- ○ I believe in science.
- ○ Something-ism (I believe there is 'something' that transcends human beings.)
- ○ Humanistic (I'm not religious, but I believe in the strength and value of human beings.)
- ○ Atheist (I renounce any belief in a god)
- ○ Indifferent or nihilistic (I don't care or I belief in nothing)
- ○ Agnostic (I don't know, I'm still searching)
- ○ OTHER (tick the button and provide additional information in the text field below)

You can type additional information about your personal religion or philosophy of life in the text field below (optional).

| SUBMIT | CLEAR ALL RESPONSES AND GO BACK TO THE TOP |

Which of the following statements best describes your attitude to the Catholic faith?

O   The Catholic faith deserves my full support.
O   I think the Catholic faith is ok, but I remain critical of some aspects.
O   I neither have positive nor negative feelings about the Catholic faith.
O   I dislike the Catholic faith.
O   I don't know what 'Catholic faith' is.

When did you last attend a celebration of the Eucharist in your own time? Masses at school do NOT count. (Irrespective of your religious affiliation.)

O   Less than a week ago
O   Less than two weeks ago
O   Less than a month ago
O   On a Christian holy day (like Christmas, Easter, ...)
O   On a special occasion (like a wedding, a funeral, a baptism, a memorial service, ...)
O   Long ago or never before

How often do you pray to God individually? Communal prayer at school, at church, et cetera does NOT count. (Irrespective of your religious affiliation.)

O   I pray on a daily basis.
O   I pray regularly.
O   I sometimes pray, but not regularly.
O   I only pray in times of great happiness or trouble.
O   Once I did pray, but not anymore.
O   I have never prayed before.

| SUBMIT | CLEAR ALL RESPONSES AND GO BACK TO THE TOP |

End of the Profile Questionnaire.
Continue to the Doyle Questionnaire.

§4. Doyle Questionnaire

The seven-point Likert scale used in the *Doyle Questionnaire* (factual and normative level):	The 5-point Likert scale used in the *Doyle Questionnaire* (only normative level):
1 = I strongly disagree 2 = I disagree 3 = I somewhat disagree 4 = I neither agree, nor disagree 5 = I somewhat agree 6 = I agree 7 = I strongly agree	1 = a lot more 2 = more 3 = neither more, nor less 4 = less 5 = a lot less

GRID 1

1a. In my school, all people believe in God.	1234567
1b. In my ideal school, all people believe in God.	1234567

2a. In my school, people believe and think in many different ways.	1234567
2b. In my ideal school, people believe and think in many different ways.	1234567

3a. My school is a very good place to grow closer to God.	1234567
3b. My ideal school is a very good place to grow closer to God.	1234567

4a. My school helps the students to grow in the Christian faith.	1234567
4b. My ideal school helps the students to grow in the Christian faith.	1234567

NEXT

	GRID 2
5a. In my school, everybody wears the same style of clothes.	1 2 3 4 5 6 7
5b. In my ideal school, everybody wears the same style of clothes.	1 2 3 4 5 6 7
6a. My school's Catholic identity is something that I see, experience and encounter.	1 2 3 4 5 6 7
6b. My ideal school's Catholic identity is something that I see, experience and encounter.	1 2 3 4 5 6 7
7a. The school buildings, facilities and grounds contribute to my school's Catholic character.	1 2 3 4 5 6 7
7b. In my ideal school, the school buildings, facilities and grounds contribute to the school's Catholic character.	1 2 3 4 5 6 7
8a. In my school, people listen to the leadership of the Catholic church: the bishops and the pope.	1 2 3 4 5 6 7
8b. In my ideal school, people listen to the leadership of the Catholic church: the bishops and the pope.	1 2 3 4 5 6 7

NEXT

334

GRID 3

9. Do you support the Catholic identity of schools?

○ I am a strong supporter!
○ I support it.
○ I think it's OK.

} Active or passive SUPPORT
for Catholic school identity

○ I don't really care about it.
○ I oppose it.
○ I am a strong opponent!

} INDIFFERENCE or RESISTANCE
against Catholic school identity

| NEXT |

GRID 4

Here are a number of features of Catholic schools. Think about the current practice in your school, and evaluate whether you'd want the feature MORE or LESS.

10. Religious education and formation of students.	5 a lot more 4 more 3 neither more, nor less 2 less 1 a lot less
11. Celebrating faith together.	5 a lot more 4 more 3 neither more, nor less 2 less 1 a lot less
12. Reading the Bible at school.	5 a lot more 4 more 3 neither more, nor less 2 less 1 a lot less
13. Prayer at school.	5 a lot more 4 more 3 neither more, nor less 2 less 1 a lot less

(Answered by adults and students.)

| NEXT |

GRID 5

Here are a number of features of Catholic schools. Think about the current practice in your school, and evaluate whether you'd want the feature MORE or LESS.

14. Openness towards cultural diversity, including many other philosophies of life as well as Catholicism.	5 a lot more 4 more 3 neither more, nor less 2 less 1 a lot less
15. Focus on the Catholic tradition.	5 a lot more 4 more 3 neither more, nor less 2 less 1 a lot less
16. Involvement in social justice projects.	5 a lot more 4 more 3 neither more, nor less 2 less 1 a lot less
17. Catholic rituals and sacraments at school.	5 a lot more 4 more 3 neither more, nor less 2 less 1 a lot less

(Answered by adults only.)

NEXT

End of the Doyle Questionnaire.
Continue to the *Post-Critical Belief* Scale.

§5. *Post-Critical Belief* Scale, version for adults

The seven-point Likert scale used in the PCB Scale:

1 = I strongly disagree
2 = I disagree
3 = I somewhat disagree
4 = I neither agree, nor disagree
5 = I somewhat agree
6 = I agree
7 = I strongly agree

1. The Bible holds a deeper truth which can only be revealed by personal reflection.	1 2 3 4 5 6 7
2. If you want to understand the meaning of the miracle stories from the Bible, you should always place them in their historical context.	1 2 3 4 5 6 7
3. You can only live a meaningful life if you believe.	1 2 3 4 5 6 7
4. God has been defined for once and for all and therefore is unchangeable.	1 2 3 4 5 6 7
5. Faith is more of a dream which turns out to be an illusion when one is confronted with the harshness of life.	1 2 3 4 5 6 7
6. The Bible is a guide, full of signs in the search for God, and not a historical account.	1 2 3 4 5 6 7
7. Even though this goes against modern rationality, I believe Mary was truly a virgin when she gave birth to Jesus.	1 2 3 4 5 6 7
8. Too many people have been oppressed in the name of God to still make believing possible.	1 2 3 4 5 6 7
9. Each statement about God is a result of the time in which it is made.	1 2 3 4 5 6 7
10. Despite the fact that the Bible was written in a completely different historical context from ours, it retains a basic message.	1 2 3 4 5 6 7
11. Only the major religious traditions guarantee access to God.	1 2 3 4 5 6 7
12. Because Jesus is mainly a guiding principle for me, my faith in him would not be affected if it would appear that he never actually existed as a historical individual.	1 2 3 4 5 6 7
13. Ultimately, religion is a commitment without having absolute certainty.	1 2 3 4 5 6 7
14. Religion is the one thing that gives meaning to life in all its aspects.	1 2 3 4 5 6 7

15. The manner in which humans experience their relationship with God, is always coloured by the times in which they live.	1 2 3 4 5 6 7
16. The historical accuracy of the stories from the Bible is irrelevant for my faith in God.	1 2 3 4 5 6 7
17. Ultimately, there is only one correct answer to each religious question.	1 2 3 4 5 6 7
18. God is only a name for the inexplicable.	1 2 3 4 5 6 7
19. Statements about the absolute, like dogma's, always remain relative since they are proclaimed by specific people and at specific moments in time.	1 2 3 4 5 6 7
20. The world of Bible stories is so far removed from us, that it has little relevance.	1 2 3 4 5 6 7
21. Only a priest can give an answer to important religious questions.	1 2 3 4 5 6 7
22. A scientific understanding of human life and the world makes a religious understanding obsolete.	1 2 3 4 5 6 7
23. God grows together with the history of humanity and therefore is changeable.	1 2 3 4 5 6 7
24. I am well aware that my beliefs are only one possibility among so many others.	1 2 3 4 5 6 7
25. I think that Bible stories should be taken literally, as they are written.	1 2 3 4 5 6 7
26. Despite the high number of injustices Christianity has caused people, the original message of Christ is still valuable to me.	1 2 3 4 5 6 7
27. In the end, faith is nothing more that a safety net for human fears.	1 2 3 4 5 6 7
28. Secular and religious conceptions of the world give valuable answers to important questions about life.	1 2 3 4 5 6 7
29. In order to fully understand what religion is all about, you have to be an outsider.	1 2 3 4 5 6 7
30. Faith is an expression of a weak personality.	1 2 3 4 5 6 7
31. There is no absolute meaning in life, only direction-giving, which is different for each one of us.	1 2 3 4 5 6 7
32. Religious faith often is an instrument for obtaining power, and that makes it suspect.	1 2 3 4 5 6 7
33. I still call myself a Christian, even though I do not agree with a lot of things that have happened in the past in the name of Christianity.	1 2 3 4 5 6 7

PCB Scale adult version, reading key

Reading key	Survey order	Types	Survey order	Reading key	Types
PA1	3	Literal Belief	1	PA26	Post-Critical Belief
PA2	4	Literal Belief	2	PA27	Post-Critical Belief
PA3	7	Literal Belief	3	PA1	Literal Belief
PA4	11	Literal Belief	4	PA2	Literal Belief
PA5	14	Literal Belief	5	PA9	External Critique
PA6	17	Literal Belief	6	PA28	Post-Critical Belief
PA7	21	Literal Belief	7	PA3	Literal Belief
PA8	25	Literal Belief	8	PA10	External Critique
PA9	5	External Critique	9	PA18	Relativism
PA10	8	External Critique	10	PA29	Post-Critical Belief
PA11	18	External Critique	11	PA4	Literal Belief
PA12	20	External Critique	12	PA19	Relativism
PA13	22	External Critique	13	PA30	Post-Critical Belief
PA14	27	External Critique	14	PA5	Literal Belief
PA15	29	External Critique	15	PA20	Relativism
PA16	30	External Critique	16	PA31	Post-Critical Belief
PA17	32	External Critique	17	PA6	Literal Belief
PA18	9	Relativism	18	PA11	External Critique
PA19	12	Relativism	19	PA21	Relativism
PA20	15	Relativism	20	PA12	External Critique
PA21	19	Relativism	21	PA7	Literal Belief
PA22	23	Relativism	22	PA13	External Critique
PA23	24	Relativism	23	PA22	Relativism
PA24	28	Relativism	24	PA23	Relativism
PA25	31	Relativism	25	PA8	Literal Belief
PA26	1	Post-Critical Belief	26	PA32	Post-Critical Belief
PA27	2	Post-Critical Belief	27	PA14	External Critique
PA28	6	Post-Critical Belief	28	PA24	Relativism
PA29	10	Post-Critical Belief	29	PA15	External Critique
PA30	13	Post-Critical Belief	30	PA16	External Critique
PA31	16	Post-Critical Belief	31	PA25	Relativism
PA32	26	Post-Critical Belief	32	PA17	External Critique
PA33	33	Post-Critical Belief	33	PA33	Post-Critical Belief

§6. *Post-Critical Belief Scale*, version for students aged 10-18

Page 1/6

1. I believe that God is lord and master of the whole creation, because this is in the Bible in black and white.

2. Personally I don't believe that God really exists, but for some people religious belief could be valuable – and I respect that.

3. It is impossible to come close to God because God does not exist. 'God' is just a label.

4. I feel connected to God and I am glad about that.

Page 2/6

5. Ultimately, the Christian faith is more true, than the other religions. One has to have faith in Jesus Christ in order to be fully human.

6. Whether you believe in Jesus, Allah, Buddha or in nothing, doesn't make any real difference.

7. I do not really understand how intelligent people can believe in God.

8. Although I can never fully grasp who God is, I still feel that He exists and that He supports me.

Page 3/6

9. I wish that Christians try to proclaim the Gospel to all humankind.

10. One religion isn't more or less true, than the other.

11. Religion is nonsense.

12. People who want to can come closer to God, because God knows many ways to be close to people.

Page 4/6

13. I believe in a life after death because it is in the Bible and the Bible is the Word of God.

14. It doesn't really matter what you believe. In the end, it's all the same anyway.

15. God does not exist. People who believe in 'God', are a bit insane.

16. God helps me to believe in myself and in other people. God gives me strength to do my best for a better world.

Page 5/6 [*]

17. The miracle stories about Jesus did really happen. Jesus made blind people see and He made dead people come alive again. This is precisely what's so special about Jesus.

18. The miracle stories in the Bible most likely did not really happen. The Bible is a book full of stories, some of which are more believable and meaningful than others.

19. The miracle stories in the Bible did not really happen. Making blind people see and dead people come alive again, is impossible and therefore not believable.

20. The miracle stories in the Bible express that Jesus was sent by God to set people free from bad things and to give them new hope.

Page 6/6

21. When I have done something wrong, I feel guilty and then I am afraid God will punish me.

22. I understand that other people pray to God for strength, but I rely on myself.

23. God doesn't exist and therefore praying to God is meaningless.

24. I sometimes pray to God because this gives me strength.

(*) At the request of the ECSIP Steering Committee, the 24-item student version of the *PCB Scale* was reduced to 20 items by deleting this set of questions about the interpretation of miracle stories in the Bible. Statistical analysis showed that the negative effect of the deletion of these 4 items on the stability of the scale remains minimal.

PCB Scale student version, reading key

Reading key	Survey order	Types	Survey order	Reading key	Types
PT1	5	Literal Belief	1	PT5	Literal Belief
PT2	9	Literal Belief	2	PT13	Relativism
PT3	17	Literal Belief	3	PT8	External Critique
PT4	13	Literal Belief	4	PT19	Post-Critical Belief
PT5	1	Literal Belief	5	PT1	Literal Belief
PT6	21	Literal Belief	6	PT18	Relativism
PT7	23	External Critique	7	PT10	External Critique
PT8	3	External Critique	8	PT21	Post-Critical Belief
PT9	15	External Critique	9	PT2	Literal Belief
PT10	7	External Critique	10	PT15	Relativism
PT11	11	External Critique	11	PT11	External Critique
PT12	19	External Critique	12	PT24	Post-Critical Belief
PT13	2	Relativism	13	PT4	Literal Belief
PT14	22	Relativism	14	PT16	Relativism
PT15	10	Relativism	15	PT9	External Critique
PT16	14	Relativism	16	PT22	Post-Critical Belief
PT17	18	Relativism	17	PT3	Literal Belief
PT18	6	Relativism	18	PT17	Relativism
PT19	4	Post-Critical Belief	19	PT12	External Critique
PT20	24	Post-Critical Belief	20	PT23	Post-Critical Belief
PT21	8	Post-Critical Belief	21	PT6	Literal Belief
PT22	16	Post-Critical Belief	22	PT14	Relativism
PT23	20	Post-Critical Belief	23	PT7	External Critique
PT24	12	Post-Critical Belief	24	PT20	Post-Critical Belief

§7. *Melbourne Scale*, version for adults

TOPIC 1. How to recognise a Catholic school?

How does (or doesn't) your school show itself to be *Catholic*? And what's your personal opinion on Catholic education?

1a. Nothing reveals that my school is (still) Catholic. In daily school life, Christianity is not of any real significance.

1 I strongly disagree
2 I disagree
3 I somewhat disagree
4 I neither agree, nor disagree
5 I somewhat agree
6 I agree
7 I strongly agree

1b. As far as I'm concerned, Catholic schools belong to the past. Christianity doesn't need to be of any real significance in daily school life.

1 I strongly disagree
2 I disagree
3 I somewhat disagree
4 I neither agree, nor disagree
5 I somewhat agree
6 I agree
7 I strongly agree

2a. My school is Catholic, first and foremost because it offers Catholic values and norms that can be accepted by Christians as well as non-Christians.

1 I strongly disagree
2 I disagree
3 I somewhat disagree
4 I neither agree, nor disagree
5 I somewhat agree
6 I agree
7 I strongly agree

2b. I think that, first and foremost, a Catholic school should offer Catholic values and norms that can be accepted by Christians as well as non-Christians.

1 I strongly disagree
2 I disagree
3 I somewhat disagree
4 I neither agree, nor disagree
5 I somewhat agree
6 I agree
7 I strongly agree

3a. My school shows its Catholic character in its search for a renewed way to realise the Christian message of faith, hope and love in the world today.

1 I strongly disagree
2 I disagree
3 I somewhat disagree
4 I neither agree, nor disagree
5 I somewhat agree
6 I agree
7 I strongly agree

3b. I think that a Catholic school should be searching for a renewed way to realise the Christian message of faith, hope and love in the world today.

1 I strongly disagree
2 I disagree
3 I somewhat disagree
4 I neither agree, nor disagree
5 I somewhat agree
6 I agree
7 I strongly agree

4a. My school has a clear preference for the Catholic faith and therefore wants to guarantee the Catholic faith formation of all its students.

1 I strongly disagree
2 I disagree
3 I somewhat disagree
4 I neither agree, nor disagree
5 I somewhat agree
6 I agree
7 I strongly agree

4b. My 'ideal school' has a clear preference for the Catholic faith and therefore wants to guarantee the Catholic faith formation of all its students.

1 I strongly disagree
2 I disagree
3 I somewhat disagree
4 I neither agree, nor disagree
5 I somewhat agree
6 I agree
7 I strongly agree

TOPIC 2. About confessional Catholic school identity

Think about the typical Catholic school. They are decent, disciplined schools with a large population of practicing Catholics. The school generally maintains a strong connection to the Church. Celebrations of the Eucharist are held on a regular basis. There is school prayer during the course of each day. Students have the opportunity for confession once in a while. Sometimes, religious brothers and sisters or priests play a prominent role at the school. A school possessing many of these features can be described as confessional. To what extent is your school a confessional Catholic school?

5. My Catholic school still strongly resembles the confessional schools described above.

    1 I strongly disagree
    2 I disagree
    3 I somewhat disagree
    4 I neither agree, nor disagree
    5 I somewhat agree
    6 I agree
    7 I strongly agree

6. In my Catholic school it has always been considered normal that celebrations of the Eucharist take place frequently, and today this still is the case.

    1 I strongly disagree
    2 I disagree
    3 I somewhat disagree
    4 I neither agree, nor disagree
    5 I somewhat agree
    6 I agree
    7 I strongly agree

7. As in the past, my school still assumes that the Catholic faith is practised by most of its members.

    1 I strongly disagree
    2 I disagree
    3 I somewhat disagree
    4 I neither agree, nor disagree
    5 I somewhat agree
    6 I agree
    7 I strongly agree

8. Most of the following items are considered fairly normal in my school: crucifixes on the wall, religious education classes, celebrations of the Eucharist at school, a morning prayer, praying before meals, school catechesis, a priest who's working in the school.

    1 I strongly disagree
    2 I disagree
    3 I somewhat disagree
    4 I neither agree, nor disagree
    5 I somewhat agree
    6 I agree
    7 I strongly agree

TOPIC 3. Not Catholic (anymore)?

Today the identity of Catholic schools is under pressure. Some schools are losing their traditional confessional Catholic identity. This process is called 'secularisation'. Do you notice this process also in your school? And what do you think about this?

9a. My school used to be Catholic, but Christianity has slowly disappeared from school life. Thus today my school is Catholic in name only.

1 I strongly disagree
2 I disagree
3 I somewhat disagree
4 I neither agree, nor disagree
5 I somewhat agree
6 I agree
7 I strongly agree

9b. I find it no problem that Christianity is slowly disappearing from school life, because my 'ideal school' isn't Catholic anyway.

1 I strongly disagree
2 I disagree
3 I somewhat disagree
4 I neither agree, nor disagree
5 I somewhat agree
6 I agree
7 I strongly agree

10a. In my school, most people do not believe.

1 I strongly disagree
2 I disagree
3 I somewhat disagree
4 I neither agree, nor disagree
5 I somewhat agree
6 I agree
7 I strongly agree

10b. In my 'ideal school', most people would not have to be religious believers.

1 I strongly disagree
2 I disagree
3 I somewhat disagree
4 I neither agree, nor disagree
5 I somewhat agree
6 I agree
7 I strongly agree

11. My school isn't secularising at all! It is still clear to everyone that it is a Catholic school.

1 I strongly disagree
2 I disagree
3 I somewhat disagree
4 I neither agree, nor disagree
5 I somewhat agree
6 I agree
7 I strongly agree

12a. Now that its Catholic identity is threatened, my school is trying all the harder to be and to remain clearly Catholic.

1 I strongly disagree
2 I disagree
3 I somewhat disagree
4 I neither agree, nor disagree
5 I somewhat agree
6 I agree
7 I strongly agree

12b. If their Catholic identity is threatened, I think schools should try all the harder to be and to remain clearly Catholic.

1 I strongly disagree
2 I disagree
3 I somewhat disagree
4 I neither agree, nor disagree
5 I somewhat agree
6 I agree
7 I strongly agree

TOPIC 4. Let us talk about: religious education classes at school

How does your school regard religious education classes, and what is your personal opinion on this matter?

13a. Though there are still classes of religious education in my school, they rarely mention God, Jesus or the Bible.

1 I strongly disagree
2 I disagree
3 I somewhat disagree
4 I neither agree, nor disagree
5 I somewhat agree
6 I agree
7 I strongly agree

13b. In my 'ideal school', God, Jesus or the Bible needn't be mentioned anymore.

1 I strongly disagree
2 I disagree
3 I somewhat disagree
4 I neither agree, nor disagree
5 I somewhat agree
6 I agree
7 I strongly agree

14a. My school stresses the importance of religious education classes, because learning about faith promotes a Catholic way of life.

1 I strongly disagree
2 I disagree
3 I somewhat disagree
4 I neither agree, nor disagree
5 I somewhat agree
6 I agree
7 I strongly agree

14b. I wish to stress the importance of religious education classes at Catholic schools, because learning about faith promotes a Catholic way of life.

1 I strongly disagree
2 I disagree
3 I somewhat disagree
4 I neither agree, nor disagree
5 I somewhat agree
6 I agree
7 I strongly agree

15a. Religious education classes in my school try to link the students' sense of values to the Catholic faith, hoping that they become deeper believers that way.

1 I strongly disagree
2 I disagree
3 I somewhat disagree
4 I neither agree, nor disagree
5 I somewhat agree
6 I agree
7 I strongly agree

15b. I think that religious education classes should try to link the students' sense of values to the Catholic faith, hoping that they become deeper believers that way.

1 I strongly disagree
2 I disagree
3 I somewhat disagree
4 I neither agree, nor disagree
5 I somewhat agree
6 I agree
7 I strongly agree

16a. Religious education classes in my school aspire to help all students, Catholics as well as other-believers, to discover meaning in their lives and to deepen their humanity in dialogue with the Christian story.

1 I strongly disagree
2 I disagree
3 I somewhat disagree
4 I neither agree, nor disagree
5 I somewhat agree
6 I agree
7 I strongly agree

16b. I think that religious education classes should aspire to help all students, Christians as well as other-believers, to discover meaning in their lives and to deepen their humanity in dialogue with the Christian story.

1 I strongly disagree
2 I disagree
3 I somewhat disagree
4 I neither agree, nor disagree
5 I somewhat agree
6 I agree
7 I strongly agree

TOPIC 5. How to deal with diversity at school?

Today we live in a multicultural society. We live together with people from different cultures and religions. Sometimes we speak different languages. Sometimes we have different looks. We may have different habits, feelings, tastes and ideals of beauty. We have diverging political opinions, and different moral sensibilities. Most likely this *diversity* will even increase in the future. How does your son's/daughter's school deal with these differences between people, and what do you think about it?

17a. My Catholic school is worried about the increasing diversity in society, since it considers this a threat to its Catholic school identity.

1 I strongly disagree
2 I disagree
3 I somewhat disagree
4 I neither agree, nor disagree
5 I somewhat agree
6 I agree
7 I strongly agree

17b. I am worried about the increasing diversity in society, because I consider this a threat to the identity of Catholic schools.

1 I strongly disagree
2 I disagree
3 I somewhat disagree
4 I neither agree, nor disagree
5 I somewhat agree
6 I agree
7 I strongly agree

18a. My school calls for tolerance and respect for everyone, without itself being partial or biased.

1 I strongly disagree
2 I disagree
3 I somewhat disagree
4 I neither agree, nor disagree
5 I somewhat agree
6 I agree
7 I strongly agree

18b. My 'ideal school' calls for tolerance and respect for everyone, without itself being partial or biased.

1 I strongly disagree
2 I disagree
3 I somewhat disagree
4 I neither agree, nor disagree
5 I somewhat agree
6 I agree
7 I strongly agree

19a. My Catholic school reasons as follows: "A little diversity is fine. But if the differences between people at school continue to grow, then we have a problem. For then the sense of Christian values is no longer shared by all people at school."

1 I strongly disagree
2 I disagree
3 I somewhat disagree
4 I neither agree, nor disagree
5 I somewhat agree
6 I agree
7 I strongly agree

19b. I think it is important that the sense of Christian values is shared by all people at school. Thus it becomes a problem, I think, if the differences between people at school continue to grow.

1 I strongly disagree
2 I disagree
3 I somewhat disagree
4 I neither agree, nor disagree
5 I somewhat agree
6 I agree
7 I strongly agree

20a. In my Catholic school, a multiplicity of philosophies of life is positively valued and even encouraged, since it offers a chance to the other-believers – but also to the Christians at school – to form and deepen their own personal identity in conversation with the Christian story.

1 I strongly disagree
2 I disagree
3 I somewhat disagree
4 I neither agree, nor disagree
5 I somewhat agree
6 I agree
7 I strongly agree

20b. I think that Catholic schools should positively value and even encourage a multiplicity of philosophies of life, since it offers a chance to the other-believers – but also to the Christians at school – to form and deepen their own personal identity in conversation with the Christian story.

1 I strongly disagree
2 I disagree
3 I somewhat disagree
4 I neither agree, nor disagree
5 I somewhat agree
6 I agree
7 I strongly agree

TOPIC 6. Two theological viewpoints

Here are two viewpoints that both favour Catholic education, but that are nonetheless fundamentally different. Read both texts carefully and critically. Then apply them to your son's/daughter's school, and give your personal opinion.

Viewpoint 1.

Question: *How to prevent a school from becoming less Catholic amid an increasingly secular culture? How to simultaneously remain a Catholic school while doing justice to a growing group of non-Catholics at school?*

Answer: by searching for the 'greatest common denominator' between the Christian faith and student culture. We 'translate' Christianity on a student level in a way that can appeal to all. We look creatively for a Catholic middle-way between faith and culture, in which all students can still recognise themselves. More precisely we depart from the personal life experiences of young people today, and then attempt to link these to the Catholic vision. We appeal to the students' own sense of values, and then give these a deeper Christian explanation and basis. Through an education in Christian values and norms we invite the students to discover (rediscover?) and deepen their faith.

Viewpoint 2.

Question: *How to realize a Catholic school in a culture that is becoming more diverse? How to simultaniously remain a Catholic school while doing justice to a growing group of others at school, who believe differently, including those without faith?*

Answer: by bringing into conversation the many different visions that are present in the school, against the background of the Christian message. Catholic believers at school should dare, without fear or reluctance, to have the voice of Christianity sound in the middle of the diversity. In critical dialogue with the Catholic tradition, we're searching together for meaningful ways to live that are liberating for everyone. We recognise and respect each other's differences, without aiming for a 'middle path' or a 'compromise', and without the desire to 'convert' the other. Instead we create at school a forum for exchange and discussion that nurtures the identity formation of all involved, challenged by the Christian message. Traveling together with other-minded fellow people, Catholic schools discover once more how to make Jesus' message of faith, hope and love come true today.

21a. My school agrees with viewpoint 1. As a Catholic school, it is aiming for a Catholic middle path between different visions, in which all can recognise themselves.

1 I strongly disagree
2 I disagree
3 I somewhat disagree
4 I neither agree, nor disagree
5 I somewhat agree
6 I agree
7 I strongly agree

21b. I agree with viewpoint 1. I think that Catholic schools should aim for a Catholic middle path between different visions, in which all can recognise themselves.

1 I strongly disagree
2 I disagree
3 I somewhat disagree
4 I neither agree, nor disagree
5 I somewhat agree
6 I agree
7 I strongly agree

22a. My school agrees with viewpoint 2. It freely bears witness to its Catholic inspiration, and brings different viewpoints into dialogue with each other against the background of the Christian story. As such, it renders service to the identity formation of all involved – other-believers ánd Catholics themselves.

1 I strongly disagree
2 I disagree
3 I somewhat disagree
4 I neither agree, nor disagree
5 I somewhat agree
6 I agree
7 I strongly agree

22b. I agree with viewpoint 2. I think that Catholic schools should freely bear witness to their Catholic inspiration, and should bring different viewpoints into dialogue with each other against the background of the Christian story. As such, it renders service to the identity formation of all involved – other-believers ánd Catholics themselves.

1 I strongly disagree
2 I disagree
3 I somewhat disagree
4 I neither agree, nor disagree
5 I somewhat agree
6 I agree
7 I strongly agree

23a. My Catholic school rejects both visions, because it thinks we must remain faithful to the teachings of the Catholic tradition and avoid any dialogue with diversity and subsequent 'adaptation' of the Catholic faith to today's secular culture.

1 I strongly disagree
2 I disagree
3 I somewhat disagree
4 I neither agree, nor disagree
5 I somewhat agree
6 I agree
7 I strongly agree

23b. I reject both visions, because I thinks we must remain faithful to the teachings of the Catholic tradition and avoid any dialogue with diversity and subsequent 'adaptation' of the Catholic faith to today's secular culture.

1 I strongly disagree
2 I disagree
3 I somewhat disagree
4 I neither agree, nor disagree
5 I somewhat agree
6 I agree
7 I strongly agree

TOPIC 7. Why Catholic schools today?

And now the four last questions. Why do we need Catholic schools, especially today?

24a. It is my Catholic school's mission to teach young people – in all their diversity – Catholic values and norms, thereby bringing them closer to the Catholic faith.

1 I strongly disagree
2 I disagree
3 I somewhat disagree
4 I neither agree, nor disagree
5 I somewhat agree
6 I agree
7 I strongly agree

24b. The mission of Catholic schools is to teach young people – in all their diversity – Catholic values and norms, thereby bringing them closer to the Catholic faith.

1 I strongly disagree
2 I disagree
3 I somewhat disagree
4 I neither agree, nor disagree
5 I somewhat agree
6 I agree
7 I strongly agree

25a. It is my Catholic school's mission to teach young people the attitudes and skills needed to deal with diversity in a Catholic way.

1 I strongly disagree
2 I disagree
3 I somewhat disagree
4 I neither agree, nor disagree
5 I somewhat agree
6 I agree
7 I strongly agree

25b. The mission of Catholic schools is to teach young people the attitudes and skills needed to deal with diversity in a Catholic way.

1 I strongly disagree
2 I disagree
3 I somewhat disagree
4 I neither agree, nor disagree
5 I somewhat agree
6 I agree
7 I strongly agree

Melbourne Scale adult version, reading key

Factual measurement level (current practice)

Reading key	Survey order	Types	Survey order	Reading key	Types
MAF1	1a	SEC	1a	MAF1	SEC
MAF2	9a	SEC	2a	MAF11	VALED
MAF3	10a	SEC	3a	MAF16	RECONT
MAF4	13a	SEC	4a	MAF6	RECONF
MAF5	18a	SEC	5	MAF21	CONF
MAF6	4a	RECONF	6	MAF22	CONF
MAF7	12a	RECONF	7	MAF23	CONF
MAF8	14a	RECONF	8	MAF24	CONF
MAF9	17a	RECONF	9a	MAF2	SEC
MAF10	23a	RECONF	10a	MAF3	SEC
MAF11	2a	VALED	11	MAF25	CONF
MAF12	15a	VALED	12a	MAF7	RECONF
MAF13	19a	VALED	13a	MAF4	SEC
MAF14	21a	VALED	14a	MAF8	RECONF
MAF15	24a	VALED	15a	MAF12	VALED
MAF16	3a	RECONT	16a	MAF17	RECONT
MAF17	16a	RECONT	17a	MAF9	RECONF
MAF18	20a	RECONT	18a	MAF5	SEC
MAF19	22a	RECONT	19a	MAF13	VALED
MAF20	25a	RECONT	20a	MAF18	RECONT
MAF21	5	CONF	21a	MAF14	VALED
MAF22	6	CONF	22a	MAF19	RECONT
MAF23	7	CONF	23a	MAF10	RECONF
MAF24	8	CONF	24a	MAF15	VALED
MAF25	11	CONF	25a	MAF20	RECONT

Normative measurement level (ideal school)

Reading key	Survey order	Types	Survey order	Reading key	Types
MAN1	1b	SEC	1b	MAN1	SEC
MAN2	9b	SEC	2b	MAN11	VALED
MAN3	10b	SEC	3b	MAN16	RECONT
MAN4	13b	SEC	4b	MAN6	RECONF
MAN5	18b	SEC	5	-	-
MAN6	4b	RECONF	6	-	-
MAN7	12b	RECONF	7	-	-
MAN8	14b	RECONF	8	-	-
MAN9	17b	RECONF	9b	MAN2	SEC
MAN10	23b	RECONF	10b	MAN3	SEC
MAN11	2b	VALED	11	-	-
MAN12	15b	VALED	12b	MAN7	RECONF
MAN13	19b	VALED	13b	MAN4	SEC
MAN14	21b	VALED	14b	MAN8	RECONF
MAN15	24b	VALED	15b	MAN12	VALED
MAN16	3b	RECONT	16b	MAN17	RECONT
MAN17	16b	RECONT	17b	MAN9	RECONF
MAN18	20b	RECONT	18b	MAN5	SEC
MAN19	22b	RECONT	19b	MAN13	VALED
MAN20	25b	RECONT	20b	MAN18	RECONT
-	-	-	21b	MAN14	VALED
-	-	-	22b	MAN19	RECONT
-	-	-	23b	MAN10	RECONF
-	-	-	24b	MAN15	VALED
-	-	-	25b	MAN20	RECONT

§8. *Melbourne Scale*, version for students aged 10-18

Introduction

This survey, called the **Melbourne Scale**, describes different kinds of schools by telling <u>stories of school students</u>. As you will see, each of these schools deals with the Catholic religion in a different way!

 <u>Take some time to read the stories carefully.</u> Picture in your mind what sort of school it is about.

Imagine   what it must be like to go to such a school. Does it resemble your own school? What are the differences? Do you perhaps know such schools? Would you be happy in such a school?

When you have a clear understanding of the kind of school the story is about, then answer the following questions:

| Is MY SCHOOL like this ? | 1. What type of school do you have? Is the school you attend like the school described in the story? |
| Is MY IDEAL SCHOOL like this ? | 2. What type of school would you like? Would you like to go to the school described in the story? |

Please give a personal and honest answer! Don't hesitate to use the strongest options ('*I strongly agree*' or '*I strongly disagree*') if this is in fact your opinion. If there's something you don't understand, ask your teacher to help you.

 Thank you for your cooperation!

School type 1: 'Central Park School'
Motto: "Catholic schools are outdated."
Tim's school.

Meet Tim. Like most of his classmates, **Tim and his family are not religious.** Tim comes from a Catholic family and was baptized when he was a baby, BUT being Catholic, praying and going to church isn't important anymore. To Tim and most of his friends, 'having faith in God' sounds a bit strange.

Tim's school, **Central Park School**, used to be a Catholic school but, overtime, its religious identity vanished. At some point, its original name, 'St Mary of the Cross', was changed to 'Central Park School'.

St. Mary of the Cross
↓
Central Park School

In Central Park School, there are many different people with many different beliefs and lifestyles. Christianity is not common anymore. Tim finds this okay.

In Central Park School, there are no prayers at the beginning of the day and no religious celebrations for the students anymore. There are few Catholic pictures or symbols left.

In Religion classes at Central Park School, Tim learns about many different religions and beliefs. The school makes no fuss about the beliefs and lifestyles of its students.

It would be bad to limit oneself to learning ONLY about Christianity. We need to be open to other beliefs as well.

Fewer and fewer people from Central Park school believe in God, attend mass, follow church teachings, or say their prayers.

No matter what you believe, you must treat others in a tolerant and respectful way.

Everyone is welcome!
Cheers to NEUTRALITY!

Tim believes that the Catholic faith is outdated.
Therefore we don't need Catholic schools anymore.
What do YOU think?

School type 2: 'St Benedict's School'

Motto: "Catholicism is the solution for the problems in society."

Peter's school.

Every day, Peter prays to God who is in heaven, to Jesus Christ our Lord, and to the Virgin Mary, Mother of God.

Peter receives a truly Catholic education. His mother and father find this very important.

Peter's family has close ties with the local parish community. Every Sunday, they celebrate the Eucharist together.

Peter is a Catholic believer. His faith is very important to him.

Peter always tries to live by the Ten Commandments and to obey God's Holy Will. He wants God to be proud of him, not to punish him!

Peter listens to the Pope in the Vatican.

Peter is a friend of the parish priest, Father Boyle. Peter trusts the priest and listens to him, because a priest speaks in the name of the Church.

Peter knows many stories from the Holy Bible.

Peter goes to St Benedict's School, a school with a proud history as a truly Catholic school. Almost all students and teachers are Catholic in faith and practice. The school wants to be part of the holy and unchanging Roman Catholic Church.

Sometimes, people at St Benedict's are worried. Things go wrong in the world today. People don't have faith in Christ anymore. They think only about themselves instead of loving others around them. They have left the true path that Catholic believers walk. They ignore the warnings in the Bible. Sometimes they do things that displease God! Many feel lost. Society is in need, yet many reject JESUS CHRIST, OUR SAVIOUR!

The Catholic faith is declining. St Benedict's School takes a clear stand against this.

Embrace the Catholic Church and its wisdom, and have faith in Jesus Christ!

The religious education program is very important.

Everyone prays at the start of a school day. All students go to Mass every Sunday.

Often society has a bad influence on today's youth. St Benedict's offers its students a safe and protected environment.

A school must be strict about religious teachings and practice.

St Benedict's holds on to the Catholic Tradition without adapting to present-day culture.

Peter is proud to go to St Benedict's School.
It takes a stand against the decline of the Catholic faith.
The students receive a true Catholic education.

What do YOU think?

School type 3: 'Caritas Regional School'
Motto: "Be good to each other, like Jesus was good to all."
Lisa's school.

Lisa is a bright, well-mannered and kind girl from an **average Catholic family.** She's very sociable and gets along well with all her friends. She finds it important to do good for others. Lisa and her friends are involved in social justice projects. In their free time, they collect money for aid groups like the Red Cross and Caritas. Sometimes they also help out in a home for the elderly.

Lisa goes to **Caritas Regional School.** At school there's an active, vibrant, stimulating, heartening and cheerful atmosphere. Lisa is happy about this.

There are some students who are Catholic, some students of other religions and some students who have no belief at all.

What do we find <u>important</u>? (despite our differences)
THE VALUES WE ALL SHARE:

being open minded   sincerity   helping each other
being safe   **respect**   tolerance
sharing   generosity
responsibility   **peace**   compassion   care for the poor
freedom
kindness   **harmony**   telling the truth
friendliness   doing our best
care for the environment   fairness   cooperation

➲ These values are compatible with the Catholic faith!
    Q. Is this a Catholic school ?
    A. Yes, because there are **Catholic values.**

Not all have faith in Jesus Christ, but everyone shares the same **basic values and rules for living.**

The school members share a **common moral ground.**

Believers and non-believers both feel at home in the same school, because they share a **Christian way of doing things.**

Lisa says: "There's a growing lack of values in society. Sometimes people do bad things. That's why at school we learn values and rules for living. **Above all, the Catholic faith provides and grounds those much needed values!"**

Lisa is taught to do good to others. <u>WHY?</u> Because **JESUS CHRIST** taught us to do so!

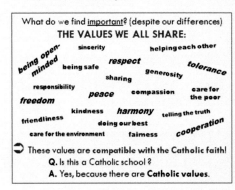

By being friendly, caring and loving, and by learning to live like Catholics, the students discover what's so good about the Catholic faith.

Ultimately, all students discover how God's Spirit is at work in their lives.

In Jesus, all are united!

Caritas Regional School teaches Catholic values and rules for living acceptable to both believers and non-believers. Lisa likes this:
"This way, my school can both be Catholic AND welcoming for other-believers."

What do YOU think?

School type 4: 'Holy Spirit School'

Motto: "Let us make the Catholic faith meaningful for people today."
Chris' school.

Chris and his family live in a big apartment building where many other families live. Chris is being raised a Catholic, but most of his neighbours' children aren't.

The inhabitants of Chris' building are a diverse and colourful bunch, with different languages and different ways, coming from many different countries all over the world.

Chris likes to meet new and different people. There is so much to learn from each other.

By meeting other people, one also learns about oneself. Through the encounter with others, Chris discovers what it means for him to be Catholic. Chris is looking for traces of God in the middle of a plural world and for new ways to live the Gospel of Jesus Christ today.

Chris goes to Holy Spirit School, a vibrant Catholic school with open doors for Christians as well as other-believers.

At Holy Spirit, the general atmosphere is tolerant, open-minded, engaging and mindful. People are attentive and willing to listen. Everyone can feel safe. There's lots of talk and discussion about the moral and religious questions of life, Christian and otherwise. There's room for criticism and different opinions. The school contributes to the personal formation of all different students. Everyone is challenged to explore one's full potential.

WHY? Because it is a *Catholic* school. All students learn about the Gospel of Jesus Christ. The Christian story is the main point of reference. Next, other stories also enter the conversation. At school, learning takes place in dialogue with the Catholic faith tradition, though sometimes also in conflict with it. Chris tries to see all sides of the story, and then decides what response would testify of true LOVE. *'What would Jesus do?'*

 At school, Christians deepen and enrich their faith, while other-believers are called to be mindful of their personal identity and responsible for their life choices.

It's like writing a new chapter in the book of the ongoing Christian story. The journey of God and humanity continues!

Holy Spirit School is a Catholic school that embraces diversity in its search for a renewed and contemporary Catholic profile. It wants to make the Catholic faith recognizable, believable and meaningful for young people today.   What do YOU think?

School type 5: 'Holy Trinity School'

Motto: "Simply a Catholic school, just like old times."

Maria's school.

Though the world is changing, there are Catholic schools that <u>pass by the change</u> and keep on doing what they always have done. A good example: **Holy Trinity School**.

Holy Trinity Catholic school has always been an uncomplicated, traditional, typically Catholic school – and it still is.

Almost every student and teacher belongs to the Catholic faith community. At school, the students simply learn how to live a good Catholic life.

The atmosphere at school is quiet and pleasant. There are no difficult questions here, no doubts and no discussions about the school's Catholic character.

It is clear to everyone that Holy Trinity is a typically Catholic school, just like it was in the old days. People don't worry about the future.

Maria is a typical student at Holy Trinity. She is being raised in a close, strongly Catholic family. Every Sunday Maria attends Mass together with her family. She is well acquainted with the local Catholic community. Maria says a prayer before her meals. At bedtime, her father reads a story from the Holy Bible. For Maria, all this is very normal.

In religious education classes, the students learn about the Bible, Jesus and God.

The school's pastoral care program is well-established.

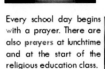

Regularly the parish priest, Father Peterson, visits Maria's school. Maria respects the priest.

It is normal that all students receive sacraments like the Eucharist, Reconciliation and Confirmation.

Every school day begins with a prayer. There are also prayers at lunchtime and at the start of the religious education class.

Once a week Father Peterson celebrates Mass at school. Maria and her friends attend the school masses. "If you're a Catholic, you regularly receive Holy Communion – it's as simple as that."

This is what Catholic schools are all about.
Let's not worry about the changes in society that put into question Catholic identity.

**Maria thinks her school should just stay as it has always been:
a faithful, carefree Catholic school just like old times, true and simple.**

What do YOU Think?

§9. *Victoria Scale*, version for adults

1a. My school looks creatively and with an open mind for good ways to be Catholic in the midst of contemporary culture.

 1 I strongly disagree
 2 I disagree
 3 I somewhat disagree
 4 I neither agree, nor disagree
 5 I somewhat agree
 6 I agree
 7 I strongly agree

1b.My 'ideal school' should look creatively and with an open mind for good ways to be Catholic in the midst of contemporary culture.

 1 I strongly disagree
 2 I disagree
 3 I somewhat disagree
 4 I neither agree, nor disagree
 5 I somewhat agree
 6 I agree
 7 I strongly agree

2a. My school holds the opinion that it is not the Catholic faith that should adapt itself to contemporary culture, but that contemporary culture should be adapted to Catholicism.

 1 I strongly disagree
 2 I disagree
 3 I somewhat disagree
 4 I neither agree, nor disagree
 5 I somewhat agree
 6 I agree
 7 I strongly agree

2b. I believe that the truth offered by Catholicism is more fundamental and fulfilling than the views of other religions or philosophies of life.

 1 I strongly disagree
 2 I disagree
 3 I somewhat disagree
 4 I neither agree, nor disagree
 5 I somewhat agree
 6 I agree
 7 I strongly agree

3a. In my school a preference for Christianity is being replaced by a respectful dialogue between different philosophies of life.

 1 I strongly disagree
 2 I disagree
 3 I somewhat disagree
 4 I neither agree, nor disagree
 5 I somewhat agree
 6 I agree
 7 I strongly agree

3b. In my ideal school a preference for Christianity is to be replaced by a respectful dialogue between different philosophies of life.

 1 I strongly disagree
 2 I disagree
 3 I somewhat disagree
 4 I neither agree, nor disagree
 5 I somewhat agree
 6 I agree
 7 I strongly agree

4a. In my school, religion is an individual, private matter that doesn't figure in daily school life.

 1 I strongly disagree
 2 I disagree
 3 I somewhat disagree
 4 I neither agree, nor disagree
 5 I somewhat agree
 6 I agree
 7 I strongly agree

4b. I'd like to go to a school where religion is an individual, private matter that doesn't figure in daily school life.

 1 I strongly disagree
 2 I disagree
 3 I somewhat disagree
 4 I neither agree, nor disagree
 5 I somewhat agree
 6 I agree
 7 I strongly agree

358

5a. If it were possible, my Catholic school would prefer all its students and teachers to be Catholic in faith and practice.

1 I strongly disagree
2 I disagree
3 I somewhat disagree
4 I neither agree, nor disagree
5 I somewhat agree
6 I agree
7 I strongly agree

5b. I'd love to go to a school where all students and teachers were Catholic in faith and practice.

1 I strongly disagree
2 I disagree
3 I somewhat disagree
4 I neither agree, nor disagree
5 I somewhat agree
6 I agree
7 I strongly agree

6a. Welcoming all open-minded people – Catholics and other believers alike – is a key feature of the Catholic identity of my school.

1 I strongly disagree
2 I disagree
3 I somewhat disagree
4 I neither agree, nor disagree
5 I somewhat agree
6 I agree
7 I strongly agree

6b. My 'ideal school' realises its Catholic identity precisely by respecting and valuing people being different.

1 I strongly disagree
2 I disagree
3 I somewhat disagree
4 I neither agree, nor disagree
5 I somewhat agree
6 I agree
7 I strongly agree

7a. In my school, respecting and valuing many philosophical views and lifestyles (including the non-Catholic!) is considered to be more important than safeguarding a Catholic school identity.

1 I strongly disagree
2 I disagree
3 I somewhat disagree
4 I neither agree, nor disagree
5 I somewhat agree
6 I agree
7 I strongly agree

7b. I think that respecting and valuing many philosophical views and lifestyles at school (including the non-Catholic!) is more important than safeguarding a Catholic school identity.

1 I strongly disagree
2 I disagree
3 I somewhat disagree
4 I neither agree, nor disagree
5 I somewhat agree
6 I agree
7 I strongly agree

8a. In my school, many different philosophical views and lifestyles co-exist, without people taking notice of each other.

1 I strongly disagree
2 I disagree
3 I somewhat disagree
4 I neither agree, nor disagree
5 I somewhat agree
6 I agree
7 I strongly agree

8b. In my 'ideal school', many different philosophical views and lifestyles should be allowed to co-exist, without people getting too much involved with each other.

1 I strongly disagree
2 I disagree
3 I somewhat disagree
4 I neither agree, nor disagree
5 I somewhat agree
6 I agree
7 I strongly agree

9a. According to my school, the Catholic faith offers a very meaningful and valuable message that should be heard by all, but without expecting all students to become Catholics.

1 I strongly disagree
2 I disagree
3 I somewhat disagree
4 I neither agree, nor disagree
5 I somewhat agree
6 I agree
7 I strongly agree

9b. My 'ideal school' presents the Catholic faith as a very meaningful and valuable message that should be heard by all, but without expecting all students to become Catholics.

1 I strongly disagree
2 I disagree
3 I somewhat disagree
4 I neither agree, nor disagree
5 I somewhat agree
6 I agree
7 I strongly agree

10a. In my school, openly presenting non-Catholic views and practices is regarded as a possible threat to its own Catholic mission.

1 I strongly disagree
2 I disagree
3 I somewhat disagree
4 I neither agree, nor disagree
5 I somewhat agree
6 I agree
7 I strongly agree

10b. I think a Catholic school should avoid non-Catholic views and practices because they could undermine its Catholic mission.

1 I strongly disagree
2 I disagree
3 I somewhat disagree
4 I neither agree, nor disagree
5 I somewhat agree
6 I agree
7 I strongly agree

11a. My school is a neutral institution that allows students to freely make their own choices concerning philosophical and religious beliefs.

1 I strongly disagree
2 I disagree
3 I somewhat disagree
4 I neither agree, nor disagree
5 I somewhat agree
6 I agree
7 I strongly agree

11b. My 'ideal school' is a neutral institution that allows students to freely make their own choices concerning philosophical and religious beliefs.

1 I strongly disagree
2 I disagree
3 I somewhat disagree
4 I neither agree, nor disagree
5 I somewhat agree
6 I agree
7 I strongly agree

12a. People in my school don't openly question each other's philosophy of life, since they'd rather not be overly involved with the lives of others.

1 I strongly disagree
2 I disagree
3 I somewhat disagree
4 I neither agree, nor disagree
5 I somewhat agree
6 I agree
7 I strongly agree

12b. I'd like to go to a school that doesn't openly question my philosophy of life and where I am not expected to be overly involved with the lives of others.

1 I strongly disagree
2 I disagree
3 I somewhat disagree
4 I neither agree, nor disagree
5 I somewhat agree
6 I agree
7 I strongly agree

PAGE 4/5

13a. People in my school are searching for what it means to live as Catholics in today's multicultural society. Therefore they greatly value dialogue with other philosophical views.

1 I strongly disagree
2 I disagree
3 I somewhat disagree
4 I neither agree, nor disagree
5 I somewhat agree
6 I agree
7 I strongly agree

13b. People in my 'ideal school' are searching for what it means to live as Catholics in today's multicultural society. To achieve this, dialogue with other philosophical views should be greatly valued.

1 I strongly disagree
2 I disagree
3 I somewhat disagree
4 I neither agree, nor disagree
5 I somewhat agree
6 I agree
7 I strongly agree

14a. My Catholic school pays little attention to the philosophical views of individuals. Individuals are simply expected to adhere to the Catholic vision of the school as a whole.

1 I strongly disagree
2 I disagree
3 I somewhat disagree
4 I neither agree, nor disagree
5 I somewhat agree
6 I agree
7 I strongly agree

14b. In my opinion, the aim of religious education classes should always be: to turn all students into better, Catholic believers.

1 I strongly disagree
2 I disagree
3 I somewhat disagree
4 I neither agree, nor disagree
5 I somewhat agree
6 I agree
7 I strongly agree

15a. In my school, a strong focus on Catholic school identity is considered to undermine the school's efforts to live together with people that are different.

1 I strongly disagree
2 I disagree
3 I somewhat disagree
4 I neither agree, nor disagree
5 I somewhat agree
6 I agree
7 I strongly agree

15b. I think that a strong focus on Catholic school identity should be avoided, because it undermines living together with people that are different.

1 I strongly disagree
2 I disagree
3 I somewhat disagree
4 I neither agree, nor disagree
5 I somewhat agree
6 I agree
7 I strongly agree

16a. My school allows every individual to freely go his/her separate way, as long as one doesn't hinder another.

1 I strongly disagree
2 I disagree
3 I somewhat disagree
4 I neither agree, nor disagree
5 I somewhat agree
6 I agree
7 I strongly agree

16b. I think that every individual at school should be allowed to freely go his/her separate way, as long as one doesn't hinder another.

1 I strongly disagree
2 I disagree
3 I somewhat disagree
4 I neither agree, nor disagree
5 I somewhat agree
6 I agree
7 I strongly agree

PAGE 5/5

17a. According to my Catholic school, the meaning and purpose of Catholic faith can only be fully realised through an active and open dialogue with other religions and philosophical views.

    1 I strongly disagree
    2 I disagree
    3 I somewhat disagree
    4 I neither agree, nor disagree
    5 I somewhat agree
    6 I agree
    7 I strongly agree

17b. The truth of Christianity isn't fixed, but is to be rediscovered and made real through a continuous search for it.

    1 I strongly disagree
    2 I disagree
    3 I somewhat disagree
    4 I neither agree, nor disagree
    5 I somewhat agree
    6 I agree
    7 I strongly agree

18a. My school defends the Catholic lifestyle against other sets of beliefs that are considered to be of less value.

    1 I strongly disagree
    2 I disagree
    3 I somewhat disagree
    4 I neither agree, nor disagree
    5 I somewhat agree
    6 I agree
    7 I strongly agree

18b. My 'ideal school' should defend the Catholic lifestyle against other sets of beliefs that , I think, are of less value.

    1 I strongly disagree
    2 I disagree
    3 I somewhat disagree
    4 I neither agree, nor disagree
    5 I somewhat agree
    6 I agree
    7 I strongly agree

19a. My school has no preference for the truth of the Catholic faith. It believes it is more important to respect the personal truth of each individual.

    1 I strongly disagree
    2 I disagree
    3 I somewhat disagree
    4 I neither agree, nor disagree
    5 I somewhat agree
    6 I agree
    7 I strongly agree

19b. I think that a school shouldn't have a preference for the truth of the Catholic faith. It is more important to respect the personal truth of each individual.

    1 I strongly disagree
    2 I disagree
    3 I somewhat disagree
    4 I neither agree, nor disagree
    5 I somewhat agree
    6 I agree
    7 I strongly agree

20a. In my school the Catholic faith is of no relevance. Each person in the school community chooses for themselves what to believe.

    1 I strongly disagree
    2 I disagree
    3 I somewhat disagree
    4 I neither agree, nor disagree
    5 I somewhat agree
    6 I agree
    7 I strongly agree

20b. I think that the Catholic faith shouldn't be of any relevance at school. Each person in the school community should be free to determine for him/herself what to believe.

    1 I strongly disagree
    2 I disagree
    3 I somewhat disagree
    4 I neither agree, nor disagree
    5 I somewhat agree
    6 I agree
    7 I strongly agree

Victoria Scale adult version, reading key

Factual measurement level (current practice)

Reading key	Survey order	Types	Survey order	Reading key	Types
VAF1	5a	MONOLOGUE	1a	VAF8	DIALOGUE
VAF2	2a	MONOLOGUE	2a	VAF2	MONOLOGUE
VAF3	10a	MONOLOGUE	3a	VAF15	COLOURFUL
VAF4	14a	MONOLOGUE	4a	VAF16	COLOURLESS
VAF5	18a	MONOLOGUE	5a	VAF1	MONOLOGUE
VAF6	6a	DIALOGUE	6a	VAF6	DIALOGUE
VAF7	9a	DIALOGUE	7a	VAF13	COLOURFUL
VAF8	1a	DIALOGUE	8a	VAF18	COLOURLESS
VAF9	13a	DIALOGUE	9a	VAF7	DIALOGUE
VAF10	17a	DIALOGUE	10a	VAF3	MONOLOGUE
VAF11	11a	COLOURFUL	11a	VAF11	COLOURFUL
VAF12	19a	COLOURFUL	12a	VAF20	COLOURLESS
VAF13	7a	COLOURFUL	13a	VAF9	DIALOGUE
VAF14	15a	COLOURFUL	14a	VAF4	MONOLOGUE
VAF15	3a	COLOURFUL	15a	VAF14	COLOURFUL
VAF16	4a	COLOURLESS	16a	VAF17	COLOURLESS
VAF17	16a	COLOURLESS	17a	VAF10	DIALOGUE
VAF18	8a	COLOURLESS	18a	VAF5	MONOLOGUE
VAF19	20a	COLOURLESS	19a	VAF12	COLOURFUL
VAF20	12a	COLOURLESS	20a	VAF19	COLOURLESS

Factual measurement level (current practice)

Reading key	Survey order	Types	Survey order	Reading key	Types
VAN1	5a	MONOLOGUE	1a	VAN8	DIALOGUE
VAN2	2a	MONOLOGUE	2a	VAN2	MONOLOGUE
VAN3	10a	MONOLOGUE	3a	VAN15	COLOURFUL
VAN4	14a	MONOLOGUE	4a	VAN16	COLOURLESS
VAN5	18a	MONOLOGUE	5a	VAN1	MONOLOGUE
VAN6	6a	DIALOGUE	6a	VAN6	DIALOGUE
VAN7	9a	DIALOGUE	7a	VAN13	COLOURFUL
VAN8	1a	DIALOGUE	8a	VAN18	COLOURLESS
VAN9	13a	DIALOGUE	9a	VAN7	DIALOGUE
VAN10	17a	DIALOGUE	10a	VAN3	MONOLOGUE
VAN11	11a	COLOURFUL	11a	VAN11	COLOURFUL
VAN12	19a	COLOURFUL	12a	VAN20	COLOURLESS
VAN13	7a	COLOURFUL	13a	VAN9	DIALOGUE
VAN14	15a	COLOURFUL	14a	VAN4	MONOLOGUE
VAN15	3a	COLOURFUL	15a	VAN14	COLOURFUL
VAN16	4a	COLOURLESS	16a	VAN17	COLOURLESS
VAN17	16a	COLOURLESS	17a	VAN10	DIALOGUE
VAN18	8a	COLOURLESS	18a	VAN5	MONOLOGUE
VAN19	20a	COLOURLESS	19a	VAN12	COLOURFUL
VAN20	12a	COLOURLESS	20a	VAN19	COLOURLESS

§10. *Victoria Scale*, version for students aged 10-18

Monologue School

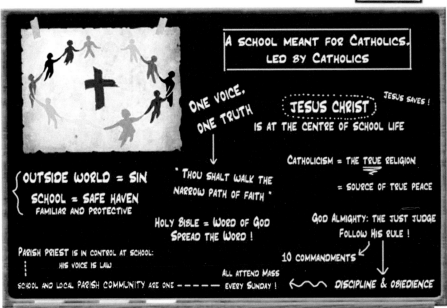

1a. Is the school you attend like the school described in the picture?	1b. Would you like to go to the school described in the picture?
1 = I strongly disagree 2 = I disagree 3 = I somewhat disagree 4 = I neither agree, nor disagree 5 = I somewhat agree 6 = I agree 7 = I strongly agree	1 = I strongly disagree 2 = I disagree 3 = I somewhat disagree 4 = I neither agree, nor disagree 5 = I somewhat agree 6 = I agree 7 = I strongly agree

Dialogue School

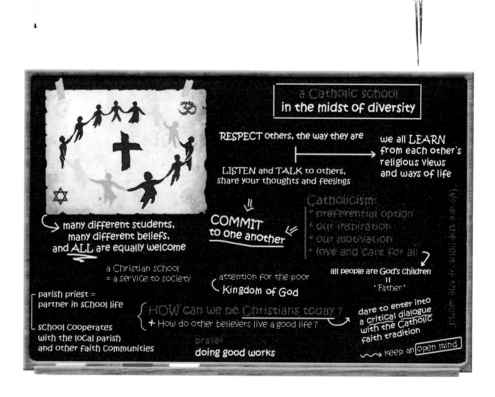

2a. Is the school you attend like the school described in the picture?	2b. Would you like to go to the school described in the picture?
1 = I strongly disagree 2 = I disagree 3 = I somewhat disagree 4 = I neither agree, nor disagree 5 = I somewhat agree 6 = I agree 7 = I strongly agree	1 = I strongly disagree 2 = I disagree 3 = I somewhat disagree 4 = I neither agree, nor disagree 5 = I somewhat agree 6 = I agree 7 = I strongly agree

Colourful School

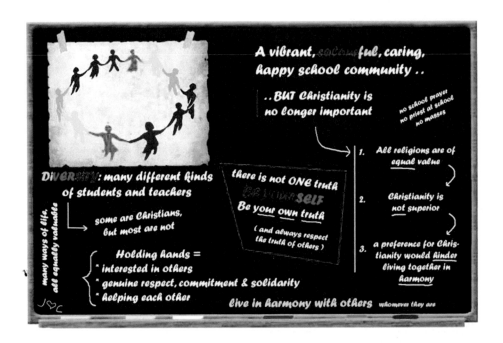

3a. Is the school you attend like the school described in the picture?	3b. Would you like to go to the school described in the picture?
1 = I strongly disagree 2 = I disagree 3 = I somewhat disagree 4 = I neither agree, nor disagree 5 = I somewhat agree 6 = I agree 7 = I strongly agree	1 = I strongly disagree 2 = I disagree 3 = I somewhat disagree 4 = I neither agree, nor disagree 5 = I somewhat agree 6 = I agree 7 = I strongly agree

Colourless School

4a. Is the school you attend like the school described in the picture?	4b. Would you like to go to the school described in the picture?
1 = I strongly disagree 2 = I disagree 3 = I somewhat disagree 4 = I neither agree, nor disagree 5 = I somewhat agree 6 = I agree 7 = I strongly agree	1 = I strongly disagree 2 = I disagree 3 = I somewhat disagree 4 = I neither agree, nor disagree 5 = I somewhat agree 6 = I agree 7 = I strongly agree

§11. Evaluation Questions

The following two evaluation questions, to be scored on a seven-point Likert scale, are always added to the *Doyle Questionnaire*, the *PCB Scale*, the *Melbourne Scale* and the *Victoria Scale* – both to the student and the adult versions:

1. The questions in this survey made sense to me.	2. I liked completing this survey.
1 I strongly disagree 2 I disagree 3 I somewhat disagree 4 I neither agree, nor disagree 5 I somewhat agree 6 I agree 7 I strongly agree	1 I strongly disagree 2 I disagree 3 I somewhat disagree 4 I neither agree, nor disagree 5 I somewhat agree 6 I agree 7 I strongly agree

This way we collect valuable feedback both about the data collection process and the reliability of the collected data. The same questions apply to all respondent groups, which makes it possible to compare their feedback.

The most important evaluation question is the first one, namely whether or not the questions in the survey made sense to the respondents. If many indicate that they couldn't make sense of the questions, then the results ought to be treated with care. Fortunately, that rarely happens.

ECSIP 2012 Statistics

Participating schools in the ECSIP 2012 Research

E-number	School name, location	Diocese	Type	Student sample	Adult sample	Total sample
E1016	Assumption College, Kilmore	Melbourne	7-12	194	95	289
E1019	St Joseph's School, Hawthorn	Melbourne	P-6	40	60	100
E1026	St Mary's School, Lancefield	Melbourne	P-6	36	31	67
E1034	St Paul's School, Coburg	Melbourne	P-6	54	27	81
E1038	Our Lady of Mount Carmel School, Sunbury	Melbourne	P-6	54	27	81
E1048	St Augustine's School, Yarraville	Melbourne	P-6	60	39	99
E1057	St Patrick's School, Geelong West	Melbourne	P-6	46	66	112
E1066	St Aloysius College, Melbourne North	Melbourne	7-12	232	68	300
E1074	St John's School, Heidelberg	Melbourne	P-6	72	30	102
E1081	Sacred Heart School, Sandringham	Melbourne	P-6	82	69	151
E1084	St Margaret Mary's School, Brunswick North	Melbourne	P-6	43	43	86
E1086	St Brigid's School, Healesville	Melbourne	P-6	28	60	88
E1087	St Mary's School, Malvern East	Melbourne	P-6	87	41	128
E1088	Holy Rosary School, Kensington	Melbourne	P-6	13	38	51
E1093	St Columba's School, Elwood	Melbourne	P-6	40	33	73
E1094	Our Lady of the Rosary, Kyneton	Melbourne	P-6	80	35	115
E1104	Our Lady of Lourdes School, Prahran East	Melbourne	P-6	11	16	27
E1119	Our Lady Help of Christians School, Eltham	Melbourne	P-6	55	41	96
E1122	St Gabriel's School, Reservoir	Melbourne	P-6	49	33	82
E1124	St Joseph's School, Black Rock	Melbourne	P-6	47	56	103
E1129	Holy Eucharist School, Malvern East	Melbourne	P-6	49	24	73
E1131	St Anne's School, Kew East	Melbourne	P-6	2	36	38
E1133	St Francis Xavier's School, Montmorency	Melbourne	P-6	65	39	104
E1138	Santa Maria College, Northcote	Melbourne	7-12	284	102	386
E1141	St John the Baptist School, Ferntree Gully	Melbourne	P-6	85	34	119
E1147	St Joseph's School, Springvale	Melbourne	P-6	219	111	330
E1151	St Bernard's School, Coburg East	Melbourne	P-6	73	57	130
E1154	St Oliver Plunkett's School, Pascoe Vale	Melbourne	P-6	107	33	140
E1162	Salesian College, Chadstone	Melbourne	7-12	376	177	553
E1172	Holy Spirit School, Thornbury East	Melbourne	P-6	62	48	110
E1175	Sacred Heart School, St Albans	Melbourne	P-6	96	69	165
E1176	St Thomas The Apostle School, Blackburn	Melbourne	P-6	82	34	116
E1182	St Peter's School, Clayton	Melbourne	P-6	48	30	78
E1184	Holy Family School, Bell Park	Melbourne	P-6	71	46	117
E1187	Mother of God School, Ardeer	Melbourne	P-6	41	15	56
E1192	St Paul's School, Sunshine West	Melbourne	P-6	99	81	180
E1198	Holy Family School, Mount Waverley	Melbourne	P-6	94	63	157
E1199	St Gerard's School, Dandenong North	Melbourne	P-6	83	39	122
E1200	Our Lady of Perpetual Succour School, Surrey Hills	Melbourne	P-6	40	76	116
E1207	St Joseph's School, Yarra Junction	Melbourne	P-6	56	70	126
E1208	St Stephen's School, Reservoir East	Melbourne	P-6	22	21	43
E1211	Our Lady of the Nativity School, Aberfeldie	Melbourne	P-6	67	53	120
E1215	St Dominic's School, Broadmeadows	Melbourne	P-6	71	52	123
E1219	St Christopher's School, Glen Waverley	Melbourne	P-6	41	40	81
E1224	St Matthew's School, Fawkner North	Melbourne	P-6	95	77	172
E1228	St Thomas More's School, Belgrave	Melbourne	P-6	56	37	93
E1229	St Christopher's School, Airport West	Melbourne	P-6	79	63	142
E1235	Mount St Joseph Girls' College, Altona	Melbourne	7-12	345	225	570
E1247	Avila College, Mount Waverley	Melbourne	7-12	565	253	818
E1248	St Philip's School, Blackburn North	Melbourne	P-6	47	55	102
E1253	St Monica's College, Epping	Melbourne	7-12	409	128	537
E1258	St Macartan's School, Mornington	Melbourne	P-6	96	120	216

E1263	John Paul College - O J Olsen Memorial, Frankston	Melbourne	7-12	298	83	381
E1284	St John's School, Thomastown East	Melbourne	P-6	75	32	107
E1287	St Dominic's School, Melton	Melbourne	P-6	47	54	101
E1289	Holy Spirit School, Ringwood North	Melbourne	P-6	6	55	61
E1314	Our Lady's School, Craigieburn	Melbourne	P-6	143	64	207
E1320	St Andrew's School, Clayton South	Melbourne	P-6	81	42	123
E1321	St Thomas More's School, Mount Eliza	Melbourne	P-6	83	49	132
E1323	St Simon's School, Rowville	Melbourne	P-6	110	69	179
E1324	Queen of Peace Primary School, Altona Meadows	Melbourne	P-6	164	74	238
E1325	Our Lady Star of the Sea School, Ocean Grove	Melbourne	P-6	103	71	174
E1330	St Anthony's School, Lara	Melbourne	P-6	78	49	127
E1333	St Mary MacKillop Primary School, Keilor Downs	Melbourne	P-6	226	65	291
E1346	Holy Trinity Primary School, Eltham North	Melbourne	P-6	104	63	167
E1361	St Peter Julian Eymard, Mooroolbark	Melbourne	P-6	104	105	209
E1362	Galilee, Melbourne South	Melbourne	P-6	63	48	111
E1369	Caroline Chisholm Catholic College, Braybrook	Melbourne	7-12	389	170	559
E1371	Thomas Carr College, Tarneit	Melbourne	7-12	539	126	665
E1374	Lumen Christi School, Point Cook	Melbourne	P-6	112	101	213
E1375	Christ the Priest School, Caroline Springs	Melbourne	P-6	82	47	129
E1391	Stella Maris, Point Cook West	Melbourne	P-6	88	77	165
E1396	St Francis de Sales, Lynbrook	Melbourne	P-6	44	66	110
E2001	St Patrick's College, Ballarat	Ballarat	7-12	630	104	734
E2002	St Patrick's School, Ballarat	Ballarat	P-6	51	96	147
E2008	St Mary's School, Donald	Ballarat	P-6	20	28	48
E2018	St Joseph's School, Charlton	Ballarat	P-6	14	15	29
E2029	St Patrick's School, Port Fairy	Ballarat	P-6	34	47	81
E2038	St Columba's School, Ballarat North	Ballarat	P-6	72	77	149
E2040	St Mary's School, Swan Hill	Ballarat	P-6	158	105	263
E2042	St Brendan's School, Coragulac	Ballarat	P-6	14	16	30
E2044	St Brigid's College, Horsham	Ballarat	7-12	202	59	261
E2060	St Mary's School, Robinvale	Ballarat	P-8	92	78	170
E2062	Sacred Heart School, Colac	Ballarat	P-6	99	64	163
E2064	Our Lady Help of Christians School, Wendouree	Ballarat	P-6	26	29	55
E2069	All Saints Parish School, Portland South	Ballarat	P-6	68	56	124
E2074	Emmanuel College Inc., Warrnambool	Ballarat	7-12	0	128	128
E4010	St Joseph's School, Korumburra	Sale	P-6	16	18	34
E4015	St Joseph's School, Trafalgar	Sale	P-6	32	11	43
E4017	St Kieran's School, Moe	Sale	P-6	34	17	51
E4018	Marist-Sion College, Warragul	Sale	7-12	688	83	771
E4027	St Mary's School, Maffra	Sale	P-6	57	28	85
E4033	Don Bosco School, Narre Warren	Sale	P-6	88	66	154
E4038	Mary MacKillop School, Narre Warren North	Sale	P-6	109	53	162
E4039	St Catherine's Primary School, Berwick South	Sale	P-6	118	84	202
E4044	St Brigid's School, Officer	Sale	P-6	40	54	94

Profile Questionnaire statistics

Average age

RG	Respondent groups	n total	Average age total	n PRIM	Average age PRIM	n SEC	Average age SEC
RG1	Students y5-6	5460	10.8	5460	10.8	0	.
RG2	Students y7-8	2035	12.7	33	13.2	2002	12.7
RG3	Students y9-10	1472	14.7	0	.	1472	14.7
RG4	Students y11-12	1417	16.8	0	.	1417	16.8
RG5	Students tertiary education	0	.	0	.	0	.
RG6	Teachers	2399	42.7	1479	42.5	920	42.9
RG7	School leadership	1050	45.3	711	45.7	339	44.7
RG8	CEO members	0	.	0	.	0	.
RG9	Parents	2469	41.9	1952	40.7	517	46.3
RG10	Individual users	0	.	0	.	0	.
RG11	Students year 7-10	3676	12.9	34	12.9	3642	12.9
RG12	Students year 9-12	3074	14.8	0	.	3074	14.8
RG13	Secondary college students	5185	13.7	34	12.9	5151	13.7
RG14	Students	10853	12.0	5702	10.4	5151	13.7
RG15	School staff	3531	42.5	2252	42.3	1279	42.7
RG16	School staff and parents	6046	41.9	4245	41.2	1801	43.6
RG17	School leadership and parents	3594	42.0	2725	41.1	869	45.0
RG18	Educational policy makers	1079	44.1	732	44.3	347	43.6
RG19	Adults	6046	41.9	4245	41.2	1801	43.6
RG20	Adults	6046	41.9	4245	41.2	1801	43.6
RG21	All respondents	16302	23.5	9635	24.3	6667	22.4

Age frequencies and percentages per respondent group

Age	RG1	RG2	RG3	RG4	RG6	RG7	RG9
1							
2							
3							
4							
5	2						
6	18						
7	13						
8	28						
9	67		1	1			
10	1578		1				
11	2807	9					
12	932	807		3			
13	14	948	5	1			
14	1	266	652				
15		4	627	3			
16			185	496			
17		1	1	730			
18				177			
19				4	2		
20				2	2		1
21				8	1		
22				31		1	
23				52	1	1	
24				58	1	2	
25				81	5	1	
26				74	12	1	
27				55	19	5	
28				67	17	5	
29				53	18	11	
30				65	22	12	
31				55	19	17	
32				41	18	35	

Age	RG1	RG2	RG3	RG4	RG6	RG7	RG9
1							
2							
3							
4							
5	0.04						
6	0.33						
7	0.24						
8	0.51						
9	1.23		0.07	0.07			
10	28.90		0.07				
11	51.41	0.44					
12	17.07	39.66		0.21			
13	0.26	46.58	0.34	0.07			
14	0.02	13.07	44.29				
15		0.20	42.60	0.21			
16			12.57	35.00			
17		0.05	0.07	51.52			
18				12.49			
19				0.28	0.08		
20				0.14	0.08		0.04
21					0.33	0.10	
22					1.29		0.04
23					2.17	0.10	0.04
24					2.42	0.10	0.08
25					3.38	0.48	0.04
26					3.08	1.14	0.04
27					2.29	1.81	0.20
28					2.79	1.62	0.20
29					2.21	1.71	0.45
30					2.71	2.10	0.49
31					2.29	1.81	0.69
32					1.71	1.71	1.42

33					36	23	45	33					1.50	2.19	1.82
34					42	25	69	34					1.75	2.38	2.79
35					45	25	93	35					1.88	2.38	3.77
36					39	19	118	36					1.63	1.81	4.78
37					43	20	122	37					1.79	1.90	4.94
38					41	22	140	38					1.71	2.10	5.67
39					50	33	152	39					2.08	3.14	6.16
40					64	42	181	40					2.67	4.00	7.33
41					62	26	184	41					2.58	2.48	7.45
42					62	39	200	42					2.58	3.71	8.10
43					59	41	168	43					2.46	3.90	6.80
44					64	35	154	44					2.67	3.33	6.24
45					68	33	130	45					2.83	3.14	5.27
46					67	31	149	46					2.79	2.95	6.03
47					79	39	100	47					3.29	3.71	4.05
48					64	43	81	48					2.67	4.10	3.28
49					63	36	76	49					2.63	3.43	3.08
50					80	29	71	50					3.33	2.76	2.88
51					73	35	39	51					3.04	3.33	1.58
52					68	35	37	52					2.83	3.33	1.50
53					67	29	15	53					2.79	2.76	0.61
54					56	48	12	54					2.33	4.57	0.49
55					75	45	12	55					3.13	4.29	0.49
56					57	27	5	56					2.38	2.57	0.20
57					51	25	2	57					2.13	2.38	0.08
58					44	31	6	58					1.83	2.95	0.24
59					45	16	6	59					1.88	1.52	0.24
60					53	16	3	60					2.21	1.52	0.12
61					34	11	2	61					1.42	1.05	0.08
62					20	17		62					0.83	1.62	
63					20	5		63					0.83	0.48	
64					19	6		64					0.79	0.57	
65					13	1	3	65					0.54	0.10	0.12
66					10	2		66					0.42	0.19	
67					6	1	1	67					0.25	0.10	0.04
68					8	1		68					0.33	0.10	
69					3	2		69					0.13	0.19	
70					4			70					0.17		
71								71							
72								72							
73					1			73					0.04		
74								74							
75								75							
76							1	76							0.04
77								77							
78								78							
79								79							
80								80							
81								81							
82								82							
83								83							
84						1		84						0.10	
85								85							
86								86							
87								87							
88								88							
89								89							
90								90							
91								91							
92								92							
93								93							
94								94							
95								95							
96								96							
97								97							
98								98							
99						2		99						0.19	
100								100							
	5460	2035	1472	1417	2399	1050	2469		100	100	100	100	100	100	100

Support for the Catholic Faith

What's your attitude to the Catholic faith?

Catholic support	Frequency	Percentage
The Catholic faith deserves my full support.	5206	30.8%
I think the Catholic faith is ok, but I remain critical of some aspects.	8033	47.5%
I neither have positive nor negative feelings about the Catholic faith.	2579	15.3%
I dislike the Catholic faith.	396	2.3%
I don't know what 'Catholic faith' is.	282	1.7%
nmiss	403	2.4%
	16899	100%

Catholic support	Students y5-6		Students y7-8		Students y9-10		Students y11-12	
	Freq.	Percent	Freq.	Percent	Freq.	Percent	Freq.	Percent
The Catholic faith deserves my full support.	2388	42.1%	520	24.6%	282	18.0%	177	11.7%
I think the Catholic faith is ok, but I remain critical of some aspects.	2191	38.7%	900	42.6%	632	40.4%	666	44.1%
I neither have positive nor negative feelings about the Catholic faith.	704	12.4%	498	23.6%	469	30.0%	455	30.2%
I dislike the Catholic faith.	91	1.6%	73	3.5%	86	5.5%	114	7.6%
I don't know what 'Catholic faith' is.	84	1.5%	90	4.3%	48	3.1%	37	2.5%
nmiss	210	3.7%	30	1.4%	48	3.1%	60	4.0%
	5668	100%	2111	100%	1565	100%	1509	100%

Catholic support	Teachers		Leadership		Parents	
	Freq.	Percent	Freq.	Percent	Freq.	Percent
The Catholic faith deserves my full support.	707	28.8%	373	34.6%	759	30.2%
I think the Catholic faith is ok, but I remain critical of some aspects.	1499	61.1%	634	58.8%	1511	60.1%
I neither have positive nor negative feelings about the Catholic faith.	207	8.4%	50	4.6%	196	7.8%
I dislike the Catholic faith.	12	0.5%	3	0.3%	17	0.7%
I don't know what 'Catholic faith' is.	6	0.2%	6	0.6%	11	0.4%
nmiss	21	0.9%	13	1.2%	21	0.8%
	2452	100%	1079	100%	2515	100%

Catholic support	Melbourne		Ballarat		Sandhurst		Sale	
	Freq.	Percent	Freq.	Percent	Freq.	Percent	Freq.	Percent
The Catholic faith deserves my full support.	4255	32.9%	547	23.0%	0	.	404	25.3%
I think the Catholic faith is ok, but I remain critical of some aspects.	6156	47.6%	1193	50.1%	0	.	684	42.9%
I neither have positive nor negative feelings about the Catholic faith.	1792	13.9%	484	20.3%	0	.	303	19.0%
I dislike the Catholic faith.	226	1.7%	76	3.2%	0	.	94	5.9%
I don't know what 'Catholic faith' is.	185	1.4%	48	2.0%	0	.	49	3.1%
nmiss	309	2.4%	32	1.3%	0	.	62	3.9%
	12923	100%	2380	100%	0	.	1596	100%

Church Praxis

When did you last attend a celebration of the Eucharist in your own time? (Masses at school do not count.)

Church praxis	Frequency	Percentage
Less than a week ago.	3440	20.4%
Less than two weeks ago.	1665	9.9%
Less than a month ago.	2257	13.4%
On a Christian holy day.	3056	18.1%
On a special occasion.	3500	20.7%
Long ago or never before.	2576	15.2%
nmiss	405	2.4%
	16899	100%

Church praxis	Students y5-6		Students y7-8		Students y9-10		Students y11-12	
	Freq.	Percent	Freq.	Percent	Freq.	Percent	Freq.	Percent
Less than a week ago.	1199	21.2%	314	14.9%	206	13.2%	172	11.4%
Less than two weeks ago.	668	11.8%	138	6.5%	73	4.7%	66	4.4%
Less than a month ago.	736	13.0%	215	10.2%	132	8.4%	152	10.1%
On a Christian holy day.	941	16.6%	392	18.6%	339	21.7%	335	22.2%
On a special occasion.	1044	18.4%	509	24.1%	352	22.5%	344	22.8%
Long ago or never before.	870	15.3%	511	24.2%	415	26.5%	380	25.2%
nmiss	210	3.7%	32	1.5%	48	3.1%	60	4.0%

Church praxis	Teachers		Leadership		Parents	
	Freq.	Percent	Freq.	Percent	Freq.	Percent
Less than a week ago.	562	22.9%	428	39.7%	559	22.2%
Less than two weeks ago.	290	11.8%	154	14.3%	276	11.0%
Less than a month ago.	433	17.7%	166	15.4%	423	16.8%
On a Christian holy day.	407	16.6%	133	12.3%	509	20.2%
On a special occasion.	546	22.3%	138	12.8%	567	22.5%
Long ago or never before.	193	7.9%	47	4.4%	160	6.4%

nmiss	21	0.9%	13	1.2%	21	0.8%
	2452	100%	1079	100%	2515	100%

Church praxis	Melbourne		Ballarat		Sandhurst		Sale	
	Freq.	Percent	Freq.	Percent	Freq.	Percent	Freq.	Percent
Less than a week ago.	2770	21.4%	380	16.0%	0	.	290	18.2%
Less than two weeks ago.	1298	10.0%	225	9.5%	0	.	142	8.9%
Less than a month ago.	1752	13.6%	327	13.7%	0	.	178	11.2%
On a Christian holy day.	2401	18.6%	427	17.9%	0	.	228	14.3%
On a special occasion.	2618	20.3%	543	22.8%	0	.	339	21.2%
Long ago or never before.	1775	13.7%	444	18.7%	0	.	357	22.4%
nmiss	309	2.4%	34	1.4%	0	.	62	3.9%
	12923	100%	2380	100%	0	.	1596	100%

Personal Prayer Life

How often do you pray to God individually?
(Communal prayer at school, at church, et cetera does NOT count.)

Personal Prayer Life	Frequency	Percentage
I pray on a daily basis.	3401	20.1%
I pray regularly.	3409	20.2%
I sometimes pray, but not regularly.	4474	26.5%
I only pray in times of great happiness or trouble.	2811	16.6%
Once I did pray, but not anymore.	1399	8.3%
I have never prayed before.	999	5.9%
nmiss	406	2.4%
	16899	100%

Personal Prayer Life	Students y5-6		Students y7-8		Students y9-10		Students y11-12	
	Freq.	Percent	Freq.	Percent	Freq.	Percent	Freq.	Percent
I pray on a daily basis.	1280	22.6%	340	16.1%	206	13.2%	167	11.1%
I pray regularly.	1323	23.3%	310	14.7%	155	9.9%	120	8.0%
I sometimes pray, but not regularly.	1518	26.8%	513	24.3%	340	21.7%	318	21.1%
I only pray in times of great happiness or trouble.	916	16.2%	455	21.6%	352	22.5%	359	23.8%
Once I did pray, but not anymore.	261	4.6%	237	11.2%	257	16.4%	266	17.6%
I have never prayed before.	160	2.8%	224	10.6%	207	13.2%	219	14.5%
nmiss	210	3.7%	32	1.5%	48	3.1%	60	4.0%
	5668	100%	2111	100%	1565	100%	1509	100%

Personal Prayer Life	Teachers		Leadership		Parents	
	Freq.	Percent	Freq.	Percent	Freq.	Percent
I pray on a daily basis.	626	25.5%	312	28.9%	470	18.7%
I pray regularly.	591	24.1%	307	28.5%	603	24.0%
I sometimes pray, but not regularly.	698	28.5%	282	26.1%	805	32.0%
I only pray in times of great happiness or trouble.	283	11.5%	89	8.2%	357	14.2%
Once I did pray, but not anymore.	155	6.3%	50	4.6%	173	6.9%
I have never prayed before.	78	3.2%	26	2.4%	85	3.4%
nmiss	21	0.9%	13	1.2%	22	0.9%
	2452	100%	1079	100%	2515	100%

Personal Prayer Life	Melbourne		Ballarat		Sandhurst		Sale	
	Freq.	Percent	Freq.	Percent	Freq.	Percent	Freq.	Percent
I pray on a daily basis.	2852	22.1%	304	12.8%	0	.	245	15.4%
I pray regularly.	2770	21.4%	399	16.8%	0	.	240	15.0%
I sometimes pray, but not regularly.	3420	26.5%	666	28.0%	0	.	388	24.3%
I only pray in times of great happiness or trouble.	2065	16.0%	460	19.3%	0	.	286	17.9%
Once I did pray, but not anymore.	924	7.2%	278	11.7%	0	.	197	12.3%
I have never prayed before.	582	4.5%	239	10.0%	0	.	178	11.2%
nmiss	310	2.4%	34	1.4%	0	.	62	3.9%
	12923	100%	2380	100%	0	.	1596	100%

Doyle Questionnaire statistics

Variable	Item
D21F	In my school, all people believe in God.
D21N	In my ideal school, all people believe in God.
D22F	In my school, people believe and think in many different ways.
D22N	In my ideal school, people believe and think in many different ways.
D23F	My school is a very good place to grow closer to God.
D23N	My ideal school is a very good place to grow closer to God.
D24F	My school helps the students to grow in the Christian faith.
D24N	My ideal school helps the students to grow in the Christian faith.
D25F	In my school, everybody wears the same style of clothes.
D25N	In my ideal school, everybody wears the same style of clothes.
D26F	My school's Catholic identity is something that I see, experience and encounter.
D26N	My ideal school's Catholic identity is something that I see, experience and encounter.
D27F	The school buildings, facilities and grounds contribute to my school's Catholic character.
D27N	In my ideal school, the school buildings, facilities and grounds contribute to the school's Catholic character.
D28F	In my school, people listen to the leadership of the Catholic church: the bishops and the pope.
D28N	In my ideal school, people listen to the leadership of the Catholic church: the bishops and the pope.
DC1N	religious education and formation of students
DC2N	celebrating faith together
DC3N	reading the Bible at school
DC4N	prayer at school
DC7N	openness towards cultural diversity, including many other philosophies of life as well as Catholicism
DC8N	focus on the Catholic tradition
DC9N	involvement in social justice projects
DC12N	Catholic rituals and sacraments at school
DE2	The questions in this survey made sense to me.
DE4	I liked completing this survey.

Variable	Mean	Std Dev	Variance	Min	Max	N	Quart 1	Median	Quart 2	Lower 99% CL	Upper 99% CL	t Value	Pr > |t|
D21F	4.271	1.751	3.065	1	7	16168	3	5	6	4.235	4.306	310.18	<.0001
D21N	4.712	1.763	3.109	1	7	16166	4	5	6	4.676	4.747	339.76	<.0001
D22F	6.036	1.016	1.032	1	7	16166	6	6	7	6.015	6.056	755.37	<.0001
D22N	6.016	1.110	1.231	1	7	16164	6	6	7	5.994	6.039	689.28	<.0001
D23F	5.578	1.248	1.558	1	7	16166	5	6	6	5.553	5.603	568.13	<.0001
D23N	5.423	1.451	2.107	1	7	16232	5	6	6	5.394	5.453	476.05	<.0001
D24F	5.758	1.156	1.335	1	7	16233	5	6	7	5.735	5.782	634.88	<.0001
D24N	5.488	1.438	2.069	1	7	16233	5	6	7	5.458	5.517	486.05	<.0001
D25F	5.792	1.567	2.456	1	7	16097	5	6	7	5.760	5.824	468.91	<.0001
D25N	4.863	1.997	3.987	1	7	16097	4	6	7	4.823	4.904	309.02	<.0001
D26F	5.530	1.207	1.456	1	7	16097	5	6	6	5.505	5.554	581.46	<.0001
D26N	5.373	1.407	1.979	1	7	16096	4	6	6	5.345	5.402	484.64	<.0001
D27F	5.269	1.367	1.868	1	7	16097	5	6	6	5.241	5.297	489.1	<.0001
D27N	5.156	1.512	2.287	1	7	16051	4	6	6	5.125	5.187	431.97	<.0001
D28F	5.111	1.399	1.958	1	7	16053	4	5	6	5.083	5.140	462.75	<.0001
D28N	5.050	1.536	2.360	1	7	16052	4	5	6	5.018	5.081	416.43	<.0001
DC1N	3.181	0.773	0.597	1	5	15984	3	3	4	3.166	3.197	520.52	<.0001
DC2N	3.340	0.822	0.676	1	5	15979	3	3	4	3.324	3.357	513.7	<.0001
DC3N	3.151	0.914	0.835	1	5	15980	3	3	4	3.133	3.170	435.9	<.0001
DC4N	3.328	0.857	0.735	1	5	15979	3	3	4	3.310	3.345	490.81	<.0001
DC7N	3.604	0.728	0.530	1	5	5862	3	4	4	3.579	3.628	378.9	<.0001
DC8N	3.234	0.624	0.389	1	5	5861	3	3	4	3.213	3.255	396.74	<.0001
DC9N	3.712	0.719	0.517	1	5	5860	3	4	4	3.688	3.736	395.32	<.0001
DC12N	3.215	0.614	0.377	1	5	5861	3	3	3	3.195	3.236	401.14	<.0001
DE2	5.429	1.365	1.862	1	7	15957	5	6	6	5.401	5.457	502.54	<.0001
DE4	4.506	1.769	3.129	1	7	15957	4	5	6	4.470	4.542	321.75	<.0001

PCB Scale statistics

Variable	Item
LB_T	[scale means for Literal Belief, all students]
EC_T	[scale means for External Critique, all students]
REL_T	[scale means for Relativism, all students]
PCB_T	[scale means for Post-Critical Belief, all students]
LB_A	[scale means for Literal Belief, all adults]
EC_A	[scale means for External Critique, all adults]
REL_A	[scale means for Relativism, all adults]
PCB_A	[scale means for Post-Critical Belief, all adults]
PT1_3	Ultimately, the Christian faith is more true, than the other religions. One has to have faith in Jesus Christ in order to be fully human.
PT2_3	I wish that Christians try to proclaim the Gospel to all humankind.
PT3_3	The miracle stories about Jesus did really happen. Jesus made blind people see and He made dead people come alive again. This is precisely what's so special about Jesus.
PT4_3	I believe in a life after death because it is in the Bible and the Bible is the Word of God.
PT5_3	I believe that God is lord and master of the whole creation, because this is in the Bible in black and white.
PT6_3	When I have done something wrong, I feel guilty and then I am afraid God will punish me.
PT7_3	God doesn't exist and therefore praying to God is meaningless.
PT8_3	It is impossible to come close to God because God does not exist. 'God' is just a label.
PT9_3	God does not exist. People who believe in 'God', are a bit insane.
PT10_3	I do not really understand how intelligent people can believe in God.
PT11_3	Religion is nonsense.
PT12_3	The miracle stories in the Bible did not really happen. Making blind people see and dead people come alive again, is impossible and therefore not believable.
PT13_3	Personally I don't believe that God really exists, but for some people religious belief could be valuable – and I respect that.
PT14_3	I understand that other people pray to God for strength, but I rely on myself.
PT15_3	One religion isn't more or less true, than the other.
PT16_3	It doesn't really matter what you believe. In the end, it's all the same anyway.
PT17_3	The miracle stories in the Bible most likely did not really happen. The Bible is a book full of stories, some of which are more believable and meaningful than others.
PT18_3	Whether you believe in Jesus, Allah, Buddha or in nothing, doesn't make any real difference.
PT19_3	I feel connected to God and I am glad about that.
PT20_3	I sometimes pray to God because this gives me strength.
PT21_3	Although I can never fully grasp who God is, I still feel that He exists and that He supports me.
PT22_3	God helps me to believe in myself and in other people. God gives me strength to do my best for a better world.
PT23_3	The miracle stories in the Bible express that Jesus was sent by God to set people free from bad things and to give them new hope.
PT24_3	People who want to can come closer to God, because God knows many ways to be close to people.
PA1	You can only live a meaningful life if you believe.
PA2	God has been defined for once and for all and therefore is unchangeable.
PA3	Even though this goes against modern rationality, I believe Mary was truly a virgin when she gave birth to Jesus.
PA4	Only the major religious traditions guarantee access to God.
PA5	Religion is the one thing that gives meaning to life in all its aspects.
PA6	Ultimately, there is only one correct answer to each religious question.
PA7	Only a priest can give an answer to important religious questions.
PA8	I think that Bible stories should be taken literally, as they are written.
PA9	Faith is more of a dream which turns out to be an illusion when one is confronted with the harshness of life.
PA10	Too many people have been oppressed in the name of God to still make believing possible.
PA11	God is only a name for the inexplicable.
PA12	The world of Bible stories is so far removed from us, that it has little relevance.
PA13	A scientific understanding of human life and the world makes a religious understanding obsolete.
PA14	In the end, faith is nothing more than a safety net for human fears.
PA15	In order to fully understand what religion is all about, you have to be an outsider.
PA16	Faith is an expression of a weak personality.
PA17	Religious faith often is an instrument for obtaining power, and that makes it suspect.
PA18	Each statement about God is a result of the time in which it is made.
PA19	Because Jesus is mainly a guiding principle for me, my faith in him would not be affected if it would appear that he never actually existed as a historical individual.
PA20	The manner in which humans experience their relationship with God, is always coloured by the times in which they live.
PA21	Statements about the absolute, like dogma's, always remain relative since they are proclaimed by specific people and at specific moments in time.
PA22	God grows together with the history of humanity and therefore is changeable.
PA23	I am well aware that my beliefs are only one possibility among so many others.
PA24	Secular and religious conceptions of the world give valuable answers to important questions about life.
PA25	There is no absolute meaning in life, only direction-giving, which is different for each one of us.
PA26	The Bible holds a deeper truth which can only be revealed by personal reflection.
PA27	If you want to understand the meaning of the miracle stories from the Bible, you should always place them in their historical context.
PA28	The Bible is a guide, full of signs in the search for God, and not a historical account.
PA29	Despite the fact that the Bible was written in a completely different historical context from ours, it retains a basic message.
PA30	Ultimately, religion is a commitment without having absolute certainty.
PA31	The historical accuracy of the stories from the Bible is irrelevant for my faith in God.
PA32	Despite the high number of injustices Christianity has caused people, the original message of Christ is still valuable to me.
PA33	I still call myself a Christian, even though I do not agree with a lot of things that have happened in the past in the name of Christianity.
PE2	The questions in this survey made sense to me.
PE4	I liked completing this survey.

Variable	Mean	Std Dev	Variance	Min	Max	N	Quart 1	Median	Quart 2	Lower 99% CL	Upper 99% CL	t Value	Pr > |t|
LB_T	4.3385	1.3825	1.9113	1	7	8974	3.4	4.55	5.4	4.3009	4.3761	297.28	<.0001
EC_T	2.4600	1.3405	1.7970	1	7	8974	1.4	2.2	3.2	2.4236	2.4965	173.85	<.0001
REL_T	4.3923	1.1825	1.3983	1	7	8974	3.6	4.4	5.2	4.3602	4.4245	351.88	<.0001
PCB_T	5.2573	1.4202	2.0171	1	7	8974	4.6	5.6	6.4	5.2186	5.2959	350.66	<.0001
LB_A	3.2041	1.0488	1.1000	1	7	5257	2.5	3.125	3.875	3.1669	3.2414	221.5	<.0001
EC_A	2.7859	0.9301	0.8651	1	7	5257	2.111	2.667	3.333	2.7528	2.8189	217.17	<.0001
REL_A	4.6742	0.6937	0.4812	1	7	5257	4.25	4.75	5.125	4.6496	4.6989	488.54	<.0001
PCB_A	5.2232	0.7013	0.4918	1	7	5257	4.75	5.25	5.625	5.1983	5.2481	540	<.0001
PT1_3	3.8118	1.8307	3.3513	1	7	9733	2	4	5	3.7640	3.8596	205.42	<.0001
PT2_3	4.2840	1.6370	2.6797	1	7	9674	4	4	6	4.2411	4.3268	257.4	<.0001
PT3_3	.	.	.	.	.	0	.	.	.	.	.	.	
PT4_3	4.9365	1.7346	3.0090	1	7	9617	4	5	6	4.8909	4.9820	279.08	<.0001
PT5_3	4.8378	1.9038	3.6243	1	7	9813	4	5	6	4.7883	4.8873	251.73	<.0001
PT6_3	3.7840	1.8604	3.4610	1	7	9562	2	4	5	3.7350	3.8331	198.9	<.0001
PT7_3	2.3982	1.6633	2.7666	1	7	9562	1	2	4	2.3544	2.4421	140.99	<.0001
PT8_3	2.6947	1.7646	3.1137	1	7	9813	1	2	4	2.6488	2.7406	151.28	<.0001
PT9_3	2.2214	1.5889	2.5247	1	7	9617	1	2	3	2.1796	2.2631	137.1	<.0001
PT10_3	3.1876	1.7422	3.0354	1	7	9734	2	3	4	3.1421	3.2331	180.51	<.0001
PT11_3	2.4090	1.7189	2.9547	1	7	9674	1	2	4	2.3640	2.4541	137.85	<.0001
PT12_3	.	.	.	.	.	0	.	.	.	.	.	.	
PT13_3	3.7257	2.0553	4.2244	1	7	9813	2	4	6	3.6722	3.7791	179.57	<.0001
PT14_3	4.2447	1.6700	2.7890	1	7	9562	3	4	6	4.2007	4.2887	248.54	<.0001
PT15_3	5.1194	1.6476	2.7145	1	7	9674	4	5	6	5.0762	5.1625	305.62	<.0001
PT16_3	4.2896	1.7893	3.2016	1	7	9617	3	4	6	4.2426	4.3366	235.1	<.0001
PT17_3	.	.	.	.	.	0	.	.	.	.	.	.	
PT18_3	4.6132	1.8392	3.3828	1	7	9734	3	5	6	4.5652	4.6612	247.46	<.0001
PT19_3	5.1850	1.7283	2.9870	1	7	9812	4	6	7	5.1400	5.2299	297.17	<.0001
PT20_3	4.8952	1.7482	3.0563	1	7	9562	4	5	6	4.8492	4.9413	273.81	<.0001
PT21_3	5.2964	1.6646	2.7708	1	7	9734	4	6	7	5.2529	5.3399	313.92	<.0001
PT22_3	5.1947	1.6964	2.8779	1	7	9617	4	6	7	5.1501	5.2392	300.29	<.0001
PT23_3	.	.	.	.	.	0	.	.	.	.	.	.	
PT24_3	5.3982	1.4450	2.0881	1	7	9674	4	6	7	5.3603	5.4360	367.43	<.0001
PA1	3.7778	1.8436	3.3990	1	7	5604	2	4	5	3.7144	3.8413	153.4	<.0001
PA2	3.6671	1.7564	3.0850	1	7	5594	2	4	5	3.6066	3.7277	156.16	<.0001
PA3	4.3417	1.8517	3.4288	1	7	5590	3	4	6	4.2779	4.4055	175.31	<.0001
PA4	2.5895	1.4413	2.0772	1	7	5583	1	2	4	2.5398	2.6392	134.25	<.0001
PA5	4.4283	1.7174	2.9495	1	7	5573	3	5	6	4.3690	4.4876	192.49	<.0001
PA6	2.5691	1.4018	1.9650	1	7	5568	2	2	3	2.5207	2.6176	136.36	<.0001
PA7	2.1249	1.2447	1.5492	1	7	5557	1	2	3	2.0819	2.1679	127.26	<.0001
PA8	2.4948	1.4866	2.2100	1	7	5542	1	2	3	2.4433	2.5462	124.93	<.0001
PA9	2.9519	1.5139	2.2918	1	7	5594	2	3	4	2.8998	3.0041	145.84	<.0001
PA10	3.4945	1.5996	2.5588	1	7	5590	2	4	5	3.4393	3.5496	163.33	<.0001
PA11	3.2292	1.5454	2.3883	1	7	5568	2	3	4	3.1758	3.2825	155.92	<.0001
PA12	2.8954	1.3588	1.8463	1	7	5557	2	3	4	2.8485	2.9424	158.85	<.0001
PA13	2.7312	1.3756	1.8922	1	7	5547	2	2	4	2.6836	2.7788	147.88	<.0001
PA14	2.9394	1.5802	2.4970	1	7	5542	2	2	4	2.8847	2.9941	138.48	<.0001
PA15	2.4473	1.1530	1.3293	1	7	5533	2	2	3	2.4074	2.4873	157.89	<.0001
PA16	1.7541	1.0695	1.1437	1	7	5534	1	1	2	1.7170	1.7911	122.01	<.0001
PA17	3.2734	1.6201	2.6248	1	7	5530	2	3	5	3.2173	3.3296	150.25	<.0001
PA18	4.6034	1.3260	1.7584	1	7	5590	4	5	6	4.5577	4.6491	259.55	<.0001
PA19	4.1920	1.6875	2.8475	1	7	5582	3	4	6	4.1338	4.2502	185.6	<.0001
PA20	5.1326	1.2821	1.6438	1	7	5573	5	5	6	5.0884	5.1769	298.86	<.0001
PA21	4.2462	1.2488	1.5596	1	7	5557	4	4	5	4.2030	4.2893	253.46	<.0001
PA22	4.5333	1.4928	2.2284	1	7	5547	4	5	6	4.4816	4.5849	226.18	<.0001
PA23	5.7298	1.2875	1.6578	1	7	5547	5	6	7	5.6852	5.7743	331.44	<.0001
PA24	4.7976	1.2226	1.4948	1	7	5533	4	5	6	4.7552	4.8399	291.88	<.0001
PA25	4.0360	1.7798	3.1676	1	7	5530	2	4	6	3.9743	4.0977	168.63	<.0001
PA26	5.0564	1.3473	1.8151	1	7	5604	4	5	6	5.0100	5.1028	280.95	<.0001
PA27	4.9773	1.4140	1.9993	1	7	5604	4	5	6	4.9287	5.0260	263.52	<.0001
PA28	4.5828	1.5717	2.4703	1	7	5594	4	5	6	4.5286	4.6369	218.08	<.0001
PA29	5.8434	0.9848	0.9699	1	7	5582	5	6	6	5.8095	5.8774	443.3	<.0001
PA30	5.1764	1.4732	2.1704	1	7	5573	4	6	6	5.1255	5.2272	262.3	<.0001
PA31	4.8242	1.4816	2.1952	1	7	5568	4	5	6	4.7730	4.8753	242.96	<.0001
PA32	5.6651	1.1907	1.4179	1	7	5542	5	6	6	5.6239	5.7063	354.18	<.0001
PA33	5.3083	1.5256	2.3276	1	7	5530	5	6	6	5.2555	5.3612	258.74	<.0001
PE2	5.0760	1.5106	2.2818	1	7	15070	4	5	6	5.0443	5.1077	412.52	<.0001
PE4	4.2614	1.8320	3.3564	1	7	15070	3	4	6	4.2229	4.2998	285.54	<.0001

380

Pearson Correlation Coefficients, student respondents, n=8974
Prob > |r| under H0: Rho=0

	LB_T	EC_T	REL_T	PCB_T
LB_T	1	-0.55718	-0.39043	0.76804
		<.0001	<.0001	<.0001
EC_T	-0.55718	1	0.46164	-0.75268
	<.0001		<.0001	<.0001
REL_T	-0.39043	0.46164	1	-0.38349
	<.0001	<.0001		<.0001
PCB_T	0.76804	-0.75268	-0.38349	1
	<.0001	<.0001	<.0001	

Pearson Correlation Coefficients, adult respondents, n=5257
Prob > |r| under H0: Rho=0

	LB_A	EC_A	REL_A	PCB_A
LB_A	1	-0.08861	-0.19196	0.12252
		<.0001	<.0001	<.0001
EC_A	-0.08861	1	0.2094	-0.30864
	<.0001		<.0001	<.0001
REL_A	-0.19196	0.2094	1	0.34749
	<.0001	<.0001		<.0001
PCB_A	0.12252	-0.30864	0.34749	1
	<.0001	<.0001	<.0001	

Pearson Correlation Coefficients, student respondents
Prob > |r| under H0: Rho=0
Number of Observations

	PT1	PT2	PT4	PT5	PT6	PT7	PT8	PT9	PT10	PT11
PT1	1	0.54346	0.44541	0.50737	0.31955	-0.20849	-0.20807	-0.16319	0.05246	-0.20643
		<.0001	<.0001	<.0001	<.0001	<.0001	<.0001	<.0001	<.0001	<.0001
	9733	9671	9614	9731	9559	9559	9731	9614	9733	9671
PT2	0.54346	1	0.55714	0.58891	0.34233	-0.3589	-0.34671	-0.30952	-0.0719	-0.36077
	<.0001		<.0001	<.0001	<.0001	<.0001	<.0001	<.0001	<.0001	<.0001
	9671	9674	9616	9672	9561	9561	9672	9616	9671	9674
PT4	0.44541	0.55714	1	0.67233	0.38771	-0.50238	-0.48711	-0.45208	-0.19946	-0.47384
	<.0001	<.0001		<.0001	<.0001	<.0001	<.0001	<.0001	<.0001	<.0001
	9614	9616	9617	9615	9562	9562	9615	9616	9614	9616
PT5	0.50737	0.58891	0.67233	1	0.38105	-0.52562	-0.51894	-0.46791	-0.19158	-0.50291
	<.0001	<.0001	<.0001		<.0001	<.0001	<.0001	<.0001	<.0001	<.0001
	9731	9672	9615	9813	9560	9560	9813	9615	9732	9672
PT6	0.31955	0.34233	0.38771	0.38105	1	-0.24135	-0.22853	-0.19997	-0.02148	-0.23687
	<.0001	<.0001	<.0001	<.0001		<.0001	<.0001	<.0001	0.0357	<.0001
	9559	9561	9562	9560	9562	9562	9560	9562	9559	9561
PT7	-0.20849	-0.3589	-0.50238	-0.52562	-0.24135	1	0.69381	0.7772	0.42645	0.73364
	<.0001	<.0001	<.0001	<.0001	<.0001		<.0001	<.0001	<.0001	<.0001
	9559	9561	9562	9560	9562	9562	9560	9562	9559	9561
PT8	-0.20807	-0.34671	-0.48711	-0.51894	-0.22853	0.69381	1	0.66007	0.44479	0.66606
	<.0001	<.0001	<.0001	<.0001	<.0001	<.0001		<.0001	<.0001	<.0001
	9731	9672	9615	9813	9560	9560	9813	9615	9732	9672
PT9	-0.16319	-0.30952	-0.45208	-0.46791	-0.19997	0.7772	0.66007	1	0.45604	0.72557
	<.0001	<.0001	<.0001	<.0001	<.0001	<.0001	<.0001		<.0001	<.0001
	9614	9616	9616	9615	9562	9562	9615	9617	9614	9616
PT10	0.05246	-0.0719	-0.19946	-0.19158	-0.02148	0.42645	0.44479	0.45604	1	0.42528
	<.0001	<.0001	<.0001	<.0001	0.0357	<.0001	<.0001	<.0001		<.0001
	9733	9671	9614	9732	9559	9559	9732	9614	9734	9671
PT11	-0.20643	-0.36077	-0.47384	-0.50291	-0.23687	0.73364	0.66606	0.72557	0.42528	1
	<.0001	<.0001	<.0001	<.0001	<.0001	<.0001	<.0001	<.0001	<.0001	
	9671	9674	9616	9672	9561	9561	9672	9616	9671	9674
PT13	-0.19345	-0.25913	-0.35377	-0.40632	-0.13934	0.43045	0.53106	0.38617	0.30516	0.41172
	<.0001	<.0001	<.0001	<.0001	<.0001	<.0001	<.0001	<.0001	<.0001	<.0001
	9731	9672	9615	9813	9560	9560	9813	9615	9732	9672
PT14	-0.1589	-0.24415	-0.31346	-0.32952	-0.14236	0.44175	0.41912	0.37027	0.29646	0.38207
	<.0001	<.0001	<.0001	<.0001	<.0001	<.0001	<.0001	<.0001	<.0001	<.0001
	9559	9561	9562	9560	9562	9562	9560	9562	9559	9561
PT15	-0.16914	-0.01713	-0.00017	-0.01559	-0.01123	-0.04062	0.02782	-0.05104	-0.00242	-0.02564
	<.0001	0.092	0.9866	0.1252	0.2721	<.0001	0.0062	<.0001	0.8122	0.0117
	9671	9674	9616	9672	9561	9561	9672	9616	9671	9674
PT16	-0.11999	-0.12627	-0.16534	-0.17801	-0.06715	0.27813	0.30589	0.26506	0.26351	0.27657
	<.0001	<.0001	<.0001	<.0001	<.0001	<.0001	<.0001	<.0001	<.0001	<.0001
	9614	9616	9616	9615	9562	9562	9615	9617	9614	9616
PT18	-0.16193	-0.11406	-0.10499	-0.12138	-0.04163	0.14812	0.2047	0.11625	0.14958	0.1438
	<.0001	<.0001	<.0001	<.0001	<.0001	<.0001	<.0001	<.0001	<.0001	<.0001
	9733	9671	9614	9732	9559	9559	9732	9614	9734	9671
PT19	0.4326	0.56278	0.6551	0.71053	0.38502	-0.62365	-0.62032	-0.5634	-0.27159	-0.59745
	<.0001	<.0001	<.0001	<.0001	<.0001	<.0001	<.0001	<.0001	<.0001	<.0001
	9731	9672	9615	9812	9560	9560	9812	9615	9732	9672
PT20	0.36548	0.47226	0.58191	0.56775	0.40898	-0.54683	-0.49733	-0.46852	-0.21624	-0.49697
	<.0001	<.0001	<.0001	<.0001	<.0001	<.0001	<.0001	<.0001	<.0001	<.0001
	9559	9561	9562	9560	9562	9562	9560	9562	9559	9561
PT21	0.337	0.47217	0.56175	0.57999	0.35077	-0.56258	-0.51725	-0.51008	-0.21218	-0.52186
	<.0001	<.0001	<.0001	<.0001	<.0001	<.0001	<.0001	<.0001	<.0001	<.0001
	9733	9671	9614	9732	9559	9559	9732	9614	9734	9671
PT22	0.42673	0.56027	0.66545	0.68756	0.42292	-0.6186	-0.58499	-0.55781	-0.26187	-0.58953
	<.0001	<.0001	<.0001	<.0001	<.0001	<.0001	<.0001	<.0001	<.0001	<.0001
	9614	9616	9616	9615	9562	9562	9615	9617	9614	9616
PT24	0.3321	0.48831	0.56903	0.56722	0.3122	-0.54283	-0.49821	-0.50868	-0.24578	-0.51525
	<.0001	<.0001	<.0001	<.0001	<.0001	<.0001	<.0001	<.0001	<.0001	<.0001
	9671	9674	9616	9672	9561	9561	9672	9616	9671	9674

	PT13	PT14	PT15	PT16	PT18	PT19	PT20	PT21	PT22	PT24
PT1	-0.19345	-0.1589	-0.16914	-0.11999	-0.16193	0.4326	0.36548	0.337	0.42673	0.3321
	<.0001	<.0001	<.0001	<.0001	<.0001	<.0001	<.0001	<.0001	<.0001	<.0001
	9731	9559	9671	9614	9733	9731	9559	9733	9614	9671
PT2	-0.25913	-0.24415	-0.01713	-0.12627	-0.11406	0.56278	0.47226	0.47217	0.56027	0.48831
	<.0001	<.0001	0.092	<.0001	<.0001	<.0001	<.0001	<.0001	<.0001	<.0001
	9672	9561	9674	9616	9671	9672	9561	9671	9616	9674
PT4	-0.35377	-0.31346	-0.00017	-0.16534	-0.10499	0.6551	0.58191	0.56175	0.66545	0.56903
	<.0001	<.0001	0.9866	<.0001	<.0001	<.0001	<.0001	<.0001	<.0001	<.0001
	9615	9562	9616	9616	9614	9615	9562	9614	9616	9616
PT5	-0.40632	-0.32952	-0.01559	-0.17801	-0.12138	0.71053	0.56775	0.57999	0.68756	0.56722
	<.0001	<.0001	0.1252	<.0001	<.0001	<.0001	<.0001	<.0001	<.0001	<.0001
	9813	9560	9672	9615	9732	9812	9560	9732	9615	9672
PT6	-0.13934	-0.14236	-0.01123	-0.06715	-0.04163	0.38502	0.40898	0.35077	0.42292	0.3122
	<.0001	<.0001	0.2721	<.0001	<.0001	<.0001	<.0001	<.0001	<.0001	<.0001
	9560	9562	9561	9562	9559	9560	9562	9559	9562	9561
PT7	0.43045	0.44175	-0.04062	0.27813	0.14812	-0.62365	-0.54683	-0.56258	-0.6186	-0.54283
	<.0001	<.0001	<.0001	<.0001	<.0001	<.0001	<.0001	<.0001	<.0001	<.0001
	9560	9562	9561	9562	9559	9560	9562	9559	9562	9561
PT8	0.53106	0.41912	0.02782	0.30589	0.2047	-0.62032	-0.49733	-0.51725	-0.58499	-0.49821
	<.0001	<.0001	0.0062	<.0001	<.0001	<.0001	<.0001	<.0001	<.0001	<.0001
	9813	9560	9672	9615	9732	9812	9560	9732	9615	9672
PT9	0.38617	0.37027	-0.05104	0.26506	0.11625	-0.5634	-0.46852	-0.51008	-0.55781	-0.50868
	<.0001	<.0001	<.0001	<.0001	<.0001	<.0001	<.0001	<.0001	<.0001	<.0001
	9615	9562	9616	9617	9614	9615	9562	9614	9617	9616
PT10	0.30516	0.29646	-0.00242	0.26351	0.14958	-0.27159	-0.21624	-0.21218	-0.26187	-0.24578
	<.0001	<.0001	0.8122	<.0001	<.0001	<.0001	<.0001	<.0001	<.0001	<.0001
	9732	9559	9671	9614	9734	9732	9559	9734	9614	9671
PT11	0.41172	0.38207	-0.02564	0.27657	0.1438	-0.59745	-0.49697	-0.52186	-0.58953	-0.51525
	<.0001	<.0001	0.0117	<.0001	<.0001	<.0001	<.0001	<.0001	<.0001	<.0001
	9672	9561	9674	9616	9671	9672	9561	9671	9616	9674
PT13	1	0.38695	0.13605	0.28671	0.24581	-0.4253	-0.34308	-0.29297	-0.41175	-0.28764
		<.0001	<.0001	<.0001	<.0001	<.0001	<.0001	<.0001	<.0001	<.0001
	9813	9560	9672	9615	9732	9812	9560	9732	9615	9672
PT14	0.38695	1	0.14417	0.32789	0.22632	-0.38504	-0.36028	-0.28642	-0.3801	-0.27753
	<.0001		<.0001	<.0001	<.0001	<.0001	<.0001	<.0001	<.0001	<.0001
	9560	9562	9561	9562	9559	9560	9562	9559	9562	9561
PT15	0.13605	0.14417	1	0.2453	0.33267	0.02944	0.02548	0.09639	0.0346	0.13092
	<.0001	<.0001		<.0001	<.0001	0.0038	0.0127	<.0001	0.0007	<.0001
	9672	9561	9674	9616	9671	9672	9561	9671	9616	9674
PT16	0.28671	0.32789	0.2453	1	0.4429	-0.19231	-0.16127	-0.11459	-0.18357	-0.10017
	<.0001	<.0001	<.0001		<.0001	<.0001	<.0001	<.0001	<.0001	<.0001
	9615	9562	9616	9617	9614	9615	9562	9614	9617	9616
PT18	0.24581	0.22632	0.33267	0.4429	1	-0.11776	-0.09338	-0.03101	-0.11109	-0.02711
	<.0001	<.0001	<.0001	<.0001		<.0001	<.0001	0.0022	<.0001	0.0077
	9732	9559	9671	9614	9734	9732	9559	9734	9614	9671
PT19	-0.4253	-0.38504	0.02944	-0.19231	-0.11776	1	0.67989	0.68834	0.7905	0.65066
	<.0001	<.0001	0.0038	<.0001	<.0001		<.0001	<.0001	<.0001	<.0001
	9812	9560	9672	9615	9732	9812	9560	9732	9615	9672
PT20	-0.34308	-0.36028	0.02548	-0.16127	-0.09338	0.67989	1	0.60499	0.7085	0.56049
	<.0001	<.0001	0.0127	<.0001	<.0001	<.0001		<.0001	<.0001	<.0001
	9560	9562	9561	9562	9559	9560	9562	9559	9562	9561
PT21	-0.29297	-0.28642	0.09639	-0.11459	-0.03101	0.68834	0.60499	1	0.67708	0.58807
	<.0001	<.0001	<.0001	<.0001	0.0022	<.0001	<.0001		<.0001	<.0001
	9732	9559	9671	9614	9734	9732	9559	9734	9614	9671
PT22	-0.41175	-0.3801	0.0346	-0.18357	-0.11109	0.7905	0.7085	0.67708	1	0.66197
	<.0001	<.0001	0.0007	<.0001	<.0001	<.0001	<.0001	<.0001		<.0001
	9615	9562	9616	9617	9614	9615	9562	9614	9617	9616
PT24	-0.28764	-0.27753	0.13092	-0.10017	-0.02711	0.65066	0.56049	0.58807	0.66197	1
	<.0001	<.0001	<.0001	<.0001	0.0077	<.0001	<.0001	<.0001	<.0001	
	9672	9561	9674	9616	9671	9672	9561	9671	9616	9674

Pearson Correlation Coefficients, adult respondents
Prob > |r| under H0: Rho=0
Number of Observations

	PA1	PA2	PA3	PA4	PA5	PA6	PA7	PA8	PA9	PA10	PA11
PA1	1	0.52133	0.43445	0.30655	0.54718	0.36511	0.23803	0.30936	-0.04439	-0.01314	-0.06262
		<.0001	<.0001	<.0001	<.0001	<.0001	<.0001	<.0001	0.0009	0.326	<.0001
	5604	5594	5589	5581	5572	5566	5555	5540	5594	5589	5566
PA2	0.52133	1	0.46856	0.37372	0.43815	0.46651	0.2988	0.41374	0.07413	0.04336	-0.04753
	<.0001		<.0001	<.0001	<.0001	<.0001	<.0001	<.0001	<.0001	0.0012	0.0004
	5594	5594	5589	5581	5572	5566	5555	5540	5594	5589	5566
PA3	0.43445	0.46856	1	0.19764	0.45741	0.2861	0.17989	0.30703	-0.16661	-0.12071	-0.21035
	<.0001	<.0001		<.0001	<.0001	<.0001	<.0001	<.0001	<.0001	<.0001	<.0001
	5589	5589	5590	5582	5573	5567	5556	5541	5589	5590	5567
PA4	0.30655	0.37372	0.19764	1	0.23607	0.44707	0.42618	0.37993	0.26623	0.19419	0.1521
	<.0001	<.0001	<.0001		<.0001	<.0001	<.0001	<.0001	<.0001	<.0001	<.0001
	5581	5581	5582	5583	5573	5567	5556	5541	5581	5582	5567
PA5	0.54718	0.43815	0.45741	0.23607	1	0.27388	0.16674	0.21621	-0.17573	-0.14578	-0.15291
	<.0001	<.0001	<.0001	<.0001		<.0001	<.0001	<.0001	<.0001	<.0001	<.0001
	5572	5572	5573	5573	5573	5567	5556	5541	5572	5573	5567
PA6	0.36511	0.46651	0.2861	0.44707	0.27388	1	0.41076	0.42534	0.16796	0.14058	0.17096
	<.0001	<.0001	<.0001	<.0001	<.0001		<.0001	<.0001	<.0001	<.0001	<.0001
	5566	5566	5567	5567	5567	5568	5557	5542	5566	5567	5568
PA7	0.23803	0.2988	0.17989	0.42618	0.16674	0.41076	1	0.39096	0.23173	0.18351	0.18405
	<.0001	<.0001	<.0001	<.0001	<.0001	<.0001		<.0001	<.0001	<.0001	<.0001
	5555	5555	5556	5556	5556	5557	5557	5542	5555	5556	5557
PA8	0.30936	0.41374	0.30703	0.37993	0.21621	0.42534	0.39096	1	0.20344	0.17223	0.08864
	<.0001	<.0001	<.0001	<.0001	<.0001	<.0001	<.0001		<.0001	<.0001	<.0001
	5540	5540	5541	5541	5541	5542	5542	5542	5540	5541	5542
PA9	-0.04439	0.07413	-0.16661	0.26623	-0.17573	0.16796	0.23173	0.20344	1	0.4748	0.35863
	0.0009	<.0001	<.0001	<.0001	<.0001	<.0001	<.0001	<.0001		<.0001	<.0001
	5594	5594	5589	5581	5572	5566	5555	5540	5594	5589	5566
PA10	-0.01314	0.04336	-0.12071	0.19419	-0.14578	0.14058	0.18351	0.17223	0.4748	1	0.33828
	0.326	0.0012	<.0001	<.0001	<.0001	<.0001	<.0001	<.0001	<.0001		<.0001
	5589	5589	5590	5582	5573	5567	5556	5541	5589	5590	5567
PA11	-0.06262	-0.04753	-0.21035	0.1521	-0.15291	0.17096	0.18405	0.08864	0.35863	0.33828	1
	<.0001	0.0004	<.0001	<.0001	<.0001	<.0001	<.0001	<.0001	<.0001	<.0001	
	5566	5566	5567	5567	5567	5568	5557	5542	5566	5567	5568
PA12	-0.12413	-0.06384	-0.25289	0.14939	-0.24453	0.12006	0.24983	0.11442	0.42996	0.42013	0.33389
	<.0001	<.0001	<.0001	<.0001	<.0001	<.0001	<.0001	<.0001	<.0001	<.0001	<.0001
	5555	5555	5556	5556	5556	5557	5557	5542	5555	5556	5557
PA13	-0.09336	0.02811	-0.19099	0.24703	-0.21928	0.19632	0.29241	0.20962	0.45967	0.42143	0.35825
	<.0001	0.0364	<.0001	<.0001	<.0001	<.0001	<.0001	<.0001	<.0001	<.0001	<.0001
	5545	5545	5546	5546	5546	5547	5547	5542	5545	5546	5547
PA14	-0.14204	-0.08023	-0.2646	0.16401	-0.2779	0.12104	0.20771	0.1589	0.50319	0.42704	0.41747
	<.0001	<.0001	<.0001	<.0001	<.0001	<.0001	<.0001	<.0001	<.0001	<.0001	<.0001
	5540	5540	5541	5541	5541	5542	5542	5542	5540	5541	5542
PA15	0.02211	0.03959	-0.11351	0.23504	-0.10501	0.21678	0.30649	0.21842	0.35427	0.31096	0.30945
	0.1001	0.0032	<.0001	<.0001	<.0001	<.0001	<.0001	<.0001	<.0001	<.0001	<.0001
	5531	5531	5532	5532	5532	5533	5533	5533	5531	5532	5533
PA16	-0.05555	-0.00631	-0.15003	0.23012	-0.17142	0.20043	0.30158	0.20132	0.38032	0.30645	0.31177
	<.0001	0.6389	<.0001	<.0001	<.0001	<.0001	<.0001	<.0001	<.0001	<.0001	<.0001
	5532	5532	5533	5533	5533	5534	5534	5534	5532	5533	5534
PA17	-0.18604	-0.20916	-0.30467	-0.012	-0.30714	0.0064	0.03517	-0.01903	0.30789	0.32233	0.30141
	<.0001	<.0001	<.0001	0.3724	<.0001	0.6342	0.0089	0.1572	<.0001	<.0001	<.0001
	5527	5527	5528	5528	5528	5529	5529	5529	5527	5528	5529

	PA12	PA13	PA14	PA15	PA16	PA17	PA18	PA19	PA20	PA21	PA22
PA1	-0.12413	-0.09336	-0.14204	0.02211	-0.05555	-0.18604	-0.02198	0.07568	0.04773	-0.005	-0.13719
	<.0001	<.0001	<.0001	0.1001	<.0001	<.0001	0.1004	<.0001	0.0004	0.7093	<.0001
	5555	5545	5540	5531	5532	5527	5589	5580	5572	5555	5545
PA2	-0.06384	0.02811	-0.08023	0.03959	-0.00631	-0.20916	-0.06246	0.08196	-0.03318	-0.03077	-0.28558
	<.0001	0.0364	<.0001	0.0032	0.6389	<.0001	<.0001	<.0001	0.0133	0.0218	<.0001
	5555	5545	5540	5531	5532	5527	5589	5580	5572	5555	5545
PA3	-0.25289	-0.19099	-0.2646	-0.11351	-0.15003	-0.30467	-0.10599	0.01359	-0.02299	-0.03625	-0.17082
	<.0001	<.0001	<.0001	<.0001	<.0001	<.0001	<.0001	0.31	0.0861	0.0069	<.0001
	5556	5546	5541	5532	5533	5528	5590	5581	5573	5556	5546
PA4	0.14939	0.24703	0.16401	0.23504	0.23012	-0.012	0.03623	0.09539	0.02746	0.00468	-0.0841
	<.0001	<.0001	<.0001	<.0001	<.0001	0.3724	0.0068	<.0001	0.0404	0.7272	<.0001
	5556	5546	5541	5532	5533	5528	5582	5582	5573	5556	5546
PA5	-0.24453	-0.21928	-0.2779	-0.10501	-0.17142	-0.30714	-0.06381	0.07308	0.11937	0.02262	-0.11656
	<.0001	<.0001	<.0001	<.0001	<.0001	<.0001	<.0001	<.0001	<.0001	0.0918	<.0001
	5556	5546	5541	5532	5533	5528	5573	5573	5573	5556	5546
PA6	0.12006	0.19632	0.12104	0.21678	0.20043	0.0064	0.00353	0.07552	-0.01366	0.01224	-0.15769
	<.0001	<.0001	<.0001	<.0001	<.0001	0.6342	0.7921	<.0001	0.3082	0.3618	<.0001
	5557	5547	5542	5533	5534	5529	5567	5567	5567	5557	5547
PA7	0.24983	0.29241	0.20771	0.30649	0.30158	0.03517	0.02872	0.10461	-0.00686	0.05143	-0.02286
	<.0001	<.0001	<.0001	<.0001	<.0001	0.0089	0.0323	<.0001	0.6092	0.0001	0.0887
	5557	5547	5542	5533	5534	5529	5556	5556	5556	5557	5547
PA8	0.11442	0.20962	0.1589	0.21842	0.20132	-0.01903	-0.03946	0.03656	-0.07111	-0.03152	-0.14407
	<.0001	<.0001	<.0001	<.0001	<.0001	0.1572	0.0033	0.0065	<.0001	0.0189	<.0001
	5542	5542	5542	5533	5534	5529	5541	5541	5541	5542	5542
PA9	0.42996	0.45967	0.50319	0.35427	0.38032	0.30789	0.20804	0.10792	0.04945	0.02273	0.04883
	<.0001	<.0001	<.0001	<.0001	<.0001	<.0001	<.0001	<.0001	0.0002	0.0903	0.0003
	5555	5545	5540	5531	5532	5527	5589	5580	5572	5555	5545
PA10	0.42013	0.42143	0.42704	0.31096	0.30645	0.32233	0.26901	0.10554	0.079	0.03695	0.03885
	<.0001	<.0001	<.0001	<.0001	<.0001	<.0001	<.0001	<.0001	<.0001	0.0059	0.0038
	5556	5546	5541	5532	5533	5528	5590	5581	5573	5556	5546
PA11	0.33389	0.35825	0.41747	0.30945	0.31177	0.30141	0.21336	0.15696	0.10397	0.17924	0.09877
	<.0001	<.0001	<.0001	<.0001	<.0001	<.0001	<.0001	<.0001	<.0001	<.0001	<.0001
	5557	5547	5542	5533	5534	5529	5567	5567	5567	5557	5547
PA12	1	0.51512	0.48061	0.36799	0.40478	0.34898	0.1466	0.05224	0.00975	0.00987	0.04636
		<.0001	<.0001	<.0001	<.0001	<.0001	<.0001	<.0001	0.4676	0.4621	0.0006
		5557	5547	5542	5533	5534	5529	5556	5556	5556	5557	5547
PA13	0.51512	1	0.49573	0.3968	0.44347	0.31889	0.1273	0.05541	-0.01016	0.01039	0.02372
	<.0001		<.0001	<.0001	<.0001	<.0001	<.0001	<.0001	0.4492	0.439	0.0774
	5547	5547	5542	5533	5534	5529	5546	5546	5546	5547	5547
PA14	0.48061	0.49573	1	0.40099	0.45853	0.42232	0.19293	0.07423	0.05368	0.07447	0.06507
	<.0001	<.0001		<.0001	<.0001	<.0001	<.0001	<.0001	<.0001	<.0001	<.0001
	5542	5542	5542	5533	5534	5529	5541	5541	5541	5542	5542
PA15	0.36799	0.3968	0.40099	1	0.49334	0.32707	0.1178	0.07323	0.03068	0.05495	0.04352
	<.0001	<.0001	<.0001		<.0001	<.0001	<.0001	<.0001	0.0225	<.0001	0.0012
	5533	5533	5533	5533	5533	5529	5532	5532	5532	5533	5533
PA16	0.40478	0.44347	0.45853	0.49334	1	0.37232	0.08349	0.03954	-0.05056	0.0172	-0.01619
	<.0001	<.0001	<.0001	<.0001		<.0001	<.0001	0.0033	0.0002	0.2008	0.2286
	5534	5534	5534	5533	5534	5529	5533	5533	5533	5534	5534
PA17	0.34898	0.31889	0.42232	0.32707	0.37232	1	0.18474	0.00732	0.07291	0.0836	0.08567
	<.0001	<.0001	<.0001	<.0001	<.0001		<.0001	0.5863	<.0001	<.0001	<.0001
	5529	5529	5529	5529	5529	5530	5528	5528	5528	5529	5529

	PA23	PA24	PA25	PA26	PA27	PA28	PA29	PA30	PA31	PA32	PA33
PA1	-0.24272	0.15204	-0.21145	0.37164	0.13459	0.03657	0.20492	-0.12714	0.07669	0.22721	-0.01906
	<.0001	<.0001	<.0001	<.0001	<.0001	0.0062	<.0001	<.0001	<.0001	<.0001	0.1566
	5545	5531	5527	5604	5604	5594	5580	5572	5566	5540	5527
PA2	-0.27995	0.07282	-0.18095	0.29354	0.04859	0.00299	0.17779	-0.14215	0.01978	0.15459	-0.08323
	<.0001	<.0001	<.0001	<.0001	0.0003	0.8233	<.0001	<.0001	0.1402	<.0001	<.0001
	5545	5531	5527	5594	5594	5594	5580	5572	5566	5540	5527
PA3	-0.24059	0.18135	-0.21557	0.35126	0.01634	-0.02087	0.32384	-0.12774	0.087	0.32679	0.01767
	<.0001	<.0001	<.0001	<.0001	0.222	0.1188	<.0001	<.0001	<.0001	<.0001	0.189
	5546	5532	5528	5589	5589	5589	5581	5573	5567	5541	5528
PA4	-0.18822	-0.01165	-0.0406	0.06594	-0.01069	0.02081	-0.04787	-0.03582	-0.07643	-0.08358	-0.16183
	<.0001	0.3865	0.0025	<.0001	0.4248	0.1201	0.0003	0.0075	<.0001	<.0001	<.0001
	5546	5532	5528	5581	5581	5581	5582	5573	5567	5541	5528
PA5	-0.21577	0.26714	-0.23001	0.39509	0.1199	0.0322	0.32896	-0.00475	0.14159	0.36531	0.06845
	<.0001	<.0001	<.0001	<.0001	<.0001	0.0162	<.0001	0.7227	<.0001	<.0001	<.0001
	5546	5532	5528	5572	5572	5572	5573	5573	5567	5541	5528
PA6	-0.24401	-0.0018	-0.07437	0.11512	0.00403	0.02949	-0.02618	-0.09858	0.00702	-0.0274	-0.12639
	<.0001	0.8938	<.0001	<.0001	0.7635	0.0278	0.0508	<.0001	0.6004	0.0414	<.0001
	5547	5533	5529	5566	5566	5566	5567	5567	5568	5542	5529
PA7	-0.13484	-0.03798	0.02773	0.02906	-0.04113	0.03267	-0.09143	-0.03031	-0.03995	-0.10422	-0.11773
	<.0001	0.0047	0.0392	0.0303	0.0022	0.0149	<.0001	0.0239	0.0029	<.0001	<.0001
	5547	5533	5529	5555	5555	5555	5556	5556	5557	5542	5529
PA8	-0.21498	-0.06207	-0.07341	0.09329	-0.07142	-0.12202	-0.03424	-0.14422	-0.11344	-0.05441	-0.15674
	<.0001	<.0001	<.0001	<.0001	<.0001	<.0001	0.0108	<.0001	<.0001	<.0001	<.0001
	5542	5533	5529	5540	5540	5540	5541	5541	5542	5542	5529
PA9	0.01807	-0.23297	0.18484	-0.19553	-0.03541	0.09632	-0.274	0.07521	-0.12138	-0.33711	-0.14565
	0.1785	<.0001	<.0001	<.0001	0.0081	<.0001	<.0001	<.0001	<.0001	<.0001	<.0001
	5545	5531	5527	5594	5594	5594	5580	5572	5566	5540	5527
PA10	0.04833	-0.20933	0.13458	-0.18746	-0.0558	0.07177	-0.24971	0.04213	-0.15691	-0.30739	-0.11214
	0.0003	<.0001	<.0001	<.0001	<.0001	<.0001	<.0001	0.0017	<.0001	<.0001	<.0001
	5546	5532	5528	5589	5589	5589	5581	5573	5567	5541	5528
PA11	0.10457	-0.09989	0.18982	-0.14684	-0.00271	0.11804	-0.20706	0.13393	-0.0108	-0.22604	-0.06157
	<.0001	<.0001	<.0001	<.0001	0.8396	<.0001	<.0001	<.0001	0.4205	<.0001	<.0001
	5547	5533	5529	5566	5566	5566	5567	5567	5568	5542	5529
PA12	0.05048	-0.28543	0.19131	-0.34614	-0.10953	0.02476	-0.4311	0.03205	-0.10418	-0.43508	-0.1236
	0.0002	<.0001	<.0001	<.0001	<.0001	0.065	<.0001	0.0169	<.0001	<.0001	<.0001
	5547	5533	5529	5555	5555	5555	5556	5556	5557	5542	5529
PA13	0.01477	-0.27229	0.16223	-0.269	-0.10363	0.01528	-0.37084	0.01091	-0.17325	-0.415	-0.18493
	0.2714	<.0001	<.0001	<.0001	<.0001	0.2551	<.0001	0.4165	<.0001	<.0001	<.0001
	5547	5533	5529	5545	5545	5545	5546	5546	5547	5542	5529
PA14	0.08496	-0.22817	0.25632	-0.28676	-0.07638	0.03393	-0.33737	0.08323	-0.14768	-0.42467	-0.13287
	<.0001	<.0001	<.0001	<.0001	<.0001	0.0115	<.0001	<.0001	<.0001	<.0001	<.0001
	5542	5533	5529	5540	5540	5540	5541	5541	5542	5542	5529
PA15	-0.01973	-0.12593	0.14567	-0.13729	-0.03358	0.03834	-0.26761	-0.00402	-0.0796	-0.25482	-0.13171
	0.1423	<.0001	<.0001	<.0001	0.0125	0.0043	<.0001	0.7649	<.0001	<.0001	<.0001
	5533	5533	5529	5531	5531	5531	5532	5532	5533	5533	5529
PA16	-0.06975	-0.16566	0.14556	-0.22728	-0.1021	0.02248	-0.36432	-0.02959	-0.12038	-0.37834	-0.18691
	<.0001	<.0001	<.0001	<.0001	<.0001	0.0946	<.0001	0.0277	<.0001	<.0001	<.0001
	5534	5533	5529	5532	5532	5532	5533	5533	5534	5534	5529
PA17	0.12011	-0.11297	0.29409	-0.23322	0.00925	0.06527	-0.27064	0.10522	-0.08081	-0.26473	0.01448
	<.0001	<.0001	<.0001	<.0001	0.4918	<.0001	<.0001	<.0001	<.0001	<.0001	0.2818
	5529	5529	5530	5527	5527	5527	5528	5528	5529	5529	5530

	PA1	PA2	PA3	PA4	PA5	PA6	PA7	PA8	PA9	PA10	PA11
PA18	-0.02198	-0.06246	-0.10599	0.03623	-0.06381	0.00353	0.02872	-0.03946	0.20804	0.26901	0.21336
	0.1004	<.0001	<.0001	0.0068	<.0001	0.7921	0.0323	0.0033	<.0001	<.0001	<.0001
	5589	5589	5590	5582	5573	5567	5556	5541	5589	5590	5567
PA19	0.07568	0.08196	0.01359	0.09539	0.07308	0.07552	0.10461	0.03656	0.10792	0.10554	0.15696
	<.0001	<.0001	0.31	<.0001	<.0001	<.0001	<.0001	0.0065	<.0001	<.0001	<.0001
	5580	5580	5581	5582	5573	5567	5556	5541	5580	5581	5567
PA20	0.04773	-0.03318	-0.02299	0.02746	0.11937	-0.01366	-0.00686	-0.07111	0.04945	0.079	0.10397
	0.0004	0.0133	0.0861	0.0404	<.0001	0.3082	0.6092	<.0001	0.0002	<.0001	<.0001
	5572	5572	5573	5573	5573	5567	5556	5541	5572	5573	5567
PA21	-0.005	-0.03077	-0.03625	0.00468	0.02262	0.01224	0.05143	-0.03152	0.02273	0.03695	0.17924
	0.7093	0.0218	0.0069	0.7272	0.0918	0.3618	0.0001	0.0189	0.0903	0.0059	<.0001
	5555	5555	5556	5556	5556	5557	5557	5542	5555	5556	5557
PA22	-0.13719	-0.28558	-0.17082	-0.0841	-0.11656	-0.15769	-0.02286	-0.14407	0.04883	0.03885	0.09877
	<.0001	<.0001	<.0001	<.0001	<.0001	<.0001	0.0887	<.0001	0.0003	0.0038	<.0001
	5545	5545	5546	5546	5546	5547	5547	5542	5545	5546	5547
PA23	-0.24272	-0.27995	-0.24059	-0.18822	-0.21577	-0.24401	-0.13484	-0.21498	0.01807	0.04833	0.10457
	<.0001	<.0001	<.0001	<.0001	<.0001	<.0001	<.0001	<.0001	0.1785	0.0003	<.0001
	5545	5545	5546	5546	5546	5547	5547	5542	5545	5546	5547
PA24	0.15204	0.07282	0.18135	-0.01165	0.26714	-0.0018	-0.03798	-0.06207	-0.23297	-0.20933	-0.09989
	<.0001	<.0001	<.0001	0.3865	<.0001	0.8938	0.0047	<.0001	<.0001	<.0001	<.0001
	5531	5531	5532	5532	5532	5533	5533	5533	5531	5532	5533
PA25	-0.21145	-0.18095	-0.21557	-0.0406	-0.23001	-0.07437	0.02773	-0.07341	0.18484	0.13458	0.18982
	<.0001	<.0001	<.0001	0.0025	<.0001	<.0001	0.0392	<.0001	<.0001	<.0001	<.0001
	5527	5527	5528	5528	5528	5529	5529	5529	5527	5528	5529
PA26	0.37164	0.29354	0.35126	0.06594	0.39509	0.11512	0.02906	0.09329	-0.19553	-0.18746	-0.14684
	<.0001	<.0001	<.0001	<.0001	<.0001	<.0001	0.0303	<.0001	<.0001	<.0001	<.0001
	5604	5594	5589	5581	5572	5566	5555	5540	5594	5589	5566
PA27	0.13459	0.04859	0.01634	-0.01069	0.1199	0.00403	-0.04113	-0.07142	-0.03541	-0.0558	-0.00271
	<.0001	0.0003	0.222	0.4248	<.0001	0.7635	0.0022	<.0001	0.0081	<.0001	0.8396
	5604	5594	5589	5581	5572	5566	5555	5540	5594	5589	5566
PA28	0.03657	0.00299	-0.02087	0.02081	0.0322	0.02949	0.03267	-0.12202	0.09632	0.07177	0.11804
	0.0062	0.8233	0.1188	0.1201	0.0162	0.0278	0.0149	<.0001	<.0001	<.0001	<.0001
	5594	5594	5589	5581	5572	5566	5555	5540	5594	5589	5566
PA29	0.20492	0.17779	0.32384	-0.04787	0.32896	-0.02618	-0.09143	-0.03424	-0.274	-0.24971	-0.20706
	<.0001	<.0001	<.0001	0.0003	<.0001	0.0508	<.0001	0.0108	<.0001	<.0001	<.0001
	5580	5580	5581	5582	5573	5567	5556	5541	5580	5581	5567
PA30	-0.12714	-0.14215	-0.12774	-0.03582	-0.00475	-0.09858	-0.03031	-0.14422	0.07521	0.04213	0.13393
	<.0001	<.0001	<.0001	0.0075	0.7227	<.0001	0.0239	<.0001	<.0001	0.0017	<.0001
	5572	5572	5573	5573	5573	5567	5556	5541	5572	5573	5567
PA31	0.07669	0.01978	0.087	-0.07643	0.14159	0.00702	-0.03995	-0.11344	-0.12138	-0.15691	-0.0108
	<.0001	0.1402	<.0001	<.0001	<.0001	0.6004	0.0029	<.0001	<.0001	<.0001	0.4205
	5566	5566	5567	5567	5567	5568	5557	5542	5566	5567	5568
PA32	0.22721	0.15459	0.32679	-0.08358	0.36531	-0.0274	-0.10422	-0.05441	-0.33711	-0.30739	-0.22604
	<.0001	<.0001	<.0001	<.0001	<.0001	0.0414	<.0001	<.0001	<.0001	<.0001	<.0001
	5540	5540	5541	5541	5541	5542	5542	5542	5540	5541	5542
PA33	-0.01906	-0.08323	0.01767	-0.16183	0.06845	-0.12639	-0.11773	-0.15674	-0.14565	-0.11214	-0.06157
	0.1566	<.0001	0.189	<.0001	<.0001	<.0001	<.0001	<.0001	<.0001	<.0001	<.0001
	5527	5527	5528	5528	5528	5529	5529	5529	5527	5528	5529

387

	PA12	PA13	PA14	PA15	PA16	PA17	PA18	PA19	PA20	PA21	PA22
PA18	0.1466	0.1273	0.19293	0.1178	0.08349	0.18474	1	0.09556	0.31809	0.24114	0.16773
	<.0001	<.0001	<.0001	<.0001	<.0001	<.0001		<.0001	<.0001	<.0001	<.0001
	5546	5546	5541	5532	5533	5528	5590	5581	5573	5556	5546
PA19	0.05224	0.05541	0.07423	0.07323	0.03954	0.00732	0.09556	1	0.05248	0.07739	0.15939
	<.0001	<.0001	<.0001	<.0001	0.0033	0.5863	<.0001		<.0001	<.0001	<.0001
	5556	5546	5541	5532	5533	5528	5581	5582	5573	5556	5546
PA20	0.00975	-0.01016	0.05368	0.03068	-0.05056	0.07291	0.31809	0.05248	1	0.21193	0.12207
	0.4676	0.4492	<.0001	0.0225	0.0002	<.0001	<.0001	<.0001		<.0001	<.0001
	5556	5546	5541	5532	5533	5528	5573	5573	5573	5556	5546
PA21	0.00987	0.01039	0.07447	0.05495	0.0172	0.0836	0.24114	0.07739	0.21193	1	0.10498
	0.4621	0.439	<.0001	<.0001	0.2008	<.0001	<.0001	<.0001	<.0001		<.0001
	5557	5547	5542	5533	5534	5529	5556	5556	5556	5557	5547
PA22	0.04636	0.02372	0.06507	0.04352	-0.01619	0.08567	0.16773	0.15939	0.12207	0.10498	1
	0.0006	0.0774	<.0001	0.0012	0.2286	<.0001	<.0001	<.0001	<.0001	<.0001	
	5547	5547	5542	5533	5534	5529	5546	5546	5546	5547	5547
PA23	0.05048	0.01477	0.08496	-0.01973	-0.06975	0.12011	0.18024	0.09199	0.16199	0.14661	0.31928
	0.0002	0.2714	<.0001	0.1423	<.0001	<.0001	<.0001	<.0001	<.0001	<.0001	<.0001
	5547	5547	5542	5533	5534	5529	5546	5546	5546	5547	5547
PA24	-0.28543	-0.27229	-0.22817	-0.12593	-0.16566	-0.11297	0.05054	0.02993	0.15698	0.14901	0.02438
	<.0001	<.0001	<.0001	<.0001	<.0001	<.0001	0.0002	0.026	<.0001	<.0001	0.0698
	5533	5533	5533	5533	5533	5529	5532	5532	5532	5533	5533
PA25	0.19131	0.16223	0.25632	0.14567	0.14556	0.29409	0.13717	0.10737	0.08057	0.08685	0.22282
	<.0001	<.0001	<.0001	<.0001	<.0001	<.0001	<.0001	<.0001	<.0001	<.0001	<.0001
	5529	5529	5529	5529	5529	5530	5528	5528	5528	5529	5529
PA26	-0.34614	-0.269	-0.28676	-0.13729	-0.22728	-0.23322	0.00666	0.06561	0.10272	0.06396	-0.03005
	<.0001	<.0001	<.0001	<.0001	<.0001	<.0001	0.6189	<.0001	<.0001	<.0001	0.0252
	5555	5545	5540	5531	5532	5527	5589	5580	5572	5555	5545
PA27	-0.10953	-0.10363	-0.07638	-0.03358	-0.1021	0.00925	0.25576	0.01952	0.21218	0.14691	0.05521
	<.0001	<.0001	<.0001	0.0125	<.0001	0.4918	<.0001	0.1449	<.0001	<.0001	<.0001
	5555	5545	5540	5531	5532	5527	5589	5580	5572	5555	5545
PA28	0.02476	0.01528	0.03393	0.03834	0.02248	0.06527	0.18484	0.17143	0.13559	0.11374	0.10365
	0.065	0.2551	0.0115	0.0043	0.0946	<.0001	<.0001	<.0001	<.0001	<.0001	<.0001
	5555	5545	5540	5531	5532	5527	5589	5580	5572	5555	5545
PA29	-0.4311	-0.37084	-0.33737	-0.26761	-0.36432	-0.27064	-0.00268	0.06694	0.12715	0.08291	0.01664
	<.0001	<.0001	<.0001	<.0001	<.0001	<.0001	0.8411	<.0001	<.0001	<.0001	0.2153
	5556	5546	5541	5532	5533	5528	5581	5582	5573	5556	5546
PA30	0.03205	0.01091	0.08323	-0.00402	-0.02959	0.10522	0.19359	0.17944	0.23323	0.14988	0.18919
	0.0169	0.4165	<.0001	0.7649	0.0277	<.0001	<.0001	<.0001	<.0001	<.0001	<.0001
	5556	5546	5541	5532	5533	5528	5573	5573	5573	5556	5546
PA31	-0.10418	-0.17325	-0.14768	-0.0796	-0.12038	-0.08081	0.00368	0.1806	0.09229	0.10167	0.0932
	<.0001	<.0001	<.0001	<.0001	<.0001	<.0001	0.7839	<.0001	<.0001	<.0001	<.0001
	5557	5547	5542	5533	5534	5529	5567	5567	5567	5557	5547
PA32	-0.43508	-0.415	-0.42467	-0.25482	-0.37834	-0.26473	0.00997	0.04083	0.14236	0.12219	0.04827
	<.0001	<.0001	<.0001	<.0001	<.0001	<.0001	0.4583	0.0024	<.0001	<.0001	0.0003
	5542	5542	5542	5533	5534	5529	5541	5541	5541	5542	5542
PA33	-0.1236	-0.18493	-0.13287	-0.13171	-0.18691	0.01448	0.06071	0.07042	0.12731	0.08069	0.11476
	<.0001	<.0001	<.0001	<.0001	<.0001	0.2818	<.0001	<.0001	<.0001	<.0001	<.0001
	5529	5529	5529	5529	5529	5530	5528	5528	5528	5529	5529

388

	PA23	PA24	PA25	PA26	PA27	PA28	PA29	PA30	PA31	PA32	PA33
PA18	0.18024	0.05054	0.13717	0.00666	0.25576	0.18484	-0.00268	0.19359	0.00368	0.00997	0.06071
	<.0001	0.0002	<.0001	0.6189	<.0001	<.0001	0.8411	<.0001	0.7839	0.4583	<.0001
	5546	5532	5528	5589	5589	5589	5581	5573	5567	5541	5528
PA19	0.09199	0.02993	0.10737	0.06561	0.01952	0.17143	0.06694	0.17944	0.1806	0.04083	0.07042
	<.0001	0.026	<.0001	<.0001	0.1449	<.0001	<.0001	<.0001	<.0001	0.0024	<.0001
	5546	5532	5528	5580	5580	5580	5582	5573	5567	5541	5528
PA20	0.16199	0.15698	0.08057	0.10272	0.21218	0.13559	0.12715	0.23323	0.09229	0.14236	0.12731
	<.0001	<.0001	<.0001	<.0001	<.0001	<.0001	<.0001	<.0001	<.0001	<.0001	<.0001
	5546	5532	5528	5572	5572	5572	5573	5573	5567	5541	5528
PA21	0.14661	0.14901	0.08685	0.06396	0.14691	0.11374	0.08291	0.14988	0.10167	0.12219	0.08069
	<.0001	<.0001	<.0001	<.0001	<.0001	<.0001	<.0001	<.0001	<.0001	<.0001	<.0001
	5547	5533	5529	5555	5555	5555	5556	5556	5557	5542	5529
PA22	0.31928	0.02438	0.22282	-0.03005	0.05521	0.10365	0.01664	0.18919	0.0932	0.04827	0.11476
	<.0001	0.0698	<.0001	0.0252	<.0001	<.0001	0.2153	<.0001	<.0001	0.0003	<.0001
	5547	5533	5529	5545	5545	5545	5546	5546	5547	5542	5529
PA23	1	0.04556	0.21149	-0.0744	0.07312	0.08829	0.00667	0.25177	0.08077	0.03698	0.15136
		0.0007	<.0001	<.0001	<.0001	<.0001	0.6192	<.0001	<.0001	0.0059	<.0001
	5547	5533	5529	5545	5545	5545	5546	5546	5547	5542	5529
PA24	0.04556	1	-0.06512	0.32161	0.21041	0.11299	0.3347	0.08675	0.1781	0.37667	0.15241
	0.0007		<.0001	<.0001	<.0001	<.0001	<.0001	<.0001	<.0001	<.0001	<.0001
	5533	5533	5529	5531	5531	5531	5532	5532	5533	5533	5529
PA25	0.21149	-0.06512	1	-0.12602	-0.0281	0.10603	-0.10521	0.1935	0.01785	-0.11727	0.06159
	<.0001	<.0001		<.0001	0.0367	<.0001	<.0001	<.0001	0.1844	<.0001	<.0001
	5529	5529	5530	5527	5527	5527	5528	5528	5529	5529	5530
PA26	-0.0744	0.32161	-0.12602	1	0.2868	0.1249	0.42164	-0.00398	0.15221	0.42207	0.13495
	<.0001	<.0001	<.0001		<.0001	<.0001	<.0001	0.7663	<.0001	<.0001	<.0001
	5545	5531	5527	5604	5604	5594	5580	5572	5566	5540	5527
PA27	0.07312	0.21041	-0.0281	0.2868	1	0.10386	0.19127	0.10465	0.07717	0.22488	0.12322
	<.0001	<.0001	0.0367	<.0001		<.0001	<.0001	<.0001	<.0001	<.0001	<.0001
	5545	5531	5527	5604	5604	5594	5580	5572	5566	5540	5527
PA28	0.08829	0.11299	0.10603	0.1249	0.10386	1	0.12464	0.1788	0.17405	0.10638	0.10492
	<.0001	<.0001	<.0001	<.0001	<.0001		<.0001	<.0001	<.0001	<.0001	<.0001
	5545	5531	5527	5594	5594	5594	5580	5572	5566	5540	5527
PA29	0.00667	0.3347	-0.10521	0.42164	0.19127	0.12464	1	0.09116	0.21037	0.52684	0.19754
	0.6192	<.0001	<.0001	<.0001	<.0001	<.0001		<.0001	<.0001	<.0001	<.0001
	5546	5532	5528	5580	5580	5580	5582	5573	5567	5541	5528
PA30	0.25177	0.08675	0.1935	-0.00398	0.10465	0.1788	0.09116	1	0.11761	0.07888	0.14747
	<.0001	<.0001	<.0001	0.7663	<.0001	<.0001	<.0001		<.0001	<.0001	<.0001
	5546	5532	5528	5572	5572	5572	5573	5573	5567	5541	5528
PA31	0.08077	0.1781	0.01785	0.15221	0.07717	0.17405	0.21037	0.11761	1	0.24337	0.16042
	<.0001	<.0001	0.1844	<.0001	<.0001	<.0001	<.0001	<.0001		<.0001	<.0001
	5547	5533	5529	5566	5566	5566	5567	5567	5568	5542	5529
PA32	0.03698	0.37667	-0.11727	0.42207	0.22488	0.10638	0.52684	0.07888	0.24337	1	0.30592
	0.0059	<.0001	<.0001	<.0001	<.0001	<.0001	<.0001	<.0001	<.0001		<.0001
	5542	5533	5529	5540	5540	5540	5541	5541	5542	5542	5529
PA33	0.15136	0.15241	0.06159	0.13495	0.12322	0.10492	0.19754	0.14747	0.16042	0.30592	1
	<.0001	<.0001	<.0001	<.0001	<.0001	<.0001	<.0001	<.0001	<.0001	<.0001	
	5529	5529	5530	5527	5527	5527	5528	5528	5529	5529	5530

Internal consistencies, student respondents, Literal Belief

Cronbach Coefficient Alpha

Variables	Alpha
Raw	0.816651
Standardised	0.818683

Cronbach Coefficient Alpha with Deleted Variable

Deleted variable	Raw Variables			Standardised Variables	
	Correlation with Total	Alpha		Correlation with Total	Alpha
PT1	0.576092	0.790083		0.578295	0.792369
PT2	0.661335	0.766949		0.661769	0.767573
PT4	0.675219	0.760989		0.673985	0.763858
PT5	0.706321	0.749019		0.70906	0.753068
PT6	0.43933	0.830485		0.438815	0.831572

Pearson Correlation Coefficients
Prob > |r| under H0: Rho=0
Number of Observations

	PT1	PT2	PT4	PT5	PT6
PT1	1	0.54346	0.44541	0.50737	0.31955
		<.0001	<.0001	<.0001	<.0001
	9733	9671	9614	9731	9559
PT2	0.54346	1	0.55714	0.58891	0.34233
	<.0001		<.0001	<.0001	<.0001
	9671	9674	9616	9672	9561
PT4	0.44541	0.55714	1	0.67233	0.38771
	<.0001	<.0001		<.0001	<.0001
	9614	9616	9617	9615	9562
PT5	0.50737	0.58891	0.67233	1	0.38105
	<.0001	<.0001	<.0001		<.0001
	9731	9672	9615	9813	9560
PT6	0.31955	0.34233	0.38771	0.38105	1
	<.0001	<.0001	<.0001	<.0001	
	9559	9561	9562	9560	9562

Internal consistencies, student respondents, External Critique

Cronbach Coefficient Alpha

Variables	Alpha
Raw	0.881146
Standardised	0.882739

Cronbach Coefficient Alpha with Deleted Variable

Deleted variable	Raw Variables		Standardised Variables	
	Correlation with Total	Alpha	Correlation with Total	Alpha
PT7	0.800569	0.835626	0.802271	0.837469
PT8	0.739866	0.849774	0.740179	0.852349
PT9	0.796669	0.837936	0.797637	0.838594
PT10	0.495459	0.906273	0.495449	0.9071
PT11	0.770099	0.842397	0.771947	0.844787

Pearson Correlation Coefficients
Prob > |r| under H0: Rho=0
Number of Observations

	PT7	PT8	PT9	PT10	PT11
PT7	1	0.69381	0.7772	0.42645	0.73364
		<.0001	<.0001	<.0001	<.0001
	9562	9560	9562	9559	9561
PT8	0.69381	1	0.66007	0.44479	0.66606
	<.0001		<.0001	<.0001	<.0001
	9560	9813	9615	9732	9672
PT9	0.7772	0.66007	1	0.45604	0.72557
	<.0001	<.0001		<.0001	<.0001
	9562	9615	9617	9614	9616
PT10	0.42645	0.44479	0.45604	1	0.42528
	<.0001	<.0001	<.0001		<.0001
	9559	9732	9614	9734	9671
PT11	0.73364	0.66606	0.72557	0.42528	1
	<.0001	<.0001	<.0001	<.0001	
	9561	9672	9616	9671	9674

Internal consistencies, student respondents, Relativism / Awareness of Contingency

Cronbach Coefficient Alpha

Variables	Alpha
Raw	0.657053
Standardised	0.657559

Cronbach Coefficient Alpha with Deleted Variable

Deleted variable	Raw Variables		Standardised Variables	
	Correlation with Total	Alpha	Correlation with Total	Alpha
PT13	0.386067	0.620705	0.387015	0.616344
PT14	0.4091	0.606133	0.399548	0.610552
PT15	0.305316	0.649043	0.30663	0.65247
PT16	0.494161	0.564993	0.494398	0.56528
PT18	0.465919	0.577834	0.469775	0.577278

Pearson Correlation Coefficients
Prob > |r| under H0: Rho=0
Number of Observations

	PT13	PT14	PT15	PT16	PT18
PT13	1	0.38695	0.13605	0.28671	0.24581
		<.0001	<.0001	<.0001	<.0001
	9813	9560	9672	9615	9732
PT14	0.38695	1	0.14417	0.32789	0.22632
	<.0001		<.0001	<.0001	<.0001
	9560	9562	9561	9562	9559
PT15	0.13605	0.14417	1	0.2453	0.33267
	<.0001	<.0001		<.0001	<.0001
	9672	9561	9674	9616	9671
PT16	0.28671	0.32789	0.2453	1	0.4429
	<.0001	<.0001	<.0001		<.0001
	9615	9562	9616	9617	9614
PT18	0.24581	0.22632	0.33267	0.4429	1
	<.0001	<.0001	<.0001	<.0001	
	9732	9559	9671	9614	9734

Internal consistencies, student respondents, Post-Critical Belief

Cronbach Coefficient Alpha

Variables	Alpha
Raw	0.907152
Standardised	0.906989

Cronbach Coefficient Alpha with Deleted Variable

Deleted variable	Raw Variables		Standardised Variables	
	Correlation with Total	Alpha	Correlation with Total	Alpha
PT19	0.827401	0.873022	0.824786	0.873651
PT20	0.736839	0.893357	0.733785	0.893044
PT21	0.736038	0.892852	0.735391	0.892708
PT22	0.837321	0.870913	0.835266	0.871368
PT24	0.702041	0.900086	0.701806	0.89968

Pearson Correlation Coefficients
Prob > |r| under H0: Rho=0
Number of Observations

	PT19	PT20	PT21	PT22	PT24
PT19	1	0.67989	0.68834	0.7905	0.65066
		<.0001	<.0001	<.0001	<.0001
	9812	9560	9732	9615	9672
PT20	0.67989	1	0.60499	0.7085	0.56049
	<.0001		<.0001	<.0001	<.0001
	9560	9562	9559	9562	9561
PT21	0.68834	0.60499	1	0.67708	0.58807
	<.0001	<.0001		<.0001	<.0001
	9732	9559	9734	9614	9671
PT22	0.7905	0.7085	0.67708	1	0.66197
	<.0001	<.0001	<.0001		<.0001
	9615	9562	9614	9617	9616
PT24	0.65066	0.56049	0.58807	0.66197	1
	<.0001	<.0001	<.0001	<.0001	
	9672	9561	9671	9616	9674

Internal consistencies, adult respondents, Literal Belief

Cronbach Coefficient Alpha

Variables	Alpha
Raw	0.814936
Standardised	0.815922

Cronbach Coefficient Alpha with Deleted Variable

Deleted variable	Raw Variables		Standardised Variables	
	Correlation with Total	Alpha	Correlation with Total	Alpha
PA1	0.603156	0.783024	0.58675	0.787199
PA2	0.658737	0.773864	0.650407	0.777847
PA3	0.510918	0.798436	0.493598	0.800501
PA4	0.482834	0.800552	0.502049	0.799313
PA5	0.51949	0.795928	0.494665	0.800351
PA6	0.561892	0.790861	0.575308	0.788857
PA7	0.425786	0.807643	0.442731	0.807576
PA8	0.50647	0.79743	0.519809	0.796803

Pearson Correlation Coefficients
Prob > |r| under H0: Rho=0
Number of Observations

	PA1	PA2	PA3	PA4	PA5	PA6	PA7	PA8
PA1	1	0.52133	0.43445	0.30655	0.54718	0.36511	0.23803	0.30936
		<.0001	<.0001	<.0001	<.0001	<.0001	<.0001	<.0001
	5604	5594	5589	5581	5572	5566	5555	5540
PA2	0.52133	1	0.46856	0.37372	0.43815	0.46651	0.2988	0.41374
	<.0001		<.0001	<.0001	<.0001	<.0001	<.0001	<.0001
	5594	5594	5589	5581	5572	5566	5555	5540
PA3	0.43445	0.46856	1	0.19764	0.45741	0.2861	0.17989	0.30703
	<.0001	<.0001		<.0001	<.0001	<.0001	<.0001	<.0001
	5589	5589	5590	5582	5573	5567	5556	5541
PA4	0.30655	0.37372	0.19764	1	0.23607	0.44707	0.42618	0.37993
	<.0001	<.0001	<.0001		<.0001	<.0001	<.0001	<.0001
	5581	5581	5582	5583	5573	5567	5556	5541
PA5	0.54718	0.43815	0.45741	0.23607	1	0.27388	0.16674	0.21621
	<.0001	<.0001	<.0001	<.0001		<.0001	<.0001	<.0001
	5572	5572	5573	5573	5573	5567	5556	5541
PA6	0.36511	0.46651	0.2861	0.44707	0.27388	1	0.41076	0.42534
	<.0001	<.0001	<.0001	<.0001	<.0001		<.0001	<.0001
	5566	5566	5567	5567	5567	5568	5557	5542
PA7	0.23803	0.2988	0.17989	0.42618	0.16674	0.41076	1	0.39096
	<.0001	<.0001	<.0001	<.0001	<.0001	<.0001		<.0001
	5555	5555	5556	5556	5556	5557	5557	5542
PA8	0.30936	0.41374	0.30703	0.37993	0.21621	0.42534	0.39096	1
	<.0001	<.0001	<.0001	<.0001	<.0001	<.0001	<.0001	
	5540	5540	5541	5541	5541	5542	5542	5542

Internal consistencies, adult respondents, External Critique

Cronbach Coefficient Alpha

Variables	Alpha
Raw	0.848231
Standardised	0.852742

Cronbach Coefficient Alpha with Deleted Variable

Deleted variable	Raw Variables		Standardised Variables	
	Correlation with Total	Alpha	Correlation with Total	Alpha
PA9	0.603015	0.828336	0.600283	0.834514
PA10	0.555541	0.833989	0.550291	0.839573
PA11	0.494704	0.840373	0.492312	0.845342
PA12	0.606382	0.828442	0.606961	0.833832
PA13	0.625496	0.826424	0.629099	0.831561
PA14	0.670415	0.820539	0.669858	0.827339
PA15	0.5294	0.83671	0.538184	0.840787
PA16	0.57324	0.83405	0.58042	0.836534
PA17	0.488461	0.84186	0.490753	0.845496

Pearson Correlation Coefficients
Prob > |r| under H0: Rho=0
Number of Observations

	PA9	PA10	PA11	PA12	PA13	PA14	PA15	PA16	PA17
PA9	1	0.4748	0.35863	0.42996	0.45967	0.50319	0.35427	0.38032	0.30789
		<.0001	<.0001	<.0001	<.0001	<.0001	<.0001	<.0001	<.0001
	5594	5589	5566	5555	5545	5540	5531	5532	5527
PA10	0.4748	1	0.33828	0.42013	0.42143	0.42704	0.31096	0.30645	0.32233
	<.0001		<.0001	<.0001	<.0001	<.0001	<.0001	<.0001	<.0001
	5589	5590	5567	5556	5546	5541	5532	5533	5528
PA11	0.35863	0.33828	1	0.33389	0.35825	0.41747	0.30945	0.31177	0.30141
	<.0001	<.0001		<.0001	<.0001	<.0001	<.0001	<.0001	<.0001
	5566	5567	5568	5557	5547	5542	5533	5534	5529
PA12	0.42996	0.42013	0.33389	1	0.51512	0.48061	0.36799	0.40478	0.34898
	<.0001	<.0001	<.0001		<.0001	<.0001	<.0001	<.0001	<.0001
	5555	5556	5557	5557	5547	5542	5533	5534	5529
PA13	0.45967	0.42143	0.35825	0.51512	1	0.49573	0.3968	0.44347	0.31889
	<.0001	<.0001	<.0001	<.0001		<.0001	<.0001	<.0001	<.0001
	5545	5546	5547	5547	5547	5542	5533	5534	5529
PA14	0.50319	0.42704	0.41747	0.48061	0.49573	1	0.40099	0.45853	0.42232
	<.0001	<.0001	<.0001	<.0001	<.0001		<.0001	<.0001	<.0001
	5540	5541	5542	5542	5542	5542	5533	5534	5529
PA15	0.35427	0.31096	0.30945	0.36799	0.3968	0.40099	1	0.49334	0.32707
	<.0001	<.0001	<.0001	<.0001	<.0001	<.0001		<.0001	<.0001
	5531	5532	5533	5533	5533	5533	5533	5533	5529
PA16	0.38032	0.30645	0.31177	0.40478	0.44347	0.45853	0.49334	1	0.37232
	<.0001	<.0001	<.0001	<.0001	<.0001	<.0001	<.0001		<.0001
	5532	5533	5534	5534	5534	5534	5533	5534	5529
PA17	0.30789	0.32233	0.30141	0.34898	0.31889	0.42232	0.32707	0.37232	1
	<.0001	<.0001	<.0001	<.0001	<.0001	<.0001	<.0001	<.0001	
	5527	5528	5529	5529	5529	5529	5529	5529	5530

Internal consistencies, adult respondents, Relativism / Awareness of Contingency

Cronbach Coefficient Alpha

Variables	Alpha
Raw	0.536899
Standardised	0.548271

Cronbach Coefficient Alpha with Deleted Variable

Deleted variable	Raw Variables			Standardised Variables	
	Correlation with Total	Alpha		Correlation with Total	Alpha
PA18	0.333585	0.476986		0.343718	0.485878
PA19	0.174724	0.537504		0.16936	0.545561
PA20	0.298172	0.489692		0.316511	0.495542
PA21	0.276439	0.497125		0.289759	0.504916
PA22	0.331316	0.473977		0.32169	0.493713
PA23	0.339838	0.476043		0.333177	0.489638
PA24	0.091121	0.551197		0.106121	0.565924
PA25	0.225532	0.519266		0.218215	0.529369

Pearson Correlation Coefficients
Prob > |r| under H0: Rho=0
Number of Observations

	PA18	PA19	PA20	PA21	PA22	PA23	PA24	PA25
PA18	1	0.09556	0.31809	0.24114	0.16773	0.18024	0.05054	0.13717
		<.0001	<.0001	<.0001	<.0001	<.0001	0.0002	<.0001
	5590	5581	5573	5556	5546	5546	5532	5528
PA19	0.09556	1	0.05248	0.07739	0.15939	0.09199	0.02993	0.10737
	<.0001		<.0001	<.0001	<.0001	<.0001	0.026	<.0001
	5581	5582	5573	5556	5546	5546	5532	5528
PA20	0.31809	0.05248	1	0.21193	0.12207	0.16199	0.15698	0.08057
	<.0001	<.0001		<.0001	<.0001	<.0001	<.0001	<.0001
	5573	5573	5573	5556	5546	5546	5532	5528
PA21	0.24114	0.07739	0.21193	1	0.10498	0.14661	0.14901	0.08685
	<.0001	<.0001	<.0001		<.0001	<.0001	<.0001	<.0001
	5556	5556	5556	5557	5547	5547	5533	5529
PA22	0.16773	0.15939	0.12207	0.10498	1	0.31928	0.02438	0.22282
	<.0001	<.0001	<.0001	<.0001		<.0001	0.0698	<.0001
	5546	5546	5546	5547	5547	5547	5533	5529
PA23	0.18024	0.09199	0.16199	0.14661	0.31928	1	0.04556	0.21149
	<.0001	<.0001	<.0001	<.0001	<.0001		0.0007	<.0001
	5546	5546	5546	5547	5547	5547	5533	5529
PA24	0.05054	0.02993	0.15698	0.14901	0.02438	0.04556	1	-0.06512
	0.0002	0.026	<.0001	<.0001	0.0698	0.0007		<.0001
	5532	5532	5532	5533	5533	5533	5533	5529
PA25	0.13717	0.10737	0.08057	0.08685	0.22282	0.21149	-0.06512	1
	<.0001	<.0001	<.0001	<.0001	<.0001	<.0001	<.0001	
	5528	5528	5528	5529	5529	5529	5529	5530

Internal consistencies, adult respondents, Post-Critical Belief

Cronbach Coefficient Alpha

Variables	Alpha
Raw	0.617294
Standardised	0.642263

Cronbach Coefficient Alpha with Deleted Variable

Deleted variable	Raw Variables		Standardised Variables	
	Correlation with Total	Alpha	Correlation with Total	Alpha
PA26	0.377996	0.567116	0.408487	0.591016
PA27	0.279778	0.595065	0.286694	0.623681
PA28	0.23946	0.610067	0.233595	0.637357
PA29	0.457269	0.560407	0.475792	0.572169
PA30	0.18928	0.622253	0.179576	0.650926
PA31	0.290295	0.592629	0.293169	0.62199
PA32	0.492548	0.541111	0.520401	0.559359
PA33	0.298461	0.590617	0.304101	0.619124

Pearson Correlation Coefficients
Prob > |r| under H0: Rho=0
Number of Observations

	PA26	PA27	PA28	PA29	PA30	PA31	PA32	PA33
PA26	1	0.2868	0.1249	0.42164	-0.00398	0.15221	0.42207	0.13495
		<.0001	<.0001	<.0001	0.7663	<.0001	<.0001	<.0001
	5604	5604	5594	5580	5572	5566	5540	5527
PA27	0.2868	1	0.10386	0.19127	0.10465	0.07717	0.22488	0.12322
	<.0001		<.0001	<.0001	<.0001	<.0001	<.0001	<.0001
	5604	5604	5594	5580	5572	5566	5540	5527
PA28	0.1249	0.10386	1	0.12464	0.1788	0.17405	0.10638	0.10492
	<.0001	<.0001		<.0001	<.0001	<.0001	<.0001	<.0001
	5594	5594	5594	5580	5572	5566	5540	5527
PA29	0.42164	0.19127	0.12464	1	0.09116	0.21037	0.52684	0.19754
	<.0001	<.0001	<.0001		<.0001	<.0001	<.0001	<.0001
	5580	5580	5580	5582	5573	5567	5541	5528
PA30	-0.00398	0.10465	0.1788	0.09116	1	0.11761	0.07888	0.14747
	0.7663	<.0001	<.0001	<.0001		<.0001	<.0001	<.0001
	5572	5572	5572	5573	5573	5567	5541	5528
PA31	0.15221	0.07717	0.17405	0.21037	0.11761	1	0.24337	0.16042
	<.0001	<.0001	<.0001	<.0001	<.0001		<.0001	<.0001
	5566	5566	5566	5567	5567	5568	5542	5529
PA32	0.42207	0.22488	0.10638	0.52684	0.07888	0.24337	1	0.30592
	<.0001	<.0001	<.0001	<.0001	<.0001	<.0001		<.0001
	5540	5540	5540	5541	5541	5542	5542	5529
PA33	0.13495	0.12322	0.10492	0.19754	0.14747	0.16042	0.30592	1
	<.0001	<.0001	<.0001	<.0001	<.0001	<.0001	<.0001	
	5527	5527	5527	5528	5528	5529	5529	5530

Factor analysis, student respondents

Initial Factor Method: Principal Components
Prior Communality Estimates: ONE
Eigenvalues of the Correlation Matrix: Total = 20 Average = 1

	Eigenvalue	Difference	Proportion	Cumulative
1	8.49799357	6.42760951	0.4249	0.4249
2	2.07038405	0.38091004	0.1035	0.5284
3	1.68947401	0.92638691	0.0845	0.6129
4	0.7630871	0.02625701	0.0382	0.651
5	0.73683009	0.05368215	0.0368	0.6879
6	0.68314794	0.04111078	0.0342	0.722
7	0.64203716	0.0347526	0.0321	0.7541
8	0.60728456	0.04132399	0.0304	0.7845
9	0.56596058	0.05102339	0.0283	0.8128
10	0.51493719	0.0782852	0.0257	0.8386
11	0.436652	0.02283551	0.0218	0.8604
12	0.41381649	0.0129461	0.0207	0.8811
13	0.40087039	0.01654879	0.02	0.9011
14	0.3843216	0.05800542	0.0192	0.9203
15	0.32631618	0.01016919	0.0163	0.9367
16	0.31614699	0.03364861	0.0158	0.9525
17	0.28249838	0.02627886	0.0141	0.9666
18	0.25621951	0.04551608	0.0128	0.9794
19	0.21070343	0.00938465	0.0105	0.9899
20	0.20131879		0.0101	1

3 factors will be retained by the NFACTOR criterion.

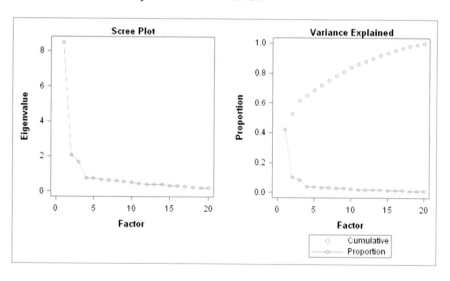

Eigenvectors

	1	2	3
PT1	0.16505	0.23544	0.41012
PT2	0.21906	0.23264	0.22179
PT4	0.26094	0.15856	0.09056
PT5	0.27077	0.15003	0.11766
PT6	0.15385	0.23251	0.16005
PT7	-0.27398	0.15484	0.20462
PT8	-0.26441	0.19799	0.12478
PT9	-0.25436	0.17652	0.25359
PT10	-0.1415	0.34698	0.24713
PT11	-0.26267	0.15396	0.19331
PT13	-0.1909	0.23599	-0.07356
PT14	-0.17792	0.2485	-0.07777
PT15	-0.00449	0.24646	-0.49881
PT16	-0.11169	0.39754	-0.25691
PT18	-0.07311	0.34968	-0.4111
PT19	0.29703	0.10833	0.00127
PT20	0.26117	0.12561	0.01065
PT21	0.25891	0.15615	-0.08676
PT22	0.29544	0.12606	0.00319
PT24	0.25357	0.15498	-0.10882

Factor Pattern

	Factor1	Factor2	Factor3
PT19	0.86588	0.15587	0.00165
PT22	0.86126	0.18139	0.00415
PT5	0.78934	0.21587	0.15293
PT20	0.76136	0.18074	0.01385
PT4	0.76068	0.22815	0.11771
PT21	0.75477	0.22468	-0.11276
PT24	0.7392	0.223	-0.14145
PT2	0.63859	0.33474	0.28828
PT6	0.4485	0.33455	0.20804
PT14	-0.51865	0.35756	-0.10108
PT13	-0.55651	0.33956	-0.09561
PT9	-0.74148	0.25399	0.32961
PT11	-0.76571	0.22153	0.25126
PT8	-0.77079	0.28489	0.16219
PT7	-0.7987	0.2228	0.26596
PT16	-0.32558	0.57202	-0.33393
PT10	-0.41248	0.49926	0.32122
PT1	0.48113	0.33877	0.53307
PT18	-0.21313	0.50315	-0.53434
PT15	-0.01308	0.35462	-0.64836

Variance Explained by Each Factor

	Factor1	Factor2	Factor3
	8.4979936	2.0703841	1.689474

Final Communality Estimates: Total = 12.257852

PT1	PT2	PT4	PT5	PT6	PT7	PT8	PT9	PT10	PT11
0.63041	0.60296	0.64454	0.69305	0.35636	0.75830	0.70159	0.72295	0.52258	0.69853

PT13	PT14	PT15	PT16	PT18	PT19	PT20	PT21	PT22	PT24
0.43414	0.40707	0.54629	0.54472	0.58411	0.77404	0.61252	0.63287	0.77468	0.61616

Rotation Method: Varimax

Orthogonal Transformation Matrix

	1	2	3
1	0.73437	-0.6655	-0.13342
2	0.59155	0.53115	0.60659
3	0.33282	0.52438	-0.78374

Rotated Factor Pattern

	Factor1	Factor2	Factor3
PT2	0.76292	-0.09602	-0.10809
PT5	0.75827	-0.33045	-0.09423
PT22	0.74116	-0.47465	-0.00813
PT4	0.73275	-0.32333	-0.05535
PT1	0.73114	0.13928	-0.27649
PT19	0.72863	-0.49259	-0.02227
PT20	0.67064	-0.40342	-0.00280
PT21	0.64966	-0.44209	0.12397
PT24	0.62769	-0.44767	0.14750
PT6	0.59651	-0.01169	-0.01995
PT9	-0.28458	0.80121	-0.00534
PT7	-0.36623	0.78935	0.03327
PT11	-0.34765	0.75901	0.03962
PT8	-0.34355	0.74933	0.14854
PT10	0.09933	0.70813	0.10613
PT13	-0.23964	0.50058	0.35515
PT14	-0.20301	0.48208	0.36532
PT18	-0.03672	0.12889	0.75243
PT15	-0.01562	-0.14292	0.72500
PT16	-0.01186	0.34540	0.65213

Variance Explained by Each Factor

Factor1	Factor2	Factor3
5.4946204	4.8124056	1.9508257

Factor analysis, adult respondents

Initial Factor Method: Principal Components
Prior Communality Estimates: ONE
Eigenvalues of the Correlation Matrix: Total= 33 Average = 1

	Eigenvalue	Difference	Proportion	Cumulative
1	6.00854104	1.88251069	0.1821	0.1821
2	4.12603035	1.19378703	0.125	0.3071
3	2.93224332	1.65080405	0.0889	0.396
4	1.28143927	0.22899828	0.0388	0.4348
5	1.052441	0.03872233	0.0319	0.4667
6	1.01371866	0.06841969	0.0307	0.4974
7	0.94529897	0.05346194	0.0286	0.5261
8	0.89183703	0.0394079	0.027	0.5531
9	0.85242913	0.01652424	0.0258	0.5789
10	0.83590489	0.0425046	0.0253	0.6042
11	0.79340029	0.03149806	0.024	0.6283
12	0.76190223	0.00909457	0.0231	0.6514
13	0.75280766	0.02945271	0.0228	0.6742
14	0.72335495	0.04207973	0.0219	0.6961
15	0.68127522	0.01658197	0.0206	0.7167
16	0.66469325	0.00980455	0.0201	0.7369
17	0.65488871	0.01752261	0.0198	0.7567
18	0.63736609	0.01972157	0.0193	0.776
19	0.61764452	0.02854867	0.0187	0.7948
20	0.58909585	0.02549443	0.0179	0.8126
21	0.56360142	0.01255803	0.0171	0.8297
22	0.55104339	0.02599388	0.0167	0.8464
23	0.52504951	0.00982544	0.0159	0.8623
24	0.51522407	0.00362458	0.0156	0.8779
25	0.5115995	0.01952378	0.0155	0.8934
26	0.49207572	0.01172514	0.0149	0.9083
27	0.48035058	0.01597602	0.0146	0.9229
28	0.46437456	0.01242465	0.0141	0.937
29	0.45194992	0.01468481	0.0137	0.9507
30	0.43726511	0.02196793	0.0133	0.9639
31	0.41529718	0.01645152	0.0126	0.9765
32	0.39884566	0.02183469	0.0121	0.9886
33	0.37701097		0.0114	1

4 factors will be retained by the NFACTOR criterion.

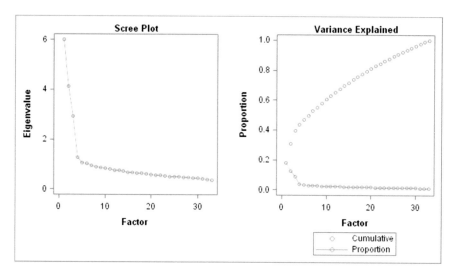

Eigenvectors

	1	2	3	4
PA1	-0.12455	0.32279	0.08019	-0.04042
PA2	-0.08076	0.36709	0.01459	0.00376
PA3	-0.18626	0.27166	0.00068	0.05759
PA4	0.07919	0.31623	0.05925	0.0371
PA5	-0.19956	0.26241	0.10562	0.01639
PA6	0.04624	0.34621	0.04479	0.05197
PA7	0.10941	0.28733	0.07201	0.15017
PA8	0.05742	0.32781	-0.03788	0.0251
PA9	0.26186	0.10407	0.10159	-0.01825
PA10	0.24025	0.08833	0.10462	-0.10718
PA11	0.21602	0.04013	0.19068	0.03065
PA12	0.28918	0.03934	0.01883	0.02979
PA13	0.28698	0.10017	0.0156	0.0013
PA14	0.29917	0.03701	0.0851	-0.03265
PA15	0.22718	0.13152	0.08377	0.00268
PA16	0.26024	0.11456	0.00486	0.00963
PA17	0.23153	-0.07156	0.1146	-0.1178
PA18	0.08728	-0.0322	0.3202	-0.3412
PA19	0.02517	0.04335	0.21981	0.4726
PA20	-0.00937	-0.02542	0.31591	-0.29065
PA21	0.00989	-0.02232	0.27181	-0.16857
PA22	0.04071	-0.15607	0.2167	0.24777
PA23	0.04221	-0.22403	0.21454	0.08983
PA24	-0.17757	0.01784	0.20888	-0.09442
PA25	0.13738	-0.11593	0.16671	0.21112
PA26	-0.21698	0.14387	0.17927	-0.07222
PA27	-0.08018	0.00199	0.25089	-0.41074
PA28	0.00302	-0.01172	0.26725	0.16024
PA29	-0.25448	0.03286	0.18084	0.03335
PA30	0.02304	-0.11282	0.28819	0.13896
PA31	-0.10476	-0.02516	0.19304	0.36623
PA32	-0.275	0.01767	0.19819	0.01308
PA33	-0.10347	-0.10868	0.19154	0.09428

Factor Pattern

	Factor1	Factor2	Factor3	Factor 4
PA14	0.73334	0.07517	0.14572	-0.03696
PA12	0.70884	0.07991	0.03224	0.03372
PA13	0.70345	0.20347	0.02671	0.00147
PA9	0.64188	0.2114	0.17396	-0.02066
PA16	0.6379	0.23271	0.00831	0.0109
PA10	0.58891	0.17942	0.17915	-0.12133
PA17	0.56754	-0.14536	0.19624	-0.13335
PA15	0.55687	0.26714	0.14345	0.00304
PA11	0.52952	0.08151	0.32651	0.03469
PA25	0.33675	-0.23547	0.28546	0.23899
PA24	-0.43527	0.03624	0.35769	-0.10689
PA26	-0.53186	0.29224	0.30698	-0.08176
PA29	-0.62379	0.06675	0.30967	0.03775
PA32	-0.67409	0.03588	0.33938	0.0148
PA2	-0.19795	0.74566	0.02498	0.00426
PA6	0.11334	0.70324	0.0767	0.05883
PA8	0.14075	0.66586	-0.06486	0.02841
PA1	-0.30531	0.65567	0.13732	-0.04576
PA4	0.19411	0.64236	0.10145	0.04199
PA7	0.2682	0.58365	0.12331	0.16999
PA3	-0.45656	0.55182	0.00117	0.0652
PA5	-0.48916	0.53302	0.18085	0.01856
PA23	0.10348	-0.45505	0.36737	0.10168
PA18	0.21394	-0.06541	0.5483	-0.38624
PA20	-0.02296	-0.05164	0.54096	-0.32902
PA30	0.05647	-0.22917	0.49349	0.1573
PA21	0.02424	-0.04534	0.46544	-0.19083
PA28	0.00741	-0.02381	0.45763	0.18139
PA22	0.09979	-0.31702	0.37107	0.28048
PA33	-0.25363	-0.22077	0.32799	0.10672
PA19	0.0617	0.08806	0.3764	0.53498
PA31	-0.25678	-0.0511	0.33056	0.41458
PA27	-0.19653	0.00404	0.42961	-0.46496

Variance Explained by Each Factor

Factor1	Factor2	Factor3	Factor 4
6.008541	4.1260303	2.9322433	1.2814393

Final Communality Estimates: Total = 14.348254

PA1	PA2	PA3	PA4	PA5	PA6	PA7	PA8	PA9	PA10	PA11
0.54407	0.59584	0.51720	0.46236	0.55644	0.51674	0.45668	0.46820	0.48739	0.42583	0.39485

PA12	PA13	PA14	PA15	PA16	PA17	PA18	PA19	PA20	PA21	PA22
0.51101	0.53695	0.56604	0.40205	0.46126	0.39952	0.49987	0.43944	0.40408	0.25570	0.32682

PA23	PA24	PA25	PA26	PA27	PA28	PA29	PA30	PA31	PA32	PA33
0.36308	0.33014	0.30745	0.46920	0.43939	0.24295	0.49089	0.32399	0.34969	0.57108	0.23203

Rotation Method: Varimax

Orthogonal Transformation Matrix

	1	2	3	4
1	0.98054	-0.17541	-0.08816	-0.00087
2	0.17027	0.97131	-0.03722	-0.16179
3	0.08838	0.12334	0.73098	0.66532

Rotated Factor Pattern

	Factor1	Factor2	Factor3	Factor4
PA14	0.74629	-0.04144	0.06404	0.05721
PA13	0.7267	0.07769	-0.05106	-0.01469
PA12	0.71009	-0.03928	-0.06469	0.03247
PA9	0.68162	0.11208	0.07666	0.06592
PA16	0.66539	0.11629	-0.06619	-0.02473
PA10	0.6289	0.0806	0.15433	0.00122
PA15	0.60407	0.17981	0.04377	0.05395
PA11	0.56051	0.03013	0.16551	0.22887
PA17	0.55465	-0.23025	0.18891	0.0564
PA24	-0.38456	0.14468	0.37071	0.15459
PA26	-0.44121	0.4066	0.31565	0.09783
PA29	-0.57449	0.21633	0.25337	0.22329
PA32	-0.62548	0.19648	0.29618	0.23137
PA2	-0.06511	0.76251	0.00509	-0.10075
PA1	-0.17368	0.70265	0.13381	-0.04781
PA6	0.23519	0.6787	-0.01985	-0.01997
PA5	-0.37368	0.62775	0.14295	0.04804
PA3	-0.35633	0.62292	-0.02348	-0.04059
PA8	0.24447	0.61699	-0.1038	-0.13031
PA4	0.30692	0.60671	0.00477	-0.006
PA7	0.36616	0.55255	-0.07009	0.11127
PA23	0.05221	-0.40438	0.20765	0.39206
PA27	-0.13466	0.04357	0.64537	-0.05352
PA18	0.26321	-0.07314	0.64534	0.09369
PA20	0.03023	-0.01324	0.62168	0.12849
PA21	0.06515	-0.01051	0.46871	0.1779
PA19	0.08645	0.17614	-0.09505	0.62603
PA31	-0.24857	0.07881	-0.01394	0.53057
PA22	0.06496	-0.25082	0.08474	0.5025
PA30	0.05341	-0.15546	0.258	0.48001
PA28	0.03609	0.05067	0.21219	0.44052
PA25	0.30536	-0.228	0.02626	0.40191
PA33	-0.26174	-0.11852	0.19822	0.33194

Variance Explained by Each Factor

Factor1	Factor2	Factor3	Factor 4
5.921713	4.1357152	2.2041926	2.0866332

Melbourne Scale statistics

Variable	Item
SecF_T	Institutional Secularisation, factual level, all students
ReconfF_T	Institutional Reconfessionalisation, factual level, all students
ValedF_T	Christian Values Education, factual level, all students
RecontF_T	Recontextualisation, factual level, all students
ConfF_T	Confessional school, factual level, all students
SecN_T	Institutional Secularisation, normative level, all students
ReconfN_T	Institutional Reconfessionalisation, normative level, all students
ValedN_T	Christian Values Education, normative level, all students
RecontN_T	Recontextualisation, normative level, all students
SecF_A	[scale means for Institutional Secularisation, factual measurement level, all adults]
ReconfF_A	[scale means for Institutional Reconfessionalisation, factual measurement level, all adults]
ValedF_A	[scale means for Christian Values Education, factual measurement level, all adults
RecontF_A	[scale means for Recontextualisation, factual measurement level, all adults
ConfF_A	[scale means for Confessional school, factual measurement level, all adults
SecN_A	[scale means for Institutional Secularisation, normative measurement level, all adults]
ReconfN_A	[scale means for Institutional Reconfessionalisation, normative measurement level, all adults]
ValedN_A	[scale means for Christian Values Education, normative measurement level, all adults
RecontN_A	[scale means for Recontextualisation, normative measurement level, all adults
MAF1_2	Nothing reveals that my school is (still) Catholic. In daily school life, Christianity is not of any real significance.
MAF2_2	My school used to be Catholic, but Christianity has slowly disappeared from school life. Thus today my school is Catholic in name only.
MAF3_2	In my school, most people do not believe.
MAF4_2	Though there are still classes of religious education in my school, they rarely mention God, Jesus or the Bible.
MAF5_2	My school calls for tolerance and respect for everyone, without itself having any preference.
MAF6_2	My school has a clear preference for the Catholic faith and therefore wants to guarantee the Catholic faith formation of all its students.
MAF7_2	Now that its Catholic identity is threatened, my school is trying all the harder to be and to remain clearly Catholic.
MAF8_2	My school stresses the importance of religious education classes, because learning about faith promotes a Catholic way of life.
MAF9_2	My Catholic school is worried about the increasing diversity in society, since it considers this a threat to its Catholic school identity.
MAF10_2	My Catholic school thinks we must remain faithful to the teachings of the Catholic tradition and avoid any 'adaptation' of the Catholic faith to today's secular culture.
MAF11_2	My school is Catholic, first and foremost because it offers Catholic values and norms that can be accepted by Christians as well as non-Christians.
MAF12_2	Religious education classes in my school try to link the students' sense of values to the Catholic faith, hoping that they become deeper believers that way.
MAF13_2	My Catholic school reasons as follows: "A little diversity is fine. But if the differences between people at school continue to grow, then we have a problem. For then the sense of Christian values is no longer shared by all people at school."
MAF14_2	As a Catholic school, my school is aiming for a Catholic middle path between different visions, in which all can recognise themselves.
MAF15_2	It is my Catholic school's mission to teach young people – in all their diversity – Catholic values and norms, thereby bringing them closer to the Catholic faith.
MAF16_2	My school shows its Catholic character in its search for a renewed way to realise the Christian message of faith, hope and love in the world today.
MAF17_2	Religious education classes in my school aspire to help all students, Catholics as well as other-believers, to discover meaning in their lives and to deepen their humanity in dialogue with the Christian story.
MAF18_2	In my Catholic school, a multiplicity of philosophies of life is positively valued and even encouraged, since it offers a chance to the other-believers – but also to the Christians at school – to form and deepen their own personal identity in conversation with the Christian story.
MAF19_2	My school freely bears witness to its Catholic inspiration, and brings different viewpoints into dialogue with each other against the background of the Christian story. As such, it renders service to the identity formation of all involved – other-believers ánd Catholics themselves.
MAF20_2	In my Catholic school's mission to teach young people the attitudes and skills needed to deal with diversity in a Catholic way.
MAF21_2	My Catholic school still strongly resembles the confessional schools of the past.
MAF22_2	In my Catholic school it has always been considered normal that celebrations of the Eucharist take place frequently, and today this still is the case.
MAF23_2	As in the past, my school still assumes that the Catholic faith is practised by most of its members.
MAF24_2	Most of the following items are considered fairly normal in my school: crucifixes on the wall, religious education classes, celebrations of the Eucharist at school, a morning prayer, praying before meals, school catechesis, a priest who's working in the school.
MAF25_2	My school isn't secularising at all! It is still clear to everyone that my school is Catholic.
MAN1_2	As far as I'm concerned, Catholic schools belong to the past. Christianity doesn't need to be of any real significance in daily school life.
MAN2_2	I find it no problem that Christianity is slowly disappearing from school life, because my 'ideal school' isn't Catholic anyway.
MAN3_2	In my 'ideal school', most people would not have to be religious believers.
MAN4_2	In my 'ideal school', God, Jesus or the Bible needn't be mentioned anymore.
MAN5_2	My 'ideal school' calls for tolerance and respect for everyone, without itself having any preference.
MAN6_2	My 'ideal school' has a clear preference for the Catholic faith and therefore wants to guarantee the Catholic faith formation of all its students.
MAN7_2	If their Catholic identity is threatened, I think schools should try all the harder to be and to remain clearly Catholic.
MAN8_2	I wish to stress the importance of religious education classes at Catholic schools, because learning about faith promotes a Catholic way of life.
MAN9_2	I am worried about the increasing diversity in society, because I consider this a threat to the identity of Catholic schools.
MAN10_2	I think we must remain faithful to the teachings of the Catholic tradition and avoid any 'adaptation' of the Catholic faith to today's secular culture.
MAN11_2	I think that, first and foremost, a Catholic school should offer Catholic values and norms that can be accepted by Christians as well as non-Christians.
MAN12_2	I think that religious education classes should try to link the students' sense of values to the Catholic faith, hoping that they become deeper believers that way.
MAN13_2	I think it is important that the sense of Christian values is shared by all people at school. Thus it becomes a problem, I think, if the differences between people at school continue to grow.
MAN14_2	I think that Catholic schools should aim for a Catholic middle path between different visions, in which all can recognise themselves.
MAN15_2	The mission of Catholic schools is to teach young people – in all their diversity – Catholic values and norms, thereby bringing them closer to the Catholic faith.
MAN16_2	I think that a Catholic school should be searching for a renewed way to realise the Christian message of faith, hope and love in the world today.
MAN17_2	I think that religious education classes should aspire to help all students, Christians as well as other-believers, to discover meaning in their lives and to deepen their humanity in dialogue with the Christian story.

MAN18_2	I think that Catholic schools should positively value and even encourage a multiplicity of philosophies of life, since it offers a chance to the other-believers – but also to the Christians at school – to form and deepen their own personal identity in conversation with the Christian story.
MAN19_2	I think that Catholic schools should freely bear witness to their Catholic inspiration, and should bring different viewpoints into dialogue with each other against the background of the Christian story. As such, it renders service to the identity formation of all involved – other-believers ánd Catholics themselves.
MAN20_2	The mission of Catholic schools is to teach young people the attitudes and skills needed to deal with diversity in a Catholic way.
ME2	The questions in this survey made sense to me.
ME4	I liked completing this survey.

Variable	Mean	Std Dev	Variance	Min	Max	N	Quart 1	Median	Quart 2	Lower 99% CL	Upper 99% CL	t Value	Pr > |t|
SecF_T	2.474	1.574	2.477	1	7	7323	1	2	4	2.427	2.522	134.54	<.0001
ReconfF_T	4.531	1.530	2.342	1	7	7247	4	5	6	4.485	4.577	252.06	<.0001
ValedF_T	5.065	1.391	1.936	1	7	7177	4	5	6	5.023	5.108	308.46	<.0001
RecontF_T	4.782	1.296	1.680	1	7	7114	4	5	6	4.742	4.821	311.14	<.0001
ConfF_T	4.427	1.490	2.220	1	7	7081	3	5	5	4.381	4.473	250.01	<.0001
SecN_T	3.157	1.787	3.195	1	7	7323	2	3	4	3.103	3.211	151.14	<.0001
ReconfN_T	3.854	1.805	3.257	1	7	7247	2	4	5	3.799	3.908	181.79	<.0001
ValedN_T	5.016	1.538	2.365	1	7	7177	4	5	6	4.969	5.062	276.31	<.0001
RecontN_T	4.397	1.466	2.150	1	7	7114	4	4	5	4.352	4.442	252.93	<.0001
SecF_A	2.149	0.845	0.715	1	7	5205	1.5	2	2.5	2.119	2.179	183.39	<.0001
ReconfF_A	4.236	0.695	0.484	1.4	7	5205	3.8	4.2	4.6	4.211	4.261	439.48	<.0001
ValedF_A	5.075	0.645	0.416	1.8	7	5205	4.6	5	5.4	5.051	5.098	567.77	<.0001
RecontF_A	5.383	0.734	0.539	1	7	5205	5	5.4	5.8	5.357	5.410	529.09	<.0001
ConfF_A	5.325	1.002	1.004	1	7	5205	4.8	5.4	6	5.289	5.361	383.45	<.0001
SecN_A	2.249	1.008	1.015	1	7	5205	1.5	2	2.75	2.213	2.285	161.03	<.0001
ReconfN_A	4.276	0.899	0.808	1	7	5205	3.8	4.4	4.8	4.243	4.308	343.14	<.0001
ValedN_A	5.209	0.727	0.529	1	7	5205	4.8	5.2	5.67	5.184	5.235	516.71	<.0001
RecontN_A	5.570	0.677	0.458	1	7	5205	5.2	5.6	6	5.545	5.594	593.49	<.0001
MAF1_2	1.962	1.172	1.374	1	7	5396	1	2	2	1.921	2.004	122.96	<.0001
MAF2_2	2.061	1.186	1.406	1	7	5378	1	2	2	2.019	2.102	127.42	<.0001
MAF3_2	2.650	1.331	1.772	1	7	5377	2	2	4	2.603	2.696	145.96	<.0001
MAF4_2	2.102	1.250	1.562	1	7	5366	1	2	2	2.058	2.146	123.2	<.0001
MAF5_2	5.889	1.179	1.390	1	7	5345	6	6	7	5.848	5.931	365.24	<.0001
MAF6_2	5.505	1.228	1.508	1	7	5396	5	6	6	5.462	5.548	329.27	<.0001
MAF7_2	4.297	1.526	2.328	1	7	5378	4	4	6	4.244	4.351	206.56	<.0001
MAF8_2	5.711	1.115	1.242	1	7	5366	5	6	6	5.672	5.750	375.32	<.0001
MAF9_2	2.715	1.357	1.842	1	7	5345	2	2	4	2.667	2.763	146.23	<.0001
MAF10_2	2.898	1.357	1.841	1	7	5252	2	3	4	2.850	2.946	154.78	<.0001
MAF11_2	5.986	1.089	1.186	1	7	5396	6	6	7	5.948	6.024	403.73	<.0001
MAF12_2	5.640	1.072	1.149	1	7	5366	5	6	6	5.602	5.678	385.49	<.0001
MAF13_2	3.478	1.586	2.516	1	7	5345	2	4	5	3.422	3.534	160.31	<.0001
MAF14_2	4.457	1.402	1.965	1	7	5253	4	4	6	4.407	4.507	230.42	<.0001
MAF15_2	5.685	1.009	1.018	1	7	5244	5	6	6	5.649	5.721	408.07	<.0001
MAF16_2	5.678	1.062	1.127	1	7	5396	5	6	6	5.640	5.715	392.79	<.0001
MAF17_2	5.837	1.020	1.041	1	7	5366	5	6	7	5.801	5.873	419.17	<.0001
MAF18_2	4.962	1.250	1.563	1	7	5345	4	5	6	4.918	5.006	290.22	<.0001
MAF19_2	4.661	1.290	1.663	1	7	5253	4	5	6	4.615	4.707	261.94	<.0001
MAF20_2	5.630	1.028	1.056	1	7	5244	5	6	6	5.593	5.666	396.73	<.0001
MAF21_2	4.912	1.640	2.690	1	7	5386	4	5	6	4.854	4.969	219.76	<.0001
MAF22_2	5.562	1.273	1.619	1	7	5386	5	6	6	5.517	5.607	320.78	<.0001
MAF23_2	4.792	1.603	2.570	1	7	5386	4	5	6	4.736	4.848	219.39	<.0001
MAF24_2	5.739	1.198	1.436	1	7	5386	5	6	7	5.697	5.781	351.51	<.0001
MAF25_2	5.493	1.381	1.907	1	7	5378	5	6	6	5.445	5.542	291.76	<.0001
MAN1_2	1.881	1.129	1.275	1	7	5396	1	2	2	1.841	1.920	122.32	<.0001
MAN2_2	2.186	1.330	1.769	1	7	5378	1	2	3	2.140	2.233	120.54	<.0001
MAN3_2	3.069	1.642	2.695	1	7	5378	2	3	4	3.011	3.126	137.09	<.0001
MAN4_2	2.038	1.234	1.523	1	7	5366	1	2	2	1.994	2.081	120.97	<.0001
MAN5_2	6.250	1.063	1.131	1	7	5345	6	7	7	6.212	6.287	429.73	<.0001
MAN6_2	5.167	1.519	2.308	1	7	5396	4	6	6	5.114	5.221	249.83	<.0001
MAN7_2	5.276	1.327	1.762	1	7	5378	4	6	6	5.229	5.323	291.48	<.0001
MAN8_2	5.530	1.253	1.569	1	7	5366	5	6	6	5.486	5.574	323.39	<.0001
MAN9_2	2.657	1.555	2.420	1	7	5345	1	2	4	2.602	2.712	124.89	<.0001
MAN10_2	2.664	1.411	1.992	1	7	5252	2	2	4	2.614	2.714	136.8	<.0001
MAN11_2	6.030	1.079	1.164	1	7	5396	6	6	7	5.992	6.068	410.63	<.0001
MAN12_2	5.588	1.223	1.496	1	7	5366	5	6	6	5.545	5.631	334.65	<.0001
MAN13_2	4.062	1.651	2.724	1	7	5345	3	4	5	4.004	4.121	179.94	<.0001
MAN14_2	4.477	1.507	2.270	1	7	5253	4	5	6	4.424	4.531	215.4	<.0001
MAN15_2	5.746	1.018	1.036	1	7	5244	5	6	6	5.710	5.782	408.88	<.0001
MAN16_2	5.650	1.152	1.327	1	7	5396	5	6	6	5.610	5.691	360.34	<.0001
MAN17_2	6.043	0.974	0.949	1	7	5366	6	6	7	6.008	6.077	454.3	<.0001
MAN18_2	5.398	1.224	1.498	1	7	5345	5	6	6	5.355	5.441	322.41	<.0001
MAN19_2	4.907	1.328	1.763	1	7	5252	4	5	6	4.860	4.954	267.82	<.0001
MAN20_2	5.693	1.040	1.082	1	7	5244	5	6	6	5.656	5.730	396.35	<.0001
ME2	4.943	1.563	2.444	1	7	14314	4	5	6	4.909	4.976	378.25	<.0001
ME4	3.995	1.852	3.430	1	7	14314	2	4	6	3.955	4.035	258.08	<.0001

Pearson Correlation Coefficients, student respondents
Prob > |r| under H0: Rho=0
Number of Observations

	SecF	ReconfF	ValedF	RecontF	ConfF	SecN	ReconfN	ValedN	RecontN
SecF	1	-0.12262	-0.09782	-0.11179	-0.04328	0.43909	-0.06806	-0.14181	-0.10237
		<.0001	<.0001	<.0001	0.0003	<.0001	<.0001	<.0001	<.0001
	7323	7245	7177	7112	7080	7323	7245	7177	7112
ReconfF	-0.12262	1	0.10271	0.20933	0.38007	-0.09292	0.51973	0.06252	0.13751
	<.0001		<.0001	<.0001	<.0001	<.0001	<.0001	<.0001	<.0001
	7245	7247	7176	7112	7080	7245	7247	7176	7112
ValedF	-0.09782	0.10271	1	0.27866	0.07166	-0.0888	0.06991	0.4612	0.22024
	<.0001	<.0001		<.0001	<.0001	<.0001	<.0001	<.0001	<.0001
	7177	7176	7177	7112	7080	7177	7176	7177	7112
RecontF	-0.11179	0.20933	0.27866	1	0.20414	-0.07234	0.13155	0.1991	0.47941
	<.0001	<.0001	<.0001		<.0001	<.0001	<.0001	<.0001	<.0001
	7112	7112	7112	7114	7081	7112	7112	7112	7114
ConfF	-0.04328	0.38007	0.07166	0.20414	1	-0.08577	0.34641	0.08705	0.18004
	0.0003	<.0001	<.0001	<.0001		<.0001	<.0001	<.0001	<.0001
	7080	7080	7080	7081	7081	7080	7080	7080	7081
SecN	0.43909	-0.09292	-0.0888	-0.07234	-0.08577	1	-0.33126	-0.10158	-0.16425
	<.0001	<.0001	<.0001	<.0001	<.0001		<.0001	<.0001	<.0001
	7323	7245	7177	7112	7080	7323	7245	7177	7112
ReconfN	-0.06806	0.51973	0.06991	0.13155	0.34641	-0.33126	1	0.2152	0.35464
	<.0001	<.0001	<.0001	<.0001	<.0001	<.0001		<.0001	<.0001
	7245	7247	7176	7112	7080	7245	7247	7176	7112
ValedN	-0.14181	0.06252	0.4612	0.1991	0.08705	-0.10158	0.2152	1	0.40197
	<.0001	<.0001	<.0001	<.0001	<.0001	<.0001	<.0001		<.0001
	7177	7176	7177	7112	7080	7177	7176	7177	7112
RecontN	-0.10237	0.13751	0.22024	0.47941	0.18004	-0.16425	0.35464	0.40197	1
	<.0001	<.0001	<.0001	<.0001	<.0001	<.0001	<.0001	<.0001	
	7112	7112	7112	7114	7081	7112	7112	7112	7114

Pearson Correlation Coefficients, student respondents, n=5205
Prob > |r| under H0: Rho=0

	SecF	ReconfF	ValedF	RecontF	ConfF	SecN	ReconfN	ValedN	RecontN
SecF	1	-0.1112	-0.23661	-0.39574	-0.4499	0.45359	-0.06613	-0.1654	-0.25523
		<.0001	<.0001	<.0001	<.0001	<.0001	<.0001	<.0001	<.0001
ReconfF	-0.1112	1	0.36639	0.0838	0.30908	-0.08877	0.50182	0.27722	0.0404
	<.0001		<.0001	<.0001	<.0001	<.0001	<.0001	<.0001	0.0036
ValedF	-0.23661	0.36639	1	0.36663	0.32001	-0.26251	0.40423	0.69224	0.24863
	<.0001	<.0001		<.0001	<.0001	<.0001	<.0001	<.0001	<.0001
RecontF	-0.39574	0.0838	0.36663	1	0.3158	-0.37762	0.22752	0.36636	0.66091
	<.0001	<.0001	<.0001		<.0001	<.0001	<.0001	<.0001	<.0001
ConfF	-0.4499	0.30908	0.32001	0.3158	1	-0.20088	0.19608	0.21422	0.16196
	<.0001	<.0001	<.0001	<.0001		<.0001	<.0001	<.0001	<.0001
SecN	0.45359	-0.08877	-0.26251	-0.37762	-0.20088	1	-0.49998	-0.40313	-0.32588
	<.0001	<.0001	<.0001	<.0001	<.0001		<.0001	<.0001	<.0001
ReconfN	-0.06613	0.50182	0.40423	0.22752	0.19608	-0.49998	1	0.52995	0.11031
	<.0001	<.0001	<.0001	<.0001	<.0001	<.0001		<.0001	<.0001
ValedN	-0.1654	0.27722	0.69224	0.36636	0.21422	-0.40313	0.52995	1	0.31426
	<.0001	<.0001	<.0001	<.0001	<.0001	<.0001	<.0001		<.0001
RecontN	-0.25523	0.0404	0.24863	0.66091	0.16196	-0.32588	0.11031	0.31426	1
	<.0001	0.0036	<.0001	<.0001	<.0001	<.0001	<.0001	<.0001	

Pearson Correlation Coefficients, adult respondents.
Prob > |r| under H0: Rho=0
Number of Observations

	MAF1	MAF2	MAF3	MAF4	MAF5	MAF6	MAF7	MAF8	MAF9	MAF10
MAF1	1	0.44923	0.28927	0.34454	-0.22679	-0.2175	-0.06053	-0.29294	0.21814	0.18114
		<.0001	<.0001	<.0001	<.0001	<.0001	<.0001	<.0001	<.0001	<.0001
	5396	5378	5377	5366	5344	5396	5378	5366	5344	5249
MAF2	0.44923	1	0.42135	0.37696	-0.246	-0.25561	-0.05159	-0.37058	0.22616	0.15254
	<.0001		<.0001	<.0001	<.0001	<.0001	0.0002	<.0001	<.0001	<.0001
	5378	5378	5377	5366	5344	5378	5378	5366	5344	5249
MAF3	0.28927	0.42135	1	0.2748	-0.17974	-0.2092	-0.05575	-0.28551	0.18785	0.09458
	<.0001	<.0001		<.0001	<.0001	<.0001	<.0001	<.0001	<.0001	<.0001
	5377	5377	5377	5366	5344	5377	5377	5366	5344	5249
MAF4	0.34454	0.37696	0.2748	1	-0.18642	-0.14842	-0.0472	-0.32464	0.21408	0.16245
	<.0001	<.0001	<.0001		<.0001	<.0001	0.0005	<.0001	<.0001	<.0001
	5366	5366	5366	5366	5344	5366	5366	5366	5344	5249
MAF5	-0.22679	-0.246	-0.17974	-0.18642	1	0.12811	0.05078	0.2491	-0.23937	-0.21072
	<.0001	<.0001	<.0001	<.0001		<.0001	0.0002	<.0001	<.0001	<.0001
	5344	5344	5344	5344	5345	5344	5344	5344	5345	5250
MAF6	-0.2175	-0.25561	-0.2092	-0.14842	0.12811	1	0.17317	0.36689	-0.02412	-0.00456
	<.0001	<.0001	<.0001	<.0001	<.0001		<.0001	<.0001	0.0779	0.741
	5396	5378	5377	5366	5344	5396	5378	5366	5344	5249
MAF7	-0.06053	-0.05159	-0.05575	-0.0472	0.05078	0.17317	1	0.16807	0.13665	0.01934
	<.0001	0.0002	<.0001	0.0005	0.0002	<.0001		<.0001	<.0001	0.1613
	5378	5378	5377	5366	5344	5378	5378	5366	5344	5249
MAF8	-0.29294	-0.37058	-0.28551	-0.32464	0.2491	0.36689	0.16807	1	-0.08475	-0.10341
	<.0001	<.0001	<.0001	<.0001	<.0001	<.0001	<.0001		<.0001	<.0001
	5366	5366	5366	5366	5344	5366	5366	5366	5344	5249
MAF9	0.21814	0.22616	0.18785	0.21408	-0.23937	-0.02412	0.13665	-0.08475	1	0.26009
	<.0001	<.0001	<.0001	<.0001	<.0001	0.0779	<.0001	<.0001		<.0001
	5344	5344	5344	5344	5345	5344	5344	5344	5345	5250
MAF10	0.18114	0.15254	0.09458	0.16245	-0.21072	-0.00456	0.01934	-0.10341	0.26009	1
	<.0001	<.0001	<.0001	<.0001	<.0001	0.741	0.1613	<.0001	<.0001	
	5249	5249	5249	5249	5250	5249	5249	5249	5250	5252
MAF11	-0.31294	-0.32499	-0.23391	-0.22688	0.26903	0.29237	0.08359	0.35352	-0.12619	-0.14921
	<.0001	<.0001	<.0001	<.0001	<.0001	<.0001	<.0001	<.0001	<.0001	<.0001
	5396	5378	5377	5366	5344	5396	5378	5366	5344	5249
MAF12	-0.26654	-0.31002	-0.27264	-0.2742	0.24697	0.37223	0.18227	0.50574	-0.11222	-0.1141
	<.0001	<.0001	<.0001	<.0001	<.0001	<.0001	<.0001	<.0001	<.0001	<.0001
	5366	5366	5366	5366	5344	5366	5366	5366	5344	5249
MAF13	0.11267	0.11795	0.09927	0.13638	-0.17102	0.06173	0.11066	-0.00227	0.41839	0.22045
	<.0001	<.0001	<.0001	<.0001	<.0001	<.0001	<.0001	0.8682	<.0001	<.0001
	5344	5344	5344	5344	5345	5344	5344	5344	5345	5250
MAF14	0.0506	0.03516	0.03819	0.05667	0.0513	-0.01267	-0.00661	0.01443	0.03996	-0.06591
	0.0002	0.0108	0.0056	<.0001	0.0002	0.3587	0.6319	0.2957	0.0038	<.0001
	5250	5250	5250	5250	5251	5250	5250	5250	5251	5252
MAF15	-0.24948	-0.28595	-0.24912	-0.18962	0.22038	0.35379	0.11748	0.39708	-0.08891	-0.0773
	<.0001	<.0001	<.0001	<.0001	<.0001	<.0001	<.0001	<.0001	<.0001	<.0001
	5243	5243	5243	5243	5244	5243	5243	5243	5244	5244
MAF16	-0.31275	-0.35605	-0.28325	-0.21734	0.31662	0.35762	0.11113	0.37221	-0.16347	-0.16815
	<.0001	<.0001	<.0001	<.0001	<.0001	<.0001	<.0001	<.0001	<.0001	<.0001
	5396	5378	5377	5366	5344	5396	5378	5366	5344	5249
MAF17	-0.3022	-0.34145	-0.28768	-0.30943	0.35781	0.25295	0.10621	0.4282	-0.22839	-0.23371
	<.0001	<.0001	<.0001	<.0001	<.0001	<.0001	<.0001	<.0001	<.0001	<.0001
	5366	5366	5366	5366	5344	5366	5366	5366	5344	5249
MAF18	-0.093	-0.11165	-0.12308	-0.09748	0.27907	0.07077	0.04104	0.15732	-0.15921	-0.24367
	<.0001	<.0001	<.0001	<.0001	<.0001	<.0001	0.0027	<.0001	<.0001	<.0001
	5344	5344	5344	5344	5345	5344	5344	5344	5345	5250
MAF19	-0.08284	-0.11786	-0.11024	-0.09497	0.17609	0.11897	0.06503	0.15841	-0.11377	-0.26749
	<.0001	<.0001	<.0001	<.0001	<.0001	<.0001	<.0001	<.0001	<.0001	<.0001
	5250	5250	5250	5250	5251	5250	5250	5250	5251	5252
MAF20	-0.22558	-0.22643	-0.21916	-0.17509	0.27265	0.28485	0.12429	0.35798	-0.08332	-0.12392
	<.0001	<.0001	<.0001	<.0001	<.0001	<.0001	<.0001	<.0001	<.0001	<.0001
	5243	5243	5243	5243	5244	5243	5243	5243	5244	5244

408

MAF21	-0.16651	-0.28861	-0.22491	-0.14738	0.14035	0.27441	0.12007	0.25225	-0.04287	-0.00913
	<.0001	<.0001	<.0001	<.0001	<.0001	<.0001	<.0001	<.0001	0.0017	0.5085
	5386	5378	5377	5366	5344	5386	5378	5366	5344	5249
MAF22	-0.25647	-0.345	-0.27219	-0.22359	0.19667	0.31263	0.12186	0.34901	-0.07224	-0.0509
	<.0001	<.0001	<.0001	<.0001	<.0001	<.0001	<.0001	<.0001	<.0001	0.0002
	5386	5378	5377	5366	5344	5386	5378	5366	5344	5249
MAF23	-0.07155	-0.18595	-0.26285	-0.07088	0.05872	0.28179	0.05637	0.2339	0.03477	0.09927
	<.0001	<.0001	<.0001	<.0001	<.0001	<.0001	<.0001	<.0001	0.011	<.0001
	5386	5378	5377	5366	5344	5386	5378	5366	5344	5249
MAF24	-0.22506	-0.34217	-0.2506	-0.19973	0.18388	0.28069	0.11112	0.32214	-0.04925	-0.03854
	<.0001	<.0001	<.0001	<.0001	<.0001	<.0001	<.0001	<.0001	0.0003	0.0052
	5386	5378	5377	5366	5344	5386	5378	5366	5344	5249
MAF25	-0.27117	-0.38385	-0.29467	-0.22596	0.21405	0.27419	0.16552	0.34781	-0.12803	-0.06927
	<.0001	<.0001	<.0001	<.0001	<.0001	<.0001	<.0001	<.0001	<.0001	<.0001
	5378	5378	5377	5366	5344	5378	5378	5366	5344	5249

	MAF11	MAF12	MAF13	MAF14	MAF15	MAF16	MAF17	MAF18	MAF19	MAF20
MAF1	-0.31294	-0.26654	0.11267	0.0506	-0.24948	-0.31275	-0.3022	-0.093	-0.08284	-0.22558
	<.0001	<.0001	<.0001	0.0002	<.0001	<.0001	<.0001	<.0001	<.0001	<.0001
	5396	5366	5344	5250	5243	5396	5366	5344	5250	5243
MAF2	-0.32499	-0.31002	0.11795	0.03516	-0.28595	-0.35605	-0.34145	-0.11165	-0.11786	-0.22643
	<.0001	<.0001	<.0001	0.0108	<.0001	<.0001	<.0001	<.0001	<.0001	<.0001
	5378	5366	5344	5250	5243	5378	5366	5344	5250	5243
MAF3	-0.23391	-0.27264	0.09927	0.03819	-0.24912	-0.28325	-0.28768	-0.12308	-0.11024	-0.21916
	<.0001	<.0001	<.0001	0.0056	<.0001	<.0001	<.0001	<.0001	<.0001	<.0001
	5377	5366	5344	5250	5243	5377	5366	5344	5250	5243
MAF4	-0.22688	-0.2742	0.13638	0.05667	-0.18962	-0.21734	-0.30943	-0.09748	-0.09497	-0.17509
	<.0001	<.0001	<.0001	<.0001	<.0001	<.0001	<.0001	<.0001	<.0001	<.0001
	5366	5366	5344	5250	5243	5366	5366	5344	5250	5243
MAF5	0.26903	0.24697	-0.17102	0.0513	0.22038	0.31662	0.35781	0.27907	0.17609	0.27265
	<.0001	<.0001	<.0001	0.0002	<.0001	<.0001	<.0001	<.0001	<.0001	<.0001
	5344	5344	5345	5251	5244	5344	5344	5345	5251	5244
MAF6	0.29237	0.37223	0.06173	-0.01267	0.35379	0.35762	0.25295	0.07077	0.11897	0.28485
	<.0001	<.0001	<.0001	0.3587	<.0001	<.0001	<.0001	<.0001	<.0001	<.0001
	5396	5366	5344	5250	5243	5396	5366	5344	5250	5243
MAF7	0.08359	0.18227	0.11066	-0.00661	0.11748	0.11113	0.10621	0.04104	0.06503	0.12429
	<.0001	<.0001	<.0001	0.6319	<.0001	<.0001	<.0001	0.0027	<.0001	<.0001
	5378	5366	5344	5250	5243	5378	5366	5344	5250	5243
MAF8	0.35352	0.50574	-0.00227	0.01443	0.39708	0.37221	0.4282	0.15732	0.15841	0.35798
	<.0001	<.0001	0.8682	0.2957	<.0001	<.0001	<.0001	<.0001	<.0001	<.0001
	5366	5366	5344	5250	5243	5366	5366	5344	5250	5243
MAF9	-0.12619	-0.11222	0.41839	0.03996	-0.08891	-0.16347	-0.22839	-0.15921	-0.11377	-0.08332
	<.0001	<.0001	<.0001	0.0038	<.0001	<.0001	<.0001	<.0001	<.0001	<.0001
	5344	5344	5345	5251	5244	5344	5344	5345	5251	5244
MAF10	-0.14921	-0.1141	0.22045	-0.06591	-0.0773	-0.16815	-0.23371	-0.24367	-0.26749	-0.12392
	<.0001	<.0001	<.0001	<.0001	<.0001	<.0001	<.0001	<.0001	<.0001	<.0001
	5249	5249	5250	5252	5244	5249	5249	5250	5252	5244
MAF11	1	0.32539	-0.04308	0.04763	0.31548	0.47567	0.35719	0.22252	0.17117	0.29004
		<.0001	0.0016	0.0006	<.0001	<.0001	<.0001	<.0001	<.0001	<.0001
	5396	5366	5344	5250	5243	5396	5366	5344	5250	5243
MAF12	0.32539	1	-0.01087	0.02508	0.42708	0.40619	0.53229	0.21713	0.19623	0.38719
	<.0001		0.4268	0.0692	<.0001	<.0001	<.0001	<.0001	<.0001	<.0001
	5366	5366	5344	5250	5243	5366	5366	5344	5250	5243
MAF13	-0.04308	-0.01087	1	0.03413	0.02707	-0.0498	-0.08806	-0.12688	-0.07327	0.01223
	0.0016	0.4268		0.0134	0.05	0.0003	<.0001	<.0001	<.0001	0.376
	5344	5344	5345	5251	5244	5344	5344	5345	5251	5244
MAF14	0.04763	0.02508	0.03413	1	0.05896	0.04162	0.02277	0.11802	-0.23562	0.04885
	0.0006	0.0692	0.0134		<.0001	0.0026	0.099	<.0001	<.0001	0.0004
	5250	5250	5251	5253	5244	5250	5250	5251	5253	5244
MAF15	0.31548	0.42708	0.02707	0.05896	1	0.35356	0.3683	0.16265	0.1668	0.57111
	<.0001	<.0001	0.05	<.0001		<.0001	<.0001	<.0001	<.0001	<.0001
	5243	5243	5244	5244	5244	5243	5243	5244	5244	5244
MAF16	0.47567	0.40619	-0.0498	0.04162	0.35356	1	0.46678	0.29487	0.23306	0.35597
	<.0001	<.0001	0.0003	0.0026	<.0001		<.0001	<.0001	<.0001	<.0001
	5396	5366	5344	5250	5243	5396	5366	5344	5250	5243
MAF17	0.35719	0.53229	-0.08806	0.02277	0.3683	0.46678	1	0.33363	0.26919	0.39208
	<.0001	<.0001	<.0001	0.099	<.0001	<.0001		<.0001	<.0001	<.0001

	5366	5366	5344	5250	5243	5366	5366	5344	5250	5243
MAF18	0.22252	0.21713	-0.12688	0.11802	0.16265	0.29487	0.33363	1	0.26702	0.23093
	<.0001	<.0001	<.0001	<.0001	<.0001	<.0001	<.0001		<.0001	<.0001
	5344	5344	5345	5251	5244	5344	5344	5345	5251	5244
MAF19	0.17117	0.19623	-0.07327	-0.23562	0.1668	0.23306	0.26919	0.26702	1	0.2065
	<.0001	<.0001	<.0001	<.0001	<.0001	<.0001	<.0001	<.0001		<.0001
	5250	5250	5251	5253	5244	5250	5250	5251	5253	5244
MAF20	0.29004	0.38719	0.01223	0.04885	0.57111	0.35597	0.39208	0.23093	0.2065	1
	<.0001	<.0001	0.376	0.0004	<.0001	<.0001	<.0001	<.0001	<.0001	
	5243	5243	5244	5244	5244	5243	5243	5244	5244	5244
MAF21	0.21748	0.22403	0.0222	0.00594	0.24347	0.2341	0.21417	0.0955	0.09218	0.19685
	<.0001	<.0001	0.1046	0.667	<.0001	<.0001	<.0001	<.0001	<.0001	<.0001
	5386	5366	5344	5250	5243	5386	5366	5344	5250	5243
MAF22	0.2818	0.31538	-0.01374	-0.0087	0.31043	0.31518	0.28489	0.13887	0.14398	0.25314
	<.0001	<.0001	0.3154	0.5284	<.0001	<.0001	<.0001	<.0001	<.0001	<.0001
	5386	5366	5344	5250	5243	5386	5366	5344	5250	5243
MAF23	0.14724	0.16655	0.0561	0.0726	0.18665	0.16582	0.10458	0.00865	0.00236	0.12395
	<.0001	<.0001	<.0001	<.0001	<.0001	<.0001	<.0001	0.5275	0.8642	<.0001
	5386	5366	5344	5250	5243	5386	5366	5344	5250	5243
MAF24	0.2438	0.30089	-0.0093	0.02091	0.27977	0.27016	0.27608	0.12109	0.12435	0.23823
	<.0001	<.0001	0.4968	0.1298	<.0001	<.0001	<.0001	<.0001	<.0001	<.0001
	5386	5366	5344	5250	5243	5386	5366	5344	5250	5243
MAF25	0.28997	0.2686	-0.04168	-0.00982	0.26215	0.29585	0.29348	0.09318	0.10259	0.19765
	<.0001	<.0001	0.0023	0.4768	<.0001	<.0001	<.0001	<.0001	<.0001	<.0001
	5378	5366	5344	5250	5243	5378	5366	5344	5250	5243

	MAF21	MAF22	MAF23	MAF24	MAF25
MAF1	-0.16651	-0.25647	-0.07155	-0.22506	-0.27117
	<.0001	<.0001	<.0001	<.0001	<.0001
	5386	5386	5386	5386	5378
MAF2	-0.28861	-0.345	-0.18595	-0.34217	-0.38385
	<.0001	<.0001	<.0001	<.0001	<.0001
	5378	5378	5378	5378	5378
MAF3	-0.22491	-0.27219	-0.26285	-0.2506	-0.29467
	<.0001	<.0001	<.0001	<.0001	<.0001
	5377	5377	5377	5377	5377
MAF4	-0.14738	-0.22359	-0.07088	-0.19973	-0.22596
	<.0001	<.0001	<.0001	<.0001	<.0001
	5366	5366	5366	5366	5366
MAF5	0.14035	0.19667	0.05872	0.18388	0.21405
	<.0001	<.0001	<.0001	<.0001	<.0001
	5344	5344	5344	5344	5344
MAF6	0.27441	0.31263	0.28179	0.28069	0.27419
	<.0001	<.0001	<.0001	<.0001	<.0001
	5386	5386	5386	5386	5378
MAF7	0.12007	0.12186	0.05637	0.11112	0.16552
	<.0001	<.0001	<.0001	<.0001	<.0001
	5378	5378	5378	5378	5378
MAF8	0.25225	0.34901	0.2339	0.32214	0.34781
	<.0001	<.0001	<.0001	<.0001	<.0001
	5366	5366	5366	5366	5366
MAF9	-0.04287	-0.07224	0.03477	-0.04925	-0.12803
	0.0017	<.0001	0.011	0.0003	<.0001
	5344	5344	5344	5344	5344
MAF10	-0.00913	-0.0509	0.09927	-0.03854	-0.06927
	0.5085	0.0002	<.0001	0.0052	<.0001
	5249	5249	5249	5249	5249
MAF11	0.21748	0.2818	0.14724	0.2438	0.28997
	<.0001	<.0001	<.0001	<.0001	<.0001
	5386	5386	5386	5386	5378
MAF12	0.22403	0.31538	0.16655	0.30089	0.2686
	<.0001	<.0001	<.0001	<.0001	<.0001
	5366	5366	5366	5366	5366
MAF13	0.0222	-0.01374	0.0561	-0.0093	-0.04168
	0.1046	0.3154	<.0001	0.4968	0.0023
	5344	5344	5344	5344	5344
MAF14	0.00594	-0.0087	0.0726	0.02091	-0.00982

	0.667	0.5284	<.0001	0.1298	0.4768
	5250	5250	5250	5250	5250
MAF15	0.24347	0.31043	0.18665	0.27977	0.26215
	<.0001	<.0001	<.0001	<.0001	<.0001
	5243	5243	5243	5243	5243
MAF16	0.2341	0.31518	0.16582	0.27016	0.29585
	<.0001	<.0001	<.0001	<.0001	<.0001
	5386	5386	5386	5386	5378
MAF17	0.21417	0.28489	0.10458	0.27608	0.29348
	<.0001	<.0001	<.0001	<.0001	<.0001
	5366	5366	5366	5366	5366
MAF18	0.0955	0.13887	0.00865	0.12109	0.09318
	<.0001	<.0001	0.5275	<.0001	<.0001
	5344	5344	5344	5344	5344
MAF19	0.09218	0.14398	0.00236	0.12435	0.10259
	<.0001	<.0001	0.8642	<.0001	<.0001
	5250	5250	5250	5250	5250
MAF20	0.19685	0.25314	0.12395	0.23823	0.19765
	<.0001	<.0001	<.0001	<.0001	<.0001
	5243	5243	5243	5243	5243
MAF21	1	0.56251	0.38817	0.42083	0.29956
		<.0001	<.0001	<.0001	<.0001
	5386	5386	5386	5386	5378
MAF22	0.56251	1	0.38277	0.52971	0.35317
	<.0001		<.0001	<.0001	<.0001
	5386	5386	5386	5386	5378
MAF23	0.38817	0.38277	1	0.35132	0.2324
	<.0001	<.0001		<.0001	<.0001
	5386	5386	5386	5386	5378
MAF24	0.42083	0.52971	0.35132	1	0.29986
	<.0001	<.0001	<.0001		<.0001
	5386	5386	5386	5386	5378
MAF25	0.29956	0.35317	0.2324	0.29986	1
	<.0001	<.0001	<.0001	<.0001	
	5378	5378	5378	5378	5378

Pearson Correlation Coefficients, adult respondents.
Prob > |r| under H0: Rho=0
Number of Observations

	MAN1	MAN2	MAN3	MAN4	MAN5	MAN6	MAN7	MAN8	MAN9	MAN10
MAN1	1	0.55064	0.38787	0.50776	-0.09922	-0.33479	-0.37101	-0.44341	0.03017	0.11776
		<.0001	<.0001	<.0001	<.0001	<.0001	<.0001	<.0001	0.0274	<.0001
	5396	5378	5378	5366	5344	5396	5378	5366	5344	5249
MAN2	0.55064	1	0.47146	0.54444	-0.03921	-0.41465	-0.43213	-0.50187	-0.04085	0.04878
	<.0001		<.0001	<.0001	0.0041	<.0001	<.0001	<.0001	0.0028	0.0004
	5378	5378	5378	5366	5344	5378	5378	5366	5344	5249
MAN3	0.38787	0.47146	1	0.43423	0.01668	-0.36686	-0.36203	-0.40601	-0.10491	-0.01661
	<.0001	<.0001		<.0001	0.2228	<.0001	<.0001	<.0001	<.0001	0.229
	5378	5378	5378	5366	5344	5378	5378	5366	5344	5249
MAN4	0.50776	0.54444	0.43423	1	-0.095	-0.34905	-0.3792	-0.50005	-0.00377	0.10244
	<.0001	<.0001	<.0001		<.0001	<.0001	<.0001	<.0001	0.783	<.0001
	5366	5366	5366	5366	5344	5366	5366	5366	5344	5249
MAN5	-0.09922	-0.03921	0.01668	-0.095	1	-0.01722	0.04513	0.08037	-0.21479	-0.22331
	<.0001	0.0041	0.2228	<.0001		0.2081	0.001	<.0001	<.0001	<.0001
	5344	5344	5344	5344	5345	5344	5344	5344	5345	5250
MAN6	-0.33479	-0.41465	-0.36686	-0.34905	-0.01722	1	0.47535	0.52329	0.1993	0.10422
	<.0001	<.0001	<.0001	<.0001	0.2081		<.0001	<.0001	<.0001	<.0001
	5396	5378	5378	5366	5344	5396	5378	5366	5344	5249
MAN7	-0.37101	-0.43213	-0.36203	-0.3792	0.04513	0.47535	1	0.53933	0.19261	0.03788
	<.0001	<.0001	<.0001	<.0001	0.001	<.0001		<.0001	<.0001	0.0061
	5378	5378	5378	5366	5344	5378	5378	5366	5344	5249
MAN8	-0.44341	-0.50187	-0.40601	-0.50005	0.08037	0.52329	0.53933	1	0.13276	0.00686
	<.0001	<.0001	<.0001	<.0001	<.0001	<.0001	<.0001		<.0001	0.6192
	5366	5366	5366	5366	5344	5366	5366	5366	5344	5249
MAN9	0.03017	-0.04085	-0.10491	-0.00377	-0.21479	0.1993	0.19261	0.13276	1	0.28443
	0.0274	0.0028	<.0001	0.783	<.0001	<.0001	<.0001	<.0001		<.0001
	5344	5344	5344	5344	5345	5344	5344	5344	5345	5250
MAN10	0.11776	0.04878	-0.01661	0.10244	-0.22331	0.10422	0.03788	0.00686	0.28443	1
	<.0001	0.0004	0.229	<.0001	<.0001	<.0001	0.0061	0.6192	<.0001	
	5249	5249	5249	5249	5250	5249	5249	5249	5250	5252
MAN11	-0.2919	-0.26789	-0.16097	-0.24634	0.16272	0.25488	0.27255	0.32127	-0.01218	-0.12193
	<.0001	<.0001	<.0001	<.0001	<.0001	<.0001	<.0001	<.0001	0.3735	<.0001
	5396	5378	5378	5366	5344	5396	5378	5366	5344	5249
MAN12	-0.41302	-0.42892	-0.34202	-0.42548	0.12055	0.47636	0.46835	0.6275	0.08177	-0.04153
	<.0001	<.0001	<.0001	<.0001	<.0001	<.0001	<.0001	<.0001	<.0001	0.0026
	5366	5366	5366	5366	5344	5366	5366	5366	5344	5249
MAN13	-0.10471	-0.13345	-0.17475	-0.11047	-0.09782	0.27682	0.25721	0.23181	0.39835	0.2127
	<.0001	<.0001	<.0001	<.0001	<.0001	<.0001	<.0001	<.0001	<.0001	<.0001
	5344	5344	5344	5344	5345	5344	5344	5344	5345	5250
MAN14	0.06343	0.06393	0.08543	0.06563	0.04031	-0.00768	-0.01719	-0.01676	0.03581	-0.04925
	<.0001	<.0001	<.0001	<.0001	0.0035	0.578	0.2131	0.2248	0.0095	0.0004
	5250	5250	5250	5250	5251	5250	5250	5250	5251	5252
MAN15	-0.35089	-0.3544	-0.26648	-0.33257	0.11636	0.39802	0.3895	0.47935	0.06395	-0.01491
	<.0001	<.0001	<.0001	<.0001	<.0001	<.0001	<.0001	<.0001	<.0001	0.2804
	5243	5243	5243	5243	5244	5243	5243	5243	5244	5244
MAN16	-0.18115	-0.16373	-0.0878	-0.18371	0.17269	0.19351	0.16347	0.20892	-0.0602	-0.16258
	<.0001	<.0001	<.0001	<.0001	<.0001	<.0001	<.0001	<.0001	<.0001	<.0001
	5396	5378	5378	5366	5344	5396	5378	5366	5344	5249
MAN17	-0.39623	-0.37716	-0.27371	-0.43713	0.2277	0.2872	0.34626	0.4522	-0.07145	-0.20279
	<.0001	<.0001	<.0001	<.0001	<.0001	<.0001	<.0001	<.0001	<.0001	<.0001
	5366	5366	5366	5366	5344	5366	5366	5366	5344	5249
MAN18	-0.02795	0.01682	0.09544	-0.02925	0.27185	-0.05982	-0.03048	0.00982	-0.22162	-0.30794
	0.0411	0.2191	<.0001	0.0325	<.0001	<.0001	0.0259	0.473	<.0001	<.0001
	5344	5344	5344	5344	5345	5344	5344	5344	5345	5250
MAN19	-0.15087	-0.1201	-0.0495	-0.15075	0.11284	0.10405	0.12353	0.15799	-0.09692	-0.28765
	<.0001	<.0001	0.0003	<.0001	<.0001	<.0001	<.0001	<.0001	<.0001	<.0001
	5249	5249	5249	5249	5250	5249	5249	5249	5250	5252
MAN20	-0.32975	-0.33422	-0.24744	-0.32132	0.1555	0.34881	0.35412	0.46429	0.04537	-0.06923
	<.0001	<.0001	<.0001	<.0001	<.0001	<.0001	<.0001	<.0001	0.001	<.0001
	5243	5243	5243	5243	5244	5243	5243	5243	5244	5244

MAN11	MAN12	MAN13	MAN14	MAN15	MAN16	MAN17	MAN18	MAN19	MAN20	MAN11
-0.2919	-0.41302	-0.10471	0.06343	-0.35089	-0.18115	-0.39623	-0.02795	-0.15087	-0.32975	-0.2919
<.0001	<.0001	<.0001	<.0001	<.0001	<.0001	<.0001	0.0411	<.0001	<.0001	<.0001
5396	5366	5344	5250	5243	5396	5366	5344	5249	5243	5396
-0.26789	-0.42892	-0.13345	0.06393	-0.3544	-0.16373	-0.37716	0.01682	-0.1201	-0.33422	-0.26789
<.0001	<.0001	<.0001	<.0001	<.0001	<.0001	<.0001	0.2191	<.0001	<.0001	<.0001
5378	5366	5344	5250	5243	5378	5366	5344	5249	5243	5378
-0.16097	-0.34202	-0.17475	0.08543	-0.26648	-0.0878	-0.27371	0.09544	-0.0495	-0.24744	-0.16097
<.0001	<.0001	<.0001	<.0001	<.0001	<.0001	<.0001	<.0001	0.0003	<.0001	<.0001
5378	5366	5344	5250	5243	5378	5366	5344	5249	5243	5378
-0.24634	-0.42548	-0.11047	0.06563	-0.33257	-0.18371	-0.43713	-0.02925	-0.15075	-0.32132	-0.24634
<.0001	<.0001	<.0001	<.0001	<.0001	<.0001	<.0001	0.0325	<.0001	<.0001	<.0001
5366	5366	5344	5250	5243	5366	5366	5344	5249	5243	5366
0.16272	0.12055	-0.09782	0.04031	0.11636	0.17269	0.2277	0.27185	0.11284	0.1555	0.16272
<.0001	<.0001	<.0001	0.0035	<.0001	<.0001	<.0001	<.0001	<.0001	<.0001	<.0001
5344	5344	5345	5251	5244	5344	5344	5345	5250	5244	5344
0.25488	0.47636	0.27682	-0.00768	0.39802	0.19351	0.2872	-0.05982	0.10405	0.34881	0.25488
<.0001	<.0001	<.0001	0.578	<.0001	<.0001	<.0001	<.0001	<.0001	<.0001	<.0001
5396	5366	5344	5250	5243	5396	5366	5344	5249	5243	5396
0.27255	0.46835	0.25721	-0.01719	0.3895	0.16347	0.34626	-0.03048	0.12353	0.35412	0.27255
<.0001	<.0001	<.0001	0.2131	<.0001	<.0001	<.0001	0.0259	<.0001	<.0001	<.0001
5378	5366	5344	5250	5243	5378	5366	5344	5249	5243	5378
0.32127	0.6275	0.23181	-0.01676	0.47935	0.20892	0.4522	0.00982	0.15799	0.46429	0.32127
<.0001	<.0001	<.0001	0.2248	<.0001	<.0001	<.0001	0.473	<.0001	<.0001	<.0001
5366	5366	5344	5250	5243	5366	5366	5344	5249	5243	5366
-0.01218	0.08177	0.39835	0.03581	0.06395	-0.0602	-0.07145	-0.22162	-0.09692	0.04537	-0.01218
0.3735	<.0001	<.0001	0.0095	<.0001	<.0001	<.0001	<.0001	<.0001	0.001	0.3735
5344	5344	5344	5251	5244	5344	5344	5345	5250	5244	5344
-0.12193	-0.04153	0.2127	-0.04925	-0.01491	-0.16258	-0.20279	-0.30794	-0.28765	-0.06923	-0.12193
<.0001	0.0026	<.0001	0.0004	0.2804	<.0001	<.0001	<.0001	<.0001	<.0001	<.0001
5249	5249	5250	5252	5244	5249	5249	5250	5252	5244	5249
1	0.32801	0.07514	0.08437	0.304	0.29553	0.35173	0.18889	0.12459	0.28305	1
	<.0001	<.0001	<.0001	<.0001	<.0001	<.0001	<.0001	<.0001	<.0001	
5396	5366	5344	5250	5243	5396	5366	5344	5249	5243	5396
0.32801	1	0.18731	0.00132	0.4485	0.27034	0.49852	0.09522	0.18453	0.42452	0.32801
<.0001		<.0001	0.9235	<.0001	<.0001	<.0001	<.0001	<.0001	<.0001	<.0001
5366	5366	5344	5250	5243	5366	5366	5344	5249	5243	5366
0.07514	0.18731	1	0.04448	0.19215	0.01772	0.07897	-0.18357	-0.03649	0.15846	0.07514
<.0001	<.0001		0.0013	<.0001	0.1952	<.0001	<.0001	0.0082	<.0001	<.0001
5344	5344	5345	5251	5244	5344	5344	5345	5250	5244	5344
0.08437	0.00132	0.04448	1	0.0385	0.01428	0.00734	0.12289	-0.24131	0.03503	0.08437
<.0001	0.9235	0.0013		0.0053	0.3008	0.5947	<.0001	<.0001	0.0112	<.0001
5250	5250	5251	5253	5244	5250	5250	5251	5252	5244	5250
0.304	0.4485	0.19215	0.0385	1	0.18041	0.36016	0.04736	0.14822	0.59046	0.304
<.0001	<.0001	<.0001	0.0053		<.0001	<.0001	0.0006	<.0001	<.0001	<.0001
5243	5243	5244	5244	5244	5243	5243	5244	5244	5244	5243
0.29553	0.27034	0.01772	0.01428	0.18041	1	0.31206	0.19389	0.16528	0.19162	0.29553
<.0001	<.0001	0.1952	0.3008	<.0001		<.0001	<.0001	<.0001	<.0001	<.0001
5396	5366	5344	5250	5243	5396	5366	5344	5249	5243	5396
0.35173	0.49852	0.07897	0.00734	0.36016	0.31206	1	0.23928	0.24231	0.37988	0.35173
<.0001	<.0001	<.0001	0.5947	<.0001	<.0001		<.0001	<.0001	<.0001	<.0001
5366	5366	5344	5250	5243	5366	5366	5344	5249	5243	5366
0.18889	0.09522	-0.18357	0.12289	0.04736	0.19389	0.23928	1	0.21218	0.09519	0.18889
<.0001	<.0001	<.0001	<.0001	0.0006	<.0001	<.0001		<.0001	<.0001	<.0001
5344	5344	5345	5251	5244	5344	5344	5345	5250	5244	5344
0.12459	0.18453	-0.03649	-0.24131	0.14822	0.16528	0.24231	0.21218	1	0.17994	0.12459
<.0001	<.0001	0.0082	<.0001	<.0001	<.0001	<.0001	<.0001		<.0001	<.0001
5249	5249	5250	5252	5244	5249	5249	5250	5252	5244	5249
0.28305	0.42452	0.15846	0.03503	0.59046	0.19162	0.37988	0.09519	0.17994	1	0.28305
<.0001	<.0001	<.0001	0.0112	<.0001	<.0001	<.0001	<.0001	<.0001		<.0001
5243	5243	5244	5244	5244	5243	5243	5244	5244	5244	5243

Pearson Correlation Coefficients, adult respondents
Prob > |r| under H0: Rho=0
Number of Observations

	MAF1	MAF2	MAF3	MAF4	MAF5	MAF6	MAF7	MAF8	MAF9	MAF10
MAN1	0.53824	0.32281	0.23955	0.26143	-0.21458	-0.17639	-0.03887	-0.22943	0.18079	0.18409
	<.0001	<.0001	<.0001	<.0001	<.0001	<.0001	0.0044	<.0001	<.0001	<.0001
	5396	5378	5377	5366	5344	5396	5378	5366	5344	5249
MAN2	0.30769	0.34913	0.29871	0.27841	-0.17629	-0.18598	-0.04847	-0.25939	0.13516	0.13607
	<.0001	<.0001	<.0001	<.0001	<.0001	<.0001	0.0004	<.0001	<.0001	<.0001
	5378	5378	5377	5366	5344	5378	5378	5366	5344	5249
MAN3	0.18606	0.21099	0.31873	0.17944	-0.11314	-0.15347	-0.04587	-0.20412	0.0567	0.0608
	<.0001	<.0001	<.0001	<.0001	<.0001	<.0001	0.0008	<.0001	<.0001	<.0001
	5378	5378	5377	5366	5344	5378	5378	5366	5344	5249
MAN4	0.27117	0.24744	0.22257	0.37175	-0.19381	-0.13769	-0.03572	-0.24181	0.16494	0.17239
	<.0001	<.0001	<.0001	<.0001	<.0001	<.0001	0.0089	<.0001	<.0001	<.0001
	5366	5366	5366	5366	5344	5366	5366	5366	5344	5249
MAN5	-0.15536	-0.1639	-0.08632	-0.12448	0.60043	0.08055	0.02762	0.16199	-0.17224	-0.15643
	<.0001	<.0001	<.0001	<.0001	<.0001	<.0001	0.0434	<.0001	<.0001	<.0001
	5344	5344	5344	5344	5345	5344	5344	5344	5345	5250
MAN6	-0.10614	-0.08927	-0.13787	-0.08605	0.10507	0.57111	0.14545	0.23785	0.01967	-0.01195
	<.0001	<.0001	<.0001	<.0001	<.0001	<.0001	<.0001	<.0001	0.1504	0.3866
	5396	5378	5377	5366	5344	5396	5378	5366	5344	5249
MAN7	-0.1471	-0.15299	-0.15621	-0.12212	0.15989	0.26779	0.31374	0.2867	-0.00423	-0.06359
	<.0001	<.0001	<.0001	<.0001	<.0001	<.0001	<.0001	<.0001	0.7571	<.0001
	5378	5378	5377	5366	5344	5378	5378	5366	5344	5249
MAN8	-0.19923	-0.20054	-0.23534	-0.20861	0.2079	0.28268	0.1503	0.51763	-0.05818	-0.09212
	<.0001	<.0001	<.0001	<.0001	<.0001	<.0001	<.0001	<.0001	<.0001	<.0001
	5366	5366	5366	5366	5344	5366	5366	5366	5344	5249
MAN9	0.15628	0.19381	0.1414	0.14602	-0.12388	-0.0039	0.10135	-0.03707	0.60797	0.18454
	<.0001	<.0001	<.0001	<.0001	<.0001	0.7754	<.0001	0.0067	<.0001	<.0001
	5344	5344	5344	5344	5345	5344	5344	5344	5345	5250
MAN10	0.18123	0.17175	0.07815	0.16217	-0.13343	-0.01393	0.02295	-0.09058	0.23999	0.62228
	<.0001	<.0001	<.0001	<.0001	<.0001	0.313	0.0963	<.0001	<.0001	<.0001
	5249	5249	5249	5249	5250	5249	5249	5249	5250	5252
MAN11	-0.21719	-0.20126	-0.15781	-0.16187	0.19502	0.23361	0.06927	0.26466	-0.1008	-0.1375
	<.0001	<.0001	<.0001	<.0001	<.0001	<.0001	<.0001	<.0001	<.0001	<.0001
	5396	5378	5377	5366	5344	5396	5378	5366	5344	5249
MAN12	-0.19833	-0.17746	-0.19862	-0.17497	0.19869	0.29648	0.1367	0.36399	-0.06802	-0.12884
	<.0001	<.0001	<.0001	<.0001	<.0001	<.0001	<.0001	<.0001	<.0001	<.0001
	5366	5366	5366	5366	5344	5366	5366	5366	5344	5249
MAN13	0.02394	0.06967	0.03629	0.07073	-0.02808	0.11627	0.08622	0.06517	0.25836	0.12321
	0.0802	<.0001	0.008	<.0001	0.0401	<.0001	<.0001	<.0001	<.0001	<.0001
	5344	5344	5344	5344	5345	5344	5344	5344	5345	5250
MAN14	0.04109	-0.00213	0.01467	0.02305	0.04602	0.01667	0.01619	0.04228	0.03976	-0.04418
	0.0029	0.8771	0.288	0.0949	0.0009	0.2271	0.2409	0.0022	0.004	0.0014
	5250	5250	5250	5250	5251	5250	5250	5250	5251	5252
MAN15	-0.20923	-0.20727	-0.19355	-0.16871	0.1995	0.31582	0.11516	0.35269	-0.06025	-0.07033
	<.0001	<.0001	<.0001	<.0001	<.0001	<.0001	<.0001	<.0001	<.0001	<.0001
	5243	5243	5243	5243	5244	5243	5243	5243	5244	5244
MAN16	-0.13068	-0.11744	-0.06453	-0.08926	0.14352	0.21819	0.08752	0.17034	-0.08402	-0.13379
	<.0001	<.0001	<.0001	<.0001	<.0001	<.0001	<.0001	<.0001	<.0001	<.0001
	5396	5378	5377	5366	5344	5396	5378	5366	5344	5249
MAN17	-0.26423	-0.24146	-0.19219	-0.2584	0.27035	0.2341	0.07495	0.33266	-0.18364	-0.21172
	<.0001	<.0001	<.0001	<.0001	<.0001	<.0001	<.0001	<.0001	<.0001	<.0001
	5366	5366	5366	5366	5344	5366	5366	5366	5344	5249
MAN18	-0.07599	-0.08554	-0.06101	-0.09354	0.14882	0.06001	0.01186	0.09696	-0.15121	-0.18412
	<.0001	<.0001	<.0001	<.0001	<.0001	<.0001	0.3859	<.0001	<.0001	<.0001
	5344	5344	5344	5344	5345	5344	5344	5344	5345	5250
MAN19	-0.09148	-0.09207	-0.09591	-0.07975	0.12332	0.09627	0.05686	0.11925	-0.1128	-0.23455
	<.0001	<.0001	<.0001	<.0001	<.0001	<.0001	<.0001	<.0001	<.0001	<.0001
	5249	5249	5249	5249	5250	5249	5249	5249	5250	5252
MAN20	-0.18399	-0.16053	-0.18319	-0.15325	0.21603	0.25661	0.11002	0.31619	-0.06251	-0.11155
	<.0001	<.0001	<.0001	<.0001	<.0001	<.0001	<.0001	<.0001	<.0001	<.0001
	5243	5243	5243	5243	5244	5243	5243	5243	5244	5244

	MAF11	MAF12	MAF13	MAF14	MAF15	MAF16	MAF17	MAF18	MAF19	MAF20
MAN1	-0.29097	-0.26652	0.07366	0.04148	-0.30228	-0.29748	-0.32607	-0.13778	-0.11759	-0.29539
	<.0001	<.0001	<.0001	0.0026	<.0001	<.0001	<.0001	<.0001	<.0001	<.0001
	5396	5366	5344	5250	5243	5396	5366	5344	5250	5243
MAN2	-0.26323	-0.2799	0.04801	0.03877	-0.30672	-0.30629	-0.32774	-0.13816	-0.12178	-0.28875
	<.0001	<.0001	0.0004	0.005	<.0001	<.0001	<.0001	<.0001	<.0001	<.0001
	5378	5366	5344	5250	5243	5378	5366	5344	5250	5243
MAN3	-0.16471	-0.22749	-0.02457	0.05602	-0.23305	-0.22262	-0.24839	-0.07368	-0.06164	-0.22847
	<.0001	<.0001	0.0725	<.0001	<.0001	<.0001	<.0001	<.0001	<.0001	<.0001
	5378	5366	5344	5250	5243	5378	5366	5344	5250	5243
MAN4	-0.24895	-0.28384	0.04948	0.04329	-0.27496	-0.25582	-0.35582	-0.13897	-0.11395	-0.26351
	<.0001	<.0001	0.0003	0.0017	<.0001	<.0001	<.0001	<.0001	<.0001	<.0001
	5366	5366	5344	5250	5243	5366	5366	5344	5250	5243
MAN5	0.15013	0.15843	-0.12609	0.03057	0.13365	0.14494	0.19528	0.16254	0.07777	0.16211
	<.0001	<.0001	<.0001	0.0267	<.0001	<.0001	<.0001	<.0001	<.0001	<.0001
	5344	5344	5345	5251	5244	5344	5344	5345	5251	5244
MAN6	0.22319	0.30238	0.10544	0.02318	0.33386	0.29954	0.23575	0.10695	0.10921	0.31169
	<.0001	<.0001	<.0001	0.0931	<.0001	<.0001	<.0001	<.0001	<.0001	<.0001
	5396	5366	5344	5250	5243	5396	5366	5344	5250	5243
MAN7	0.23401	0.30819	0.09964	0.00053	0.33137	0.26855	0.30227	0.14525	0.11957	0.31744
	<.0001	<.0001	<.0001	0.9697	<.0001	<.0001	<.0001	<.0001	<.0001	<.0001
	5378	5366	5344	5250	5243	5378	5366	5344	5250	5243
MAN8	0.30142	0.47185	0.05588	0.01664	0.42394	0.35031	0.40753	0.19059	0.15918	0.41804
	<.0001	<.0001	<.0001	0.2279	<.0001	<.0001	<.0001	<.0001	<.0001	<.0001
	5366	5366	5344	5250	5243	5366	5366	5344	5250	5243
MAN9	-0.03609	-0.03693	0.4122	0.07038	0.00915	-0.0543	-0.08267	-0.06287	-0.06068	0.01429
	0.0083	0.0069	<.0001	<.0001	0.5078	<.0001	<.0001	<.0001	<.0001	0.3007
	5344	5344	5345	5251	5244	5344	5344	5345	5251	5244
MAN10	-0.1229	-0.08637	0.19831	-0.01975	-0.03952	-0.08527	-0.17417	-0.16002	-0.19409	-0.06019
	<.0001	<.0001	<.0001	0.1525	0.0042	<.0001	<.0001	<.0001	<.0001	<.0001
	5249	5249	5250	5252	5244	5249	5249	5250	5252	5244
MAN11	0.56388	0.29751	-0.02739	0.07097	0.27532	0.40173	0.28787	0.19375	0.12534	0.26237
	<.0001	<.0001	0.0452	<.0001	<.0001	<.0001	<.0001	<.0001	<.0001	<.0001
	5396	5366	5344	5250	5243	5396	5366	5344	5250	5243
MAN12	0.28611	0.63539	0.03099	0.01259	0.40262	0.33571	0.42612	0.19661	0.16968	0.37479
	<.0001	<.0001	0.0235	0.3616	<.0001	<.0001	<.0001	<.0001	<.0001	<.0001
	5366	5366	5344	5250	5243	5366	5366	5344	5250	5243
MAN13	0.04128	0.07672	0.51612	0.06012	0.14455	0.05712	0.05054	-0.02026	-0.00677	0.13432
	0.0025	<.0001	<.0001	<.0001	<.0001	<.0001	0.0002	0.1386	0.6239	<.0001
	5344	5344	5345	5251	5244	5344	5344	5345	5251	5244
MAN14	0.06489	0.02437	0.03665	0.7161	0.04691	0.05392	0.02207	0.09526	-0.145	0.04416
	<.0001	0.0775	0.0079	<.0001	0.0007	<.0001	0.1098	<.0001	<.0001	0.0014
	5250	5250	5251	5253	5244	5250	5250	5251	5253	5244
MAN15	0.27662	0.38475	0.03721	0.05406	0.7857	0.32045	0.32919	0.15026	0.15564	0.53202
	<.0001	<.0001	0.007	<.0001	<.0001	<.0001	<.0001	<.0001	<.0001	<.0001
	5243	5243	5244	5244	5244	5243	5243	5244	5244	5244
MAN16	0.21406	0.21592	-0.01193	0.00378	0.16934	0.34185	0.23525	0.14148	0.12495	0.16583
	<.0001	<.0001	0.3833	0.7841	<.0001	<.0001	<.0001	<.0001	<.0001	<.0001
	5396	5366	5344	5250	5243	5396	5366	5344	5250	5243
MAN17	0.32771	0.42187	-0.05648	0.01493	0.34162	0.36426	0.65064	0.26433	0.19418	0.33672
	<.0001	<.0001	<.0001	0.2795	<.0001	<.0001	<.0001	<.0001	<.0001	<.0001
	5366	5366	5344	5250	5243	5366	5366	5344	5250	5243
MAN18	0.14084	0.14366	-0.16887	0.09344	0.0788	0.14507	0.18482	0.53229	0.15537	0.10322
	<.0001	<.0001	<.0001	<.0001	<.0001	<.0001	<.0001	<.0001	<.0001	<.0001
	5344	5344	5345	5251	5244	5344	5344	5345	5251	5244
MAN19	0.13186	0.16658	-0.07716	-0.18516	0.14638	0.15184	0.22593	0.19786	0.65951	0.16188
	<.0001	<.0001	<.0001	<.0001	<.0001	<.0001	<.0001	<.0001	<.0001	<.0001
	5249	5249	5250	5252	5244	5249	5249	5250	5252	5244
MAN20	0.26452	0.34564	0.0259	0.04343	0.52408	0.31139	0.34096	0.18772	0.17831	0.80349
	<.0001	<.0001	0.0607	0.0017	<.0001	<.0001	<.0001	<.0001	<.0001	<.0001
	5243	5243	5244	5244	5244	5243	5243	5244	5244	5244

	MAF21	MAF22	MAF23	MAF24	MAF25
MAN1	-0.10798	-0.16242	-0.00466	-0.16367	-0.1862
	<.0001	<.0001	0.7324	<.0001	<.0001
	5386	5386	5386	5386	5378
MAN2	-0.15159	-0.18962	-0.06258	-0.1877	-0.17948
	<.0001	<.0001	<.0001	<.0001	<.0001
	5378	5378	5378	5378	5378
MAN3	-0.11936	-0.14141	-0.09216	-0.11975	-0.13284
	<.0001	<.0001	<.0001	<.0001	<.0001
	5378	5378	5378	5378	5378
MAN4	-0.08733	-0.14161	0.00795	-0.13153	-0.14561
	<.0001	<.0001	0.5603	<.0001	<.0001
	5366	5366	5366	5366	5366
MAN5	0.08101	0.1079	0.022	0.11793	0.15505
	<.0001	<.0001	0.1078	<.0001	<.0001
	5344	5344	5344	5344	5344
MAN6	0.16493	0.18526	0.13657	0.15232	0.12852
	<.0001	<.0001	<.0001	<.0001	<.0001
	5386	5386	5386	5386	5378
MAN7	0.16899	0.18799	0.09443	0.17357	0.25966
	<.0001	<.0001	<.0001	<.0001	<.0001
	5378	5378	5378	5378	5378
MAN8	0.1908	0.22789	0.11868	0.20301	0.19957
	<.0001	<.0001	<.0001	<.0001	<.0001
	5366	5366	5366	5366	5366
MAN9	-0.01238	-0.02305	0.02154	-0.02982	-0.07756
	0.3656	0.092	0.1154	0.0292	<.0001
	5344	5344	5344	5344	5344
MAN10	-0.01308	-0.03231	0.09458	-0.00312	-0.08055
	0.3433	0.0192	<.0001	0.8214	<.0001
	5249	5249	5249	5249	5249
MAN11	0.1475	0.18757	0.09384	0.16924	0.19274
	<.0001	<.0001	<.0001	<.0001	<.0001
	5386	5386	5386	5386	5378
MAN12	0.13837	0.19116	0.07776	0.19741	0.15074
	<.0001	<.0001	<.0001	<.0001	<.0001
	5366	5366	5366	5366	5366
MAN13	0.03146	0.03942	0.04886	0.03333	-0.01366
	0.0215	0.0039	0.0004	0.0148	0.3181
	5344	5344	5344	5344	5344
MAN14	0.034	0.03905	0.11371	0.0412	0.02208
	0.0138	0.0047	<.0001	0.0028	0.1096
	5250	5250	5250	5250	5250
MAN15	0.18292	0.23165	0.12214	0.19779	0.19334
	<.0001	<.0001	<.0001	<.0001	<.0001
	5243	5243	5243	5243	5243
MAN16	0.06736	0.08833	-0.00043	0.09908	0.11666
	<.0001	<.0001	0.9745	<.0001	<.0001
	5386	5386	5386	5386	5378
MAN17	0.13239	0.19918	0.04161	0.19703	0.20543
	<.0001	<.0001	0.0023	<.0001	<.0001
	5366	5366	5366	5366	5366
MAN18	0.04646	0.08892	0.02116	0.07593	0.06596
	0.0007	<.0001	0.122	<.0001	<.0001
	5344	5344	5344	5344	5344
MAN19	0.06575	0.09933	-0.03315	0.07716	0.06573
	<.0001	<.0001	0.0163	<.0001	<.0001
	5249	5249	5249	5249	5249
MAN20	0.14678	0.19034	0.08838	0.17394	0.16319
	<.0001	<.0001	<.0001	<.0001	<.0001
	5243	5243	5243	5243	5243

Internal consistencies, adult respondents, Institutional Secularisation, factual level

Cronbach Coefficient Alpha

Variables	Alpha
Raw	0.687969
Standardised	0.691715

Cronbach Coefficient Alpha with Deleted Variable

Deleted variable	Raw Variables		Standardised Variables	
	Correlation with Total	Alpha	Correlation with Total	Alpha
MAF1	0.472843	0.622469	0.477423	0.625573
MAF2	0.567576	0.562354	0.568404	0.565853
MAF3	0.42547	0.655639	0.426376	0.657535
MAF4	0.429171	0.649665	0.431964	0.65409

Pearson Correlation Coefficients
Prob > |r| under H0: Rho=0
Number of Observations

	MAF1	MAF2	MAF3	MAF4
MAF1	1	0.44923	0.28927	0.34454
		<.0001	<.0001	<.0001
	5396	5378	5377	5366
MAF2	0.44923	1	0.42135	0.37696
	<.0001		<.0001	<.0001
	5378	5378	5377	5366
MAF3	0.28927	0.42135	1	0.2748
	<.0001	<.0001		<.0001
	5377	5377	5377	5366
MAF4	0.34454	0.37696	0.2748	1
	<.0001	<.0001	<.0001	
	5366	5366	5366	5366

Internal consistencies, adult respondents, Institutional Secularisation, normative level

Cronbach Coefficient Alpha

Variables	Alpha
Raw	0.775606
Standardised	0.788714

Cronbach Coefficient Alpha with Deleted Variable

Deleted variable	Raw Variables			Standardised Variables	
	Correlation with Total	Alpha		Correlation with Total	Alpha
MAN1	0.58451	0.725257		0.595406	0.73732
MAN2	0.650145	0.683932		0.658481	0.704905
MAN3	0.52123	0.772363		0.519266	0.774857
MAN4	0.608857	0.708846		0.616145	0.726795

Pearson Correlation Coefficients
Prob > |r| under H0: Rho=0
Number of Observations

	MAN1	MAN2	MAN3	MAN4
MAN1	1	0.55064	0.38787	0.50776
		<.0001	<.0001	<.0001
	5396	5378	5378	5366
MAN2	0.55064	1	0.47146	0.54444
	<.0001		<.0001	<.0001
	5378	5378	5378	5366
MAN3	0.38787	0.47146	1	0.43423
	<.0001	<.0001		<.0001
	5378	5378	5378	5366
MAN4	0.50776	0.54444	0.43423	1
	<.0001	<.0001	<.0001	
	5366	5366	5366	5366

Internal consistencies, adult respondents, Institutional Reconfessionalisation, factual level

Cronbach Coefficient Alpha

Variables	Alpha
Raw	0.331403
Standardised	0.332871

Cronbach Coefficient Alpha with Deleted Variable

Deleted variable	Raw Variables		Standardised Variables	
	Correlation with Total	Alpha	Correlation with Total	Alpha
MAF6	0.212429	0.241918	0.233607	0.220363
MAF7	0.219691	0.223696	0.22648	0.226894
MAF8	0.144769	0.297228	0.153249	0.291899
MAF9	0.146841	0.295755	0.125771	0.315326
MAF10	0.085751	0.348468	0.073293	0.358647

Pearson Correlation Coefficients
Prob > |r| under H0: Rho=0
Number of Observations

	MAF6	MAF7	MAF8	MAF9	MAF10
MAF6	1	0.17317	0.36689	-0.02412	-0.00456
		<.0001	<.0001	0.0779	0.741
	5396	5378	5366	5344	5249
MAF7	0.17317	1	0.16807	0.13665	0.01934
	<.0001		<.0001	<.0001	0.1613
	5378	5378	5366	5344	5249
MAF8	0.36689	0.16807	1	-0.08475	-0.10341
	<.0001	<.0001		<.0001	<.0001
	5366	5366	5366	5344	5249
MAF9	-0.02412	0.13665	-0.08475	1	0.26009
	0.0779	<.0001	<.0001		<.0001
	5344	5344	5344	5345	5250
MAF10	-0.00456	0.01934	-0.10341	0.26009	1
	0.741	0.1613	<.0001	<.0001	
	5249	5249	5249	5250	5252

Internal consistencies, adult respondents, Institutional Reconfessionalisation, normative level

Cronbach Coefficient Alpha

Variables	Alpha
Raw	0.617242
Standardised	0.624504

Cronbach Coefficient Alpha with Deleted Variable

Deleted variable	Raw Variables		Standardised Variables	
	Correlation with Total	Alpha	Correlation with Total	Alpha
MAN6	0.496471	0.49156	0.515219	0.498401
MAN7	0.476514	0.51183	0.488334	0.513037
MAN8	0.461323	0.523638	0.468411	0.52373
MAN9	0.301659	0.603037	0.297958	0.610058
MAN10	0.165044	0.661743	0.15204	0.676946

Pearson Correlation Coefficients
Prob > |r| under H0: Rho=0
Number of Observations

	MAN6	MAN7	MAN8	MAN9	MAN10
MAN6	1	0.47535	0.52329	0.1993	0.10422
		<.0001	<.0001	<.0001	<.0001
	5396	5378	5366	5344	5249
MAN7	0.47535	1	0.53933	0.19261	0.03788
	<.0001		<.0001	<.0001	0.0061
	5378	5378	5366	5344	5249
MAN8	0.52329	0.53933	1	0.13276	0.00686
	<.0001	<.0001		<.0001	0.6192
	5366	5366	5366	5344	5249
MAN9	0.1993	0.19261	0.13276	1	0.28443
	<.0001	<.0001	<.0001		<.0001
	5344	5344	5344	5345	5250
MAN10	0.10422	0.03788	0.00686	0.28443	1
	<.0001	0.0061	0.6192	<.0001	
	5249	5249	5249	5250	5252

Internal consistencies, adult respondents, Christian Values Education, factual level

Cronbach Coefficient Alpha

Variables	Alpha
Raw	0.330491
Standardised	0.406967

Cronbach Coefficient Alpha with Deleted Variable

Deleted variable	Raw Variables		Standardised Variables	
	Correlation with Total	Alpha	Correlation with Total	Alpha
MAF11	0.234863	0.227457	0.285155	0.292253
MAF12	0.2876	0.187808	0.34704	0.240521
MAF13	0.005853	0.45588	0.002864	0.499899
MAF14	0.067416	0.372623	0.067229	0.456445
MAF15	0.33289	0.162282	0.37992	0.212069

Pearson Correlation Coefficients
Prob > |r| under H0: Rho=0
Number of Observations

	MAF11	MAF12	MAF13	MAF14	MAF15
MAF11	1	0.32539	-0.04308	0.04763	0.31548
		<.0001	0.0016	0.0006	<.0001
	5396	5366	5344	5250	5243
MAF12	0.32539	1	-0.01087	0.02508	0.42708
	<.0001		0.4268	0.0692	<.0001
	5366	5366	5344	5250	5243
MAF13	-0.04308	-0.01087	1	0.03413	0.02707
	0.0016	0.4268		0.0134	0.05
	5344	5344	5345	5251	5244
MAF14	0.04763	0.02508	0.03413	1	0.05896
	0.0006	0.0692	0.0134		<.0001
	5250	5250	5251	5253	5244
MAF15	0.31548	0.42708	0.02707	0.05896	1
	<.0001	<.0001	0.05	<.0001	
	5243	5243	5244	5244	5244

Internal consistencies, adult respondents, Christian Values Education, normative level

Cronbach Coefficient Alpha

Variables	Alpha
Raw	0.452283
Standardised	0.506622

Cronbach Coefficient Alpha with Deleted Variable

Deleted variable	Raw Variables		Standardised Variables	
	Correlation with Total	Alpha	Correlation with Total	Alpha
MAN11	0.296383	0.367671	0.327967	0.417666
MAN12	0.365838	0.310739	0.412392	0.359614
MAN13	0.190806	0.449806	0.197136	0.501222
MAN14	0.062454	0.535602	0.063434	0.578996
MAN15	0.394725	0.31643	0.421474	0.353169

Pearson Correlation Coefficients
Prob > |r| under H0: Rho=0
Number of Observations

	MAN11	MAN12	MAN13	MAN14	MAN15
MAN11	1	0.32801	0.07514	0.08437	0.304
		<.0001	<.0001	<.0001	<.0001
	5396	5366	5344	5250	5243
MAN12	0.32801	1	0.18731	0.00132	0.4485
	<.0001		<.0001	0.9235	<.0001
	5366	5366	5344	5250	5243
MAN13	0.07514	0.18731	1	0.04448	0.19215
	<.0001	<.0001		0.0013	<.0001
	5344	5344	5345	5251	5244
MAN14	0.08437	0.00132	0.04448	1	0.0385
	<.0001	0.9235	0.0013		0.0053
	5250	5250	5251	5253	5244
MAN15	0.304	0.4485	0.19215	0.0385	1
	<.0001	<.0001	<.0001	0.0053	
	5243	5243	5244	5244	5244

Internal consistencies, adult respondents, Recontextualisation, factual level

Cronbach Coefficient Alpha

Variables	Alpha
Raw	0.675729
Standardised	0.686939

Cronbach Coefficient Alpha with Deleted Variable

Deleted variable	Raw Variables		Standardised Variables	
	Correlation with Total	Alpha	Correlation with Total	Alpha
MAF16	0.484759	0.602092	0.496565	0.612484
MAF17	0.535916	0.582777	0.545621	0.590186
MAF18	0.403184	0.63923	0.402117	0.653682
MAF19	0.344269	0.670017	0.341828	0.678817
MAF20	0.416479	0.631259	0.426409	0.643301

Pearson Correlation Coefficients
Prob > |r| under H0: Rho=0
Number of Observations

	MAF16	MAF17	MAF18	MAF19	MAF20
MAF16	1	0.46678	0.29487	0.23306	0.35597
		<.0001	<.0001	<.0001	<.0001
	5396	5366	5344	5250	5243
MAF17	0.46678	1	0.33363	0.26919	0.39208
	<.0001		<.0001	<.0001	<.0001
	5366	5366	5344	5250	5243
MAF18	0.29487	0.33363	1	0.26702	0.23093
	<.0001	<.0001		<.0001	<.0001
	5344	5344	5345	5251	5244
MAF19	0.23306	0.26919	0.26702	1	0.2065
	<.0001	<.0001	<.0001		<.0001
	5250	5250	5251	5253	5244
MAF20	0.35597	0.39208	0.23093	0.2065	1
	<.0001	<.0001	<.0001	<.0001	
	5243	5243	5244	5244	5244

Internal consistencies, adult respondents, Recontextualisation, normative level

Cronbach Coefficient Alpha

Variables	Alpha
Raw	0.572585
Standardised	0.586747

Cronbach Coefficient Alpha with Deleted Variable

Deleted variable	Raw Variables		Standardised Variables	
	Correlation with Total	Alpha	Correlation with Total	Alpha
MAN16	0.324628	0.520697	0.33341	0.537022
MAN17	0.465625	0.454625	0.476078	0.455591
MAN18	0.283933	0.54573	0.281059	0.565083
MAN19	0.30548	0.537597	0.30614	0.551758
MAN20	0.311802	0.52804	0.32635	0.540862

Pearson Correlation Coefficients
Prob > |r| under H0: Rho=0
Number of Observations

	MAN16	MAN17	MAN18	MAN19	MAN20
MAN16	1	0.31206	0.19389	0.16528	0.19162
		<.0001	<.0001	<.0001	<.0001
	5396	5366	5344	5249	5243
MAN17	0.31206	1	0.23928	0.24231	0.37988
	<.0001		<.0001	<.0001	<.0001
	5366	5366	5344	5249	5243
MAN18	0.19389	0.23928	1	0.21218	0.09519
	<.0001	<.0001		<.0001	<.0001
	5344	5344	5345	5250	5244
MAN19	0.16528	0.24231	0.21218	1	0.17994
	<.0001	<.0001	<.0001		<.0001
	5249	5249	5250	5252	5244
MAN20	0.19162	0.37988	0.09519	0.17994	1
	<.0001	<.0001	<.0001	<.0001	
	5243	5243	5244	5244	5244

Internal consistencies, adult respondents, Confessional School, factual level

Cronbach Coefficient Alpha

Variables	Alpha
Raw	0.747188
Standardised	0.755562

Cronbach Coefficient Alpha with Deleted Variable

Deleted variable	Raw Variables		Standardised Variables	
	Correlation with Total	Alpha	Correlation with Total	Alpha
MAF21	0.576381	0.677874	0.580092	0.690644
MAF22	0.644273	0.659674	0.64699	0.665354
MAF23	0.454374	0.728195	0.453287	0.736182
MAF24	0.546437	0.695421	0.551425	0.701211
MAF25	0.384924	0.746273	0.389192	0.758039

Pearson Correlation Coefficients
Prob > |r| under H0: Rho=0
Number of Observations

	MAF21	MAF22	MAF23	MAF24	MAF25
MAF21	1	0.56251	0.38817	0.42083	0.29956
		<.0001	<.0001	<.0001	<.0001
	5386	5386	5386	5386	5378
MAF22	0.56251	1	0.38277	0.52971	0.35317
	<.0001		<.0001	<.0001	<.0001
	5386	5386	5386	5386	5378
MAF23	0.38817	0.38277	1	0.35132	0.2324
	<.0001	<.0001		<.0001	<.0001
	5386	5386	5386	5386	5378
MAF24	0.42083	0.52971	0.35132	1	0.29986
	<.0001	<.0001	<.0001		<.0001
	5386	5386	5386	5386	5378
MAF25	0.29956	0.35317	0.2324	0.29986	1
	<.0001	<.0001	<.0001	<.0001	
	5378	5378	5378	5378	5378

Factor analysis, adult respondents, factual level

Initial Factor Method: Principal Components
Prior Communality Estimates: ONE
Eigenvalues of the Correlation Matrix: Total = 24 Average = 1

	Eigenvalue	Difference	Proportion	Cumulative
1	6.10947286	4.03251754	0.2546	0.2546
2	2.07695532	0.51071203	0.0865	0.3411
3	1.56624329	0.34145506	0.0653	0.4064
4	1.22478822	0.02831768	0.051	0.4574
5	1.19647054	0.22528751	0.0499	0.5072
6	0.97118303	0.09616422	0.0405	0.5477
7	0.87501882	0.03287066	0.0365	0.5842
8	0.84214815	0.04156667	0.0351	0.6193
9	0.80058148	0.02001494	0.0334	0.6526
10	0.78056654	0.04958755	0.0325	0.6851
11	0.73097899	0.04536862	0.0305	0.7156
12	0.68561037	0.05073765	0.0286	0.7442
13	0.63487273	0.02411529	0.0265	0.7706
14	0.61075743	0.01225761	0.0254	0.7961
15	0.59849983	0.04114671	0.0249	0.821
16	0.55735312	0.01309436	0.0232	0.8442
17	0.54425876	0.02654327	0.0227	0.8669
18	0.51771549	0.0033902	0.0216	0.8885
19	0.5143253	0.02643348	0.0214	0.9099
20	0.48789181	0.02527584	0.0203	0.9302
21	0.46261597	0.03445855	0.0193	0.9495
22	0.42815742	0.03317061	0.0178	0.9674
23	0.39498681	0.0064391	0.0165	0.9838
24	0.38854771		0.0162	1

4 factors will be retained by the NFACTOR criterion.

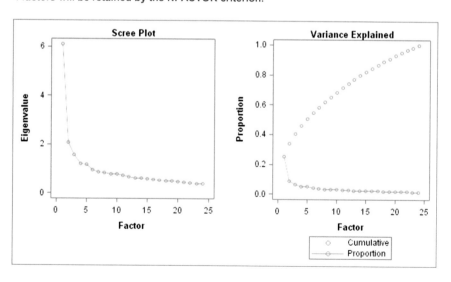

Eigenvectors

	1	2	3	4
MAF1	-0.21451	0.13375	0.17981	0.27597
MAF2	-0.25522	0.06238	0.27188	0.17194
MAF3	-0.21218	0.0301	0.22711	0.09387
MAF4	-0.19096	0.15548	0.19734	0.27206
MAF6	0.21795	0.18966	0.09522	-0.09997
MAF7	0.08514	0.18359	0.21407	-0.21422
MAF8	0.27008	0.05481	0.09466	-0.15361
MAF9	-0.10761	0.40675	0.26239	-0.11288
MAF10	-0.09929	0.3876	-0.05043	-0.19752
MAF11	0.23587	-0.05314	0.09746	0.00209
MAF12	0.26707	0.00228	0.22189	-0.10319
MAF13	-0.04171	0.38851	0.29062	-0.18237
MAF14	0.0042	0.05697	0.13552	0.48661
MAF15	0.24769	0.06154	0.243	-0.02894
MAF16	0.26581	-0.07101	0.15348	0.04076
MAF17	0.27009	-0.16056	0.18117	0.00434
MAF18	0.13971	-0.23355	0.2513	0.40064
MAF19	0.13021	-0.20327	0.19842	0.00762
MAF20	0.22961	-0.00655	0.32204	0.00752
MAF21	0.20834	0.26142	-0.21393	0.26895

Factor Pattern

	Factor1	Factor2	Factor3	Factor4
MAF17	0.66759	-0.23139	0.22673	0.0048
MAF8	0.66757	0.07898	0.11847	-0.17
MAF12	0.66012	0.00328	0.27769	-0.1142
MAF16	0.65702	-0.10234	0.19208	0.04511
MAF22	0.62549	0.31578	-0.24525	0.24218
MAF15	0.61223	0.08869	0.30412	-0.03203
MAF11	0.583	-0.07658	0.12198	0.00231
MAF24	0.57116	0.29234	-0.21582	0.21937
MAF20	0.56752	-0.00944	0.40303	0.00832
MAF25	0.55657	0.11455	-0.20152	-0.09489
MAF6	0.53871	0.27333	0.11916	-0.11063
MAF21	0.51497	0.37676	-0.26773	0.29765
MAF19	0.32184	-0.29295	0.24832	0.00844
MAF4	-0.47201	0.22407	0.24697	0.30109
MAF3	-0.52445	0.04338	0.28422	0.10389
MAF1	-0.53022	0.19276	0.22503	0.30542
MAF2	-0.63085	0.0899	0.34025	0.19028
MAF9	-0.26598	0.5862	0.32838	-0.12493
MAF13	-0.1031	0.55991	0.36371	-0.20183
MAF10	-0.24541	0.5586	-0.06312	-0.2186
MAF23	0.38147	0.48537	-0.2653	0.29175
MAF7	0.21045	0.26459	0.26791	-0.23708
MAF14	0.01038	0.0821	0.16961	0.53853
MAF18	0.34533	-0.33658	0.3145	0.44339

Variance Explained by Each Factor

Factor1	Factor2	Factor3	Factor4
6.1094729	2.0769553	1.5662433	1.2247882

Final Communality Estimates: Total = 10.977460

MAF1	MAF2	MAF3	MAF4	MAF6	MAF7	MAF8	MAF9	MAF10	MAF11
0.46220	0.55802	0.36850	0.42465	0.39135	0.24227	0.49482	0.53780	0.42402	0.36063

MAF12	MAF13	MAF14	MAF15	MAF16	MAF17	MAF18	MAF19	MAF20	MAF21
0.52591	0.49714	0.32563	0.47619	0.48107	0.55065	0.52804	0.25113	0.48467	0.56741

MAF22	MAF23	MAF24	MAF25
0.60975	0.53660	0.50639	0.37250

Rotation Method: Varimax

Orthogonal Transformation Matrix

	1	2	3	4
1	0.7297	0.5498	-0.39069	-0.11236
2	-0.19559	0.54438	0.17141	0.79751
3	0.65519	-0.45156	0.48326	0.36506
4	0.00259	0.44437	0.76449	-0.467

Rotated Factor Pattern

	Factor1	Factor2	Factor3	Factor4
MAF17	0.68096	0.14083	-0.18724	-0.17901
MAF20	0.68005	0.12859	-0.02221	0.07194
MAF12	0.66269	0.18858	-0.21044	0.08315
MAF15	0.62856	0.23332	-0.1015	0.12792
MAF16	0.62541	0.23883	-0.14692	-0.10638
MAF8	0.54886	0.28099	-0.31999	0.11062
MAF18	0.52503	0.06165	0.29835	-0.39948
MAF11	0.52032	0.22479	-0.18019	-0.08313
MAF19	0.45487	-0.09091	-0.04951	-0.18308
MAF6	0.41742	0.342	-0.19061	0.25262
MAF21	0.12743	0.74139	-0.03845	0.00586
MAF22	0.2346	0.73416	-0.12363	-0.02108
MAF23	0.01035	0.7234	0.02899	0.11112
MAF24	0.21876	0.66811	-0.10963	-0.01226
MAF25	0.25144	0.4172	-0.36774	-0.00043
MAF1	-0.27637	-0.15248	0.58243	0.15282
MAF4	-0.22566	-0.11526	0.57235	0.18128
MAF2	-0.25449	-0.36699	0.57177	0.17793
MAF14	0.10404	0.21312	0.50368	-0.12527
MAF3	-0.20468	-0.34691	0.42911	0.14876
MAF13	0.05303	-0.00581	0.15772	0.68514
MAF9	-0.09391	-0.03092	0.26758	0.6756
MAF10	-0.33025	0.10052	-0.00599	0.5521
MAF7	0.27673	0.03341	-0.08864	0.39589

Variance Explained by Each Factor

	Factor1	Factor2	Factor3	Factor4
	4.0048493	3.0235005	2.0751593	1.8739506

Factor analysis, adult respondents, normative level

Initial Factor Method: Principal Components
Prior Communality Estimates: ONE
Eigenvalues of the Correlation Matrix: Total = 19 Average = 1

	Eigenvalue	Difference	Proportion	Cumulative
1	5.63358466	3.42542252	0.2965	0.2965
2	2.20816214	0.86285069	0.1162	0.4127
3	1.34531145	0.2386012	0.0708	0.4835
4	1.10671025	0.18983153	0.0582	0.5418
5	0.91687872	0.08484	0.0483	0.59
6	0.83203872	0.11249823	0.0438	0.6338
7	0.71954049	0.02809488	0.0379	0.6717
8	0.69144561	0.03907538	0.0364	0.7081
9	0.65237022	0.03670367	0.0343	0.7424
10	0.61566655	0.03539352	0.0324	0.7748
11	0.58027303	0.00806745	0.0305	0.8054
12	0.57220558	0.03892592	0.0301	0.8355
13	0.53327966	0.02892261	0.0281	0.8636
14	0.50435705	0.02944458	0.0265	0.8901
15	0.47491247	0.02337214	0.025	0.9151
16	0.45154032	0.03409016	0.0238	0.9389
17	0.41745017	0.01594712	0.022	0.9608
18	0.40150305	0.05873315	0.0211	0.982
19	0.34276989		0.018	1

3 factors will be retained by the NFACTOR criterion.

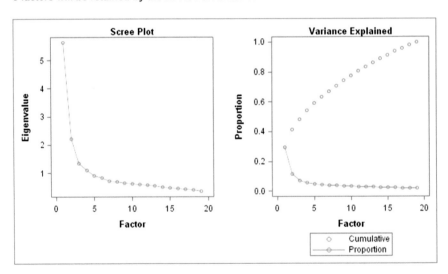

Eigenvectors

	1	2	3
MAN1	-0.28049	0.05332	0.22909
MAN2	-0.29712	-0.03297	0.24892
MAN3	-0.24085	-0.13419	0.283
MAN4	-0.28785	0.03461	0.24531
MAN6	0.27703	0.17994	0.05709
MAN7	0.28573	0.13897	0.02296
MAN8	0.33363	0.07478	0.01723
MAN9	0.05002	0.42997	0.19388
MAN10	-0.03762	0.45718	0.03846
MAN11	0.20776	-0.15393	0.26916
MAN12	0.31544	-0.0087	0.08622
MAN13	0.12352	0.36736	0.21181
MAN14	-0.01327	-0.00537	0.59067
MAN15	0.27607	0.01328	0.19255
MAN16	0.153	-0.22304	0.20367
MAN17	0.27538	-0.21196	0.05887
MAN18	0.03391	-0.43357	0.26641
MAN19	0.11376	-0.28731	-0.19436
MAN20	0.2663	-0.03949	0.19422

Factor Pattern

	Factor1	Factor2	Factor3
MAN8	0.79187	0.11112	0.01999
MAN12	0.74871	-0.01293	0.10001
MAN7	0.67818	0.20651	0.02663
MAN6	0.65753	0.26738	0.06621
MAN15	0.65527	0.01974	0.22333
MAN17	0.65361	-0.31498	0.06828
MAN20	0.63207	-0.05868	0.22527
MAN11	0.49311	-0.22874	0.31219
MAN16	0.36315	-0.33143	0.23624
MAN3	-0.57165	-0.19941	0.32824
MAN1	-0.66576	0.07923	0.26572
MAN4	-0.68323	0.05144	0.28453
MAN2	-0.70522	-0.04899	0.28872
MAN10	-0.08928	0.67936	0.04461
MAN9	0.11871	0.63893	0.22488
MAN13	0.29317	0.54589	0.24568
MAN19	0.27001	-0.42694	-0.22544
MAN18	0.08048	-0.64428	0.30901
MAN14	-0.0315	-0.00798	0.68511

Variance Explained by Each Factor

Factor1	Factor2	Factor3
5.6335847	2.2081621	1.3453114

Final Communality Estimates: Total = 9.187058

MAN1	MAN2	MAN3	MAN4	MAN6	MAN7	MAN8	MAN9	MAN10	MAN11
0.52011	0.58309	0.47429	0.55039	0.50822	0.50329	0.63980	0.47289	0.47149	0.39294

MAN12	MAN13	MAN14	MAN15	MAN16	MAN17	MAN18	MAN19	MAN20
0.57073	0.44430	0.470427	0.479644	0.29753	0.53107	0.51706	0.30600	0.45370

Rotation Method: Varimax

Orthogonal Transformation Matrix

	1	2	3
1	0.94995	0.00441	0.31237
2	0.1	0.94299	-0.31743
3	-0.29596	0.33278	0.89536

Rotated Factor Pattern

	Factor1	Factor2	Factor3
MAN8	0.75744	0.11493	0.22998
MAN12	0.68034	0.0244	0.32752
MAN7	0.65701	0.2066	0.17014
MAN6	0.63177	0.27708	0.1798
MAN17	0.56919	-0.27141	0.36528
MAN15	0.55835	0.09583	0.39838
MAN20	0.5279	0.02242	0.41776
MAN3	-0.66013	-0.08133	0.17863
MAN1	-0.70316	0.1602	0.0048
MAN4	-0.7281	0.14017	0.02501
MAN2	-0.76028	0.04677	0.05377
MAN9	0.11011	0.67787	0.03561
MAN10	-0.03008	0.65509	-0.2036
MAN13	0.26037	0.59783	0.13826
MAN19	0.28052	-0.47643	0.01802
MAN14	-0.23349	0.22033	0.60611
MAN18	-0.07943	-0.50437	0.50633
MAN11	0.35316	-0.10963	0.50616
MAN16	0.24192	-0.23232	0.43016

Variance Explained by Each Factor

	Factor1	Factor2	Factor3
	5.2237086	2.1126737	1.850676

Victoria Scale statistics

Variable	Item
MonoF_T	Monologue School, factual level, all students
DiaF_T	Dialogue School, factual level, all students
ColfulF_T	Colourful School, factual level, all students
CollessF_T	Colourless School, factual level, all students
MonoN_T	Monologue School, normative level, all students
DiaN_T	Dialogue School, normative level, all students
ColfulN_T	Colourful School, normative level, all students
CollessN_T	Colourless School, normative level, all students
MonoF_A	[scale means for Monologue School, factual measurement level, all adults]
DiaF_A	[scale means for Dialogue School, factual measurement level, all adults]
ColfulF_A	[scale means for Colourful School, factual measurement level, all adults
CollessF_A	[scale means for Colourless School, factual measurement level, all adults
MonoN_A	[scale means for Monologue School, normative measurement level, all adults]
DiaN_A	[scale means for Dialogue School, normative measurement level, all adults]
ColfulN_A	[scale means for Colourful School, normative measurement level, all adults]
CollessN_A	[scale means for Colourless School, normative measurement level, all adults]
VAF1_2	If it were possible, my Catholic school would prefer all its students and teachers to be Catholic in faith and practice.
VAF2_2	My school holds the opinion that it is not the Catholic faith that should adapt itself to contemporary culture, but that contemporary culture should be adapted to Catholicism.
VAF3_2	In my school, openly presenting non-Catholic views and practices is regarded as a possible threat to its own Catholic mission.
VAF4_2	My Catholic school pays little attention to the philosophical views of individuals. Individuals are simply expected to adhere to the Catholic vision of the school as a whole.
VAF5_2	My school defends the Catholic lifestyle against other sets of beliefs that are considered to be of less value.
VAF6_2	Welcoming all open-minded people – Catholics and other believers alike – is a key feature of my school's Catholic identity.
VAF7_2	According to my school, the Catholic faith offers a very meaningful and valuable message that should be heard by all, but without expecting all students to become Catholics.
VAF8_2	My school looks creatively and with an open mind for good ways to be Catholic in the midst of contemporary culture.
VAF9_2	People in my school are searching for what it means to live as Catholics in today's multicultural society. Therefore they greatly value dialogue with other philosophical views.
VAF10_2	According to my Catholic school, the meaning and purpose of Catholic faith can only be fully realised through an active and open dialogue with other religions and philosophical views.
VAF11_2	My school is a neutral institution that allows students to freely make their own choices concerning philosophical and religious beliefs.
VAF12_2	My school has no preference for the truth of the Catholic faith. It believes it is more important to respect the personal truth of each individual.
VAF13_2	In my school, respecting and valuing many philosophical views and lifestyles (including the non-Catholic!) is considered to be more important than safeguarding a Catholic school identity.
VAF14_2	In my school, a strong focus on Catholic school identity is considered to undermine the school's efforts to live together with people that are different.
VAF15_2	In my school a preference for Christianity is being replaced by a respectful dialogue between different philosophies of life.
VAF16_2	In my school, religion is an individual, private matter that doesn't figure in daily school life.
VAF17_2	My school allows every individual to freely go his/her separate way, as long as one doesn't hinder another.
VAF18_2	In my school, many different philosophical views and lifestyles co-exist, without people taking notice of each other.
VAF19_2	In my school the Catholic faith is of no relevance. Each person in the school community chooses for themselves what to believe.
VAF20_2	People in my school don't openly question each other's philosophy of life, since they'd rather not be overly involved with the lives of others.
VAN1_2	I'd love to go to a school where all students and teachers were Catholic in faith and practice.
VAN2_2	I believe that the truth offered by Catholicism is more fundamental and fulfilling than the views of other religions or philosophies of life.
VAN3_2	I think a Catholic school should avoid non-Catholic views and practices because they could undermine its Catholic mission.
VAN4_2	In my opinion, the aim of religious education classes should always be: to turn all students into better, Catholic believers.
VAN5_2	My 'ideal school' should defend the Catholic lifestyle against other sets of beliefs that, I think, are of less value.
VAN6_2	My 'ideal school' realises its Catholic identity precisely by respecting and valuing people being different.
VAN7_2	My 'ideal school' presents the Catholic faith as a very meaningful and valuable message that should be heard by all, but without expecting all students to become Catholics.
VAN8_2	My 'ideal school' should look creatively and with an open mind for good ways to be Catholic in the midst of contemporary culture.
VAN9_2	People in my 'ideal school' are searching for what it means to live as Catholics in today's multicultural society. To achieve this, dialogue with other philosophical views should be greatly valued.
VAN10_2	The truth of Christianity isn't fixed, but is to be rediscovered and made real through a continuous search for it.
VAN11_2	My 'ideal school' is a neutral institution that allows students to freely make their own choices concerning philosophical and religious beliefs.
VAN12_2	I think that a school shouldn't have a preference for the truth of the Catholic faith. It is more important to respect the personal truth of each individual.
VAN13_2	I think that respecting and valuing many philosophical views and lifestyles at school (including the non-Catholic!) is more important than safeguarding a Catholic school identity.
VAN14_2	I think that a strong focus on Catholic school identity should be avoided, because it undermines living together with people that are different.
VAN15_2	In my ideal school a preference for Christianity is to be replaced by a respectful dialogue between different philosophies of life.
VAN16_2	I'd like to go to a school where religion is an individual, private matter that doesn't figure in daily school life.
VAN17_2	I think that every individual at school should be allowed to freely go his/her separate way, as long as one doesn't hinder another.
VAN18_2	In my 'ideal school', many different philosophical views and lifestyles should be allowed to co-exist, without people getting too much involved with each other.
VAN19_2	I think that the Catholic faith shouldn't be of any relevance at school. Each person in the school community should be free to determine for him/herself what to believe.
VAN20_2	I'd like to go to a school that doesn't openly question my philosophy of life and where I am not expected to be overly involved with the lives of others.
VE2	The questions in this survey made sense to me.
VE4	I liked completing this survey.

Variable	Mean	Std Dev	Variance	Min	Max	N	Quart 1	Median	Quart 2	Lower 99% CL	Upper 99% CL	t Value	Pr > |t|
MonoF_T	3.914	1.606	2.579	1	7	7298	3	4	5	3.878	3.951	208.25	<.0001
DiaF_T	5.171	1.272	1.617	1	7	7270	4	5	6	5.142	5.200	346.75	<.0001
ColfulF_T	3.470	1.671	2.792	1	7	7247	2	3	5	3.432	3.509	176.79	<.0001
CollessF_T	3.172	1.610	2.593	1	7	7234	2	3	4	3.135	3.209	167.55	<.0001
MonoN_T	3.474	1.790	3.205	1	7	7298	2	4	5	3.433	3.515	165.8	<.0001
DiaN_T	4.909	1.533	2.351	1	7	7270	4	5	6	4.874	4.944	272.97	<.0001
ColfulN_T	4.058	1.771	3.137	1	7	7247	3	4	5	4.017	4.098	195.01	<.0001
CollessN_T	3.656	1.750	3.062	1	7	7234	2	4	5	3.616	3.696	177.7	<.0001
MonoF_A	3.735	0.925	0.855	1	7	4797	3.2	3.8	4.4	3.709	3.762	279.75	<.0001
DiaF_A	5.061	0.765	0.585	1.2	7	4797	4.6	5	5.6	5.039	5.083	458.49	<.0001
ColfulF_A	3.251	0.904	0.818	1	7	4797	2.6	3.2	3.8	3.226	3.277	249.06	<.0001
CollessF_A	3.362	0.833	0.694	1	6.6	4797	2.8	3.4	4	3.338	3.385	279.54	<.0001
MonoN_A	3.396	1.182	1.397	1	7	4797	2.6	3.4	4.2	3.362	3.429	198.94	<.0001
DiaN_A	5.549	0.736	0.542	1	7	4797	5.2	5.6	6	5.528	5.569	521.89	<.0001
ColfulN_A	3.517	1.170	1.369	1	7	4797	2.6	3.6	4.4	3.484	3.550	208.15	<.0001
CollessN_A	3.498	1.073	1.151	1	7	4797	2.8	3.4	4.2	3.468	3.529	225.88	<.0001
VAF1_2	4.284	1.651	2.727	1	7	5147	3	4	6	4.239	4.329	186.11	<.0001
VAF2_2	3.700	1.380	1.906	1	7	5154	3	4	4	3.663	3.738	192.45	<.0001
VAF3_2	3.288	1.415	2.002	1	7	5137	2	3	4	3.249	3.327	166.56	<.0001
VAF4_2	3.679	1.532	2.347	1	7	5126	2	4	5	3.637	3.721	171.91	<.0001
VAF5_2	3.841	1.395	1.945	1	7	5116	3	4	5	3.802	3.879	196.97	<.0001
VAF6_2	5.217	1.275	1.626	1	7	5147	5	5	6	5.183	5.252	293.54	<.0001
VAF7_2	5.462	1.204	1.450	1	7	5137	5	6	6	5.429	5.495	325.1	<.0001
VAF8_2	5.625	1.066	1.137	1	7	5154	5	6	6	5.596	5.654	378.74	<.0001
VAF9_2	4.481	1.279	1.637	1	7	5126	4	4	5	4.446	4.516	250.76	<.0001
VAF10_2	4.336	1.256	1.578	1	7	5116	4	4	5	4.301	4.370	246.85	<.0001
VAF11_2	3.429	1.472	2.166	1	7	5136	2	3	5	3.389	3.470	166.99	<.0001
VAF12_2	3.137	1.352	1.827	1	7	5116	2	3	4	3.100	3.174	166	<.0001
VAF13_2	3.716	1.499	2.247	1	7	5147	2	4	5	3.675	3.757	177.84	<.0001
VAF14_2	2.981	1.335	1.782	1	7	5126	2	3	4	2.945	3.018	159.92	<.0001
VAF15_2	3.286	1.309	1.712	1	7	5154	2	3	4	3.250	3.322	180.3	<.0001
VAF16_2	2.295	1.226	1.504	1	7	5154	1	2	3	2.261	2.328	134.31	<.0001
VAF17_2	4.215	1.417	2.009	1	7	5126	3	4	5	4.176	4.254	212.92	<.0001
VAF18_2	3.998	1.396	1.949	1	7	5147	3	4	5	3.960	4.036	205.47	<.0001
VAF19_2	2.519	1.373	1.884	1	7	5116	2	2	3	2.482	2.557	131.27	<.0001
VAF20_2	4.027	1.382	1.910	1	7	5136	3	4	5	3.989	4.065	208.83	<.0001
VAN1_2	3.562	1.756	3.083	1	7	5147	2	3	5	3.514	3.610	145.54	<.0001
VAN2_2	3.834	1.620	2.626	1	7	5154	2	4	5	3.790	3.878	169.85	<.0001
VAN3_2	2.832	1.478	2.184	1	7	5136	2	2	4	2.792	2.873	137.35	<.0001
VAN4_2	3.449	1.605	2.575	1	7	5126	2	3	5	3.405	3.493	153.87	<.0001
VAN5_2	3.491	1.597	2.550	1	7	5116	2	4	5	3.447	3.534	156.34	<.0001
VAN6_2	5.781	1.075	1.156	1	7	5147	5	6	6	5.752	5.811	385.8	<.0001
VAN7_2	5.527	1.280	1.639	1	7	5137	5	6	6	5.492	5.562	309.45	<.0001
VAN8_2	5.945	1.010	1.019	1	7	5154	6	6	7	5.917	5.972	422.69	<.0001
VAN9_2	5.010	1.291	1.666	1	7	5126	4	5	6	4.975	5.046	277.88	<.0001
VAN10_2	5.144	1.247	1.555	1	7	5116	4	5	6	5.110	5.178	295.08	<.0001
VAN11_2	3.872	1.705	2.907	1	7	5136	2	4	5	3.825	3.919	162.75	<.0001
VAN12_2	3.621	1.553	2.412	1	7	5116	2	4	5	3.578	3.663	166.75	<.0001
VAN13_2	3.953	1.656	2.743	1	7	5147	3	4	5	3.908	3.998	171.24	<.0001
VAN14_2	2.799	1.344	1.806	1	7	5126	2	2	4	2.762	2.836	149.13	<.0001
VAN15_2	3.565	1.588	2.521	1	7	5154	2	4	5	3.521	3.608	161.16	<.0001
VAN16_2	2.587	1.497	2.242	1	7	5153	2	2	3	2.547	2.628	124.03	<.0001
VAN17_2	4.471	1.561	2.436	1	7	5125	3	5	6	4.428	4.514	205.08	<.0001
VAN18_2	4.114	1.556	2.422	1	7	5146	3	4	5	4.072	4.157	189.65	<.0001
VAN19_2	2.844	1.571	2.467	1	7	5116	2	2	4	2.801	2.887	129.52	<.0001
VAN20_2	3.696	1.529	2.339	1	7	5136	2	4	5	3.654	3.738	173.21	<.0001
VE2	5.000	1.551	2.406	1	7	13959	4	5	6	4.974	5.026	380.82	<.0001
VE4	4.125	1.860	3.459	1	7	13960	3	4	6	4.094	4.155	262.03	<.0001

Pearson Correlation Coefficients, student respondents
Prob > |r| under H0: Rho=0
Number of Observations

	MonoF_T	DiaF_T	ColfulF_T	CollessF_T	MonoN_T	DiaN_T	ColfulN_T	CollessN_T
MonoF_T	1	0.144	0.07866	0.13289	0.65395	0.10222	-0.03914	0.04265
		<.0001	<.0001	<.0001	<.0001	<.0001	0.0009	0.0003
	7298	7270	7246	7234	7298	7270	7246	7234
DiaF_T	0.144	1	0.04019	-0.04928	0.12606	0.49433	-0.01047	-0.07421
	<.0001		0.0006	<.0001	<.0001	<.0001	0.3729	<.0001
	7270	7270	7246	7234	7270	7270	7246	7234
ColfulF_T	0.07866	0.04019	1	0.45106	0.09546	-0.01423	0.50865	0.24972
	<.0001	0.0006		<.0001	<.0001	0.2258	<.0001	<.0001
	7246	7246	7247	7234	7246	7246	7247	7234
CollessF_T	0.13289	-0.04928	0.45106	1	0.14202	-0.07375	0.21431	0.52884
	<.0001	<.0001	<.0001		<.0001	<.0001	<.0001	<.0001
	7234	7234	7234	7234	7234	7234	7234	7234
MonoN_T	0.65395	0.12606	0.09546	0.14202	1	0.30378	-0.11175	-0.02911
	<.0001	<.0001	<.0001	<.0001		<.0001	<.0001	0.0133
	7298	7270	7246	7234	7298	7270	7246	7234
DiaN_T	0.10222	0.49433	-0.01423	-0.07375	0.30378	1	0.01491	-0.09687
	<.0001	<.0001	0.2258	<.0001	<.0001		0.2044	<.0001
	7270	7270	7246	7234	7270	7270	7246	7234
ColfulN_T	-0.03914	-0.01047	0.50865	0.21431	-0.11175	0.01491	1	0.43061
	0.0009	0.3729	<.0001	<.0001	<.0001	0.2044		<.0001
	7246	7246	7247	7234	7246	7246	7247	7234
CollessN_T	0.04265	-0.07421	0.24972	0.52884	-0.02911	-0.09687	0.43061	1
	0.0003	<.0001	<.0001	<.0001	0.0133	<.0001	<.0001	
	7234	7234	7234	7234	7234	7234	7234	7234

Pearson Correlation Coefficients, adult respondents, n=4797
Prob > |r| under H0: Rho=0

	MonoF_A	DiaF_A	ColfulF_A	CollessF_A	MonoN_A	DiaN_A	ColfulN_A	CollessN_A
MonoF_A	1	-0.35229	-0.04149	0.06997	0.4409	-0.20904	0.07964	0.13404
		<.0001	0.0041	<.0001	<.0001	<.0001	<.0001	<.0001
DiaF_A	-0.35229	1	0.13666	-0.0179	-0.08116	0.52744	-0.02332	-0.08429
	<.0001		<.0001	0.2151	<.0001	<.0001	0.1062	<.0001
ColfulF_A	-0.04149	0.13666	1	0.57167	0.03356	-0.05932	0.59858	0.43579
	0.0041	<.0001		<.0001	0.0201	<.0001	<.0001	<.0001
CollessF_A	0.06997	-0.0179	0.57167	1	0.00045	-0.0657	0.458	0.65548
	<.0001	0.2151	<.0001		0.9753	<.0001	<.0001	<.0001
MonoN_A	0.4409	-0.08116	0.03356	0.00045	1	-0.14936	-0.37095	-0.27115
	<.0001	<.0001	0.0201	0.9753		<.0001	<.0001	<.0001
DiaN_A	-0.20904	0.52744	-0.05932	-0.0657	-0.14936	1	-0.09201	-0.14208
	<.0001	<.0001	<.0001	<.0001	<.0001		<.0001	<.0001
ColfulN_A	0.07964	-0.02332	0.59858	0.458	-0.37095	-0.09201	1	0.73252
	<.0001	0.1062	<.0001	<.0001	<.0001	<.0001		<.0001
CollessN_A	0.13404	-0.08429	0.43579	0.65548	-0.27115	-0.14208	0.73252	1
	<.0001	<.0001	<.0001	<.0001	<.0001	<.0001	<.0001	

434

Pearson Correlation Coefficients, adult respondents.
Prob > |r| under H0: Rho=0
Number of Observations

	VAF1	VAF2	VAF3	VAF4	VAF5	VAF6	VAF7	VAF8	VAF9	VAF10
VAF1	1	0.15759	0.22232	0.21882	0.22932	-0.23426	-0.12978	-0.01719	-0.03585	-0.12526
		<.0001	<.0001	<.0001	<.0001	<.0001	<.0001	0.2175	0.0103	<.0001
	5147	5147	5136	5125	5115	5147	5136	5147	5125	5115
VAF2	0.15759	1	0.22518	0.17463	0.21612	-0.05587	-0.05715	-0.07754	-0.04251	-0.06777
	<.0001		<.0001	<.0001	<.0001	<.0001	<.0001	<.0001	0.0023	<.0001
	5147	5154	5136	5125	5115	5147	5136	5154	5125	5115
VAF3	0.22232	0.22518	1	0.31621	0.27131	-0.20218	-0.23913	-0.19302	-0.1363	-0.13297
	<.0001	<.0001		<.0001	<.0001	<.0001	<.0001	<.0001	<.0001	<.0001
	5136	5136	5137	5126	5116	5136	5137	5136	5126	5116
VAF4	0.21882	0.17463	0.31621	1	0.23252	-0.22688	-0.18643	-0.24794	-0.2898	-0.20762
	<.0001	<.0001	<.0001		<.0001	<.0001	<.0001	<.0001	<.0001	<.0001
	5125	5125	5126	5126	5116	5125	5126	5125	5126	5116
VAF5	0.22932	0.21612	0.27131	0.23252	1	-0.08764	-0.05736	-0.0657	-0.00291	-0.02672
	<.0001	<.0001	<.0001	<.0001		<.0001	<.0001	<.0001	0.8354	0.056
	5115	5115	5116	5116	5116	5115	5116	5115	5116	5116
VAF6	-0.23426	-0.05587	-0.20218	-0.22688	-0.08764	1	0.30806	0.25002	0.22804	0.24295
	<.0001	<.0001	<.0001	<.0001	<.0001		<.0001	<.0001	<.0001	<.0001
	5147	5147	5136	5125	5115	5147	5136	5147	5125	5115
VAF7	-0.12978	-0.05715	-0.23913	-0.18643	-0.05736	0.30806	1	0.27484	0.19196	0.1796
	<.0001	<.0001	<.0001	<.0001	<.0001	<.0001		<.0001	<.0001	<.0001
	5136	5136	5137	5126	5116	5136	5137	5136	5126	5116
VAF8	-0.01719	-0.07754	-0.19302	-0.24794	-0.0657	0.25002	0.27484	1	0.30524	0.17326
	0.2175	<.0001	<.0001	<.0001	<.0001	<.0001	<.0001		<.0001	<.0001
	5147	5154	5136	5125	5115	5147	5136	5154	5125	5115
VAF9	-0.03585	-0.04251	-0.1363	-0.2898	-0.00291	0.22804	0.19196	0.30524	1	0.32244
	0.0103	0.0023	<.0001	<.0001	0.8354	<.0001	<.0001	<.0001		<.0001
	5125	5125	5126	5126	5116	5125	5126	5125	5126	5116
VAF10	-0.12526	-0.06777	-0.13297	-0.20762	-0.02672	0.24295	0.1796	0.17326	0.32244	1
	<.0001	<.0001	<.0001	<.0001	0.056	<.0001	<.0001	<.0001	<.0001	
	5115	5115	5116	5116	5116	5115	5116	5115	5116	5116
VAF11	-0.14093	0.04028	-0.03787	-0.07907	-0.05371	0.19777	0.09622	0.00071	0.06413	0.16597
	<.0001	0.0039	0.0066	<.0001	0.0001	<.0001	<.0001	0.9596	<.0001	<.0001
	5135	5135	5136	5126	5116	5135	5136	5135	5126	5116
VAF12	-0.07162	0.06447	0.04503	0.01792	-0.04038	0.07602	-0.03466	-0.0801	-0.02041	0.11902
	<.0001	<.0001	0.0013	0.2	0.0039	<.0001	0.0132	<.0001	0.1445	<.0001
	5115	5115	5116	5116	5116	5115	5116	5115	5116	5116
VAF13	-0.17027	0.00032	-0.06902	-0.08604	-0.09668	0.28826	0.09493	0.03591	0.07352	0.19108
	<.0001	0.9817	<.0001	<.0001	<.0001	<.0001	<.0001	0.01	<.0001	<.0001
	5147	5147	5136	5125	5115	5147	5136	5147	5125	5115
VAF14	0.05429	0.14989	0.23508	0.20404	0.16265	-0.05217	-0.15444	-0.17626	-0.08583	0.01694
	0.0001	<.0001	<.0001	<.0001	<.0001	0.0002	<.0001	<.0001	<.0001	0.2258
	5125	5125	5126	5126	5116	5125	5126	5125	5126	5116
VAF15	-0.05951	0.10302	0.06834	0.01166	-0.00662	0.09977	-0.02781	-0.05589	0.0229	0.15352
	<.0001	<.0001	<.0001	0.4039	0.6361	<.0001	0.0463	<.0001	0.1011	<.0001
	5147	5154	5136	5125	5115	5147	5136	5154	5125	5115
VAF16	-0.03926	0.11448	0.15525	0.12824	0.05999	-0.01894	-0.13453	-0.23443	-0.08283	0.03172
	0.0048	<.0001	<.0001	<.0001	<.0001	0.1743	<.0001	<.0001	<.0001	0.0233
	5147	5154	5136	5125	5115	5147	5136	5154	5125	5115
VAF17	-0.05188	0.00253	-0.0603	-0.04286	-0.04708	0.16486	0.14692	0.0524	0.02998	0.14638
	0.0002	0.8566	<.0001	0.0021	0.0008	<.0001	<.0001	0.0002	0.0318	<.0001
	5125	5125	5126	5126	5116	5125	5126	5125	5126	5116
VAF18	-0.062	0.03625	0.02645	0.04186	0.00888	0.16658	0.1039	-0.01599	0.01833	0.09874
	<.0001	0.0093	0.0581	0.0027	0.5253	<.0001	<.0001	0.2515	0.1895	<.0001
	5147	5147	5136	5125	5115	5147	5136	5147	5125	5115
VAF19	-0.0793	0.08977	0.10353	0.0976	0.02452	0.01216	-0.09253	-0.20095	-0.1036	0.04848
	<.0001	<.0001	<.0001	<.0001	0.0795	0.3845	<.0001	<.0001	<.0001	0.0005
	5115	5115	5116	5116	5116	5115	5116	5115	5116	5116
VAF20	0.0599	0.07735	0.15233	0.26078	0.07757	-0.03377	-0.02687	-0.14669	-0.21774	-0.08591
	<.0001	<.0001	<.0001	<.0001	<.0001	0.0155	0.0541	<.0001	<.0001	<.0001
	5135	5135	5136	5126	5116	5135	5136	5135	5126	5116

	VAF11	VAF12	VAF13	VAF14	VAF15	VAF16	VAF17	VAF18	VAF19	VAF20
VAF1	-0.14093	-0.07162	-0.17027	0.05429	-0.05951	-0.03926	-0.05188	-0.062	-0.0793	0.0599
	<.0001	<.0001	<.0001	0.0001	<.0001	0.0048	0.0002	<.0001	<.0001	<.0001
	5135	5115	5147	5125	5147	5147	5125	5147	5115	5135
VAF2	0.04028	0.06447	0.00032	0.14989	0.10302	0.11448	0.00253	0.03625	0.08977	0.07735
	0.0039	<.0001	0.9817	<.0001	<.0001	<.0001	0.8566	0.0093	<.0001	<.0001
	5135	5115	5147	5125	5154	5154	5125	5147	5115	5135
VAF3	-0.03787	0.04503	-0.06902	0.23508	0.06834	0.15525	-0.0603	0.02645	0.10353	0.15233
	0.0066	0.0013	<.0001	<.0001	<.0001	<.0001	<.0001	0.0581	<.0001	<.0001
	5136	5116	5136	5126	5136	5136	5126	5136	5116	5136
VAF4	-0.07907	0.01792	-0.08604	0.20404	0.01166	0.12824	-0.04286	0.04186	0.0976	0.26078
	<.0001	0.2	<.0001	<.0001	0.4039	<.0001	0.0021	0.0027	<.0001	<.0001
	5126	5116	5125	5126	5125	5125	5126	5125	5116	5126
VAF5	-0.05371	-0.04038	-0.09668	0.16265	-0.00662	0.05999	-0.04708	0.00888	0.02452	0.07757
	0.0001	0.0039	<.0001	<.0001	0.6361	<.0001	0.0008	0.5253	0.0795	<.0001
	5116	5116	5115	5116	5115	5115	5116	5115	5116	5116
VAF6	0.19777	0.07602	0.28826	-0.05217	0.09977	-0.01894	0.16486	0.16658	0.01216	-0.03377
	<.0001	<.0001	<.0001	0.0002	<.0001	0.1743	<.0001	<.0001	0.3845	0.0155
	5135	5115	5147	5125	5147	5147	5125	5147	5115	5135
VAF7	0.09622	-0.03466	0.09493	-0.15444	-0.02781	-0.13453	0.14692	0.1039	-0.09253	-0.02687
	<.0001	0.0132	<.0001	<.0001	0.0463	<.0001	<.0001	<.0001	<.0001	0.0541
	5136	5116	5136	5126	5136	5136	5126	5136	5116	5136
VAF8	0.00071	-0.0801	0.03591	-0.17626	-0.05589	-0.23443	0.0524	-0.01599	-0.20095	-0.14669
	0.9596	<.0001	0.01	<.0001	<.0001	<.0001	0.0002	0.2515	<.0001	<.0001
	5135	5115	5147	5125	5154	5154	5125	5147	5115	5135
VAF9	0.06413	-0.02041	0.07352	-0.08583	0.0229	-0.08283	0.02998	0.01833	-0.1036	-0.21774
	<.0001	0.1445	<.0001	<.0001	0.1011	<.0001	0.0318	0.1895	<.0001	<.0001
	5126	5116	5125	5126	5125	5125	5126	5125	5116	5126
VAF10	0.16597	0.11902	0.19108	0.01694	0.15352	0.03172	0.14638	0.09874	0.04848	-0.08591
	<.0001	<.0001	<.0001	0.2258	<.0001	0.0233	<.0001	<.0001	0.0005	<.0001
	5116	5116	5115	5116	5115	5115	5116	5115	5116	5116
VAF11	1	0.34694	0.31793	0.17732	0.29871	0.25848	0.34439	0.27017	0.36056	0.17501
		<.0001	<.0001	<.0001	<.0001	<.0001	<.0001	<.0001	<.0001	<.0001
	5136	5116	5135	5126	5135	5135	5126	5135	5116	5136
VAF12	0.34694	1	0.32629	0.29371	0.34633	0.31868	0.27504	0.22353	0.45165	0.16941
	<.0001		<.0001	<.0001	<.0001	<.0001	<.0001	<.0001	<.0001	<.0001
	5116	5116	5115	5116	5115	5115	5116	5115	5116	5116
VAF13	0.31793	0.32629	1	0.17903	0.36361	0.25673	0.22382	0.31635	0.27223	0.08756
	<.0001	<.0001		<.0001	<.0001	<.0001	<.0001	<.0001	<.0001	<.0001
	5135	5115	5147	5125	5147	5147	5125	5147	5115	5135
VAF14	0.17732	0.29371	0.17903	1	0.25137	0.28669	0.05048	0.13658	0.30009	0.17202
	<.0001	<.0001	<.0001		<.0001	<.0001	0.0003	<.0001	<.0001	<.0001
	5126	5116	5125	5126	5125	5125	5126	5125	5116	5126
VAF15	0.29871	0.34633	0.36361	0.25137	1	0.35801	0.18571	0.23993	0.31669	0.11932
	<.0001	<.0001	<.0001	<.0001		<.0001	<.0001	<.0001	<.0001	<.0001
	5135	5115	5147	5125	5154	5154	5125	5147	5115	5135
VAF16	0.25848	0.31868	0.25673	0.28669	0.35801	1	0.14026	0.22176	0.42278	0.18898
	<.0001	<.0001	<.0001	<.0001	<.0001		<.0001	<.0001	<.0001	<.0001
	5135	5115	5147	5125	5154	5154	5125	5147	5115	5135
VAF17	0.34439	0.27504	0.22382	0.05048	0.18571	0.14026	1	0.30142	0.24232	0.14864
	<.0001	<.0001	<.0001	0.0003	<.0001	<.0001		<.0001	<.0001	<.0001
	5126	5116	5125	5126	5125	5125	5126	5125	5116	5126
VAF18	0.27017	0.22353	0.31635	0.13658	0.23993	0.22176	0.30142	1	0.23272	0.20571
	<.0001	<.0001	<.0001	<.0001	<.0001	<.0001	<.0001		<.0001	<.0001
	5135	5115	5147	5125	5147	5147	5125	5147	5115	5135
VAF19	0.36056	0.45165	0.27223	0.30009	0.31669	0.42278	0.24232	0.23272	1	0.19107
	<.0001	<.0001	<.0001	<.0001	<.0001	<.0001	<.0001	<.0001		<.0001
	5116	5116	5115	5116	5115	5115	5116	5115	5116	5116
VAF20	0.17501	0.16941	0.08756	0.17202	0.11932	0.18898	0.14864	0.20571	0.19107	1
	<.0001	<.0001	<.0001	<.0001	<.0001	<.0001	<.0001	<.0001	<.0001	
	5136	5116	5135	5126	5135	5135	5126	5135	5116	5136

Pearson Correlation Coefficients, adult respondents.
Prob > |r| under H0: Rho=0
Number of Observations

	VAN1	VAN2	VAN3	VAN4	VAN5	VAN6	VAN7	VAN8	VAN9	VAN10
VAN1	1	0.45723	0.3958	0.46027	0.39115	-0.19807	-0.11496	0.12122	0.00919	-0.09055
		<.0001	<.0001	<.0001	<.0001	<.0001	<.0001	<.0001	0.5107	<.0001
	5147	5147	5135	5125	5115	5147	5136	5147	5125	5115
VAN2	0.45723	1	0.35532	0.40139	0.43119	-0.10126	-0.02426	0.12948	-0.01735	-0.10493
	<.0001		<.0001	<.0001	<.0001	<.0001	0.0821	<.0001	0.2142	<.0001
	5147	5154	5135	5125	5115	5147	5136	5154	5125	5115
VAN3	0.3958	0.35532	1	0.40341	0.34672	-0.24804	-0.20034	-0.05497	-0.16233	-0.18118
	<.0001	<.0001		<.0001	<.0001	<.0001	<.0001	<.0001	<.0001	<.0001
	5135	5135	5136	5126	5116	5135	5136	5135	5126	5116
VAN4	0.46027	0.40139	0.40341	1	0.35941	-0.14134	-0.13724	0.03327	-0.06516	-0.1021
	<.0001	<.0001	<.0001		<.0001	<.0001	<.0001	0.0172	<.0001	<.0001
	5125	5125	5126	5126	5116	5125	5126	5125	5126	5116
VAN5	0.39115	0.43119	0.34672	0.35941	1	-0.13902	-0.02894	0.06771	-0.02671	-0.06736
	<.0001	<.0001	<.0001	<.0001		<.0001	0.0385	<.0001	0.0561	<.0001
	5115	5115	5116	5116	5116	5115	5116	5115	5116	5116
VAN6	-0.19807	-0.10126	-0.24804	-0.14134	-0.13902	1	0.31818	0.32526	0.25972	0.25834
	<.0001	<.0001	<.0001	<.0001	<.0001		<.0001	<.0001	<.0001	<.0001
	5147	5147	5135	5125	5115	5147	5136	5147	5125	5115
VAN7	-0.11496	-0.02426	-0.20034	-0.13724	-0.02894	0.31818	1	0.33599	0.2743	0.21229
	<.0001	0.0821	<.0001	<.0001	0.0385	<.0001		<.0001	<.0001	<.0001
	5136	5136	5136	5126	5116	5136	5137	5136	5126	5116
VAN8	0.12122	0.12948	-0.05497	0.03327	0.06771	0.32526	0.33599	1	0.30344	0.25332
	<.0001	<.0001	<.0001	0.0172	<.0001	<.0001	<.0001		<.0001	<.0001
	5147	5154	5135	5125	5115	5147	5136	5154	5125	5115
VAN9	0.00919	-0.01735	-0.16233	-0.06516	-0.02671	0.25972	0.2743	0.30344	1	0.2846
	0.5107	0.2142	<.0001	<.0001	0.0561	<.0001	<.0001	<.0001		<.0001
	5125	5125	5126	5126	5116	5125	5126	5125	5126	5116
VAN10	-0.09055	-0.10493	-0.18118	-0.1021	-0.06736	0.25834	0.21229	0.25332	0.2846	1
	<.0001	<.0001	<.0001	<.0001	<.0001	<.0001	<.0001	<.0001	<.0001	
	5115	5115	5116	5116	5116	5115	5116	5115	5116	5116
VAN11	-0.27995	-0.21986	-0.14055	-0.14225	-0.18646	0.08046	0.02004	-0.17476	-0.0455	-0.01538
	<.0001	<.0001	<.0001	<.0001	<.0001	<.0001	0.1511	<.0001	0.0011	0.2714
	5135	5135	5136	5126	5116	5135	5136	5135	5126	5116
VAN12	-0.23671	-0.23004	-0.09352	-0.1045	-0.19871	0.03831	-0.08219	-0.18721	-0.1092	-0.00926
	<.0001	<.0001	<.0001	<.0001	<.0001	0.0061	<.0001	<.0001	<.0001	0.5076
	5115	5115	5116	5116	5116	5115	5116	5115	5116	5116
VAN13	-0.33741	-0.27376	-0.21651	-0.18894	-0.23861	0.14246	0.03363	-0.12586	-0.02577	0.05582
	<.0001	<.0001	<.0001	<.0001	<.0001	<.0001	0.0159	<.0001	0.0651	<.0001
	5147	5147	5135	5125	5115	5147	5136	5147	5125	5115
VAN14	-0.1512	-0.12867	0.03957	-0.01227	-0.07102	-0.11833	-0.1569	-0.26945	-0.16842	-0.11948
	<.0001	<.0001	0.0046	0.3797	<.0001	<.0001	<.0001	<.0001	<.0001	<.0001
	5125	5125	5126	5126	5116	5125	5126	5125	5126	5116
VAN15	-0.21809	-0.20647	-0.08415	-0.08691	-0.17374	0.02424	-0.07783	-0.16438	-0.03645	0.00771
	<.0001	<.0001	<.0001	<.0001	<.0001	0.082	<.0001	<.0001	0.0091	0.5813
	5147	5154	5135	5125	5115	5147	5136	5154	5125	5115
VAN16	-0.23616	-0.21752	-0.02308	-0.08789	-0.13852	-0.12503	-0.16811	-0.3473	-0.17861	-0.10856
	<.0001	<.0001	0.0981	<.0001	<.0001	<.0001	<.0001	<.0001	<.0001	<.0001
	5147	5153	5135	5125	5115	5147	5136	5153	5125	5115
VAN17	-0.20328	-0.15514	-0.14356	-0.09906	-0.13657	0.11574	0.07972	-0.06028	-0.02804	0.1091
	<.0001	<.0001	<.0001	<.0001	<.0001	<.0001	<.0001	<.0001	0.0447	<.0001
	5124	5124	5125	5125	5116	5124	5125	5124	5125	5116
VAN18	-0.22473	-0.15858	-0.10606	-0.0779	-0.11031	0.10941	0.04682	-0.09499	-0.04109	0.03431
	<.0001	<.0001	<.0001	<.0001	<.0001	<.0001	0.0008	<.0001	0.0033	0.0141
	5146	5146	5135	5125	5115	5146	5136	5146	5125	5115
VAN19	-0.25009	-0.21216	-0.06312	-0.08463	-0.15769	-0.06508	-0.12139	-0.28836	-0.14701	-0.09046
	<.0001	<.0001	<.0001	<.0001	<.0001	<.0001	<.0001	<.0001	<.0001	<.0001
	5115	5115	5116	5116	5116	5115	5116	5115	5116	5116
VAN20	-0.04126	-0.02417	0.09273	0.08249	0.01759	-0.04987	-0.04863	-0.11709	-0.18161	-0.05442
	0.0031	0.0833	<.0001	<.0001	0.2085	0.0003	0.0005	<.0001	<.0001	<.0001
	5135	5135	5136	5126	5116	5135	5136	5135	5126	5116

	VAN11	VAN12	VAN13	VAN14	VAN15	VAN16	VAN17	VAN18	VAN19	VAN20
VAN1	-0.27995	-0.23671	-0.33741	-0.1512	-0.21809	-0.23616	-0.20328	-0.22473	-0.25009	-0.04126
	<.0001	<.0001	<.0001	<.0001	<.0001	<.0001	<.0001	<.0001	<.0001	0.0031
	5135	5115	5147	5125	5147	5147	5124	5146	5115	5135
VAN2	-0.21986	-0.23004	-0.27376	-0.12867	-0.20647	-0.21752	-0.15514	-0.15858	-0.21216	-0.02417
	<.0001	<.0001	<.0001	<.0001	<.0001	<.0001	<.0001	<.0001	<.0001	0.0833
	5135	5115	5147	5125	5154	5153	5124	5146	5115	5135
VAN3	-0.14055	-0.09352	-0.21651	0.03957	-0.08415	-0.02308	-0.14356	-0.10606	-0.06312	0.09273
	<.0001	<.0001	<.0001	0.0046	<.0001	0.0981	<.0001	<.0001	<.0001	<.0001
	5136	5116	5135	5126	5135	5135	5125	5135	5116	5136
VAN4	-0.14225	-0.1045	-0.18894	-0.01227	-0.08691	-0.08789	-0.09906	-0.0779	-0.08463	0.08249
	<.0001	<.0001	<.0001	0.3797	<.0001	<.0001	<.0001	<.0001	<.0001	<.0001
	5126	5116	5125	5126	5125	5125	5125	5125	5116	5126
VAN5	-0.18646	-0.19871	-0.23861	-0.07102	-0.17374	-0.13852	-0.13657	-0.11031	-0.15769	0.01759
	<.0001	<.0001	<.0001	<.0001	<.0001	<.0001	<.0001	<.0001	<.0001	0.2085
	5116	5116	5115	5116	5115	5115	5116	5115	5116	5116
VAN6	0.08046	0.03831	0.14246	-0.11833	0.02424	-0.12503	0.11574	0.10941	-0.06508	-0.04987
	<.0001	0.0061	<.0001	<.0001	0.082	<.0001	<.0001	<.0001	<.0001	0.0003
	5135	5115	5147	5125	5147	5147	5124	5146	5115	5135
VAN7	0.02004	-0.08219	0.03363	-0.1569	-0.07783	-0.16811	0.07972	0.04682	-0.12139	-0.04863
	0.1511	<.0001	0.0159	<.0001	<.0001	<.0001	<.0001	0.0008	<.0001	0.0005
	5136	5116	5136	5126	5136	5136	5125	5136	5116	5136
VAN8	-0.17476	-0.18721	-0.12586	-0.26945	-0.16438	-0.3473	-0.06028	-0.09499	-0.28836	-0.11709
	<.0001	<.0001	<.0001	<.0001	<.0001	<.0001	<.0001	<.0001	<.0001	<.0001
	5135	5115	5147	5125	5154	5153	5124	5146	5115	5135
VAN9	-0.0455	-0.1092	-0.02577	-0.16842	-0.03645	-0.17861	-0.02804	-0.04109	-0.14701	-0.18161
	0.0011	<.0001	0.0651	<.0001	0.0091	<.0001	0.0447	0.0033	<.0001	<.0001
	5126	5116	5125	5126	5125	5125	5125	5125	5116	5126
VAN10	-0.01538	-0.00926	0.05582	-0.11948	0.00771	-0.10856	0.1091	0.03431	-0.09046	-0.05442
	0.2714	0.5076	<.0001	<.0001	0.5813	<.0001	<.0001	0.0141	<.0001	<.0001
	5116	5116	5115	5116	5115	5115	5116	5115	5116	5116
VAN11	1	0.48037	0.43433	0.3544	0.40289	0.4145	0.43148	0.39045	0.49145	0.2939
		<.0001	<.0001	<.0001	<.0001	<.0001	<.0001	<.0001	<.0001	<.0001
	5136	5116	5135	5126	5135	5135	5125	5135	5116	5136
VAN12	0.48037	1	0.45599	0.43376	0.44615	0.45274	0.38391	0.36128	0.56798	0.30341
	<.0001		<.0001	<.0001	<.0001	<.0001	<.0001	<.0001	<.0001	<.0001
	5116	5116	5115	5116	5115	5115	5116	5115	5116	5116
VAN13	0.43433	0.45599	1	0.37016	0.46512	0.39857	0.32539	0.45062	0.42219	0.2031
	<.0001	<.0001		<.0001	<.0001	<.0001	<.0001	<.0001	<.0001	<.0001
	5135	5115	5147	5125	5147	5147	5124	5146	5115	5135
VAN14	0.3544	0.43376	0.37016	1	0.38732	0.45579	0.23686	0.29238	0.48214	0.28067
	<.0001	<.0001	<.0001		<.0001	<.0001	<.0001	<.0001	<.0001	<.0001
	5126	5116	5125	5126	5125	5125	5125	5125	5116	5126
VAN15	0.40289	0.44615	0.46512	0.38732	1	0.45933	0.27525	0.34074	0.4287	0.21183
	<.0001	<.0001	<.0001	<.0001		<.0001	<.0001	<.0001	<.0001	<.0001
	5135	5115	5147	5125	5154	5153	5124	5146	5115	5135
VAN16	0.4145	0.45274	0.39857	0.45579	0.45933	1	0.27578	0.35272	0.53536	0.31397
	<.0001	<.0001	<.0001	<.0001	<.0001		<.0001	<.0001	<.0001	<.0001
	5135	5115	5147	5125	5153	5153	5124	5146	5115	5135
VAN17	0.43148	0.38391	0.32539	0.23686	0.27525	0.27578	1	0.37488	0.35461	0.24944
	<.0001	<.0001	<.0001	<.0001	<.0001	<.0001		<.0001	<.0001	<.0001
	5125	5116	5124	5125	5124	5124	5125	5124	5116	5125
VAN18	0.39045	0.36128	0.45062	0.29238	0.34074	0.35272	0.37488	1	0.3404	0.32511
	<.0001	<.0001	<.0001	<.0001	<.0001	<.0001	<.0001		<.0001	<.0001
	5135	5115	5146	5125	5146	5146	5124	5146	5115	5135
VAN19	0.49145	0.56798	0.42219	0.48214	0.4287	0.53536	0.35461	0.3404	1	0.29627
	<.0001	<.0001	<.0001	<.0001	<.0001	<.0001	<.0001	<.0001		<.0001
	5116	5116	5115	5116	5115	5115	5116	5115	5116	5116
VAN20	0.2939	0.30341	0.2031	0.28067	0.21183	0.31397	0.24944	0.32511	0.29627	1
	<.0001	<.0001	<.0001	<.0001	<.0001	<.0001	<.0001	<.0001	<.0001	
	5136	5116	5135	5126	5135	5135	5125	5135	5116	5136

Pearson Correlation Coefficients
Prob > |r| under H0: Rho=0
Number of Observations

	VAF1	VAF2	VAF3	VAF4	VAF5	VAF6	VAF7	VAF8	VAF9	VAF10
VAN1	0.55393	0.13563	0.1218	0.0617	0.15015	-0.13877	-0.0978	0.05593	0.00693	-0.07166
	<.0001	<.0001	<.0001	<.0001	<.0001	<.0001	<.0001	<.0001	0.6201	<.0001
	5147	5147	5136	5125	5115	5147	5136	5147	5125	5115
VAN2	0.15748	0.30715	0.09772	0.00009	0.19706	-0.00143	-0.0249	0.09782	0.04783	-0.02931
	<.0001	<.0001	<.0001	0.9948	<.0001	0.9181	0.0743	<.0001	0.0006	0.0361
	5147	5154	5136	5125	5115	5147	5136	5154	5125	5115
VAN3	0.18668	0.18986	0.45964	0.14677	0.17401	-0.12842	-0.16392	-0.02767	-0.08791	-0.10731
	<.0001	<.0001	<.0001	<.0001	<.0001	<.0001	<.0001	0.0474	<.0001	<.0001
	5135	5135	5136	5126	5116	5135	5136	5135	5126	5116
VAN4	0.24241	0.16579	0.20364	0.19089	0.18251	-0.09261	-0.1329	0.04109	-0.01458	-0.04195
	<.0001	<.0001	<.0001	<.0001	<.0001	<.0001	<.0001	0.0033	0.2967	0.0027
	5125	5125	5126	5126	5116	5125	5126	5125	5126	5116
VAN5	0.16929	0.17269	0.15404	0.05738	0.6162	-0.01195	-0.01627	0.0285	0.02127	-0.00881
	<.0001	<.0001	<.0001	<.0001	<.0001	0.3929	0.2447	0.0415	0.1283	0.5288
	5115	5115	5116	5116	5116	5115	5116	5115	5116	5116
VAN6	-0.13394	-0.1046	-0.16505	-0.11721	-0.07988	0.42735	0.24409	0.20443	0.17313	0.15764
	<.0001	<.0001	<.0001	<.0001	<.0001	<.0001	<.0001	<.0001	<.0001	<.0001
	5147	5147	5136	5125	5115	5147	5136	5147	5125	5115
VAN7	-0.1321	-0.06364	-0.19972	-0.11913	-0.04642	0.25441	0.63979	0.16718	0.14642	0.143
	<.0001	<.0001	<.0001	<.0001	0.0009	<.0001	<.0001	<.0001	<.0001	<.0001
	5136	5136	5126	5137	5116	5136	5137	5136	5126	5116
VAN8	0.01759	-0.02233	-0.11849	-0.08078	-0.00586	0.15797	0.22122	0.42851	0.16774	0.101
	0.207	0.109	<.0001	<.0001	0.6751	<.0001	<.0001	<.0001	<.0001	<.0001
	5147	5154	5136	5125	5115	5147	5136	5154	5125	5115
VAN9	-0.00131	-0.0542	-0.11183	-0.13042	-0.0077	0.10434	0.17281	0.13844	0.55861	0.21075
	0.9251	0.0001	<.0001	<.0001	0.5821	<.0001	<.0001	<.0001	<.0001	<.0001
	5125	5125	5126	5126	5116	5125	5126	5125	5126	5116
VAN10	-0.04589	-0.0881	-0.11477	-0.06579	0.00059	0.12985	0.18405	0.135	0.18495	0.30104
	0.001	<.0001	<.0001	<.0001	0.9663	<.0001	<.0001	<.0001	<.0001	<.0001
	5115	5115	5116	5116	5116	5115	5116	5115	5116	5116
VAN11	-0.06988	0.0338	0.06018	0.07868	-0.0031	0.0928	0.03053	-0.08105	-0.01085	0.09078
	<.0001	0.0154	<.0001	<.0001	0.8243	<.0001	0.0287	<.0001	0.4374	<.0001
	5135	5135	5136	5126	5116	5135	5136	5135	5126	5116
VAN12	-0.0347	0.05519	0.08977	0.12968	0.00937	0.02394	-0.05907	-0.13269	-0.06574	0.0764
	0.0131	<.0001	<.0001	<.0001	0.5029	0.0869	<.0001	<.0001	<.0001	<.0001
	5115	5115	5116	5116	5116	5115	5116	5115	5116	5116
VAN13	-0.10243	0.01674	0.02629	0.0555	-0.02733	0.14081	0.00844	-0.06667	0.0202	0.12468
	<.0001	0.2299	0.0596	<.0001	0.0506	<.0001	0.5455	<.0001	0.1483	<.0001
	5147	5147	5136	5125	5115	5147	5136	5147	5125	5115
VAN14	0.00285	0.12272	0.2267	0.2085	0.10975	-0.07254	-0.17236	-0.22005	-0.09752	0.01887
	0.8386	<.0001	<.0001	<.0001	<.0001	<.0001	<.0001	<.0001	<.0001	0.1771
	5125	5125	5126	5126	5116	5125	5126	5125	5126	5116
VAN15	-0.01961	0.07939	0.14255	0.1368	0.0338	0.00864	-0.06538	-0.14243	-0.02438	0.07201
	0.1595	<.0001	<.0001	<.0001	0.0156	0.5356	<.0001	<.0001	0.081	<.0001
	5147	5154	5136	5125	5115	5147	5136	5154	5125	5115
VAN16	0.01417	0.08525	0.19832	0.17775	0.06347	-0.07552	-0.13033	-0.23309	-0.1043	-0.00357
	0.3093	<.0001	<.0001	<.0001	<.0001	<.0001	<.0001	<.0001	<.0001	0.7986
	5147	5153	5136	5125	5115	5147	5136	5153	5125	5115
VAN17	-0.04183	0.00693	0.01358	0.05872	0.0019	0.0836	0.07759	-0.02997	-0.0281	0.09446
	0.0027	0.62	0.3309	<.0001	0.8917	<.0001	<.0001	0.0319	0.0443	<.0001
	5124	5124	5125	5125	5116	5124	5125	5124	5125	5116
VAN18	-0.04546	0.05066	0.07968	0.11656	0.03531	0.09273	0.01675	-0.08495	-0.0199	0.0706
	0.0011	0.0003	<.0001	<.0001	0.0115	<.0001	0.2301	<.0001	0.1543	<.0001
	5146	5146	5136	5125	5115	5146	5136	5146	5125	5115
VAN19	-0.05067	0.07005	0.14275	0.17774	0.03657	-0.02423	-0.09797	-0.19201	-0.08616	0.03539
	0.0003	<.0001	<.0001	<.0001	0.0089	0.0831	<.0001	<.0001	<.0001	0.0114
	5115	5115	5116	5116	5116	5115	5116	5115	5116	5116
VAN20	0.03264	0.08939	0.16942	0.22088	0.06747	-0.01389	-0.03966	-0.11334	-0.14778	-0.04288
	0.0193	<.0001	<.0001	<.0001	<.0001	0.3197	0.0045	<.0001	<.0001	0.0022
	5135	5135	5136	5126	5116	5135	5136	5135	5126	5116

	VAF11	VAF12	VAF13	VAF14	VAF15	VAF16	VAF17	VAF18	VAF19	VAF20
VAN1	-0.02265	-0.01859	-0.08248	0.05015	0.017	-0.00144	-0.04603	-0.07776	-0.03408	0.04956
	0.1045	0.1838	<.0001	0.0003	0.2227	0.9175	0.001	<.0001	0.0148	0.0004
	5135	5115	5147	5125	5147	5147	5125	5147	5115	5135
VAN2	0.03878	0.00689	-0.01443	0.0531	0.055	0.0128	-0.01304	-0.03131	-0.00864	0.01708
	0.0054	0.6221	0.3008	0.0001	<.0001	0.3581	0.3508	0.0247	0.5367	0.2211
	5135	5115	5147	5125	5154	5154	5125	5147	5115	5135
VAN3	0.03788	0.08015	-0.01919	0.18063	0.07789	0.1054	-0.03343	-0.01145	0.10819	0.11352
	0.0066	<.0001	0.1692	<.0001	<.0001	<.0001	0.0167	0.4119	<.0001	<.0001
	5136	5116	5135	5126	5135	5135	5126	5135	5116	5136
VAN4	0.05042	0.07534	-0.0031	0.20174	0.08619	0.09294	-0.00237	-0.01343	0.07106	0.09649
	0.0003	<.0001	0.8246	<.0001	<.0001	<.0001	0.8651	0.3363	<.0001	<.0001
	5126	5116	5125	5126	5125	5125	5126	5125	5116	5126
VAN5	0.02798	0.03461	-0.01696	0.10639	0.03927	0.06964	0.00849	-0.01214	0.05101	0.08132
	0.0454	0.0133	0.2252	<.0001	0.005	<.0001	0.5436	0.3853	0.0003	<.0001
	5116	5116	5116	5116	5115	5115	5116	5115	5116	5116
VAN6	0.02408	-0.0515	0.10271	-0.15439	-0.05021	-0.14464	0.08484	0.05257	-0.11561	-0.03288
	0.0844	0.0002	<.0001	<.0001	0.0003	<.0001	<.0001	0.0002	<.0001	0.0185
	5135	5115	5147	5125	5147	5147	5125	5147	5115	5135
VAN7	0.06199	-0.04984	0.06908	-0.12458	-0.04071	-0.10486	0.10475	0.0798	-0.08958	-0.02045
	<.0001	0.0004	<.0001	<.0001	0.0035	<.0001	<.0001	<.0001	<.0001	0.1429
	5136	5116	5136	5126	5136	5136	5126	5136	5116	5136
VAN8	-0.05501	-0.11411	-0.02211	-0.15668	-0.07409	-0.20029	0.00287	-0.03952	-0.17239	-0.04288
	<.0001	<.0001	0.1128	<.0001	<.0001	<.0001	0.8373	0.0046	<.0001	0.0021
	5135	5115	5147	5125	5154	5154	5125	5147	5115	5135
VAN9	-0.03686	-0.1137	-0.02668	-0.1334	-0.0434	-0.12312	-0.00591	-0.01947	-0.13156	-0.10859
	0.0083	<.0001	0.0561	<.0001	0.0019	<.0001	0.6724	0.1633	<.0001	<.0001
	5126	5116	5125	5126	5125	5125	5126	5125	5116	5126
VAN10	-0.03242	-0.04476	0.04222	-0.12465	-0.01747	-0.10023	0.10918	0.04285	-0.11676	-0.02606
	0.0204	0.0014	0.0025	<.0001	0.2116	<.0001	<.0001	0.0022	<.0001	0.0623
	5116	5116	5115	5116	5115	5115	5116	5115	5116	5116
VAN11	0.60569	0.27747	0.22315	0.20431	0.22381	0.21967	0.28691	0.2533	0.2909	0.18669
	<.0001	<.0001	<.0001	<.0001	<.0001	<.0001	<.0001	<.0001	<.0001	<.0001
	5136	5116	5135	5126	5135	5135	5126	5135	5116	5136
VAN12	0.24452	0.54763	0.24568	0.26071	0.26071	0.25818	0.22785	0.22454	0.36159	0.16449
	<.0001	<.0001	<.0001	<.0001	<.0001	<.0001	<.0001	<.0001	<.0001	<.0001
	5116	5116	5115	5116	5115	5115	5116	5115	5116	5116
VAN13	0.206	0.24482	0.59056	0.19125	0.25601	0.21321	0.18833	0.28883	0.20627	0.07363
	<.0001	<.0001	<.0001	<.0001	<.0001	<.0001	<.0001	<.0001	<.0001	<.0001
	5135	5115	5147	5125	5147	5147	5125	5147	5115	5135
VAN14	0.18246	0.29185	0.19949	0.49396	0.25596	0.33623	0.10905	0.16091	0.34545	0.14889
	<.0001	<.0001	<.0001	<.0001	<.0001	<.0001	<.0001	<.0001	<.0001	<.0001
	5126	5116	5125	5126	5125	5125	5126	5125	5116	5126
VAN15	0.16989	0.24148	0.23368	0.23133	0.5421	0.29146	0.14162	0.18034	0.23213	0.11808
	<.0001	<.0001	<.0001	<.0001	<.0001	<.0001	<.0001	<.0001	<.0001	<.0001
	5135	5115	5147	5125	5154	5154	5125	5147	5115	5135
VAN16	0.15454	0.24234	0.17723	0.26878	0.22258	0.53158	0.11764	0.17767	0.31606	0.17456
	<.0001	<.0001	<.0001	<.0001	<.0001	<.0001	<.0001	<.0001	<.0001	<.0001
	5135	5115	5147	5125	5153	5153	5125	5147	5115	5135
VAN17	0.27072	0.23274	0.15455	0.09482	0.1288	0.13125	0.72322	0.26578	0.21969	0.15108
	<.0001	<.0001	<.0001	<.0001	<.0001	<.0001	<.0001	<.0001	<.0001	<.0001
	5125	5116	5124	5125	5124	5124	5125	5124	5116	5125
VAN18	0.20935	0.20824	0.2524	0.18424	0.184	0.20968	0.25117	0.58456	0.19898	0.19105
	<.0001	<.0001	<.0001	<.0001	<.0001	<.0001	<.0001	<.0001	<.0001	<.0001
	5135	5115	5146	5125	5146	5146	5125	5146	5115	5135
VAN19	0.26412	0.34246	0.21328	0.28599	0.22665	0.33678	0.20727	0.21704	0.57732	0.17237
	<.0001	<.0001	<.0001	<.0001	<.0001	<.0001	<.0001	<.0001	<.0001	<.0001
	5116	5116	5115	5116	5115	5115	5116	5115	5116	5116
VAN20	0.22006	0.217	0.13071	0.23074	0.14134	0.21519	0.17032	0.2228	0.21336	0.55678
	<.0001	<.0001	<.0001	<.0001	<.0001	<.0001	<.0001	<.0001	<.0001	<.0001
	5136	5116	5135	5126	5135	5135	5126	5135	5116	5136

Internal consistencies, adult respondents, Monologue School, factual level

Cronbach Coefficient Alpha

Variables	Alpha
Raw	0.591219
Standardised	0.594042

Cronbach Coefficient Alpha with Deleted Variable

Deleted variable	Raw Variables		Standardised Variables	
	Correlation with Total	Alpha	Correlation with Total	Alpha
VAF1	0.316149	0.557221	0.315875	0.557232
VAF2	0.290006	0.565197	0.29276	0.569356
VAF3	0.406615	0.505194	0.407289	0.507484
VAF4	0.364957	0.526343	0.365536	0.530566
VAF5	0.367944	0.526075	0.368681	0.528849

Pearson Correlation Coefficients
Prob > |r| under H0: Rho=0
Number of Observations

	VAF1	VAF2	VAF3	VAF4	VAF5
VAF1	1	0.15759	0.22232	0.21882	0.22932
		<.0001	<.0001	<.0001	<.0001
	5147	5147	5136	5125	5115
VAF2	0.15759	1	0.22518	0.17463	0.21612
	<.0001		<.0001	<.0001	<.0001
	5147	5154	5136	5125	5115
VAF3	0.22232	0.22518	1	0.31621	0.27131
	<.0001	<.0001		<.0001	<.0001
	5136	5136	5137	5126	5116
VAF4	0.21882	0.17463	0.31621	1	0.23252
	<.0001	<.0001	<.0001		<.0001
	5125	5125	5126	5126	5116
VAF5	0.22932	0.21612	0.27131	0.23252	1
	<.0001	<.0001	<.0001	<.0001	
	5115	5115	5116	5116	5116

Internal consistencies, adult respondents, Monologue School, normative level

Cronbach Coefficient Alpha

Variables	Alpha
Raw	0.769561
Standardised	0.769371

Cronbach Coefficient Alpha with Deleted Variable

Deleted variable	Raw Variables		Standardised Variables	
	Correlation with Total	Alpha	Correlation with Total	Alpha
VAN1	0.581762	0.712816	0.581389	0.712808
VAN2	0.559325	0.720834	0.557319	0.721258
VAN3	0.500615	0.740828	0.50038	0.740825
VAN4	0.549611	0.724267	0.54902	0.724146
VAN5	0.511368	0.737297	0.511003	0.737219

Pearson Correlation Coefficients
Prob > |r| under H0: Rho=0
Number of Observations

	VAN1	VAN2	VAN3	VAN4	VAN5
VAN1	1	0.45723	0.3958	0.46027	0.39115
		<.0001	<.0001	<.0001	<.0001
	5147	5147	5135	5125	5115
VAN2	0.45723	1	0.35532	0.40139	0.43119
	<.0001		<.0001	<.0001	<.0001
	5147	5154	5135	5125	5115
VAN3	0.3958	0.35532	1	0.40341	0.34672
	<.0001	<.0001		<.0001	<.0001
	5135	5135	5136	5126	5116
VAN4	0.46027	0.40139	0.40341	1	0.35941
	<.0001	<.0001	<.0001		<.0001
	5125	5125	5126	5126	5116
VAN5	0.39115	0.43119	0.34672	0.35941	1
	<.0001	<.0001	<.0001	<.0001	
	5115	5115	5116	5116	5116

Internal consistencies, adult respondents, Dialogue School, factual level

Cronbach Coefficient Alpha

Variables	Alpha
Raw	0.620320
Standardised	0.622038

Cronbach Coefficient Alpha with Deleted Variable

Deleted variable	Raw Variables		Standardised Variables	
	Correlation with Total	Alpha	Correlation with Total	Alpha
VAF6	0.390532	0.557726	0.391915	0.559789
VAF7	0.356563	0.575053	0.359625	0.576178
VAF8	0.380442	0.565674	0.380705	0.565516
VAF9	0.397762	0.55381	0.40008	0.555593
VAF10	0.348993	0.579507	0.344217	0.583884

Pearson Correlation Coefficients
Prob > |r| under H0: Rho=0
Number of Observations

	VAF6	VAF7	VAF8	VAF9	VAF10
VAF6	1	0.30806	0.25002	0.22804	0.24295
		<.0001	<.0001	<.0001	<.0001
	5147	5136	5147	5125	5115
VAF7	0.30806	1	0.27484	0.19196	0.1796
	<.0001		<.0001	<.0001	<.0001
	5136	5137	5136	5126	5116
VAF8	0.25002	0.27484	1	0.30524	0.17326
	<.0001	<.0001		<.0001	<.0001
	5147	5136	5154	5125	5115
VAF9	0.22804	0.19196	0.30524	1	0.32244
	<.0001	<.0001	<.0001		<.0001
	5125	5126	5125	5126	5116
VAF10	0.24295	0.1796	0.17326	0.32244	1
	<.0001	<.0001	<.0001	<.0001	
	5115	5116	5115	5116	5116

Internal consistencies, adult respondents, Dialogue School, normative level

Cronbach Coefficient Alpha

Variables	Alpha
Raw	0.656751
Standardised	0.663192

Cronbach Coefficient Alpha with Deleted Variable

Deleted variable	Raw Variables			Standardised Variables	
	Correlation with Total	Alpha		Correlation with Total	Alpha
VAN6	0.425968	0.598992		0.42907	0.605517
VAN7	0.413699	0.603514		0.420223	0.609613
VAN8	0.452565	0.590687		0.453455	0.594116
VAN9	0.411843	0.604692		0.412288	0.613268
VAN10	0.364273	0.627088		0.365024	0.634683

Pearson Correlation Coefficients
Prob > |r| under H0: Rho=0
Number of Observations

	VAN6	VAN7	VAN8	VAN9	VAN10
VAN6	1	0.31818	0.32526	0.25972	0.25834
		<.0001	<.0001	<.0001	<.0001
	5147	5136	5147	5125	5115
VAN7	0.31818	1	0.33599	0.2743	0.21229
	<.0001		<.0001	<.0001	<.0001
	5136	5137	5136	5126	5116
VAN8	0.32526	0.33599	1	0.30344	0.25332
	<.0001	<.0001		<.0001	<.0001
	5147	5136	5154	5125	5115
VAN9	0.25972	0.2743	0.30344	1	0.2846
	<.0001	<.0001	<.0001		<.0001
	5125	5126	5125	5126	5116
VAN10	0.25834	0.21229	0.25332	0.2846	1
	<.0001	<.0001	<.0001	<.0001	
	5115	5116	5115	5116	5116

Internal consistencies, adult respondents, Colourful School, factual level

Cronbach Coefficient Alpha

Variables	Alpha
Raw	0.670309
Standardised	0.671429

Cronbach Coefficient Alpha with Deleted Variable

Deleted variable	Raw Variables		Standardised Variables	
	Correlation with Total	Alpha	Correlation with Total	Alpha
VAF11	0.417423	0.62245	0.416027	0.624176
VAF12	0.48983	0.589679	0.490246	0.590109
VAF13	0.435904	0.613851	0.435451	0.615404
VAF14	0.315188	0.664678	0.31871	0.666635
VAF15	0.467803	0.600731	0.466918	0.600977

Pearson Correlation Coefficients
Prob > |r| under H0: Rho=0
Number of Observations

	VAF11	VAF12	VAF13	VAF14	VAF15
VAF11	1	0.34694	0.31793	0.17732	0.29871
		<.0001	<.0001	<.0001	<.0001
	5136	5116	5135	5126	5135
VAF12	0.34694	1	0.32629	0.29371	0.34633
	<.0001		<.0001	<.0001	<.0001
	5116	5116	5115	5116	5115
VAF13	0.31793	0.32629	1	0.17903	0.36361
	<.0001	<.0001		<.0001	<.0001
	5135	5115	5147	5125	5147
VAF14	0.17732	0.29371	0.17903	1	0.25137
	<.0001	<.0001	<.0001		<.0001
	5126	5116	5125	5126	5125
VAF15	0.29871	0.34633	0.36361	0.25137	1
	<.0001	<.0001	<.0001	<.0001	
	5135	5115	5147	5125	5154

Internal consistencies, adult respondents, Colourful School, normative level

Cronbach Coefficient Alpha

Variables	Alpha
Raw	0.784836
Standardised	0.785695

Cronbach Coefficient Alpha with Deleted Variable

Deleted variable	Raw Variables		Standardised Variables	
	Correlation with Total	Alpha	Correlation with Total	Alpha
VAN11_2	0.555635	0.747556	0.553743	0.748346
VAN12_2	0.611027	0.728163	0.611279	0.729225
VAN13_2	0.576991	0.739416	0.574886	0.741385
VAN14_2	0.503665	0.763232	0.504949	0.764123
VAN15_2	0.565343	0.743168	0.565341	0.744537

Pearson Correlation Coefficients
Prob > |r| under H0: Rho=0
Number of Observations

	VAN11_2	VAN12_2	VAN13_2	VAN14_2	VAN15_2
VAN11_2	1	0.48037	0.43433	0.3544	0.40289
		<.0001	<.0001	<.0001	<.0001
	5136	5116	5135	5126	5135
VAN12_2	0.48037	1	0.45599	0.43376	0.44615
	<.0001		<.0001	<.0001	<.0001
	5116	5116	5115	5116	5115
VAN13_2	0.43433	0.45599	1	0.37016	0.46512
	<.0001	<.0001		<.0001	<.0001
	5135	5115	5147	5125	5147
VAN14_2	0.3544	0.43376	0.37016	1	0.38732
	<.0001	<.0001	<.0001		<.0001
	5126	5116	5125	5126	5125
VAN15_2	0.40289	0.44615	0.46512	0.38732	1
	<.0001	<.0001	<.0001	<.0001	
	5135	5115	5147	5125	5154

Internal consistencies, adult respondents, Colourless School, factual level

Cronbach Coefficient Alpha

Variables	Alpha
Raw	0.596046
Standardised	0.598369

Cronbach Coefficient Alpha with Deleted Variable

Deleted variable	Raw Variables		Standardised Variables	
	Correlation with Total	Alpha	Correlation with Total	Alpha
VAF16	0.375739	0.530896	0.377794	0.530575
VAF17	0.320129	0.55894	0.316383	0.563294
VAF18	0.374459	0.528528	0.372391	0.533505
VAF19	0.4218	0.502196	0.429967	0.50176
VAF20	0.27446	0.582362	0.275179	0.584535

Pearson Correlation Coefficients
Prob > |r| under H0: Rho=0
Number of Observations

	VAF16	VAF17	VAF18	VAF19	VAF20
VAF16	1	0.14026	0.22176	0.42278	0.18898
		<.0001	<.0001	<.0001	<.0001
	5154	5125	5147	5115	5135
VAF17	0.14026	1	0.30142	0.24232	0.14864
	<.0001		<.0001	<.0001	<.0001
	5125	5126	5125	5116	5126
VAF18	0.22176	0.30142	1	0.23272	0.20571
	<.0001	<.0001		<.0001	<.0001
	5147	5125	5147	5115	5135
VAF19	0.42278	0.24232	0.23272	1	0.19107
	<.0001	<.0001	<.0001		<.0001
	5115	5116	5115	5116	5116
VAF20	0.18898	0.14864	0.20571	0.19107	1
	<.0001	<.0001	<.0001	<.0001	
	5135	5126	5135	5116	5136

Internal consistencies, adult respondents, Colourless School, normative level

Cronbach Coefficient Alpha

Variables	Alpha
Raw	0.721891
Standardised	0.721999

Cronbach Coefficient Alpha with Deleted Variable

Deleted variable	Raw Variables		Standardised Variables	
	Correlation with Total	Alpha	Correlation with Total	Alpha
VAN16	0.52705	0.656931	0.526409	0.656636
VAN17	0.435821	0.69257	0.434794	0.692897
VAN18	0.491179	0.670601	0.490981	0.670878
VAN19	0.545546	0.648188	0.54719	0.648152
VAN20	0.406801	0.703196	0.40716	0.703474

Pearson Correlation Coefficients
Prob > |r| under H0: Rho=0
Number of Observations

	VAN16	VAN17	VAN18	VAN19	VAN20
VAN16	1	0.27578	0.35272	0.53536	0.31397
		<.0001	<.0001	<.0001	<.0001
	5153	5124	5146	5115	5135
VAN17	0.27578	1	0.37488	0.35461	0.24944
	<.0001		<.0001	<.0001	<.0001
	5124	5125	5124	5116	5125
VAN18	0.35272	0.37488	1	0.3404	0.32511
	<.0001	<.0001		<.0001	<.0001
	5146	5124	5146	5115	5135
VAN19	0.53536	0.35461	0.3404	1	0.29627
	<.0001	<.0001	<.0001		<.0001
	5115	5116	5115	5116	5116
VAN20	0.31397	0.24944	0.32511	0.29627	1
	<.0001	<.0001	<.0001	<.0001	
	5135	5125	5135	5116	5136

Factor analysis, adult respondents, factual level

Initial Factor Method: Principal Components
Prior Communality Estimates: ONE
Eigenvalues of the Correlation Matrix: Total = 20 Average = 1

	Eigenvalue	Difference	Proportion	Cumulative
1	3.49333066	0.510554	0.1747	0.1747
2	2.98277666	1.54313467	0.1491	0.3238
3	1.43964199	0.22892897	0.072	0.3958
4	1.21071302	0.28780311	0.0605	0.4563
5	0.92290991	0.0596565	0.0461	0.5025
6	0.86325341	0.03974535	0.0432	0.5456
7	0.82350805	0.0376183	0.0412	0.5868
8	0.78588975	0.05798682	0.0393	0.6261
9	0.72790294	0.01816171	0.0364	0.6625
10	0.70974122	0.01987632	0.0355	0.698
11	0.6898649	0.02680877	0.0345	0.7325
12	0.66305613	0.01569953	0.0332	0.7656
13	0.6473566	0.01740379	0.0324	0.798
14	0.62995282	0.00949953	0.0315	0.8295
15	0.62045328	0.01934534	0.031	0.8605
16	0.60110794	0.02052112	0.0301	0.8906
17	0.58058682	0.01264161	0.029	0.9196
18	0.56794521	0.02129822	0.0284	0.948
19	0.54664699	0.0532853	0.0273	0.9753
20	0.49336169		0.0247	1

3 factors will be retained by the NFACTOR criterion.

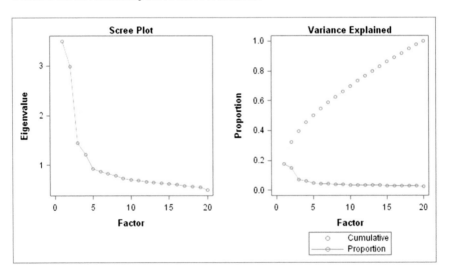

Eigenvectors

	1	2	3
VAF1	-0.06618	-0.24213	0.37104
VAF2	0.0929	-0.17935	0.37352
VAF3	0.08553	-0.33015	0.25946
VAF4	0.07117	-0.36244	0.08984
VAF5	0.02256	-0.215	0.49782
VAF6	0.09499	0.34308	0.1383
VAF7	-0.01689	0.3059	0.18856
VAF8	-0.10935	0.29992	0.30707
VAF9	-0.03751	0.2927	0.37749
VAF10	0.10051	0.27951	0.24057
VAF11	0.328	0.14442	-0.01168
VAF12	0.35713	0.02663	-0.06852
VAF13	0.30976	0.18537	-0.01793
VAF14	0.26676	-0.17505	0.11474
VAF15	0.33171	0.03764	0.04077
VAF16	0.33469	-0.10953	-0.07488
VAF17	0.24896	0.14758	0.03695
VAF18	0.2799	0.08075	0.07884
VAF19	0.36816	-0.06126	-0.12734
VAF20	0.20292	-0.15985	-0.02937

Factor Pattern

	Factor1	Factor2	Factor3
VAF19	0.6881	-0.10579	-0.15279
VAF12	0.6675	0.04599	-0.08221
VAF16	0.62555	-0.18917	-0.08985
VAF15	0.61997	0.06501	0.04892
VAF11	0.61305	0.24942	-0.01401
VAF13	0.57895	0.32015	-0.02152
VAF18	0.52314	0.13946	0.0946
VAF14	0.49859	-0.30232	0.13768
VAF17	0.46532	0.25489	0.04434
VAF20	0.37927	-0.27608	-0.03523
VAF6	0.17754	0.59252	0.16594
VAF7	-0.03158	0.52832	0.22624
VAF8	-0.20438	0.51798	0.36844
VAF9	-0.07011	0.50551	0.45293
VAF10	0.18785	0.48273	0.28865
VAF3	0.15987	-0.57019	0.31132
VAF4	0.13303	-0.62596	0.1078
VAF5	0.04217	-0.37133	0.5973
VAF2	0.17363	-0.30974	0.44817
VAF1	-0.12369	-0.41818	0.4452

Variance Explained by Each Factor

	Factor1	Factor2	Factor3
	3.4933307	2.9827767	1.439642

Final Communality Estimates: Total = 9.187058

VAF1	VAF2	VAF3	VAF4	VAF5	VAF6	VAF7	VAF8	VAF9	VAF10
0.38837	0.32694	0.44760	0.42114	0.49643	0.41014	0.33130	0.44582	0.46560	0.35164

VAF11	VAF12	VAF13	VAF14	VAF15	VAF16	VAF17	VAF18	VAF19	VAF20
0.43823	0.45443	0.43814	0.35894	0.39099	0.43518	0.28346	0.30207	0.50802	0.22131

Rotation Method: Varimax

Orthogonal Transformation Matrix

	1	2	3
1	0.99286	-0.05566	0.1055
2	0.10724	0.80378	-0.58519
3	-0.05223	0.59232	0.80401

Rotated Factor Pattern

	Factor1	Factor2	Factor3
VAF19	0.67982	-0.21383	0.01166
VAF12	0.67196	-0.04888	-0.02259
VAF11	0.63615	0.15805	-0.09254
VAF15	0.61996	0.04672	0.06669
VAF13	0.61027	0.21236	-0.14357
VAF16	0.60549	-0.24009	0.10446
VAF18	0.52942	0.13901	0.04964
VAF17	0.48702	0.20523	-0.06442
VAF14	0.45541	-0.1892	0.34021
VAF20	0.3488	-0.26389	0.17324
VAF9	-0.03906	0.6785	0.06095
VAF8	-0.16661	0.64595	-0.02845
VAF6	0.23115	0.56466	-0.19459
VAF7	0.01349	0.56041	-0.1306
VAF10	0.2232	0.54853	-0.03059
VAF5	-0.02915	0.05299	0.70198
VAF3	0.08132	-0.28281	0.60084
VAF1	-0.1909	-0.06554	0.58961
VAF2	0.11576	0.00683	0.55991
VAF4	0.05932	-0.44668	0.46701

Variance Explained by Each Factor

	Factor1	Factor2	Factor3
	3.4818564	2.4429551	1.9909378

Factor analysis, adult respondents, normative level

Initial Factor Method: Principal Components
Prior Communality Estimates: ONE
Eigenvalues of the Correlation Matrix: Total = 20 Average = 1

	Eigenvalue	Difference	Proportion	Cumulative
1	5.05746892	2.18729212	0.2529	0.2529
2	2.87017679	1.15009046	0.1435	0.3964
3	1.72008634	0.78080151	0.086	0.4824
4	0.93928482	0.12346309	0.047	0.5294
5	0.81582173	0.06334091	0.0408	0.5701
6	0.75248082	0.01977817	0.0376	0.6078
7	0.73270265	0.02823207	0.0366	0.6444
8	0.70447058	0.0327423	0.0352	0.6796
9	0.67172828	0.0549467	0.0336	0.7132
10	0.61678158	0.02234614	0.0308	0.7441
11	0.59443545	0.01611463	0.0297	0.7738
12	0.57832082	0.00110033	0.0289	0.8027
13	0.57722048	0.04041169	0.0289	0.8315
14	0.53680879	0.01178353	0.0268	0.8584
15	0.52502526	0.02060523	0.0263	0.8846
16	0.50442003	0.01755109	0.0252	0.9099
17	0.48686893	0.0163366	0.0243	0.9342
18	0.47053234	0.01908306	0.0235	0.9577
19	0.45144928	0.05753318	0.0226	0.9803
20	0.3939161		0.0197	1

3 factors will be retained by the NFACTOR criterion.

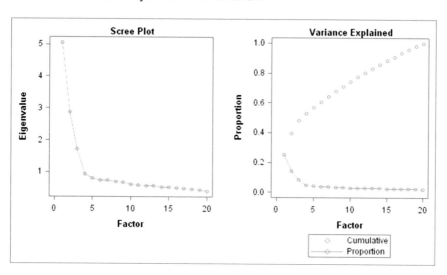

452

Eigenvectors

	1	2	3
VAN1	-0.22962	0.26367	0.24714
VAN2	-0.20622	0.23536	0.3152
VAN3	-0.11963	0.36794	0.16931
VAN4	-0.13485	0.31015	0.32215
VAN5	-0.17186	0.24656	0.30098
VAN6	0.02554	-0.34941	0.26557
VAN7	-0.03108	-0.31862	0.27975
VAN8	-0.15351	-0.26005	0.36055
VAN9	-0.07022	-0.29113	0.24018
VAN10	-0.00671	-0.28949	0.23481
VAN11	0.30986	0.00279	0.14071
VAN12	0.32142	0.06188	0.1076
VAN13	0.31013	-0.06909	0.10112
VAN14	0.26733	0.19209	0.03765
VAN15	0.28788	0.04367	0.09449
VAN16	0.3078	0.16335	-0.03294
VAN17	0.24363	-0.04796	0.2419
VAN18	0.26319	-0.00535	0.24099
VAN19	0.3248	0.12839	0.03396
VAN20	0.18398	0.17324	0.23269

Factor Pattern

	Factor1	Factor2	Factor3
VAN19	0.73044	0.21751	0.04453
VAN12	0.72284	0.10483	0.14113
VAN13	0.69744	-0.11705	0.13262
VAN11	0.69684	0.00473	0.18454
VAN16	0.69221	0.27675	-0.04321
VAN15	0.64741	0.07398	0.12392
VAN14	0.6012	0.32543	0.04937
VAN18	0.59188	-0.00907	0.31607
VAN17	0.5479	-0.08125	0.31726
VAN20	0.41376	0.29349	0.30518
VAN2	-0.46376	0.39873	0.41339
VAN1	-0.51639	0.4467	0.32413
VAN3	-0.26904	0.62334	0.22205
VAN4	-0.30327	0.52544	0.42251
VAN5	-0.38649	0.41772	0.39474
VAN10	-0.0151	-0.49045	0.30796
VAN9	-0.15791	-0.49322	0.31501
VAN7	-0.06989	-0.53979	0.3669
VAN6	0.05743	-0.59196	0.3483
VAN8	-0.34522	-0.44057	0.47287

Variance Explained by Each Factor

Factor1	Factor2	Factor3
5.0574689	2.8701768	1.7200863

Final Communality Estimates: Total = 9.187058

VAN1	VAN2	VAN3	VAN4	VAN5	VAN6	VAN7	VAN8	VAN9	VAN10
0.57126	0.54495	0.51025	0.54657	0.47968	0.47503	0.43087	0.53688	0.36743	0.33561

VAN11	VAN12	VAN13	VAN14	VAN15	VAN16	VAN17	VAN18	VAN19	VAN20
0.51966	0.55340	0.51771	0.46979	0.43997	0.55761	0.40744	0.45030	0.58283	0.35047

Rotation Method: Varimax

Orthogonal Transformation Matrix

	1	2	3
1	0.89686	-0.42135	-0.13456
2	0.18849	0.63929	-0.7455
3	0.40015	0.64324	0.65278

Rotated Factor Pattern

	Factor1	Factor2	Factor3
VAN12	0.72451	-0.14677	-0.0833
VAN19	0.71392	-0.14008	-0.23137
VAN11	0.6997	-0.17189	0.02317
VAN13	0.6565	-0.28339	0.07999
VAN16	0.65569	-0.14253	-0.32767
VAN18	0.65559	-0.05188	0.13344
VAN15	0.64417	-0.14578	-0.06138
VAN14	0.62029	-0.01352	-0.29128
VAN17	0.60302	-0.07873	0.19395
VAN20	0.54852	0.2096	-0.07526
VAN4	-0.00388	0.73547	-0.0751
VAN2	-0.17535	0.71623	0.035
VAN1	-0.24923	0.71165	-0.05195
VAN5	-0.10993	0.68381	-0.00172
VAN3	-0.03494	0.6547	-0.28355
VAN8	-0.20344	0.16798	0.68358
VAN6	0.0793	-0.1786	0.66094
VAN7	-0.01762	-0.07963	0.65132
VAN9	-0.10854	-0.04615	0.59457
VAN10	0.01724	-0.10909	0.56869

Variance Explained by Each Factor

	Factor1	Factor2	Factor3
	4.4453851	2.7826416	2.4197053

Intercorrelations between the three multi-variate attitude scales

Correlations between the PCB Scale and the Melbourne Scale, factual level

Pearson Correlation Coefficients
Prob > |r| under H0: Rho=0
Number of Observations

	SecF	ReconfF	ValedF	RecontF	ConfF
LB	0.01082	0.24802	0.25776	0.15535	0.18143
	0.4446	<.0001	<.0001	<.0001	<.0001
	4994	4994	4994	4994	4994
EC	0.29694	0.05091	-0.10455	-0.27366	-0.05543
	<.0001	0.0003	<.0001	<.0001	<.0001
	4994	4994	4994	4994	4994
REL	-0.03883	-0.00676	0.07121	0.1192	0.01548
	0.0061	0.6327	<.0001	<.0001	0.2741
	4994	4994	4994	4994	4994
PCB	-0.1671	0.02735	0.17016	0.28875	0.05141
	<.0001	0.0533	<.0001	<.0001	0.0003
	4994	4994	4994	4994	4994

Correlations between the PCB Scale and the Melbourne Scale, normative level

Pearson Correlation Coefficients
Prob > |r| under H0: Rho=0
Number of Observations

	SecN	ReconfN	ValedN	RecontN
LB	-0.32585	0.52242	0.33888	0.01339
	<.0001	<.0001	<.0001	0.4803
	4996	4996	4996	4996
EC	0.57285	-0.25233	-0.19856	-0.29263
	<.0001	<.0001	<.0001	<.0001
	4996	4996	4996	4996
REL	0.08835	-0.13612	0.04791	0.20514
	<.0001	<.0001	0.0004	<.0001
	4996	4996	4996	4996
PCB	-0.35551	0.11068	0.30742	0.39416
	<.0001	<.0001	<.0001	<.0001
	4996	4996	4996	4996

Correlations between the PCB Scale and the Victoria Scale, factual level

Pearson Correlation Coefficients
Prob > |r| under H0: Rho=0
Number of Observations

	MonoF	DiaF	ColfulF	CollessF
LB	0.14203	0.05341	0.15552	0.06148
	<.0001	0.0003	<.0001	<.0001
	4667	4667	4667	4667
EC	0.15645	-0.1144	0.30835	0.31544
	<.0001	<.0001	<.0001	<.0001
	4667	4667	4667	4667
REL	-0.02035	0.14668	0.0255	0.05772
	0.1645	<.0001	0.0815	<.0001
	4667	4667	4667	4667
PCB	-0.04723	0.21447	-0.14662	-0.11137
	0.0012	<.0001	<.0001	<.0001
	4667	4667	4667	4667

Correlations between the PCB Scale and the Victoria Scale, normative level

Pearson Correlation Coefficients
Prob > |r| under H0: Rho=0
Number of Observations

	MonoN	DiaN	ColfulN	CollessN
LB	0.59301	-0.11705	-0.21712	-0.18544
	<.0001	<.0001	<.0001	<.0001
	4625	4625	4625	4625
EC	-0.19248	-0.21615	0.54735	0.53508
	<.0001	<.0001	<.0001	<.0001
	4625	4625	4625	4625
REL	-0.18457	0.29741	0.13547	0.11539
	<.0001	<.0001	<.0001	<.0001
	4625	4625	4625	4625
PCB	0.12120	0.40556	-0.29368	-0.26652
	<.0001	<.0001	<.0001	<.0001
	4625	4625	4625	4625

Correlations between the Melbourne Scale, factual level and the Victoria Scale, factual level

Pearson Correlation Coefficients
Prob > |r| under H0: Rho=0
Number of Observations

	SecF	ReconfF	ValedF	RecontF	ConfF
MonoF	0.10659	0.39203	0.13499	-0.23988	0.0755
	<.0001	<.0001	<.0001	<.0001	<.0001
	4755	4755	4755	4755	4755
DiaF	-0.19666	-0.04706	0.19024	0.56731	0.14335
	<.0001	0.0012	<.0001	<.0001	<.0001
	4755	4755	4755	4755	4755
ColfulF	0.36328	-0.05904	-0.04874	-0.08879	-0.17695
	<.0001	<.0001	0.0008	<.0001	<.0001
	4755	4755	4755	4755	4755
CollessF	0.39908	-0.06437	-0.08487	-0.1924	-0.2039
	<.0001	<.0001	<.0001	<.0001	<.0001
	4755	4755	4755	4755	4755

Correlations between the Melbourne Scale, normative level and the Victoria Scale, factual level

Pearson Correlation Coefficients
Prob > |r| under H0: Rho=0
Number of Observations

	SecN	ReconfN	ValedN	RecontN
MonoF	0.10788	0.17497	0.09203	-0.1274
	<.0001	<.0001	<.0001	<.0001
	4755	4755	4755	4755
DiaF	-0.15775	0.03407	0.16215	0.35872
	<.0001	0.0188	<.0001	<.0001
	4755	4755	4755	4755
ColfulF	0.23979	-0.02516	-0.0035	-0.14855
	<.0001	0.0827	0.8091	<.0001
	4755	4755	4755	4755
CollessF	0.29527	-0.06802	-0.06138	-0.14637
	<.0001	<.0001	<.0001	<.0001
	4755	4755	4755	4755

**Correlations between the Melbourne Scale, factual level
and the Victoria Scale, normative level**

Pearson Correlation Coefficients
Prob > |r| under H0: Rho=0
Number of Observations

	SecF	ReconfF	ValedF	RecontF	ConfF
MonoN	0.01571	0.33873	0.3199	0.09896	0.13405
	0.2787	<.0001	<.0001	<.0001	<.0001
	4755	4755	4755	4755	4755
DiaN	-0.17417	-0.06698	0.13606	0.3882	0.03521
	<.0001	<.0001	<.0001	<.0001	0.0152
	4755	4755	4755	4755	4755
ColfulN	0.27706	-0.06388	-0.1713	-0.24763	-0.10598
	<.0001	<.0001	<.0001	<.0001	<.0001
	4755	4755	4755	4755	4755
CollessN	0.28165	-0.02802	-0.14369	-0.26792	-0.08802
	<.0001	0.0533	<.0001	<.0001	<.0001
	4755	4755	4755	4755	4755

**Correlations between the Melbourne Scale, normative level
and the Victoria Scale, normative level**

Pearson Correlation Coefficients
Prob > |r| under H0: Rho=0
Number of Observations

	SecN	ReconfN	ValedN	RecontN
MonoN	-0.37070	0.66964	0.42512	-0.01418
	<.0001	<.0001	<.0001	0.3356
	4733	4733	4733	4733
DiaN	-0.24669	-0.00697	0.18993	0.54100
	<.0001	0.6137	<.0001	<.0001
	4733	4733	4733	4733
ColfulN	0.62205	-0.45695	-0.26438	-0.18706
	<.0001	<.0001	<.0001	<.0001
	4733	4733	4733	4733
CollessN	0.59691	-0.36207	-0.23095	-0.21606
	<.0001	<.0001	<.0001	<.0001
	4733	4733	4733	4733

ECSIP picture album

Group photo of the ECSIP team posing with the CEO staff members responsible for religious education and Catholic school identity during the two-week CEO Staff Training in Leuven. Picture taken at the Faculty Club Restaurant in Leuven, 5 February 2009.

Prof. Dr. Didier Pollefeyt (promotor of the ECSIP, standing in the middle) and his predecessor Prof. Dr. Herman Lombaerts, posing with the officers responsible for Religious Education in the Catholic Education Offices of the four dioceses of Victoria. Leuven, 5 February 2009.

Learning to analyse, describe, interpret and evaluate the ECSIP results bears a similarity to learning to read *X-ray pictures*. It requires a thorough knowledge of the 'anatomy' of both Catholic educational organisations and the empirical instruments used to picture it.

The skills needed to *assess* school identity should be acquainted by all who engage with it as a first step and a prerequisite to a meaningful and successful process of *enhancing* the Catholic identity of schools.

Top left: **Mr. Tony Byrne**, Coordinating Manager, Religious Education and Catholic Identity in the *Catholic Education Office Melbourne* (CEOM) and member of the *ECSIP Steering Committee*.

Top right: **Prof. Dr. Didier Pollefeyt**, Vice President for Education KU Leuven, full professor at the *Faculty of Theology and Religious Studies*, Chair of the *Center for Academic Teacher Training* and promotor of the ECSIP Project.

Bottom right: **Drs. Jan Bouwens**, scientific collaborator and research assistant to Didier Pollefeyt, appointed to the ECSIP Project since 2007.

The pictures were taken in the *Natural Evolution* section of the *Melbourne Museum* during a leisure visit on 28 August 2010.

These photographs show a group of secondary school students from Mary MacKillop College Swan Hill, completing the ECSIP surveys in the computer room on 25 May 2010 as part of the *ECSIP 2010 Trial*.

The pictures were taken by Gina Bernasconi, Education Officer for secondary colleges in the *Catholic Education Office Ballarat* (reproduced with permission).

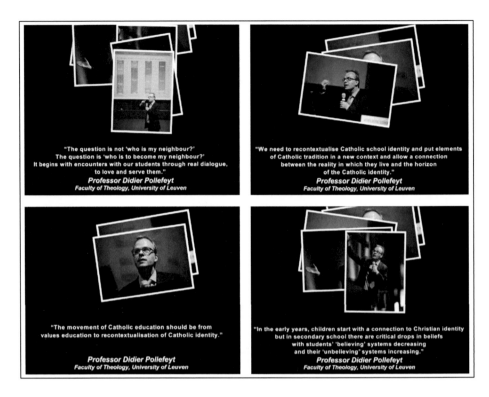

Pictures and quotes from Prof. Didier Pollefeyt's keynote lecture at the *National Catholic Education Convention* in Adelaide, Australia in September 2011.

Screenshots taken from the official NCEC website, http://www.nceconv2011.com.au/ (access 29-11-2011).

On Friday 7 March 2014, the ECSIP Project was presented in Rome by prof. Didier Pollefeyt to the Vatican *Congregation for Catholic Education (for Educational Institutions)* in the presence of the prefect of the Congregation, Cardinal Zenon Grocholewski. The ECSIP research was very well received.

Also present at the meeting were:
- André-Joseph Léonard, archbishop of Mechelen-Brussel
- Johan Bonny, bishop of Antwerp
- Rik Torfs, Rector Magnificus of the KU Leuven
- representatives of the governing association of the KU Leuven.

Top left: Polish-born Cardinal Zenon Grocholewski, Prefect of the *Congregation for Catholic Education* and Grand Chancellor of the *Pontifical Gregorian University*, presides over the meeting.

Top right: Prof. Didier Pollefeyt, Vice President for Education KU Leuven, presents the ECSIP Project to the assembled dignitaries.

Bottom left: In the middle of the picture is Mgr Johan Bonny, bishop of Antwerp, mandated to oversee Catholic education in Flanders, Belgium.

Bottom right: Cardinal Grocholewski responds to the ECSIP presentation. On the right hand side of the picture is prof. Rik Torfs, current Rector of the KU Leuven.

Selected bibliography

ARBUCKLE, G. A., *Catholic Identity or Identities? Refounding Ministries in Chaotic Times*, Collegeville, MN, Liturgical Press, 2013.

BAARDA, B. & DE GOEDE, M., *Basisboek Methoden en Technieken. Handleiding voor het opzetten van onderzoek*, Groningen, Stenfert Kroese, 2001.

BARNES, P. L., *Education, Religion and Diversity. Developing a new model of religious education*, London - New York, Routledge, 2014.

BEST, J., *Damned Lies and Statistics. Untangling Numbers from the Media, Politicians, and Activists*, Berkeley – Los Angeles – London, University of California Press, 2001.

BILLIET J., LOOSVELDT G. & WATERPLAS L., *Het Survey-Onderzoek Onderzocht. Sociologische Studies en Documenten*, Leuven, Leuven University Press, 1984.

BILLIET, J. & WAEGE (ed.), H., *Een samenleving onderzocht. Methoden van sociaal-wetenschappelijk onderzoek*, 2de druk, Antwerpen, De Boeck nv, 2006.

BOEVE, L., *Interrupting Tradition. An Essay on Christian Faith in a Postmodern Context* (*Louvain Theological and Pastoral Monographs* 30), Leuven, Peeters, 2002.

BOEVE, L., *The Identity of a Catholic University in Post-Christian European Societies: Four Models*, in *Louvain Studies* 31 (2006), 238-258.

BOEVE, L., *Beyond Correlation Strategies. Teaching Religion in a Detraditionalised and Pluralised Context*, in H. LOMBAERTS & D. POLLEFEYT (ed.), *Hermeneutics and Religious Education* (BETL 180), Leuven, Peeters, 2004, 233-254.

BOEVE, L., *God Interrupts History: Theology in a Time of Upheaval* , London - New York, Continuum, 2007.

BOEVE, L., *Systematic Theology, Truth and History: Recontextualisation*, in M. Lamberigts, L. Boeve & T. Merrigan (eds), *Orthodoxy: Process and Product* (BETL, 227), Leuven: Peeters Press, 2009, 27-44.

Church Documents on Catholic Education 1965-2002, Australian Edition, Strathfield NSW, St Pauls Publications, 2004.

CONGREGATION FOR CATHOLIC EDUCATION (FOR INSTITUTES OF STUDY), signed by ZENON GROCHOLEWSKI & ANGELO VINCENZO ZANI, *Educating to Intercultural Dialogue in Catholic Schools. Living in Harmony for a Civilization of Love* (22 October 2013); http://www.vatican.va/roman_curia/congregations/ccatheduc/documents/rc_c on_ccatheduc_doc_20131028_dialogo-interculturale_en.html (access 15 May 2014).

DILLEN, A. & POLLEFEYT, D. (ed.), *Children's Voices. Children's Perspectives in Ethics, Theology and Religious Education* (BETL, 230), Leuven, Peeters, 2009.

DIXON, R. E., *The Catholic Community in Australia* (Australia's Religious Communities), Adelaide, Openbook Publishers, 2005.

DUNCAN, D. J. & RILEY, D., *Leadership in Catholic Education. Hope for the Future*, Sydney, HarperCollinsPublishers, 2002.

DURIEZ, B., FONTAINE, R.J. & HUTSEBAUT, D., *A Further Elaboration of the Post-Critical Belief Scale: Evidence for the Existence of Four Different Approaches to Religion in Flanders-Belgium*, in *Psychologica Belgica* 40-3 (2000) 153-181.

DURIEZ, B., HUTSEBAUT, D. et al, *An Introduction to the Post-Critical Belief Scale. Internal Structure and External Relationships*, in *Psyke & Logos* 28 (2007) 767-793.

ENGEBRETSON, K., *Catholic Schools and the Future of the Church*, New York - London, Bloomsbury, 2014.

FONTAINE, J. R. J., DURIEZ, B., LUYTEN, P. & HUTSEBAUT, D., *The internal structure of the Post-Critical Belief Scale. Personality and Individual Differences*, 2003.

FOWLER, F.J.JR, *Survey Research Methods* (Applied Social Research Methods Series, 1), 4th edition, Los Angeles – London – New Delhi – Singapore – Washington DC, Sage, 2009.

GROOME, T. H., *Educating for Life. A Spiritual Vision for Every Teacher and Parent*, New York, The Crossroad Publishing Company, 2001.

HENRIKSEN J.O., *Difficult Normativity. Normative Dimensions in Research on Religion and Theology*, Frankfurt, Peter Lang, 2011.

HERMANS, C. & VAN VUYGT, J. (ed.), *Identiteit door de tijd. Reflectie op het confessionele basisonderwijs in een geseculariseerde en multiculturele samenleving*, Den Haag, ABKO, 1997.

HOLOHAN, G. J., *Australian Religious Education – Facing the Challenges. A Discussion on Evangelisation, Catechesis and Religious Education Questions Raised for Parishes and Catholic Schools by the General Directory for Catechesis*, Canberra, National Catholic Education Commission (NCEC), 1999.

HUGHES, P., *Putting Life Together. Findings from Australian Youth Spirituality Research*, Fairfield, Fairfield Press, 2007.

HUTSEBAUT, D., *Post-Critical Belief. A New Approach to the Religious Attitude Problem*, in *Journal of Empirical Theology* 9/2 (1996) 48-66.

KEERSMAEKERS, P., VAN KERCKHOVEN M. & VANSPEYBROECK K. (ed.), *Dialoogschool in Actie! Mag Ik er Zijn Voor U?*, Antwerpen, Halewijn / VSKO / VVKHO, 2013, 49-60.

KRYSINSKA, K., DE ROOVER, K., BOUWENS, J., CEULEMANS, E., CORVELEYN, J., DEZUTTER, J., DURIEZ, B., HUTSEBAUT, D., & POLLEFEYT, D., *Measuring Religious Attitudes in (Post-)Secularised Western European Context: Recent Changes in the Underlying Dimensions of the Post-Critical Belief Scale*, in *International Journal for the Psychology of Religion* (in press).

LOMBAERTS, H. & POLLEFEYT, D., *Hermeneutics and Religious Education* (BETL, 180), Leuven, Peeters, 2004.

LOOSVELDT G., SWYNGEDOUW M. & CAMBRÉ B., *Measuring meaningful data in social research*, Leuven - Voorburg, Acco, 2007.

METTEPENNINGEN, J., *Welke kerk? Vandaag en morgen*, Leuven, Davidsfonds, 2011.

METTEPENNINGEN, J., Toegepaste Blijde Boodschap. Waarom geloven mij (en anderen) gelukkig maakt, Tielt, Lannoo, 2012.

MOORE D.S. & MCCABE G.P., *Statistiek in de Praktijk. Theorieboek*, 5de herziene druk, Den Haag, Sdu Uitgevers bv, 2006 (repr. 2007).

MORTELMANS, D., *Handboek kwalitatieve onderzoeksmethoden*, Acco, Leuven & Voorburg, 2007.

MOYAERT, M., *Een zekere fragiliteit? Interreligieuze dialoog en de spanning tussen openheid en identiteit* (unpublished doctoral dissertation, KU Leuven), Leuven, 2007.

MOYAERT, M. & POLLEFEYT, D., *De Pedagogie tussen Maakbaarheid en Verbeelding*, in *Ethische Perspectieven* 14 (2004) 87-93.

O'LOUGHLIN, F., *This Time of the Church*, Mulgrave, Garratt Publishing, 2012.

POLLEFEYT, D., *Het Leven Doorgeven. Religieuze Traditie in de Katholieke Godsdienstpedagogiek. Ontwikkelingen en Toekomstperspectieven*, in H. VAN CROMBRUGGE & W. MEIJER (ed.), *Pedagogiek en Traditie. Opvoeding en Religie*, Tielt, LannooCampus, 2004, 133-149.

POLLEFEYT, D., *Interreligious Learning* (BETL, 201), Leuven, Peeters, 2007.

POLLEFEYT, D., HUTSEBAUT, D., LOMBAERTS, H., DE VLIEGER, M., DILLEN, A., MAEX, J. & SMIT, W., *Godsdienstonderwijs Uitgedaagd. Jongeren en (Inter)Levensbeschouwelijke Vorming in Gezin en Onderwijs. Opzet, Methode en Resultaten van Empirisch Onderzoek bij Leerkrachten Rooms-Katholieke Godsdienst en Leerlingen van de Derde Graad Secundair Onderwijs in Vlaanderen* (Instrumenta Theologica, 26), Leuven, 2004.

POLLEFEYT, D., *The Difference of Alterity. A Religious Pedagogy for an Interreligious and Interideological World*, in J. DE TAVERNIER *et al.* (ed.), *Responsibility, God and Society. Theological Ethics in Dialogue. Festschrift Roger Burggraeve* (BETL, 217), Leuven, Peeters, 2008, 305-330.

POLLEFEYT, D. & BAEKE, G., *Developing the Identity of Catholic Schools. Report First Stage of the Research* (unpublished interim research report, KU Leuven), Leuven, augustus 2007, 406 p.

POLLEFEYT, D., & BOUWENS, J., *Framing the Identity of Catholic Schools. Empirical Methodology for Quantitative Research of the Catholic Identity of an Education Institute*, in *International Studies in Catholic Education* 2-2 (2010) 193-211.

POLLEFEYT, D., *Hoe aan onze (Klein)Kinderen Uitleggen dat Sinterklaas (niet) Bestaat*, in *Over levensbeschouwelijke en religieuze maturiteit*, H-ogelijn 17-1 (2009) 31-35.

POLLEFEYT, D. & BIERINGER, R., *The Role of Biblical and Religious Education Reconsidered. Risks and Challenges in Teaching the Bible*, in R. BIERINGER & M. ELSBERND (ed.), *Normativity of the Future. Reading Biblical and Other Authoritative Texts in an Eschatological Perspective*, Leuven-Paris-Walpole (MA), Peeters, 2010.

POLLEFEYT, D. & BOUWENS, J., *The Post-Critical Belief Scale, the Melbourne Scale and the Victoria Scale 'for dummies'* (unpublished interpretation manuals of the typological scales of the *Enhancing Catholic School Identity Project*, KU Leuven), Leuven, February, 2009.

POLLEFEYT, D., & BOUWENS, J., *Dialogue as the Future. A Catholic Answer to the 'Colourisation' of the Educational Landscape*, English translation of the Dutch article: *Dialoog als Toekomst. Een Katholiek Antwoord op de Verkleuring van het Onderwijslandschap*, in P. KEERSMAEKERS, M. VAN KERCKHOVEN & K. VANSPEYBROECK (ed.), *Dialoogschool in Actie! Mag Ik er Zijn Voor U?*, Antwerpen, Halewijn / VSKO / VVKHO, 2013, 49-60.

RAES, P., *Katholiek of kwaliteit? Over de identiteit van een katholieke school*, Kapellen, Pelckmans, 2006.

RAPLEY, T., *Doing Conversation, Discourse and Document Analysis*, 2 ed., London, Sage, 2009.

RICHARDS, L., *Handling Qualitative Data*, London - Thousand Oaks - New Delhi, Sage Publications, 2005.

SAROGLOU, V. & HUTSEBAUT, D., *Religion et développement humaine: Questions psychologiques [Religion and human development: Psychological questions]*, Paris, L'Harmattan, 2001.

SLOTBOOM, A., *Statistiek in Woorden. Een Gebruiksvriendelijke Beschrijving van de Meest Voorkomende Statistische Termen en Technieken,* vierde druk, Groningen, Wolters-Noordhoff, 2008.

STOOP I., BILLIET J., KOCH A. & FITZGERALD R., *Improving survey response. Lessons learned from the European Sociale Survey*, New York, John Wiley & Sons, 2010.

SWINTON, J. & MOWAT, H., *Practical Theology and Qualitative Research*, London, SCM Press, 2006.

TER HORST, W., *Wijs Me De Weg. Mogelijkheden voor een Christelijke Opvoeding in een Post-Christelijke Samenleving*, Kampen, Kok, 1995.

VAN DER VEN, J.A. & M. SCHRERER-RATH, M. (ed.), *Normativity and Empirical Research in Theology* (Empirical Studies in Theology), Leiden, Brill, 2004.

WULFF, D.M., *Psychology and Religion. Classic and Contemporary Views*, New York, Wiley, 1991 & 1997.